FLYING BY NIGHT
SCOTTISH WITCHES
AND FAIRIES

By

SHEILA A McGREGOR

Volume 6 of
'Culture and Language' Series

Tis the land where Macbeth met the witches,
(And aften I've met them mysel',)
At the time when he speered at the limmers,
'How far is't to Forres, come tell'
My witches, unlike those of Shakspeare,

Had no beards at all on their chins,
But were strapping, braw, good-looking hizzies,
Weel made, and weel set on their pins.

William Hay (1794-1854), *The Bonnie Land o' Moray*

FLYING BY NIGHT:
SCOTTISH WITCHES AND FAIRY FOLK

This book is a DIY guide to the wonderful world of the witch. It is full of spells, ancient lore and vanished magic but underneath, always, it is full of the most surprising reality. Some of the discoveries explored in the following pages are as plain as a pikestaff; others are still only shadowy suggestions which are the starting-point for much more work. However, as far as possible in a single volume, here is a mound of material to mine for gold.

Some of these new ideas are, I contend, proven beyond reasonable doubt, (such as the equivalence of the historical witch with the imaginary but pervasive Scottish 'fairy'). More contentious is the perception that the archaic Gaelic of the witches' testimonies, source of much confusion and invention, was changed into meaningless and fantastic English by recording clerks and other writers who spoke only English. Confusion at the clerical interface was a very important source of inspiration for nonsensical magical beliefs. The clerk, who has no Gaelic, asks a question of the illiterate witch who has little or no English and a very shaky idea of what her trial entails. The clerk makes his record in English, garbling the original Gaelic into phonetic English. By this process of mis-translation, an original hunting metaphor meaning 'as fast as possible' is transmuted into a belief that witches (and fairies) flew by night to their meetings. This line of evolution is easy and convincing to demonstrate and forms a reliable explanation wherever we find 'supernatural' nonsense in the records. It was not, after all, the stuff of dreams.

Other facets of the argument laid out in the following pages lie further beyond firm proof. The most significant and elusive of these is the equivalence of fairies and, by extension, witches, with hunters, a society we might define as night-fliers, since men hunted by moonlight. The two ends of the equation are time and again brought close, but fail to overlap in any single source. However, this identification provides a satisfactory explanation of all sorts of otherwise incomprehensible aspects of Scottish fairy lore.

If fairies were hunters, or a memory of hunters, this would also provide the basis of a satisfactory explanation for the supernatural aspects of religious fiction, which can be viewed as attempts, widely distributed in time and space to explain obsolete aspects of long-lost oral learning to do with hunting and beacon lore. Themselves subjects which are beyond the scope of this book.

However there is a mass of indeterminate material which points in the same direction. A good example of deduction and speculation which falls short of proven fact but which has a very wide distribution is the dragon story. Typically, a little boy starts it all off. Puzzled by the passing mention in adult conversation of something he does not understand, he asks his father, "Daddy, what is a dragon?" His father explains that it was a large beast which belched flames and smoke and devastated the surrounding countryside with its poisonous breath. In other words, it was an active volcano. But, the father reassures his son, there are no more dragons. Even so, the little boy persists. "Why are there no more dragons?" From then on, the tale evolves backwards by repeated question and speculative answer until it arrives at the starting point: Once upon a time there was a king's son who left home to seek his fortune. He killed the last of the dragons – as men later killed wild pigs by catching them in nets – and was thus rewarded with the hand of the princess and half the kingdom.

In Scotland – and perhaps universally – the grains of obsolete fact which inspired this kind of tale – which is notably matrilocal – are words and phrases which relate to hunting or to beacon lore. Like other large and violent animals, the dragon can only be killed by a prince or hunt-leader; it is caught in a net like a wild ox or wild boar; it is rendered harmless by the spent malt from the Christmas ale – all these details identify a background in a hunting society, also the archaic background to the witch cult and the fairy romances.

In 1584 Reginald Scott wrote *The Discouerie of Witchcraft* in order, so he hoped, to show that the lewd dealings attributed to witches and witchmongers had no basis in fact. I have written *The Night-Fliers* to show that they did, and what it was.

This book is dedicated to the pagan healers, midwives, wise women and wise men of Scotland, who were put to death by ignorant and prejudiced men in the years following the Reformation. Their crime was to observe their old religion, a benign faith which made their tedious lives possible to endure. It was written to perpetuate the memory of the deer-hunters who were among the first victims of modern times.

Note: Source materials, particularly where listing or referring to named persons, offer variable spellings, often for the same person and often in a single document. In early documents, no uniformity of spelling was recognised. Where referring to original or quoted sources, the author often replicates the spellings as recorded in the source documents.

CONTENTS

* * *

ACT OF MARY QUEEN OF SCOTS
AGAINST WITCHCRAFT

Queen Marie – Ninth Parliament

IV of June, 1563

73. Anentis Witchcraftes.

'Item– For sa meikle as the Queen's Majesty, and the three estates in this present Parliament, being informed that the heavie and abominable superstition used by divers of the lieges of this realm by using of witchcrafts, sorcerie, and necromancie, and credence given thereto in times by-gone, against the law of God; and for avoiding and away-putting of all such vain superstition in times to come, it is statute, and ordained by the Queen's Majesty, and the three estates aforesaid – that no manner of persone or persones, of what-sum-ever estait, degree or condition they be of, take upon hand in onie times hereafter to use onie manner of witchcraft, sorcerie, or necromancie, not give themselves forth to have onie such craft or knowledge thereof, their-throw abusan the people; nor than onie such users or abusers foresaid, of witchcraft, sorcerie, or necromancie, under the pain of death, as well to be execute against the user, abuser, as the seeker of the response or consultation. And this is to be put in execution by the justice, sheriffs, stewards, bailies, lords of regalites and royalties, their deputies, and other ordinary judges competent within this realm, with all vigour, and they have power to execute the same.'

Chronicles of Strathearn 1896, 337-8.

INTRODUCTION

WHAT IT WAS TO BE A WITCH

In 1590 an Aberdeenshire witch was accused of being 'ane notirouse and commowne Wiche in the cuntrie; and cane do all thingis, and hes done all mischeifis, that deuilrie or Wichcraft cane devyse, in abstracking of mennis lyffis, wemennis milk, bestis milk, and bewisching of bestis as well as menne' (Pitcairn I, 208-209).

Witches were blamed when anything went wrong. In Dysart, Fife, in 1691, Euphan Logan said that when her brewings went wrong, she could blame no person but Margaret Halket. She abused Margaret, called her a witch, and physically attacked her in an attempt to 'get blood of her' (Simpkins 1914, 100). When a rat got into the works of a mill at Anstruther, Fife, 1701, this was blamed on a local beggar-woman. Just after being refused alms at Anstruther Mill, where James Osten was grinding his pease, Elizabeth Dick said that she saw the meal change to a red colour, but after she said 'God be in the miln', the rest of the meal came down white. The account suggests that red meal was not unusual. The miller cleaned out the mess with a handful of sheeling-seeds (bran or unhusked grain), and after a little while the meal came back to its normal colour (Simpkins 1914, 101).

Witches were blamed when they did nothing. Jean Lachlane of Carnwath (1644) was found guilty of working cures even when not bodily present (RPC 152-3). The defence in the case of Margaret Wallace of Glasgow in 1622 argued that she had not used any of the standard tools of the witch and thus could not have been practising witchcraft: 'Witchcraft can nocht be accomplischet as Witchcraft, bot be characteris, signes, croces, poysonet watteris, poysonet herbis, ruittis, vennemous oyles, woirdis, speiches, by incalling and invocatioun of the name of Sathan, quha, without the quhilks, or only of thame, Witchcraft can nocht be accompleischet.' The self-evident logic of this did not impress the jury. Margaret had been a witch without even knowing it herself (Pitcairn iii, 513).

If the cow or the child died the witch had deceived the people by claiming to be a healer and was sentenced to death. If the cow or the child got better it was by the witch's devillish art, and doom was again pronounced: 'Thow hes confessit that thow never chairmed aither beast or bodie bot thy chairmes maid thame ever the better. This thow did also by the devillis helpe as ane notorious witch, and *this thou canst not deny*' (RPC 154).

CHAPTER 1: MURRAY AND AFTER

There is at present nothing to show how much of the Witches Mass (in which the bread, the wine, and the candles were black) derived from the Christian ritual and how much belonged to the Dianic cult; it is, however, possible that the witches' service was the earlier form and influenced the Christian.

Margaret Murray 1921, 14-15.

In the following pages I have endeavoured to show the witch as she really was – an evil liver: a social pest and parasite: the devotee of a loathly and obscene creed: an adept at poisoning, blackmail, and other creeping crimes: a member of a powerful secret organisation inimical to Church and State: a blasphemer in word and deed, swaying the villagers by terror and superstition: a charlatan and a quack sometimes: a bawd: an abortionist: the dark counsellor of lewd court ladies and adulterous gallants: a minister to vice and inconceivable corruption, battening upon the filth and foulest passions of the age.

Montague Summers 1926, 48.

During the First World War the polymath, Margaret Alice Murray, noted for her competence, intelligence, tenacity and longevity, was unable to continue with her work as an archaeologist in Egypt and found herself with time on her hands. In 1921, when she was 58, she published a comprehensive study of European witchcraft entitled *The Witch-Cult in Western Europe - a Study in Anthropology.* She found that 'the cult appears to have been the same throughout Western Europe' and concluded that it was 'obviously' a survival of a benign fertility religion based on the worship of a horned god. Some felt she had gone beyond what was justified by the evidence but in general her views were recognised to be true and remained the accepted view on European witchcraft until she died in 1963 a few months after her hundredth birthday.

The challenge thrown at his feet by Miss Murray was picked up promptly by Montague Summers, a religious eccentric who is best known for his study of vampires. Summers had joined the Church of Rome and passed himself off as a Roman Catholic priest after his career in the Church of England came to an ignominious halt. He attacked Murray's view of the cult, claiming that witchcraft was pure evil and a work of the Anti-Christ (1926). But his position is closer to Miss Murray's than either might imagine, for her god of the witches is the next man's devil, complete with horns, tail and cloven hooves. Both accepted the reality of the evidence and its universal validity, though they differed in their interpretations. Murray pushed the evidence for uniformity somewhat further than it goes and did not allow for the influence of written sources in post-Reformation Europe; Summers was passionate about his Christian identity and exaggerated the evils of witchcraft, to the detriment of his argument. But he showed, inadvertently, that there is very little in popular worship in Catholic countries that cannot be attributed to the same pagan rituals and beliefs that one finds in the witch cult.

A strong thread in this tissue of continuity is the proliferation of powerful Black Virgins. Summers was a devoted worshipper of these dark old Ladies. He dedicated *The History of Witchcraft* to 'his friend Patrick and to

> Loreto and Our Lady's Holy House, as also of Our Lady's miraculous Picture at Campocavallo, Our Lady of Pompeii, La Consolata of Turin, Consolatrix Afflictorum in S. Caterina ai Funari at Rome, la Santissima Vergine del Parto of S. Agostino, the Madona della Strada at the Gesù, La Nicopeja of San Marco at Venice, Notre-Dame-de-Bonne-Nouvelle of Rennes, Notre-Dame de Grande Puissance of Lamballe, and all the Italian and French Madonnas at whose shrines we have worshipped.'

It is probable that, had Summers and his friend Patrick lived in Scotland in the latter part of the sixteenth century, they would have been sentenced to death for communing with that devilische sprit, the Queen of Elfhame.

Between the Devil and the deep, the matter of witchcraft rested for many years, and still rests despite a steady flow of historical and pseudo-historical studies. The currently fashionable approach is making little progress, as it depends on the denial of the supernatural elements which are the key to the subject. Professor Norman Cohn was one of those who rejected the supernatural evidence. In 1975 he launched an attack on Miss Murray and her 'society of the witches'. He disagreed with her interpretation of the facts and dismissed most of her evidence, which she quoted from original documents, as 'impossible'. He also made the very grave accusation that she had omitted bits of the evidence when it suited her argument (Cohn 1975, 102-125). He claimed that he had found 'in half a dozen instances', a discrepancy between what Murray quotes with what she passes over in silence (1975, 110). This 'passing over in silence' of significant evidence would amount to academic fraud and would of course invalidate her argument. In any case her theory did not suit Cohn who, as a historian of the holocaust, had a different view of witches, seeing them as innocent victims, on a par with the hapless Jews. His accusation appears to be serious but it is in fact very easy to refute.

For if one takes a few minutes to examine his 'half a dozen instances', one finds that in her approach to European witchcraft Murray was quite fearless and totally honest, as she was in everything she did. Cohn's allegations of wilful omission are unfounded. Like any historian faced with the unwieldy volume of material relating to witchcraft in Europe, Murray was selective but she avoids none of the 'impossible' aspects of the evidence. Her presentation of the evidence is comprehensive, balanced and omits nothing of importance. Had Cohn taken half a minute to look for his missing bits of evidence in Murray's capacious index, he would have found them all listed under the most appropriate topic. She did not offer any explanation of supernatural events but neither did she reject them as 'impossible'. She covers the Scottish evidence so adequately that one can deduce all the significant facts from *The Witch Cult in Western Europe*, without reference to any other source. One may disagree with her theory about the old religion and the horned god but one cannot fault her treatment of the evidence. Since the point is important, not only to her reputation but to my argument, I will go through Cohn's half a dozen instances.

Cohn notes as a sinister fact that in a lengthy quote from the trial of Helen Guthrie of Forfar in 1661, Murray omits to say that the witches, in the company of the Devil in the shape of a great horse, went down to Barrie where they tried to sink a ship. Not so. On page 69 we read that when the Forfar witches tried to sink a ship 'the divell wes there present with them all, in the shape of ane great horse'.

Cohn then says: 'It comes as no surprise to learn that another member of the group [Isobel Shirie of Forfar] was accustomed to turn herself into a horse, shod with horse-shoes, and in that guise transport her fellow witches, and even the Devil himself, to and from the sabbat - with the result that the following day she was confined to bed with sore hands' (1975, 112). Had Cohn checked Murray's index under 'Forfar' or referred to the transcript of the trial (she gives the reference), he would have learned that the story about horses and horseshoes was reported by Agnes Spark, another of the accused, who said it was a rumour she had heard in the coven. It was, in fact, a joke. As Murray notes, the Devil of the Forfar coven called Isobel Shirie his 'Horse' because she was his messenger and went to fetch people to the meetings (Murray 1921, 103, 236). 'Horse' appears to have been an affectionate nick-name. Apparently she had sore hands on the day after a coven meeting but this was not because she had been shod as a horse.

Cohn detected another sinister dash (-) which he imagined to mark missing words, in Murray's citation of the evidence given by Isobel Gowdie of Auldearn in Moray who was tried in 1662 (1975, 113). The passage refers to shape-changing and to riding on horses made of straws or bean-stalks (Murray 1921, 141-142) and Murray quotes it in full under the head of flying (1921, 105-106). She can hardly be said to have avoided shape-changing or flying as she devotes six pages of *The Witch-Cult* to the various animal shapes assumed by the Devil, and eleven pages to witches' flying on straws or otherwise (Murray 1921, 65-70, 100-106). Isobell Gowdie's testimony is of great interest and great value but it is also extremely long and contains a great deal of duplication. Not even Murray could quote it all, but she has unerringly selected the most significant parts (Murray 1921, 69, 183).

Cohn then complains that Miss Murray omitted to say that when the Forfar witches stole ale from John Benny's house, they went in 'through at a little hole like bees and took the substance of the ale . . .' (1975, 112). This is true but I am not sure why he finds it significant. 'Like bees' means to gain stealthy entry through a small opening. Because they did not like John Benny they probably replaced the stolen beer with their own urine, as Isobell Gowdie said they did in Moray: 'When we goe to any hous, we tak meat and drink; and we fill wp the barrellis with owr own pish again' (Pitcairn 1833, 603-4). In this case Murray can hardly be said to omitted something of importance.

Finally, and this reflects rather on the standards of his own research, Cohn claims that Isobell Gowdie in 1662 drew on existing local fairy lore, and that her evidence is therefore second-hand and worthless (Cohn 1975, 113). But there was no local fairy lore in Moray in 1662 other than the genuine scraps known to individual witches. The earliest known fairy fiction is a story dating from 1695. Anyone who investigates the history of the rather silly night-flying stories that passed for fairy lore in seventeenth-century Britain, must know that this sequence of events should be reversed.

Professor Cohn does not identify the fairy lore in question but it is no doubt the famous formula, 'Horse and hattock!' which Isobell said she used when she set off on a journey: 'Quhan we wold ryd, we tak windle-strawes or been-stakes, and put them betwixt owr foot and say thryse, Horse and Hattock . . . and immediately we flie away whair euir we wold' (Pitcairn 1833, 604). 'Horse and Hattock' is a good example of archaic Gaelic converted to nonsensical English, its real meaning hidden behind puns and the expectation of supernatural nonsense. A plausible phonetic equivalent for 'Horse and hattock!' is G. *ursainn-chata* 'ranks of an army in battle order' (Dwelly 1910, 1001). In its original setting it was a call for troops of hunters to gather at the muster.

Isobell Gowdie's cryptic phrase appears in only one local fairy tale of any importance, the story of the Fairy Cup of Duffus. All the relevant information is given by Pitcairn. Its literary history started in 1695, more than thirty years after the trial. The hero of the piece is said to be an ancestor of the family of Duffus, in Moray, not far from Auldearn. The story was written by Mr Steward who went to school in Forres and at the end of the seventeenth century was tutor to the eldest son of James, second Lord Duffus (d.1705) and, as he says in a letter to the English publisher John Aubrey, it was inspired by an old silver cup in the possession of the family. This story and another even more trivial were sent by Mr Steward to John Aubrey in March 1695. Norman Cohn believed this story was the origin of 'Horse and Hattock!' in the witch trial but the trial was a generation earlier. Aubrey checked with the Lord Duffus, who thought the story was nonsense, and published the letter anyway in his *Miscellanies*, a collection of silly superstitions and tall tales, under the heading 'Transportation by an Invisible Power' (vol. xiv, 94-95). Mr Steward wrote:

> 'As soon as I read your letter of May 24 I called to mind a story which I heard long ago, concerning one of the Lord Duffus (in the shire of Murray) his predecessors, of whom it is reported that upon a time, when he was walking abroad in the fields near his own house, he was suddenly carried away and found the next day at Paris in the French King's cellar with a silver cup in his hand; that being brought into the King's presence and question'd by him, Who he was? And how he came hither? He told his name, his country and the place of his residence, and that on such a day of the month (which proved to be the day immediately preceding), being in the fields, he heard the noise of a whirl-wind and of voices crying Horse and Hattock (this is the Word, which the Fairies are said to use when they remove from any place) whereupon he cried (Horse and Hattock) also, and was immediately caught up and transported through the air, by the Fairies, to that place... There was an old silver-cup in his Lordship's possession still, which is called the Fairy Cup; but has nothing engraven upon it except the Arms of the Family.' (From a letter to John Aubrey dated 25 March 1695; edition of 1784, 209-210).

Earlier and later variants on this story are known from different parts of Scotland and will be discussed under the heading of Fake Folklore, but the spelling 'Hattock' for *chathach* appears only twice, in the transcript of Isobel Gowdie's evidence in 1662 and the Duffus story of 1695. This suggests that Mr Steward copied from a transcript of the trial, which was no doubt preserved at Duffus. The story of the Fairy Cup is a genteel, mildly humorous dining-out yarn, based very loosely on a grain of truth. It is not local folklore, as Cohn perhaps imagined but he had an ulterior motive in reducing Isobell's testimony to local folklore. He was uncomfortable with her testimony: it did not not sit well with his 'inner demon' theory and it contained apparent nonsense which he could not explain. When we turn to Gaelic, we find an exact and appropriate explanation.

As we will see, trials of coven witches began in 1621 at Inverkeithing, West Fife, and later at Crook of Devon, Forfar, Alloa, Bute, Moray and elsewhere. Certain aspects of coven magic were not derived from an ancient native fertility religion but from experiments in necromancy. Sometimes it is evident that their leaders or Devils were members of the educated elite. We know these new-fangled Devils were not Gaelic speakers because they gave their witches English aliases instead of the old Gaelic spirit names used by healers and others. The Auldearn witches had names like Able and Stout, Nearest the Wind, Through the Corn-yaird and Ower the Dyke With It, which are inventive but not authentic. In Forfar and in Crook of Devon certain witches were called Alyson, The White Witch, The Pretty Dancer, Horse, and Beelzebub (Reid 1899, 242-243; Anderson 1888, 249). In contrast Gaelic by-names belong to an earlier world of hunting magic: Shuddak, a witch-name in Aberdeen in 1597 is G. *siodhach* 'a fairy, one of the fairy folk'; Trachak, another witch-name from Aberdeenshire recorded in 1597, is G. *dreachach* 'fair, handsome'; Toppock, alias of Elizabeth Steven in Lothian in use as late as 1629, is G. *tapaidh* 'clever, bold, heroic'.

In contrast to the worshipful approach of traditional witches these educated Devils were preoccupied with evil powers, personal advancement and the destruction of their enemies. However they inherited and perpetuated many of the ritual aspects of the sabbat, the music, the dancing, the choice of meeting place in an old kirk or at a prehistoric beacon site, the wax or clay dollies, the shape-changing, and the ritual intercourse by which the witch raised her powers and those of her community. It is not always possible to separate pagan tradition from book-lore, as many aspects of learned witchcraft (and of Christian worship) derive from a similar body of pagan belief but it is important to recognise that these two levels, the native and the imported, existed in Scotland. Isobell Gowdie in Moray was typical in using both the archaic pagan imagery of the local fairyfolk or hunters and the black magic, designed to harm or kill, which she learned from her master, the 'Devil'.

The subject of Cohn's *Europe's Inner Demons* is not witchcraft so much as genocide. Before Cohn began to write he had already made up his mind that witchcraft as an organised force did not exist, that the persecution of witches had no rational basis, that they (like the Jews) were innocent victims of daemonic forces of social and economic repression. This belief was fundamental to his belief in a pan-European psychopathy. However Cohn's starting position required him to reject all the apparently supernatural evidence without discussion, arguing that 'stories which contain manifestly impossible elements ought not to be accepted as evidence for physical events' (1975, 124). It is ironic that he investigated the demons which he believed were responsible in the twentieth century in Europe for the deaths of millions of innocent people on the basis of their religion and culture, but scoffed at the evidence for a very similar if numerically less important purge in Scotland in the seventeenth century which was also based on a difference of religion and culture.

Cohn's criticisms and his general approach – in particular his rejection of the supernatural evidence – have been found convenient by subsequent writers who also find themselves unable to explain the supernatural aspects of the evidence of the trials and other sources and who repeat what he wrote without checking the facts for themselves. One recent writer said that 'Much of this inaccurate interpretation is the result of the work of Margaret Murray... Murray chose her evidence selectively and subjectively, and omitted any details that did not correspond to, or contradicted, her ideas' (Millar 2004, 79). This is not true and five minutes with Murray's book is enough to show it is not true. Those who choose their evidence selectively and subjectively, leaving out the details that they cannot explain or understand, are Norman Cohn and his followers. Murray's research was logical and scientific, if now dated. She is the only writer so far who has tackled the entire spread of evidence and reduced it to logical order, ready for the next advance in understanding. The perpetuation of this old slander against her in 2004 is sad evidence for the decline in academic standards since 1921.

Cohn rejected the supernatural evidence as manifestly impossible but it is difficult to have confidence in an argument which requires one, as a first step, to reject most of the evidence. In fact the 'impossible' elements in Scottish witchcraft can be explained quite readily when one makes the reasonable assumption that the supernatural does not exist in fact, though it might exist in the imagination of every person in a society. Like Isobell's imaginary little horse, these impossible elements describe something mundane which, like much in Gaelic, is described in picturesque language. The Gaels like to use puns, metaphors and exaggeration. We still say 'I must fly!' when we depart on foot, but in a hurry. The first step in understanding what a witch meant is to believe it has rational meaning. For centuries the public has preferred to believe supernatural and nonsensical, the fake folklore; but they cannot blame the witches for that.

The potential for at last making sense of the Scottish evidence makes it all the more unfortunate that Kirstie Larner followed Cohn so closely in her historical study of the Scottish witch-hunts (1981). However she did not attempt to explain what witchcraft was, only how it was perceived and treated. This is a proper approach for a historian but of limited value. The problem was that she, like Cohn, did not know what to do with the irrational evidence. She could neither accept it nor explain it and so chose to reject it, particularly the fairy elements, which she dismissed as 'dreams, nightmares, and collective fantasies' (1981, 152). This led her into the same illogical position as Cohn. How can one reject the evidence for a supernatural dimension in Scottish witchcraft, and then deny that witchcraft in Scotland had any cultic significance? Larner's most useful contribution was perhaps to define the three essentials for a witch-hunt as a peasant economy, a peasantry who believed in witches, and an educated class who believed in the Devil (1981, 193). If we add linguistic confusion, this defines the situation in Scotland in the seventeenth century.

In summary, Murray based her conclusions on an objective catalogue of all the evidence. She did not venture to explain the supernatural elements, but she records them conscientiously, showing that they were widely spread and so (one can deduce) of considerable age. Montague Summers rejected nothing but believed in the Devil as a literal supernatural force, and did not try to explain anything. Cohn and Larner ignored the supernatural elements of witchcraft as though they did not exist. They all leave unanswered questions. Why did people believe in witches? What *was* a witch? How can we explain the supernatural aspects of the evidence?

It is perhaps only in Scotland that the two strands of European witch-craft – the pagan religious features and the learned features – survive side by side. Before c.1650 Gaelic was still the native tongue of most rural people in Lowland Scotland, unrecorded but persistent. Most of the accused came from Lowland areas along the Highland Border, where Gaelic lingered among the peasantry long after education in English was not only available but desirable. Educated men wrote and thought in English and, from their reading, from James VI downwards, they were convinced of guilt before asking a witch a question. There was often great confusion at the clerical interface.

CHAPTER TWO: HOW OLD ARE THEY?

An unaccountable correspondence pervades the confessions of sorcery throughout Europe.

J.G. Dalyell, 1835, 660.

Far away in a timeless world, the beautiful gopis dance at night around Krishna. They go with him on moonlit nights to the meadow near the village where they dance the circle dance. His attraction is such that when they were summoned, they abandoned whatever they were doing – even churning butter, nursing a baby or dressing themselves – and run to meet him (Gosh 1965, 104). The Dark One and his favourite, the White Maiden, are at the centre of the ring, he playing the flute while the others dance round them, now in pairs, now all holding hands. Each of the gopis, as they dance, desires Krishna and believes herself to be loved by him. His abundance is such that he is able to satisfy all the milk-maids at the same time.

Like the gopis, the witches of Europe were summoned to the ring by a Black Man, they danced at night around him and they enjoyed a sexual experience with him. The sexual aspects of the encounter were the main purpose of the dance. The speed with which witches flew to the sabbat was legendary. These are common themes throughout Europe and beyond. In Scotland an older symbolism survived, for the Dark One at the centre of the ring was the bonfire, a dark rough construction of brushwood, charcoal, pitch and bones, while the White Maiden is fire or flame, who dances when the bonfire is lit from the ashes.

One of the most striking aspects of witchcraft in Europe is the impression of a consistent, widespread and very old reality which is reinforced by the geographical spread of the recorded witch-hunts and which might have been forgotten eventually without the records of the trials. All writers on witchcraft quote promiscuously from the evidence of trials in Scotland, England, France, Germany, and elsewhere in Europe. Larner confirms that there was no particularly Calvinistic form of witch belief in Scotland (1981, 158).

To hunt for witches or persecute witches does not mean that they exist but that people believe that they do. In Europe this belief was well-founded. Necromancy and other forms of heterodox spiritual belief had been outlawed in the sixth century in Christian Visigothic Spain but persisted through the next thousand years; they persist today. Trials for sorcery began in France, England and Germany in the fourteenth century, and in Switzerland and Italy in the fifteenth century. In Scotland witchcraft became a capital crime in 1563 and remained so until 1736. The last legal execution for witchcraft in Western Europe was that of Anna Goelid in Switzerland in 1782 but two alleged witches were burned in Poland in 1793. The Irish statute was not repealed until 1821 (Summers 1926, 46, note) while what was possibly the last legal case to involve traditional witchcraft in Britain was heard in November 1871 at Stornoway, Lewis, the most remote of the Gaelic-speaking areas of the British Isles. All those involved in this case were Gaelic-speaking natives of the island. Murdo Morison, a crofter, sued Angus Graham, another crofter, for defamation. Angus had accused Murdo and his wife of having, by means of witchcraft, 'stolen the substance out of the milk of his cows'. Angus not only admitted having made this allegation but repeated it in court. He was found guilty, fined five shillings, and ordered to pay costs (Shaw 1988, 48). The case was probably unusual only in reaching court. A belief in witchcraft or something very similar survives today wherever a rural population keeps cows. I have seen a pentacle cut into the concrete doorstep of a byre in Creuse, central France, to protect the cows against witchcraft.

There was one later atypical case. The Scottish medium Helen Duncan (1898-1956), who was born in Perthshire, was the last person to be jailed under the 1735 Witchcraft Act but this was a political pretext. In 1944 she claimed to have conjured up the spirit of a sailor killed when HMS Barham was sunk in 1941. This made public the sinking of the ship, which was supposed to be a military secret, and the British authorities were afraid she might reveal other military secrets, in particular their plans for the Normandy landings which were then at an advanced stage. She was convicted of 'pretending to raise spirits from the dead' and sentenced to nine months in prison.

The Act was repealed in 1951.

A great deal of what we know about witchcraft in Europe comes from the efforts of the various Christian Churches to abolish it. Without this active and persistent opposition we might now view pagan practices as harmless folk-rituals or childish games but they had serious aspects, as the Church knew. In Scotland the main rituals took place at Hallowe'en, at Beltane and at other salient points of the year (latterly the Quarter Days) when worshippers danced round a bonfire. Where after all is the harm in lighting a bonfire and eating, drinking, singing bawdy songs and dancing bawdy dances? It becomes more explicit when the bones of the dead are burned in the fire and when the dancers are led by a man impersonating a wild bull or stag, with whom they have ritual sex. Thousands – perhaps hundreds of thousands – of women died in Europe for doing nothing more.

The repeated bans confirm that pagan rites persisted through the centuries. As a force against the old religion the Church appears to have been totally ineffectual. In 589 the third council of Toledo stated that the whole of Spain was still affected by sorcery and once again tried to ban necromancy, the chanting of funeral dirges, singing immodest songs and taking part in unbecoming dances at Church festivals, and other abuses which had crept into the liturgy of the Church. St Eligius (c.600) tried to ban dancing and capering (miming the sexual act), and the singing of carols and diabolical or obscene songs at St John's feast at Midsummer (24 June) (Pearson 1897, II, 17). The pagan midsummer feast persisted and so did all the others.

The *Forum Iudicum* of Receswinth (654) punished the use of magic to injure the person or property of another. One of its laws was directed against enchanters and invokers of tempests, who by incantations were said to bring down storms upon the vineyards and crops of others, and who invoked the Devil and thereby disturbed men's minds. Visigothic law, more lenient, laid down that those who robbed a coffin for a magical purpose were to be fined twelve solidi, which was to be given to the heirs of the deceased. This covered necromancy in its original form, which Isidore defines as uttering incantations over a corpse in the belief that the dead person would arise, and utter words of prophecy or give answer to questions put to it. Isidore goes on to add that since the demons, who are always associated with idolatry and magic, love blood, the necromancer in performing his magical rites always used blood mixed with water. Among the Greeks and Romans the evocation of the dead took place in caverns and near rivers and lakes where communication with the abodes of the dead was thought to be easier. A comparable ritual among the Gaels, reported by Dwelly (1901), was the *taghairm*: the prophet or wise man was wrapped in the hide of a recently-slain ox, a question was posed, and he was left for several hours in the recess of a waterfall to consult the spirits.

Despite various bans, in the seventh century the witches of Galicia still held their sabbats at night in the mountains. St Valerius (c.630-695) who was abbot of the monastery of San Pedro de Montes, had previously lived for many years as a hermit in the Galician wilderness and once chanced on a nocturnal meeting in the forest, which was conducted by a priest, 'forgetful of his sacred calling' and which featured the usual unbecoming songs and dances. He does not define this meeting as a sabbat or even as a religious exercise, but a group of people led by a priest, who meet in a forest at night to sing sexually-explicit songs while dancing indecent dances is beyond any doubt performing a pagan ritual cognate with a sabbat. Valerius does not mention the sexual rite but it is implicit. He describes another meeting he had with some peasants who were practising idolatrous worship on the top of a mountain. As he was at that time in the mountains not far from Astorga, they were perhaps devotees of Jupiter Candamius, a Celt-Iberian sky god who was worshipped on Mount Candanedo, on the border of Asturias and León. Gods worshipped on mountain-tops are found as far as the Middle East, Ceylon and China; they were originally signal beacons.

Problems at parish level persisted in Spain and elsewhere. In the eighth century Boniface made it illegal for 'choruses of laymen and maidens to sing and feast in the churches' but his impact was limited. In the ninth century Benedictus Levita ordered that when the people come to church, 'they shall only do there what belongs to the service of God ... these dances and capers, the disgraceful and lewd songs, must not be performed either in the church-yards or the houses of God, nor in any other place, because they remain from the custom of the heathens' (Pearson 1897, II, 17).

Spanish bishops tried to ban soothsaying, divination and sorcery, believing (as the Reformed Church did in Scotland a thousand years later) that witches could raise devils by means of nocturnal sacrifices in order to drive men insane and that sorcerers or charmers had the power to invoke tempests, damage vineyards and crops, and injure or kill men and domestic animals and destroy their fertility. But the authority of the Church was illusory and the native cult continued to enjoy massive support.

In the face of such popular belief, the Spanish Church inevitably developed its own black magic. Its priests performed requiem masses for persons still alive to provoke their deaths and went through other sacrilegious rituals designed to force God to punish their enemies: 'The invocation of the powers of the Devil by the sorcerer was simply the other side of the coin to the appeal for heavenly intercession by the saint' (King 1972, 145-148; McKenna 1938, chapter 5).

A thousand years later Karl Pearson in *Chances of Death* (1897) had much to say about the way pagan religion was manifested in Germany. He describes a ritual performed by men dressed as stags and other men dressed as women. 'Remarkable in the same respect is the "playing of the stag", to which reference occurs in a number of penitential books and homilies. Men on New Year's Day clothed themselves in the skin of a stag, with its horns upon their heads, and were accompanied by other men dressed in women's clothing. In this costume, with licentious songs and drinking, they proceeded to the doors of the churches, where they danced and sung with extraordinary antics' (Pearson 1897, II, 19). 'In Northumbria, a man was dressed in the hide of an ox recently slaughtered for winter provisions' [at Martinmas]. This practice had been denounced in 614 (Hutchinson, *View of Northumberland*, 1776). In other countries, at New Year, country people dressed in the skins and heads of cattle, implying horns (Dalyell 1835, 499).

Pearson also describes obscene bridal dances. To the horror of the Kirk Session, obscene bridal dances were performed c.1600 in the 'reformit citie' of Aberdeen and young men dressed as women and young women wearing masks danced together through the streets of the town (Turreff 1859, 24). Reformed or not, the Church had an antipathy to the joys of sex so cheerfully embraced by the average citizen.

Their difficulty of course was that one cannot distinguish between witches, who, as initiated followers of the Devil, had a religious interest in bonfires, dancing, eating and drinking, and ritual sex, and revellers with a secular interest in bonfires, dancing, eating and drinking, and orgiastic sex. What after all *was* the difference between popular celebrations and witchcraft, between gross indecency and pagan sexual mores? Lay celebrations like those described in many old sources contain all the elements of a sabbat, including deregulated sex on feast days, at the Quarter days, or at the bridal season of the year. It was one of the perks that kept society going.

CHAPTER 3:
'THE COMMON USAGE OF THE COUNTRY'

WITCHCRAFT IN SCOTLAND

Previous to the passing of the statute of June, 1563, there is but scant mention of witchcraft in Scotland.

George Black, 1938, 9

To anyone who wants to understand the origins of European witchcraft the Scottish evidence is of great relevance. For in Scotland the dense mat of history sometimes fails to felt into a single solid fabric and allows us to disentangle a few of the threads that belong to an older pattern. Archaic survival is typical of the country, enforced by its isolation at the northern end of a long island, its cold wet climate, its mountainous topography and its Gaelic language. Mesolithic and even older practices survived in the Highlands and Islands until very recently (see *Possibly Palaeolithic* in this series).

One element of which, however, only fragments have survived is the religion practised by Scotland's hunters. Its oldest aspect was the worship of fire personified as a Maiden or Cailleach and it appears to have persisted into the post-Reformation period. However the natives were not literate and left no liturgies or scriptures. But we know that G. *cail* means 'to burn' and that the Flame Maiden in her various forms is a fundamental element in European mythology. In the Upper Palaeolithic she evolved into the fat and fertile Mother who controlled the herds of deer and cattle on which hunters depended and who is depicted in European art as far away as the Urals and as far back as we can go in the history of European settlement. It seems probable that the Cailleach came to Scotland with the first settlers fourteen thousand years ago.

In the Christian era her cult began to face opposition. The monk who compiled the Chronicle of Lanercost was scandalised by the ritual performed at Inverkeithing in 1282.

'About this time, in Easter Week the parish priest of Inverkeithing named John revived the profane rites of Priapus, collecting young girls

18

from the villages and compelling them to dance in circles to Father Bacchus. When he had these females in a troop, out of sheer wantonness he led the dance, carrying in front on a pole a representation of the human organs of reproduction and singing and dancing himself like a mime, he viewed them all and stirred them to lust by obscene language. Those who held respectable matrimony in honour were scandalised by such a shameless performance...' Stevenson (1839, 109).

John the priest defended his actions to the Bishop by claiming that this kind of festival was the common usage of the country, which implies that despite the presence of the Church, Scotland was still a pagan country. The Bishop evidently accepted this argument as John was still priest in Inverkeithing a year later when he was killed in a brawl. It is probable that this Easter dance with its phallic Devil, dancing maidens and orgiastic sex was intended to bring luck to the community, as the very similar sabbat of the witches brought luck, and that John and his maidens would have been found guilty of witchcraft had they danced in the kirkyard three hundred years later. The scandalous choral songs or Minnelieder are also recorded in Germany where they had been banned as far back as 600 AD (Pearson 1897, 17).

The same Chronicle reports a second example of pagan activity in medieval Scotland, at Fenton, probably in East Lothian, in 1268, when a plague was decimating the cattle. The peasants made needfire, traditionally a cleansing ritual; they set up statues of Priapus in the fields; they dipped a dog's testicles in water and they sprinkled the enchanted water on the affected cattle. The Chronicle does not say that they burned the bones of dead cattle in the fire but it is probable that they did, for in 1102 the Synod of Westminster had banned the use of animal bones as a charm against disease in cattle in identical circumstances (Watkins 2007, 89).

The Gaels used a similar rite involving needfire to purify cattle before they moved to their summer pastures at Beltane. Dwelly (1901, 81-82) quotes from Armstrong's *Dictionary of Perthshire Gaelic*.

'On the first of May was held a great Druidical festival in favour of the god Belus. On this day fires were kindled on the mountain tops for the purposes of sacrifice; and between these fires the cattle were driven, to preserve them from contagion till next May-day. On this day it was usual to extinguish all the hearth fires, in order that they should be re-kindled from this purifying flame'.

Needfire, G. *tein-eigin* 'fire by friction, forced fire or fire of necessity', was considered by the Gaels to be 'an antidote against the plague and murrain and all infectious diseases among cattle'. Water heated by such a fire was also effective. Dwelly (1901, 943) adds that needfire was last used for healing in

North Uist c.1829, in Arran c.1820, in Helmsdale (Caithness) c.1818, and in Reay (Caithness) c.1830. As always, we can date the advance of the Reformed Kirk by the abandonment of native belief.

Another common remedy for cattle murrain was to transfer the illness away from the remaining healthy beasts by burying a sick one and having the others walk over it. This was done at East Barns, East Lothian, in 1629, when the farmer's wife, Isobel Young, was found guilty of witchcraft and executed.

From Highland Perthshire comes a report of an even more extreme remedy.

> 'There is a tradition that, once upon a time, when a pestilence raged among the cattle on the south side of Loch Tay, the people seized a poor wandering man who happened to come the way, bound him hand and foot, and placed him in the ford of Ardtalnaig burn. They made all the cattle pass over his body until his life was crushed out. It is said that he was buried on the knoll now occupied by the graveyard. This tale carries us back to the time of human sacrifices.' (Gillies 1938, 385).

The justification for the Scottish witch-hunts was the belief, shared by those who believed themselves to be victims of witchcraft and by those who described themselves as witches, that a witch possessed supernatural powers which (by the logic of the Church) she got from the Devil. As Dalyell put it, 'The word of the Scottish sorcerers was held to proceed under the immediate auspices of Satan. Thus, says King James, some "he teacheth how to make pictures in waxe, that by the rostinge thereof, the persones that they beare the name of, may be continuallie dryed awaie by continuall sicknesse." While the sorcerer roasts the image, Satan is occupied with the original; the substance of vitality escapes by perspiration, and digestion is impeded, so that "hee at last shall vanish awaie as his picture will doe at the fire"... The immediate agency of Satan was thought essential towards impregnating the type of sorcery with lethal efficacy' (Dalyell 1835, 337).

The outcome of individual cases often depended on whether a witch was seen as benevolent or malevolent by her neighbours and that depended on social, theological and individual circumstances. Those who used magic to heal provided a service which was valued by the entire community and, like much modern medicine, their methods seem to have been successful as often as not. But in hard times, after the witch-hunts began, poor people, living at bare subsistence, blamed the local witch, sometimes long after the event, for anything and everything that had gone wrong with them and their households, for causing the death of people and livestock, raising storms, wrecking ships, making cows run dry, spoiling butter, taking the good out of brew-tubs, dye-vats, middens and fields of oats, and alienating the affections of their spouses.

So much could go wrong in a peasant household that the belief that a witch had power over life or death must often have seemed to be justified.

Witchcraft was their way of explaining disaster, as fairies were in Ireland, one difference being that fairies were understood to be supernatural and beyond the reach of any law. On the other hand, domestic disasters, large or small, were often claimed as an achievement by a local witch. In 1662 Helen Guthrie, a member of the Forfar coven, boasted at her trial that she had been a very wicked woman and that 'when shoe gave her malisone to any persone or creature it usually lighted' (Anderson 1888, 246). This power implied the help of Satan and defined her as a witch.

If there was agreement about the power of the witch to kill or cure, there was no agreement about the Devil. The Kirk certainly believed it was involved in a battle against devil-worship – which in a sense was nothing but the truth – and consistently defined the leader of a coven as Sathan or the Devil but the scriptural Devil was very different from the Devil of the witches. All trials of coven witches from 1620 onwards confirm that the coven was under the rule of a master whom the witches called their Lord but they also reveal the influence of educated men dabbling in the black arts and recruiting local charmers and healers to use as a workforce.

As they were seldom prosecuted, very little is known of these local 'Devils' but they were certainly members of the educated elite. One might guess that after the Reformation they educated abroad, in the Low Countries or in Italy, where they had picked up an interest in witchcraft with their Latin grammar. The Devil at Auldearn taught his witches the words of charms or curses – in English, not in Gaelic – and rehearsed them until they got them right. He also supervised the making of the clay dolls and the witch-pokes, made and distributed the elf-arrows, and told the witches whom to shoot. All of this he could have learned from books. Apart from ritual intercourse his concern with the coven appears to have been with the practical details, whom to attack and how. Whatever the area of expertise and power of a coven leader might be he had no supernatural powers, however much the credulous might believe he was the Devil incarnate. But the work of a coven relied far more on the contribution made by those of its witches who had traditional learning than any novel elements imported by their masters. For their adherence to their master many women and a few men went in their thousands to be wirreit at the stake and have their bodies burnt to ashes but on the few occasions when the Kirk did have the dark gentleman in their grasp they were strangely reluctant to persecute him.

It is clear, from the testimony of witches as far apart as Bute and Moray that many basic elements of coven magic, such as clay dollies, witch-pokes, charms and elf-arrows, belonged to a pre-coven body of traditional learning which individual witches brought with them when recruited into the coven. Such techniques were part of a native pool of magical lore, not novel inventions or book-learning. Up to 1650 or so it appears that knowledge of magical processes was still passed down orally and usually by women to their pupils, from mothers to daughters, and quite often from wives to husbands. Less often, and notably among the fairy folk, the lore was passed to men such as Thom Reid, William Simpson, Andro Man, Alexander Drummond, John Brugh and John Stewart.

The use of magic to curse individuals was not an innovation of the coven masters but it appears to have been their main activity. Wise women and warlocks had offered a service to the community as a whole, curing rather than cursing, but, if the Devil at Auldearn in Moray is at all typical, the coven masters were preoccupied with cursing their local enemies and using magic for their destruction. It appears that the charms and rituals used for cursing were originally used, with more moral authority, to guard against disaster. In the Highlands protective magic was universal. It was worked on the Eve of every Quarter, to remove the evil influences that might have accumulated in the previous period and prepare against those to be inflicted in the following months. Farm wives and dairy-maids performed rituals and pronounced charms to protect cattle, cure illness, enhance the fertility of animals and crops, give sailors a fine wind, make the milk flow, the butter churn and the beer brew. These 'saining' rituals appear to have persisted in every part of Scotland that remained free from the control of the Reformed Kirk into the nineteenth century.

The disappearance of domestic magic may be connected to the fact that the tolerance or indifference manifested at Inverkeithing in the thirteenth century vanished abruptly in 1560 when religious control passed into the hands of a small number of narrow-minded zealots, whose education and knowledge of the Bible did not prevent their being as superstitious as their parishioners. Having achieved the downfall of the Catholic establishment, the Reformed Church then directed its 'pith and fury' to eradicating paganism or devil-worship. The Kirk believed in the power of the Devil much more fervently than it believed in the power of God but its ministers were evidently alarmed to find a popular pagan religion flourishing in their parishes. In 1563 the Scottish parliament passed an act against witchcraft and dealing with witches: 'All who used witchcraft, sorcery, necromancy, or pretended skill therein, and all consulters of witches and sorcerers, should be punished capitally' (Erskine's Institutes, 706.) Healers used devilish powers when they worked successfully and deceived the public; it was as evil for a witch to cure a person by magic as to kill him as both powers derived from the Devil and obstructed the work of God. Unfortunately God seldom provided a better alternative.

The Act of 1563 did not provoke a panic. At that date witches were certainly active in every community but there was little action against them until the hysterical campaign by King James VI in 1590. After listening for several months to the superstitious fears of his new Danish brother-in-law, Christian IV, and surviving multiple attempts by Scottish witches on his sacred person and his new queen, it was perhaps not surprising that he became an active persecutor of witches. The failure of his cousin Bothwell's campaign against him, which tried every form of magic known to witch, showed as clearly as any logical person might wish that their powers were futile and that witchcraft did not work. But James was a credulous man with little or no common sense and preferred to succumb to horror, fear, the thrill of the sensational, and the delights of reported torture. He believed that as God's holy representative he was leading a holy crusade. In November 1590 an English spy reported that 'the King and Counsaill is occupied with the examinacions of sundry witches taken in this contrye, and confessing bothe the great nombres and the names of their fellowes; and also strange and odiouse factes done by them.' In December 1590 the King was still 'busy examining witches, who confess many strange things' (Calendar of State Papers relating to Scotland, v.10, 425, 434, quoted by Black 1938, 23). In 1590 there were few voices of reason raised in Scotland. The Privy Council, the courts, the national church and the elite naturally followed the king's lead. Under torture most people will confess 'strange things'.

In 1590 the population of Lowland Scotland was divided between a very small educated Anglophone elite and an illiterate rural population. This closely parallels the structure of the later covens. Outwith the reach of the capital, their isolation and ignorance were considerable. But the elite and their tenants interacted in some unexpected ways: as one historian has noted, 'operative magic of one kind or another permeated Scottish society from top to bottom and continued to do so despite the Kirk's attempts to eradicate both the operation and the beliefs which made operation feasible' (Maxwell-Stuart 2001, 145).

One episode revealed by the trials of the North Berwick witches in 1590 shows how close the landed class was to the witches and midwives who worked its lands. When Barbara Naper complained to the great witch Agnes Sampson that 'a man callit Archie had done hir grit wrang' and that she wanted to be avenged of him (Pitcairn 1833 i, 240), she was not talking about her husband, Archibald Douglas, but about the eighth earl of Angus, whose name was also Archibald Douglas. The earl died, perhaps of dolly-magic but probably of poison, in 1588. There was easy access to the doomed man through Agnes Sampson who had treated his third wife, Jean Lyon, daughter of John Lyon, ninth Lord Glamis, for vomiting when she was pregnant. Richard Graham, a warlock, was called to treat the Earl when he fell ill, as magic was suspected but he refused to help when he heard that the Earl himself was suspected of dabbling in magic. One did not want the magic to rebound on oneself.

The most striking achievement of the witch-hunt begun by James VI in 1590 was not the extirpation of witches but a great heightening of public interest in the procedures revealed by the trials and the spread of information both factual and fictional in published sources, including *Daemonologie*, a learned work written by James VI himself in 1597. The trials with their primitive legal basis were very detrimental to Scottish culture. Despite its backward economy, at the end of the sixteenth century Scotland had been on its way to Enlightenment. It had four universities (at St Andrews, Glasgow, Aberdeen and Edinburgh) and its scholars went to study in Italy, Flanders and Germany. Now their foreign tours often led not to enlightenment but to an interest in the occult: Francis Stewart and his cousin James are two early examples. Demonology became a fashionable study with what was promised to be a practical aspect if one could only learn the right procedures and spells. From their foreign studies the elite brought back recipes, charms and magical procedures which circulated among the like-minded and prompted experiments in the field. Necromancy evolved into an experimental science which promised great powers to anyone who could discover the right recipes. One of the first uses of the new printing technology was to feed popular demand for sensational stories about witches as the new presses made it possible to print cheap and lurid broadsheets such as *Newes from Scotland*. Among the illiterate the more sensational aspects of the trials spread by word of mouth and such melodramatic concepts very soon began to affect those who gave evidence and those who interrogated the suspects.

Before there were covens

It is not possible to distinguish with certainty between trials of individual coven witches and individual healers but we can at least say that between 1590 and 1615 the majority of those accused of witchcraft were not members of covens but local wise women, midwives or charmers, who had learnt their lore from older witches, from their relatives or from the fairy folk (Black 1938). They worked alone, or in conjunction with one or two others, or with a family member. They were condemned to death for deceiving the public by using traditional charms and rituals, including herbal remedies, Catholic prayers, and charm-stones to treat sick people and animals. A minority were 'bad women', elderly and demented, who cursed their neighbours and were naturally blamed when misfortune fell.

But in the testimonies of these poor women, who rarely had enough to eat and sometimes owned little more than the clothes that they stood up in, we can glimpse the outlines of a virtually unknown religion which owes nothing to the Anti-Christ and reaction by a suppressed peasantry to the discipline of the Kirk. To say so is to reverse the order of events. One might however argue that the Church was justified in its attempts to suppress witchcraft, though its methods were reprehensible. But local ministers had little by way of guidance. The ritual aspects of this pagan religion in Scotland are very strange even today. To whom did witches dedicate themselves if not to the Devil? Was he the Devil of Scripture, or not? Why was it ungodly to dance around a bonfire? Why were witches generally women?

For several centuries the Kirk at home and abroad did its best to control the most persistent pagan folk practices but despite the executions it fought a losing battle. In Perth in 1591 the presbytery pronounced a ban on 'filthy and ungodly singing about the Mayis on Sunday evening after the sermon' but the filthy singing continued and so did visits to holy wells by large and unruly groups of young people, particularly on 1 May. In 1592 despite the official abolition of Christmas the Session was still faced with the need to discipline 'the abuses that fall out in the time of Yule'. This may seen relatively harmless but no more than five years after these cheerful and cheeky Christmas celebrations, several dozen women and a man were strangled and their bodies burnt for the crime of dancing at Hallowe'en in public in the centre of Aberdeen.

If this was intended to be a deterrent it did not work. In 1646 the Session at Slains in northern Aberdeenshire was still trying to ban the lighting of bonfires at Beltane, Midsummer, Hallowe'en and Yule. But we might wonder where is the devilish aspect of these events? Why did the people continue to light fires and dance, despite the terrible penalties enforced by the Reformed Kirk?

Some of those put to death for witchcraft in Aberdeenshire in the great purge of 1597 were accused of little more. The principal complaint against Thomas Leyis of Aberdeen, executed in that year, was that he had led the revels in the town at Hallowe'en, dancing round the Fish Cross and up and down the Meal Market. From his trial it is clear that the Hallowe'en celebration in Aberdeen was a long-established communal or folk activity. There was nothing secretive about it. The witches of Aberdeen had probably danced in the same way at the same place at Hallowe'en for hundreds if not thousands of years. This is suggested by local geography, for the Fish Cross stood on St Katherine's Hill, a fairy mound once used by hunters as the site of a landing light which once guided coastal traffic into the mouth of the river Dee. There is a link here between the original use of the site and the celebration but it is practical, not religious, let alone sacriligeous.

Nonetheless between sixty and seventy women were executed in Aberdeen in the 1590s. Today all of them look more like independent healers and charmers than coven witches. Considerable detail survives of several trials (published in the first Spalding Club Miscellany in 1841). Half of them came from the rural parishes of Cromar, Aboyne, Lumphanan and Kincardine O'Neill in Strathdee, an area of no more than ten miles square. The rest came in penny numbers from New Deer, Kinnadie, Methlick, Newburgh, Kintore, Dyce and Aberdeen itself. Most of Aberdeenshire was untouched by the witch-hunts but Andro Man of Banff and several women there were also tried in 1597. They were not only charmers but fairy folk or pagans in the old Gaelic tradition.

As so often the arrests in Lumphanan were largely due to one inspired man, the minister, Mr John Ross who was responsible for putting thirty witches to death. The campaign began in 1590 when two 'great witches', Janet Grant alias

Gradoch (G. *gràdhag* 'esteemed, loved, admired') in Colquhatstane and Janet Clark alias *Spalding* in Blalach, together with five or six others, were accused on flimsy evidence of killing several people, destroying sixteen head of cattle, and raising the Devil to get his advice on a cure. They were also accused of trying to kill the Laird of Craigievar, William Forbes (1566-1633), and his son (Pitcairn i, 206-9), no doubt on behalf of an unnamed customer.

But in 1597 the most common accusation was that they had celebrated Hallowe'en in 1596 by dancing with the Devil round a standing stone at Craigleauch 'beacon hill', now Craiglich (NO5305) near Lumphanan. Evidence for a local coven at this date is given in full below but fails to be convincing: there was only the one meeting, the oath was administered by a senior witch, not by a Devil, the group appears to be composed of related and friendly healers and charmers. A curious feature of several confessions is that the Devil was present but *invisible*. Depending on interpolations by court officials and clerks the story gathers and sheds details as it goes along, many of them found also in *Newes from Scotland* but not, on the whole, typical of the testimonies of coven witches.

Six witches were tried together on 4 April 1597. They had danced round a standing-stone at Hallowe'en.

1 Margrat Og was accused of dancing with Margaret Bean (previously tried and burned as a witch) and her own two daughters (Issobell and Beatrix Robbie) and certain others, around a great stone, 'under the conduct of Sathan, your maister' (SCM 1841, I, 144). 'Sathan' was apparently present but only as an invisible force or influence.

2 Helene Rogie was at the same deuilische dance with her mother, the late Margaret Bain 'with the rest of your consorts, the Deuil your maister, beand present' (SCM 1841, I, 147). At this point copious new details are added.

3 Jonat Lucas was accused of dancing at Craigleauch with eight others, 'being in companie and societie with thy maister the Deuill, of quhome thow leirnit all thy sorcerie ... where thou and they was vnder the conduct of thy maister the Deuill, danceing in ane ring, and he playing melodiously vpone ane instrument, *albeit invisibilie to yow*, ... and that the Deuill your maister causit ilkane of yow kiss his arse, and the Deuill your maister, beand in the likeness of ane beist, had carnall [deal] with ilk ane of yow, and this thow can nocht deny' (SCM 1841, I, 149).

4 and 5 Jonat Davidsone and Issobell Oige were accused in similar terms of being with others 'at the deuilische dance about ane grey stane at the Hill of Cragleauche, accompaneit with vmquhil Margaret Bayne,

and the Deuill thy maister, he being playing to the and thame, he *onvisabill*, and at that tyme he had deill with the, in forme of ane beist and causit the and thame all kiss his arse etc.' (SCM 1841, I, 151, 152).

6 Beatrix Robbie's dittay appears to be by a different writer and refers only to 'their dansing altogidder about a gryt stane, a lang space, and the Devill your maister, playing afoir ye' (SCM 1841, I, 153). The Devil has now made an appearance as a musician.

Only one other sighting or presence of the Devil is noted for this district: he is said to have appeared in likeness of a horse to the late Margaret Bane (SCM 1841, I, 157).

The dittays are very clearly not the words of the witches but those of a literate man, the minister or the session clerk: only a man of superior education would write in 1597 that the Devil 'played melodiously vpone ane instrument'. This does not rule out the presence of a Devil who took part in the Hallowe'en revels, as Thomas Leys did in Aberdeen. There must have been such a person. But a Devil, invisible or not, is not quite enough to constitute a coven, particularly when the lore was still passed down from mother to daughter and from great witches to their novices.

As noted, the more salacious details appear to be borrowed from the inventive account of the North Berwick witches in *Newes from Scotland*. But even if we accept all these details, the picture revealed by the trials in Strathdee is not quite that of a coven. A coven had a recognised Lord or master, a literate man who applied an oath of loyalty which replaced Christian baptism, who gave the new witch a new name, and who enforced attendance at regular meetings or sabats. What we seem to lack at Craigleauch in 1596 is the element of control. All we can claim is a meeting at the Quarter at an old beacon site of seven or eight related witches, mothers and daughters, who danced and had ritual intercourse with a man disguised as an animal. This would justify a charge of witchcraft and may unlock part of the puzzle. It is not yet a coven but suggests the kind of low-key local organisation that preceded and contributed substantially to the new covens.

It made little difference whether a woman accused of witchcraft confessed or not. It was enough that a sufficient number of people believed that she was a witch: 'Being habit and repute a witch, that is, general credulity in her supernatural powers, was enough without any evil deed in confirmation' (Dalyell 1835, 630). An example was the attack on Isobel Grierson of Prestonpans (1607) by David Seaton, baillie in Tranent, who was leader of the Assise or jury which heard the evidence. Seaton had been a notorious persecutor of local witches since 1590, when he was responsible for burning nine women at Haddington in the aftermath of the attempt on the life of James VI. At that time he is said to have tortured his own servant, Geillis Duncan, to reveal the source of her healing abilities (*Newes from Scotland* 1591, 8-9). In 1607 he began again by accusing Isobel Grierson of causing illness and death among the families at his salt-works. Her dittay contains not one plausible fact. Before she was executed on Castlehill in Edinburgh Isobel responded with a splendid curse: 'May the faggotis of Hell lycht on thee, and Hell's caldrane may thou seith in!' (Dalyell 1833, 33). Pitcairn thought the proceedings at her trial were 'perhaps the most absurd on record' (1833, 523-6) but this did not save her from death.

The civil powers in Scotland were better-educated and, on the whole, more enlightened than the ministers and elders of the Kirk. The lack of understanding, education and privilege of those who were accused of witchcraft was recognised by a leading judge, Sir George Mackenzie (1636-1691). He was known as Bluidy Mackenzie for his ruthless persecution of Covenanters but he was surprisingly sympathetic towards poor women accused of witchcraft. He wrote:

> 'Those poor persons who are ordinarily accused of this Crime are poor ignorant creatures, and oft times Women who understand not the nature of what they are accused of; and may mistake their own fears and apprehensions for Witchcraft; of which I shall give you two instances, one of a poor weaver who after he had confessed Witchcraft being asked how he saw the Devil, he answered, Like flies dancing about the candle. Another of a Woman, who asked seriously when she was accused, if a Woman might be a Witch and not know it? ... These poor creatures, when they are defamed, become confounded with fear, and the close prison in which they are kept, and so starved for want of meat and sleep, either of which wants is enough to disorder reason the strongest, that hardly wiser and more serious people than they, would escape distraction.'

Sir George Mackenzie 1678, 45, quoted by Dalyell 1835, 630.

Dalyell adds: 'Yet persons of elevated rank, some occupying the highest stations, and others whose learning was in advance of their era, were also endangered by such charges... Being habit and repute a witch; that is, general credulity in her supernatural powers, was enough without any evil deed in confirmation.'

Several aspects of witchcraft show how claims of evil-doing can lead to evil being done. Certain of the Catholic clergy invented a Black Mass which involved a number of ingenious perversions. They account for Montague Summers' passionate denunciation of the witch as 'an evil liver; a social pest and parasite; the devotee of a loathly and obscene creed ... battening upon the filth and foulest passions of the age' (1926, xvi). He overlooks the point that, without the Church as *agent provocateur*, such perversions serve no purpose. We do not find them in Reformed Scotland where there is nothing more extreme than the pact with the Devil. We know of only one 'black' service at which the Devil in cap and gown (the Earl of Bothwell again) preached the sermon in a parody of the Sunday-morning service (Larner 1981, 170). Infant sacrifice in Scotland was probably more common than the very rare recorded examples imply but it had nothing to do with a reaction against Christianity.

We are justified in calling the appearance of covens a movement as despite its small scale, throughout Lowland Scotland methods of recruitment, organisation and activities of every known coven are very similar. The majority of the covens were in small ports on the Firth of Forth. From West Fife the coven movement appears to have spread north to Forfar, Aberdeenshire and Moray and south to Lothian and the Borders, often but not always on the coast. It is not so clear why large areas remain blank. Have we not found the evidence or has it been destroyed? Did local magistrates and ministers refuse to persecute harmless individuals but dealt humanely with the occasional wicked witch? Or were the witches and their master the dominant force, protected by his elite status and by the public popularity of the old cult, as they appear to have been in Moray?

The idea that a witch was a poor peasant or a derelict widow-woman is an over-simplification. Bessie Dunlop's husband travelled from Ayrshire to Leith in Midlothian to buy meal. Isobell Gowdie's husband raised cattle which he sold at market. Had healers continued to use their enchanted stones in harmless healing rituals and abstained from digging up dead babies and making them into pies and pokes (Forfar, 1661), had witches limited their activities to meeting in secret at the raiths of the year to copulate with a man impersonating an animal and refused to further the ambitions of the elite, had James VI been sensible, there might have been no witch hunts. This would have been better for Scotland but then of course we would know nothing about the old religion and its rituals which were a feature of life for a very long time before 1282 and the spring dance at Inverkeithing. It was however unfortunate that witchcraft became a popular hobby among the landed gentry who moved its focus from saining and curing to evil and the destruction of their enemies, and themselves remained unscathed.

It has become fashionable to write off the activities of coven witches as if they were poor deluded women and not really evil but it is clear from their testimonies that once they had learned to be bad, they were as bad as they could be whether they were trying to kill the minister with elf-shot, destroying their neighbours with witch-pokes, trampling down crops, or cursing male infants. They did not always achieve the intended evil but it was not for want of trying. Unfortunately, when Scottish witches moved from curing to embrace black magic and tried to kill their neighbours by spells and magic, they created a situation which neither their neighbours, their landlords, the local kirk sessions, nor the justiciary could afford to ignore.

Witchcraft finally dwindled into a lot of old wives' tales. This was probably not because of persecution – it is difficult to enforce new ways in an illiterate peasantry – but because it did not work. The witches were rewarded with fairy gold but within twenty-four hours it had changed to horse muck (Isobell again). Their masters were equally frustrated in their attempts to kill off their enemies by remote control. Robert Wilson of the Crook of Devon coven was said to complain that 'Sathan promised you both silver and gold whilk ye said ye never got; and also said that Sathan gave you both meat and drink sundry times, but it did you never good. And sin syne ye was Sathan's servant that ye was never able to buy yourself a pair of shoone' (Reid 1899, 231). Nicolas Lawson of Pittenweem, confessed in 1704 that when she had renounced her baptism the Devil promised her a good milk cow, but 'he never gave it' (Dunbar 1865, 266). Isobell Adam, another of the Pittenweem coven, said the Devil had told her he knew she was discontent with her lot and that in his service she should get riches as much as she could wish (Dunbar 1865, 267). Instead she was tortured on the orders of the court; her ultimate fate is not known.

While it lasted the beliefs and sheer animosity of the witch covens presented a real threat to the established Church and to the structure of rural society where one could choose one's friends but had to live with one's neighbours.

The purges of the seventeenth century were marred by the use of torture. The Reformed Church made a strenuous effort to root out an alternative religion based on devil-worship but, as Black says, 'there is no excuse for the clergy, who, from education and training, ought to have known better. Unfortunately the majority of the clergy of the period were just about as ignorant as was the mass of the people, and were bound hand and foot to the superstitions of the age, many of them, without doubt, the result of their teachings on demonology' (1938, 19).

In Scotland we can begin to distinguish between an older native tradition which was passed down orally among the local healers and charmers, and the same practices used by local covens recruited by a learned man with personal motives. Healers and charmers were generally found guilty of cheating the public while coven witches were accused of demonology and sorcery and 'divilische practizes'.

Another development provoked by the witch-hunts of the 1590s was the spread of covens organised on a similar pattern and led by educated men who shared Bothwell's hope of harnessing the power of the Devil to achieve their political and personal ends. This movement evolved in part out of an earlier tradition where large numbers of local witches assemble by word of mouth to achieve a specific purpose for a member of the local aristocracy. An example is the great assembly of wise men and women who came together in Easter Ross in 1577 to work for Katherine Ross, Lady Fowlis, making clay dolls, shooting with elf-arrows and (less traditionally but more effectively) brewing up a bucket of beer laced with rat poison. Considerations of right and wrong seem to have played no part in anyone's calculations from the judiciary downwards. Several of the witches were executed in the Chanonry in 1577 but Katherine Ross was not tried until 1590 when she was acquitted, despite her certain guilt.

Another example is the number of witches from Lismore and Morven who were consulted by Campbell of Ardkinglass in 1590. The witches who gathered in North Berwick Kirk to listen to Francis Stewart, also in 1590, also came from a wide area, some apparently by boat. Bothwell appears to have been familiar with the operation of European covens and the more salacious episodes were probably added by James VI. The witches in the case stuck to their traditional methods including a wax pictour and spells and rituals involving knuckle bones, cats and iron.

Gaelic

By the sixteenth century there had been other significant changes in Scotland. In the thirteenth century most of Lowland Scotland, including Inverkeithing, was still Gaelic in its language and pastoral in its culture. By 1563 the Lowland population had adopted arable farming, though still with a strong pastoral bias, and most of them now spoke English of a kind. It is uncertain to what extent Gaelic persisted as an oral language but it was certainly used at the time of the trials in most of the areas where witch trials were held, including Bute, Alloa, Aberdeenshire and Moray. The by-name *Gradoch,* for G. *gràdhag* 'esteemed, loved, admired', given to a new initiate, is typical of many.

Whether or not our witches still spoke Gaelic, their immediate ancestors had been Gaels and most of the trials took place in areas close to the Highland border. The names of the six men and twenty-six women tried for witchcraft in Easter Ross in 1577 are given in Gaelic form, with Gaelic aliases. They were accused of making images of butter and clay and shooting them with elf-arrows, as we find also in Moray and Bute in the next century. When we look for a Gaelic element in the evidence, we find the same kind of archaic survival as in Highland folklore: a pure archaic Gaelic badly garbled in translation into English. In the Highlands itself, trials for witchcraft seem to have been rare, not because the Highlanders did not indulge in superstitious practices, but because before 1700 the reformed Church did not have the resources to colonise and police the Gaelic-speaking areas. Consequently evidence from the Highlands is of a different kind.

CHAPTER 4: THE HORNED GOD

God seems to have had nothing to do but watch the Devil.

J.D. Dalyell 1835, 253.

Today the Devil is usually shown to be part human, part goat, reflecting his role in a fertility cult, and he may also have claws, wings, blazing eyes and a long scaly tail. Some of this he shares with that other fiery monster, the Dragon. The link between Devil and Dragon is of some age; in the Revelation of St John the Divine, 12:9, the Devil was seen as a great dragon; we read: 'So the great dragon was cast out, that old serpent, called the Devil and Satan, which deceiveth the whole world; he was cast out into the earth, and his angels were cast out with him'. As they knew in Scotland, Dragons are female and at the oldest level they represent the Flame Maiden or Virgin Mother. The Black Man – a great fire – was the Dragon's whelp; he may have been rough and fiery but had neither horns nor goat's feet. A Black Man like Ciaran was also a saint. So it seems as though two images come together in Scottish tradition: the native Black Man and the imported Horned God. Of the two the Black Man is by far the most popular and widespread.

Larner thought worship of the Devil was 'rather rare' in Scotland (1981, 151), which is true but it rather depends on how one defines 'worship' and 'Devil'. The efforts of the Kirk to suppress covens and their celebration of the quarterly festivals was due to the fact that members of covens took an oath of allegiance to the Devil (or so it was claimed by those who persecuted them) and worshipped him at the sabbat by dancing, singing lewd songs, and performing ritual sex with a man dressed to represent an animal. This could certainly be defined as Devil-worship. However it is less clear who or what the Devil worshipped at the sabbat was. There is reasonable unanimity about his animal disguise – seldom if ever as a horned beast but often as a humble dog – and confusion about his identity. Was there a Horned God in Scotland?

Some people at the time of the Reformation certainly thought so. A story popular with the Catholic faction told that John Knox and his secretary went into the churchyard of St Andrew's intending to raise some saints but that, by a mistake in their conjurations, they raised the great fiend himself. Knox's secretary was so frightened by Satan's great horns, goggle eyes, and long tail that he went mad, and shortly afterwards died, but Knox was built of sterner stuff (Mackay 1841, vol.2, 129). But a search for this horned figure in Scottish witchcraft does not add to this picture. A goat with great horns is absent from the Scottish cult. Admittedly at Auldearn, their Master 'vold be lyk a stirk, a bull, a deir, a rae or a dowg, &c.' (Pitcairn iii, 613) but the use of a dog skin does suggest that the leader of a Scottish coven wore whatever was available, with or without horns; that the significant point about his disguise was to mark his role as a male animal. The age and separate evolution of Scottish pagan lore is suggested by the fact that the goat plays no part in it. There seems to have been no horned god in Scotland before 1590 and Wright's woodcut.

When we look at ancestral images of the Devil the theme is not horns but fire. All the traditional Devils – Lucifer, Satan, Beelzebub, Heilal, Baal and Belial – have fiery names and were worshipped in mountain-top sanctuaries which had once served as strategic signal stations and beacon sites, as a good many still do. The managed use of fire as a means of communication was once very widespread in Europe, the Middle East, Ceylon, and the Far East but everywhere there was a progression from the practical to the irrational, from the use of a signal beacon to control a communal hunt to religious devotion.

Horns come with the fertility cult and may not have reached Scotland. The Devil who dances in the cave of the Trois Freres, Ariege, in southwest France, is probably not a shaman, as Breuil thought, but a witch-priest. He wears an animal skin complete with antlers and what might be a horse's tail. His phallus is not erect but 'well-developed', carefully drawn and deliberately exposed. He may be as much as twelve thousand years old (Bahn 1997, 63) and he would have been recognised as their Lord by any member of a seventeenth century Scottish coven, with his animal pelt and unnatural member. There is a second 'sorcerer' in the same cave system, also dancing and playing some kind of flute.

Some time later he has become the more or less benevolent god Pan with his pipes. The name Pan is found in Gaelic as *ban* 'light, white', in archaic terms: 'fire'. The Greek Pan is half man, half goat. He has the head, horns, beard and feet of a goat, an erect phallus and a goat's short tail but the rest of his body and his hands are human. He is sexually undiscriminating and very active. Originally Pan was the god of the wild herds and hunting in the wild woods, where pipes and horns were used to send signals and spread information, before sheep spread into the mountains and the old hunting god was adopted by or chased out by shepherds. A vase from Early Classical Greece shows Pan chasing a shepherd, suggesting that sheep were not universally popular.

A similar creature, but a ram rather than a billy-goat, was Robin Goodfellow, the wild man of the English woods. In a pamphlet published in London c.1588, Robin is shown, in the words of Robert Graves, as an 'ithyphallic god of the witches with young ram's horns sprouting from his forehead, ram's legs, a witches' besom over his left shoulder, a lighted candle in his right hand. Behind him in a ring dance a coven of men and women witches in Puritan costume...' (1961, 396). The woodcut for the first edition was more detailed than later versions. By 1628 Robin's huge member of 1588 was veiled by a curtain of fleece. Robin, like a robber, was a hunter, which is why the red-breast is a robin.

The Hebrew Devil was called HYLL or Heilel, translated as 'morning star' but Heilel is any shining thing such as a guiding light or signal beacon. Hebrew *heilel ben shakhar* is 'Lucifer, son of the morning'. That Heilel was a fire is clear from Job: 'Its snorting throws out flashes of light; its eyes are like the red glow of dawn' (Job 41:18) and 'O that I could be as I was in the months now gone, in the days when God watched over me, when he caused his lamp to shine upon my head, and by his light I walked through darkness' (Job 29:2-3). Heilel has the same root as Ger. *hell* 'shining, brilliant' and E. *hell*, once a paradise of heat for people living in a very cold climate.

A related name for a fiery devil is Beelzebub or Baal, a root found also as G. *bal* 'lord, the sun, fire', G. *Bealltuinn* 'May day', G. *beoll* 'fire' and Gr. *helios* 'the sun'. The HL name HYLL is a reduced (aspirated) version of the BL names. Another old BL god, Belial, the most evil of the fallen angels, was banished from the Christian Bible. He is equated with Sammael, Archangel of Death, who was the consort of Adam's first wife, Lilith. These are all 'fire' names: Lilith was a Flame Maiden or Cailleach (E. *lily* is like a flame), G. *aingeal* means 'bright fire; messenger'. G. *diabhol* 'devil' means 'fire-god', from G. *dia* 'god' and G. *beoll* 'fire'. G. *diabhol* is a compound made up of *Dia* 'god' and *bol* or *bal* 'fire', as in G. *bal* 'Lord, the sun', *beol* 'ashes with live embers'; *Bealltuinn* 'May Day', and Sc. *balefire* 'bonfire, warning beacon'.

The most important beacon in the Middle East was on Mount Hermon which has been sacred in turn to Canaanites, Israelites, Greeks, Itureans, Christians and Muslims. In Judges 3:3 it is called Baal-Hermon 'the beacon fire of Hermon', and devotees to Pan had a santuary there (Neusner and Green 1999, 287). The reason for its importance is its outlook: whoever controlled the beacon on Hermon controlled communications throughout the Middle East. When the Devil took Jesus up into an exceeding high mountain and showed him 'all the kingdoms of the world' (Matthew 4:1-11) this is not an imaginary scene but the view from the top of Mount Hermon. What the Devil offered was the means to secular control, the beacon on Hermon or fire, personified as an angel (G. *aingeal* 'bright fire').

Turning to the other sex (but fire spreads and reproduces and in fire mythology the sexes and the generations are very confused) the Sybil was worshipped in a cave on a peak in Italy from which one could see both the Adriatic and the Mediterranean Seas. 'Sybil' is a compound of a BL name, perhaps 'gathering fire'. Prophecy is an attribute of beacons as they notify watchers of forthcoming events.

An archaic Gnostic tradition worshipped the Serpent as the source of knowledge and believed that Lucifer 'light-bearer' was created by Sophia (Knowledge). The Serpent is linked to the Horned God by that rare animal, the ram-horned snake. Despite its horns, serpents, dragons and worms like fire are always female, like Knowledge, and usually mothers. The Serpent in the Garden was a Maiden.

The identity of the Serpent as wisdom persisted in medieval Europe where serpents and maidens intertwine in Romanesque churches. Perhaps the most beautiful is the glorious maiden who nurses two serpents on the west gable of the great eleventh-century abbey church of St-Jouin-de-Marnes, looking out over the plains of Deux Sevres in France. The sexual imagery in Romanesque churches is from similar sources: it shows sharp teeth like a deer-trap, staring eyes watching for the beacon, exaggerated male and female organs, flaming leaves and flowers – all pagan symbols for good luck which were still patent among hunters in the Middle Ages, and found permanent expression in stone.

With the spread of Christian belief the Devil came to be identified with the Serpent of Eden and he (or she) became the epitome of evil who turned Man against God. In the New Testament he is responsible for the Temptation of Jesus. Scripture does not provide the Devil with any physical attributes and medieval paintings of devils show groups of deformed small creatures, naked and vulnerable imps. When new technology made printed sources such as *Newes from Scotland* and *Robin Goodfellow* available to a wider public, sensationalism took over and the Devil rapidly acquired his fearsome modern shape as a larger-than-life black man with horns, wings, a hairy body, clawed feet, red eyes and a tail which is long like the serpent's or short like the goat's. This image owes nothing to Scripture and very little to medieval demons but may have been inspired by Pan whose image was familiar in Europe.

The growth of the fantasy

In Scotland his origins were more pedestrian. It was an open secret at the time that the Devil who preached in North Berwick Kirk at Hallowe'en 1590, and who hoped to sink the ship carrying King James VI home from Denmark by witchcraft, was Francis Stewart, fifth Earl of Bothwell, the King's cousin. At that time he was aged twenty-eight or thereabouts and is described as a tall thin man with a dark beard. The sensational nature of this case and the intervention of the King himself means that very little written about witchcraft in Scotland after 1590 is reliable; conversely it shows in some detail how the image of the Devil changed over the years.

We start with the description given by Barbara Naipar. At her trial in 1590, she said the Devil was a gentleman wearing a black gown and a black hat (Pitcairn 1833. iii, 240, note). On 27 January 1591, when Agnes Sampson described the same person on the same occasion, she is reported to have said that 'the dewill stert up in the pulpett, lyk ane mekle blak man, with ane blak beard stikand out lyk ane gettis baird, and ane hie ribbet nois, lyk the beik of ane halk, with ane lang rumpill; cled in ane blak tatie goune; and ane ewill favorit scull bonnett on his heid; haifand ane blak buik in his hand' (Pitcairn 1833, iii, 246): 'the Devil stood up in the pulpit, like a tall black man, with a black beard sticking out like a goat's beard, and a high ribbed nose like the beak of a hawk, with a long tail; dressed in a shabby black gown; and an ugly skull cap on his head; having a black book in his hand'. Whether these embellishments were invented by the witch or by the recording clerk or even by the King, in a few weeks the Devil had gained a black beard like a goat's, a beaked nose like that of a hawk, a long tail, and a black book.

By 1591 when William Wright's sensational woodcut was used to illustrate *Newes from Scotland,* there had been further developments. The Devil preaching to the witches from the pulpit of North Berwick kirk is now a black creature with dramatic wings, clawed hands, and well-developed horns. We cannot comment on his nether parts as they are hidden behind the pulpit, no doubt to avoid provoking lust among readers. Even Montague Summers, who believed in the Devil as a living force, recognised that the image in the *Newes* had been inspired by a theatrical costume and was not a materialisation of supernatural forces (1925, 9-10). As early as 1617 a devil with horns and claws was a standard character in London plays such as John Webster's *The White Devil* and Thomas Dekker's *If This Be Not A Good Play, the Devil Is in It* (Wikipedia).

Sir James Melville provides another imaginary version of events at North Berwick in his *Memoirs* (written between 1603 and his death in 1617). 'Now efter that the deuell had endit his admonitions, he cam down out of the pulpit, and caused all the company to com and kiss his ers, quhilk they said was cauld lyk yce; his body was hard lyk yrn, as they thocht that handled him; his faice was terrible, his nose lyk the bek of an egle, gret bourning eyn; his handis and legis wer herry, with clawes upon his handis and feit lyk the griffon, and spak with a how voice!' (Pitcairn 1833, iii, 240). This is a good imaginary effort but fails to mention wings or a serpentine tail!

The woodcut showing the Devil preaching to the witches in North Berwick church was one of the earliest images to circulate in post-Reformation Scotland. Its impact on the popular imagination is difficult to imagine but must have been considerable. As an image of evil, it could hardly be improved upon; this black and hairy Devil was still inspiring sermons threatening hellfire and tales of the supernatural in the nineteenth century. Many people at the time, having no basis for comparison, believed the Devil was real. If literal belief is now rare, the spurious details are still regarded as genuine folklore, but they too are nothing more than sensational journalism. To retrace our steps, the wise women who gathered at North Berwick at Hallowe'en 1590 saw a tall thin bearded man, whom they knew to be Francis Bothwell, wearing a black cap and a black cloak and carrying a book. Everything else is fake folklore, invented to gratify the public demand for sensational detail and the profits of the book-sellers.

In particular the woodcut must have shaped the view of an evil Devil in the minds of the Reformed clergy. Some of the details may have come from Denmark where James VI had spent some months in 1589 to celebrate his marriage to the Protestant princess Anne. Seeking out and destroying witches was an obsession of his new brother-in-law Christian IV who no doubt told James how to recognise and deal with the menace.

Reality was very different from the King's imaginary fiend. Pearson (1897, vol.2, 22-23) quotes a statement by a German witch: 'Had she a sweetheart-devil? (*Buhlteufeln*). "Yes! The Sniveller." Did she not fear this devil? "No, he was only a sweetheart-devil." Was there a difference between a sweetheart-devil and other devils? "Why, of course! The sweetheart-devil was not a real devil, only a witch's sweetheart like the Sniveller, who was old Zimmerpeterle's son.' Pearson's witch shows that the witch-gatherings were real meetings, to which the women took with them a symbol of the old hearth or home goddess, a broom or in some cases a fire-fork (*Feuergabel*), and that the devils were real men of the neighbourhood. There are no supernatural elements.

The Devil and the coven

In Scotland after 1590 there arose two divergent images of the Devil. The first makes a brief appearance in the New Testament as the Tempter of Christ. His Scriptural nonentity was eked out with fantastic details and presented to the people as the Anti-Christ, a supernatural bogeyman. The Devil was also the name given by the Church to the leader of a coven, which the Church justified by arguing that as witches lived outwith the control of the Church they were therefore under the influence of Satan their Master who was always present with them, even when he was invisible. To his witches this so-called 'Devil' was simply their master, whom the Auldearn witches treated with scant repect but addressed as 'Our Lord'. He was an undeniably human figure whom they knew to be a man, both at the coven meetings and when they met him in daily life. They readily admitted to the existence of this Lord who had caused them to reject their baptism and follow him, but they did not believe he was in any way supernatural. This coven-Devil was seldom horned and was equipped with an artificial penis or *fascinum* which he wore at coven meetings and which is described by many different witches as being cold, hard and unnatural. No examples are known to survive. The witches often described their Devil as a coarse or shaggy black man, 'very rough', by which it seems that at the sabbat he wore the pelt of an animal such as a cat, a dog or a bull. Sometimes his costume was complete with horns, tail and cloven hooves but these appendages seem to have varied according to the animal who provided the hide. When William Barton, a warlock, and his wife went with others to a meeting in the Pentland Hills in 1655, the Devil of the Kirkliston witches, who can hardly be said to have kept a low profile, went before them in the likeness of a rough tanny dog playing on a pair of pipes. The tune he played was 'The silly bit chicken, gar cast it a pickle and it will grow meikle'. He carried a candle in his bottom under his tail (the dog's tail) 'which played ey wig wag wig wag' (Sinclair 1685, 163).

The Scriptural and the pagan images had little in common and this must have led to bewilderment on the part of coven witches accused of supernatural dealing with the Anti-Christ. One must wonder to what extent the Kirk Sessions believed they were engaged in a battle with supernatural forces. However it is curious that they were evidently reluctant to punish the masters of the covens, though they had no hesitation about executing whole covens of witches. Did they believe that their own fictions had physical existence, like the fiend that John Knox is said to have raised in the churchyard?

The leaders of covens were probably more interested in experimental and practical black magic than in dancing, feasting, dressing up or ritual copulation but they needed to keep their witches obedient, devoted and, above all, empowered and this required regular sabbats following set procedures. Some of these devils were more advanced than others. According to Sir James Melville, Francis Stewart had reduced witchcraft to an experimental science. When his witches assembled at North Berwick Kirk he quizzed them about 'what skaith they had done, whow many they had won to their oppinion sen ther last meting, what succes the melting of the pictour had tane, and sic vain toyes'. He or his Registrar, John Fean, noted the names of those attending and made notes in the black book.

The Devil confused

Sir George Mackenzie (1636-1691) was among the first to recognise openly that the Devil was imaginary and the witch-hunts were a scandal. One poor woman had asked him, when she was accused, if a woman might be a witch and not know it (Scott 1830, 293) and the answer was Yes, certainly, if her neighbours accused her of being a witch. Many women accused of Devil-worship had no idea who or what was meant by 'Satan'. Even when he was understood by all concerned to be the male person who led a coven and in no way supernatural or more powerful than the witches themselves, the replies obtained point to confusion. That the accused were confused about the identity of the Devil is everywhere apparent and is a striking measure of their limited command of English, their innocence of the charges brought against them and the Church's failure to control the situation.

In one series of trials at Dalkeith in 1661 we can deduce that the women have honestly tried to answer the leading question: 'When did you last have sex with the Devil?' 'Under pressure the women would work out that if they had indeed had carnal dealing with the Devil it must be most likely to have been any extramarital intercourse in which they had indulged: the halfling lad in the barn, or the man in the kirkland in Dunsyre. In the absence of any such encounter it must have been in the shape of their husbands' (Larner 1981, 147-8). Isobel Smith confessed that she was alone gathering heather when she fell in with 'ane braw gentleman'; Jonet Watson met 'ane prettie boy, in grein clothes'; Helene Casse 'met with the Devill in the liknes of a man with greine cloaths in the links of Dudingstone qr he wes gathering sticks amongst the whines'; Isobel Ramsay met a pleasant young man who asked politely where she lived, and 'how does the minister', and before they separated, gave her sixpence with which she bought meal. Her next meeting with the Devil was in her own house in her own bed and in the likeness of her own husband (Murray 1921, 37-40). 'The clerks' habit of speaking of every person of the other sex with whom the witches had sexual intercourse at the Sabbath as a 'Devil' has led to much confusion. The various 'devil's described do not present a very impressive appearance' (Murray 1921, 183).

In describing the Devil, light is a common theme, probably because a Gaelic speaker would deduce that a *Diabhol* or *Sàtan* had something to do with fire. In at least three cases in Lothian the Devil is described as a lantern or torch. Agnes Sampsoun said that in 1590 she sailed out of North Berwick harbour in a boat like 'ane chimnay', the Devil going before them like 'ane ruk of hay' (Pitcairn 235). Catherine Wallace and Janet Straton of Prestonpans also described the Devil as a truss of hay (Pitcairn 1833, vol.1, 398; Larner 1981, 147). A truss of hay was normally set alight to send a signal or to acknowledge a signal. Was this 'Devil' perhaps a navigation light on a small boat?

Sir George Mackenzie told of a poor weaver who described the devil enigmatically 'like flies dancing about the candle' (Scott *Letters*, 1830, 293). In the popular account of the trial of John Cunningham, known as Feane or Fian, at Prestonpans in East Lothian in 1590 the court alleged that Satan had promised John Cunningham to 'rais ane mist, and cast the kingis Majestie in England.' To achieve the mist Satan took a thing 'lyke to ane fute ball, quhilk apperit to the said Johnne lyk a wisp, and caist the same in the see, quhilk causit ane vapour and ane reik [smoke] to ryis.' A wisp is another word for a small bunch of dried grass but this context appears to describe a lantern or a container for some smoking material (Dalyell 1835, 245-6). Janet Boyman of Edinburgh in 1572 thought the Devil was a whirlwind (Larner 1981, 147), which means only that he passed by very quickly: the metaphor is more often associated with the passage of a gang of fairies.

As is invariably the case with supernatural invention in Scotland, confusion about the nature of the Devil arises out of a loss of sense or a misleading change of meaning at the interface between a clerk educated in English and a woman who fails to understand his questions. The resulting confusion can often be resolved by working back through known examples in Gaelic; but what are we to make of the witch in Strathtay who avowed that she saw Satan on his way to a meeting at Tullypowrie in the form of a cart-wheel describing a figure of eight? (Kennedy 1927, 50).

Charmers and Covens

Trial documents for the period up to 1620 show no certain evidence for organised covens but reveal a busy network of independent healers and charmers, men and women, who often collaborated locally on difficult cases. Most were tried singly charged with witchcraft and sorcery but sometimes a family group or a married couple were tried together. Black (1938) names fifty-seven witches who were tried in Aberdeenshire in the years 1596-1597. All, as far as one can judge, were independent practitioners, though as noted above the minister of Lumphanan once or twice mentions a shadowy or invisible Devil (SCM 1841, I, 84-194). Given the absence of corroboration he appears to be a figment raised by the prosecution on the grounds that all witchcraft was by definition devilish.

We know very little about the relationship between local charmers and the local coven. Sometimes a charmer or warlock was recruited into the coven. The Warlock of Fossaway, John Brugh, who was tried in 1643, was for most of his life an independent charmer of good reputation. He had been taught by a traditional great witch, Naunce Nicklerich, sister-daughter to Nik Neveing, a famous witch who belonged to a famous family of witches who were perhaps based in St Andrews. John owned two enchanted stones and was in demand for his cures over a wide area. But at his trial he confessed to helping Satan to dig up three bodies in the kirkyard of Glendevon and another at the Kirk of Muckart to put the rotting flesh above the doors of a byre and a stable to curse the animals (Reid 1899, 197). This was certainly satanic business, not John's. It is not common to find a charmer in the native tradition who works malefice with a Devil of the new type, as appears to be the case here. The Carnwath witch Jean Lachlane at her trial in 1643 confessed that she had been a charmer for twenty years before she met the Devil and joined his coven (RPC ii, 148) but four Midlothian healers – Christian Lewingstoun, Bessie Aitken, Christian Saidler and Janet Stewart – who were tried together in 1597 appear to be typical of the majority in that they were never part of an organised coven and had no dealings with the Devil.

Very few men were ever charged with witchcraft and even fewer were (perhaps) leaders of covens – Thomas Brown of Pittenweem, tried in 1705, is perhaps an example (Black 1938, 82). But the prosecution in compiling its evidence seems to have used the term 'Devil' for any male witch regardless of his status or function. Many covens, including Pittenweem, had one or two male officers who kept the roll and administered the membership. In 1590 John Cunningham or Fian was the Devil's registrar or secretary in East Lothian and kept a record of those who attended meetings at North Berwick (Pitcairn 1833, III, 209). According to different testimonies, it appears that meetings at Crook of Devon in 1662 were attended by seven different 'devils' whose functions are not known but may have been social or recreational: Lucifer, perhaps their master, who rode a horse and wore *fulyairt* (worn-out) clothes and a Spanish cloak; Samuel, who had grey clothes, a blue bonnet and a beard; Charles, a bonnie young lad with a blue bonnet; Simon, a man in dun-coloured clothes; another man called Thomas Roy; a young fellow with a dusty-coloured coat; and David Mahoun, an uncouth man with black clothes and a hood (Reid 1899, 219-252). At Auldearn, according to Isobell, every witch of her coven of thirteen had her 'spreit' or minor Devil who served her (their names are listed below). Despite being in English, their nick-names are appropriate to fairy folk or hunters and may represent English versions of old Gaelic names. Isobell said there were many other 'Devils' waiting on the Master Devil but 'he is bigger and mor awfull than the rest of the Divellis and they all reverence him'. Perhaps to scotch any idea that they were imaginary or ghosts Isobell added that she recognised all of them 'quhan they appeir lyk a man' (Pitcairn 1833, III, 606, 614). Intercourse or 'dealing' at the sabbat with anyone other than the Devil is seldom reported (Larner 1981, 151) but in a cult devoted to fertility this may perhaps be taken as given. We know ten of the thirteen names of the minor Devils of the Auldearn coven. Murray reported that French witches also danced with their lovers wearing blue, yellow or black clothing (1921, 232). The Auldearn names appear to provide a rare glimpse of pagan hunting rituals. The spelling and, of course, the form of the names, is as reported by the clerk and not necessarily as deponed by the witch. Three names are missing.

1 Hendrie Laing.

2 Mak Hector or MacKeeler, a young man in grass-green.

3 Robert the Jackis, an aged man in dune who is 'glaikit and gowkit'. Sc. *jack* was a kind of leather armour.

4 Robert the Rule, who wore sadd [dark]-dun. Perhaps G. *ruladh* 'slaughtering'.

5 Rorie, who wore yellow. *Ruairidh* was 'facetiously applied to the fox'.

6 The Roring Lyon, in sea-green. The lion, as a great hunter and as a pun on G. *lion* 'gin, snare' and 'fill, replenish, satiate' was a very old and very popular hunting pun.

7 Sanders, the Read Reiver, in black. Sandie was a name of the Lowland Devil and appears to mean 'hunter' or 'he who gathers'.

8 Swein, in grass-green. Archaic Gaelic *samh* 'to gather' + *ain* 'fire'.

9 Thieff of Hell. A thief or robber in any archaic context is a hunter.

10 Thomas a Fearie. G. *faire* 'to keep watch'. A hunter.

As noted the Devils or Lords of the Scottish covens seem to have been educated men of a prosperous class – members of the rural elite – for whom it was an entertaining and occasionally profitable business to run a coven. The witches at Auldearn addressed their Devil as 'Our Lord' but according to Isobell, 'Som tymis, among owr selwis, we wold be calling him "Blak Johne", or the lyk, and he wold ken it, and heir ws weill aneughe; and he ewin then com to ws, and say "I ken weill anewgh what ye wer sayeing of me!" And then he vold beat and buffet ws werie sor' (Pitcairn 1833, III, 613). Moray appears to have been a stronghold of the coven movement as the Auldearn coven is only one of three in the same area. From what Isobell tells us, it is evident that the Auldearn coven at least was modelled on Continental and particularly on French examples (cf Murray 1921, 183, 232). That the master was not a Gaelic speaker we can deduce from the fact that he did not give his witches traditional Gaelic aliases but invented English names such as Through the Corn-Yaird, and Ower the Dyke With It, picturesque but without deeper meaning. He taught his witches the words of various spells which they recited kneeling before him, with their hair over their faces, their hands raised and their eyes fixed on his face. Was this the local tradition or had he read about this method in a book? He used a selected few to make clay models of the male children of the Laird of Park (they died) and to make a witch-poke to cause the death of Mr Harie Forbes, the local minister (he did not die but demitted his charge in 1663, moved to England, and was still alive there in 1678).

There is only one Scottish mention of a disguise. The dittay against Barbara Napier (1590), which is otherwise reliable, alleges that at North Berwick at Hallowe'en in 1590, when the witches danced in the kirkyard, John Fein led the ring *musselit* or masked (Pitcairn 1833, I, 246). It is probable that those involved in hunting magic (the fairy folk in their dances) imitated the stag and the chain of hunters, as Scottish country dancers still do. However to say that the leader of a coven or a coven witch appeared 'in the likeness' of an animal does not imply any supernatural change of shape but only that he wore an animal skin to show he was on official coven business. The Devil at Auldearn appears to have worn the skin of any animal except the goat. Isobell Gowdie stated that at one time or another he had taken the shape of a cat, a dog, a stirk, a bull, a deer, a roe deer, a dog, and a horse (Pitcairn 1833, III,

613). This explains how Isobell could honestly state that he wore sometimes boots and sometimes shoes, and had cloven feet. Isobell also might go about 'in the likeness' of a hare, a cat, a dog or even a crow when on official business.

That the animal costume made a great impact on the inexperienced is evident from Guernsey in 1617 where a new witch met the Devil in the form of a dog, as she thought. But he had two great horns sticking up, his front paws seemed to her like hands, and when he swore her in he stood up on his hind legs.

We can deduce that the purpose of masks and animal skins was not to conceal the identity of the wearer, as the leader of a local coven and all its members were well-known to each other, but to identify him as the leader of a coven and to equip him for his ritual function. Witches of both sexes repeatedly say that his penis (or his body, or his hand) was unnaturally cold, that his kiss was a cold kiss, his semen was like ice, and his voice was muffled, hollow or rough (Murray 1921, 63-65). That he used an artificial penis is evident but none of the Scottish testimonies mention horns. The reason is probably not doctrinal but a shortage of suitable skins in the poor parts of the country.

The wearing of an animal skin by the Devil explains the Church's opposition to guisers at Hallowe'en and New Year, as they also wore skins, in this case to identify themselves as hunters. The practice of dressing a man in the hide of an ox was denounced in Northumbria in 1614 but was still reported from the Hebrides c.1900. At Hogmanay and perhaps at other times, a man known as the *Gillean Callaig* was dressed in the hide of a bull, complete with horns, hooves and tail, and perambulated through the township while his followers beat on the hide with sticks like a drum. In Lochaber a hide was worn by one man while the others beat at it with sticks, shouting 'Calluin of the yellow sack of hide' (McNeill 1961, III, 89). Guisers were originally hunters collecting a levy of food to sustain them until the hunt began. As noted, the sabbat was intended to bring good luck to hunters.

The conclusion has to be that there were no significant links between the Devil of the Christian Bible and the Lord of the covens. Apart from one lurid and quite recent woodcut there is no trace in Scotland of a pagan god with or without horns. Power rests with the Lady, who is so far invisible. This includes the power to chose her consort. The Fairy King or Devil danced in the shape of a stag but he never claimed to be a god or to have more than delegated powers. For the rule of the Devil over the covens we have to wait until 1590 when, thanks to the efforts made by James VI to suppress the witch cult, certain members of the elite began to be interested in this potential source of power and influence.

The great fallacy and injustice of the witch hunts arises from the fact that the Church saw the Devil in a supernatural or religious light, complete with wings, horns and claws. He was the Tempter, the Anti-Christ, the source of all evil. But witches joined the covens because they had been promised a modest prosperity, understood as enough to eat or nice clothes. Intercourse with their master was the essential feature, but they often treated him with scant respect and their comments on the poor quality of the food and other benefits he provided are of a piece with their comments on his hard, cold member. The Devil did not seem to go out of his way to attract their gratitude but they accepted his promises of prosperity and knowledge and sometimes of revenge and believed he was offering an opportunity to better their lives. They may have believed that their fertility ritual was for the greater benefit of their communities but this is a shadowy deduction based on their willingness to serve as witches despite the risks and lack of obvious benefits.

In the narrow view of the Kirk, the case against witches in Scotland came to focus on two legal transactions: the witches' renunciation of their baptism and their pact with the Devil. Very few of those accused can have had any clear idea of what this implied in theological terms but these two allegations are repeated in many trials in very similar terms and came to be the factors that defined a witch.

The Satanic bond and promise of material prosperity are reported from an earlier date. Thom Reid who tried to persuade Bessie Dunlop (tried in 1576) to join the fairy folk was the King of Faerie, not the master of a coven. At their third meeting he 'promeist her bayth geir, horsis, and ky [cattle], and vthir graith, gif scho wald denye her Christindome, and the faith sche tuke at the funt-stane'. When she still refused, he became 'sumthing angrie' and said 'Seis thow nocht me, baith meith-worth, claith-worth, and gude aneuch lyke in persoun; and suld make hir far better nor euer sche was'. But Bessie was already well-enough endowed with worldly goods, though as vulnerable as anyone else to bad luck, illness and the death of her stock. She was nevertheless involved in the fairy world. She had been instructed in the secret recipes for ointments, herbs, poisons, rituals, incantations and charms that were the stock-in-trade of native healers and specifically of fairy folk by her fairy master, Thom Reid. 'Quhen sundrie personnes cam to hir to seik help for thair beist, thair kow or yow, or for ane barne that was tane away with ane evill blast of wind, or elf-grippit, sche gait and sperit at Thom'. Her role as a fairy healer was played down in the trial record but it went beyond normal routine remedies. The child that was taken away by an evil blast of wind or elf-grippit, had been taken by the fairies. Bessie, like Andro Thom and Alesoun Piersoun, was at home in the fairy world and in touch with the ghosts of the dead. With her belief in the afterlife the prospect of her own death might not have been as dramatic as one might now imagine.

In Scotland many aspects of the old religion remain obscure but from certain of the earlier trials (Bessie Dunlop, Alesoune Piersoun, Andro Man) and from the much later but geographically removed trial of Donald McIlmichal, we can make a clear distinction between fairy folk and the coven movement, between the rule of the Queen and the rule of the Devil. They might co-exist, as they did at Darnaway, but one represented the old order of hunting magic and the other the new coven movement and we may imagine there was conflict between them. The old religion dwindled as hunting died out and gave rise to very few trials. After 1600 in the Lowlands (a century later in the Highlands) the Fairy Queen receded into fake folklore in which some fragments of her original power are embedded.

Appendix to Chapter 4: Names for the Devil

Oh thou! whatever title suit thee, Auld Hornie, Satan, Nick, or Clootie...

The original meaning of the word 'devil', as a Black Man or as lord of the animals, is fire. It is not surprising to find the Devil presiding over the magical aspects of hunting as he rules over Hell, the great fiery place. The Devil did not like church bells because they replaced his beacon as a source of information and system of control. Church bells were effective against lightning; but they were also effective against pagan beacons. This is confirmed by the story of St Quentin, who lamed the Devil at Llanblethian in the Vale of Glamorgan, Wales (Bord 2004, 114). Any lame or one-legged god or hero personifies a beacon on his pole. St Quentin is celebrated by the Church on 31 October, Samhain, no doubt at one time a hunt gathering at Llanblethian.

Names for God were limited to The Almighty, The Best, The Guid, and The Wye and they were not in popular use. There is a remarkable contrast with the plethora of irreverent and even affectionate names for the Devil, both in Gaelic and in English, suggesting that he was a familiar, respected and reassuring figure. They show a good many links with archaic Gaelic and with hunting but none with the Anti-Christ of the Presbyterians. They have little to do with the self-styled 'Lord' of the coven, but:-

Many of the Lowland names would be appropriate nicknames for the leader or guidman of a witch coven but the Highland names (below) appear to refer more directly to a horned or hairy animal such as a bull or a stag. The prevalence of witch belief in Lowland Scotland suggest that these names arose among peasants whose immediate ancestors had spoken Gaelic and who were much more familiar with the pagan cult of the deer hunters than with the Christian faith. They suggest a horned guidman who was responsible for hunting magic at local level. There appear to be no names referring to the devil's most prominent organ but they may remain to be recognised.

Black Lad, The. In archaic Gaelic, *an gille dubh*, 'servant of the deer'. An Gille dubh was the son of the Maiden, at Kilmallie. The witches of Auldearn talked about their devil disrespectfully as the Black Man.

Bobbie, Auld. Rob or Robin 'robber, hunter', a common name among witches and demons.

Chiel or **Chield, Auld**. Scots *chiel* 'lad' may be linked to G. *chùil* 'nook (deer trap)', as Hule. Sc. *chiel* and E. *child* may have been names for a young hunter.

Cloutie, Cloots or **Auld Cloutie**. Scots *cloot* 'hoof' reflecting G. *clùid* 'nook (deer trap)', both having a cloven shape.

Donald, Auld. 'From having assumed the shape of a Highlander'. More probably from G. *damh* 'stag'.

Gillatrypes. An obscene dance popular with witches in Moray. Probably 'servant of the herds'.

Grapus. G. *grib* 'griffon', E. *grab*, *grip*. G. and Sc. *grap* or *grape* 'three-tined fork' is a hunter's trident, once made of reindeer antler. The *Krampus* were guisers disguised as horned devils who paraded on St Nicolas (5-6 December) in parts of rural Austria.

Guidman, The. G. *guidhe* 'beseeching, praying, intercession'. The Guidman's Croft or Acre was a piece of wild ground (residual deer forest) devoted to the Devil. Andrew Man (d.1598) dedicated several such reserves or wards to 'the hynd knicht quhom thow confessis to be a spreit, and puttis four stanis in the four nokis of the ward, and charmes the samen, and theirby haillis the guidis, and preservis thame from the lunsaucht [lung disease] and all vther diseasis, and thow forbiddis to cast faill or divett [cut turf] thereon, or put plewis therin; and this thow did in the Manis of Innes, in the Manis of Caddell, and in dyvers vtheris places.' (SCM I, 120).

Halyman. The Halyman's Rig, like the Guidman's Croft, was left uncultivated in his honour but it was originally the plot of the guid mennis or fairies. Halyman is similar to Wallaway (a Shetland devil), Walliman and Wallidraggle. All probably derive from G. *gal* 'flame, kindred, slaughter, valour', so 'hunter'. The original guidmen were fairies and in the plural.

Hynd Knicht: see The Guidman.

Hind Etin was a fairy in a ballad. Perhaps G. *cinneadh* 'clan, tribe, kin' and *aodhan* 'fire'. The Red Etin was a giant (a beacon).

Hangie, Auld. G. *caingeann* 'prayer, supplication'.

Hornie, Auld Hornie. The Devil as a horned beast. The only example of a horned devil.

Hule. G. *chùil* 'nook (deer trap)'. Perhaps the same as Halyman (above).

Mahoun. Mohammed was believed to be an evil pagan god.

Mishanter, The. G. *mi-sheun* 'ill-luck, misfortune'. A curse: 'Go to the mishanter!'

Nick, Auld Nick. Is this G. *nighean* 'daughter'?

Nickieben. A female name, G. *nighean* 'daughter' + *ban* 'fire'. cf the witch alias NicNiven and the common 'devil' name Auld Nick.

Plotcock. 'wee Pluto'.

Robin son of Artes, known in Ireland in the fourteenth century (Murray 1921, 154). G. *art, airt* 'God'.

Rougie, Auld. G. *ruaig* 'pursuit, hunt, chase'. Sc. *ruggair* 'depredator (hunter)'. Sc. *rugging* 'conveys the idea of rapacity in seizing and carrying off the property of others'. The *rugged* property was originally deer belonging to the Cailleach.

Ruffie, Auld. Sc. *ruffy* 'tallow candle, blaze used for fishing by night'.

Sandie, Auld Sandie. G. *seantaidh* 'primeval, primitive (hunting lore)'.

Sim, Simmie. G. *simid* 'mallet, beetle', used by hunters to stun animals prior to cutting their throats.

Smith, The Auld. G. *gobhainn* 'smith' is a regular pun on *gamhainn* 'stag, stirk'.

Sorra, The. This is more likely to be G. *soraidh* 'success, health, happiness' than E. *sorrow*.

Suitie, Sawtan, Sathan. A Biblical name, found in the Book of Job, where God speaks out of a whirlwind. The Gaels would understood it as *samh* 'to gather' + *teine* 'fire'.

Tary, The. G. *tarbh* 'bull' or *tòir* 'pursuit, chase'.

Thief, the Auld Thief, the Muckle Thief. A thief was conventionally a hunter.

Thrummy or **Thrummy-Caip**. Scots 'shaggy cap', made of thrums or weavers' ends. Ellen Gray when in prison in Aberdeen was visited by 'an agit man, beirdit, with a quhyt gown and a thrummit hatt'. He told her she was 'ane evill trublit woman, who should forgif all creature and trust in God and a good assise'. He sounds more like a prison chaplain than a visitor from the Pit.

Wallaway or **Wallowae**, a name for the Devil in Shetland. Perhaps G. *galabhas* from *gal* 'flame' + *bàs* 'death', 'hunter', now 'glutton, flatterer' in a typical late inversion of the original sense. Wallowae is also cognate to *Gilledubh* 'servant of the deer'; perhaps a *gille* tended a fire. In Sanday c.1750 he was 'de muckle black Wallawa'.

Walliman, another version of the name of the Devil in Orkney. G. *gal* 'flame, kindred, slaughter, valour'. The same as Halyman, a Lowland name for the devil (below).

Wee Man, The.

Wirricow or **Wurricoe**, a demon or bogle. G. *mire-chatha* 'battle-frenzy'. G. *mire* 'play, pastime; mirth, sportiveness, merriment, rapture, ecstasy' describes the feelings aroused by the sabbat and by the hunt.

Gaelic names for the Devil (Campbell, 2001, 160 and other sources)

Like his virgin mother the Cailleach, the Devil, with his his blackness, roughness and burning eyes is an evolved personification of a hunt beacon. When he is vanquished in a Gaelic folk-tale he flies up the chimney in a puff of smoke or disappears in a flame of fire. Only two of those listed are Biblical in origin. It appears that the link between the Devil and the Adversary was not made by the Gaels until the Reformation. Several others are generic concepts for evil or misfortune which might be translated as 'Devil' in English but do not carry the same weight in Gaelic. G. *braman* 'misadventure', *breamas* 'mischief, mischance', *donas* 'mischief, harm, bad luck' and *mi-sheun* 'ill-luck, misfortune' are used in curses which mean 'Bad luck take you!' but which might be translated as 'Go to the devil!' Where the hero of a Lowland tale confronts and outwits a sinister black man with cloven feet, horns and a tail, his Gaelic counterpart faces a *duin-uasal* 'gentleman' or a 'shifty' or 'pranky' lad who plays tricks on him.

Abharsair. E. *adversary*. Biblical rather than traditional.

Aibhisteir, An t- 'the one from the abyss', from *aibheis* 'an abyss, a depth' (the pit of Hell). Biblical.

Ainspiorad, An t- 'the bad spirit'.

Andras 'fury, devil'. G. *dreos* 'blaze'.

Aon fhear mor, An 'the one big one'.

Art, the father of an Irish devil. Said to mean 'god'.

Balkin 'lord of the northern mountains'; a beacon. According to Reginald Scot (1584), Balkin was an urisk in Sutherland, Caithness and the adjacent islands, 'who was reputed to be a giant and the father of the fairies.' He also says that the fairies of Orkney spoke an archaic form of Gaelic. Balkin is a diminutive of AG. *bal* 'fire' and of G. *ball* 'penis'. Giants are invariably beacons; the 'father' of the fairies was a hunt beacon.

Bidein 'biter', the serpent. G. *bid* 'fence, hedge' suggests the older meaning is 'deer-trap'.

Bochdainn 'poverty; trouble; mischief; bad luck; mishap'. G. *bochd* 'fire'.

Bodach 'old churl, bogle'. G. *bod* 'penis'.

Bradaidh 'thief; a hunter'.

Braman 'misadventure, mischief'.

Brian 'angel' (bright fire); archangel; god; god of evil'. Equated with the Black Lad of Kilmallie, Son of the Bones, a son of the Maiden who conceived him when impregnated by the ashes of dead men's bones. He is also said to be the son of Bride. Brian was also the name of St Michael's white horse. Brian was perhaps the most important manifestation of the Devil among the Gaels but was displaced or destroyed by the Archangel Michael.

Ciseal, from G. *cìs* 'homage, reverence'.

Connan 'hunting fire'. Kilichonan in Rannoch. G. *connan* 'lust' is secondary, hence *aisling chonnain* 'sexual dream'. Cill Chonain in north Skye (NG2261) was a beacon site close to Dun Borrafiach ('fire of the deer'), a broch (NG2363). A traditional verse, 'The Three Winds', links Connan with fire.

Dana 'the evil one'. As *Donas*.

Deamhan E. *demon*. G. *deamh* 'want, deficiency'.

Diabhal G. *dia* 'god' + AG. *bal* 'fire'. cf Lucifer 'light bearer'.

Dithean 'killer', from G. *dith* 'die, perish'.

Dolas mor, An 'great sorrow'.

Domhnall Dubh 'Black Donald', for AG. *domhnach* 'deer forest' + *dubh* 'deer'.

Donas 'wickedness, misfortune, bad luck' probably a recent evolution from G. *dòmhnaich* 'deer forest, domain, world'. The witch alias Cassindonisch or *Cas-an donais* from Easter Ross (1577), said to mean 'Devil's foot' (Sutherland, 1977, 132) but closer to 'hunt of the forest or domain'.

Droch Spioraid, An 'the bad spirit'.

Fear dubh, Am 'black man' or 'man of the deer'.

Fear nach abair mi, Am 'the one I will not mention'.

Fear nach fhiach, Am 'the worthless one'.

Fear ud, Am 'yon one'.

Gille dubh 'servant of the deer'; the Black Lad.

Gille neumh 'holy lad' or 'servant of the deer sanctuary' (Campbell, vol. II, 318). 'A pranky man', full of tricks.

Glisoganach 'the shimmering one' of Strathtay. A Black Man or bonfire. He was tall and dark and had a single glittering eye (Kennedy, 1927, 46) which identifies him as a beacon.

Goillin or **Goiline**, an Irish term for the Devil. Related to G. *goileam* 'to kindle fire', *goill* 'war, fight (hunt)', *goilean* 'greedy-gut'.

Mac an Rusgaich 'lad of the frays'. G. *ruisgeanta* 'fond of fighting (hunting)'.

Mac Mallachd 'the hairy lad', perhaps referring to a wild bull; also found as Mac mollachd 'the son of cursing' or G. *mol* 'assembly, gathering'. *Mac* may be *magh* 'plain' referring to the deer forest.

Mogh, **Magh** or **Mabh** 'the chief fairy in Ireland'.

Muc Mhór Dhubh 'the big black pig' (Mackenzie 1935, 52), perhaps originally 'the big deer forest'. The equivalence of *magh* 'deer forest' and *muc* 'pig, devil' might explain the pork taboo in the Highlands. The Devil usually had a horse's hoof but sometimes he had a pig's trotter (Campbell, 1900, 290-2).

Muisean 'a mean or sordid fellow, ramscallion (hunter)'.

Piullaidh, for *peallaidh*, in Lewis. 'The hairy one' (Mackenzie 1935, 234).

Reabhach 'crafty, tricky person'.

an Riabhach mòr 'the great brindled one' identifies him as a stag.

Rosad, An 'the mean mischievous one'.

CHAPTER 5: COVENS AND SABBATS

Consider this entry from the Presbytery Book of Strathbogie, dated 4 February 1649. 'The Kirk officer of Echt in Aberdeenshire, James Arthour, was accused of singing New Yeir soungis on New Year's Eve through sundry houses and farmtouns and was suspended from his position and subsequently condemned to stand in penance before the congregation for this superstitious old custom' (John Stuart (ed.) (1843). Preface, xiii).

Or this old custom. The baking of sour cakes on the eve of St Luke's by fair-folk in Rutherglen in Lanarkshire presisted until 1822 (McNeill 1961, III, 21-22). This ceremonial baking had many of the features of a sabbat: six or eight women who meet at night, a woman known as the Queen or Bride, who toasts the cakes and her maidens. They all have ritual names such as Todler, Hodler, Mrs Baker, Best Maid etc. They sing the usual bawdy songs while beating out the cakes. In addition, St Luke's Fair on 18 October is close to Old Hallowe'en (on 20 October) and the Quarter Day.

The covens which were targeted by the authorities in Lowland Scotland in the seventeenth century have perhaps attracted more attention than they justify, at least in terms of identifying the origins of witchcraft and how it was manifested in Scotland. It is proposed here that the covens were not part of an age-old pagan tradition but a relatively recent development showing Continental influence and grafted on to the native cult. There was no central organisation that we know of but the covens nevertheless followed a similar pattern in every place, so much so that we can talk about a movement. Its leaders were English-speaking and educated, a fact that explains the absence of covens from the Highlands. Had covens been part of native Gaelic pagan tradition we would find them all over Scotland, in the Highlands as well as the Lowlands and Borders and at a much earlier date. But we do not. It seems they are not prehistoric. In fact we can probably trace the rise of covens in Scotland to the witch-craze spread by James VI.

Not everyone shared the King's horror of witches. It would seem on the contrary that quite a number of people shared Boswell's hopes of harnessing their imagined occult powers and turning them to their own use. The change can be traced through the trials. Before c.1620 most of the witches tried in Scotland were midwives, charmers or healers who worked independently or cooperated in a loose local network. They were accused of duping the public. After 1620 there is a change from solitary witches to collectives or covens who are accused of being in thrall to the Devil. We will come back to the signs of this change.

The coven is found only in those parts of Scotland controlled by an English-speaking elite: the Lowlands and for a variable distance into the more accessible parts of the Highlands, from Bute to Moray. As the same English-speaking elite controlled the Church and the courts and had established the infrastructure needed to administer the trial process it was only a matter of time before the covens were targeted by the church or by enemies of the local Master. One man's occult experiment was another man's devilish sorcery.

As noted already, at the Reformation in 1560 most Scots were still Gaelic-speaking and the northwards progress of English under the impetus of the Reformed Church, which produced the great divide between the English Lowlands and the Gaelic Highlands, had barely reached the Forth. We can confirm the persistent use of Gaelic in Lothian by the use of Gaelic honorific names given to new witches at their initiation. Up to the end of the sixteenth century, Gaelic witch-names such as Cane 'bright', Fian 'hunter', Gray-meal 'herd beacon', Knell 'shapely', Likkit 'light', and Wallydraggle 'comely, good-looking' were still in use in Lothian. They appear from their content to have been honorific names used within the cult when it was still devoted to hunting magic. After this date they are replaced by mundane 'coven' names such as The Pretty Dancer, Beelzebug or Christian.

There was a precedent for the covens. Before witches were recruited into covens dedicated to working for a single Master, from time to time a larger group was recruited by word of mouth to work for a member of the elite, sometimes under the overall control of a master man or warlock. One such gathering took place in Easter Ross in 1577 to work for Katherine Ross, Lady Munro, who wanted to kill off two inconvenient in-laws. The leading members of her consortium appear to have been Maggie Bawdem, the Great Witch of Chanonry, and the seer Kenneth Odhar. In addition some twenty-four more witches and warlocks from around Tain and Castle Fowlis were involved. Katherine Ross was tried in 1590 but acquitted.

A similar recruitment took place in East Lothian in 1590 when a large number of witches from Keith, Longniddry, Prestonpans, Saltoun, Tranent and other places gathered at North Berwick to support the efforts of Francis, Earl of Bothwell, to drown King James VI and his new bride, Anne of Denmark. Bothwell ran his conventicle of women with the help of John Cunningham, a local school-master, as his secretary. According to their different skills these women raised the wind, made a wax dolly, made witch-pokes, tried sark magic, and cast spells involving cats and iron. Bothwell made a poor show. First he forgot to bring the wax model, and then he forgot to call Cunningham by his new nickname, Rob the Rowar, which had been assigned to him as Master of the Rows, or Rolls (Scott 130, 313). With a Master like Bothwell there was no hope of success. He justified their low opinion by fleeing abroad and abandoning them to the fatal petulance and cruelty of King James.

These two gatherings have the appearance of a coven but they were temporary alliances focussed on a single outcome. Had they succeeded in their purpose the witches would no doubt have returned to their private practices in their home villages. We hear very little about successful plots. But it is not until 1621 that we find the first trial of what looks very like members of a coven, defined as a regularly established band of witches, recruited for life, who meet quarterly or more often, who were bound by oath to their master or Lord, and who practiced ritual sex. Every coven follows this same pattern despite the apparent absence of any central authority or Grand Master who might impose a general standard for organisation or discipline. Nor is there any publication other than the King's own *Daemonologie* (1596) which might have been used as a guide. This uniformity suggests that esoteric knowledge was passed from one Master to another at secretive meetings.

The Coven

The first certain trial of coven witches probably took place at Inverkeithing in Fife in 1621 and was followed in the next ten years by several more. After 1630 trials of independent local healers and charmers become less frequent as they are sent to their deaths or driven underground while trials of coven witches increase. The growth of covens over this period must be related to the fact that during the same period (1600-1629) no fewer than thirty-three male charmers or healers were tried individually. Were these wise men always there? Were they taking up positions vacated by coven witches? Or is this a sign of some upheaval in the organisation of the pagan religion in Scotland, such as the abandonment of hunting magic?

Occasionally a healer trained under the old regime was recruited by a local Devil into a new-style coven. One such was Helen Guthrie, a leading member of the Forfar coven, who had been taught by Jonet Galloway who lived near Kirriemuir. Helen confessed 'that she was ane witch a long tyme since and that she went abroad with the Egyptians she being a witch then'. In other words, she had been trained by the fairy folk. Another healer who worked with a coven was John Brugh, the Warlock of Fossaway (Reid 1899, 195-208), who had helped the local Devil to dig up dead bodies in local churchyards. He was strangled and burnt but the Devil got off scot free.

The information is incomplete but it supports the proposal that organised covens came into being soon after 1590, when local gentlemen with an interest in necromancy copied Francis Stewart and began to recruit teams of local witches to work for them. They organised their new covens according to standard features, notably the demonic pact and the sabbat ritual, which circulated among them. These men were not traditional warlocks but educated men who may have learned their witchcraft from a book or from each other. The Devil at Inverkeithing in 1649 was described by Margaret Mairtine as being 'in the likeness of a gentle man'. The Devil at Auldearn was also a gentleman whom his witches addressed as 'Lord'. Whatever the origins of these shadowy individuals there is no common ground between the Devil who tempted Jesus (Matthew 4:11) and the so-called 'Devils' of the Scottish covens. The discrepancy between the Devil's popular image as *Auld Clootie* or *Auld Nick* and the Devil of Scripture suggests that there was in Scotland an older and more sympathetic figure.

There appear to have been relatively few covens in Scotland. From the trials we can identify twenty-three with varying degrees of certainty: Aberdeen, Aberdour, Alloa, Bo'ness, Bute, Crook of Devon (Fossaway), Dalkeith, Dunning, Eyemouth, Findo-Gask, Forfar, Inverkeithing, Kirkliston, Lanark, Lothian (at least two), Melrose, Moray (where there were three), Selkirk, Torryburn and Wemyss. There were almost certainly others as the trial records seldom distinguish between coven witches and small groups of local charmers.

Trials of probable coven witches and their leaders from 1600 to 1629

Twelve trials account for ten Devils, four probable Officers, and eighty-five women.

1621 Inverkeithing, Fife. Six women; the Devil was probably John Young. It is something of a coincidence that this trial took place in Inverkeithing where an earlier John and his maidens had danced in the kirkyard in 1282.

1622 Aberdour, Fife. Five women; the Devil is not named.

1623 Inverkeithing, Fife. John Young, probably the Devil, was tried with twelve women.

1624 Bo'ness, West Lothian. Three women confessed to carnal knowledge of the Devil, but he is not identified.

1624 Torryburn and Culross, Fife. Alexander Clerk and four women.

1624 Eyemouth, Berwickshire. Alexander Liddle and two women.

1624 West Lothian. William Falconer and five women, one of them his wife.

1626 Aberdeen. Four men (John Davie, John Propter, William Young and John Findlaw) and fifteen women. With the further arrests of 1627 they include all the members of a coven based in Aberdeen and several independent charmers from rural areas.

1626 Wemyss, Fife. Patrick Landrok and three women.

1627 Aberdeen. Walter Baird and four women.

1628 Midlothian. William Watt and seven women.

1629 Lanark. John Greinscheills, James Frame, seventeen witches and two vagabonds, all accused of charming, enchantment, laying-on and taking-off of sickness, and other devilish practices.

Early covens

The first recognisable coven comes to light at Inverkeithing in West Fife in 1621, with the trial of six women accused of witchcraft, sorcery, the use of charms, etc. One of them, Margaret Chatto, 'wes the principall persone in all thair conventionis and meitingis with the divill and most familiar with him'. In the words of her prosecutor, she confessed 'her divilische practizes and the giving ovir of hir selff, saull and body to the divil' (RPC). Two years later ten more women were apprehended. By then four women and one man, Johnne Young, had fled 'thus taking the guilt upon them'. He may have been their Master. This makes a total of sixteen women and one man.

Despite this disaster a new generation arose and in 1649 another nineteen Inverkeithing women including Margaret Henderson, Lady Pittathro, sister to the Laird of Fordel, were arrested after 'sundry persons', notably the parish minister, Mr Walter Duncan, had accused them of communing with the Devil. The wives of certain magistrats were included in the denunciation but could not be tried at first as their husbands refused to apprehend them. Lady Pittathro fled to Edinburgh but was recaptured and soon after was found dead in her cell in the Tolbooth, a fate generally seen as the Devil taking care of his own. She escaped burning and was buried at Inverkeithing in the churchyard where John and his maidens had danced almost four hundred years before. Mr Duncan evidently saw these women as agents of the Anti-Christ but, like John the priest in 1282, they probably believed they were performing an essential rite of communal blessing.

In 1597 the witches of Lumphanan in southern Aberdeenshire confessed to meeting other women at the Hallowe'en dance but the Devil played a very minor part in their dittays. At Michaelmas 1626 began a second upsurge in the persecution of witches in Aberdeenshire. Half of them were still local healers but we can identify thirteen witches, a probable Devil and a probable Officer making up a coven based in Aberdeen. This comes a generation after the execution of Margaret Bane, her son Thomas Leyis and many others for dancing in the town at Hallowe'en, the Devil again being absent. In 1626 the witches of Aberdeen confess to meeting at regular sabbats at certain fixed places. The difference is significant. Nevertheless without the kind of detailed evidence made available by reliable transcripts of the trials, there is little to distinguish the trial of a coven from a trial of local healers rounded up by the local Kirk Session. The fate of the Aberdeen coven shows up a fundamental weakness of the coven system, as one member could and often did betray all the others.

The burning of forty witches in Fife in 1643 has left not a single name but included witches from Anstruther, Dysert, Culross, Pittenweem and St Andrews. The numbers involved suggest several more covens in coastal Fife. As late as 1704 seven more coven witches were imprisoned at Pittenweem: Beatrix Laing, Isobell Adam, Nicolas Lawson, Jane Cornfoot (killed by the mob), Thomas Brown (starved to death in prison), Margaret Wallace and Margaret Jack. Another thriving coven survived into the eighteenth century at Torryburn, another small port in West Fife, despite at least two earlier burnings. Lilias Adie claimed to be the last survivor. She died in prison in 1704 and was buried 'within floodmark between Torryburn and Torrie' where her ghost would not know which way to turn and could do no harm (Black 1938, 82). By her own account she had attended a hundred meetings of twenty or thirty witches, 'whereof none are now living but herself'. The last sabbat she was at was in August 1701, where there were sixteen or eighteen. She called the Devil 'a villain that promised her many good things when she engaged with him, but never gave her anything but misery and poverty' (Simpkins 1914, 103).

It has been argued, convincingly, that the evil witch is a reflex of a polarised religious system which recognised only God and the Devil (Larner 1981, 8-9). In such a dualistic scheme, any powers or practices which do not originate with the Church must come from the Devil, and anyone who uses them, whatever their intentions or achievements, must be in league with the Devil and against Christ. From this it is a short step to deduce that the witch had made a pact with the Devil. In court coven witches were pressed to admit to such pacts and readily did so, though it is probable that they did not share the Church's view of what was implied.

Martin thought this concept first appeared after the trials of the North Berwick witches in 1590 (2002, 78) but it did not come from James VI. Martin also believed that in early trials it 'was often mingled with fairy lore' citing Andro Man in 1597 and Patrick Lowrie in 1605; but Andro and Patrick were fairy folk who owed their allegiance to the Queen of Elphane, though the court may have made it into a demonic pact. But the use of a very similar oath by a witch in Aberdeenshire suggests an older native history both for the demonic oath and for the 'Devil'.

One of the most interesting facts to emerge from the Aberdeenshire trials is the accusations made against Helen Frasser of Foveran in coastal Aberdeenshire in 1597 that she had administered an oath to Christane Hendersoune, telling her to put one hand to the crown of her head and the other to the sole of her foot, and deliver up whatever was between them to the Devil, and she should want for nothing that she would know or desire (SCM I, 107). The same oath was used in later times by the master of a coven when recruiting a new witch. What is not certain is what is meant by the Devil in a pagan oath or to what extent this term reflects the witch's statement. To whom did these witches imagine they were dedicating themselves? In both the cases mentioned above, the answer appears to be that the court identified the Queen with the Devil. Murray notes that 'The Queen of Elphin, or Elfhame, is sometimes called the Devil' (1921, 44). This is specifically so in 1605, when Patrick Lowrie and Janet Hunter were celebrating Hallowe'en on Lowdon Hill 'quhair thair appeirit to thame ane devillische Spreit, in liknes of ane woman, and callit hir selff Helen Mcbrune' (Pitcairn 1833, ii, 478).

Evidently the old dedicatory formula was adopted by the new coven masters, feeling their way into uncharted and possibly dangerous territory, and anxious to do the right thing. They also asked the new witch to reject the Trinity and her Christian baptism and often gave her a new name (Murray 1921, 82). When he baptised Janet Breadheid at Auldearn c.1640, the Devil bit her shoulder, sucked out her blood and spat it out again on her head. He also gave her a new name, Christian (Pitcairn iii, 617), which must surely be a joke.

Another aspect of the demonic pact which was taken over from the earlier pagan oath was the promise, often broken, that the new witch 'should want for nothing that she would know or desire.' This suggests that some form of social security operated within the coven, though to judge by frequent complaints perhaps it did not operate very well. One of the accused at Crook of Devon complained that he was still waiting for his money (Reid, 1899, 231). Both Janet Briedhead and Isobell Gowdie of Auldearn said that the money the Devil gave them was worthless – 'within fowr and twantie houris it vold be horse-muke', as Isobell put it (Pitcairn 1833 iii, 613). In a world of neglect, uncertainty and disappointment it must have been a great comfort to a poor woman to believe that someone accepted responsibility for her and granted her personal value, at a price. The Queen of Elphen in Banff made a similar promise when she recruited Andro Man as a young boy: he would become a healer of every disease except stand deid, and would be 'weill entertenit' but predicted that he would have to beg for his bread at the end of his life (SCM I, 119).

The best-organised coven that we know of was at Auldearn in Moray which was already working in 1643 and before 1662 had expanded to three separate groups at Auldearn, Darnaway and Elgin. Two of the Auldearn witches, Isobell Gowdie and Janet Braidheid, seem to have decided in 1662 that they had been wicked for long enough and gave themselves up. Had they not had this crise de conscience, had Isobell not been such a satisfactory witness, and had the local notary not been such an indefatigable scribe, we would know nothing whatsoever about witchcraft in Moray in the seventeenth century and very little about how a coven functioned. Isobell and Janet were manifestly guilty on multiple counts and executed but as far as one can judge their coven continued to function. There was no wholesale extermination although Janet named thirty-nine witches who once met at Nairn. They did a good job (had they not exterminated the Hays of Park?) and were well protected.

Isobell said: 'Ther ar threttein persones in my Coven'. The coven of twelve with a Master is seen as an anti-Christian feature but Christianity did not invent the witches' dozen. In fact the number of witches at a sabbat varied considerably and does not seem to have had any particular significance. Reports of the meetings of the Forfar coven name only seven or eight attending each time out of a possible total of twenty known witches (Anderson 1888, 246-255) but Forfar appears to have been badly managed and demoralised.

On the other hand the covens of Moray were very well run. Janet Braidheid of Auldearn at her trial in 1662 described a Great Meeting which had taken place many years earlier in Nairn (Pitcairn 1833, iii 615-617). She named thirty-nine women in addition to the Devil and three men who were 'Ruleris'. This Devil appears to have been active, ambitious and well-organised. There can be no doubt that he was a member of a powerful local family, untouchable by the secular authorities or by the Church, whose local minister, Mr Harry Forbes, was targeted with many others and able (which was more unusual) to keep his witches safe. We can locate the homes of thirty-seven of them on the modern map. All of the women like herself were the wives of small tenant farmers. Seventeen lived in Auldearn itself, and the rest in the area between the river Nairn and the Meikle Burn which appears to have been the boundary between the coven at Auldearn and another at Darnaway, seat of the Earls of Moray. Isobell Gowdie reported a memorable joint meeting when the Auldearn coven and 'the other coven' met at the Downie Hillock, near Darnaway; they were entertained by the Fairy King and Queen and given more food than they could eat.

The trial documents show that sabbats were held at many 'local and specific' places in the countryside, in private houses, at remote places where they could be certain of not being disturbed. They also met at parish churches including those of Alloa, Auldearn, Carnwath, Elgin, Forfar, Lanark, Nairn and North Berwick. Many of their meeting-places were prehistoric beacon sites or Fairy Knolls used as ritual centres by local hunters, such as the Hill of Cragleauche near Lumphanan in Deeside, the Binn of Cullen in Banffshire, the Knock of Alves near Forres, Banffshire, the Downie Hillock at Darnaway, Gibson's Craig in Fossaway, the Horn in Stenton parish, the Hill of Earlseat in Nairn, and St Katherine's Hill in Aberdeen where poor Thomas Leyis once danced at Hallowe'en. The witches of Carnwath met in the High Kirk of Lanark, in the church of Carnwath, at Niveinseat 'witches' seat', and at Tormonquheill. Neither Niveinseat nor Tormonquheill can now be located but Niven derives from G. *naomh* 'sanctified, set apart' and is used of a deer forest; NcNiven 'daughter of the deer forest' was a common name for a witch. Tormonquheill may be derived from G. *toir* 'to hunt' and *monadh* 'upland'.

At Hallowe'en in 1605, Patrick Lowrie and three women met Helen McBrune on Loudon Hill, a prominent rock in northern Ayrshire. The name is the same as Sc. *lowe* 'blaze'. From its summit one has an extensive view over the Firth of Clyde to the island of Arran. The pagan folk of Cromar and Lumphanan danced at Hallowe'en at Craiglich 'beacon rock', another place with an immense view, where they danced round a great stone (SCM 1841. I, 144). There were thirteen witches at a meeting in the kirkyard of Forfar but 'they daunsed a whyle togidder till they were skaired by some people coming by and that thereupon they were fryghted and fled suddenly' (Anderson 1888, 246-255). The most impressive demonstration of continuity is found in the parish of Fossaway, where the Crook of Devon coven met at Gibson's Craig (NS982975), where there is a place called Palace Brae. This was once the home of the Murrays of Tullibardine, later Earls of Atholl (OSA c.1790), where they gathered their tenants for a deer-drive. A traditional ball game was played at Ball Green, part of Palace Brae. Ball games including bowls, golf and shinty were played by hunters as they waited for the drive to start.

Witches also gathered on Minchmuir, a hill near Peebles, where Mr Williamson of Cardrona carried off the Devil's book from witches dancing there. When they gave chase he gave it back to them, and so had nothing to show for his adventure but a good story (Murray 1921, 197). Fairies or hunters also congregated on Minchmuir but could be propitiated by an offering of cheese thrown into the Cheese Well (Scott 1931, 315-6), a typical scrap of fake lore (G. *cas* is another archaic word for a hunt).

All these sites were traditional. Witches who met at parish churches were not impious intruders performing a travesty of Christian worship but pagan worshippers who persisted in using local beacon sites despite their adoption as strategic centres by the Church. They continued to gather at the traditional sites used by their hunting ancestors long before Christianity. Their persistent use of the same old sites makes it abundantly plain that every aspect of the sabbat was older than Christianity, and that the music, dancing, miming and suggestive songs were all designed to encourage participation by initiates in the sexual act, particularly at the quarters, to bring good luck.

The impression we get from the trials is that before 1600, before the Reformed clergy had their attention drawn to the presence of the Anti-Christ in their parishes, and, above all, before James VI had become hysterical about the presence of the Anti-Christ in his kingdom, witches had worked their magic openly to the general benefit of the community (as many were skilled midwives and others used effective herbal remedies), and that the main ritual centred on the meetings at the appointed places at the reaths or seasons of the year. As the Kirk spread over Lowland Scotland, it must have everywhere encountered these local groups who appear to have made no secret of their activities.

As an example of life as a coven witch, Jonet Watsone's experience is probably typical.

'Dalkeith, Midlothian, June 1661. Confession of Jonet Watsone accused of Witchcraft.'

> From the original in the collection of the
> Society of Antiquaries of Scotland.

'Jonet Watsone confessed, that in Apryle last bypast, or thairby, she come home to hir awne house [from the funeral of Lady Dalhousie], being verrie grieved and angrie at it, wished to have amendse of Jean Bughane. Upone the which the Devill apeired unto her, in the liknes of ane prettie boy, in grein clothes; and asked, 'What aild her? And what amendse she wold have, he should give her.' And at that tyme the Devill gaive hir his markis; and went away from hir in the liknes of ane blak doug:– And constantlie, for thrie dayis thereffter, ther was a great bee come to her; and upone ane morning, when she was cheinging her schirt, it did sit down upone her shoulder (she being naked) wher she had one of the markis.

'As also, about the tyme of the last Baille-ffyre night [Beltane, 30 April], she was at a Meitting in Newtoun-dein with the Devill, who had grein cloathes upon him, and a blak hatt upone his head; wher she denyd Christ, and took her self to be the servant of the Deivill. Wherfor she acknoweledged that she was, from her heart, sorrowfull for the doeing of it. And likewise, he then gave her a new name, and called her 'Weill-dancing Jenot' – and promised her money at the nixt Meitting.

'And also, that upone ane uther night, the Deivill was very heavie upon her in her bed. As also, she confessed that Bessie Moffit, Elspeth Grahame, and Jenot Mikeljohn come to her house, and tooke her away to that Meating; when they all danced togither: At which tyme, when she renunced her baptisme, the Deivill laid his hand upon her head, and bad her 'give all ower to him that was under his hand' and she did so. Quhilk haill premisses she confessed, in presens of the under-sub-scryvers, without compulsion.

61

'W. Calderwood (Minister of Dalkeith), William Scott (Bailie of Dalkeith), And. Macmillone witness and eight more witnesses.'

Jonet Watsone had little chance of surviving. At least twenty of her coven were arrested and most or all were sentenced to be strangled and burnt, a punishment that seems now to be totally out of proportion to the alleged crime. In 1662 every member of the coven at Crook of Devon in Kinross-shire was arrested and charged with witchcraft. 'Each of the accused supports and corroborates the others, at least to that extent, as well as in their statement that midnight meetings of the "covin", at which they and others were present, were held at various places in the neighbourhood. They also corroborate the statements made by the others that a person met them at these meetings whom they believed to be Satan, and that they at his request renounced their baptism and "engaged themselves to be his servant by putting one of their hands on the crown of their head and the other under the sole of their foot, and delivering all betwixt them over to him"'. The Master provided meat and drink, a piper played, and they danced. He was 'uniformly ardent in his attentions to the witches' (Anderson 1888, 216).

In some groups two or three men regularly attended the sabbats to act as officers and at some meetings at Auldearn there were equal numbers of men and women. We get occasional glimpses of groups of men wearing green or brown clothes, perhaps fairy folk wearing plaids in a muted or 'hunting' tartan, who were controlled by the Queen of Elfane. Sabbats took place on the eves of the Quarter Days or Reaths of the year, strictly speaking 1 May, 1 August, 1 November and 1 February, but the Forfar witches met at Candlemas (2 February), Ruidday (3 May), Lambesmas or Lammas (1 August) and at Hallowmas (31 October) (Anderson, 1888, 258). Minor meetings took place on other dates which were intimated at the previous meeting, or notified in person by the Devil or his 'horse', the messenger of the coven. This is reminiscent of the scheme of worship in the Reformed Kirk, with its weekly services and three or four Communion seasons in the year. In some covens a roll was kept, attendance was enforced, progress was monitored, and backsliders were punished, just as they were in the Reformed Kirk.

It has been an article of faith for centuries that witches, like fairies, met on the reaths of the year but since the sabbat took place at night it is evident that its dates, like those of important hunts, must have been related to the lunar cycle. The word 'reath' comes from G. *raidhe* 'quarter of the year' which is linked to G. *raidhe* 'rank of soldiers (hunters)', *raidhe* 'intercession' and E. *raid* 'a sudden assault or attack, originally by horsemen (a hunt)'. G. *sabaid* is 'fight, fray', also a hunt, suggesting that the Reath or Quarter was once the date of an important hunt, at or near a full moon, for which a blessing was sought at the sabbat.

Women joined by invitation or were introduced by relatives already in the coven: Janet Breidhead was introduced by her husband, John Taylor. Tracing family relationships is made difficult by the fact that women in Scotland continued to be known on marriage by their maiden names but sometimes married couples and their adult children were all members of a coven, the women as witches and the husband as an officer. Women generally presented their daughters when they reached twelve. The Devil at Forfar was reluctant to take little Janet Howit as she was too young: 'What sall I doe with such a little bairn as this?' He appears to have been under an obligation to accept her all the same but the Devil at Forfar was rather ineffectual.

Some women claimed that they had been reluctant to join. Membership of a coven seems to have been, at least in part, a burden, undertaken out of a sense of duty or responsibility to the community as a whole. Sex with the Devil was often unpleasant but it was necessary. It seems to have been very uncommon for a husband to object to his wife's activities, which suggests that he felt his wife's involvement in the local coven was of value to the family, or at least that it was her own affair.

The sabbat seems to have been similar everywhere whether the witches were rich or poor: they ate, drank, danced lewd dances, sang lewd songs, and had intercourse with the Devil. One of the company played the pipes or the Jew's harp, or they all sang to provide the music. Sometimes the food provided was very little and not very good: the witches at Crook of Devon complained that their Devil gave them 'rough bread and sour drink' (Reid, 1899, 248). Sometimes they took their allotted share of a crop and divided it up. Sometimes they stole food and drink from their neighbours. The Devil in his animal guise copulated with each of the witches who reported that his member was very large, very hard and as cold as ice. Then they walked through the moonlit night back to their marital beds, where the besom or milking stool they had left in it (Pitcairn 1833, 604) confirmed that their domestic responsibilities were in abeyance.

The sabbat as celebrated by the covens preserves all the elements of an archaic fertility cult deeply rooted in Scottish society and, from its landscape associations, tied to hunting. It probably did good and, if it did no good, it did not normally do harm. The Reformed Church must accept responsibility for changing the sabbat ritual from a harmless practice to a criminal activity whose practitioners had evil intentions and believed themselves capable of evil acts. The Church argued that witches were evil even when they were successful as healers and midwives since they operated without its sanction. By this logic, charmers and healers were as guilty as necromancers, poisoners and murderers, and were to suffer the same penalties. After the Reformation, wise women and wise men who had studied their craft and worked to cure or control disease and remedy disaster, were tortured and burnt alongside women who had murdered their own babies to make magic ointment and who claimed, perhaps with truth, to have killed their neighbours and their neighbours' children.

When the Church looked for witches they found them everywhere. In Langendorf in Germany in 1492, all but two of the women were accused of witchcraft. Things in some parts of Scotland in 1650 were almost as bad: 'At a little Village within two Miles [of Berwick], two Men and three Women were burnt for Witches, and nine more were to be burnt, the Village consisting but of fourteen Families, and there were as many witches... That twenty more were to be burnt within six miles of that place and all their Goods are forfeited to the King and the Lords' (Black 1938, 61). Witchcraft in its original form was very much a religion of the folk, a household religion, a source of blessing in hard times, and they were loathe to give it up.

The chapters that follow investigate a number of interwoven themes such as archaic Gaelic, hunting, fire, ritual sex, the Black Man and the White Lady. All of these are aspects of the old religion, laid out by Robert Graves in *The White Goddess*, but cast by him into a different mould. The Lady did not demand human sacrifice: the 'men' who died were her deer. The Lady's responsibility for the herds explains how she was at the same time the fertile Maiden whose children were the deer, the generous Mother who allowed her deer to be sacrificed, and the Hag who oversaw their death. In an older incarnation, she was fire, without which no man, woman or child could survive. This radical error is typical of a priesthood which had inherited the images and the lore of an older religion but no longer understood what they meant. Graves defined iconotrophy as the reinterpretation of such obsolete images; it also happens in ritual language where it gives rise to fake folklore.

The sabbat was not the reaction of a deprived peasantry to over-strict discipline by repressive ministers. Parish records certainly show that the Church tried to ban Yule and Easter, Hallowe'en bonfires, pilgrimages, visits to wells, suggestive songs and dances, carol singing, mumming, guising, capering, cross-dressing, and plays and were keenly alive to the sin of fornication but they also show that all these amusements continued from one generation to the next. As they did in Visigothic Spain, the antipathies of the Church are a reliable marker for the pagan practices of an earlier date.

Today evangelical Protestants are still preoccupied with the Church's old confrontation with the witch cult and its Devil, whether they recognise this or not. They should remember 2 Samuel 6, 12-20. When David brought the Ark to Zion, he worshipped God by sacrificing fat cattle, distributing bread, meat, and wine to every person present, leaping and dancing with all his might to the music of the trump, and exposing himself in an indecent manner. He would have been very popular as the master of a Scottish coven.

CHAPTER 6: CARNAL DEALING

In fertility cults it is one of the chief features, not only symbolizing the fertilizing power in the whole animate world, but, in the belief of the actors, actually assisting it and promoting its effects.

Margaret Murray (1921, 175).

In the century of the Scottish witch mania, which ran from 1570 to 1670, thousands of illiterate women from all parts of Lowland Scotland, the majority living in isolated hamlets and small farms, were accused and found guilty of being witches. A majority of those whose testimony has survived gave consistent and detailed accounts of having sex with the Devil. Many of these accounts, in English, were preserved for posterity by the Scottish legal system. Some suppose that these accounts were invented by the accused woman or by credulous clerks but there are a great many of these accounts and they are widespread, consistent and detailed. They are also a necessary aspect of everything else that is known of the witch cult in Scotland.

Most of the women agree that they had sex with the Devil and describe the experience in remarkably similar terms. In most cases carnal dealing took place during a sabbat and other women were involved but sometimes there is no sign of a coven. Janet Barker, tried in 1643, was a servant in Edinburgh to whom the Devil promised a red wylliecott or a kirtle. She 'had dyvers tymes carnall copulatioun with the devill both in hir awin littill chope, and in the said unquhile Jonet Cransoun hir hous, and had ado with him in hir naiket bed, quha was heavie abone hir lyk an ox and nocht lyk ane uther man'. It is possible that an unknown man took advantage of her but it was what she expected of the Devil. In most cases carnal dealing was an aspect of the sabbat and other women gave corroborative evidence.

According to Manie Haliburton at Dirleton in 1649, the Devil came to her house in likeness of a man, calling himself a physician, and sold her ointment to treat her daughter. When he came again it was early in the morning, when she was still in bed. He lay down with her 'and had carnall copulatioun with hir, his nature being cold: He desyreit her to renunce Christ and hir baptisme, and become his servand; quhilk scho did' (Pitcairn 1833, III, 109-110). In 1661, Janet Watsone of Dalkeith confessed that the Devil laid his hand on her head and bade her 'give all ower to him that was vnder his hand', and she did so. 'Vpone ane vther night, the Devil was verie heavie vpon her in her bed' (RPC, 1661). Intercourse with the Devil often sounds more like a penance than a pleasure.

Isobel Shyrie and Jonet Stout of the Forfar coven, interrogated in 1662, confessed that they 'had carnale copulation with the divill at Petterden' (Anderson, 1888, 251). Isobel Smith, also of the Forfar coven, confessed to many meetings with the Devil. 'Ane on the head off the hill off Fineheaven while shee was alone gathering heather hee appeared to her lik ane braw gentleman ... and that tyme they made their covenant and he kissed her and lay with her as shee thought and his mouth and breath wer wery cold and his body lyk clay' (Anderson, 1888, 256). The coldness might relate to an artificial phallus and seems to be a diagnostic feature.

A similar account is given by Isobell Gowdie of Auldearn in Moray in 1662. The clerk, the notary John Innes, sometimes cut her testimony short but on the topic of carnal dealing he made a copious report in duplicate. A few days after her initiation in Auldearn Kirk, she said, the Devil came to her in the New Wards of Inshoch, a place not far from her home at Lochloy, and 'ther had carnall cowpulatioun with me. He wes a werie meikle blak roch man. He will lye as hewie wpon ws, quhan he hes carnall dealling with ws, lyk an malt-secke. His members are exceeding great and long; no man's memberis ar so long and bigg as they ar. He wold be amongst ws lyk a weath [wild] horse amongst mears...' She describes renouncing her baptism, dedicating her whole body to the Devil, and having intercourse with him and her account makes it plain that sexual intercourse was not just a regular part of the sabbat but its culmination, the key to the whole event. She repeats that the Devil 'was a meikle, black, roch man, werie cold' and she found 'his nature als cold within me as spring-well-water... He wold lye with ws in presence of all the multitud; heither haid we nor he any kynd of shame; bot especiallie he hes no shame with him at all. He wold lye and hawe carnall dealling with all, at euerie tym, as he pleased. He wold haw carnall dealling with ws in the shape of a deir, or in any vther shap that he that he wold be in. We wold never refuse him. He wold come to my hows-top in the shape of a crow, or lyk a deir, or in any vther shap, now and then. I wold ken his woice, at the first heiring of it, and wold goe furth to him and haw carnall cowpulatioun with him. The youngest and lwstiest women will haw werie great pleasour in their carnall cowpulatioun with him, yea much mor than with their awin husbandis; and they will haw a exceiding great desir of it with him, als much as he can haw to them, and mor; and never think shame of it. He is abler for ws that way than any man can be (Alace! that I sould compair him to ane man!) onlie he ves heavie lyk a malt-seck; a hudg nature, verie cold, as yce' (Pitcairn 1833, 603, 610).

Lilias Adie of Torryburn in Fife, who died in prison in 1704, was the last of her generation of witches but reports a comparable ritual. She declared under oath that when she renounced her baptism the Devil put one hand on the crown of her head and the other on the soles of her feet, and she said that all was the devil's between the crown of her head and the soles of her feet; and then the devil lay with her carnally; and that his skin was cold, and his colour black and pale, he had a hat on his head, and his feet were cloven like the feet of a stirk (Simpkins, 1914, 102-104). Sometimes it seems the clerk could not prevent himself from embellishing the record.

In 1644 Margaret Watson and Jean Lachland of Carnwath in the bleak uplands of Lanarkshire told the court they had 'enterit in covenant withe Sathan' and renounced their baptism, giving 'thair soule and bodie totallie to his service' (RPC 1643). Margaret claimed that 'he appeired to the thryse, the first tyme lyke ane blak man and gripped the about the left pape and then had carnall deale with the, and thow decerned his nature to be cold'.

In Irvine, Ayrshire, in 1650, Margaret Cooper, Janet Robison and Catherine Montgomerie confessed to 'the renunciation of their baptism, carnal copulation with the Devil and the taking of a new name from him' (NSA Ayrshire, 1845, 632-633). In Moray, giving her testimony in 1662, Janet Braidheid said that she had been recruited into the cult twenty years earlier by her husband, John Taylor, and his mother Elspet Nishie. She went with them at night to a Great Meeting in the Kirk of Nairn, where she saw the Devil in the reader's desk with a book in his hand and thirty-nine other members (whom she names). After the Devil had had intercourse with all the women, she was presented to him by her husband, who was at that time officer to the Auldearn coven. She put one hand to the sole of her feet and the other to the crown of her head and renounced her baptism and all between her two hands to the Devil. Then the Devil marked her in the shoulder and 'suked out my blood with his mowth, at that place; he spowted it in his hand, and sprinkled it on my head. He baptised me thairvith, in his awin nam, "Christian". And than immediatlie thairefter they all returned each to ther awin howssis' (Pitcairn 1833, III, 615). A few days later he 'cam to me to my hows, quhan my husband was furth in the morning, at the plewgh ... and he did lye with me in the naked bed and had carnall cowpulation with me...' He came again eight days later, then twenty days later, and for a third time within the next twenty days and lay with her each time. He presumably waited for an auspicious date, perhaps a full moon. The timing corresponds to one lunar month of twenty-eight days and a period of forty days which is one and a half lunations. He gave her a piece of money which turned red. The Devil 'was a meikle, roch, blak man, cloven-footed, werie cold; and I fand his nature within me als cold as spring-well-water' – then the clerk repeats Isobell Gowdie's testimony almost word for word (Pitcairn 1833, III, 616-618).

Sometimes the sex-for-power equation is explicit. Isobel Smith, one of the Forfar coven tried in 1662, became a witch because she had a score to settle with James Gray, bowman or cattle-man to my Lord Spynie. The Devil promised to help her: 'they made their covenant and he kissed her and lay with her as shee thought and his mouth and breath wer wery cold and his body lyk clay' (Kinloch 1848, 115, 129, 132; Murray 1921, 64).

From the evidence given independently by witches in every part of the trial area, from Bute to Moray, it is clear that the focus of coven ritual in Lowland Scotland was on sexual magic, specifically on ritual intercourse at the raiths of the year or on special occasions. Karl Pearson established that the German *Mailehn*, a local marriage-ritual where the village maidens were auctioned off, was 'a fossil of what was once a communal sex-festival – the evening gathering in the woods for the choice of temporary mates' (1897, II, 407-412). It was an aspect of the great spring-festivals. This brings us back to Easter 1283 at Inverkeithing and the spring festival organised by the priest named John who 'revived the profane worship of Priapus, collecting young girls from the village and compelling them to dance in circles to Father Bacchus' (Stevenson 1839, 109). He almost certainly did more than that.

Pearson describes the selection of the May Queen as 'a fossil of the old worship of the goddess of fertility' (1897, 408). She was not originally a chaste virgin but 'the woman arrayed in purple and scarlet, decked with gold, seated on a scarlet beast and having a golden cup in her hand' (Revelation 17). As the representative of the goddess of fertility the woman arrayed in purple and scarlet is worshipped by the whole community. In her red robes she is also the personification of the purifying fires that marked the festivals. In comparison, the sexual rites in Scotland were humble and impoverished – the Queen of Elphane appeared in white homespun, not in purple – but their frequency and fidelity, confirmed in one report after another, not only in the spring but at every quarter, were remarkable. John the priest was evidently justified in claiming that his ritual was the common use of the country.

And yet Larner did not think carnal dealing was a very important aspect of Scottish witchcraft (1981, 148).

'Although sexual intercourse, usually called "carnal dealing" to empha- sise that there was nothing imaginary about it, was an almost essential ingredient in female accounts of the Pact, it cannot be said that details of sexual relationships were an important part of Scottish demonic beliefs).'

Levack dismissed sexual magic in a paragraph (1987, 46-47).

'Descriptions of sexual activity at the sabbath also varied, reflecting dif- ferences in the erotic imagination of both the accusers and the accused. Sometimes there were reports of sexual commerce between witches and demons, but at others there were allegations of widespread sexual promiscuity among the witches themselves.'

This could hardly be further from the truth. However one approaches the witch cult, 'carnal dealing' is the key to its purpose and origins. No doubt many people found their imaginations stimulated by what they heard in court or read in the broadsheets – it would still grab headlines today – but this does not reduce its significance. As for being a product of over-heated eroticism, the descriptions are, if anything, passion-killers.

At the sabbats, the Devil provided food and drink and he ate and drank and danced with the rest. He might whistle or sing or play the pipes to provide the music (Murray 1925, 38, 138; Larner 1981, 153). However there is no doubt that his primary purpose was to copulate with the female witches. Witches from covens in all parts of Lowland Scotland state in very similar terms that they copulated with the devil at the sabbat and saw other witches doing so. It was the primary ritual.

Murray attributed the undue prominence given in the trial evidence to dealing with the Devil to prurience on the part of the inquisitors but it is probable that everyone involved was well aware of the importance of inter-course with the Devil. It was the focal point of the cult and the culmination of the sabbat. We should hardly be surprised to find simulated intercourse with a god or goddess as the focus of a religion evolved by hunters. There is no need to argue the point: hunting was the original context of all Gaelic culture. Ritual sex was used as a magical method of increasing the fertility of the herds and of generating good luck. It was the climax of the quarterly meetings when the Devil normally had sexual intercourse with all the witches present except for pregnant women and pre-pubertal girls whose fertility was still latent.

Nevertheless Pearson's spring rites did not limit sex to the Devil; the whole reproductive community, male and female, was involved in these festivals, a pattern found at the Hebridean Oda (discussed in a later chapter). It appears to be the older native pattern. We must also explain who or what the Devil of the old religion was, if he was not the Anti-Christ of the Church.

Another problem is why, if intercourse with the Devil is so important, do certain witches fail to mention it in their accounts of the sabbat? Did it not happen? Were they told not to mention it or has some later editor altered the text? Selective editing is very likely. At Crook of Devon, instead of describing the Devil's unnaturally cold member (of which we hear plenty elsewhere) the witches referred to his unnaturally cold *hand*. Instead of having sexual inter-course with his witches in the normal way, this gentleman *shook their hands*. At Forfar, the record suggests that sex was a regular part of the sabbats, that the witches were told not to mention it but to use 'kissing' as a euphemism but sometimes forgot. So accounts from Forfar are confused: 'The divill kissed hir selfe that night and that it was ane cold kisse... Jonet Stout confest ... that she had carnal copulation with the divill at Petterden... That night the said Isabel Shirrie went aside fra hir for some tyme, and that the divill (as she supposed) had then carnal copulation with hir... The divill kist them all except herself and that he kist her hand onlie...' (Anderson 1888, 246-262; see Note).

69

If it were true it would barely affect the Scottish picture but Jonet Stout or the clerk lets slip that the Devil's 'cold kiss' is a euphemism for more significant sexual activity. Such evasion only serves to emphasise the importance of 'dealing' and its general acceptance as an important feature of the evidence. In most cases the clerk is quite prepared to call a member a member, if unnaturally hard and cold. Witches after all were country-wives who describe, and no doubt experienced, sex in a very matter-of-fact way. What makes it more impressive is that they reported their experiences in remarkably similar terms regardless of date or district. The importance of carnal dealing can also be judged from the fact that it concluded the initiation ceremony, following on from the point where the witch dedicated everything from the top of her head to the soles of her feet to the Devil.

Despite the absence of surviving examples or any other direct evidence it is abundantly evident that leaders of Scottish covens must have used an artificial penis. Both Murray and Summers took for granted that the leader of the coven used a *fascinum*, a device made of leather, strips of cloth, horn, wax, or some similar material. The 'little bundle' has a long history of use in copulatory rituals in a congregation, like that of the coven, where it was manifestly impossible for one man to 'comply with the requirements of so many women', as Murray puts it (1921, 178). This element of the pagan fertility rite was so typical that it gave rise to the word *fascination*, meaning 'witchcraft'. To be fascinated or penetrated by the Devil is to be bewitched which again suggests that ritual intercourse was believed to empower women.

Summers claimed that the Vestals of Rome who maintained the sacred fire 'favoured a phallic superstition' akin to that of the *fascinum* (1925, 99). Pliny mentions that among the sacred objects entrusted to them was a *fascinus* and that the function of fertility was represented by the image of a male sex organ (*Natural History* xxviii. 7, 39). The fecundating power of sacred fire is confirmed in Latin mythology when Ocresia becomes pregnant after sitting upon a phallus that appeared among the ashes on the altar of the god Vulcanus. A comparable legend is preserved at Kilmallie on Loch Eil where the Cailleach conceives the Black Lad after exposing herself to the ashes of a fire made of human bones. The early Church banned the use of the *fascinus* as a sexual aid, a good indication of its importance in pagan circles. The Reformed Church was particularly zealous in its campaign against unlicenced sex.

The use of an artificial phallus explains why it is repeatedly noted that the Devil's member and his ejaculate were cold. Isobell Gowdie and Janet Braidheid in identical words 'fand his nature als cold within me as spring-well-water ... He is abler for ws that way than any man can be ... a hudg nature, verie cold, as yce' (Pitcairn 1833, III, 603, 611). When Bessie Lacost of Stenton lay with the Devil she 'thought that his bodie was harder and colder than a man' (Larner 1981, 150). The same circumstances are reported from England: Widow Bush of Barton, Suffolk, said that he was 'colder than man, and heavier, and could not perform nature as man' (Murray 1921, 181). This contraption was evidently part of the animal disguise or hidden under the coat of skins that the leader of the coven wore when in his official capacity.

It seems clear that the sex act with the Devil was symbolic or ritualistic, perhaps no more than a token gesture, not a natural event, though Isobell Gowdie told the court that the youngest and lustiest women had very great pleasure in copulating with the devil, 'much mor than with their awin husbandis'. It is equally probable that the Devil did not undertake this sexual rite for his personal pleasure. In the context of the sabbat he was not a man but an animal. There were exceptions. Little Janet Hewit of the Forfar coven, who had a talent for being in the wrong place at the wrong time, once saw the Devil having carnal copulation with her mother at a place called Newmanhill hard by Forfar, about midnight. When the Devil had ridden off, 'hir mother forbade her to tell hir father of what shoe had seen that night' (Anderson 1888, 248). There were evidently rules against non-ritual intercourse.

It has been proposed that ointments containing aconite, hemlock and belladonna were used by witches to give the illusion of flying, and so perhaps they did, but the primary purpose of these ointments may rather have been to dull or confuse the senses in preparation for ritual intercourse, for the carnal copulation of Scottish witches as recorded by the courts seems to have been a joyless, perhaps even unpleasant affair, undertaken as a duty, not for pleasure, despite what Isobell confessed. The technique evidently varied from place to place and was sometimes painful. In the Basses Pyrénées it took place behind a screen and the women cried out as though they were in great pain and came back bleeding (Murray 1921, 180-1). In view of the symbolic links between the shedding of blood by hunters and the deer trap seen in metaphorical terms as the vulva of the Cailleach, it is possible that bleeding was deliberately provoked.

An early but unreliable reference to the activities of witches in Scotland is the broadsheet *Newes from Scotland*, published as 'A True Discourse of the apprehension of sundrie Witches lately taken in Scotland' in 1590-91 (Pitcairn 1833, III, 74). This document was either written by James VI or under his supervision and it is a strange mixture of fact and fantasy. On the one hand we are expected to believe that on Allhallow Even 1590 Agnes Sampson and two hundred other witches went to sea, each one in a riddle or sieve, and sailed, drinking and making merry, to the Kirk of North Berwick and on the other that when they got there they danced a reel while Geillis Duncane played on the trump or Jew's harp and all sang together: 'Commer goe ye before, commer goe ye. Gif ye will not goe before, commer let me'. It is an unstable mixture of truth and fantasy: Geillis Duncane probably did play on the Jew's harp but there were at most forty witches, perhaps only twenty and they travelled in the normal way, by boat.

The same mixture is found in its account of Bothwell's dealing with his witches. If two hundred witches going to sea in two hundred sieves are as unreal as a nursery tale, the claim of carnal usage by Bothwell is equally unreal: 'Quhen the Devill did recyeve them for his servauntes, and that they had vowed themselves unto him, then hee woulde carnally use them, albeit to their litle pleasure, in respect to his colde nature; and would do the like at sundry other times' (Pitcairn 1590-91, 219). Bothwell, the Devil in the case, was unlikely to have had intercourse however nominal or mechanical with any of his witches, nor do any of them claim that he did, but James must have learned by then that 'dealing' was a standard element of witch practice.

Certain trials in Aberdeenshire in 1597 reveal a similar admixture of fantasy to a plain tale. We are told that at Hallowe'en 1597 eight healers, all women, gathered at Craigleauch Hill (now Craiglich, NO 5305), between Warthill and Lochmanse, when they danced all together for a long time in a ring round a great stone, under the direction of Satan, who provided the music. They were all accused of unlawful intercourse with the Devil: 'the deuill your master, beand in the liknes of a beast, had carnall deall with ilk ane of yow'. This has been added at the very end of the dittay against Jonet Lucas (SCM 1841, I, 149) and appears to be an afterthought or improvement. In the next two dittays, Jonat Davidsone and Issobell Oige are individually accused of having sexual dealings with the Devil (SCM, 1841, I, 151-2). The sexual rite is certainly possible as Hallowe'en was a major sabbat. However when we compare the various dittays the evidence for intercourse with a Devil present in person tends to dwindle away. John Ros, minister of Lumphanan, who was the moving spirit in these trials, accused the women of being 'under the direction' of Satan but the physical presence of the fiend in their revels is questionable. In the following two dittays, against Jonat Davidsone and Issobell Oige, there is no more mention of carnal dealing and in Jonat Davidsone's dittay the Devil has become 'onvisibill' (SCM 1841, I, 151). There appears to have been discussion of the point among the judges, with the minister making a retreat and the clerk recording only established facts in these two cases. This now reduces allegations of carnal dealing from eight to one. The original story of sexual dealings with the Devil in likeness of a beast is probably an unfounded allegation by John Ros, the minister, once again influenced by written sources and imported sensation. 1597 is in any case very early for a coven governed by a Devil but the minister appears to have known all about how they operated.

The most likely source of the minister's expectations was *Newes from Scotland* whose original Scottish edition was produced in 1591. It deals with the attack on His Majesty's life in the previous year and its contents were closely supervised by James VI, if he did not actually write them. The relevant passage (in both editions) says: 'Moreouer the said Witches being demaunded how the Diuell would vse them when he was in their company, they confessed that when the Diuell did receiue them for his seruants, and that they had vowed themselues vnto him, then he would Carnally vse them, albeit to their little pleasure, in respect of his colde nature: and would doo the like at sundry other times'. This might be seen as proof that the demonic pact validated by carnal use was known in Scotland at the time of these trials c.1600. The demonic pact (however the Devil was envisaged) was certainly known in Scotland before the great witch-hunts, as we have found it administered by one witch to another, but we know that James had information from Continental sources which he acquired in Denmark.

This still leaves one question: was ritual intercourse using an artificial penis part of earlier pagan practice in Scotland? This is not yet clear but in the dwindling evidence for a native Devil it is perhaps not important. We should also remember that 'the Devil' in the context of the *Newes* was Bothwell and the witches who vow themselves to work with him are not supernatural creatures but the charmers, healers and midwives of East Lothian who met him in North Berwick. But James was anxious to demonise all those involved and often strays far from the facts (which tend to demonise the King). In that case the pact, the ritual sex and the cold body all refer to the Earl, are limited to this one mention in the *Newes,* and may be invented. However as we will see the Oda of the West involves sexual activity using what looks very like a *fascinum.*

But there is no sign of sex, ritual or otherwise, at Hallowe'en in Aberdeen in 1597 in the case against Thomas Leyis, son of a notorious wise woman. He was sentenced to death for having led the ring at a Hallowe'en revel in Aberdeen, for guising and dancing, and for being a notorious witch. The dance seems to have been a public event. There is no mention of a pact or of sex, nor did the baillies identify him as the Devil (SCM, 1841, I, 97-101).

We can perhaps distinguish the fertility rite from the many communal revels which are known throughout Europe and which hark back to preparations for a hunt – including the wearing of animal skins or some other disguise, the blackened faces for the night hunt, and begging for food to sustain the hunters. Sex is seldom if ever mentioned in the context of hunting but given its importance in the related hunting cult it would be strange if the Hallowe'en celebrations did not involve sex. Karl Pearson describes 'the Playing of the Stag', a type of hunting play with surrogate women, celebrated at New Year. A man dressed in the skin of a stag, with its antlers and cloven hooves still attached, went round the community accompanied by other men wearing women's clothing. 'In this costume, with licentious songs and drinking, they proceeded to the doors of the churches, where they danced and sung with extraordinary antics.' Similar celebrations with men dressed as women took place in various places at Twelfth Night, May Day and Midsummer Day, all seasonal markers and fire festivals. The old religious rites with their choral dances and lascivious songs were pleasurable events (Pearson 1897, II, 19). This mingling of fun with religious observance, so foreign to the Reformed mentality, persisted in the Hallowe'en guising which was still popular in post-war Scotland. Boys dressed as girls and girls as boys, wearing old clothes turned inside out as a disguise and their faces blackened like hunters. They sang to entertain the householder and were rewarded with durable rations, no longer cheese and oatcakes but apples, nuts and sweets. In the Outer Hebrides at midwinter, the *Gillean Callaig* was dressed in the hide of a bull, complete with horns, hooves and tail which had been kept since Martinmas and perambulated through the township while his followers beat on the hide with sticks (McNeill 1961, III, 89).

The Church adopted many aspects of the preceding pagan religion including its sites, its calendar, its saints, its prayers, its chants and its sacraments. The communal meal, once the communal feast after the hunt, persisted, with wine and bread replacing ale and meat. Christmas carols derive from the sexually-explicit choral love-songs sung to provide music for dancing. But for some reason the Church drew a firm line at orgiastic sex or at any sex outside marriage and made marriage into a sacrament. They banned sex for priests altogether. Dancing was banned as its movements are inherently wanton when they are not deliberately obscene, and pagan dances were as obscene as they could be.

Despite this detailed, persistent and consistent evidence for real or simulated sex as the key to witchcraft, Larner saw nothing more in the sabbat than the reaction of a deprived peasantry to over-strict discipline by repressive ministers, 'jollifications for eating, drinking and dancing of which in Scotland at least peasants were in real life deprived' (1981, 200). She makes the sabbat sound like a Sunday School treat. Smout, more to the point, remarked that it is 'not at all easy to understand why the reformers concentrated on the prosecution of sexual offenders; it was a quite unscriptural emphasis'. Why, he wondered, did they not attack the Biblical sins of hypocrisy, greed, pride and mendacity, whose prevalence within the Church of Rome had been the main cause of the Reformation (and which were by no means extinct in the Reformed version), but came down very hard on the apparently harmless indulgence by the common folk in 'riotous cheer, banqueting, immoderate dancing and whoredom'? (Smout 1970, 82-3).

But the Church's opposition to riotous cheer and in particular to unlicensed sex makes perfect sense when we accept that unlicensed sex was the primary sacrament of the witch cult. We would expect the Kirk to know this only too well as soon as it began to concern itself with its parish responsibilities. It became well informed about the activities of witches from the reports given to the General Assembly by its parish ministers and must have been surprised and alarmed by the spread of organised covens, set up in direct competition and often poaching on the membership. Many Christians are still preoccupied with the fight against the perceived evils of dancing and fornication, not to mention the Demon Drink, without realising they are not spreading Christianity but only reacting to the rituals of the old religion. In Auldearn the witches reacted to persecution in predictable fashion by working with their Lord to bring about the death of Mr Harie Forbes, the parish minister. If they did not succeed it was not for want of trying (Pitcairn 1833, III, 609-610, 612, 615). Mr Forbes knew for a fact that riotous cheer, banqueting, immoderate dancing and whoredom were works of the Devil; he knew the Devil personally.

Like all religious beliefs, those of the witch cult were irrational and the powers claimed by witches were illusory but when we accept that the main purpose of the witch cult was to generate fertility and prosperity by ritual copulation between a horned beast and a group of dedicated women, the purpose of the coven, its shaggy master, the sabbats, the witch-hunts and the repressive activities of the Reformed Church in Scotland all fall into place. They may be to some extent derivative, influenced by imported sources, as we find a very different picture beyond the Highland Line, as we will see, but fertility magic certainly influenced what we find in the trials of coven witches in Lowland Scotland.

Women did not seek intercourse with the devil for pleasure, even less for lust, but endured it as a source of blessing, a ritual which generated supernatural powers and guaranteed prosperity, or, more simply, brought good luck to the witch, her family and her community. Her ability to acquire power by this act is the only possible explanation of the fact that witches were women, that witchcraft was a woman's business, and that carnal dealing was part of the ritual. The Church's objection to the copulatory aspects of the sabbat was not to the pleasures of the flesh but to their religious nature.

CHAPTER 7:
WITCHCRAFT IN ABERDEENSHIRE

Aberdeen can serve as a model for the history of witchcraft in Lowland Scotland. John Stuart in his preface to the first Spalding Club Miscellany (1841, 49) notes that the history of witchcraft in northeast Scotland previous to 1590 is not well known, but 'it is probable that no case of importance had been tried, as no earlier notice on the subject occurs in the Records of the Town Council of the Burgh, which commence in 1397.' He attributes the sharp upsurge in trials after 1590 to 'the well-known predilection of King James VI for inquiries into the mysteries of futurity'.

George Black notes only one earlier trial, in 1536, when Agnes *alias* Lanie Scot was convicted of using magical arts (1938, 21). Then on 18 June 1590, the Chronicle of Aberdeen notes that 'Barbara Card, wiche, was bryntt on the Hedownis Hill' (SCM 1842, II, 65) and on 17 August 1590 two 'great vitches', Janet Grant alias *Gradoch* in Colquhatstane and Janet Clark alias *Spaldarg* in Blalak were strangled and burnt on the Castle Hill of Edinburgh for 'certane crymes of wichcraft'. On the following day, also in Edinburgh, Marion Bruce in Auldrain (Old Rayne) and Bessie Paull in the Cromar are mentioned as fugitives (Pitcairn 1833, I, 206-8). Then, again, for a few years there is silence but the forces of outraged piety are gathering.

The main campaign against witches in Aberdeenshire began in 1595 and continued into 1598. Despite the numbers involved (more than seventy are thought to have been executed), all the known trials are those of individuals or small groups rather than members of covens. Public interest was considerable: one of the expenses caused by the execution of Margaret Clerk or Bane in 1597 was 'for caring [carrying] of four sparris to withstand the press of the people, quhairof there was tua broken.' In September 1597, the Provost, Baillies and Council of the city compensated William Dunn, Dean of Guild, for losses incurred through neglect of his business in the discharge of his civic duties, as well as 'his extraordinarie takin panis in the burning of the gryt numer of the witches brunt this yeir, and on the four pirattis, and bigging of the port on the brig of Dee, repairing of the grey freris kirk and stepill thairof.' It was all in the day's darg.

The accused women seem to have been well-known locally as healers, charmers, wise women and midwives who were suddenly rounded up, tried and executed after practising peacefully for many years with the support of their communities. There are no demonic pacts and only very elusive accusations of ritual sex in Aberdeenshire at this time. The Devil occasionally lurks in the background as a Devilish spirit but he may be wishful thinking on the part of the ministers. In 1597 he makes an improbable appearance to Ellen Gray in the prison at Slains in the form of an aged bearded man wearing a white gown and a thrummit hat, who advises her to depend on God and a good jury (SCM 1841, I, 127).

A feature of the 1596-7 trials is the variation of accusations made against individual witches which suggests uncertainty or differing opinions on the part of the authorities. Isobel Cockie of Kintore was accused of cursing and curing. Helene Frasser of Foveran was found guilty of cursing, curing and odd behaviour. Janet Wischert of Aberdeen who had been a witch for thirty years was accused of thirteen cases of the evil eye, two failed cures, and three allegations. In addition she had a bad reputation and her neighbours were afraid of her. In several cases a woman was stated without other complaint to be 'a common vitche be oppin voce and common fame'. All of them were strangled and burnt.

The main complaint against Thomas Leyis, Jonet Wischert's son, is that he led the traditional celebrations in Aberdeen town centre by dancing with many others around the Market Cross and in the Meal Market, at midnight on Hallowe'en, 1596. He was denounced by Kathren Mitchell, the widow of a burgess, whom he hit, because she was slow and spoiled the dance. (Does this suggest that the dance was magical?) His other crime was to be the son of a great witch. The Devil was present at the Cross, or so it was said, but if so he was not one of those arrested.

The dittay or accusation against Thomas Leyis places his fate firmly within the daily life of the town. (All exerpts from Stuart 1848.)

'Follows the particular dittey and accusatioun gewin in aganis Thomas Leyis sone to John Leyis, stabler, for his being ane commoun witche and sorcerar, wsing the tred and craft thairof be perswasioun of the Dewill, as followis:–

Imprimis, Wpoun Hallowewin last bypast, att tuelff houris at ewin or thairby, thow the said Thomas Leyis, accompaneit withe vmquhill Jonett Wischert, Issobel Coky, Issobell Manteithe, Kathren Mitchell, relict of vmquhill Charles Dwn, litster, sorceraris and witches, withe ane gryit number of vtheris witches, come to the mercatt and fische croce of Aberdene, under the conduct and gyding of the Dewill, present withe yow, all in company, playing befoir yow on his kynd of instrumentis: Ye all dansit about baythe the saidis croces, and the meill mercatt ane lang space of tyme; in the quhilk Dewillis dans, thow the said Thomas was formest and led the ring, and dang the said Kathren Mitchell, becaus scho spillit your dans, and ran nocht sa fast about as the rest. Testifeit be the said Kathrin Mitchell, quha was present withe the at the tyme forsaid, dansing withe the Dewill.'

The court of Justiciarie was held in the Tolbooth of Aberdeen on 23 February 1596 with Alexander Rutherfuird, provost; Mr Alexander Cullen and Alexander Jaffray, baillies, justices in that part, and an assize of twenty-one townsmen including several elders, a mariner, a stabler, and a butcher.

'The said day, Thomas Leis, sone to Johne Leis, staibler in Abirdenen, was accusit as a commoun notorious witche, in vsing of witchecraft and sorcerie, thir dyvers yeirs bygane, as at gryt lenth is contenit in his ditay: Quhilk, being denyit be the said Thomas, was referrit to the knauledge of the assise abouevritten, chosin, sworne and admittit.

James Steuart chosin chancellar. The haill assis, in ane voce, for the maist pairt [except thrie, to vit, Thomas Douglas, Patrick Huntar, and William Mar] be the mouth of James Stewart, chancellor, convictis and fyllis Thomas Leis in the first poynt, that he was the ringleader of the dans on a Hallow evin last, about the croce, and in vther thrie speciall poyntis, and as a notorious witche be oppin voce and common fame.

Item, the 23d Feb 1597, for peattis, tar barrelis, fir, and coallis, to burn the said Thomas, and to Jon Justice for his fie in executing him £2 13 4'

It cost much more to burn Janet Wischert and Isobel Cocker in 1596.

'Item, for twenty loads of peattis to burn them	£2 0 0
Item, for ane boll of coillis	1 4 0
Item, for four tar barrelis	1 6 8
Item, for fir and win [dry] barrellis	0 16 8
Item, for a staik, and dressing of it	0 16 0
Item, for four fadomes of towis	4 0 0
Item, for careing the peattis, coallis and barrelis to the hill	0 13 4
Item, to Jon Justice for their execution	0 13 4'

Isobel Monteith hanged herself in prison but was punished nonetheless:

'Item, for trailling Monteithe through the streits of the toun in ane cart, quha hangit herself in prison, and eirding [burying] of her £ 0 10 0.'

At least sixty people were executed for witchcraft at this period in Aberdeen. Ten were banished. As mentioned, Isobel Monteith hung herself in prison. Of Kathren Mitchell no more is known. But healers and charmers retained their popularity. So many people visited John Gordon when he was in the church lock-up to ask his advice and have his blessing that the Town Council felt obliged to ban the practice. His popularity is a measure of the importance of traditional witchcraft in Scotland in the late sixteenth century. It also suggests that the witch trials did nothing to turn those in need from having recourse to local healers.

Aberdeen, 2 September 1596 (Stuart 1848, 144-5)

'The quhilk day, the counsall considering that thair is a gryt resort of the inhabitants of this burght, bayth men and women, daylie to ane Johne Gordone, alias Williamsone, presentlie detenit in captivitie in the kirk wolt, as a manifest and oppin witche, quha continewallie, quhill he was laitlie apprehendit and tane, gawe himself out as a dum man, and speris athe sad Johne dyvers and sindrie thingis werray preiudiciall to the commoun pepill, quha has bene, and is yit, daylie seducit and deludit be him, to the gryt dishonour of God, theirfor ordanit proclamatioun to be maid the morne, be the drum passand throw the haill rewis of the toune, that na inhabitant within this burght presume nor tak upon hand to confer to, nor speak with, the said Johne in tyme cumming in any sort, certifeing six as sal be fun and notit conferring with him, sall be causit mak publict repentance in sack cloth, besyd the danger of the kingis lawis to be execut on thame with all rigour, conforme to the actis of parliament; and siclyk ordanis ane commissioun to be send for to his Maiestie, to be direct to the schireff, or sitting and haulding justice on him, conforme to the lawis of this realme, for his witchcraft.'

After the last victims were put to death early in 1598, the pace of persecution slowed for a few years, there being no doubt a dearth of potential victims. However folk memory is long and persistent but also does not rapidly absorb new ideas and before long Aberdeenshire saw a new generation of witches in the hinterland of the town and a new coven in Aberdeen itself.

1601 Aberdeen: Walter Ronaldstone (perhaps related to Margaret Ronaldson, Aberdeen 1627).

1607 Banchory: Isabell Smith, accused of using a 'wolne thred and a slewof' [sleeve], elements in a common cure.

1613 Aberdeen: Margaret Reoch, a vagabond (a fairy woman), sometime in Lumfannan.

The following items appear in the Town's accounts (Stuart 1848)

'Item, peyit for ane commission anent ye witches   £ 6 13 4

For a barrow to carie ye cripple witches   0 6 0

To Alex. Ramsy debursit be him for interteining ye witches   1 4 2 3 4

To Mr Andro Clerk for his pains in wrytting ye dittays on ye witches and sitting as clerk in ye commission   6 13 4'

These ghastly events are interspersed with accounts for municipal junketing, for 'saluting of doctor forbes at his home-cuming', for poems 'presentit to ye provest on ye praise of aberdein', for the reception of Lord Marischall and Lord Erskine, for municipal wine for Bishop Murray, and wines and spices for the Earl Enzie.

A new attack on witches in Aberdeenshire began at Michaelmas 1626. Between 1626 and 1627 twenty-six are named in the Commissions issued by the Privy Council, including thirteen witches, a probable Devil and a probable officer belonging to a coven based in Aberdeen (including Futtie and Whitestripes). The rest are widely scattered: Ellon is fifteen miles from Aberdeen, Alford and Lumphanan are twenty-five miles away, Aboyne thirty miles. This coven does not seem to have survived the purge.

1626, 14 December: Issobell Leslie and Cummer Muttoun in Aberdeen; Johne Propter and William Young in Allon [Ellon]; Agnes Forbes and her sister in Whitestrypis; Johnne Findlaw in Wester Beltie; Gowane Andersoun in Awfuird [Alford]; Marioun Quhyte in Stradowne; Elspet Herald in Birkinbad; Margaret Turnour in Tulliowne; Helen spouse to Alexander Reid and Margaret spouse to Johnne McConnochie in Aboyne; Margaret Cleroch in Lomquhannane; Jonnet Robbie in Newmilne of Auchlossin (RPC).

1627, 23 January: Jonnet Dovertie, Agnes Carle and John Davie in Aberdeen; Margaret Durie, Annabell Cattenheid and Nanse (Agnes) Durie in Futtie (RPC).

1627, 25 April: Walter Baird (perhaps the Devil as he has a Commission to himself), accused of 'the crymes of witchcraft, sorcerie, useing of charmes and inchantmentis and utheris divillische practizes', Margaret Ronaldson, Agnes Watt, Issobell Smyth in Futtie, Margaret Udny in Aberdeen (RPC).

The last cases

1629 Helen Knight in Grange, in the parish of Petterugie, Margaret Strath in Auchereis, Alexander Hay in Kinmudie, tried for witchcraft.

1630 Andrew Abel in Hill of Tillicarie, fugitive (RPC).

1630 Marion Hardie, a vagabond (one of the fairy folk), born in Elgin but arrested in Aberdeen where she was strangled and burnt, having confessed that she and Margaret Lumsden, Mallie Cowper, and Marion Rodgie came from Fraserburgh in May 'and conveennand with the devill at the water mouth of Dee beside the blockehous, plotted the death of Richard Cadenheids boate in Futtie, kuist ane nomber of stones in the water mouth when the boat wes comming in, quhairthrow and by thair divilish inchantments, the said Richard and all his companie died, ane man excepted. And sicluke she confest that she accompanied [by several other women] being all conveened togidder in one companie at the devills command be Mathow Wills wyfe her instigatioun, destroyed ane boate belonging to Peterheid quhairin there perished or died twelffe or threttein persons' (RPB). Magic is missing but this fandangle was apparently taken seriously by the Bishop, Provost and Bailies of Aberdeen who heard the case.

1630 Margaret Anderson in Ally and Thomas Grig at the Burn of Auchly, suspected of witchcraft; sentence not known (RPC).

1630 James Hall was accused of charming; 'nothing more is known of this case (Black 1938, 45).

1630 Margaret Rid and Janet Currie at Crimond 'long suspected of witchcraft'; to be tried (RPC).

1631 John Phillip, vagabond (one of the last of the fairy folk of Banff) found guilty of witchcraft and sorcerie (RPC). For Preip the Witch see the Presbytery Book of Strathbogie 1843, 5).

1636 Margaret Fraser, Aberdeen, a suspected witch, broke ward and fled. 1650: reported dead.

By 1650 the panic was almost over. The people reverted to their old healers and persisted with their superstitious revels when men dress as women and dance to bring luck to the town. Changed times are evident in the case of Issobell Malcolme, a wise and clever woman who for twenty years had helped women in childbed and cured sick children in Strathbogie. She was summoned in 1637 to appear before the presbytery. She was again summoned for charming in 1640 and 1644. Her ladies were evidently grateful.

At Botary, Apryl 12, 1637 (Turreff 1871).

'Issobell Malcolme, parishioner of Botarye, sumonded to this daye for charming, compeared, and confessed that she had been in use of charming this twenty yeeres, and, being requyred to name some of those whome she had charmed, she named Jeane Rutherfuird, spouse to James Gordoune, in Torrisoyle, and [...] Innes, spouse to Johne Ogilvye of Miltoune; she confessed that she had charmed both these gentlewemen for the bairne bed; and siclyke, she confessed that she had charmed ane chylde's sore eye in Bade, within the parish of Ruven. The censure of the said Issobell was continued in hope that she should be found yet more guiltye.'

Not with a bang but a whimper

1642 Christane Rind and Thomas Duff of Botary were summoned for sending for Issobell Malcolme in Glasse, supposed to be a witch, for consulting with her, and receiving charms and directions from her. The said Christane compeared not.

1643 Janet Maconachie of Botarie was accused of witchcraft.

1644 Patrick Malcolmie of Botary was found guilty of sorcery but fled the country.

1649 Isoble Kelman of Aberdeen, said to be a known charmer but 'against whom ther was no proofe'.

1650 Margaret Ogg of Insch accused of witchcraft. Her case was remitted to the Synod.

1669 Margret Abernethy, Margret Dury in Fuittie, Issobell Spens, Robert Shevies of Aberdeen (RPC). All were probably executed. The Kirk Session lamented that witchcraft was 'much abounding in all pairtes of the country'.

1676 Isabel Davidson of Belhelvie, accused of charming, drowned herself.

1703 Robert Bainzie, a church elder, of Oyne, was accused of charming.

APPENDIX
A provisional list of all those tried for witchcraft in Aberdeenshire 1590-1597.

So far 78 individuals have been identified.

Alshenour, Catherine: known only from the expenses of her execution (SCM 1841, I, preface 53).

Bane, Margaret in Lumphanan, 1597: see Clerk or Bane.

Barroun, Isobel 1596. Burnt with Christen Mitchell and Bessie Thom. One of those who danced around the Fish Croce, Aberdeen, at Hallowe'en 1596 (SCM 1841, I, 168-170).

Bessie Roy 'nurreych', accused of taking away a woman's milk and tried in Fetternear in 1590 but acquitted (Pitcairn 1833, I, 207-209).

Bruce, Marion in Auldrain, fugitive in 1590 (Pitcairn 1833, I, 208).

Burnett, Isobel, the gudwyfe of Cloak, widow of Thomas Forbes of Cloak, and Elspet Forbes hir dochter were exempted from the charge of witchcraft by direction of the king. 5m NE of Aboyne (SCM 1841, I, 163-164).

Card, Barbara: see Keand.

Clark, Janet, alias *Spaldairg*, in Blalach (Lumphanan), sister of Margaret Clark or Bane – 'the mother of all vitches'. G. *spall* 'to beat' + *dearg* 'red, red-hot'. Burnt in Edinburgh 1590 (SCM 1841, I, 158; Pitcairn I, 206).

Cleraucht, Margaret in Lumphanan, acquitted 25 April 1597 (SCM 1841, I, 183).

Clerk or Bane, Margaret in Lumphanan, 1597, sister of Janet Clark '*Spaldarg*' (SCM 1841, I, 156-162).

Cockie, Isobel 1597, wife of John Duff in Kintore. Leader of the ring after Thomas Leyis when the witches danced in Aberdeen at Hallowe'en 1596. Taught others for forty years (SCM 1841, I, preface, 52).

Davidson, Janet, banished owt of the shirrefdome in 1597 (SCM 1841, I, 150-151, 156).

Degeddes, Janet, an associate of Katherine Gerard in NE Aberdeenshire (SCM I1841, 174-175, 177).

Douglas, Janet, known only from the expenses incurred by her execution (SCM 1841, I, preface, 53).

Ego, Thomas, fugitive, husband of Bessie Paul, in Blelak 1597 (SCM 1841, I, 182-184).

Elder, Moriss, his wife at Hill of Chattie, Banff, 1597, was named by Andro Man.

Fergus, Catherine, executed with Isobel Strauthaquhin alias *Scudder* or *Sculdr* in Dyce. Perhaps her daughter; 1595-1597 (SCM 1841, I, 177-182).

Fernsche, Catherine of the parish of Coldstone, 3 m. W Tarland, Cromar (SCM 1841, I, 187-188).

Ferries or Fergus, Catherine, probably Lumphanan, 1597 (SCM 1841, I, 184).

Fidlar, Gilbert, in Auchmacoy, son-in-law of Janet Leisk at Fortrieford; acquitted 1597 (SCM 1841, I, 137-138).

Findley, Elspeth in Blelak, 6m.W of Aboyne (SCM 1841, I, 182-184).

Forbes, Agnes in Wester Kincardine. Kincardine O'Neil is 4m. E Aboyne (SCM 1841, I, 184-185).

Forbes, Isobel in Glenmullocht, Lumphanan, 1597: acquitted (SCM 1841, I, 183).

Fram or Fren, Agnes, accused by Mr John Ros, minister at Lumphanan. At Auchlossin (2m south of Lumphanan), 1597 (SCM 1841, I, 182-184, 191-2).

Fraser, Helen 1597, at Aikinshill, at Foveran. Condemned as 'a rank vitche be oppin voce and commoun fame' (SCM I, 105-110) and executed.

Fynnie, Malie in the Blairtoun of Balhelueis. Belhelvie, parish 8m N Aberdeen (SCM 1841, I, 106.)

Gerard, Catherine, daughter of Hellie Pennie, 1597. Associated with Christian Reid in NW Aberdeenshire (SCM 1841, I, 174-177).

Grant, Jonet alias *Gradoch*, in Colquhatstane, Aberdeen, executed in Edinburgh, 1590 with Jonet Clark. In addition to being 'commoune notorous Wichis' they were accused of causing the death of the Laird of Craigievar, his son and others. Pitcairn vol 1, part 2, 206-209. Colquhatstane is now Coldstone (NO4404), *Kilchodistan* in 1342 (Alexander 1952, 223).

Grant, Marion, widow of John Huchoun of Acheldie, in Methlick, 1597. Christsonday taught her several spells 'in the name of the Father, Sone, and Haly Ghaist, and Chrystsonday'. She admitted that 'The Devill, thy maister, quhome thow termes Christsonday, causit the dans sindrie tymes with him and with Our Ladye, quha, as thow sayes, was a fine woman, cled in a quhyt walicot' (SCM 1841, I, 170-2).

Gray, Elspeth in Findlater, Banff. Named by Andro Man but not known to have been tried.

Gray, Ellen, Slains, 1597. Convicted as 'ane commoun viche'. An associate of Agnes Wobster in NE Aberdeenshire (SCM 1841, I, 125-128).

Guisset, Janet, probably Cromar, 1597. Under Laird of Abergeldie (SCM 1841, I, 184-185).

Henderson, Christen, henwife in Foveran, recruited by Helen Fraser, 1597 (SCM 1841, I, 107).

Henderson, Elspeth, known only from the expenses incurred by her execution (SCM 1841, I, preface, 53).

Innes, Margaret, associate of Christen Michell (SCM 1841, I, 164-165, 170).

Keand or Card, Barbara, alias Leslie, wiche, 'was bryntt on the Hedownis Hill' on 18 June 1590 (SCM 1842, II, 65).

Leisk, Janet in Fortrieford, sister of Isobel Leisk, 1597. Acquitted (SCM 1841, I, 134-137).

Leslie, Barbara: see Keand.

Leyis, John, husband of Jonet Wishert, and his daughters Elspet, Jonet and Violat, Aberdeen 1596: absolved and banished (SCM 1841, I, 102-104).

Leyis, Thomas, son of Jonet Wischert, in Aberdeen 1596, lived with Elspet Reid, led the ring when the witches danced about the Fish Cross in Aberdeen (SCM 1841, I, 93).

Lucas, Janet in Pitmurchie. 2m SE Lumphanan, 5m NE Aboyne (SCM 1841, I, 147-149, 156).

Makkie, Helen alias *Suppak*, Kintore; died in prison 1597 (SCM 1841, I, 114, preface p. 52).

Malcolme, Isobel, Botary, Aberdeenshire, midwife and charmer, 1637-1642 (Turreff 1859, 15).

Man, Andro, Banff. A wise man in the old Gaelic tradition. He lived at Tarbruich, Banff (NJ 4863), on the south side of the Bin of Cullen, site of a coastal beacon. Strangled and burnt 1598 (SCM 1841, I, 117-125).

Menteith, Isobel, Aberdeen, hanged herself in prison, 1596. She had danced around the Fish Croce of Aberdeen at Hallowe'en 1596 (SCM 1841, I, preface, 52).

Mergie, consort of Ellen Gray, 1597; fugitive (SCM 1841, I, 127).

Miller, Christian, an associate of Katherine Gerard in NE Aberdeenshire (SCM 1841, I, 174-175, 177).

Mitchell, Christian, Aberdeen, 1597. Widow of a burgess of Aberdeen. One of those who danced around the Fish Croce at Hallowe'en 1596 (SCM 1841, I, 164-5).

Mitchell, Kathren, widow of Charles Dwn, litster, Aberdeen. She was danged by Thomas Leis because she spoiled the Hallowe'en dance in Aberdeen by being slow (SCM 1841, I, 97-98).

Moinness, Elspeth, known as Erss Elspett, from the Highlands. An associate of Katherine Gerard in NE Aberdeenshire (SCM 1841, I, 175).

Mutche, Meriorie in Corstane, 1597, spouse of William Ross. Acquitted (SCM 1841, I, 131-133).

Og, James in Lumphanan, cast a curse on his neighbour's crops and livestock, 1597 (SCM 1841, I, 190).

Og, Margaret, spouse to John Robbie in Marywall. Marywell, 4m SE

Aboyne. She and her daughters Beatrix and Isobel Robbie went to Criagleauch on Hallowe'en last where with others they danced round a great stone (SCM 1841, I, 142-145, 154).

Oige, Isobel, wife of Johne Dauidsone in Blelak, 1597. Lumphanan coven (SCM 1841, I, 151-152, 155).

Paul, Bessie, wife of Thomas Ego in Blelak 1597. Cromar (SCM I, 182-184; Pitcairn 208).

Pennie, Hellie, mother of Katherine Gerard, burnt at Slains in 1597 (SCM 1841, I, 174-175, 177).

Reauche, Margaret in Wodfeidill; probably Cromar (SCM 1841, I, 185).

Reid, Christian, vagabond (fairy woman). She cast a spell on a mill at Fedderat, near New Deer 'in the name of God and Christsunday'. Also at Slains, NE Aberdeenshire (SCM 1841, I, 172-4).

Riauch, Margaret in Green Cottis (SCM 1841, I, 191).

Richie, Isobel, wife of John Bayne, 1597, at Cloak (Lumphanan) (SCM 1841, I, 140-142, 154).

Robbie, Beatrix, daughter to Margaret Og, Marywell, near Aboyne. Banished (SCM 1841, I, 152-153, 155).

Robbie, Isobel, Lumphanan, 1597. She was often seen in the shape of a hare. A daughter of Margaret Og and John Robbie, Marywall (SCM 1841, I, 185, 191).

Roger or Rogie, Helen, daughter to the late Margaret Baine, wife of John Strachan in Finderak (Lumphanan), 1597 (SCM 1841, I, 145-147, 153).

Saythe, Margaret or Maggy, Banff, named by Andro Man who said that she 'hes bein this sex yeris in cumpany with the weychis with Cryistsunday'. 1597 (SCM 1841, I, 125).

Sherare, Margaret, in Kincardyne (near K O'Neill, 4m E Aboyne) (SCM I, 184-185).

Shuddak, one of those who danced around the Fish Cross and Meil Market of Aberdeen at Hallowe'en 1596 (SCM 1841, I, 115). G. *siodhach* 'a fairy, one of the fairy folk (a hunter)'.

Skein, Malie wife of Couper Watsoun, who taught Helen Fraser in Foveran (SCM 1841, I, 105).

Smelie, Agnes, known only from the expenses incurred by her execution (SCM 1841, I, preface 52).

Smith, Janet in Cushnie, 5 m. SW Alford. Cromar coven (SCM 1841, I, 185).

Smithe, Elspeth in Tillilair (Coull, 3m NW Aboyne (SCM 1841, I, 184-185).

Smyth, Margaret, associate of Katherine Gerard in NE Aberdeenshire, 1597 (SCM 1841, I, 174-175, 177).

Strathauchyn, Elspeth in Warthiel, fugitive. Wartle, parish of Lumphanan (SCM 1841, I, 182-184).

Strauthaquhin, Isobel alias *Scudder*, and hir dochter, 1597, Dyce (SCM 1841, I, 177-182).

Taiss, Beak, Burnside of Logie, in Logiemar, Cromar. Fugitive, 1597 (SCM 1841, I, 182, 188).

Thom, Bessie, 1597, in Aberdeen. One of those who danced around the Fish Croce at Hallowe'en 1596. (SCM 1841, I, 166-7, 170). Convicted.

Wischert, Jonet, a great witch, spouse of John Leyis and mother of Thomas, Elspet, Jonet and Vilat Leyis, Aberdeen 1596. One of those who danced around the Fish Croce at Hallowe'en 1596. Burnt with Isobel Cockie very soon after this event. See John Leyis (SCM 1841, I, 83-102).

Wobster, Agnes, in Ludcairnie (NK0243), 1597. Complaints against her came from clients in Auchtidonald (NK0147), Coynach (NJ 9944), Elrik (NJ 9440), and Jock's Hill (NJ 9544). Associated with Helen Gray in Slains (SCM 1841, I, 128-130).

Wood, Marion, known as Erss Marion or the 'Catnes norrische'. In NE Aberdeenshire with Katherine Gerard, Christian Reid and Marioun Grant, 1597 (SCM 1841, I, 176).

Over the period from 1590 to the end only a dozen men were tried. Three fled and one was acquitted.

CHAPTER 8: HIGHLANDS AND LOWLANDS: WITCHCRAFT IN PERTHSHIRE

When compared with other parts of Scotland, it is hard to find anything particularly unique or distinctive about Gaelic witch beliefs.

Liz Henderson 2008, 118

Perthshire is a convenient place to study the contrast between the Highland and the Lowland attitude to witchcraft. By the seventeenth century the county was already divided into a Gaelic-speaking and an English-speaking part, the dividing line running east-west between Monzie, a Highland parish, and Crieff, a Lowland town with a church, a school and a weaving industry. Breadalbane, further west in Highland Perthshire, was an important feudal estate whose jurisdiction ran from Aberfeldy to the Argyll border. It incorporated the Highland parishes of Kenmore, Killin, Weem and Dull.

Highland Perthshire

The records of the Breadalbane Baron Court give us a measure of how insignificant witchcraft was in this very large and populous Highland area. Between 1622 and 1757 the authorities dealt with only six cases dealing with what might be described as witchcraft, though they steadfastly avoided the use of the term (Gillies 1938, 260, 346-352). No-one was strangled or burnt.

There is no reason to think that belief in the power of magical processes was less deep-rooted among the population of Breadalbane than in other parts of the Highlands, or that the population were more or less pious, but there were no recorded panics, no hunting out of suspects. Benevolent domestic magic involving charmings, sainings, healings and blessings was certainly common and probably universal (according to MacGregor, 1891, and many similar compilations) but is not mentioned at all. Official policy appears to have been to dampen down and ignore any local belief in magic.

In Killin there is an artificial hillock behind the school, marked by a standing-stone and known as *Tom nan Aingeil* 'the hillock of the fire'. Baron Courts were once held there which leads one to think it had been a fairy hillock or outlook post used by hunters. The hunters had vanished but the soil of the mound was still believed to have magical qualities. In 1622 Donald Taillour McGillechrist in Morenish on north Lochtayside sued a woman called McVane who had taken a pock (a poke or bag) of earth from *Tom nan Aingeil* and brought it first to the house of a man called McOlean and then to Donald's house, 'whereby since then the pursuer's gear had not luckit with him, and his corn grew not'. The Court rejected the complaint but it also banned all future use of the pock of earth 'seeing it inclined to no good but to an evil custom' (Gillies 1938, 260).

Nothing of relevance is then reported until 15 September 1700. 'It was enacted this day that because the Session was troubled with people suggested to use enchantments, any who were found to use any charms should be reported guilty of witchcraft' (Gillies 1938, 307). The threat appears to have worked. No doubt enchantments continued to be used and the population continued to believe in their efficacity but no complaints were made until 1730 when a woman from Port of Loch Tay complained that a neighbouring couple had accused her of witchcraft; all three were rebuked.

In 1736 witchcraft ceased to be a crime in Scotland but this did not change the picture in Breadalbane. In 1747 Margaret Robertson of Rhevucky harboured a grudge that Patrick Tossach's former croft had been given to Archibald Cameron and cursed the new tenant in no uncertain terms, wishing him 'Ill meeting and ill flitting, that ill might he thrive, and that he might be drowned by sea or water'. The day that Cameron took over the croft, Margaret was seen down at the lochside apparently working magic with her rock and spindle. She denied that but again beseeched that 'the devil take them in the air that are the instruments of Patrick Tossach's removal'. The Session unanimously found her guilty of praying curses and imprecations but not guilty of witchcraft. She was sentenced to stand in church for three consecutive Sundays to be rebuked by the congregation for sin and scandal. Archibald Cameron was rebuked for causing a scandal.

Still in 1747, Janet and Margaret McIntaggart, two servant lassies, confessed that after the substance of their milk had been taken away (in other words, their milk-ewes had gone dry), they were advised by a certain woman to milk three drops from their neighbours' sheep into an egg shell as a charm to recover their own milk. Margaret had gone round all the neighbouring houses with the egg shell and milk concealed in her breast and her efforts had been successful. The girls were rebuked, examined, exhorted and dismissed.

Domestic magic no doubt persisted through this period but is rarely reported. At Shian in Glenquaich in 1753 on 1 May, Janet McNicol, a servant, was seen 'carrying out some unusual and unbecoming practices very early on Beltane morning', crossing and recrossing a burn three times, then going down the burn, and picking up sticks which she had left at the foot of an ash tree. Another neighbour alleged that her mistress had cut some hairs from her cow's tail and tied them up in a cloth. The local belief was that they were stealing their neighbours' milk. The mistress was rebuked and told not to deal any more with charms and her servant had to stand before the congregation for three Sundays in penance (Gillies 1938, 348).

Lastly, in 1757 Duncan McNucator claimed that Anne McNucator, known to posterity as the Witch of Lawers, was a witch, as he had seen her doing odd things at Beltane. She denied this and no action was taken against her. It seems that the accusation arose out of a family squabble as Anne disapproved of Duncan's wife. This was the last case involving witchcraft in Breadalbane (Gillies 1938, 350).

To summarise, in this large area at the heart of the southern Highland, the court dealt with six cases involving witchcraft or magic in a period of one hundred and thirty-five years in a population of twenty thousand (Webster's Census, 1755; OSA, 1790). Most of the cases reflect a quarrel with neighbours or family. The worst punishment was to do penance by standing before the congregation for three consecutive Sundays and it seems to have been effective.

Thomas Pennant visited Breadalbane in 1769. He noted that Perthshire 'still retains some of its ancient customs and superstitions'; that witchcraft had died out after 1736 but the people still believe in ghosts (1769, 108-9). Surreptitious magical activity certainly continued in Pennant's day, as women continued to teach charms and rituals to their daughters and their maids, most of them designed to maintain the all-important supplies of milk. The ritual known as 'gathering the dew' probably persisted into the twentieth century. Gillies (1938, 351-2) gives instructions: 'Go out early on Beltane morning and draw a hair rope over the neighbour's dewy grass, saying *Bainne an te so shios, bainne an te so shuas 'na mo ghogan fhien,* "The milk of that cow down, the milk of that cow up, in my own great coggie". Then all the neighbour's milk will come to you'. This procedure was witnessed at Morenish about 1890. At the end of the nineteenth century it was still customary on Beltane morning in many of the remote glens of Perthshire to throw ashes and a live peat over one's head, repeating a secret charm for good luck. 'The strictest secrecy was observed, lest news of the ritual should reach the ear of the minister' (McNeill 1959, 2, 64).

In 1938 Wiliam Gillies (the parish minister) wrote that belief in the malign influences of the evil eye had persisted until recently. 'The cure for animals so affected was to take water in God's name from a stream over which the living passed and the dead were carried, put it in a pail along with a silver coin, and then sprinkle the water in the ears and over the backs of the ailing animals. The residue of the water was given to the animals to drink, and if the coin was found to adhere to the bottom of the pail, the cure was supposed to be complete. Cows were protected from the influences of the evil eye by tying a pin of rowan wood to their tails. People also believed that evil spells could be cast upon the cream in the churns so that butter would not come, however long it was churned... In order to counteract the spell they put silver in the form of a coin or an ornament into the churn' (Gillies 1938, 352). The real problem was usually that the cream was too cold.

Lowland Perthshire

When we move the short distance south and east into Lowland Perthshire, we find a very different picture, and yet the people were from the same race and observed the same form of religion though they spoke a different language. George Black in his *Calendar* (1938) gives the historical references to trials for witchcraft in Lowland Perthshire, both in the city of Perth and in the country districts. Between 1577 and 1662, which marked the virtual end of the witch-hunts, he recorded twenty-three court cases, most of them involving more than one person and leading to multiple executions. Most of the victims were charmers and healers but in 1662 three covens come into focus, at Crook of Devon, at Findo-Gask, and at Dunning and at least thirty coven witches were found guilty and put to death. Only one probable 'Devil' was arrested: Robert Wilson in Crook of Devon in 1622. After 1643 activity is in the country districts.

> 1577 Kildeis (Culdees at Muthil, Strathearn): Violat Mar was 'dilaitit of the using of sorcerie, witchcraft, and incantatioune with invocatioune of spreittis' to destroy the Regent the Earl of Morton. All the co-conspirators are from western Strathearn: John Murray [5th] of Strowan, Grizel Bruce his spouse, William Scotland in Strowan, Bessie Corbie servant to Lady there, Robert Bruce of Clackmannan, John Galloway in Little Coig, William Reid there, John Eldar in Drummond Eistir, Charles Fultoun and Elizabeth Mar, sister to Violat Mar (Treasurer's Accounts vol.20, 6 Oct. 1576, 181; Pitcairn 1833, I, 76-77; Reid 1899, 179-181). Violat, probably a professional charmer (or poisoner) of fairy stock, was found guilty but her execution is not noted; nor is there any information about co-conspirators.
>
> 1580 Perth town: a witch (perhaps Janet Gowrie) was banished from the town.
>
> 1581 Perth town: Bessie Robertson was accused of witchcraft.
>
> 1582 Perth town: a woman in the Meal Vennel was suspected of witchcraft; she was probably a healer or midwife.
>
> 1598 Perth town: Janet Robertson, Marion Macause and Bessie Ireland were burnt on the South Inch for witchcraft.

1612 Perth town: Commission to try Janet Campbell and ... Robertson for witchcraft.

1615 Crieff, apocryphal. The story of Kate McNiven, the Witch of Monzie, is discussed below.

1615 Dunblane: Watty Bryis and Jonnet Murriache were examined by the Bishop and confessed to Divers charges of witchcraft, sorcery and enchantment. Probably husband-and-wife.

1615 Perth town: The Erskine case did not involve witchcraft but poison which was supplied by a wise woman.

1618 Logie: Bessie Finlayson was suspected of witchcraft.

1620 Perth town: James Stewart was suspected of witchcraft and sorcery (Book of Perth).

1623 Perth town: Issobell Haldane, Margaret Ormscleugh, Janet Trail or Trall, three healers with fairy links were tried and executed.

1628 Perth town: Bessie Wright was accused of being a witch and abusar of the people.

1629 Auchterarder: Alexander Drummond, warlock, of Auchterarder was tried at the High Court and found guilty of sorcerie, witchcraft, charming and curing illness. He was strangled and burnt at the Market Cross of Edinburgh (Reid 1899, 67-75).

1629 Dunblane: Johne Hog and Margaret Nicoleson his wife were examined by Bishop on charges of witchcraft.

1641 Culross and Glendevon: three witches who met with John Brugh are named in his dittay as Catharene Mitchell of Culros, Margaret Kinard in Glendevon and Margaret Cowane.

1643 Fossoway (also known as Crook of Devon), in Kinross-shire but geographically part of Perthshire: John Brugh 'the Warlock of Fossoway' was a successful charmer who used 'twa inchantit stanes' but in 1641 he had met with Satan in various graveyards 'at quhilkis tymes ther was taine up thrie severall dead corps, ane of thame being an servand man named John Chrystiesone; the uther corps, tane up at the Kirk of Mukhart, the flesch of quhilk corps was put above the byre and stable dure headis.' This is the first mention of a Devil in this part of Scotland. The Court was puzzled by John's role in this disgraceful proceedings but argued that this meeting constituted a demonic pact (Reid 1899, 202). John was strangled and burned.

1643 Perth town: Agnes Stoddard, Thomas Rob and Jean Rob, tried together, were probably healers, perhaps husband, wife and daughter.

1650 Dunblane: Helen McClew of Kippen used a witch bag to curse cattle. Barbara Drummond, also accused of witchcraft, was tried with her (Fergusson 1907, 65).

1662 Abernethy: Elspeth Young, Jonet Crystie and Margaret Mathie, all confessed to be witches. Abernethy (NO 1816) is 18 km (11 miles) east of Dunning (NO 0214).

1662 Dunning: Trial of nine women belonging to a probable coven: Issobell McKendley, Espeth Reid, Anna Law, Jonet Toyes, Agnes Hutsone and Issobell Goold in Dunning, Helen Ilson and Margret Crose in Forteviot and Jonet Airth in Aberuthven, all suspected of witchcraft. Forteviot (NO 9518) is 3 miles (5 km) from Dunning on the north side of the Ochils which is only 4 km (2.5 miles) from Aberuthven (NN 9815) and only 16 km (9 miles) from Crook of Devon (NO 0400) on the south side of the Ochils.

1662 Findo-Gask: Trial of six women belonging to another probable coven: Janet Rob in Woodhead of Findogask, Janet Mertin in Nethergask, Jonet Allan in Overgask, Jonet Young, Jonet Bining and Agnes Ramsay in Clathimore, all suspected of witchcraft. Findo-Gask (NO 0020) is on the north side of the river Earn opposite Dunning and Aberuthven (NN9815).

1662 Methven: (a) Commission to try Janet Gilivory and Kathrin Scoby guilty of witchcraft; (b) Commission to try Elspeth Jonstoun a self-confessed witch.

1662 Crook of Devon (Fossoway), Kinross on the borders of Perthshire. This coven was active in 1643 when John Brugh helped Satan to make witch-pokes (above). Agnes and Janet were perhaps his daughters. Eleven people were tried and executed: Agnes Murie, Bessie Henderson, Isabella Rutherford, Robert Wilson (almost certainly the Devil), Bessie Neil, Margaret Lister, Janet Paton, Agnes Brugh, Agnes Pittendreich (respited on account of pregnancy), Janet Brugh and, three months later, Christian Grieve. Margaret Hoggan aged 79 apparently died before she was convicted. Reid comments: 'We do not know from the Records of any such wholesale holocaust of witches in Scotland as took place at Crook of Devon. The account is a dreadful one, and shows what an amount of credulity and terror had seized upon the inhabitants of this country parish' (1899, 217). Fossoway is south of the Ochils and open to Lowland rather than Highland influences.

1715 Perth town: in a mad late flourish, Margaret Ogilvy and Sarah Johnson were tried, condemned and burnt on the North Inch of Perth (Cowan 1904, vol.2, 132-133).

One entry which does not belong here is the 1662 trial of William Cowan at Innerwick. Black thought this was Innerwick in Glenlyon in Highland Perthshire, but in fact it is the parish of Innerwick in East Lothian. There was no persecution of witches in Highland Perthshire.

In Breadalbane witchcraft was restricted to charming and saining and only exceptionally used to curse. There are no covens or Devils. But only a few miles to the south, the authorities believed healers and charmers were in a pact with the Devil, which was a capital offence. The contrast between Lowland Perthshire and Breadalbane is not due to inherited ethnic differences or even to local belief but may be related to the greater freedom of action enjoyed by the authorities, particularly the Reformed Church, in the Low country and their ready access to the courts in Edinburgh. Superstitious beliefs about witches circulating in the literate Lowlands also contributed to the periodic panics. Any written sources were of course in English, not in Gaelic.

It appears from the pogroms of 1662 that by then covens had spread from Crook of Devon – where the earliest coven in the area appears c.1640 – north through the Ochils to Dunning and Findo-Gask in Strathearn. The organisation of covens is so similar in all these places, as in Lowland Scotland as a whole, that we must infer that information spread from one 'Devil' to the next by word of mouth. The Lowlands of Perthshire were also more open to 'learned' influences coming ultimately from Continental Europe.

The difference between the two areas is unlikely to be due to ethnic differences as the whole of Perthshire had been Gaelic-speaking only a few generations earlier. In the seventeenth century Scotland's population was divided between the growing number whose native vernacular was Gaelic but who spoke at least a little English and the much greater number who still spoke nothing but Gaelic, but even those who spoke English were only a few generations away from their Gaelic roots. Surnames show the process very well. There was a considerable expatriate Highland population in the Lowlands. Almost sixty per cent of the North Berwick witches in 1590 used surnames that identify them as coming from the Perthshire Highlands: these names include Brown (the anglicised version of Dunn), Buchanan, Campbell, Clark (from MacIlclerich), Cowan (from MacCowan or MacEwan), Cunningham,

Duncan, Dunn, Graham, Gray, Grierson (from MacGhrioghair), Gylloun, Logan, MacCalyan, MacGill, Nicolson (from MacNicol), Paterson (from MacIlphatrick), Robson (from MacRobert), Shaw, Thomson (from MacOmish), White (from MacIlvane) and Wright (from MacIntyre). We will come back to these names in the next chapter.

Many of these names were adopted by members of Clan Gregor, a notoriously archaic body which kept up the old religion and which was, perhaps in consequence, picked out for particularly vindictive treatment by James VI. The last Act he signed before departing for the flesh-pots of London had for its purpose the extirpation of the Clan. It was second only to his fear of witches. Such surnames show that a major migration from Highland to Lowland was under way even before the forced resettlement which James devised in 1603. Their location in East Lothian suggests they had come south with droves of cattle and settled along the drove routes. Droving with London market as the prize was highly profitable. The Fletchers of Saltoun who had reached East Lothian by way of Dundee from Glenorchy and were established as burgesses at Cockermouth in Cumbria before 1567, were an early part of this migration of Highlanders displaced by feudal incomers after c.1500. The influence of such people on local witchcraft is unknown but was not negligible and may have been enormous. Apart from a few witches who are said to be 'Erse' or Gaelic-speakers, one sign of Gaelic influence is the persistent use of traditional Gaelic witch-names in Lothian.

But in Breadalbane there is no sign of covens, black magic or the Devil. The Campbells of Breadalbane were forward-looking, astute and pragmatic; one cannot imagine the Earl of Breadalbane consulting a local witch when faced with a problem, or to supply him with magical protection in a dangerous journey, though other members of the Highland elite did so. Highlanders of all classes had links with fairy folk or charmers but there was no Devil lurking at the end of the house, as far as one can judge.

One answer for the marked difference between Highland and Lowland Perthshire is that it followed the difference between an evolving society open to legal, literate and religious manipulation and a non-literate native culture of an extremely conservative nature. In other terms, there was no room in the Highlands for an alien witch-cult because the position was taken by an older and more congenial system. Instead of covens of witches riding by night on their broomsticks we have processions of fairy folk.

Lest it be thought that the lack of witchcraft in Breadalbane was exceptional, a very similar picture emerges from *The Records of the Presbyteries of Inverness and Dingwall* (Mackay (ed.) 1896). These also were Gaelic-speaking Highland districts and more open to foreign ideas than Breadalbane. It is true that the Munros of Foulis in Ross-shire, a short distance to the north, were steeped in witchcraft – but they were in every way exceptional. (Katherine Ross, Lady Munro of Foulis, was tried and acquitted in Edinburgh in 1590. In

1577 she had employed twenty-six local witches to rid herself of her sister-in-law and step-son by shooting at dollies and then by rat poison.)

The Kirk Sessions did not condone witches, charming, healing and cursing, let alone rat poison and murder, and they spoke out against charming and quite harmless superstitions like pouring milk on a fairy mound to appease the fairies who 'in Christian times became the representatives of the former spirits of the earth', putting a poke of herbs in the milk to keep it safe, or 'turning the sieve and the shears' to raise the Devil, but they did not react with violence to this usurpation even though their attempts to prevent such activities did not meet with much success (Mackay, 1896, xxxix). They seem to have been reasonable people faced with a universal folk belief and knew they had as much hope of reforming it as of preventing fornication.

Witches on a hill in Atholl

Anyone who looks in the Highlands for covens meeting at midnight finds instead fabulous tales of bands of fairies making merry in fairy hills at the quarters of the year. The two have much in common. Of ritual intercourse with a horned Devil we find very little before the self-conscious fiction of the eighteenth century. The probable explanation is that instead of closed covens meeting in secret, the entire community was involved in pagan fertility rituals, undeterred by the faint presence of the Christian Church. Instead of bands of witches we had troops of fairies or deer-hunters flying over the hills to their meeting-places and hunting by the light of the full moon. When they disappeared they went so rapidly and so completely that folk memory for once was not equal to the task of explaning what had once been.

It was once claimed, admittedly by an imposter, that twenty-three hundred witches had gathered on a hill in Atholl in May 1597 (Black 1938, 26) – an exciting prospect, but it was an invention of Margaret Atken, the Great Witch of Balwearie in Fife, who for a short time saved her own life by inventing magical tales and claiming that she could identify witches simply by looking at them (Spottiswoode 1855, III, 66-67). Her imagination may have been stirred by a report of the great autumn hunt-meets at Atholl where hundreds of hunters gathered on the hills for a deer drive. They brought their dogs and enough food to sustain themselves for three or four days during which time they made a *tinchell* or human chain of beaters which enclosed an immense area of upland and drove everything with four legs – wolves and wild cats as well as deer – down to an ambush site. Deer-drives on this scale are recorded in Atholl from the time of David Lyndsay in the sixteenth century but have prehistoric antecedents. Perhaps Margaret Atken had heard them described as a *sabaid*, or hunt gathering and used her imagination. But the 2,300 witches, regrettably, are a figment.

Appendix 1 to Chapter 8: The story of Kate McNieven

The best-known Perthshire witch-story concerns Kate McNieven, said to be nurse to the Laird of Inchbrackie, Perthshire, a few miles east of Crieff. According to legend she was burned on the Knock of Crieff in 1715 for stealing a knife and fork while in the shape of a bee. This is certainly a tall tale or jape.

The name of this woman is of considerable interest. Nicneven means 'daughter of the holy place or deer forest' and it was a common and appropriate name for a witch leading processions of fairies. Scott in talking of Celtic fairy lore mentions 'a gigantic and malignant female, the Hecate of this mythology, who rode on the storm, and marshalled the rambling host of wanderers under her grim banner. This hag ... was called *Nicneven* in that later system which blended the faith of the Celts and the Goths on this subject' (Scott, 1830, 130). From this we can deduce that Nicneven is a name of the Cailleach and a hunt-beacon.

According to various sources a witch known by this name was burnt at St Andrews in 1569. A second was burned at Monzie, near Crieff, at about the same time, and a third on the Knock of Crieff in 1715. Kate McNieven's Crag at Monzie, the site of the supposed burning, is still pointed out (NN 8723). Long before any of this the Knock was a beacon site where a *cailleach* or local beacon was lit. 'To burn the witch' in Gaelic means 'to light the bonfire'. That is part of the explanation. But there is a great deal more.

In the *Flyting of Dunbar and Kennedy* (written c.1500) Dunbar pictures the great witch *Nicniven* at Hallowe'en, riding at the head of a procession of witches, fairies, sorceresses and elves (Irving and Laing 1821, 117). A similar passage in the *Flyting of Montgomery and Polwart* refers to Nicniven and the Great Witch of the Chanonry, executed there in 1577 (Dalyell 1835, 233, note).

> 'Then a cleir companie came soone after closse *Nicniven*, with her nymphs in number anew, With charmes from Caithness and Chanrie of Rosse, Whose cunning consists in casting a clew...'

The traditions attached to Kate McNieven fail to coalesce. The story of the bee is frankly fake. The Crieff historian Duncan Macara thought it was a fictional version of earlier events at Monzie with the addition of spurious fantasy and gave a local tradition which placed her death in 1715 (1881, 201). This version of events was disputed by Hugh Jamieson, minister of Monzie, who could find no mention in the Session records of Monzie of any witch-burning in 1715 (1896, 229, 333-340) or at any more propitious date. He also pointed out that in 1715 Patrick of Inchbrakie, who plays a prominent part in the legend, was not resident in Perthshire but in exile, having murdered John, the Master of Rollo, and did not return to Inchbrakie until January 1725. Jamieson also notes that McNieven is the male form; the correct female name was Kate Nik Neiving, the female form using G. *nighean* 'daughter'. Jamieson's story is different again.

'Monzie is best known in connection with the burning of a witch. The traditionary story makes out Kate McNiven to have been a nurse in the family of the Graemes of Inchbrakie, and as a proof that she was a member of the weird sisterhood, a story is told of her in connection with a visit which the Laird of Inchbrakie made to Dunning on the occasion of some festivity. According to the fashion of the time, he took with him his knife and fork. After he was seated at the dinner table he was subjected to annoyance similar to that which teased Uncle Toby – namely, the hovering of a bee about his head. To relieve himself from the tiny tormentor, he laid down his knife and fork, and attempted to beat off the insect with his hands. It soon flew out at the window; but behold! the laird's knife and fork had disappeared. They were searched for all over the table, and under the table; nowhere could they be found; but when their owner reached home and recounted his mysterious loss, Kate McNiven, who was present, straightway went and produced both articles safe and sound from their accustomed repository. It was whispered that Kate had personated the bee.

Relieved of her duties in the house of Inchbrakie – as a result, it is said, of an attempt to poison the young laird – Kate McNiven returned to her old home at the Kirkton of Monzie, where she acquired an 'uncanny' reputation. Evidence of her sorceries was collected or suborned, and through the machinations of the young laird of Inchbrakie, she was apprehended and brought to trial on a charge of witchcraft, and her guilt being conclusively established, sentence of death was passed against her. The stake was pitched and the faggots piled on the summit of the Knock of Crieff, and thither was the sorceress dragged, to suffer in presence of an immense multitude gathered from all the surrounding country ...'

Not to be left behind the Inchbrakie family have their own tradition. Writing on 25 November 25, 1895, Miss L. Graeme said:

'My mother was the wife of the second son of Inchbrakie, and I have over and over again heard her relate how, on her home-coming as a bride, my grandfather on one occasion told her the story. He spoke of Monzie having brought a witch to the notice of the authorities. She was being burnt on the Knock of Crieff, above Monzie, when the

Inchbrakie of the day, riding past, did all in his power to try and prevent the matter from being concluded, without avail. Just as the pile was being lit, she bit a blue bead from off her necklet, and spitting it at Inchbrakie, bade him guard it carefully, for so long as it was kept at Inchbrakie the lands should pass from father to son. Kate then cursed the Laird of Monzie.'

The first Graeme of Inchbrakie was a son of the first Earl of Montrose. His father gave him a charter to it and to Aberuthven, dated June 1513. The blue stone was honoured by being set in a gold ring. It seems rather elaborate for a nurserymaid, even one with an uncanny reputation, but it is typical of Lowland folk fiction to be inspired in its flights of fancy by a physical object such as a silver cup, a gold ring, an ancient flag, a brooch... The Highlands are full of peculiar and evocative little treasures. The Inchbrakie jewel

> 'is a moonstone sapphire, set in two brilliants of different shape. There is a curious bluish enamel on part of the gold, which is embossed half-way round. There is also a charm, which is said to have belonged to Kate McNiven. It is a slight iron chain with a black heart, having two cross bones in gold on the back, bearing the words 'cruelle death' on it, and attached to a death's head in the shape of a serpent's head with curious enamel.'

To pursue fact as far as it goes, that a witch known as Kate Nike Neiving was among the first to suffer as the result of the passing of the 1563 statute, is supported by the history of John Brugh of Fossoway, a healer who was tried at Edinburgh on November 24th, 1643, for practising sorcery. He was then an elderly man and it was alleged that he had obtained his knowledge from a widow woman called Neance Nikclerith who was sixty years old and was sister daughter (niece) to *Nike Neveing*, that notorious infamous witch in Monzie, who for her sorcery and witchcraft was burnt eighty years ago or thereabouts (Reid 1899, 199). This would place her death c.1560, close to 1563, when witchcraft became a capital offence in Scotland. Dalyell found another Nicnevin in the *Historie and Life of King James the Sext* (where the name is given wrongly as Nic Neville): the 'notabill sorceress callit Nicnevin— condemnit to the death and brunt at St Andrews in the year 1569' which is still within the bounds of possible dates (1835, 233). Herries in his memoirs refers to her as a 'fellow called Nick Nevin, a notable witch' (Black 1938, 21). According to the *Historie and Life of King James the Sext*, page 40, 'A notable sorceres callit Nic Neville, was condamnit to the death and byrnt' in 1569 (Dalyell 1835 233).

Appendix 2 to Chapter 8: The death of a healer: John Brugh in the Brae of Fossaway.

Toward the end of November 1643, John Brugh the Warlock of Fossoway, an elderly man and a famous healer, was tried, found guilty and executed by strangling and his body subsequently burnt at Edinburgh. For thirty-six years he had been in demand as a healer with an extensive practice both north and south of the Ochils, from Strathearn to Stirling. The use of the inflected form VcClerich in the following account suggests that he and his companions were Gaelic-speakers. The techniques they used are found widely throughout Scotland. Fossoway is on the border, on the south slopes of the Ochil Hills (NT 0202). The complete record of the trial was copied from the Books of Adjournal of the High Court of Justiciary by Alexander Reid, solicitor in Auchterarder (1899, 201-208) and is worth attention as a witness to a changing world. It has a rare sense of immediacy.

* * *

'Curia Justiciarie S.D.N. regis tenta in pretorio de Edinburgh, xxiiii Nov., 1643, per Magros Alexander Colville et Jacobus Robertoun, Justiciarios Deputatos. 'Intran eodem die.

'Johnne Brughe, indweller and parochiner of Fossoquhay. Dilatit of dyverse poyntis of sorcerie conteinit in his dittay following. Persewer Sir Thomas Hope of Craighall, Knyt Barronet, His Maj. Advocat for his hienes intreis.

'My Lord Advocat producet the dittay. The Justice efter accusatione of the pannel of the perticuler crymes of sorcerie and witchcraft specifiet in his dittay, findis the samyn relevant conviction in the perticuler articles thereof to be put to the knowledge of ane assyse, qrupone His Maj. Advocat askit instrumentis.

'Assise.

Robert Patersone, in Schanuell; Patrick Flokart of Borb; Mathow Baveridge in Nether Cairnboe; John Anderson, thair; John Hallie of Balruthrie; William Huttoun of Ballilisk Eister; John Patoun of Middle Mallilisk; James Huttoun of Waster Ballilisk; James Alexander of Waster Dounhill; William Gilcreist, in Eister Quhythill; Alexr. Chopman, in Common of Dyning; Henrie Anderson, in the Rig; William Glass, portioner of Dalquish; Hendrie Daes, in the eist side; James Greave of Leadlatione.

'My Lord Advocat askit instrumentis of the sweiring of the assise, and for verification of the dittay producet the severall and perticuler depositiones for instructing of ilk article thereof. Quhilkis persones of assise being choisen, sworne, and admitted efter accusatione of the said John Brughe of the perti-culer crymes and poyntis of dittay following, viz.: Forasmeikle as be the devyne law of Almytie God mentionat in his sacreid word, all users and practizers of witchcraft, sorcerie, charmeing, suthesaying, are ordainit to be puneished to the daithe, and by dyverse Actis of Parliament, namelie, by the 73 Act of the Parliament halden by his Maj. dairest goodame Queane Marie of good memorie: It is statut and ordainit that na manner of persone of whatsumever estait or degrie thai be of, tak upon hand to use any manner of witchcraft, sorcerie, or necromancie, nor gif thame selfis furth to have any sic craft or knawledge thairby to abuise his Maj. good people's subjectis under the payne of dead: As in the said lawis and Actis of Parliament at lenthe is contenit. Nochwithstanding whereof it is of veritie that the said John Brughe shaiking aff all feir of the Omnipotent and Almytie God, reverence or regaird to his blessed word, and to the lawis and acts of parliament of this Kingdome groun-dit thereupon, and geiving himself haillielie over to the service of Sathan, the enemie of mane's salvatione, for thir threttie sax yeiris by gane practeized, used, and exerced the devellische charmes of witchcraft and sorcerie upon dyverse persones, alsweill men as women, by onlaying of deikness, and deseass, and apptaking thereof upon ther personnes, and guids and geir, hantit and frequentit the ungodlie and damnable meetings of witches, and kepit cump-anie and trystis with the devill and thame at dyverse his appoyntit trystis; in sua far as the said John hes been ane continuall ressaver of sarkis, coller boddis, beltis and uther abuilziementis perteneing alsweill to men as women for cureing them of their seikness, urgeing thame to bring the samyn unto him, declaring himself thereby to have a mediate paktione with the devill, and, in sua doing, abuseing his Maj. leidges maist abominablie in making thame to believe that he was able to give thame health of bodies, for the quhilk he tuik from thame dyverse great sowmes of money, victualls, butter, cheise, and uther commodeteis, impoverishing thame thereby.

'And be his causing thame likewayes for ther cure and healthes to weishe thame selfis in southe ryning wateris, involving therthrow the ignorant peaple consulters with him in a second giltines qlk was auquheable to baptisme in the name of Sathan the devill playing the ape in all God's warkis, and be sua doing to draw away the heartis of God's peaple fra ther blissed creator to be cured and helped be Sathan and his infernal intrumentis; and for this effect, according to his awin confessione, has given out himself to have knawledge of dyverse sorcis of seiknes, and deseiss learned be him frome a wedow woman namit Noance VcClerith, of thrie scoir years of aidge, quha was sister dochter to Nik Neiving, that notorious and infamous witche in Monzie, quha for hir sorcerie and witchecraft was burnt four scoir of yeir since or therby.

102

'And first, the said John, understanding that James Leveingstoun of Maw had all his beistis beseit wt grevous seikness and deseass sua that ane grit number of thame daylie deit, the said Jon Brughe, accumpaneit wt the said Noance VcClerich, come to the said James Levingstoune's hous and to his byre thereof, wherein his cattell was for the tyme, and there the said John, be his devillische practeizes of sorcerie and witchcraft, causit fill a tub full of water and pat therein tua inchantit stanes, and therefter causit the haill cattell to pas by the tub full of water, and in ther by-passing sprinkled ilk ane of thame with ane wisp dipped in the said water. At quhilk tyme ane of the said goodis, not being able to gang, was be force drawin out at the byre dure, and the said John wt Nikclerith, smelling the nois thereof, said it wald not leive, caused ane holl to be maid in the maw greane qlk was put quick [alive] in the hole, and maid all the rest of the cattell therefter to goe over that place, and in this devillish maner be charmeing of the saidis goodis they were cured of ther former deseiss, and caused him therefter to cleansait his haill byres, stables, and houss upon the said croft of land, and to the said James Levingstone's great chairges and expenss, caused him build new houss in uther places for saiftie alsweill of him selff as his goods, as at lenthe is contenit in the said Jon Brughe his depositione.

'Item: The said John Brughe, be his charmeing, devilrie, and witchcraft practeized be him and be the said Nikclerich and Jon McIlvorie, his sone-in-law, thay being in his cumpanie practeized the lyk devillische cure upone certane guidis perteneing to Robert Robertsone in Leadlatione, as he had prateizet upone the goods of the said James Levingstoun of Maw, for the qulk he gat tuelff ss. for his paynes, comittit be him a twentie yeirs since or therby.

'Item: About the yeir of God 1633 or 1634 yeirs, the said John Brughe, having consavet ane deadlie heatret aganes Jon Gib of Couthe, for calling him ane witche, he be his devilrie and witchcraft, in revenge therof, slew and caused frenit to dead tua of his ploughe horse and ane of his best oxen, together wt nyne peace of horse, follis and staigis [young horses] perteneing to him.

'Item: The said John Brughe at Andermes [30 November] in anno 1634, understanding that Archibald Huttoun, elder in Cleughe, had ane number of his oxen beset wt seiknes, qlk maid thame refuis to tak any meat, the said John Brughe, for cureing of thame of that deseass, come under nyt, and be his devilrie and witchcraft, and be resaveing of ellevin od schillings wt tua peckis of meill and thrie tailzies of beiff, and using of certain charmes, and repeitting of thir wordis at three severall tymes, God put them in ther awin place; and also be applying of ane pynt of new lettin goe wirt to everie ox be his devilrie and witchcraft cured the said oxen.

'Item: for cureing at threttie yeir since or therby to the Threipmure, wtin the parochin of Fossoquhay, and ther be the said John be his devilrie and witchcraft, and be applying of wort and walgrase [water-cress] soddin togidder, and be using of certain charmes cured a staig perteneing to Thomas Gibsone, in Threipmuire, confessit by the said John Brughe to be of veritie.

'Item: At sevin yeirs since or therby the said John Brughe, having ressavit fra Agnes Murray, spous to Jon Hallie, in Balruddrie [one of the jury] certain cornes upone trust, to have been delyverit bak agane at a certain day therefter; and becaus the said Agnes for not delyvering thereof at the appoyntit day come to the said John Brughe's hous and poyndit and brocht wt her a plaid of his, he, in revenge thereof, laid ane grevous deseis be his sorcerie and witchcraft upone ane kow perteneing to the said John Hallie, qlk kow gave nothing therefter furthe of her pappis but bluid and worsum insteid of mylk.

'Item: The said John be his devilrie and witchcraft cured ane kow perteneing to John Rutherford, in Colsknow, the kow being braine wood [mad] for the tyme, be taking from hir three turnouris [tumouris?] qlk efter his rubbing thame under the lap of his cot and putting thame outthrow and inthrow his belt head, and causeing thame to be cassin in a tubfull of cleane water not suffering it to tutch the ground, and therefter to set it before the said kow and caus the kow to drink the samyn, efter the drinking thereof be the said John Brughe his sorcerie and witchcraft, the said kow was cured, for the qlk he ressaved nyne schillings.

'Item: For abuising of Henrie Young, in Bankhead, be causing him to tak tua inchantit stanes and cast the same in water, and therefer to weshe hishorse and cattell therwt, affirmeing that they had been bewitched be some evil nyebors, for the qlk he ressaved frathe said Henrie Young fourtie schillings.

'Item: For laying on of ane heavie seiknes be sorcerie and witchcraft upone Helene Young, spous to William Miller, and therefter taking the same aff the said Helene Young and laying it upone Jonet Clerk, her servand woman, qlk seiknes be his sorcerie and witchcraft was tane aff the said Jonet Clerk and cassin upone ane lamb.

'Item: for cureing by sorcerie and witchcraft of ane grit number of ky and oxen perteneing to Hendrie Crombie, the spous of Christiane Glass, relict of umqle Thomas Hendersone, in the nether tout of Collennoquhy, for the qlk cure he ressavit 40 ss. fra the said Hendrie.

'Item: For cureing be sorcerie, and witchcraft, and uther devillische charmeing of an young chyld about sevin or aught yeir auld, sone to Andrew Young, cotter in Tillierie under my Lord Burlie, being beseit wt ane grevous seiknes laid upone him be ane witch called Margaret Kinglassie, qlk bairne was cured by his sorcerie and witchcraft as said is.

'Item: For cureing of Thomas Bannatyne, ane of the fewaris of Ballado, be the said John Brughe, his sorcerie and witchcraft, and taking fra him of ane of his sarkis [shirts] and causeing him to pas thrie severall nights to a south ryning water and to wesche himself nytlie therin, and by delyvering to him of ane inchantit stane the bigness of ane dow eg, advyseing him to put the samyn in his drink, for the qlk the said John ressaved ane dollar.

'Item: For cureing be sorcerie and witchcraft of Wm. Gilcreist, the spous of Margaret Miller, be taking of his sarkis and ane bonnet mutch, togidder wt sevin or ellevin schillings in od money, and be taking a pynt of south ryning water and wesheing the said Wm. Gilcreist's feit therwt, qua was curet according thereto.

'Item: For cureing be sorcerie and witchcraft of James Hutsone, in Auchlenskie, his sone, of a grevous seiknes, qlk made him senceles, dum and speichles.

'Item: For cureing be sorcerie and witchcraft and devillishe charmeing of Jon Currie, his said ky and oxin by coming to the said Jon Currie's byre and casting ane cogful of water croce-ways upone ane of the oxin, being seik for the tyme, and therefter bureing the said ox, being dead, in a place where na man did repair, andbe that devillische meanes curet all the rest of his goods.

'Item: For cureing of ane horse be sorcerie and witchcraft perteneing to Andro Dynning in Iginser, and affirmeing to the said Andro that the seiknes was devyset for himselff.

'Item: For onlaying be sorcerie and witchcraft upone Andro Dynmure, his haill bestial, ky, horss, and oxen of dyverse deseiss and grevous seiknes, wherby his horss ran wood [mad] and drouned themsellis in the dame.

'Item: For giving to Helene Gib of ane inchantit bonnok, baiken of meill be sorcerie and witchcraft. At her reswsaving whercof directit her to weit it in water and to cast it over the goodis wtin the byre, bot at her going to the water to weit the same, the bannok falling out of her hands, brak in tua pieces, qlk was tane up be tua dogis, and swallowit be thame, qrupone that both went mad and died.

'Item: Eleven year since or therby, John Kyd, maltman in Sant Johnestoun [Perth], being heavlie deseaset wt. continewall sweating, and forgaddering wt. the said John Brughe, directit him to send a sark of his wt. a boy, whereby he might be cured, causing put the said under the dock of ane barrell, and therefter put the same upone him, and ressavet 40 ss. for the said cure, albeit he was never the better thereof. But the said John Brughe being discontent with the money, being over little, the said John, be his sorcerie and witchcraft, caused the haill meanes and money perteneing to the said John Kyd, being then wt. one thowsand pundis, togidder wt. his haill malt browin be him in drink to evanish and goe from him, so that the haill wort grew thik lyk sowings and stank lyk gutter glaur, and thereby, and be his sorcerie and witchcraft, maid him altogiffer poore.

'Item: For being in cumpanie wt. Catharene Mitchell, ane commone and notorious witch, qa was convict and execut for witchcraft at Culros in May last, Margaret Kinard in Glendoven, Margaret Cowane, wt the said John Brughe, being all convenit togedder, and having three severall meetings wt the devill in the kirk yeard of Glendovan, at qlk times there was tane up thrie severall dead corps, ane of them being ane servand man named Jon Chrystiesone. The uther corps was put above the byre and stable durehead of James and Robert Mechell, wtin the parochin of Mukhart, of purpois to destroy his cattell and

105

guidis. And the thrid meeting being wt the devil at the Rumbling Brigis about two yeir since or therby, qlkis thrie severall meittings was affirmet be the said Catharene Mitchell to be of veritie, the tyme of her criminall tryal at Culrose, and immediately before her execution, the said John Brughe being confronted wt. her at that tyme, wt. qlk confession and affirmatione, the said Catharene Mitchell went to death.

'And last, the said Jon Brughe is indytit and accusit as ane commone sorcerer, and ane keiper of cumpanie wt. witches at all their wicket conventiones and meitings, the devill being in cumpanie wt. thame, geveing directiones and instructiones to the said Jon and the remanent witches alsweill, anent cureing of sieknes and deseass upone men, women, childring, and bestiall as onlaying therof.

'The foirnamet persones of assize removet therefter furthe of Court to ane secreit place be thame selffis qr. they first electit and choyset Robert Patersone, in Schanuell, ane of ther number to be chancellor. Thairefter resonnet and voitit upone the said dittay and haill articles thereof, and being ryplie and at lenth advyset theranent, and wt. the haill depositiones and confessiones producet for verificatione of the said dittay and crymes therin contenit, reenterit agane in Court qr. they all in ane voce be the judiciall report and declaratione of the said Robert Patersone, chancellor, fand, pronuncet, and declairit the said Jon Brughe to be fyllit culpable and convict of the several and perticuler crymes of sorcerie and witchcraft mentionet in his said dittay. Qrupone his Maj. advocat askit instrumentis.

'The Justice continews the pronounceing of dome upon the former convictione to Wednesday next, the penult of November instant, and ordainit the pannell to be returned to waird, therin to remaine qll the said day.'

Dome pronuncet upon Jon Brughe, Warlok.

'The samyn twentie nyne day of November, 1643, John Brughe, indweller in the parochin of Fossoquhy, warlok, being brocht furthe of waird be the bailleis of Edr., and enterit upon pallell to heir and see dome pronuncet and sentence pronuncet againes him as he that was dewlie and orderlie convict be ane assise of dyverse poyntis of sorcerie and witchcraft specifiet in his dittay, and convictione following thereupone in ane Justice Court heldin by the saidis Justice Deputtis upone the xxiii. day of November instant, as the said convictione in the selff proporttis; the Justices, thairfoir, be the mouth of Patrick Barrie, dempster of Court, decernit and adjudget the said John Brughe to be tane to the Castell Hill of the Burgh of Edr., and ther to be wirreit at any stake qll he be dead, and therefter his bodie to be brunt in assis, as any sorcerer and warlock convict of the crymes specifiet in his dittay, qlk was pronuncet for dome.'

* * *

106

Appendix 3 to Chapter 8: The witches of Easter Ross, 1577

The Commission issued at Holyroodhouse against Catherine Ross on 25 October 1577 (Exchequer Rolls 1899, xx, 522-3) shows that at that date two different naming conventions were in use: Gaelic patronyms which were cumbersome but gave the person a detailed identity, and English surnames which required an address or some other distinguishing information. The Commission lists the names of thirty alleged witches from Easter Ross. Their names have been compiled by an English-speaking clerk using information supplied orally by a number of people with local knowledge. Women also used patronymics (using *Nic* instead of *Mac*) such as *Jonet Neyne Thomas McAllan*, 'Janet daughter of Thomas son of Allan' or *Jonetam Neyne Willelmun McClachan* 'Janet son of William McClachan'. A small minority have Lowland surnames such as Cattanach, Ross, Miller and Forbes. This is in striking contrast to a legal document of 1589 which accuses Hector Munro of Fowlis, step-son of Catherine Ross, of persecuting certain women. The background is still Easter Ross but now the accused women and the male jury all have English surnames: MacKenzie, Bain, Glas, Cuthbert, Sutherland, Innes, Ross and Mowat (MacKenzie, 1898, 65). This does not mean they had all suddenly learned to speak English.

On 25 October 1577 a Commission of Justice from Holyroodhouse was issued to Walter Urquhart, Sheriff of Cromarty, and Robert Munro of Foulis (Exchequer Rolls vol.20 1568-79, GRH 1899, 522-3). It authorised them to arrest seven men and twenty-three women charged with 'diabolical practices of magic, enchantment, murder, homicide and other offences'. Their names and locations are given below. They acted on instructions from Catherine Ross, Lady Munro, to kill her step-son and sister-in-law by casting elf-arrows at images of butter and clay and, when this failed, using ratsbane (probably hemlock). Several people were poisoned including young Lady Balnagowan. 'The last name is that of Keanoch Ower – Coinneach Odhar as written by a Lowland clerk – who is described as "the leading or principal enchantress", no doubt due to the clerk's inability to distinguish between a male and a female Gaelic name.' He and several others (including Christiane Ross Malcolmson who is not mentioned in the Commission) were tried and executed at Chanonry, probably early in 1578.

Commissio justiciarie facta Waltero Urquhart, vicecomiti de Cromertie, et Roberto Monro de Foulis, conjunctim et divisim ad querendum, perscrutandum, capiendum et apprehendendum omnes et singulas personas subscriptas de diabolicis, iniquis, et odiosis criminibus artis magice, incantationis, murthuri, homicidii, aliorumque horribilium criminum et offensionum, infra bondes comitatus Rossie et dominii de Ardmanach ac aliarum partium infra vicecomitatum de Invernes commissis, suspectus et delitatas, videlicet.

Commission of justiciary addressed to Walter Urquhart, sheriff of

Cromarty, and Robert Monro of Fowlis, jointly and severally, to search for and apprehend all or one of the various persons listed, who were accused of diabolical, iniquitous and odious practices of magic, enchantment, murder, homicide and other offences: committed within the bounds of the earldom of Ross and lordship of Ardmanach in the sheriffdom of Inverness.

A second commission was found among the Foulis papers.

Commission under the Quarter Seal appointing Lauchlin Mackintosche of Dunnachtane, Colin Mackenzie of Kintail, Robert Munro of Foulis, Walter Urquhart, Sheriff of Cromartie, Hugh alias Hughean Ross of Kilraok, and Alexander Falconar of Halkartoun, or one, two or three of them, conjunctly and severally, justiciaries within the bounds of the Earldoms of Ross and Moray and Lordship of Ardmanach, and other parts within the sheriffdoms of Innernes, Elgin, Forres and Narne, to apprehend, imprison and try Kenneth alias Kennoch Owir, principle or leader in the art of magic, [blank] Neyeane McAllester alias Loskoloukart and Marjory Miller, daughter of Robert Miller, smith in Assint, and all other men and women using and exercising the diabolical, iniquitous and odious crimes of the art of magic, sorcery and incantation within said bounds, who shall be named by the ministers within the bounds foresaid each for his own parish. At Halerudehouse 1577/8, 23 January

Names of the Easter Ross witches, 1577

The witches who worked for the elite of Clan Munro were illiterate Gaelic-speaking natives living in Easter Ross. Their names are given in three forms. There are Gaelic patronyms, Lowland surnames such as Bawden, Forbes, Miller and Ross, and witchnames (listed below). William McGilliewareycht-dane is so-called because he lived in Dune or Dane (NH6884), now Daan, near Tain, and was evidently liable to be confused with another William McGilliewareycht. Black gives the following versions of this name: Mcgillieuorie-dam, McGilliveri-dame and McGillevori-dame. He was one of those convicted and executed at the Chanonrie early in 1578.

Thomas McAnemoir McAllan McHenryk alias *Cassindonisch* [executed in 1577-78];

John McAne McThomas Cattanach;

William McGillevoir in Dune (Dane) [executed in 1577-78] (see note above);

Donald Gillevoir in Dune (Dane); Marion Neynaine McAlester alias *Loskoir Longert* 'Fire at the hunt lodge';

Christian [Marjorie?] Milla[r], dau of Robert Milla[r], smith in Assynt [executed in 1577];

Cradoch Neynane McGillechallum, also listed as Gradoche Malcolmson;

Christian McColinstoun;

Katherine Ros, dau of David Ros [of Balnagoune];

Agnes Ros, servant of said Katherine;

Agnes Neynkeard;

Marion alias Mauld Neyne Donald McAndyour in Glastulie;

Jonet Neyne Thomas McAllan;

John McNoullar [McNellan];

Jonet Moir in Mylncraighous in Ardros;

Margaret alias Mage Bawden in lie Channonrie [the Great Witch of Channonrie];

Christina Neyn Andoy McGevin in Nig;

Agnes Roy there [condemned in 1577];

Christian Chactach in Tayne;

Moriach Neyne Yraschte there;

Margaret Neyne Govin there;

Margaret Neyn Velene [NicMillan] there;

Helen Neyne Alexander McConnochie in Logy Eistir;

Kna wife of Donald McConill Leiris there;

Isabella alias Ibbie ... in Calrossie;

Alexander McKessak;

Katherine Neyne Donald Roy;

Marian Neynewin ...;

Jonet Neyne William McClachan;

Isabella alias Ibbie Forbes, materfamilias of Ordhouse;

Keannoch Owir [executed in 1578], *ductricem sey principalem incantatricem, ac super iisdem juxta leges regni justitiam administrandum ac super iisdem juxta leges regni justitiam administrandum* etc. 'leader and principal of the witches and of those persons subject to the laws of the kingdom'.

Christiane Roiss Malcolmson of Canorth is mentioned in the trial in 1590 of Catherine Ross, Lady Fowlis (Pitcairn 1833, I, 193) and listed by Black (1938, 22). She worked with Loskie Longhart to make clay dollies representing the young laird and Lady Balnagowan and was one of those who shot at them with elf arrows in her wester chalmer at 'Canorth'. These details seem to have been supplied from confession. On 28 November 1577 she was tried in the cathedral church of Ross, convicted, and burnt (Pitcairn i, 193). In the Commissions she is listed under her witch name as *Cradoch* Neynane McGillechallum or *Gradoche* Malcolmson. 'Canorth' may be a misreading of Teanord, near Castle Fowlis.

Locations of the Easter Ross witches, 1577

3 in Ardros (NH 6174), at Millhouse near Ferindonald (the Munro *duchthas*).

2 in Assynt (NH 5967), near Ferindonald.

4 in Calrossie (NH 8077), next to Glastullich, near Tain.

1 in The Channonrie (NH 7256), at Fortrose, on the south side of the Black Isle.

4 in Dane (NH 6884), now Daan, near Tain.

6 in Glastulie (NH 7976), next to Calrossie, near Tain.

2 in Logy Easter at Logie Hill (NH 7676).

2 in Nig (NH 8071), near Tain.

2 in Ordhouse, an English version of Teanord (NH 5964), next to

Castle Foulis.

4 in Tayne (NH 7881), now Tain.

1 in 'Canorth', probably Teanord or Ordhouse (NH 5964).

There were twenty witches in or near Tain, seven or eight near Castle Foulis, one isolated witch in Chanonrie on the south side of the Black Isle, and two more in Dingwall. Kennoch Owir or Coinneach Odhar may have been a vagabond like other fairy folk. According to Matheson's persuasive argument (1968) this warlock is the original of the so-called Brahan Seer, in Easter Ross, a century before his traditional date.

The pattern is very similar to that in East Lothian in 1590, where a member of the elite (the Earl of Bothwell) gathered together all the leading healers and charmers of the area, by word of mouth, using their own network, and employed them to make clay and wax models and to work other traditional magical rituals. In both cases several of the leading witches were executed and the elite person escaped justice.

CHAPTER 9: THE CLERICAL INTERFACE

This connexion of the witches and fairies opens up a very wide field; at present it is little more than speculation that the two are identical, but there is promise that the theory may be proved at some later date.

Margaret Murray 1921, 14.

The language of the trial transcripts which supply students of the Scottish supernatural with the bulk of their material is of course in the local variety of English (known as Scots) which was the language of literacy in the post-Reformation country. Quotations from this enormous mass of material are treated as though there had been in every corner of the Lowlands experienced court reporters with rapid and accurate shorthand who made a verbatim report of what the accused women actually said. This, we will see, is very far from the case. Particularly when we are given what is supposed to be a witch's description of supernatural activity but which is manifest nonsense, we can deduce a hidden source of error which we will call the clerical interface. It is a widespread phenomenon but in the particular circumstances of the trials it produces errors of a most absolute kind to be taken as sober fact. The conversion of picturesque but mundane Gaelic figures of speech into miraculous nonsense, arises out of the fact that an English-speaking clerk with no Gaelic has not been able to make sense of a witch who speaks – at least among her peers – an obsolete local dialect of Gaelic.

Contemporary references are few but there is no doubt that Gaelic lingered on in Lowland Scotland for much longer than most sources admit. Before the eleventh century Scotland was entirely Gaelic-speaking. When trade with England began with the creation of the feudal state the people in the Border counties began to use English or Scots to communicate with their neighbours. The language of the southern neighbour did not for a long time replace their own vernacular but it spread inexorably north and west through the Lowlands and into the Highlands and Islands until only Hebridean Gaelic remained.

However it seems still to have been current at the time of the witch panic (1560-1660). In Galloway, as Henderson notes, an old witch was still using Gaelic curses in the middle of the eighteenth century (2008, 15). In 1600 Gaelic as a spoken peasant vernacular was probably still common throughout Lowland Scotland. Of Gaelic Withers says that 'we may infer that the language was still spoken in Carrick and Galloway in the 1560s' (1989, 105). Sir Thomas Craig of Riccarton (1538-1608) could remember a time when 'the inhabitants of the shires of Stirling and Dumbarton spoke pure Gaelic' (Grant 1930, 56). Lowland Perthshire was bilingual in the early 1500s and Gaelic was still spoken in some recesses in the twentieth century in Aberdeenshire, Moray, Highland Perthshire and other border areas. The last native speakers of Perthshire Gaelic died in Rannoch in the 1980s. There is nothing more persistent than a vernacular spoken by a non-literate peasant population.

After the Reformation Scots was taught in schools and at universities and became increasingly important in Lowland Scotland, replacing Latin as the language of the courts and of administration. Before the end of the century English was used in courts regardless of the language of the accused. After the Reformation education in English became fashionable: in 1597 there was an *Inglis* school at Kintore, in rural Aberdeenshire. But Gaelic persisted as the vernacular among the illiterate peasant women who supplied the covens with the majority of their members, well into the seventeenth century. There are traces in Alloa and the Hillfoots, Lothian, Fife, Strathearn, Forfar, and Moray, and further north.

The earliest reliable information about the use of Gaelic in Scotland is summarised by Withers (1989, 104, Fig.7.1) but is by a century too late to cover the main period of the trials. However he shows that as late as 1698 – a century after the start of the purge – Gaelic was still the main language west of a line which extended north and east from Bute to include Lowland Perthshire, the landward half of Aberdeenshire, and the uplands of Moray, all trial locations. If we extrapolate from later trends we can see that a century earlier Gaelic persisted to the south and east of the 1698 line in Dunbartonshire, Ayrshire, Galloway, Lanarkshire, Lothian, Stirlingshire, the Hillfoots, west Fife, southeast Perthshire, Angus, most of Aberdeenshire and coastal Moray. At the time of the trials, all these areas still had a substantial Gaelic-speaking population as well as a substantial population of witches.

The direction and speed of the conversion is suggested by the similarity of three maps which cover different aspects of this question. The first is Withers' map which shows the *Gaidhealtachd* as it was in 1698, referred to already. This is very similar to MacCulloch's map which shows the separation of Highland fairies from Lowland witches (1921, 242), and both are similar to Larner's map showing the distribution of the witch-hunts (1981, 81), if one discounts the number of important cases heard at the High Court in Edinburgh. MacCulloch's map is of particular interest in confirming the occurrence of witchcraft in Highland and Lowland Perthshire analysed in chapter 8.

There were during the whole period of the witch panics only two occasions where we can be reasonably certain that Gaelic was spoken in court by fluent experts. Even then there was some uncertainty over technicalities. The first was the trial in 1677 of Donald McIlmichall, a vagabond. He was tried in the burgh of Inveraray in Argyll and found guilty of consulting with the Devil anent stolen goods 'expressly contrare to the 73 Act, Queen Mary Parl. 9'; of playing on his trumps or Jew's harp to 'unworldlie' folk when they danced on a Sabbath night; and of stealing a cow and two horses. The editor thought the 'unworldlie folk' were fairies rather than witches (MacPhail 1920, 2) but the record of the trial does not make this clear; nor does MacPhail add any useful definitions. I suspect the 'unworldlie folk' in the original examination were the *sith*, fairies or hunters, the people of the *sithean* or fairy mounds or outlook posts with which the area is so well furnished; and that the theft of the cow and two horses weighed more heavily with the court than Donald's consulting with the Devil (presumably the old man like a soldier who was in charge of the dancers). One cannot feel that Donald was unfairly treated, except by fate, and it seems clear that those who questioned him in court were at least able to understand what he said.

The second occasion was the interrogation of Margaret Campbell, widow of John Og Campbell of Cabrachan in Argyll, c.1590. The Ardkinglass affair in the early 1590s reveals how her husband, implicit in the murder of Campbell of Ardkinglass, near Inveraray in Argyll, tried to exploit the powers of local wise women for his own ends. Our information comes from the deposition given, in Gaelic, by his widow who was not apparently herself a charmer or witch. She told the court that her husband had been in the habit of consulting witches such as Katherene NicClaartie and Nichachlerich in Blairgoir when about to travel away from home. He also consulted Mary Voir Nicvolvoire vic Coil vic Neil of Lismore, who was not a witch but had the second sight, and several charmers including Euphrick Nikceoll roy of Lismore who had been taught by old Mackellar of Cruachan who had learned his charming at the Priory of Iona (MacPhail 1914, 165). The Great Witch of Iona who was consulted by kings is mentioned by Boethius lib.vi (Dalyell 1835, 494). Other local witches or wise women were Christian Nichean vic Couil Vic Gillespie in Lismore, Nichaicherne the Great Witch of Morven, and the two Nicricherts, one in Dunache and the other in Soraba. Dougal Macaurie worked charms to protect Ardkinglass's men against injury by weapons. Ardkinglass, disappointed that the assembled charmers had failed to protect him, found himself a new agent, Patrick MacQueen, said to be 'ane deboysched and depryved minister'. The witches of Argyll worked in much the same way as those of East Lothian or Easter Ross (MacPhail 1914, 159-169; Henderson 2008, 103). The names given appear to be patronymics, not honorific 'witch names'. 'Nic' (daughter of) is the female version of 'Mac' (son of).

Her statement explains how Iain Og used local charmers to protect himself; this was apparently normal behaviour. From the linguistic point of view the widow deponed in Gaelic which was translated into Scots by three reputable members of the local elite, including the Bishop of the Isles and the Dean of Lismore, who were evidently bilingual. The procedure with its safeguards suggests the court was aware of the risks attendant on unsupervised amateur translation.

The evidence suggests, if it can never prove, that the great majority of those accused of witchcraft in Scotland lived in areas where peasants like themselves still spoke Gaelic or were bilingual or at least had a residual knowledge of the old language trending rapidly towards obsolescence. In Argyll one might expect Gaelic but there are traces also in the Lowlands. The trials reveal many points of overlap. Lowland witches used Gaelic incantations, danced Highland dances, and sang indecent Gaelic songs.

There is one more source of evidence for a Gaelic presence even in Lothian well into the seventeenth century. This is the fact that many witches at that time were still known and are recorded in legal documents by honorific Gaelic cult names such as Toppock (G. *tapaidh* 'clever, bold, heroic'), Gradock (G. *gràdhag* 'esteemed, loved, admired') and Greibok (G. *gribhach* 'heroic, warlike' (see below for a list). These names were in circulation before the rise of the covens c.1600, when local witches looked after their own affairs and they persist to the end of the period. The translations suggest a link with hunting. We can use these names to track the use of Gaelic and in some cases its replacement with English. Current names show that Gaelic was still in use in Lothian in the 1590s.

Gaelic witch-names belong to an older tradition than English nicknames such as Able and Stout, Pikle Neirest the Wind and Throw-the-Cornyard (Pitcairn 1833, III, 615) or the even less impressive personal names such as 'Janet' and 'Christian' (Pitcairn 1833, III, 617) used by the master of the Auldearn coven c.1640. He was an English-speaking member of the local gentry but in 1662 when Isobell Gowdie was tried, she was still using elements of coded Gaelic which belong to an older tradition of Gaelic hunting lore. This will be discussed in the next chapter.

Finally, a less specific source of evidence for the continued use of Gaelic among Lowland witches is the form of surnames used by the courts. By 1600 surnames were established in the Lowlands but still rare in the Highlands, where a name normally consisted of a series of patronymics (A, son of B, grandson of C...) and personal descriptives. The use of a name in Gaelic form (a patronymic) is a reliable sign of a Gaelic-speaker but the form of a name depended on the clerk. An English name may point to an abbreviation invented by an English-speaking clerk. In 1576 a burgess of Perth was known by his tribal name, Gregor McGregour, when about his business in Breadalbane but he became George Johnstoun in Perth (Murray MacGregor 1898, 170). Most names c.1600 are Lowland versions of Highland names.

In the trials of the North Berwick witches (1590) half the names of the accused women are eroded or abbreviated Highland names, including Brown, Buchanan, Campbell, Clark, Cowan, Cunningham, Dunn, Gow, Graham, Gray, Grierson for MacGregor, Logan, McCalzane, McGill, Murray, Napier,

Nicholson for MacNicol, Paterson for MacPhaterick, Ramsay, Robson for Robertson, Shaw, Thomson for MacThomas, White and Wright. In addition two of the accused were said to be 'Erse' or Gaelic-speaking Highlanders who are not given their patronyms which were probably too complicated for the clerk. John Cunningham's original alias, *Fian*, is Gaelic and means 'hunter'.

At Alloa there is a suggestion that the rank and file of the coven used Gaelic as late as 1658. Margaret Talzeor confessed that she went to a meeting at midnight in Bodsmeadow when the witches danced to the music of James Kirk playing on a whistle, and immoral transactions took place. The clerk recorded that at this meeting 'their language *wes not our ordinarie language*' (Fergusson, 1907, 96). Witches are not known to have spoken with tongues so if they did not use ordinary English they must have spoken Gaelic. There is nothing to suggest this was unusual in the Hillfoots at that date. The names of thirteen members of the Alloa coven, two men and eleven women, are all given in Lowland form but they include Black, Dougal, Kirk, Millar, Paterson, Paton and Taylor which are all clerical abbreviations of Gaelic names which, as it happens, were used as aliases by members of Clan Gregor in southern Perthshire. What they called themselves we do not know. The written form of surnames at this period and for long after was decided by the clerk.

In the seventeenth century names begin to change to fit circumstances but Gaelic persists for a generation or two. This is shown by comparing two documents relating to the affairs of the Monros of Fowlis. A Commission issued at Holyroodhouse against Catherine Ross, Lady Monro, on 25 October 1577 (Exchequer Rolls 1899, xx, 522-3) shows that at that date both Gaelic and English naming conventions were in use in Easter Ross. The Commission lists the names of thirty alleged witches whose names have evidently been compiled by an English-speaking clerk using information supplied by local informants. Most of those named are known by their Gaelic patronymics (using *nighean* 'daughter') such as *Jonet Neyne Thomas McAllan*, 'Janet daughter of Thomas son of Allan' or *Jonetam Neyne Willelmun McClachan* 'Janet son of William McClachan'. A handful are given Lowland surnames such as Cattanach, Ross, Miller and Forbes. We can compare this with the names in a legal document of 1589 which accuses Hector Munro of Fowlis, step-son of Catherine Ross, of persecuting certain women. The background is still the Monro duchthas in Easter Ross and the players are the same as in 1577 but now all the accused women and the male jury have English surnames: MacKenzie, Bain, Glas, Cuthbert, Sutherland, Innes, Ross and Mowat (MacKenzie, 1898, 65). This does not mean these women had all suddenly learned to speak English.

In 1629 Gaelic was still current in this area when four women were tried there: Katharine Nein Rob Aunchtie, Marie Nein Eane Eir alias McIntoshe, Katharine Memphersoun [*lege* Nein Pherson] alias Naunchie, and Gradoche Neinechat, a grand mixture of full-blown patronymics, broken-down versions and witch aliases such as Gradoch and perhaps Naunchie and Neinechat.

One of the last witches to be tried in Nairn was Agnes Nic Ean Vane in 1662, a contemporary of Isobell Gowdie, who was certainly a Gaelic-speaker. Vane is not her surname but part of her patronym: she was the daughter of Iain Bain or John White.

The loss of Gaelic can largely be attributed to the distaste the Gaels felt for literacy and its impossible spelling system which seems to have been designed to impede progress. The Gaels seldom if ever committed their learning to writing, preferring to develop their memories, which were prodigious, but the absence of written documents in Gaelic contributed to a massive and irreversible loss of pagan material. It has also led scholars to diminish the importance of Gaelic in the history of Scotland and even to overlook its use in favour of Irish, not at all the same thing. But Gaelic is the key to the heart and soul of the Gael, to the identity and culture of the fairy-folk, and to the supernatural aspect of the evidence. Gaelic shows us how to make sense of it all.

The use of English in court hearings caused profound confusion. In several cases we can deduce that the accused did not understand the questions put to her (particularly when they referred to the Devil), and it is beyond doubt that the clerk did not always understand what a witch replied. It becomes clear that the legal documents transcribed by Pitcairn and others, including the record of Isobell Gowdie's four testimonies, are not a word-for-word transcript of what the witch said but the clerk's version, at best a bad translation and at worst an incomprehensible interpretation. In many cases these court documents have been edited, amplified and changed to make what the clerk felt was better sense. Mention of Isobell's 'little horse' is an example of a clerical interpolation: he is trying to explain what he thought she said but the horse is pure invention. Gaelic hunting shouts, which are generally in very obscure language, are treated with great suspicion as a way of raising the Devil; but it was a distant beacon that was raised to muster the troops.

However evident fantasy or illogical nonsense is useful as a sign-post. The 'impossible' evidence is invariably a mistaken interpretation or a bad translation of what the witch intended to say. The magistrates accepted almost any kind of fantasy with amazement but uncritically and had neither the knowledge nor any incentive to winkle out the truth. Where witches were concerned, since the time of James VI, any supernatural achievement was felt to be possible and added to the guilt of the accused. Both the accused and their accusers were ignorant and isolated. The Church was obsessed with demonology and had no concept of historical or scientific plausibility. The conversion of the Gaelic of the witches, whether it was pedestrian, metaphorical, dialectal, ritual, obsolete, or simply garbled, into the wild fantasies that pass for Scottish witch-lore, began in the courtrooms of Reformed Scotland, as accused women struggled to understand questions framed in a foreign language and their interlocutors struggled to make sense of their replies. It continues to the present day.

Black, like Cohn, Larner and other scholars, could only propose that the supernatural evidence was invented or imaginary. He picked out the following statement made by Margaret Watsone of Carnwath, tried at Lanark in 1644, as typical of what he called 'the *utterly unreliable* evidence of not a few confessions' (1938, 13). His selected confession was in fact a very good example of coded or metaphorical Gaelic reduced by an ignorant clerk to complete nonsense. However it is not too difficult to reconstruct an original. According to the court record, Margaret stated that at a coven meeting she and four other witches flew on a cat, a cock, a thorn tree, a bottell of straw, and a bourtrie or elder. Since nonsense is a reliable sign of archaic or metaphorical Gaelic, probably garbled or punned, this gives us five riddles to solve. The key, as always with archaic Gaelic, is to look for puns with words that relate to hunting or fire.

> 1 The *cat* in Scottish folklore is a metaphor for a troop of hunters (G. *cath*). It might also be a mistaken reading of G. *cath* 'battle, fight, strife', all coded references to a deer-drive. Since hunters always travelled very rapidly, to ride on a cat or to fly like a cat was to go as fast as a hunter.

> 2 The *cock* is a pun on G. *cog* 'war, fight' – again a deer-hunt. The same word with a related meaning is found as G. *coigchreach* 'plundering, pillaging', also a deer-hunt. This word is found in place-names such as Cockburn, Cockpen and Coigach. To ride or fly on a cock is again a reference to hunters travelling at great speed. A red cock or a black cock, usually of the humble farmyard variety, was used in magical cures.

> 3 The *thorn tree* or bramble, G. *dris*, which is the badge of a branch of Clan Maclean, is a pun on G. *greis* (W. Ross *dreis*) 'prowess, strength; battle, slaughter (hunt); hero (hunter)'. This is the third example of a hunter in a hurry to take part in a battle.

> 4 A *bottell of straw*, G. *connlach*, was set on fire to send a signal, to summon a ferry, or to acknowledge a message. As a torch it would show the way to a meeting.

> 5 The *bourtrie* or elder is G. *fearna*, an archaic word for fire.

This allows that Margaret's evidence is not 'utterly unreliable' or 'impossible' (another word much used by scholars) but full of information. To ride on a cat or a cock refers to travelling very rapidly, like a band of hunters who see a beacon signal. Witches, being a kind of hunt-support group, were used to such cant terms. The thorn-tree, G. *dris*, is a pun on a rare or obsolete word for a hunter. A bundle of straw was used as a torch when travelling by night; the elder is a punning way of saying the same thing. All that Margaret said, in essence, was that she and four other witches travelled very rapidly to the meeting-place and that two of them carried torches. The Gaels enjoyed this kind of lexical play but it does not survive translation. Her puns show that even in Lanarkshire, which is never included in the *Gaidhealtachd*, the old ritual language was still in daily use in 1644.

These solutions are of course guesswork but as they allow us to solve five riddles and provide coherent solutions we can be sure that they are close to the truth. We could reject one such solution as coincidence; two would not be much more convincing, but to find that we can link the nonsensical English of the court record in all five cases with a plausible Gaelic pun referring to the hunt suggests that we are close to the correct interpretation. This confidence is supported by the fact that all these puns have to do with hunting or with fire and provide sensible answers to some postulated question about attendance at a coven meeting. The witches must have found the whole transaction very strange and quite meaningless.

Having got so far one would like to know more. Were these five items real tokens or only figures of speech? The bottell of straw was obviously real but did Margaret and her friends normally wear a cat-skin, some black feathers, and a few twigs of thorn and elder as a kind of insignia, only when they were on official business or not at all? This list is reminiscent of the graphic story of Isobell Gowdie who was trapped in her own house by dogs while wearing a hare skin (probably badly cured) on official business. It is also reminiscent of the clan 'plant badges' which have also been dismissed as meaningless invention. A closer look at the badges associated with the more authentic native clans shows they are either kindling for a fire, such as sprigs of pine, heather, juniper, moss, rowan berries, furze, laurel leaves and dried grass, or wild herbs such as rosemary, myrtle, thyme and juniper which might have been sprinkled on a roasting haunch of venison. In both cases they are just what you would expect a hunter to carry.

But over the century of the trials, 1570-1670, as hunting died, authentic Gaelic hunting lore or fairy lore went out of use without being recorded and a great deal was lost. From surviving fragments (see *Archaic Gaelic* in this series) we know there was both religious and secular information: there were poems in praise of the Cailleach, liturgies and rituals including prayers of intercession and atonement, a hunting calendar, medical lore, plant lore, beacon lore, legal precedents and boundary lore. We may be thankful that the Reformed Church did not have sufficient Gaelic-speaking ministers to police the Highlands very strictly in the sixteenth and seventeenth centuries but the absence of trial transcripts deprives us of the detailed if often garbled information about occult practices revealed by the trials in the Lowlands. Without the trials we would now know very little about pre-Christian beliefs and practices in Scotland.

One rare claim that a pre-Christian religion persisted among the Gaels of Perthshire was made in Henry Jenner's Introduction to an edition of the *Memoirs of the Lord Viscount Dundee* (1903, xlix). When commenting on the religious background of Clan Gregor at the time of Dundee's campaigns, he says that 'in the latter part of the nineteenth century, a Macgregor, a clergyman of some distinction, had told him that down to very recent times the clan possessed a religion of its own. He could give no details of its peculiarities, as it was just out of reach; but being asked whether they were Catholics or Protestants, he replied, "No, they were neither Catholics nor Protestants; they were just Macgregors"; and from what one knows of the clan one may well believe him'. There is no other mention of this pagan religion. The relics of pre-Christian religion in Highland Perthshire are limited to the bells, bones, stones and holy books associated with the cult of St Fillan, several abandoned Annats – probably cremation grounds – and one very old yew tree in a vast enclosure. The old religion, as the clergyman said, was just out of reach (or discreetly ignored) by the late Victorians. But there was one happy exception to which we will come shortly. The solitary surviving description of a magical or pagan fertility festival in which every member of the community was involved was the Oda, latterly a kind of Michaelmas Fair. It died out in the Outer Isles and West Highlands early in the nineteenth century and is not reported from the mainland. On the eastern Lowlands religion was in the hands of the more or less pagan Culdees or Picts who are dealt with elsewhere (see *A Pagan Priesthood*, in this series).

Despite the paucity of the evidence, between the Culdees, the Picts, the Oda and the archaic Gaelic fragments, it cannot be doubted that the Gaels had a religion of their own and that the pre-coven witchcraft activity provides a surviving if faint testimony. If Queen Mary's Act of 1563 making witchcraft a crime had been strictly applied a witchfinder in the *Gaidhealtachd* would have found that though there were no covens every housewife he examined was guilty of performing magic rituals within her own home and byre. He would have found himself in a situation like that in Langedorf, Germany, where in 1492 all but two of the adult females were charged with witchcraft (Kieckhefer 1976, 145). With its limited resources it did what it could. An English observer noted that in 1650 'at a little village within two miles [of Berwick], two men and three women were burnt for witches, and nine more were to be burnt, the village consisting but of fourteen families, and there were as many witches ... Twenty more were to be burnt within six miles of that place and all their goods are forfeited to the King and the Lords...' (Whitelock 1682, 434, quoted by Black 1938, 61). There was certainly an alternative religion in Scotland which survived for longest in country places.

The absence of trials in the Highlands was in part due to a chronic shortage of Gaelic-speaking ministers to spearhead the attack but also because the necessary infrastructure of courts, clerks, lawyers, ministers, kirk sessions, prisons, hangmen and funding were rare beyond the Highland line before c.1700. In the rare corners where this administrative structure did exist within the Gaeltachd, as it did under Campbells in Rothesay and Inverarary, which were both burghs of barony in the fifteenth century, we find witch-hunts on the Lowland pattern and even some rather irregular activity by a Devil in Bute. The trials of 1662 in Rothesay reveal a very interesting transitional phase between English and Gaelic, between Lowland and Highland witchcraft, and between native practice and learned coven magic. The Devil doubles as Master of the Hunt, witches are members of a coven but also work as independent healers, and some healers use Gaelic charms that some of their patients do not understand.

We must also admit that not all the 'strange and odiouse factes' confessed in court were accidents of transmission or clerical invention. Scottish witches were guilty of many evil and scandalous practices including infanticide, cannibalism and ritual intercourse with the Devil. These practices would be difficult to believe if we did not have the evidence of the trials, and are difficult to believe even with this evidence. But were they local practices native to the country or were they alien imports? As there is no sign of infanticide, cannibalism, or ritual intercourse with a local Devil north of the Highland Line we may conclude that these extreme activities were influenced by imported and perhaps imaginary ideas. The Oda admits a *fascinum* or bundle but administered by each individual woman.

This raises the question of how we can distinguish between genuine lore and spurious invention. As mentioned above, one reliable rule is the lack of sense which appears to be inevitable whenever an English-speaker encounters archaic Gaelic. To make a pie out of a dead baby is revolting but not impossible in extreme circumstances. But if a witch flies on a cat or a cock or a bottell of straw, this is evidently nonsense and it was created in court at the clerical interface, not by the witch whose meaning (if we are right) was quite pedestrian. Such nonsense almost always represents a word or phrase of archaic Gaelic which has been misinterpreted by an English-speaking clerk, accidentally out of ignorance or to create a claim of supernatural activity and cause an effect. Whenever we come across apparent nonsense in the evidence given by a witch in the course of her trial we can reliably expect to find a rational meaning in Gaelic disguised by a pun or a bad translation into English. Very seldom is there anything very sensational among the coded material. Once we recognise that mysteries such as shape-shifting and flying by night are not incomprehensible supernatural features but errors arising from deliberate puns or nonsense arising from bad scholarship, we can begin to decode them and get closer to the reality behind the witch panics.

A second rule when interpreting archaic Gaelic is that topics are limited to hunting, fire, beacons, deer, the Cailleach. These are all associated with men, who were hunters. There was presumably a parallel world of female belief which has left even fewer traces except in the Oda which fortunately was well recorded before it was banned.

A third rule is that any violent confrontation such as a battle, war, affray, skirmish or wrangle means a hunt. G. *sabaid* now translated as 'brawl, quarrel, fight, fray or row' was originally and perhaps always a deer-hunt. Soldiers, warriors and heroes are hunters. The many Gaelic words which now refer to warfare and battles referred originally to the deer-drive which was organised on military lines. The link between hunting and warfare has been lost in English but is still alive in most European languages. In Italian, German, Dutch and French but not in English or Gaelic, words for a soldier are also those for a hunter. French *chasseur* 'hunter' is now also an infantryman or a fighter pilot. Dutch *jager* and German *Jäger* are both 'hunter' and 'rifleman, fusilier, fighter pilot'. G. *cath* 'hunt' is now translated as 'battle, fight, struggle, contest' but it was originally a deer-drive and G. *cath* 'company of soldiers' was originally a troop of hunters. The fairy raid was a deer-drive when they raided the deer-forest. As soon as we convert the impossible evidence back into Gaelic we can see that the witch is referring to hunting lore and not to improbable supernatural activities. The esoteric aspects of the witches' sabbat were to ensure luck in the subsequent hunt.

A fourth point to bear in mind is that the text transcribed and printed so carefully by Pitcairn and others is not a word-by-word transcript of what the accused woman had said but an edited version of what an English-speaking court thought she had said. They converted her statements, days or weeks after the events, into a version which made sense to them (the witch was not in a position to comment) and which gained in credibility from being officially recorded. The fact that supernatural events were described in such sources gave them credibility. If a report was clearly impossible this only added to the general conviction that a witch was able to change shape, fly, blast crops, sink ships, raise winds, spoil beer, and generally work evil 'and this thou canst not deny'.

As the seventeenth century went on, stories of the supernatural found a ready market in the burgeoning fake folklore industry. The courts were also influenced by the spurious witch-lore that had become popular entertainment and which in almost every case can be traced to confusion at the clerical interface where Gaelic metaphors and puns, lexical confusion, bad translations of Gaelic material, a negligent attitude to the truth, and commercial incentives made an unholy broth. The invention of printing, used at first for holy books, was rapidly exploited by the gutter press and led to the publication of sensational and worthless broadsheets which became a novel form of popular entertainment. It is probable that the entire population of Lowland Scotland quite rapidly became familiar with the more lurid cases. These details fed back into the accusations made by hostile witnesses, the charges brought against individual witches, and the court's interpretation of their confessions. Far from extinguishing the practices of witchcraft, the trials gave it an immense and lasting popularity. Reginald Scot was rare in his day, a sceptic who hoped to make witchcraft seem ridiculous and improbable but he was out of step with the times. At a later date a handful of the contemporary elite – notably the lawyer Sir George Mackenzie (1636-1691) – applied legal standards, common sense and a measure of common humanity to the problem of the witch-hunts and made allowances for the unbelievable aspects of the evidence. They did not understand it but they knew it was not literally true.

Appendix 1 to Chapter 9: Gaelic Witch Names

'Many witches taken there who confessed many uncouth and strange things, and how the devil gave them marks and signs with other names, as Wallidragle and the like. And[ro] Mudies wife in Tranent was called Knell...'

Patrick Anderson, History, 1596.

The Gaelic origins of witchcraft in Lowland Scotland are most clearly shown by the nicknames attributed to witches in the records, as far as Orkney and Shetland. Witches gave them to each other and some masters of covens gave a witch a new name (but in English) when she or he joined the coven, renounced her original baptism and swore to follow him. Most of the aliases given in the trial records are complimentary names such as Greibok, G. *gribhach* 'heroic, warlike', Lykeas, G. *leigheas* 'healing, curing', and Premak G. *priomhach* 'favourite'. *Loskoir Longert* 'fire of the deer trap' in Easter Ross represents an archaic vein of Gaelic hunting lore. These names are evidence for a widespread cult operating in the Gaidhealtachd which was exposed, briefly, by the trials. On the basis of these names alone, I believe that Margaret Murray was right in identifying the witch-cult as a prehistoric sacred tradition, though what we find in Scotland is probably older than even she envisaged.

The continued use of Gaelic in Lothian up to 1600 is shown by the persistence of Gaelic names such as *Fian, Knell, Toppock, Wallydraggle* and *Winzit*. These names were part of a widespread cult operating in the Gaeltachd which might have remained invisible but for the trials. The Devil generally gave a witch a new name when she or he joined a coven but such names are invariably in English. The loss of the Gaelic naming tradition can be traced to the creation of covens by men who spoke only English: there is no known case of a Devil giving a new convert a Gaelic name. In 1640 when Janet Breadheid was initiated, the Devil at Auldearn was giving his witches English names and teaching them how to curse in English (Pitcairn iii, 618). Nevertheless, to judge by elements of Isobell Gowdie's confession, Gaelic was still spoken in Moray in 1662.

The names used by the Gaelic-speakers in Easter Ross deserve special notice. Some thirty individuals were named in a Commission issued at Holyroodhouse on 25 October 1577 (Exchequer Rolls xx, 522-3, 1899).

Their names were evidently compiled by an English-speaking clerk using information supplied orally by a number of people with local knowledge. In consequence the names are given in a variety of forms. The women's names are often Gaelic patronyms such as *Jonet Neyne Thomas McAllan*, 'Janet daughter of Thomas son of Allan', or *Jonetam Neyne Willelmun McClachan* 'Janet son of William McClachan'. In Caithness in 1719 we find *Margaret Nin-Gilbert*, 'Margaret daughter of Gilbert', instead of Margaret Gilbertson. This reflect the use of Gaelic as a spoken vernacular. A few individuals use surnames of Lowland type, such as Cattanach, Ross, Miller and Forbes. There are also Gaelic aliases such as Cassindonisch and Loskoir Longert. Cradoch Neynane McGillechallum and Christian Chactach are also listed. *Cradoch* and *Chactach* are neither personal names nor surnames but appear to be witch-aliases which have replaced their owners' original names. This kind of substitution is found elsewhere. A leader of the North Berwick witches was known as John Fean or Fiene (G. *fiann* 'giant, warrior (hunter)', but his real name was John Cunningham. In Aberdeenshire, one of the witches who danced around the Fish Cross and Meil Market of Aberdeen at Hallowe'en 1596 is known only as *Shuddack*. These names underline the widespread understanding of the Gaelic idiom among the witches.

Appendix 2 to Chapter 9: Dating the survival of Gaelic

The use of a Gaelic alias in any place shows the continued use of vernacular Gaelic among its witches within the previous generation. In the southwest and perhaps also in Ayrshire a knowledge of Gaelic lingered into the eighteenth century. There was more Gaelic than appeared as the leaders of covens generally spoke English and gave English names to their witches, regardless of their native vernacular.

1597: Aberdeen. Last Gaelic name on record in 1597: English also in use by that date.

1618: Ayrshire.

1622: West Lothian.

1622: Wigtown.

1629: Easter Ross. Gaelic was spoken still here for centuries.

1629: East Lothian. English in use by 1661.

1630: Dumfriesshire. Gaelic still in use.

1631: Banff, Moray. English was in use by the elite before c.1640.

1645: Fife. Gaelic still in use.

1645: Orkney. Gaelic names on record.

1662: Bute. Gaelic was still spoken in Bute in 1662 but by then the Devil was giving his witches pedestrian names like Janet, Catherine and Mary (MacPhail 1920, 6, 12, 13).

Appendix 3 to Chapter 9: Gaelic Witch Names

Aunchtie. Katharine Nein Rob Aunchtie was tried in Easter Ross in 1629. This name is not listed by Black (1946) as a Scottish surname. Perhaps G. *anam-chaidh* 'brave'.

Bargans: 'a man called Bargans' was a fugitive from justice at Bo-ness, in Renfrew in 1650. The name is not listed by Black (1946) as a Scottish surname. It may be from G. *barg* 'red hot' (RPC 2 series, vol.8, 211-235).

Bean, the alias of Margaret Clerk executed in Aberdeen, 1597. G. *ban* 'white, bright'.

Berdock, alias used by Margaret Borthwick, Cousland, West Lothian, 1630. Perhaps G. *bearraideach* 'nimble, light, active'.

Brune, the alias of Katharene Rannald, Kilpunt, West Lothian, 1622. Mother of Barbara Home alias Winzit. Helen Mcbrune (below) may have been a local Fairy Queen.

Callioch, alias of Janet McIllwhichill in Ardoch, 1622. G. *cailleach* 'maiden'; she was perhaps the Maiden of the coven.

Cane, alias of Effie McCalzane, tried in Edinburgh in 1591 (Pitcairn 246). G. *cain* 'beloved, dear; clear, bright'.

Cassindonisch, the alias of Thomas McAnemoir McAllan McHendrik, Easter Ross, 1577. G. *cas* 'hunt', of the *dòmhnaich* 'deer forest' would be a hunting shout (cf Christsonday, below). It could also be *cas an donais* 'Devil's foot' but this is essentially meaningless.

Chactach, a probable witch-name recorded in Easter Ross in 1577: G. *chiatach* 'handsome, goodly'.

Cradoch or **Gradoch** for G. *gràdhag* 'esteemed, loved, admired'.

Dam. The first witch contacted by Katherine Ross, Lady Fowlis, was 'William McGilliewareycht-dame', William McGillievorich. This is probably not G. *damh* 'stag' but Dann or Daan, a place in Easter Ross.

Douglas, alias (or married surname?) of Barbara Napiar, Edinburgh 1590. G. *dubh* + *glas* 'deer light'.

Elva, one of the Devils in Bute in 1662. Perhaps G. *eala* 'sanctuary' or 'deer forest'. E. *elf* may have a similar origin.

Feane, Fian, alias of John Cunningham, leader of the North Berwick witches. The Fian or Feinne were legendary deer-hunters (G. *fiadh* 'deer'). The word is related to G. *fionn* 'white'.

Galdragon, Shetland. 'Fire Master'. A traditional name for a witch or sorceress (Scott). cf Wallydraggle and W. *dragon* 'leader in war' or 'hunt master'.

Goilean. G. *goileam* 'fire, fire-kindling (Dalyell 1835, 540).

Gradoch. Neynane McGillecallum in Easter Ross in 1577. Gradock, the alias of Jonet Grant, 1590, Aberdeen. Gradoche Neinechat 'Beloved Maiden of the Troop', the name of a witch in Ross-shire in 1629 (Black 1938, 45). G. *gràdhag* 'esteemed, loved, admired'.

Gray-meal, the alias of John Gordoun, 'a silly old ploughman', who was door-keeper to the North Berwick witches, 1590 and evidently a Highlander. G. *greigh* 'herd' + *meall* 'beacon hill'.

Greibok, Griebik or **Grewik**, used by two Orkney witches: Katherine Bigland in 1615 and Jonet Thomesone in 1643. G. *gribhach* 'heroic, warlike'. Grapus is a name of the devil. Both are related to G. *gribh* 'warrior (hunter)', G. *grib, griobh* 'griffon', and E. *grab, grip*.

Greysteil, nickname of Patrick, third Lord Ruthven, father of William, first Earl of Gowrie and son of the Lord Ruthven who killed Queen Mary's favourite, David Rizzio. Greysteil was the hero of a metrical romance popular in the 15th-16th centuries. A Gaelic nickname meaning 'gallant warrior'.

Hattaraick, alias of Alexander Hunter, 'an old wizard' in Haddington, 1629. G. *càtharrach* 'fighting bravely or resolutely' (Summer 1925, 135).

Hauche, alias of Marion Johnestoun, Dumfriesshire, 1630. Perhaps G. *abhach* 'sportive, humorous, joyous'.

Helen Mcbrune. The name of a spirit (perhaps the Queen of Elphane) that appeared to Patrick Lowrie and Jonet Hunter at Hallowe'en 1605, on Lowdon Hill, Ayrshire, and gave him what sounds like a knitted glove (Pitcairn ii, 478). 'Brian' is a name of the devil and means 'fire'. At Hallowe'en on Lowdon Hill we would expect the fairy folk or hunters to light a bonfire.

Huthart was a familiar or spirit who informed the female soothsayer who predicted the imminent death of James I in 1436. G. *cutharthach* or *cobhartach* 'saviour, helper, comforter'.

Klareanough, the Devil who met Janet Morisoun at Knockanrioch, Bute, in 1662. G. *clàr-aodhanach* 'broad-faced' refers to a widely-visible fire (G. *aodh* 'fire'). A comparable word is *clàireineach* said to mean 'dwarf', but perhaps a small fire. The first element is related to G. *clearc* 'radiant, bright', E. *clear*, E. *clarion*, a type of trumpet used to send a signal. Isobell Gowdie said that the Fairy King at the Downie Hills was 'broad-faced'. This may have been the name of a beacon. The name Knockanrioach seems to be obsolete but in 1573 it was granted to Marion Fairlie, widow of Sheriff John Stewart together with Little Barone (NS0764) and Gartnakeilly (also NS0764), which are both a mile west of Rothesay. It may be the house now known as Larkhall.

Kna, Kna Donaldi 'daughter of Donald' was a witch in Easter Ross in 1577: G. *cna* 'good, bountiful, gracious, precious, merciful' (attributes of the Cailleach).

Knell, the name given to And[rew] Mudie's wife, a witch in Tranent, 1596. G. *gnèidheil* 'shapely, well-proportioned' (Anderson Adv. mss 35.5.3).

Lanie, Agnes alias Lanie Scot, tried in Aberdeen in 1536 (Black 1938, 21). G. *laineach* 'glad, joyful, merry'.

Leiris, listed in Easter Ross in 1577 as the husband of a witch. Perhaps from G. *leir* 'destructive, terrible', applied to G. *leirist* 'slovenly woman, slut' (both applied to the Cailleach).

Likkit or **Lukit,** alias of Christian Keringtoune of Prestonpans, tried in Edinburgh in 1591 (Pitcairn 246). G. *luchaidh* 'light'.

Loskoir Longert, alias of Mariota Neymaine (or Neyeane) McAlester, Easter Ross (1577). A hunting shout meaning 'fire at the hunting lodge' with G. *loisg* 'to burn' and *longhairt* or *luncart* 'hunting lodge'.

Lykeas, G. *leigheas* 'healing, curing'. On 16 October 1673, at the trial of Jannet McNicoll in Rothesay in Bute, it was stated that the devil, a gross lepper-faced man, gave her a new name of Mary Lykeas.

Micol, in English literature, a name of the Queen of Elfhame who could be summoned by calling, 'Micol, Micol queen of the pygmies, come!' (Dalyell 1835, 537).

Molach, Donald Molach was a notable witch in Morvern, 18-19c. (Campbell 1902, 10). G. *mol* 'assembly, flock', so, a hunter but also *mollachd* 'curse'.

Napeas or the fairie; G. *nàbaidh* 'neighbour' (Dalyell 1835, 539). Barbara Naipar, 1590 in Edinburgh, was **Naip**, perhaps a pun on her surname.

Naunnchie, alias of Katharine Mcinphersoun, Ross-shire, 1629. Perhaps G. *naomh* 'holy, sacred' + *sith* 'deer forest'. Noance NicClerich was said to be sister's daughter to the witch of Monzie (see under Nic Niven).

NicAicherne, a witch in Morven; perhaps a beacon. Henderson, 2008, 7.

NicNiven or **Neven**, G. *nighean* 'daughter' + *naomhin* 'holy place (deer forest)'. Cognate with Nemain or Neamhain, an Irish war goddess or battle fury (a hunting goddess) and with Gaulish *Nemetona*. Nemed was the husband of Macha, another war goddess, and of Cera ('light'), and father of Starn ('light'). There is probably also a link with Nine, as in Nine Maidens, G. *naoinear* 'nine persons', indicating a holy place or deer sanctuary. Nicniven was a frequent alias in Scotland, said to identify the Fairy Queen: 'Now Nicniven is the Queen of Elphin, the Mistress of the Sabbat' (Scott 1931, 300; M. Summers 1925, 7).

Sara Neven, the name of a trow at Quarff, Shetland, in the late nineteenth century. Sara in Gaelic is Mór, archaic *mar* 'hunt'. Archaic G. *naomhin* 'holy place (deer forest)'.

Noance [Agnes?] NicClerich was sister's daughter to Nik Neiving, a notorious and infamous witch in Monzie who was burnt c.1565. She worked with John Brugh, the warlock of Fossaway (Reid, 1899, 202). Dalyell thought Nik Neiving of Monzie was the same as the witch called NicNiven who was burned at St Andros in 1569.

Kate McNieven, according to a story which has all the features of fake folklore, was nurse to the Laird of Inchbrackie, Perthshire, and was burned on the Knock of Crieff in 1715 for stealing a knife and fork while in the shape of a bee. This appears to be inspired by earlier events at Monzie with the addition of spurious fantasy (McAra 1881, 201). The date is disputed by Jamieson, minister of Monzie, in 'A southern outpost on the edge of the Highlands' (*Chronicles of Strathearn*, 1896, 333-340). Both Inchbrakie and Monzie are within two miles of Crieff. In *The Flyting of Montgomery and Polwart* Nicnevin is a generic (Irving and Laing (eds) 1821, 117). Then a cleir companie came soone after closse *Nicniven*, with her nymphs in number anew, With charmes from Caithness and Chanrie of Rosse, Whose cunning consists in casting a clew. . . Scott in talking of Celtic fairy lore mentions 'a gigantic and malignant female, the Hecate of this mythology, who rode on the storm, and marshalled the rambling host of wanderers under her grim banner. This hag . . . was called Nicneven in that later system which blended the faith of the Celts and the Goths on this subject.' (Scott, Letters, 130). In *The Flyting of Dunbar and Kennedy* Dunbar pictures her at Hallowe'en, riding at the head of witches, fairies, sorceresses, elves and ghosts.

Nun. Janet Paton 'a great witch' of the Fossaway coven was called 'the Nun', perhaps for 'the Cailleach', which can have that meaning.

Pardone, name used by Marion Peebles, Shetland, 1644 (Pitcairn 194). G. *pairtean* '(having) abilities, or powers'.

Preip the Witch that wes brunt at Banff (Presbytery Book of Strathbogie 1843, 5). Perhaps G. *breab* 'kick, prance'. Black (1938, 48) says: Wrongly thought to be the alias of John Philip, vagabond, tried and executed in Banff, 1631, but if Preip the Witch was not John Philip, then who was?

Premak, alias of Isobel Thomson, Elgin, Moray in 1596. G. *priomhach* 'favourite' (Huie 1976, 290). Wrongly given as Preinak.

Rigerum, an alias of Margaret Craige, one of the Pollockshaws witches in 1676. Perhaps from G. *ruagair* 'hunter'. It is late to find Gaelic in daily use.

Rigga, Jonet Rendall, a poor vagabond, in Orkney 1629. G. *ruaig* 'pursuit, hunt, chase'. Her Devil was called Walliman. She blamed him for all the cattle who died: 'Giff they deit Walliman did it'.

Rossina, the new name given to Agnes Murie, Fossaway, 1661. G. *ros* 'pleasant, pretty, delightful' or from G. *rosachd* 'enchantment, charm, witchcraft' (Reid 1899, 220).

Runa Rowa, alias of Annie Tailyour, Orkney 1624. G. *run* 'beloved person or object' and *ruith* 'chase, pursuit, rout (deer drive)'. 'Beloved of the Hunt' was no doubt an honorific name of the Cailleach.

Scudder or **Sculdr**, alias of Isobell Strathaquin, Aberdeen, 1597. G. *sguideir* 'slut, whore', once an honourable attribute of the Cailleach.

Seweis, a suspected witch in custody in St Andrews, 1645. G. *seamhas* 'good luck, prosperity'. This is not known as a personal name or a family name. It corresponds to Lucky or Goody.

Shuddak, one of those who danced around the Fish Cross and Meil Market of Aberdeen at Hallowe'en 1596. G. *siodhach* 'a fairy, one of the fairy folk'.

Spaldarge, alias of Jonet Clark, 1590 (S.C.M. I, 140). Perhaps G. *spio-ladair* 'teaser'. Also as **Spalding.**

Spalding. See Spaldarge.

Stovd, alias of Barbara Thomasdochter, Shetland, 1616. Jakob Jakobsen gives *støvi* 'whirl of dust'.

Suppak or **Suppok**, alias of Helene Makkie in Aberdeen, 1597. G. *sopag* 'small bundle of straw', used to make a torch or send a signal. There are several other instances of a small bundle of straw or hay in witch-lore.

Swein, a male witch in Auldearn, in grass-green. Archaic Gaelic *samh* 'to gather' + *ain* 'fire'. It is the same as *Samhain* 'Hallowe'en'.

Todlock, alias of Margaret Ranie, Orkney 1643. G. *todhail* 'destruction'.

Toppock, alias of Elizabeth Steven, a female witch in Lothian c.1629. G. *tapaidh* 'clever, bold, heroic', or *taobhach* 'friendly, kind' (Summer 1925, 135).

Trachak, a witch in Aberdeenshire, with Spaldairg, 1597. G. *dreachach* 'fair, handsome'. (Michie 1896, 38).

Wallawa, in Orkney a name of the Devil. The oath in part went: 'O Mester King o' a' that's ill, Come fill me with the warlock skill, An' I sall serve wi' all me will, in de name o' de muckle black Wallawa!' Probably the same name as Walliman (see below), an aspirated version of G. *baillie ban* meaning 'the person of the fire enclosure'.

Wallidragle, the name of a witch in Tranent, 1596 (Anderson. Adv. mss 35.5.3). G. *gal* 'flame, kindred, slaughter, valour (hunter)' or Sc. *wally* 'excellent, showy, ample' + *dreachail* 'comely, good-looking, handsome'. Probably an epithet of the hunting goddess 'the handsome one of the flame', degraded in Scots to *wallidraggle* 'slovenly woman'. It is related to the names Galdragon and Walliman, Jonet Rendall's Devil in Orkney.

Walliman, Jonet Rendall's Devil in Orkney. Perhaps from G. *baillie ban* 'of the enclosure of the fire'.

Winzit, alias of Barbara Home in Kilpont, West Lothian, 1622. G. *uinnseachadh* 'managing'.

Appendix 4 to Chapter 9: Lowland names for the Fairy Queen.

Galdragon, an obsolete Shetland word for a witch or sorceress (Scott). 'Fire-master'.

Gay Carline. A name of the Cailleach. Probably for 'Gray Carline'. The same as the following.

Gyre-Carline. She lived on human flesh, which is a view of the Cailleach as a cremation bonfire.

Helen McBrune on Lowdon Hill, Ayrshire.

NicNevin. See above.

Queen of Elphame or **Elphin** 'ruler of the hill ground or deer forest'.

Appendix 5 to Chapter 9: Scottish Witch and Devil Names derived from English

Most of these names are from the later period or reflect early contact with English-speakers. The practice of giving witches Gaelic dedicatory or 'spirit' names persisted through the sixteenth and into the seventeenth century in most of Lowland Scotland. Then Gaelic names were replaced by English names. This reflects the spread of education in English and the control of local covens by educated Devils who spoke no Gaelic. On a wider scale the change reflects the retreat of Gaelic from Lowland Scotland.

The practice of giving witches new names when they renounced their Christian baptism persisted after 1600 but in a degraded fashion. Pedestrian English names such as Margaret, David, Nan and Christian mark a break in the oral transmission of Gaelic lore, related to the spread of literacy in English, when the meaning and purpose of the Gaelic names (and no doubt many other features of the cult) were lost. This break corresponds with the spread of imported rituals and recipes learned from books and with the general spread of English at the expense of Gaelic.

Isobell Gowdie named several of the witches and ten of the thirteen devils belonging to her company at Auldearn as it was in 1662. The names she supplies are all in Scots – confirming that the Auldearn Devil was a member of the local elite who had been educated abroad, was not a Gaelic speaker, and who had acquired his interest in black magic from books. We can recognise the work of two different devils there, neither of them a Gaelic-speaker. The first, who was active c.1640, gave his witches very ordinary names such as Janet and Christian. The second had more imagination, but his names still have nothing in common with traditional Gaelic spirit names.

Able-and-Stout, alias of Bessie Hay, Auldearn, 1662.

Bandon is a figment found in the diary of Alexander Brodie of Brodie, in his entry for 30 September 1662: 'My Son went to Aldearn to see the trial of the witch *Bandon*; who adheard to her confessions, and was condemd.' His entry of 2 October: 'I heard much of her blaming Betti Hay as a teacher and partner in her witchcrafts.' Like Bessie Hay ('Able and Stout') 'Bandon' is in error for I.Gowdie. Only two members of the Auldearn coven were interrogated at that date: Isobell Gowdie and Janet Breidhead. Examination of the MS shows that Brodie made a mistake with the initial letter but corrected it without deletion to read 'IGaudie'. Apart from this it is easy to make 'owdie' out of the remaining letters.

Bawdem, the surname or alias of Maggie, the Great Witch of the Chanonrie, Easter Ross, executed 1577.

Bessie Bald, alias given to Elspet Nishe, Auldearn, 1662.

Broun, alias of Katharene Rannald in Kilpont, 1622. This is apparently not her married surname as her daughter's name was Barbara Home (see Winzie, above). Broun, as in Helen McBrune, is probably a 'fire' word and may represent Brian, a name of the Devil.

Christian, the name given to Janet Breadheid by her Devil, perhaps as early as 1640.

Hynd Knight, the Devil of Andro Man's coven, Aberdeen, 1587. cf. Hind Etin (above).

Janet, the baptismal name given to Isobell Gowdie by her Devil, some time before 1662.

Lanthorne, alias of Christian Wilson, a witch in Dalkeith, 1661.

Mak Hector or **MacKeeler** a male witch in Auldearn, a young man in grass-green.

Noblie, given as an alias of Isobel Durward, Angus, 1661. See Ouglie.

Norische or **Nurreych.** Marioun Wod, alias Erss [Highland?] Marioun, vtherwayes callit the Catnes norische (Aberdeen 1597). Bessie Roy, nurreych, Fetternear, Angus, 1590: both probably *nourrice* or wet-nurse. Was this an official position? Did they look after abducted infants?

Nun: Janet Paton, a great witch in Crook of Devon, was termed The Nun = G. *cailleach* (Reid 1899, 221).

Ower-the-Dyke-with-it, the name given to Janet Martin, Maiden of the Auldearn coven, 1662.

Pickle Nearest the Wind, name given to Margaret Wilson, Auldearn, 1662.

Rob the Rower, one of the North Berwick witches, 1590. He kept the roll or row. Robert was a popular name among devils and witches and means 'hunter' (as E. *robber*). Bobbie was a name for the Lowland Devil. This name reflects the influence of Francis Stewart, Earl of Bothwell, whose natural language appears to have been French.

Robbie o da Rees, a trow at Quarff, Shetland, late nineteenth century. The Rees may be the reaths or quarter-days.

Robert the Comptroller, the alias of Robert Grierson, North Berwick, 1590. This name has the same meaning as Rob the Rower.

Robert the Jackis, a male witch in Auldearn, 1662, an aged man in dune. For Robert see above. Sc. *jack* was a leather bag such as a saddle bag. Hunters carried provisions in leather satchels.

Robert the Rule, a male witch in Auldearn, 1662, who wore sadd-dun. For Robert see above. The second part is perhaps G. *ruladh* 'slaughtering, massacre (hunting)' but cf 'Rob the Rower'.

Rorie, a male witch in Auldearn, 1662, who wore yellow. *Ruairidh* was 'facetiously applied to the fox'. E. Dwelly 1026. A fox was one of the shape-changing animals; in other words, the Devil sometimes wore a fox-skin.

Roring Lyon, a male witch in Auldearn, in grass-green. The lion, as a great hunter and as a pun on G. *lion* 'gin, snare' and 'fill, replenish, satiate' was a very old and very popular hunting pun.

Samuel, the name used by the Devil of the Crook of Devon coven, 1662 (Reid 1899, 223).

Sanders, the Read Reiver, a male witch in Auldearn, in black. Sandie was a name of the Lowland Devil and appears to mean 'hunter'. A riever or robber was also a hunter. The root is found in G. *reubail* 'tear, mangle (kill, butcher)'. Red is perhaps G. *ruadh* 'deer'.

The Seelie Wights 'the skilful people', remembered as beautiful, happy people; G. *seilg* 'hunt'.

Serpent, the name of the leader of the coven at Inverkip, Renfrewshire. St Paul equated the serpent with the Devil.

Thieff of Hell, a male witch in Auldearn, 1662. A thief in any archaic context was a hunter. The Lowland Devil was known as the Auld Thief.

Thomas the Fearie, a male witch in Auldearn, 1662. G. *faire* 'to keep watch'. Thomas may be G. *tomhais* 'to measure, survey', which was originally done at night by aligning fires.

Throw-the-Cornyard, alias of Bessie Wilson, Auldearn, 1662.

Viceroy, the name used by Isabel Rutherford of the Crook of Devon coven, 1662.

In a notorious case that came to court in 1677 six members of an alleged coven at Pollockshaws near Glasgow were tried and condemned for attempting to cause the death of Sir George Maxwell. Their 'spirit' names are given by Sinclair in *Satan's Invisible World* (pages 4 to 10). As at Auldearn there is a change between the pedestrian English name *Landlady* and the obscure (invented?) Annippy or Enippa of 1677. Locas and Rigerum appear to be Gaelic in origin.

Ejoall or *Ejool*: the name given by the Black Man at Pollockshaws. He wore black clothes, a blue band and white hand-cuffs with hogers and his feet were cloven.

Enippa or *Annippy*: the name given to Annabil Stuart (who had just been recruited) at Pollockshaws in 1677. This may be Scots *aneabil* 'single woman, concubine' or simply a version of her own name.

Jonat: the name given to John Stuart at Pollockshaws. It is unusual to give a man a woman's name.

Landlady: the name given to Jonet Mathie, mother of Annabil Stuart, at Pollockshaws.

Locas: the witch-name of Margaret Jackson at Pollockshaws. Perhaps G. *logais* 'awkward unwieldy person'?

Rigerum: the name given to Margaret Craige at Pollockshaws. It could be from G. *ruagair* 'hunter'.

Sopha: name given to Bessie Weir at Pollockshaws. This might be intended for Greek *Sophia* 'Wisdom', who is said to have created Lucifer; if so it points to some knowledge of the Classics on the part of the local Devil.

Appendix 6 to Chapter 9: Names of the Cailleach

In the Highlands, despite her evolved identity as the goddess of deer and of life and death, and some late appearances as an evil witch, the Cailleach retained her original local identity as a tribal beacon. The following manifestations are all local beacons which were lit to announce important communal hunts (Campbell 1902, 26, 51, ff). The names shows very nicely the distinction between meaningless literal translations and the archaic original Gaelic. At one time every local hunt had its own *cailleach*; these are only a few of the local names.

Fhua Mhoir Bein Baynac was a male ghost who lived in Glenavon, Banffshire. See Clashnichd Aulnaic.

Clashnichd Aulnaic was a female ghost who lived in Glenavon, Banffshire, and who often shrieked at night because Fhua Mhoir Bein Baynac had expelled her from her home (Stewart 1822, 6-8).

Ball odhar, Kintra, Ardnamurchan: G. *beoll* 'fire', archaic G. *odhar* 'fire place' or 'deer forest'. G. *crom-odhar* 'the crook of the fireplace' or 'pot-hanger' also means 'penis', for obvious reasons.

Beire, a name of the Cailleach Bheur.

Cailleach Bheine Mhor lived in Jura at Larig Breac 'the pass of the deer'. When she saw that Mhic a Phie (a fairy man or hunter) had left her by a trick she slid down the side of Beinn an Oir on Sgriob na Cailich, the scree of the Big Woman, where you can still see her track (Campbell vol II).

Cailleach Bheur, the long-distance beacon on Ben Nevis. G. *beur* 'sharp, loud (of a signal)'. Also known as Beire, the Gyre-Carline, the Gay Carline, and Mag Moullach. She heralded winter by washing her plaid in the Corrievreacain, a whirlpool which at times can be heard at a distance of twenty miles. It takes three days for the cauldron to boil and when the washing is done 'the plaid of old Scotland is virgin white'. The Cailleach Bheur had only one eye and lived on Ben Nevis where the Maiden Bride was imprisoned over the winter. She presided over the three months from Hallowe'en to Candlemas (McNeill 1959, vol 2, 20).

Cailleach Dhomhnuill Bhric, Lawers, Lochtayside. Donald Breac's Old Wife. Said to be the name of the Witch of Lawers; probably in fact the long-distance beacon on Ben Lawers (Gillies 1938, 350). Dhomhnuill or Donald is probably G. *domhan* 'world, universe (the tribal deer forest)'. G. *breac* 'speckled' normally refers to deer. Originally a Clan Gregor beacon.

Cailliach Mhor Chlibhrich, at Reay, Caithness. Campbell gives a spurious folk tale in which she milks the hinds.

Caiseart gharbh Ni'n an Aodhair, said to be one of the sisters of Glenforsa, Mull, but this is probably two names. 'The rough foot-gear of the daughter of the herdsman (or hunter)'. A.G. *cas* 'hunt', G. *casgair* 'butcher, massacre', A.G. *garbh* 'deer (rough ones)'. Nighean an Aodhair means 'woman of the beacon site'.

Cas a mhogain riabhaich, 'foot of the brindled footless stocking'. Perhaps one of the sisters of Glenforsa, Mull, but also said to have been in Glencoe. G. *cas* 'hunt, kill', *mùgh* 'kill, destroy', *riabhaich* 'deer (brindled ones)'. *An riabhach mòr* 'the great brindled one' is the Devil, seen as a great stag.

Corrag, daughter of *Iain Buidhe*, 'Yellow John' or 'Beacon of the hunting troop'. G. *corrach* 'fetter, shackle' is probably a deer trap.

Doideag, the famous Mull witch, *Na Doideag-un Muileach*, in the plural. In one story the Doideag lived in a house at Rutha Ghuirmean near Duart, no doubt to be handy for the MacLean chief. *Doideag-un* was a children's name for snowflakes, which are said to be the Mull witches on their way. Archaic G. *dòid* 'tooth' is cognate with the English word. The name may mean 'the sharp one' referring to the penetrating power of her beacon signal.

Gentle Annie, the anything-but-gentle storm-wife of northeast Scotland. G. *ain* 'fire'.

Gorm-shùil chrotach, Cràcaig, near Portree, Skye. Not: 'blue-eye humped one'. G. *crotach* 'hump-backed' is probably G. *cròthadh* 'enclosing in a pen or trap'. Isobell Gowdie described the fairy-boys who made the elf-arrows as hump-backed which means they were hunters.

Gorm-shùil mhòr, Moy, Lochaber. She was the leader of seven 'witches', leading to the memorable image of seven old crones dancing in a circle. She was stronger than all the witches of Mull – which means that her signal took precedence over those of the Mull beacons. But there may have been another *Gorm-shùil mhòr* on Mull, for according to Fitzroy MacLean her home was on Ben More and she was the most potent of the *Doideagan Muileach* or Grizzled Ones of Mull (F. MacLean, *West Highland Tales*, 2000, 116).

Gorm-shùil, Hianish, Tiree. Like all beacons she had but a single eye. Archaic G. *gorm* 'noble', *sùil* 'beacon'.

Gyre Carline, a name of the Cailleach Bheur (McNeill 1959, vol 2, 20). She lived on human flesh: in other words the Cailleach was a cremation bonfire.

Laorag, Tiree. G. *ladhrach* 'having large hoofs or claws'. A claw is a common metaphor for a deer-trap, as a feature which grips the animal so that he cannot escape. G. *ladhar* can also mean 'the single foot of a cloven-footed animal' and would be an appropriate name for the Devil.

Luideag of the Bens. 'A slovenly woman or slattern'. All sluts and whores are the Cailleach. So was Luideag, the shaggy filly of the folk tale, who comes to the magic bridge and should not be despised.

Mac Crauford, the witch of Arran. F.M. McNeill 1959, vol 2, 20.

Mac-Mhuirich nam buadh, said to mean 'Macpherson of power'.

Mag Moullach, the beacon of Clan Grant, also in Tullochgorum (McNeill 1959, vol 2, 20). G. *magh* 'plain, deer forest'. G. *mol* 'a bald place, a beacon site'.

Maol-Odhar of Kintyre. G. *mol* 'gathering, assembly; A.G. *mol* for maol 'beacon site', literally a bare place. G. *odhar* 'dun' probably for *aodhair* 'beacon site'.

Muileatach, Muileartach or *Muireartach*. Translated as 'Western Sea' and said to be the Witch of Lochlann ('hunting trap') but probably 'of Mull' (Campbell 1902, 188). A Mull or Maol was the site of a long-distance beacon; e.g., the Mull of Galloway, the Mull of Kintyre, and the island of Mull.

Nic-ill'-Domhnuich, Tiree: 'Daughter of the servant of Domnuich'. G. *gille* 'hunter', *damh* 'stag'; the pun between *dòmhnaich* 'of the deer forest' and *Dòmhnaich* 'Sunday' is discussed in the list of witch names. It probably means 'of the deer forest'; Sunday was perhaps once a hunting day.

Nuckelavee. Douglas describes Nuckelavee as a fearsome creature, part man, part horse, with a large head, a large mouth, breath like steam from a kettle, and a single eye as red as fire (Douglas, 1894, 162). This is *Nic-ille-dhuibh* 'daughter of the black lad (deer hunter)' (cf Macgillewie for *Mac-gille-dhuibh*). Nuckelavee appears to be another name for the Cailleach as beacon. She is reported from Orkney.

Spoga buidhe: 'Yellow claws', from Meligeir on the east side of Skye. Also recorded as *Spoga buidhe ni'a Douill 'ic Cormaig* 'Yellow claws, daughter of Donald son of Cormac' which appears to be two names compounded. G. *spoga* 'deer trap', *buidhe* 'fire', *caoir* 'blaze of fire', *magh* 'plain, deer forest'.

Appendix 7 Names of English familiars.

The fantastic names given to their familiars by English witches also respond to decipherment in terms of Gaelic. They may be relics of Gaelic in England or they may have been borrowed by Victorian pseudo-folklorists from Scottish sources (cf. the Tewhit or linnet).

Elimanzar or Ilimauzar, 17c., a white dog. G. *eallach* 'battle, herd' + *maon* 'hero (hunter)' + *sar* 'noble, brave'.

Farmara 17c. cf Jarmara, 'who came in like a fat spaniel without any legs at all.'

Fillie, a white cat. G. *pealag* 'a felted cloak worn by hunters'.

Gibbe, a black cat. G. *gibeag* 'largesse, boon'.

Gille, a black cat. G. *gille* 'boy (young hunter)'.

Ginnie, 'a kitlyng or feende'. G. *gin* 'mouth (trap), E. *gin* 'trap'.

Greedigut. 17c. Grizel Greedigut. G. *greidh* 'herd of deer' + *guidhe* 'prayer'.

Hoult, 17c. who came in like a white kittling. G. *cùil* 'nook (deer trap)'. E. *holt* 'otter's den'.

Inges, a black and white cat. G. *innes* 'choice pasture for cattle or deer'.

Jarmara, a red and white cat. G. *iarmart* 'riches, offspring'.

Lierd, a red female cat or imp. G. *léireadh* 'tormenting, wounding, stealing (hunting)'.

Lightfoot, a cat. G. *lucht-fothach* 'people of the wilderness' or hunters.

Lunch, a toad. G. *luan* 'warrior (hunter)' or 'greyhound'.

Makeshift, a weasel. Perhaps G. *magh* 'field of battle, plain (hunting forest)' + *segh* 'wild ox, elk'.

Minny, a red and white dog. G. *minneachan* 'smooth place' ie, 'deer forest'.

Newes 17c. 'Like a Polecat'. G. *niomhas* 'brightness, clearness'.

Peckin the Crown 17c.

Philip, a rat. As Fillie.

Pyewackett 17c. Perhaps G. *piobach* 'having pipes'. Or was the animal pied?

Robbyn, a toad. A hunter or 'robber'.

Sack n Sugar, 17c. 'like a black Rabbet'. A cat or imp. Perhaps G. *saigheadh-shìth* 'fairy arrow'.

Suckin, a black tom cat or imp. Perhaps the diminutive of G. *saigh* 'arrow'.

Tewhit, 'a yellow bird'. In Orkney it was believed that carrying the bones of a linnet in one's clothing preserved health (Dalyell 1835, 150). The yellow bird like others listed appears to be copied from a Scottish source.

Tissy or Tyttey. G. *titheach* 'pursuing keenly'.

Tom, a toad. G. *tom* 'mound', a fairy mound where signal fires were lit.

Vinegar Tom 17c. 'like a long-legg'd Greyhound, with a head like an Oxe.' Archaic G. *fionn* 'fire' + G. *gar* 'enclosure' + G. *tom* 'knoll'.

Wynoe, a black imp. Archaic G. *fionn* 'fire'.

CHAPTER 10: FAKE FOLKLORE

'No doubt oral transmission has played its part, as well as the desperate orthographic guesswork of scribes and collectors.'

Donald Meek (1986, 44).

So lamented Professor Donald Meek, as he tried to find sense in the incomprehensible gobbledegook that is all that we have inherited of the once-great and vital knowledge known as the *Banners of the Fian*. He never did find the key but he recognised the problem and its probable causes. The same influences have shaped all archaic Gaelic texts, which became obsolete and meaningless as soon as the great deer-hunts passed away (see *Archaic Gaelic*, in this series).

Ever since trials for witchcraft began, the 'impossible' aspects of the evidence have caused great difficulties for students of Scottish witchcraft. In consequence there are now several divergent ideas of what these supernatural events might represent, ranging from drug-induced dreams and torture-induced hallucinations to the ravings of the mentally deranged and pure invention. Chambers (1858) recognised a link between the unreal elements in popular tales about witches and the unreal facts that emerged at the trials but he mistook the direction of the influence. He believed that the witches had been influenced by popular tales to believe that they had supernatural powers and that these tales were authentic folklore, passed on orally from time immemorial but having no basis in fact. In fact, the evidence as given was perfectly rational but became sensational and meaningless as it was translated from Gaelic into English. The Gaelic-English interface of the trials is the point when their testimonies were converted into the irrational nonsense of fake folklore.

The creation of a new item of fake and meaningless witch-lore took place in several stages. Most examples begin with confusion at the clerical interface. One of the best documented which acquired fame in its day is the creation of Horse and Hattock!, a meaningless phrase attributed to Isobell Gowdie of Auldearn in Moray which began life as a mundane but picturesque simile. We even know that the process began on 13 April 1662 when the witch gave her first testimony and baffled the assise of learned men who listened to her with what sounded like a story of a little horse. But Isobell did not have a horse. Using a standard dictionary we can reconstruct what she said in plain Gaelic:

she and her colleagues went to coven meetings like an *ursainn-chathach*, a band of hunters (Dwelly 1901, 1001), in other words, as fast as they could, as hunters went to the muster.

Her use of an obsolete Gaelic word referring to hunting marks the first phase. In the second phase what she said was subjected to the desperate guesswork of the local notary, John Innes, and no doubt other members of the assise, educated local men who spoke only English and who thought that they had recognised the word 'horse'. One can imagine surprise, disbelief and amazement. After much deliberation Mr Innes the notary wrote what he thought the witch had said, amended to make sense in his mind:

'I haid a little horse, and wold say, "Horse and Hattock in the Divellis name!"'

(Pitcairn 1833, III, 604).

The little horse is pure invention but it acquired a life of its own.

'Horse and Hattock!' is particularly interesting because it had a subsequent independent history as fake folklore and even, as we will see, an earlier existence. Its history in Moray began when Mr Steward of Forres, who was tutor to the family of Duffus, found this phrase in a transcript of Isobell's trial. Duffus is only a few miles from Auldearn and he was literate if not learned. One must imagine his reading through a transcript of Isobell Gowdie's trial perhaps copied by an earlier tutor and finding this curious phrase, which he worked up into a fictional but not entirely original story about a silver cup kept by the family and the alleged adventures of an early Lord of Duffus. One can imagine that the tale was intended to be a compliment to his employer, a clever after-dinner story popular with his guests. The witches of Auldearn and their Devils and covens have been replaced by the less controversial fairies. The fairies from then on are the preferred entities.

'Being in the fields, he heard the noise of a whirl-wind and of voices crying Horse and Hattock (this is the Word, which the Fairies are said to use when they remove from any place) whereupon he cried (Horse and Hattock) also, and was immediately caught up and transported through the air, by the Fairies.'

Aubrey's *Miscellany*, 1696.

This limp little tale was published by Aubrey in 1696 and went viral. Lord Duffus, approached prudently by Aubrey prior to publication, thought the story was invented.

It is unlikely that the phrase in the form 'Horse and Hattock!' was in general use in Moray before this date as in that case the author would not have needed to explain that this 'is the word which the Fairies are said to use when they remove from any place'. Nobody earlier than Mr Steward ever said anything of the sort, as far as we know.

The Duffus story is also linked to the Auldearn witch of 1662 by the spelling. It is very unlikely that the nonsensical phrase 'Horse and Hattock!' should turn up in two unrelated documents produced within a few miles of each other, using exactly the same spelling and given a very similar and totally wrong meaning thirty years apart unless they came from the same source. Isobell's Gaelic within thirty years became fake folk.

If *ursainn-chathach* was a common metaphor in Gaelic or post-Gaelic society we would expect to find other local tales each with its own phonetic variant, and we do. In Shetland when the trows want to fly to Norway they ride on bulrushes and say: 'Up horse up hedik!', according to Alan Bruford (1991, 127) or 'Horsick up haddock, weel ridden bulwand!' according to Henderson and Cowan (2001, 67, note 6). The bulrush or bulwand is G. *gobhal-luachair* 'fork-light', because the pith of the rush, soaked in fat, was carried in a forked stick to serve as a torch.

Mr Steward may have invented the story of the Fairy Cup of Duffus but he did not invent the metaphor or the genre. There was already a host of equally silly stories in circulation, inspired by fairy cups, rings, flags, horns, banquets and bridges or by a desire to attract an audience or win a night's lodging. The theme of magical night-flying goes far back. As early as the thirteenth century, Steven of Bourbon gave, as an example of the Devil's influence, the story of a priest who was invited to join the *bonae res* or Good Things in their night-flying. He rode on a beam (another riddle to solve) to a meeting where he saw many beautiful people but when he made the sign of the Cross they all vanished, leaving him naked in the wine cellar of a neighbouring lord. He narrowly escaped being hanged for a thief (Broedel 2003, 81-82). The Good Things were well-known in the thirteenth century as followers of Diana, goddess of hunters. Steward or someone he knew probably told this earlier tale which is already nonsensical.

Another version was included in the original introduction to *Newes from Scotland* in 1591 but cut from the English edition of 1592 which was aimed at a more discriminating audience (Dalyell 1835, 592). The *Newes* tells of a 'poore pedlar' travelling to Tranent in East Lothian, who 'was in a moment convayed at midnight from Scotland to Burdeaux … into a merchantes sellar there'. The magic word is not disclosed; the point of the story has been lost. At the end of the run, in 1790 Robert Burns wrote an almost identical account of a shepherd boy from Alloway, in Ayrshire, who travelled to a wine cellar in Bordeaux (Lockhart 1839, 363-4). On returning from the fold 'he fell in with a crew of men and women, who were busy pulling stems of the plant *Ragwort*. He observed that as each person pulled a *Ragwort*, he or she got astride of it and called out "Up horsie!" on which the *Ragwort* flew off, like Pegasus, through the air with its *rider...' By that time the* magic formula has become almost unrecognisable.

At an even later date Walter Scott stole Mr Steward's story, claiming it was a genuine seventeenth-century tradition concerning an ancestor of the noble family of Duffus (Scott 1931, 322-3). He even wrote a spurious Horse and Hattock! Border Ballad to quote as a heading for Chapter 8 in his novel *The Black Dwarf* (1816). But his horses kept their feet on the ground.

'Now horse and hattock, cried the Laird,
Now horse and hattock, speedilie;
They that winna ride for Telfer's kye,
Let them never look in the face o' me.'

The horse and flying crop up perhaps for the last time in the curious tale of Manus O'Malaghan and the Fairies, published in an Irish chap-book, *The Royal Hibernian Tales*, which was in circulation before 1825. This was the tale: 'In the parish of Ahoghill lived Manus O'Malaghan. As he was searching for a calf that had strayed, he heard many people talking. Drawing near, he distinctly heard them repeating, one after the other, "Get me a horse, get me a horse;" so "Get me a horse too," said Manus. He was instantly mounted on a steed, surrounded by a vast crowd of people who galloped off, taking poor Manus with them. In a short time they suddenly stopped in a large wide street, asking Manus if he knew where he was? "Faith," says he, "I do not." "You are in Spain," they said.'

In all its versions, from the court record of 1662, 'Horse and Hattock!' is a meaningless phrase which we can trace back to the misinterpretation of the Gaelic expression *ursainn-chathach* 'the gathering of the hunting troop', invented by the English-speaking notary, John Innes, when he recorded the testimony of Isobell Gowdie. 'Horse and Hattock!' is a good example of what we might call the Innes Effect which reflects confusion at the clerical interface and which was instrumental in the creation of fake folklore.

Most, perhaps all, of the supernatural elements attributed to Scottish witches were inspired by similar attempts to understand Gaelic by those unqualified to do so, both at the time of the trials and since then. Clerks and writers were encouraged in their speculations by the wide publicity given to the trials and by the subsequent and increasing popularity of tall stories in the contemporary English-speaking world. Later writers incorporated elements of Gaelic lore whenever they could but they did not always get them right. Scott in *The Bride of Lammermoor* (1819) said that witches rode on hemlock stalks (McNeill 1967, I, 195) but Burns, always more authentic, said that they rode on ragwort and he was right.

Originally fake folk was an inadvertent ignorant bumbling but with its weird lack of logic it soon became a major source of entertainment. When W.G. Stewart published *Popular Superstitions and Festive Amusements of the Highlands of Scotland* (1823) he included many absurd stories designed to entertain tourists who, then as now, thrived on stories of the supernatural. There should preferably be a silver cup, a blue stone, a flint arrowhead, a footmark in the rock, a grave-stone, a knoll or even a place-name to show as proof. In addition to the physical artefact, the audience was assured that the events about to be disclosed happened to a real person of unimpeachable probity who lived in a real place several generations earlier, or which were disclosed to the writer when a boy by his grandfather, far away and long ago.

These tales of the supernatural may be invented and phony but they are not entirely meaningless. To write off the supernatural evidence of the trials as nightmares, lies and myths which have no reality or importance, particularly when the rest of a testimony is used as a source of significant fact, devalues the entire approach. It removes a significant part of the evidence and diminishes our ability to reach the underlying reality. The 'impossible' evidence from the trials which includes such fables as night-riding, invisibility and the witch as a hare or a cat is only one part of the problem. The folk fiction of Scotland covers an impressive range of unreal concepts all of similar origins and ranging from death lights, fairy changelings, the evil eye, and the second-sight to malevolent ghosts, milking the tether, selling winds, water horses, and fairy cattle. Burns wrote in 1787 that as a child an old woman told him tales about 'devils, ghosts, fairies, brownies, witches, warlocks, spunkies, kelpies, elf-candles, dead-lights, wraiths, apparitions, cantraips, giants, enchanted towns, dragons, and other trumpery' (MacCulloch 1921, 231). By 1690 the process of popular invention was well under way as we saw at Duffus in Moray, where the local witch rushing to coven meetings in 1662 by 1690 had become a gang of supernatural fairies flying at night to France and back. Burns might reject such beliefs as trumpery but at an earlier date, during the seventeenth century, they had a real effect on the evidence which was recorded in the course of the Scottish witch-trials by affecting the expectations of the court, shaping both the questions and the content of the answers. We cannot begin to understand them without invoking the Innes Effect.

It is not always evident. In many trials there are no supernatural elements. The accused women may have addressed the court in correct English which was correctly transcribed or the clerk may have achieved a correct translation from Gaelic into English. We cannot tell. But even then in many trials the clerk has often improved his case by adding references to 'your master the Devil' or 'where Satan was present' or 'in the Devil's name'. To him the presence of the Devil could be assumed.

Nonsensical English is also found when degenerative processes work within obsolete levels of Gaelic to turn a *cath* 'hunting troop' into a *cat,* or between Gaelic and English, to turn G. *faire* 'watchman' into a fairy. The process eventually reduces archaic incantations and charms to phonetic gibberish, like a game of Chinese Whispers. As noted already, the lack of sense is a reliable pointer to obsolete or archaic Gaelic. It is also the essential feature of the fake folklore of Scotland, which we can now define as a type of supernatural fiction based on or inspired by false translations from Gaelic into English. It describes events that did not happen as though they were part of daily life. What George Black called 'the utterly unreliable nature' of many Scottish confessions can be attributed in most cases to the utter inability of an English-speaking clerk to understand Gaelic and to their expectation of hearing irrational nonsense.

Flying and shape-changing

The main supernatural abilities attributed to witches were flying and shape-changing. The claim made by witches, or made on their behâlf, that they flew from one place to another, often in the shape of a cat or a dog, is a major component of the 'myth, fantasy and nightmare' reported from the witch trials and found so distressing by historians but flying as a figure of speech is still in use: we say: 'I must fly', meaning 'I must depart with great speed', even when we are proposing to walk or take a taxi. To the Gaels the three fastest things in the world were an arrow, a beacon signal, and a troop of hunters. If a witch departed 'like a cat' she went as quickly as a troop of hunters who had seen the beacon. If the coven 'flew like cats', they flew like hunters, with all possible speed. This is what witches generally meant when they went 'like a whirlwind' (Pitcairn iii, 602). This is why fairies and witches were said to make a whizzing or humming noise when they travelled and why a buzzing noise or a small whirlwind was taken by the superstitious as evidence of passing fairies. In the story of 'The Fairies of Corrie Chaorachain' (MacDougall 1910, 126) the fairies were invisible but Donald Post could hear the murmur of their voices.

Similar metaphors for speed were used in Moray and in Lanark but the ludicrous flying cat was taken at face value. Perkins in 1616 believed that 'woman being the weaker sexe is sooner intangled by the deuills illusions with this damnable art, then the man' (Black 1938, 5) but no section of mankind was ever more credulous than the Reformed ministers of seventeenth-century Scotland. Those who write about witchcraft, if they consider this kind of evidence at all, write it off as a shared dream, a sign of insanity, or a hallucination induced by torture or drugs. But it would be unexpected for a hallucination to take a similar form in so many unrelated cases over such a period of time, particularly as those describing their experience were untravelled, uneducated peasants.

Some common sense was injected by a woman interrogated in the Rottenburger witch trials of 1600 and quoted by Karl Pearson (1897, vol.2, 22-23). 'The supposed witch was asked if she had been at a witch-dance, and replied "Yes, for she was there initiated as a witch." Who had taken her to it? "The old shepherd's wife had fetched her, and they had gone with a broom." Did she mean that they had flown through the air on a broom? "Certainly not; they had walked to Etterle, and then placed themselves across the broom, and so come to the dancing green." So they had not gone through the air? "Certainly not; that required an ointment, which ought only to be very rarely used."' In passing we might note that the fork that the Devil often carries is said by Pearson in his 1891 lecture, 'Woman as Witch', to be a *Feuergabel* or fire-fork – a two-pronged stick used to hold meat over a fire. Being forked it is also a symbol of the female sex which sooner or later appears in every pagan context.

Pearson confirmed that witches took with them to the sabbat a symbol of the old hearth or home goddess, a broom or a *Feuergabel* or fire fork, and rode the broom or fork like a hobby-horse at the dancing place. A plain stick might also be used. The witches of Sardinia carried a spindle. When Isobell Gowdie went to a coven meeting she left her broom or a three-legged stool in her bed to let her husband know where she was (Pitcairn 608). In 1324 Lady Alice Kyteler had a tube of ointment with which she greased a stick and 'ambled and galloped through thick and thin'. The purpose of the stick and the ointment was presumably sexual, not supernatural. Three recipes for flying ointment are given by Murray (1921, 279-280).

Flying on a stalk of ragwort
Let warlocks grim and withered hags
Tell how wi' you on ragweed nags
They skim the muirs and dizzy crags
Robert Burns: Address to the Deil (1785).

Ragwort, G. *buadhghallan buidhe,* is an element in the category of supernatural travel and the coded world of hunting and beacons. Its Gaelic name means 'the fire of the hunting troop', from *gal* 'fire' and *buidhe* 'hunting troop'. Its small bright flowers look like signal beacons.

Carmichael in *Carmina Gadelica* reports the fake lore. 'The ragwort or ragweed was much prized by the old people... The fairies (some say the *sluagh* 'host') sheltered beside the ragwort in stormy nights; and the fairies rode astride the ragwort in voyaging from island to island, from Alba to Erin, from Alba to Manainn, and home again' (vol. IV, 121 and note). This metaphorically describes a beacon signal linking Scotland, Ireland and the Isle of Man. The Scottish *buadhghallan* was the beacon on the Mull of Galloway, the most southerly point of Scotland, easily visible in northern Ireland and in Man. The lore suggests that prehistoric hunters braved the North Channel to hunt in Ireland or in Man.

Carmichael also gives a nonsense rhyme about G. *buacharlain,* another name for ragwort. It begins 'Fire, fire!' which identifies a hunting shout, and continues with a prayer to the Lady.

As transcribed:

A bhuacharlain! a bhuacharlain!
'S a bhean a bhuail am buacharlan!
Nan eireadh marbh na h-uaghacha,
Bhiodh cuimhn' air bualadh buacharlain.

Meaningless English version:

Thou ragwort! thou ragwort!
And thou, woman, who plied the ragwort!
If the dead of the grave should rise,
The plying of the ragwort would be remembered.

Possible recreation of the original meaning:

'The fire! The fire!
'And thou, Lady of the beacon place,
'When the slaughtered deer are replenished,
'Remember the deer drive of the beacon!'

Shape-changing

Becoming a cat is an aspect of shape-changing, a fantasy or fallacy found in the witch trials and in Gaelic and Irish fairy-lore and poetry of considerable age. Shape-changing is found in many Irish stories as a literary tour de force which allowed the bard to introduce a string of complex metaphors and puns. It was not an occult power but a play on words and as the play was forgotten it made a considerable contribution to fake folklore. In Gaelic it was known as *fath-fith* or *fith-fath*, which MacLennan defines as an occult power which rendered a person invisible and which also 'changed men into horses, bulls or stags and women into cats, hares or hinds' (1925, 155-156, quoting Carmichael, *Carmina Gadelica*).

We can judge from related words such as *fath* 'ambush', *fathach* 'monster or giant (bonfire)', *feachd* 'army, host, war (hunt)' and *fiadh* 'deer' that originally *fath-fith,* like most of the shape-changing animals, was a pun related to hunting, beacons or some related topic. Other 'shapes' appear to be attributes of the Cailleach who is also a personification of fire (G. *cail* 'to burn'). A further problem is that we are working in English and a potentially misleading translation from Gaelic stands between these 'animals' and the original Gaelic.

The complex fantasies that grew up in Gaelic around Gaelic hunting puns are poetic rather than folkloric. In one tale the Fairy Queen appears as a large yellow frog, a meaningless translation of *muile-mhàg mhór bhuidhe* (MacDougall 1910, 270). The original Gaelic was perhaps *maol mhàg mhór bhuidhe* 'great hunting-troop at the beacon site ('the bald place') of the deer forest'. This would be a hunting shout of the type passed from one homestead to the next, to alert hunters to the fact that the gathering beacon had been lit. Whatever the Gaelic originally was, the yellow frog is a lexical figment which has nothing to do with hunting or with folklore though it may have furnished some hapless scholar with a belief in the Cailleach as frog.

The list below contains four categories of shape-changing animals.

1 Old religious puns such as the hare, fox, serpent and swan which arose in Gaelic.

2 Animals introduced after contact with English, such as the cat and the horse.

3 Horned beasts such as the bull and the stag which were peculiar to the leader of the coven.

4 Cormorants, gulls and whales which are very uncommon and may reflect the continued evolution of ritual language in a Gaelic-speaking fishing community. The superstitions of fishermen concerning taboo animals such as pigs, hares, trout and salmon can be explained in similar terms.

Angel G. *aingeal* 'bright fire'. Christsonday, an angel (a hunt-beacon in Banff), appeared in white clothing.

Bee G. *beach*. There is no convincing Gaelic background. In 1661 Jonet Watsone confessed that after her initiation, she was bothered for three days after the Devil had given her her witch marks by a large bee (Pitcairn 601). This might be literal fact, or she might have said G. *beath* 'blood', as the bee sat on her shoulder where the Devil had recently marked her and drawn blood. Gelen Guthrie said that when the Forfar witches stole ale from John Benny's house, he being a brewer, they went in 'through at a little hole like bees and took the substance of the ale ...' (Kinloch 121). This is a figure of speech. According to tradition, Kate McNiven was burned at Monzie for stealing a knife and fork while in the shape of a bee but she and the bee appear to be equally spurious.

Bull Not a shape-change but a genuine disguise which might be worn by the Devil of a coven at the sabbath meeting. See also **stag**.

Cat G. *càth* 'battle (hunt); muster of soldiers (hunters)'. Very common as 'cat' in fake folklore.

Cormorant G. *geòcaire*, for G. *geòcair* 'glutton, parasite, vagabond (hunter)'. See glossary under *gochd*. Very uncommon, late or learned, but the pun appears to be genuine (Campbell 1902, 43-4; Gregor 1881). It suggests an evolving folklore among the Gaelic fishermen of the northeast coasts. See also **Whale**, from the same source.

Crow Not common; may have begun as a figment of translation (*feannag* 'crow' confused with *feannadh* 'skinning an animal').

Dog G. *cu, con*. In archaic terms 'gathering, hunting'. Very common.

Dove G. *calman* for *calm* 'champion (hunter)'. E. *dove* is also a pun on G. *dubh* 'deer'. It underlies the names of a large number of 'patron saints' and landscape features.

Eel G. *easgann* for *ess* 'death' + *ceann* 'trap, ambush'. The eel occurs in a nonsensical proverb about St Kessog's Day and in a healing rhyme (Beith 1995, 252). It may be an old pun.

Fly G. *cuileag* for *cuile* 'deer trap' or for *cailleach* 'fire'. A pun.

Foal See below under '**whelp**'.

Fox G. *sionnach* for *sion* 'brightness' or archaic G. *sion* 'to gather'. Probably a genuine pun; the fox is a common taboo animal.

Goat There is no sign of a goat in Scottish witch lore.

Gull G. *faoileag* for archaic G. *faoileag* 'beacon'. *Faoileag* is the aspirate of G. *beolach* 'ashes with hot embers', from G. *beoll* 'fire'. *Eilean nam faoileag* was the beacon island at Ardlarich, Loch Rannoch, also known as the Isle of Loch Tay and now said to mean 'Seagull Island'. (Campbell 1902, 42-3; Gregor 1881).

Hare Perhaps the oldest of all the animal shapes. G. *labhran* was apparently used as a pun on a word for lips, Lat. *labia*, in honour of the Cailleach whose vulva as a metaphor for the deer trap was regarded as sacred above all things. Also G. *pait* and G. *maigheach*.

Horse G. *cuillidh* for *cuilidh* 'sanctuary, treasure etc (deer forest, ambush site)' but most obviously for *cailleach* 'fire'. G. *cuileasg* 'horse' can also mean 'the hunting of the trap'. Isobell Gowdie's 'horse' was an English pun on *ursainn* 'muster of hunters'; she did not 'have a little horse'.

Jackdaw G. *càthag* from *càth* 'hunt'; also *càthag-fhireann* from *fireann* 'chain', so a chain of hunters or a communal hunt. Not frequent. cf **Crow**.

Lamb The devil at Aberdeen once appeared as a lamb and blettit on the witches. G. *uan* 'lamb' is a common pun on *ain* or *aodhan* 'fire' ('fire' is also found as *uaine* 'green' and *eun* 'bird'). A lamb was sacrificed at Michaelmas in the Hebrides. Its use in ritual Gaelic curiously parallels the lamb sacrifice at Easter in Christian symbolism. 'Sheep' names often derive from fire words, since sheep were protected at night by fires. The lamb in place of 'fire' is found mainly in place-names where it is likely to be a recent mistake.

Rat G. *radan* or *rodan*; a pun on G. *ràidh* 'rank of soldiers (hunters)', E. *raid, rodent*. Rare (Campbell 1902, 42; Gregor 1881).

Raven G. *fitheach*, a pun on G. *fiadh* 'deer'. Christians have seen the pagan raven as an abominable black counterpart to the white dove of the Holy Spirit but the raven has a notable religious pedigree, and the dove or *colman* also appears as a Gaelic pun for fire. Old, rare and probably an authentic Gaelic figure.

Rook G. *rocas* appears to be the English word. Not distinguished from the crow.

Sheep G. *caora*, a common pun on G. *caoir* 'blaze'. Often found in place-names. Like the Lamb (q.v.) sheep names are commonly derived from words for 'fire' as the animals were protected by fire. Not common in folklore, fake or otherwise. Hunters abominated sheep (Campbell 1902, 30-31; Gregor 1881).

Serpent G. *ribhinn* or *righinn* 'snake, young beautiful woman', from G. *ribe* 'gin, snare, ambush'. G. *nimhir* 'venomous one' is a pun on *naomh* 'sacred place' (applied to the deer forest). As a young and beautiful maiden, the snake represents fire or flames (McNeill 1959, vol. 2, 27, 135).

Stag Not a shape-change but a genuine disguise which might be worn by the Devil of a coven at the Sabbath. See also **bull**.

Swan G. *eala* punned on *eallach* 'battle (hunt), herd'. A swan or two is found in a Pictish context and in Irish fantasy literature. The pun is a good one.

Whale G. *orc* 'whale', for G. *orc* 'to kill, murder, destroy' (Campbell 1902, 44-5; Gregor 1881). Found only in coastal communities.

Whelp. In 1649 Helen Tailyeur of Eyemouth deponed that she and others went to the house of William Burnet, he being sick, in likenesses of a black hen, a little foal, and she was a quelp. G. *cuilean* 'whelp' also means 'leveret'; both move very rapidly. The name *Amad na-gCuilean* (NC3900) 'annat of the whelps or hares' is close to the confluence of the rivers Oykell and Eunag, Ross & Cromarty, Strathoykel.

The Witch as hare and other tales

The Cailleach or Great Witch was transformed in folklore into many shapes that were also familiar to witches. The hare was the most common and most powerful witch shape. It is also a pun for a hunter which is so common it operated at a literal level. If a Gaelic housewife said she had seen a *labhran* stealing the milk from her cow, her neighbour would understand that she had seen a hunter suckling one of her cows. In the summer a hungry hunter, or anyone else, would certainly suckle a cow if he could catch her and it was a common complaint that fairies stole milk. Direct suckling belongs to the Palaeolithic exploitation of free-range cows, not to the managed dairy of evolved pastoral farmers.

Witches often went as hares, which is enough in itself to identify them as devotees of the Lady. Stories of hare magic are very common in fake folklore and in real life. In 1597 it was reported that a hare that came when Helen Frazzer was living in Foveran and which was known to be the witch in disguise was seen to suckle a milk cow belonging to the late William Findley who lived on the opposite side of the burn, whereupon the cow wasted away and gave bluid instead of milk (SCM I, 1841, 107).

Also in 1597 it was alleged that Isobel Robye of Lumphanan was commonly seen in the form of a hare passing through the township, for the moment the hare vanished the witch appeared (SCM 1841, I, 191).

Hare magic depends on an archaic Gaelic pun which identifies the hare with the hunter or devotee of the Goddess. G. *labhran* 'hare' is a pun on G. *labh* (Lat. *labia*) 'lip', in honour of the Cailleach whose vulva was a metaphor for the deer trap and was sacred above all things. The pun between G. *labh* 'lip', *labhran* 'hare' (Lat. *lepus, leporis* 'hare') only becomes unreal when this word is translated into English and the hare is assumed to be a wild animal. Other aspects of this pun or metaphor are G. *liopaire* 'person with thick lips', and *leòb* 'big lips'. The big lips define a deer ambush in terms of the Cailleach's *labia*, a sexual pun or metaphor of great power which is at the heart of hunting magic.

It is an image which the Church sought to suppress by converting all the honorific titles of the Lady into obscenities. But the vulva retained its popularity as we see from the sheela-na-gig ('hunting of the deer') which is quite explicit as an image bringing good luck. A handful survive in Scotland, all of them in a Christian context, which suggests great tolerance. They survive at Taynuilt in Argyll, at Rodel in Harris, at Iona, at Kirknewton in Midlothian, and perhaps at Kildonan on Eigg where there was a very important hunt-beacon.

A similar pun links labia or lips with the leper who appears occasionally in the lives of saints. St Fillan was a 'leper' in the sense of being a hunt-beacon. He was the son of Kentigerna 'Great Lady', another name of the Maiden. It is said that the ghosts of certain McAras, being allied to witches, haunted the shores of Lochlog in the form of hares: this is an elaborate way of saying that they hunted there. Lochlog has not been identified but may be Lochloch in Atholl which was the main ambush site for the annual tinchels or deer-drives.

Another of the hare's Gaelic names is *geàrr-fhiadh* 'short deer' which is a pun on G. *gaorsach* 'wanton girl; slut, bawd, drivelling prostitute'. G. *gaorr* 'gore, filth; thrust, pierce, fight; glut' preserves a link to hunting and butchery. A comparable link is found between G. *goil* 'smoke, fume; battle (hunt); to boil' and G. *goill* 'hanging lip; shapeless mouth; distortion of mouth; war (hunt)' which again links hunting to the Lady and her private parts.

The hare was also a great inspiration for fake folklorists. A typical story about the witch as hare comes from Breadalbane. It concerns a historical person, Anne McInucator, who lived at Lawers on Lochtayside in the middle of the eighteenth century. In her life she appears to have been feared but she was never accused of witchcraft or disciplined by the Kirk Session (Gillies 1938, 350-1). And yet, after her death, the Witch of Lawers became renowned for the harm she had done, causing abortions in cows, depriving cows of their milk, blinding people, bewitching young children so that they fell into a decline, and casting spells over horses. She was said to have adopted many disguises but especially that of a hare. Her neighbour, the blacksmith Macmartain, put an end to her wicked career. On 1 May one year he noticed a large brown hare on his croft, performing curious antics and talking to herself. He recognised the voice. It was the witch trying to steal the growth of his crops. He shot her with a silver sixpence whereupon the wounded hare ran back to her own house, which she entered by the cat-hole. Later the witch was found there back in her own shape but with a wound in her leg. She became a reformed character, and was buried in the churchyard at Lawers.

Of this taradiddle only the first and the last statements have any basis in fact. Everything else is slanderous invention which could only have been written after Anne McInucator and all her posterity were safely dead. It was published in the 1920s by the Gaelic Society of Inverness as an example of Breadalbane folklore but it is nothing of the sort. It was the work of a known author, James Macdiarmid of Morenish, also on north Lochtayside, who died c.1930. The same writer invented a second story about a man McGlasserig who encountered a witch in the form of a hen in a bothy on Ben Lawers. McGlasserig allowed his dogs to worry the witch, who died but not before cursing the family which died out on Lochtayside (Gillies 1938, 362). These worthless tales, like all fake folklore, are contrived works of fiction. There is only one point of interest: it is possible that the name given to Anne McInucator by Macdiarmid, *Cailleach Dhomhnuill Bhreac* 'Donald Breac's Old Wife', is the traditional name of the beacon on Ben Lawers, which rises behind her house.

We can learn the true facts about Anne McInucator from the minutes of the local Kirk Session (Gillies 1938, 349). The only complaint against her was of using charms and enchantments to the detriment of Duncan McInucatar. On 1 May 1757, he and two others saw Anne go down to the shores of Loch Tay, fill a small bottle with muddy water, and hide it in a cairn. Her daughter Elspeth came to collect it. The Session took no action in this case, which was the last of its kind to be brought before them. Otherwise only the witch-as-hare has any foundation in fact, and that fact is to be found in the old levels of Gaelic, not in English. The true meaning of the witch-as-hare was certainly not known to James Macdiarmid.

Back to Isobell

The story told by Isobell Gowdie in 1662 takes us back to a time when to be a hare had a rather different meaning. Her 'hare' story is quite pedestrian: she wore a hare skin to signify that she was on coven business. She told the assise that the leader of her coven would send her now and then in the shape of a hare on errands to other members of the coven. She was evidently the Devil's Hare in Auldearn as Isobel Shirie was the Devil's Horse in Forfar. Early one morning while still wearing her hare disguise, she was chased by dogs belonging to the servants of Patrick Papley of Kilnhill and to escape them she ran back to her own house. The door being open, she ran in and took shelter behind a chest but the dogs followed her in and forced her to run out again and into another house, where she had time to repeat the formula.

'Hare, hare, God send thee care,
I am in an hare's likeness just now
But I shall be in a woman's likeness even now.'

Then she could change back into the shape of a woman; in other words she could take off her hare skin. The dogs, she said, sometimes bite us when we are in hares, but will not kill us. When we change out of hares we have the bites and scratches on our bodies. Her own house at Lochloy is within a few hundred metres of Kilnhill, home of Patrick Papley. The house where she took refuge was perhaps that of Issobell Nicoll, a member of her own coven who also lived in Lochloy.

Since Isobell Gowdie evidently did not change her shape, this can only mean that when she was on official business, she wore the skin of a hare and that it was attractive to dogs (Pitcairn 1833, vol. iii. 611), no doubt because it was badly cured. This story gives the incidental impression that the business of the Auldearn coven was carried out quite openly before 1662.

The charm that she used to become a hare is also on record (Pitcairn 1833, III, 607). This may be her original version, taught her by her Devil.

> 'I sall goe intill ane haire
> With sorrow, and sych, and meikle caire
> And I sall goe in the Divellis nam
> Ay whill I com hom againe.'

That witches wore the skins of cats, dogs and hares for ritual purposes is also suggested by the allegation made in 1661 by William Johnston, baron of Broughton, Peeblesshire, that the 'wmquhill Jonet Allan, who is condemned and brunt for witchcraft, did delate [accuse] Barbara Mylne, as one whom the said Jonet did once sie come in at the Wattergate in lykness of a catt, and did change her garment wnder her awin staire' (Dalyell 1835, III, 628-9). It appears that the wearing of an animal disguise was common behaviour in a witch, that it transformed her into her official or ritual person, and that a witch could be recognised by what she wore. The cat and the hare are both Gaelic hunting puns (G. *cath* 'hunt', G. *labhran* 'lips' meaning 'devotee of the Lady' or 'hunter'), and so they were appropriate shapes for human witches.

We can therefore track back from the shape-changing of the fake folktales to a factual account of a witch wearing the skin of a hare or a cat or some other animal to identify her while on the Devil's business, through the interface to the original Gaelic lore where cats and hares meant *cath* 'hunt' or 'band of hunters' and *labhran* 'a man devoted to the Cailleach'. As Gaelic culture declined and the forests passed under feudal control, the cats and hares of the English stories fed back into Gaelic tradition to give us a wild variety of Gaelic stories about malevolent cats and the witch as hare which are now studied as folklore. They are nothing of the kind. Illiterate Gaels accepted the English story as literal truth or at least as valid entertainment, beyond their capacity to understand. Once hunting lore had become obsolete, Gaelic tradition was defenceless against corruption by English.

Witch-as-hare stories show that genuine archaic elements such as the hare and the cat have many links with Gaelic fairy lore and place-names while original fiction such as 'shaking a bridle' is isolated. The fictional stories make sense only in the way that science fiction makes sense, by creating a separate world with its own rules. To harm a witch by shooting a hare with a silver bullet does not make literal sense in any context, whether in Gaelic or in English, but when a hare steals milk from a cow this is a metaphor or paraphrase meaning that during the summer a hunter survived by stealing milk, once a commonplace event.

Fairy changelings

A few allegations that appear to be incredible are in fact true. Stories of fairy changelings which catalogue the various cruel ways of getting rid of such creatures may be imaginary (or they may not) but there is certain evidence that fairy folk and witches sacrificed newborn babies to make vanishing ointment or magical pies. In the thirteenth century killing young children was attributed to the malevolent but unreal *lamiae*. Steven of Bourbon wrote it off as 'an error arising in sleep' (Broedel 2003, 125) but in Scotland the sacrifice of babies was real enough. In 1576 Bessie Dunlop gave her baby to the Queen of Fairie as the price of keeping her husband alive. We know that in 1596 a Lothian witch called Jonet Lindsay killed her baby and boiled him up to make ointment. Truth in this case is stranger and much worse than fiction.

It is also apparently true that witches and fairies shot and killed people and animals with elf-bolts. Isobell said elf-arrows had only to touch to be effective, which suggests they were poisoned. There is archaeological evidence that flint points were still made in the fifteenth century in the Shiant Islands (DES 2004, 137) and Isobell Gowdie stated that she saw elf-boys making them in Moray in the seventeenth century.

The witch trials were not the only inspirations for fake folklore. Over the generations, surviving fragments of oral lore eventually lost whatever meaning and power they once had and were remade as nonsense rhymes, fairy tales, superstitions, charms and sayings. The evolution of this nonsense was helped by unbelievably bad translations from Gaelic into English. Even Martin Martin, supposed to be a native Gaelic speaker from Skye, was evidently educated in English and fills most of his pages with invented fakery. Writers, publishers and their public from his day until the present have been willing to believe any nonsense that came out of the Highlands no matter how improbable or ludicrous it was.

Writers such as Walter Scott, who had only the sketchiest knowledge of Gaelic, began to plunder Gaelic traditions and published new versions of many old traditional stories without making any effort to establish the real facts. Perhaps with the collapse of Gaelic culture there was no-one left who knew. But instead of factual or even plausible history they generated a mass of sensational fiction of which the phony witch-lore of the trials gives us a foretaste. Even commonplace Gaelic was converted into unreal features now accepted as genuine folklore. As John Gregorson Campbell put it, 'Many tales seem to have their origin in vain attempts to stagger credulity, and in that delight which people of lively imagination sometimes take in "cramming" their more stupid fellows' (1902, 6, 16). Campbell identifies another sign of the invented story mentioned already: it is always lost in time, everyone involved is long dead, it happened far away. Improbable marvels 'are said in the south Highlands to have occurred in the north', to a named person who has just died, or to the story-teller's grandfather when a boy. But even Campbell did not recognise the link between rational Gaelic and irrational English. He himself published several stories that are an affront to his readers' intelligence and which if true would cast doubts on the sanity of his ancestors. Virtually all of the folklore that he and others collected has been created out of odds and ends of genuine Gaelic tradition which, if we are lucky, survive in footnotes.

Writers also invented nonsensical stories out of whole cloth. Sinclair, who hoped to make money out of the occult, reported that in 1684 when he was compiling *Satan's Invisible World,* a correspondent communicated to him that several years earlier, when he was a young scholar, he passed over from Bo'ness to Culross to see a witch named Helen Eliot burned at the stake. While Helen was locked in the stocks in prison the Devil came and carried her off. When flying through the air she exclaimed 'O God whither are you taking me!' and immediately the Devil let her drop whereby 'she brake her Leggs and her Belly.' Sinclair's correspondent, 'a person of great honesty and sincerity... saw the impression and dimple of her heels; as many thousands did, which continued for six or seven years upon which no Grass would ever grow' (Sinclair 1685, 207-208). This story does not even have a Gaelic metaphor to excuse it but no doubt it entertained credulous folk who were impressed by the failure of grass to grow on a stone slab.

'I haid a little horse'...

We can now make sense of other words used by Isobell Gowdie when she wished to fly.

According to her published confession, she 'wold say Horse and Hattock in the Divellis name! and we would flie upon a hie-wey. We will flie like strawes quhan we pleas; wild strawes and corne straws wil be horses to us' (Pitcairn 1833. III, 604, 608). This nonsense rests firmly on archaic Gaelic and once again has to do with the hunt. As noted, 'Horse and Hattock' is a very close phonetic rendering of G. *ursainn-athach* 'muster of champions (hunters)' or of *ursainn-chàta* 'chief; champion; ranks of an army in battle order'. Both refer to a muster of hunters and G. *ursainn* means 'ruler of a battle; ranks of an army in battle order'. The first element of G. *ursainn* is *ur* 'fire' and the second element is G. *càth* 'battle or hunt'.

So it turns out that 'Horse and Hattock!' is not after all nonsense but a call to arms or a shout used to rouse hunters when the beacon was lit, and it was evidently still used in 1662 to rouse the witches of Moray when it was time for them to gather for their sabbat. G. *ursainn* is found in English as *urchin* 'hedgehog' since the animal looks like a small army bristling with spears. The same word is found as The Hurcheon at Blairgowrie, Perthshire, an artificial mound or moot-hill where the Earls of Gowrie once gathered their followers for hunting or for war.

G. *ursainn* can also mean 'door-post'. This explains the mysterious importance of the door-post of the fairy mound, which can now be understood to mean a muster site for hunters. So 'Horse and Hattock' can be reconstructed as a hunting shout once used to alert the community to the fact that a distant beacon had been lit. It was an urgent instruction to move as rapidly as possible to the muster site. In other words they had to fly. This appears to be the origin of night-flying as a supernatural activity.

Isobell also knew a longer version (Pitcairn 1833, III, 608; Larner 1981, 152): 'Horse and Hattock, Horse and gre (*or* goe), Horse and pellattis, Ho! Ho!' which can be reconstructed as *Ursainn chata, ursainn greigh* (or *gobh*), *ursainn peilliceach, Ho! Ho!* 'Gathering of hunters, hunters of the herds (*or* with spears), hunters of the hides, Ho! Ho!' G. *peillic* is 'a covering made of skins or rough cloth' or 'a hut or booth roofed with skins'.

According to the transcript Isobell also said: 'Quhan we wold ryd, we tak windle-strawes or been-stakes, and put them betwixt owr foot and say thryse, Horse and Hattock ... and immediately we flie away whair euir we wold.' This nonsense is a further failed attempt to make sense of what she actually said. As a bunch of straw was set alight to send a signal, G. *connlach* 'straw' also means 'gathering fire'. 'To fly on a straw' means 'to go incredibly quickly', as quickly as the light of a bunch of straw. From the same source she could make a horse out of a bean-stalk. G. *pònar* 'bean' is a common pun for archaic G. *banair* 'fire enclosure', and G. *gallan* 'stalk' is a pun on G. *galan* 'flames'. The bean and the bean-stalk are wide-spread themes in nonsense stories and rhymes. In England Jack climbed up a bean-stalk to encounter a giant, the embodiment of a major bonfire. The invocation *peasair dhuitse, 's ponair dhomhsa* is literally 'peas for you and beans for me' but in the original Gaelic it was a prayer to the Lady for good luck: 'progeny for you and a fire for me'. Finally, to claim that 'All the Coeven did fflie lyk cattis', again means that they went 'as fast as hunters'.

Isobell said that the Devil sometimes arrived at her house in the form of a crow (Pitcairn 611). If she wanted to go in a crow (adopt the disguise of a crow) she said three times 'I sall goe intill a craw, With sorrow and sych and a blak thraw!' (Pitcairn iii 608). Perhaps the word she used was not G. *feannag* 'crow', though the crow has become proverbial, but G. *feannach* 'rough, hairy' which is derived from G. *feann* 'to skin, flay', and which would describe the kind of 'blak thraw' used by the Devil when on official business. There is no certainty that this happened, but a witch as crow poses a problem which is solved as soon as we look for a pun in Gaelic. A similar anomaly is her own appearance as a jackdaw (Pitcairn 605). In Gaelic a jackdaw is *cathag-fhireann*, 'hunting troop', from *cath* 'hunt' and *foireann* 'troop'. Elsewhere she says that the Devil dressed 'lyk a bull, a deir, a rae or a dowg', at the sabbat and when he was on official business.

The magic bridle

With the magic bridle we come to something different. The witch used to shake a magic bridle to change her victim into a horse. Its origins seem to be different from the branks or scold's bridle, a spiked collar which was used as a form of torture to extract information. Such an implement was kept in the jail at Forfar (Dalyell 658; Pitcairn I, 50).

Scott states that the fairies could be detected by 'the shrill ringing of their bridles' as they passed in an invisible procession (1931, 316) but he is unreliable. More often the passing of the faerie host is marked by a gust of wind, a whirlwind, or a buzz like a swarm of bees, because they went so fast (even folk-fiction should be accurate in the details). Possible puns are between G. *srian* 'bridle' (E. *rein*) and G. *sreang* 'knot', *srann* 'to make a whistling noise' and *sreann* 'whirlwind'.

Two bridles feature in the well-known story *Càth nan Eun* 'The Battle of the Birds' (Campbell 1874, I, 56) but they are something of a red herring. The king's son has to perform three impossible feats for a giant. He accomplishes the first two with the help of the giant's daughter *Mari Ruadh* ('the hunt of the red deer'). The third of these tasks is to catch a wild filly seven years on the hill. The giant gives him *srian bhriagh shoileir dearrsach* 'the brave clear shiny bridle' but *Mari Ruadh* rejects it in favour of the *sean srian dubh meirgach* 'the old black rusty bridle' hanging behind the door. When she shakes the old black rusty bridle, the wild filly comes obediently and puts her nose into it. And so the king's son wins his bride. These names are full of beacon epithets and puns but their meaning is obscure. The shiny bright bridle was *brèagh* 'splendid, showy', *soilleir* 'bright, shining' and *dèarrsach* 'bright, beaming, glittering, resplendent' while *sean srian dubh meirgach* can be interpreted to mean 'the gathering beacon of the deer-hunt'. The wild filly is the Cailleach. This story links the bridle to hunting, fairies, and hunting magic. However the tale has little in common with other 'magic bridle' stories.

The belief that a witch could use a magic bridle to change her victim into a horse was current in the remoter parts of Scotland before 1633. In that year James Sandieson of Orkney testified that when he was seriously ill Bessie Skebister and two others whom he knew not, tormented him when he was asleep, and sometimes when awake, by carrying him 'to the sea, and to the fyre, to Norroway, Yetland, and to the south – that he had ridden all thes wayes with ane brydle in his mouth' (Dalyell 1835, 591). One has no difficulty in seeing these as hallucinations or nightmares caused by a fantastic tale working on a fevered mind but Bessie Skebister was strangled and burnt.

That the same image was an established part of witch-lore in the North of England at the same date is shown by the story told in 1634 by Edmund Robinson of Pendle Forest, Lancashire who claimed, among much else, that he had seen a neighbouring woman, Mother Dickenson, change a small boy into a horse by shaking a bridle over his head and ride off on him. It was later revealed that Edmund had been coached by his father who harboured a grudge against the woman (Scott Letters, 1830, 250-252) but his father's ideas had come from a popular source and most people took the bridle story for literal truth. In other words, changing a human being into a horse by shaking a bridle at him had become an established fact in witch-fiction in the North of England by 1634.

As the seventeenth century went on, stories about night-riding became more lurid but credibility never wavered. A pamphlet published in London in 1659 tells of the 'Strange and Terrible Newes from Cambridge, being A true Relation of the Quakers bewitching of Mary Philips ... into the shape of a Bay Mare, riding her from Dinton towards the University. With the manner how she became visible again ... in her own Likeness and Shape, with her sides all rent and torn, as if they had been spur-galled ... and the Names of the Quakers brought to tryal' (Summers 1925, 333). More innocent victims died terrible deaths.

The details continued to evolve and to reach back into coven lore. In 1661 Agnes Spark of the Forfar coven reported at her trial that she heard others say that Isabel Shirie was the Devil's horse, that the Devil always rode on her, that she was shod like a mare, and that her hands were sore the next morning (Kinloch 1848, 129). In this case rationality won a rare point, as other witches explained, and the court accepted their explanation, that Isabel Shirie was called 'Horse' because she was the Devil's messenger who brought witches to meetings and ran other errands for him. Whatever caused her sore hands it was not being shod like a mare (Anderson 1888, 252).

The death of one old woman is attributed to a literal belief in the magic bridle and night-riding, though the facts have been thoroughly confused by the desire of one author after another to improve on historical fact. Janet Horne of Loth in Sutherland was executed for witchcraft in 1727 but not even her name is known with certainty. Captain Burt, an army officer posted to Inverness in 1726, gives us a contemporary account. 'In the beginning of the year 1727, two poor Highland women (mother and daughter) in the shire of Sutherland were accused of witchcraft, tried and condemned to be burnt. This proceeding was in a court held by the Deputy Sheriff. The young one made her escape out of prison, but the old woman suffered that cruel death in a pitch barrel, in June following, at Dornoch' (Burt 1822, vol.1, 230).

Malevolent invention or mental delusion is still evident in Northumberland in 1673 where Ann Armstrong claimed that a great many people had ridden her to different places where they had conversation with the devil. She alleged that Ann Driden and Ann Forster came with a bridle and bridled her and rode upon her cross-legged to a meeting at Riding Mill Bridge-end and that she reverted to human shape as soon as the bridle was taken off. On another occasion 'the informant was ridden upon by an inchanted bridle by Michael Aynsley and Margaret his wife. Which inchanted bridle, when they tooke it from her head, she stood upp in her owne proper person.' Another of her riders came in the form of a grey cat, the bridle hanging on her foot (Murray 1921, 103-4, 236).

The original story of the witch and the magic bridle is known from all over Scotland – in Dornoch, Selkirk, Tiree, Lorne – and in Ulster and a very similar story is told in Belgium, Denmark, and Iceland (Henderson 1866, 14-16; Douglas 1894, 177; Campbell 1902, 49; Cameron 1928, 108, 116-7). A young apprentice living in lodgings with his older brother is so tired every morning that he can hardly work. He eventually confesses to his brother that his landlady comes night after night to his bed, changes him into a horse by shaking a bridle at him, and gallops off on his back to her witches' meeting. His brother changes places with him, is also changed into a horse but manages to secure the bridle while the witches are carousing. He changes the wicked woman into a mare, has her shod (in the middle of the night), and rides her up and down a ploughed field until she is almost dead. Next day his wicked landlady is found in bed, with her hands and feet horribly mangled. According to local expectations, she is killed on the spot, burned alive, bled to death, or reformed. In Belgium the scene of the transformation was a large farm at Bollebeck where the farmer's wife, who was a witch, came at night, threw a bridle over the servant's head, turned him into a horse, and rode him around all night. As in other Continental examples, the bridle was thrown, not shaken. This is an important difference.

The point of the story is that the bridle must be shaken, not thrown. E. *shake* is an old term for sexual intercourse which was replaced during the eighteenth century by *shag* (Thorne 1990, 449). E. *brothel* has also changed in meaning. Before 1600 a brothel was an abandoned woman or prostitute, and her place of business was a *bordel*. 'Shaking a bridle' is therefore a double pun on 'shagging a bordel', which is to say, 'engaging in very energetic and tiring sexual activity'. Shagging a bordel, not being ridden by a witch, is why the young man was so tired every morning. 'To ride all night' still has this meaning, while 'shagged' is a picturesque way of saying 'very tired'. This explains why the witch must shake the bridle before she can ride the horse.

This story is not folklore but a Lowland bachelor story which probably evolved early in the seventeenth century, shortly before the magic bridle begins to appear in other contexts. As the Belgian version shows, its puns and innuendoes do not survive translation. The Gaels believed it literally, so that a

Rannoch man, the tailor Cumming, who was suffering from consumption, believed that his weakened state and night sweats were due to witches changing him into a horse on which they rode through the air to Edinburgh to spend the night carousing in various cellars (Campbell 1902, 48). Old nightmares die hard.

'Hag-ridden' and 'ridden by the night-mare' have comparable sexual innuendos. Ultimately the Night-Hag who rides at Hallowe'en (McNeill vol 3, 1961, 14) and the succubus and incubus of classical tradition may all be traced to the sexual metaphors which link the Cailleach and the hunter who rides long distances at night. The Lady was both a Hag and a Maiden and a hunter copulated with her for good luck. As a belief system it is symbolically sound and immensely powerful.

Recognising true facts

When Aubrey published the story of the Fairy Cup in 1690, Isobell Gowdie, who flew like a hunter to her coven meetings, had been a generation dead, most probably strangled and burnt but the witch's horse and her magic bridle were now a common feature of witch-trials and Horse and Hattock!, originally composed as a story to entertain dinner guests at Duffus, had found fame in a commercial magazine. By 1790 Robert Burns was spreading the same corrupt vision of Fairyland and Scott would soon do the same. No-one was interested in what the witch had really said. Witches were irrational, deluded, dreaming, intoxicated, deranged by torture, or mad and it did not in any case do to spoil a good tale. However Scottish witch-lore and fairy-lore are based on fact, however distorted and remote.

Things are different in the Isle of Man. The history of witchcraft there was not sensational: five women were tried, two were executed, three were admonished. Moreover they were not witches but charmers, healers or cunning folk who sold cures and curses and were seen to have misled the public. There was a demand for more and more lurid stories to satisfy tourists. And so fake facts were created to satisfy demand. 'By the early nineteenth century ... the Manx were developing and multiplying false memories of earlier treatments of witchcraft' (Hutton 2010, 157). The process was similar to the Horsie. First the genuine facts were embellished and then, as tourism was increasingly commercialised, a handful of people invented an entirely new history for witchcraft in the Isle of Man. Today visitors are told and expected to believe that the witches of Man could fly, that they made pacts with the Devil written in their own blood, and that they danced around churches. Ritual sites associated with witches have spread over the landscape. The rewards for reinventing the past range from commercial profit from tourism to the chance of becoming a self-appointed expert in a nonexistent topic.

In Scotland it is the fairies who have been the main victims. Their story as the last of the great deer-hunters is valuable and interesting but it has been reduced to frivolous fake folk. There has probably been contamination from English sources as tourist fiction was often made up in English and retold with all its fantasy in Gaelic; it was also changed as we have seen to concern fairies and ghosts rather than witches. The English origins of one well-known horror story are clear enough. Much reduced in detail it was about a tailor who undertook to confront the Devil (or Death) in a haunted burial ground while sewing a pair of trews between bed-time and cock-crow (MacDougall 1910, 34-39). The jest in the Gaelic version of this story is now obscure but originally it rested on the English pun of the tailor's response when a horrible vision arises: 'I see that, and I sew this'. The translation into Gaelic *Chi mi sin, agus fuaghidh mi so* completely misses the point. We can detect the same problem in the Gaelic version of the story of the magic bridle.

Survival

However some Gaelic tales of the supernatural contain genuine fragments of hunting lore and provide a link between fairies and witches. They are generally the less dramatic tales which may seem quite pointless but they rest on genuine memories of fairies or hunters. There is, for example, the story of Donald Post and the Fairies which goes like this. Many years ago Donald Post carried letters between Ballachulish and Fort-William. One Hallowe'en he was returning to his lodgings at Corrie Charoachain when he saw a dozen fairies leaping and dancing on the road. One of them, slender and red-haired, cried 'We will take Donald Post with us!' But another, a fine fellow, replied: 'We will not take Donald Post with us, for he is the poor post of our own farm'. Donald then happened to look up the hill above him and on the green plain on the summit he saw a large troop of fairies wheeling and dancing like the merry-dancers (*na fir-chlis*). The troop on the road also noticed this and in the twinkling of an eye had joined the other fairies on the summit of the hill (MacDougall 1910, 126-127). This is in fact a moral tale, a dreadful warning. The hill at Corrie Charoachain was evidently a muster site for local hunters and Donald, a blundering post-man, had no business being anywhere near it on Hallowe'en. Several traditional elements survive. G. *caol* 'slender, narrow' is also a deer-trap; red hair is associated with fire; fairies wheel and dance when rounding up deer; Hallowe'en was a great bonfire festival and the first hunt of the winter.

It is not uncommon to find the only authentic material in a story right at the end in the form of a little verse. In other words the tale was written to explain a surviving fragment of archaic lore. An example is the long wandering tale about Angus Mor of Tomnahurich which is not even logical by the standards of such tales. But right at the end is the traditional rhyme on which the whole thing depends. The fairies threatened to take his wife and child unless he could guess the secret of their Queen but when he got to the bridge of Easan Dubh she was there washing clothes and singing (MacDougall 1910, 132-141). The Queen is of course the Lady worshipped by hunters.

> 'S aithne dhomh 'Bheinn Mhor am Muile, I know Ben More in Mull
> 'S aithne dhomh mullach Sguirr Eige, I know the top of Scuir Eigg
> 'S aithne dhomh 'n cat a bha 'n Ulbha, I know the cat in Ulva
> Agus 'earball ris an teine. With its tail turned to the fire.

We can tell already from the words *cat* and *teine* that this little dittay is a fragment of beacon lore. Ben More in Mull and the Sgurr of Eigg are the most visible and important of all the hunt beacons in the Inner Hebrides. The *cat* that was in Ulva with its tail turned to the fire is a hungry troop of hunters waiting on that small island to see a distant beacon announcing a hunt. The washerwoman, the *bean-nighe* or 'the pure shining woman', was the Cailleach as the Queen of the Fairies.

Genuine archaic elements almost always respond to interpretation in terms of hunting lore and have links with other aspects of archaic lore such as place-names. The fake folklore and invented stories respond to decoding only insofar as they incorporate genuine archaic elements. It is for example of no significance that various characters end up in France. Those who devise fairy fiction incorporate elements of genuine lore – they are usually central to the plot – but they often get them wrong. Scott, for example, said in 'The Bride of Lammermoor' that witches rode on hemlock stalks (McNeill vol. I, 195). Witches used hemlock as an ingredient in their ointments but they rode on ragwort, as Burns knew.

To summarise, secondary fiction was deliberately created, as a by-product of the witch trials, to create a sensation in court, to entertain the public, or as a commercial venture. These stories belong within the fashionable English-speaking literary environment and often lose their point when translated into Gaelic. They have a period flavour and were probably once thought to be quite witty. They happened to real people living in real places but several generations earlier, or in a remote corner of the country. Many of these worthless stories have been published as folklore but we can quite often identify their probable author.

Irrational or supernatural events are either based on coded hunting lore or involve a degree of fabrication or delusion. This is true whatever their origin. However we explain what we find, we can at least be certain of one thing: witches did not have supernatural powers and were no more capable than anyone else of doing impossible things. Stories of wicked witches and the wicked things which they did can ultimately be traced to Christian teachings and to invention at the clerical interface. Most of the false fables date from 1700 or later, though themes such as shape-changing and flying were already in circulation in the Middle Ages. Such fictions have no relevance to the archaic origins of witch lore.

Archaic themes such as shape-changing and flying were part of a metaphorical or coded Gaelic which appears to have very old origins. It was in use among witches in Lowland Scotland in the seventeenth century and still in the nineteenth century when collectors like Campbell of Islay sometimes talk about an old Gaelic that was difficult or impossible to understand. There was in addition a store of occult knowledge, seldom divulged at the trials or later, relating to herbal medicine, poisons, the magical use of blood, sexual magic and human sacrifice.

We are left with a few scraps of authentic Gaelic. Recognition of these elements is made easier by the fact that they make no sense when translated into English and that witch lore, fairy lore and Gaelic place-names tend to use the same archaic hunting language. The astonishing thing is that many witches from Moray to Lanark were still familiar with prehistoric Gaelic hunting lore and understood its metaphors and figures of speech. There were many in seventeenth century Scotland who would have found nothing mysterious in anything Isobell Gowdie said. The Edinburgh witches who described the devil as an angel or a whirlwind or a truss of hay (Larner 1981, 147) and the Lanark witches who rode on a cock or a bourtrie were using the same coded language.

The value of fake folklore

Gaelic plays an essential part in making sense of the supernatural or 'impossible' elements of witchcraft in Scotland. The possibility of recovering archaic elements of the old religion is one reason why Scottish witchcraft and its Gaelic dimensions are relevant to any attempt to understand the origins of witchcraft. Highland Scotland retained pagan material which survived untouched by the witch-hunts and beyond the reach of the Reformed Kirk. It is, in principle, a simple business to recognise the supernatural aspects of the evidence, change them back into Gaelic, and recover their original meaning. As a starting point, a black cat was originally 'a troop of deer-hunters', for G. *dubh* 'black' means 'deer' in the old language. A wise person will avoid a *black cat* if it crosses the road, for no sensible person ever gets in the way of hunters. A black dog, *con dubh*, is 'a round-up of deer'. Black dogs and black cats were popular as disguises by witches and their Devil and suggest that some relics of older hunting ritual persisted within the covens.

As fragments of hunting lore were recorded coincidentally in the context of the witch trials, our ability to reconstruct the original with complete certainty is evidently limited. However they are supplemented by other fragments of the archaic language collected more recently. The themes are consistent. Many fragments are local hunting-shouts which were raised in a district to alert hunters that a distant beacon is alight. These shouts were evidently memorable; dozens survive. Another common theme is an incantation for success in the hunt, usually addressed to the Cailleach as a personification of fire, the guardian of the deer forest, and mother of the deer. Rarely we find a fragment of a hunting calendar or a list of important beacons.

Before 1600 and for some time after, there was a serious lack of ministers who spoke Gaelic well enough to preach in the language and who were psychologically capable of living in the Highlands among the heathen. The language barrier was created by the Kirk and it was the main reason why the Kirk found it difficult to establish control of the Highlands and, almost incidentally, why there were virtually no trials for witchcraft there. Gilles noted that after the Reformation, 'when ministers were scarce and stipends small', the parishes of Ardeonaig and Strathfillan were united to Killin and placed under one minister. Admittedly a minister was appointed to Kenmore, seat of the Earls of Breadalbane, in 1561 and to Killin in 1567 but Strathfillan did not regain its parochial status until 1774 and Ardeonaig in 1791. The parish of Lawers did not get its own minister until 1833 and the pious souls of Glenlyon had to wait until 1837 (1938, 261).

In the context of a charm it did not matter very much if the patient understood what was being said or if the charm used was incomprehensible gobbledegook. In 1662 Jonat Mann of Bute said that 'Jonat McNeill used a charme to hir bairne, being extremely sick of the diseased called the Glaik, that the said charme was in Irish [Gaelic] quhich she understood not' (MacPhail 1920, 4), but this might have been a good thing, as is said of opera. But a mutual lack of comprehension at the clerical interface had more serious consequences. At least some of the irrational elements attributed to witches in Scotland arose when evidence given in Gaelic was badly translated and then taken as literal fact. Once we realise the existence of this problem it is evident that most of the supernatural or irrational elements in the evidence are due to the use of Gaelic by the witch and English by the Court.

In consequence we must approach the evidence recorded at the Scottish trials with caution. In many cases the recording clerk has edited what he wrote, put words into the mouths of the accused, and invented fantastic explanations of words and phrases he did not understand. In addition confusion arose at the clerical interface between Gaelic and English as the majority of the accused came from areas in which the poorer people had little or no English and the clerks who composed the court records seldom understood Gaelic. A third element, dating back to the pernicious influence of James VI, was the general expectation that witches would confess to 'strange and odiouse factes'. Everyone from the parish minister down was more than willing to be astonished by what they heard. Quite often the official record incorporates elements of popular fiction such as the flying witch, the magic bridle or the witch-as-hare.

An example of the 'entertainment and titillation' typical of the period was *Satan's Invisible World Discovered*, a compilation made by George Sinclair, Professor of Natural History at the University of Glasgow. 'His visits to England on scientific matters had made him think that there was money to be made from the occult. He accordingly published in 1685 a collection of plagiarized English stories and Scottish narratives of witches, spirit possessions, and apparitions, and in February of that year successfully petitioned the Privy Council for the sole rights of publication.' *Satan's Invisible World* did not make money for its compiler who died a poor man but sold very well in later centuries, when memories of the real witch-hunts had faded, and was said to have been the second book in a peasant's library of two (Larner 1981, 32).

Frauds and hoaxes

To complete this overview of supernatural fiction we need to consider the fraudulent cases which show the power of fake folklore over the uneducated. One might argue that all claims of witchcraft are fraudulent but certain categories were regarded as valid targets: healers who made false claims, cursers and banners, coven witches who served the Devil, those who used poison.

In the fraudulent cases there were no basis for the allegations. The accusers were almost all children who fabricated their stories out of nursery tales and kitchen gossip. Their thoughtless malevolence is matched by the credulity of the authorities who took them seriously and inspired them to create more and better lies. But the malicious lies of the Throgmorton children in 1593 led to the deaths of the Samuel family, a poverty-stricken mother, father and daughter (Scott 1830, 238-242). The elaborate dream-like stories invented by the children of Mohra, Sweden, in 1669-70 were also taken seriously and led to the deaths of eighty-four innocent women (Scott 1830, 215-220).

There was no doubt about the lack of validity in the accusations made by Edmund Robinson, a ten-year-old boy who lived in Pendle Forest, Lancashire, an area which had been notorious for witches a generation earlier. There was therefore a residual layer of fake witch lore. As Scott tells it, 'about 1634, a boy called Edmund Robinson, whose father, a very poor man, dwelt in Pendle Forest, the scene of the alleged witching, declared, that while gathering bullees (wild plums, perhaps) in one of the glades of the forest, he saw two greyhounds, which he imagined to belong to gentlemen in that neighbourhood. The boy reported that, seeing nobody following them, he proposed to have a course; but though a hare was started, the dogs refused to run. On this, young Robinson was about to punish them with a switch, when one Dame Dickenson, a neighbour's wife, started up instead of the one greyhound; a little boy instead of the other.' His suspicion that she was a witch was increased when she 'pulled out of her pocket a bridle, and shook it over the head of the boy who had so lately represented the other greyhound. He was directly changed into a horse...' There is much more incredible nonsense on similar lines. His testimony led to the arrest and trial of almost twenty people at Lancaster Assizes on 24 March 1634. All but one were found guilty but the judges refused to pass sentence and referred the case to Charles I. When cross-examined in London, Edmund eventually confessed that his father had invented the entire rigmarole to settle a score with a neighbour. Despite this it appears that the accused remained in jail, where they died (Scott 1830, 250-252). Fortunately for the sanity of researchers and the reputation of real witches, this kind of malicious invention which crosses the border between truth and fantasy was rare.

Our final example of spurious folklore had a happier ending, at least in the short term. In court at Forfar in 1661 Agnes Spark stated she had heard other witches say that Isabel Shirie was the Devil's horse, that the Devil always rode on her, that she was shod with horse-shoes like a mare or a horse, and that this was why her hands were sore the next morning (Murray 1921, 103). The assise for once did not jump to ridiculous conclusions but established that the Devil called Isabel 'Horse' because she was his messenger and was responsible for taking round notice of the meetings. The only context in which she might have been ridden hard by the Devil was in their sexual relations as her daughter's testimony suggests he had an interest in her beyond the legitimate copulation at the sabbat. The rest was a joke that circulated in the coven. The joke shows that the human horse, night-flying and horse-shoes were already popular belief in Forfar by 1661 and might, if believed literally, have influenced the course of a trial, as they might have done in 1727 in Sutherland.

Sharpe (1819, 199) improved the story: the old woman had 'ridden upon her own daughter, transformed into a pony and shod by the devil, which made the girl ever after lame both in hands and feet, a misfortune entailed upon her son'. As Scott tells the same tale, 'in the year 1727, a Sheriff-depute of Sutherland, Captain David Ross of Littledean, took it upon him, in flagrant violation of the then established rules of jurisdiction, to pronounce the last sentence of death for witchcraft which was ever passed in Scotland. The victim was an insane old woman belonging to the parish of Loth, who had so little idea of her situation as to rejoice at the sight of the fire which was destined to consume her. She had a daughter lame of both hands and feet, a circumstance attributed to the witch's having been used to transform her into a pony, and get her shod by the devil' (Scott 1830, 338).

However Elizabeth, Countess of Sutherland, had written to Mr Sharpe in 1808 to say that Janet's daughter had burned her hands when a child, which had contracted her fingers. This ought to have been the last word, but contradicts the claim that her descendants have the same deformity, for which there is also anecdotal evidence. Sharpe may have invented the story of the old woman warming herself at the fire lit to consume her but this conflicts with her death in a pitch barrel. Moreover the old woman was executed in June, not normally a cold month even in Sutherland. And, as Cowan and Henderson have pointed out, when a witch was put to death she was first strangled and the fire to burn her was not usually lit until after she was dead (2002, 206). Most of this tale is fake folklore. We can rely on nothing beyond the bare facts reported by Burt. The bridle, the pony, the horse-shoes, the deformed hands and feet, the Devil and the fire, even the genetic nature of the handicap, are all borrowed from fake folklore to make a better story.

The greatest fraud of all?

Perhaps the most awful example of fake folklore is the short book or long pamphlet known as *The Secret Commonwealth of Elves, Fauns and Fairies* which was brought to the attention of the public in 1815 by Sir Walter Scott. He claimed to have found a manuscript in the Advocates' Library entitled *An Essay of The Nature and Actions of the Subterranean (and for the most part) Invisible People, heretofoir going under the name of Elves, Faunes, and Fairies, or the lyke, among the Low-Country Scots, as they are described by those who have the Second Sight; and now, to occasion further Inquiry, collected and compared by a Circumspect Inquirer residing among the Scottish-Irish in Scotland* (Scott 1830, 163 note). The manuscript has a further introductory page with appropriate Biblical quotations and is headed '*Secret Commonwealth, or, A Treatis displayeing the Chiefe Curiosities as they are in Use among the diverse of the People of Scotland to this Day; Singularities for the most Part peculiar to that Nation*, By Mr Robert Kirk, Minister at Aberfoill 1691'. (Kirk died on 14 May 1692). A reliable sign of faking of this nature is over-elaboration; its creator cannot leave well alone.

Scott's involvement was comprehensive. It was he who found the original and solitary manuscript in the Advocates' Library, c.1815, it was he who gave the pamphlet its current name, and who arranged for publication. The problem was not evident at the time but now that we know so much more about fairies (and about witches and hunters) it is clear that *The Secret Commonwealth* is not a valuable source of Perthshire fairy lore but an elaborate and sustained work of fiction in which almost nothing meshes with genuine sources whether fake or not. *The Secret Commonwealth* is not just fake folk but meaningless.

Later critics have pondered these problems. Andrew Lang says in his introduction to the 1893 edition that 'the bibliography of the following little tract is extremely obscure'. From a bibliographical point of view it is very unsatisfactory as it starts and ends with the novelist Walter Scott, who was known for faking his sources, rather than with the minister Kirk. He discovered the only manuscript, claiming that it had been written by the Rev. Robert Kirk, minister at Aberfoyle, who was a reputable scholar, but he also claimed that it had been first published by Kirk in 1691. The first problem is that there is no sign of this edition or of any edition before 1815. There is no sign at all of *The Secret Commonwealth* before the discovery of the manuscript by Scott in 1815.

This apparently was too much of a coincidence even for Scott. Before publication in 1815 he is already describing his discovery as a transcript of Mr Kirk's original manuscript. Those who create elaborate fakes often have such fun they add layer on layer. But he inserted a comment which could not be made by Kirk or by any competent Gaelic scholar. He does not give the name of the woman who had fasted for a very long time but says only that 'her Name is not intyre', which is the kind of jest or pun which an English-speaker might make about the Gaelic name McIntyre but which would hardly occur to a Gael, who would know that McIntyre is understood to mean 'son of the wright'. Scott may have realised this is an inappropriate comment as he adds in his published edition that it is 'Thus in the Manuscript which is only a Transcript of Mr Kirk's Original'. Does he mean there may have been a more authentic older version? But there is no trace of any older edition. We come back also to the fact that the earliest known source is the Advocates manuscript of 1815.

As the manuscript was unknown before 1815, perhaps it did not exist before then? Did Scott write it himself? He is the most likely candidate, quite apart from the smoking gun in his hand. He was no stranger to invention: he had made a fortune out of writing historical fiction (much of it under the pseudonym 'Waverley'). A third of his *Border Ballads* are avowedly his own work and the rest are of unknown authenticity. As the author of *Letters on Demonology and Witchcraft* (1830) Scott had the interest and the literary capacity to create a spoof of this type.

Kirk, on the other hand, was the leading Gaelic scholar of his day, born and bred in southern Perthshire, and, like his father, a minister. Everything we know of him is serious and reputable. It would be very much out of his character to have written fantastic fiction about the fairy folk. Moreover no Highlander would describe himself as living among the Scotch-Irish. 'Scots-Irish' is a dismissive English term for a speaker of Gaelic or 'Erse'. Scott, on the other hand, frequently travelled for short periods among the Scots-Irish but remained embarrassingly ignorant of Gaelic.

It is moreover curious, if *The Secret Commonwealth* was written by a leading Gaelic scholar, that it contains no Gaelic at all and describes the Highlanders from the outside. We can contrast this with the terminology and general attitude of the genuine Highlander Patrick Graham, Scott's contemporary, in his book *Sketches of Perthshire* published in 1812. Graham writes in English but gives the Gaelic form of local place-names, calls his native language 'Gaelic', and refers repeatedly to 'the Highlanders'.

There is a more subtle reason for rejecting *The Secret Commonwealth* as a genuine work of contemporary (1690) fake folklore. Its prose sounds very obscure and subtle but though it makes no sense it does not make no sense in the right kind of way to be authentic fake folklore. In this it is like the nonsense invented by the Swedish child witches about events at Blokula in 1669. This invention eventually inspired a panic which took the lives of eighty-five women and children. As with *The Secret Commonwealth*, fantastic invention was confused with reality. *The Secret Commonwealth* is accepted today as a genuine fake, in the sense of being what leading experts in the field were saying about the fairy folk in 1690, but it is not even that. It is wonderfully complex but none of its alleged facts have any archaic depth. It provides no authentic insights. It is not even a genuine fake of later centuries like the tales told by Stewart (1823) or genuine traditions like those collected by John Graham Dalyell (1835).

Another difficulty in attributing *The Secret Commonwealth* to Robert Kirk (who died in 1692) is that he and all his family and friends knew very well what 'fairies' really were, having lived all their lives among them or their descendants. Kirk was a MacGregor and MacGregors were fairy folk, in the original sense of being traditional deer-hunters who lived in the wilds. He no doubt thought of them as the *sith*. Had Kirk been inspired to write a history of the hunting culture of this area he would have given us a wonderful source of rare information but he was a pious man whose ambition was to provide a Gaelic Bible for his people. It is significant that his memorial inscription mentions his translation work and does not have a word about the fairies. I believe he would be horrified at what has been done with his reputation.

In brief, *The Secret Commonwealth* is neither authentic hunting lore (which still survived in the heartland in 1690), nor is it a contemporary tall story based however remotely on genuine lore, like the oft-repeated stories of flying to France. It was written by an educated and inventive person who knew no Gaelic and had no insight into the authentic folklore of Gaeldom. It is admittedly difficult to see what Scott would gain by writing such a spoof, apart from the secret pleasure of baffling his readers, but one could ask the same question of the palaeontologist who created Piltdown Man. Perhaps he got carried away by his secret joy in hoaxing his friends.

Another reason for suspicion has been brought to light recently by Henderson and Cowan (2001, 198) who wrote: 'The extent to which Scott fed and indeed was responsible for the creation of tradition may be indicated by the publications of one of his informants'. They point out that when Patrick Graham, like Kirk, minister of Aberfoyle and a native of southern Perthshire, published his *Sketches Descriptive of Picturesque Scenery* in 1806, mentioned above, he included much information about the supernatural but did not mention Robert Kirk. This is equally true of his earlier account of Aberfoyle in the Old Statistical Account c.1792. But Graham's *Sketches of Perthshire* (1812) shows him in contact with Scott. It not only contains a stanza from *The Lady of the Lake* to describe Kirk's fate but also the first sign of the faux story of Graham of Duchray (an ancestor of the author) failing to free Kirk from Fairyland.

Henderson and Cowan suspect that it was Patrick Graham who invented these 'traditions' but the inventive spirit in their relationship was Scott. We know that Scott fed Graham additional material for his second edition (Graham 1812, 253ff; Henderson and Cowan 2001, 198). This, I believe, was when Scott began to write *The Secret Commonwealth*. Three years later he had the incredible 'luck' to find a manuscript in the Advocates' Library which confirmed the fables he had passed to Patrick Graham.

But alas, the value of his invention as a source of fairy belief is less than zero and later he disowned his bastard child in favour of authentic history, when he wrote his *Letters on Demonology* using genuine sources. *The Secret Commonwealth* is the Piltdown Man of fairy lore but it came too late and is too clearly a work of the imagination (and a Lowland imagination at that) to do serious damage except to Scott's own reputation as a source.

The Banners of the Fian

We come back to another set of very archaic hunting names known as the Banners of the Fian. None of them have anything in common with the nicknames of the witches but respond in the same way to interpretation in terms of archaic Gaelic. E. *banner* is from the same source as G. *bann* 'proclamation' and G. *ban* 'white, pale', in archaic Gaelic, a signal fire. A banner in an archaic or poetic context may be understood as a signal used by hunters in the form of a beacon or a hunting-shout. In Gaelic a banner is *bratach*, *suaicheantas* or *meirghe*. The first two terms are heraldic. G. *bratach* is a flag; the Fairy Flag of Dunvegan is the *bratach-shith*. G. *suaicheantas* is a small flag or ensign. But G. *meirghe* has the same root as *meirle* 'robber, hunter' and can mean either 'flag, pennant etc', 'troop, band (of hunters)' or 'signal'.

Names listed below are from *The Book of the Dean of Lismore* (c.1500), Donald Meek's article, 'The Banners of the Fian' (*Cambridge Medieval Celtic Studies* 11, 29-48 (1986), and Dwelly's Gaelic dictionary (1901).

The Gaelic is archaic and fanciful, often obscure, generally open to more than one interpretation but guesswork is made more reliable by the predictable association of these names with hunting, for the Fian, whose banners they were, were deer-hunters. *Coinneal Chatha, Geal Ghreine* and many others may be hunting shouts (see below). A sun beam is a metaphor for a beacon signal. Though collected in Ireland, like the Fian these names are probably Scottish.

Aoin-Cheannach Oir. The banner of Raighne (Meek). G. *aodhan* 'fire', *ceann* 'deer trap'. *Ceann* is any round enclosure so also 'vulva'.

Aon Chosach, Aon Chasach Ruadh or **Ruagh** (Meek). G. *aodhan* 'fire'

+ *còs* 'recess (deer trap, vulva)' + *ruadh* 'red'. G. *caise* 'privy parts of a female' derives from G. *cas* 'deer trap (vulva)', related to E. *chase*.

Bearna an Réabhain. The banner of Osgar mac Garaidh (Meek). G. *beàrn* 'gap, crevice (deer trap, vulva)' of 'the crafty one' (the Lady); cf. *reabhair* 'crafty fellow', ie, a hunter.

Bhriachail-Bhròchuil: (Meek). G. *breac* 'the speckled ones (deer)' + *bròcail* 'mangle, spoil, lacerate (kill)'. Like Fr. *bric-à-brac* 'a collection of ancient objects of little value' and E. *helter-skelter, mish-mash, mixter-maxter, pell-mell, raggle-taggle, tapsalteerie, topsy-turvy* &c. it refers to the chaotic circumstances of the kill at the end of a successful deer-drive.

Brochaill 'banner of Gaul son of Morni' (Dwelly 1901, 126). G. *bròcail* 'mangle, spoil, lacerate (kill)'. As above.

Coinneal Chatha. The banner of Faolan (Meek). 'Light of the hunt'. G. *coinneal* is the same word as E. *candle*.

Craobh Fhuileach The banner of Clann Mhic Lughaich (Meek). 'Fire of blood, or of the kindred'. In archaic Gaelic *craobh* is 'fire', in modern Gaelic it is 'tree'. G. *fuil* 'blood; family, tribe', *fuileach* 'bloody, gory'.

Dealbh-Ghréine. The banner of Fionn (Meek). 'Image of the sun or fire'. The reference is to a fire as bright as the sun. See Deo-Ghreine.

Deo-Ghréine 'sun-beam' (Meek). A ray of light from a beacon. Fionn's banner. See Dealbh-Ghreine.

Dubh-Nimhe 'deer forest', the banner of Caoilte mac Reatha (Meek). G. *dubh* for *damh* 'stag' and *nimhe* 'sacred area', nemeton, exclusion zone, game preserve or deer forest.

Dun Naomhtha, the banner of Oisean (Meek). The enclosure/beacon site of the holy place/exclusion zone.

Fhionn Chosach Ruadh: see Aoin-Cheannach Oir.

Fulang Doghra 'the banner of Goll' (Meek).

Fulang Dorrain 'the banner of Fergus, that is, the banner of one who could sustain a defeat, and play a losing game when necessary' (Dwelly 1901, 464). This interpretation rests on G. *fulang* 'patience' and *dorran* 'anger'. A *fulang* was also a prehistoric cooking place or camp kitchen, found as a mound of burnt stones. G. *dorrain* is probably from *doire* 'deer forest'. The Gaels seethed their meat in the skin of the animal, using hot stones to heat the water.

Gath-Gréine (Meek). 'Sunbeam' but in archaic hunting terms 'beacon signal'. Also *Gath-Ghreine Mhic Cumhaill*.

Geal Ghreine 'Light of the sun'. To be as bright as the sun was a compliment to a fire.

Geal-Gheugach (Meek). 'Light of the deer'. G. *geug* 'young superfine female, nymph', the Cailleach, but also an archaic word for a deer or for 'a sunbeam', ie. a beacon signal. Also *Geal-gheugach Mhic Cumhaill* (Meek).

Làmh-Dhearg. The banner of Mac Ronain (Meek). 'Red hand' or perhaps 'red blade' referring to a weapon. But G. *lamhach* 'military manoevres, shooting' is 'hunting' in the older language.

Liath Luidhmeach, Liath Luineach or **Luidagach, Lia Luathnach** (Meek). G. *liath* 'grey', in archaic terms 'a light'. G. *luid* 'slovenly or filthy person' was an inverted epithet of the goddess related to *luideach* 'having long hair, like an animal'. The original meaning may be 'dressed in skins' or more simply 'deer'. G. *fogh-luidhe* 'robber, pirate (hunter)'. This might stretch as far as G. *loichead* or *loiche* 'lamp, light, torch'. See note on the witch Ludlam (below).

Lòch Luinneach. The banner of Diarmaid (Meek). G. *loch* is an old word for a V-shaped deer trap and probably also for the vulva.

Sguab Ghábhaidh. The banner of Osgar (Meek). G. *sguab* 'besom, broom', refers to a squat female, to a triangular shape, and to the Lady in the form of a vulva. Triangles play a major role in the decoration of prehistoric textiles and pottery. A candle-snuffer, G. *sguab,* is the same triangular shape. G. *gábhaidh* 'strange, wonderful, terrible, fearful' could also be an old epithet of the goddess.

Hunting shouts

Last but not least in this roundup of coded Gaelic are the hunting shouts, once sent around the neighbourhood to alert hunters to a distant beacon, were later used to 'raise the Devil', in Calvinist terms. They survive in considerable numbers as elements of fake folklore but vary very considerably in form. In his article on the Banners of the Fian (1986, 32) Professor Meek identifies the 'powerful shout' as a theme in folklore. 'In the course of his encounter, Caoilte emits a great shout which is heard in several of the most famous warrior-centres in Ireland. By this means he obtains a response from other warriors who are presumed to come to the aid of the Fian' and gives several references from Stith Thompson (1955-58) for powerful shouts, used to summon in Irish and other literatures. There is a link between the shouts and musters of hunters and also of rounding up cattle or deer. A remarkable herdsman in Irish myth sits shouting on a mountain top and cows [deer?] come from a great distance at his call (iii, 194 F679.1). A man's voice shakes the heavens in a Chinese story and a man's shout remains in the air for three days in an Irish myth. Noisy storms are giants shouting (iii, 196 F688). The Wild Hunt was heralded by the shout of the huntsmen (E501.13.5).

A bhuacharlain! Carmichael gives a nonsense rhyme about G. *buacharlain,* another name for ragwort which means 'fire plant'. It begins *A bhuacharlain! a bhuacharlain!* 'Fire, fire!' (vol. IV, 121 and note).

Banners of the Fian (see above) seem to be either the names of hunting troops, or, what was probably much the same thing, their hunting shouts. They include **Coinneal Chatha** 'light of the hunt', **Craobh Fhuileach** 'Fire of the kindred', **Dealbh-Ghréine,** 'image of the sun'. **Gath-Gréine**, now 'Sunbeam' but in archaic hunting terms 'beacon signal', **Geal Ghreine** is 'light of the sun' which is a compliment to a fire. (see above for several more examples)

Beannaich Aonghais ann san Oirrinn, the shout at Auchtubh in Balquhidder. Another word meaning 'blessed' is found in a place-name at Auchtubh at the east end of Balquhidder Glen in Perthshire. The complete name of this spot is *Beannaich Aonghais ann san Oirrinn* – said to mean 'the Blessing of Angus in the oratory' and it is said that anyone coming into Balquhidder from the east should repeat the words *Beannach Aonghais* at Auchtubh at the spot where Balquhidder glen first comes into view. However it appears to be a hunting shout. This is where a person coming into the glen from the east gets his first sight of the Kirkton where the gathering beacon was lit and where a watcher was posted to look for the beacon, the site being invisible from Auchtubh itself. The Blessing of Angus can be explained rationally as a hunting shout meaning 'The gathering beacon at the fire site!' G. *beannachd* is derived from *ban* 'fire' and *aonach* 'assembly'.

Benedicete Maikpeblis. According to Andro Man's testimony, the two magic words Benedicete and Maikpeblis conjure up Satan and dismiss him again (SCM I, 120, 124). If we take this as Gaelic, Satan can refer to a gathering fire (A.G. *sa 'to gather' and *teine* 'fire'). To conjure up Satan is to light a beacon (or summon the coven) and to dismiss him is to put it out again. *Maikpeblis* could be G. *magh* 'plain, deer forest', and *pobull* 'tribe'. In that case 'Benedicete Maikpeblis' would mean 'Gathering fire of the tribal deer forest', a hunting shout raised when the hunt beacon was lit to mobilise the troops. There has been learned editing.

Christsonday. It has been argued elsewhere that this was the translated name of the personified hunt-beacon on the Bin of Cullen in Banff in 1597. A pun with A.G. *crios* 'beacon, fire' and G. *domhan* 'the deer forest or tribal domain'. G. *dòmhnaich* 'of the deer forest' is punned with *Dòmhnaich* 'Sunday' which would give the original meaning 'Beacon of the deer forest', a hunting shout. Sundayswell, Kincardine O'Neill, is found in Strathspey as *Tobar Domhnaich*. *Domhnach* can also mean 'the Church'.

Caisteal Folais na Theine. 'Fire at Casle Fowlis' was Clan Munro's hunting shout, war-cry or slogan. The slogans of the more authentic native clans are often their hunting shouts.

Loskoir Longert, alias of Mariota Neymaine McAlester, Easter Ross (1577) is a hunting shout meaning 'fire at the hunting lodge' with G. *loisg* 'to burn' and *longhairt* or *luncart* 'hunting lodge'.

Mult dhu an carbhail ghil. Walter Scott, source of so many wildly inaccurate and misleading stories, hung a whole clan battle on a Gaelic proverb: *mult dhu an carbhail ghil,* which he said meant 'The black wedder with the white tail (should never have been lambed)' (Scott 1893.a, 121). Scott promoted the idea that the theft of this animal by two travelling tinkers was the cause of the Battle of Glen Fruin between Colquhouns and MacGregors. In fact the grievance was the theft of Colquhoun livestock by members of Clan Gregor who had been prevented from hunting. Murray MacGregor (1898, 292) pointed out that the word is not *carbhail* but *earball* 'tail, troop of hunters', as E. *tail*. The first word is not *mult* but *milt* 'gathering, raid'; *dubh* is not 'black' but 'deer'; *geal* is not 'white' but 'fire'. The final result is 'The gathering of the deer by the troop of the fire!', a hunting shout or slogan, sent around the area to alert hunters to the fact that the hunt-beacon has been lit and they must report to the muster site. It has no necessary link with Glen Fruin.

Uir! Uir! air sùil Odhrain! The old name of the island, I, is probably G. *aodh* 'light, fire'. According to a nice old story, when building his church on Iona, Columba buried Odhran alive to secure the building. After three days he had the earth removed to see how Odhran fared. He was still alive and famously uttered the words: 'Chan eil am bàs 'na iongantas, no Ifrinn mar a dh'aithrisear', which is taken to mean: 'There is no wonder in death and hell is not as it is reported'. Columba reacted with passion, calling out, according to one version *Uir! Uir! air sùil Odhrain mu'n labhair e tuilleadh còmhraidh,* said to mean 'Earth! Earth! On Oran's eye that he may blab no more' (Henderson, 1911, 282). But it is a hunting shout: 'Fire! Fire! The beacon shows the hunter the signal for a joint hunt!' Among the puns is are *aodhair* 'fiery conflagration', *ùir* 'fire', *sùil* 'beacon, signal', *muin* 'shows, points out', *tul* 'fire', and *còmhraig* 'fight, hunt)'. Odhran's Eye or *Sùil odhrain* was presumably a beacon on Mull which was visible from Iona. A hunting shout is less sensational than burying a man alive but covering a fire with earth is a good way of putting it out.

11 THE TRIALS:
HEALERS AND THEIR MAGIC

The hail assise, in ane voce ... convictis and fyllis Helene Frasser in fourtene poyntis of witchcraft and sorcerie, contenit in her dittay, and as a rank vitche be oppin voce and commoun fame.

Spalding Club Miscellany 1841, I, 110.

An oral culture is susceptible to rapid collapse and extraordinary loss but it is difficult to explain the almost complete disappearance from the collective memory of the native deer-hunters who were for so long a pervasive aspect of Scottish life. One reason was probably the novelty and popularity of the supernatural fairy tale but the main reason was the dramatic change in Gaelic society imposed by feudal law. Suddenly native hunters were banned from the forest. The decline and eclipse of Gaelic hunting lore began in the eleventh century when the hunting forests of Scotland were taken over by Malcolm Canmore and absorbed into his new feudal kingdom. As feudal law was enforced, native hunters vanished from one district after another and their leaders and other learned men died without passing on their wisdom which, in any case, was no longer of any relevance. Within a generation, in one place after another, no-one was left who had experienced at first hand the life of the *sith*. Those who were able became drovers, taking Highland cattle as far as London. To the English-speaking farmers and cattle herders who succeeded deer-hunters in Lowland Scotland, fairyland and the fairies became unreal and magical, creatures from meaningless folk tales.

One sign of the rapid loss of Gaelic hunting lore is that descriptions of fairies in folk tales vary very much. The fictional species may be slim, beautiful, sexless creatures with red or gold hair, familiar bands of local men who dance at night and who can fly through the air, large grey-haired old men reclining around a fire; fairy children are tiny shrivelled beings with voracious appetites. The supernatural fairy never passed through the mill of popular taste. According to the most authentic lore, fairies were hunters who were organised into local troops or bands; they lived in the wild and they controlled the fairy knolls or *sithean* which served as outlook posts and beacon sites. The fairies of the Scottish witch trials were of normal size, both male and female, sometimes of known parentage, and of nomadic tendencies. But they morph

178

or degenerate into the fairy folk of Scottish folklore and more recently into the magical fairies of faux fiction. Their sacred rituals survived as children's games and popular entertainment.

The most plentiful and, give or take the general tendency towards clerical intervention and improvement, the most reliable source of information about Scottish fairies is the material generated by the trials of the century 1570-1670. Transcripts provide us with case histories of many fairy charmers, and often include their charms and magical methods, their clients, and, rarely, some obscure scraps of archaic Gaelic badly translated into nonsensical English.

A second source for information about Gaelic magic is written sources such as Dalyell (1835), Gregor (1881) and Campbell (1900). They are much later and consist very largely of fake folk but it is clear from such late sources that though the practice of magic was similar throughout the country, it was more pervasive, more elaborate, more tenacious and more authentic in the Highlands, where hunting and transhumance persisted for longer, than it was among their English-speaking cousins in the Low country.

Traditional charming can be seen as an early form of experimental medicine. Healers everywhere in Scotland used variants of similar charms, rituals, incantations, plants, drugs and poisons and were constantly passing recipes to each other. Some of their methods and principles were in general use (and are summarised below) while others were trade secrets, passed by a teacher (often described as a 'fairy') to selected pupils. The most famous healers seem to have added a secret ingredient or a touch of personal power.

Much of their magic was common territory backed up by the practitioner's own powers but there were always secret details, muttered charms or secret symbols that were seen by the family but not revealed to the patient. Charms in garbled Gaelic and some old Catholic prayers were particularly valued in the Lowlands as they were incomprehensible to most patients and partook of a special magical power. The trials cut short the careers of many experienced healers but, as we saw in Aberdeenshire, people with problems of all kinds, particularly pregnant women, continued to consult charmers, and charmers continued to treat them as well as they could.

Three warlocks

As far as one can judge the men and women found guilty of witchcraft before c.1620 were not coven witches but individual wise women or warlocks who were condemned for using traditional charms, rituals, herbal remedies, magic stones, and other magical remedies to treat sick people and animals. Sometimes they work as members of larger groups but these are temporary engagements.

Later trials are from progressively remoter places, remote at any rate from the courts in Edinburgh. As the witch hunts spread such healers and many of those they had healed found it difficult to understand what they had done wrong, why after a lifetime of reputable activity there were complaints and capital charges to answer. The main charge was that they were charlatans who misled the public. Underlying was the fact that their authority did not come from the Church but in consequence from the Devil.

Three notable and experienced warlocks, Thomas Greave, Steve Malcolm and Alexander Drummond, worked along the Highland Border in the 1620s. Each had his own specialities and all of them were executed.

Thomas Greave who worked in West Fife, was tried in 1623 and found guilty of the crimes of sorcery and witchcraft. He was a skilled charmer who practised bird magic, cattle magic, circle magic, iron magic, sark magic, thread magic, water magic and number magic using the numbers 3 and 9. He used secret charms, crosses and other figures known only to himself. He cured David Chalmer in Letham by washing his shirt in south-running water and putting it back on him. He cured a woman in Ingrie near Leslie by taking the illness off her and putting it on a cow, which died. In one case he had the family break a hole through the wall of the house, on the north side of the chimney, take a hank of yarn three times out of the hole and in by the door, and then pass the sick woman nine times through the circle of the yarn. In another case a sick man was passed three times through a hank of yarn which was then burnt in a great fire giving a blue flame. He also used a hesp of yarn and water he had blessed to give Margaret Gibson's cows their milk back again. To cure a child of epilepsy he wrapped the child's head nine times in a length of cloth soaked in various ointments 'and vther inchantit matter' which he kept in a little box, at the same time uttering various charms and making signs, so that the child fell asleep and was cured when he woke. He told William Cousin, whose wife was ill, to heat the coulter of his plough and cool it in water brought from the Holy Well of Hillside. Then Thomas blessed the water and made her drink it with results that are not reported (he was in either case guilty). In one case the illness was transferred to a hen which was passed three times widdershins in at the door and out again through a hole in the north side of the house, put under the sick woman's arm-pit and carried to a large fire where it was held down and burnt alive. This resourceful and competent man cured many and cursed no-one but was still found guilty and 'wirreit and brunt in asches' (Pitcairn 1833, III, 555-557).

Stephen Malcome of Leckie, near Stirling, was tried in 1628 for using a very similar range of therapies. He had learned them from the fairy folk 'quhom he had sein in bodilie schapes in sindrie places' (Ferguson 1907, 76). He believed he could transfer illness from one person to another, or to an animal, or to running water. He believed in the efficacity of south-running water, of rubbing an elf-arrow on the body, and boiling an elf-arrow in south-running water. He charmed one of the patient's shirts using the formula: 'God be betwixt this man that aught this sark and all evills in name of the Father, the Sone and the

Holy Ghost'. Then the patient had to put on the shirt three times, repeating the same prayer, wash his body in south-running water and cast out the water used for this washing in some desert place where no Christian soul was likely to pass. He sent the patient a napkin to dry his body and instructed him to throw it under his bed. If the illness was to be laid on a beast, the beast was to be paid for by the sick person. Malcome once treated a lunatic by taking him out alone on a winter night between nine and ten o'clock and drawing a circle around him with a sword. Then he stood ready with drawn sword to repel the fairy folk who were responsible for his illness but this cure was not successful.

Also tried in 1628 was Alexander Drummond of the Kirkton of Auchterarder in Strathearn, within the Gaelic-speaking zone at the edge of the Highlands, who had worked as a healer and charmer for fifty years before he was found guilty of 'sorcerie, witchcraft, charmeing, and cureing of dyverse seiknesses and diseases' (Reid 1899, 67). The Warlock of Auchterarder was well-known and had a good reputation though few details of his cures are given. One of his more spectacular achievements was to cure insanity by burying a live cock and iron ploughshares on the boundary between two lairds' lands. He was supposed to consult the Devil and to have a familiar spirit (not a common feature of Scottish trials). A substantial part of his dittay consists of a list of the people he had cured, ranging from Walter Buchanan, burgess of Dumbarton, to the daughter of William Scotland 'and mony hundrethis of peoples, alsweill men, women and children, as beistis.' Those who gave evidence against him were not dissatisfied patients, but even Sir George Mackenzie, who was relatively enlightened, supported the guilty verdict on the grounds that Drummond had misled people, 'albeit he had never committed any malefice, but had only cured such as were diseased'. As so often in seventeenth-century Scotland there is an almost palpable conflict between rationality on the one hand and the retrogressive fear of the supernatural fostered by the Reformed Kirk. Given their dualistic view of the supernatural, the fatal defect of all healers and charmers was that they were pagans who worked without the authority of the Church.

These three warlocks worked in the Hillfoots and Strathearn, between the Highlands and the Lowlands. We know the names of many of those treated by Alexander Drummond and the majority have Highland origins. Thomson for Macomish is found in southern Perthshire, McNab in Killin, Dewar in Glendochart, Buchanan at Leny, Drummond in Strathearn. Neish, Ramsay, Walker and White were used as aliases by migrating members of Clan Gregor (McGregor unpublished); the Andersons are a branch of Clan Gregor from Glen Lyon. Patoun (like Paterson, Peat, Peters, Patullo and many similar names) is derived from the MacPhatricks of Balquhidder (Reid 1899; Black 1946). The Hays have a good feudal pedigree but all the rest have Gaelic antecedents.

Lowland charmers

As noted, female charmers are often found working in small cooperative groups, whose members passed difficult cases and good recipes to each other. Sometimes a husband and wife or a woman and her daughter worked together. The most famous healers had been trained by the great witches of the previous generation. The charmer Euphrick Nikceoll roy of Lismore, who was active in Argyll in 1590, had been taught by old Mackellar of Cruachan, who had learned his charming at the Priory of Iona. John Brugh, executed in 1643, had learned his craft from 'a wedow woman named Neance Nikclerith, of three scoir years of age, quha was sister dochter to Nik Neveing, that notorious infamous witche in Monzie'. Many others, to their own disadvantage, claimed they had learned their charms and recipes from the fairy folk who can probably be identified with the learned men and women of the Gaelic-speaking native culture who practised in many places into the seventeenth century.

The story of the four Lothian healers who were tried in 1597 is more typical of this period (Pitcairn 1833, II, 22-29). Christian Lewingstoun of Leith in Midlothian, Jonet Stewart of the Cannongait of Edinburgh, Bessie Aitkyn, also in Leith, and Christian Saidler of Blackhouse near Haddington in East Lothian were tried on charges of witchcraft, sorcery and incantation, &c. They had worked as a team using cures learned from different sources and their services were in demand throughout a wide area. As all four were tried at the same time and as two of them were called Christian this makes some details of the transcript difficult to disentangle but the main facts are not in doubt.

Christian Lewingstoun affirmed that her knowledge came from her daughter who met with the Fairie. This may mean her daughter was dead but certainly claims supernatural powers. Lewingstoun was convicted of abusing Thomas Guthray, a baker in Haddington who had complained that he was bewitched. Lewingstoun had cured him by digging a little hole under his stair and taking out a poke of black cloth containing some grains of wheat, some worsted threads of different colours, hairs and nails of men's fingers. This, she stated, was responsible for his bad luck. She threw the witch-poke to his wife who caught it in her apron and threw it on the fire like a sensible woman. It is more probable that she knew who had laid it and where it would be. She also predicted that the child to be born to the couple would be a boy, which turned out to be the case. This lucky choice was a clear sign of demonic possession.

Christian Lewingstoun and Christian Saidler were also consulted by Robert Baillie, mason in Haddington, about his wife who seemed to be bewitched. They boiled up three pints of sweet worts (fermented malt) with fresh butter and gave it to her to drink; but it did not cure her. They all had great problems with Andrew Penicuke of that Ilk, a dissolute young gentleman. When Christian Saidler and Jonet Stewart failed to cure him, they called in Christian Lewingstoun as she was a 'wyise-wyfe and a woman of skill' but the sick man was not happy with this arrangement and asked them to refer him back to Jonet Stewart and to 'craif his health at hir hand for Godis sake'. Jonet gave him a bannock made of meal and the blood of a red cock and she also tried sark magic. This was very powerful stuff and it evidently worked as Andrew lived for another six years.

Jonet Stewart treated Bessie Inglis by washing her sark and her mutch in south-running water, putting the wet shirt back on the patient at midnight while repeating three times 'In the name of the Father, the Son and the Holy Ghost', putting red-hot iron in the water, and burning straw at the four corners of the bed, as she had been taught by the late Michael Clark, blacksmith, in Lasswade. Jonet Stewart was an adventurous healer. From the Italian Johnne Damiet, a notorious enchanter and sorcerer, she had learned a cure for the *wedonympha*, an unidentified female complaint. She used ring magic: a woman had to pass three times through a garland of green woodbine which was then cut into nine pieces and thrown on the fire. She also bathed a sick person in water in which red nettles and Allessander [*Smyrnium olistatum*, also known as Alick or Wild Celery], had been boiled and used Allessander, red nettles, woodbine and fresh butter to make various ointments. She believed in washing all over with salt water and applying sheep's dung to the affected part. Her cure for the falling evil (epilepsy) was to hang a charm-stone she had got from Lady Crawford round the client's neck for five nights. Less happily she gave Robert Hunter a cure for leprosy which contained quicksilver: 'God knawis how it wes composit' but he died within twelve hours.

Bessie Aitken also used ring magic to cure women with a pain in the lungs, passing them through a girth of woodbine nine times, repeating 'This in the name of the Father, the Son, and the Holy Ghost' (which was felt to be sacriligeous). Jonet Stewart advised her to use a salve of red nettles, Allessander and woodbine seethed in butter, as she did herself. Some of their remedies were shared but others were peculiar to one person, as if the mere ritual was not enough and they had also been initiated into a magical secret.

These four women seem to have been on the whole careful and caring, much in demand and generally useful in magical and herbal cures: William Kellis swore that his wife would have died if Bessie had not come. Despite their efforts and accumulation of skills these four women were convicted of being common abusers of the people, by giving themselves out for Witches, and to understand that they had the gift of Sorcerie, able to have cured various serious diseases and illnesses, which by no natural means of physick or other lawful and Godlie ways, they were able to perform. They were guilty of deceiving the public when their cures did not work and guilty of practising witchcraft when they did. Given the standard of medical science in 1597 their achievements and methods are quite remarkable. Ultimately belief rested with their patients.

Several other witches or fairy folk from Edinburgh and East Lothian had worked together in 1590 to help the fifth Earl of Bothwell further his ambitions. He directed several of them in a unique ritual which involved a baptised cat, parts of a dead body, four small human bones, and an iron pot-hook.

Dolly magic

There was a darker side to witchcraft in Scotland. It was alleged that Bothwell taught the North Berwick witches to make wax images 'that by the rostinge thereof, the persones that they beare the name of, may be continuallie dryed awaie by continuall sicknesse' (Dalyell 1835, 337) but such little dollies were a long-established and powerful aspect of native magic, known to the Gaels as *corp-chriadhach*. Dwelly has a note on the Gaelic variety contributed by William Cameron, Poolewe, Wester Ross (1901, 254):

'When a witch desired to destroy any one to whom she had an ill-will, she often made a corpse of clay resembling the unfortunate one, and placed it in some out-of-the-way burn under a precipice, in such a way that the water trickled slowly on it. As the clay body wasted so the live body of the person it resembled was also supposed to waste away. Were the body found, it was carefully preserved, and so the spell of the witch was broken. Sometimes pins were stuck in the clay body to make the death of the doomed one more painful. Several such bodies have been found, even of late years.'

Some were made of clay to be baked and broken, others of wax or butter to be melted. Clay dolls were made by native witches in Easter Ross for Lady Foulis in 1577 to represent two of her in-laws who survived, and another was made in Lothian in 1588 to represent the Earl of Angus who died. In 1590 a wax dolly was made to represent James VI who survived, and in Moray at some time between 1640 and 1662 a clay dolly of a male infant complete with little lips was made to represent the male children of the Laird of Park, who died one after the other as soon as they were weaned. They probably suffered from an inherited gluten allergy but the witches took the credit.

The seventeen little dollies found in 1837 in a small dry cave on the northeast flank of Arthur's Seat, Edinburgh belong to this tradition. They were made of wood, carefully dressed in jackets and trousers and housed in little coffins. The coffins were carefully arranged in two tiers of eight and a third tier of one. The eight that survive are all of comparable size and style, though not identical, and were presumably made by a single person who had deposited them one by one over a long period. They are certainly magical and probably malign in their intentions and suggest witchcraft on a large and persistent scale. Suggestions of benign purpose appear to be wrong: whether a dolly was made of clay, wax, butter, wood or straw, it was never made for anything but evil.

Witch-pokes. Witches in Lothian, Forfar, Moray and the Hillfoots confessed to using parts of recently dead bodies, particularly the bodies of unbaptised infants, for magical purposes. Dead flesh was a common ingredient of a witch-poke or witch bag, one of the most powerful spells for ill-luck. The use of dead flesh was also very old and very widespread. Robbing a coffin for magical purposes was declared a crime in 654 in Visigothic Spain, and Scottish witches including John Brugh of Fossaway, Helen Guthrie of Forfar, and Isobell Gowdie of Auldearn readily confessed to robbing coffins, killing babies and cannibalism. The Forfar coven made a pie with selected parts of an unbaptised baby 'that they might eat of it, that by this meanes they might never make a confession of their witchcraft'. This is exactly paralleled by a ritual conducted by the Paris coven 'pour ne confesser iamais le secret de l'escole' (Murray 1921, 158). This suggests that necrophagy was an imported practice: all those involved were instructed by literate Devils. But it is also certain that our attitude to such activities has been shaped by the horrified reaction of the Church and nothing suggests that Scottish witches found such practices repugnant or were reluctant to follow instructions. People also believed that fairies ate human babies.

The witch-poke (G. *poca* 'bag') was relatively common in Scottish witchcraft. It combined a variety of ingredients, most of them revolting, and was reckoned the most powerful of curses. It appears to be native magic enhanced by new ideas passed around like cookery recipes. A poke might be used to curse an individual, his family, his animals or his crops. A recipe from 1597 contained only grain, coloured threads, hair and nail clippings but later witches in several places made bags containing the stomach or intestine of a sheep, or a scrap of cloth filled with human flesh, nail clippings, hair, grain, rags, and rotting meat. Witches admit to lifting dead bodies to put in pokes in places as far apart as Lanark, Crook of Devon, Forfar and Moray. The similarity of this method of cursing in widely-separated places, from the island of Bute to Moray, suggests it is native magic, of some age, with later refinements. Pitcairn notes that a similar bag, also used for cursing, was known to the Romans.

James Reid, a sorcerer in Midlothian in 1603, had learnt his craft from the Devil in Bynnie-craigs and Corstorphine Craigs (in the marshes to the west of Edinburgh). To curse a miller he took a piece of raw meat, made nine cuts in it, enchanted it by reciting a spell, and gave it to his client to bury under the door of the mill and the rest under the stable door (Pitcairn 1833, I, 421-422). In 1643 John Brugh, a healer, of Fossaway in Crook of Devon, working with the local Devil, lifted three bodies from the churchyard of Glendevon and one from the Kirk of Muckart. They put parts of the flesh above the byre and stable doors of their victims (Reid 1899, 207). In 1650 Margaret Finlasone,

Yoker, was accused of witchcraft by Robert Patersone, miller of Blaurthill. He found lying in the yard 'something like a putch tyed together with stringes of three coloures and within it three coloures of worset, a banepick and ane lead broach'. Robert then took ill, crying that he was burning, and then cold as if pricked with 'elsines'. His wife burned the poke but in two days Robert was dead (RPC, 211-212). Among the complaints against Margaret Spittell, in Earne, Menteith in 1650 was that John Bachop, when he was her neighbour, found 'in his midding yirdit like raw flesh with other crudities like unto the inmeat of an haggies' (Fergusson 1907, 63). In the case against Helen McClew from the Highland parish of Kippen, also in 1650, it was said that she quarrelled with Robert McIlchrist and shortly after he 'fand in his yard four or five sundry sorts of flesh as raters eirs pudings' and within a year and a half lost fourteen head of cattle, and fell sick himself. Helen McClew was forced to intervene, which she did by transferring the illness to another of Robert McIlchrist's cows, which 'within a short time died and Robert from the same very time began to mend' (Fergusson 1907, 65).

In Auldearn, Moray, in 1662, Isobell Gowdie confessed that her coven, directed by their Devil, had made a poke to curse a local person on four or five occasions. They made the bags under the supervision of their Devil, who taught them several revolting recipes and the appropriate spells. In the winter of 1660 the Auldearn witches made a bag to prevent the recovery of Mr Harie Forbes, the minister of Auldearn, from an illness. It contained 'the gallis, flesh and guttis of toadis, pickles of bear [grains of barley], pairingis of the naillis of fingeris and toes, the liewer of ane hair, and bittis of clowtis [rags]'. This mixture was chopped up and soaked in water, while the witches repeated a formula taught to them by the Devil (Pitcairn 609). Kirk Session minutes confirm that the minister was ill at this date but recovered. The same recipe was used against Thomas Reid and he died (Pitcairn 1833, III, 612). On another occasion, 'Dowglas and I my self met in the Kirk-yaird of Nairne, and we raised an unchristened child owt of its greaff; and at the end of Breadleyis corn-field-land just opposit to the Milne of Nairne we took the said child, with the naillis of our fingeris and toes, pikles of all sortis of grain, and blaidis of keall, and haked theim all verie small, mixed altogither; and did put a pairt thereof among the muk-heapes of Breadleyes landis, and therby took away the fruit of his cornes &c.' (Pitcairn 1833, III, 603). The third recipe is very like a haggis made of dog-meat and sheep-meat, chopped very small with an axe, and seethed for a whole morning in a pot, with water. The Devil himself stuffed the filling into a sheep's bag while the witches repeated an incantation. The contents of the bag were scattered on the ground where the Laird of Park and his sons would normally walk and it worked, for they died. To curse a midden they used the chopped flesh of an unchristened child, dog meat, sheep flesh, parings of nails &c and repeated a charm.

'We putt this intill this home
In our Lord the Divellis nam.
The first handis that handles the
Brunt and scalded sall they be!
We sall distroy hows and hald,
With the sheip and nowt [cattle] intil the fald,
And litle sal come to the fore
Of all the rest of the litle-store.'
(Pitcairn 1833, III, 613)

The lands of Park and Lochloy in the parish of Auldearn had belonged for four hundred years to a family of Hays but according to family history, the family is said to have declined in the middle of the seventeenth century and the lands passed to Brodie of Brodie (Colcock 1908). However this was not a new development in Isobell's day. Another local witch, Agnes Grant, had been executed in Elgin in 1643 for the murder of the Laird of Park and his two sons. There was evidently a feud of long standing. Isobell's co-accused, Janet Breidheid, confessed in 1662 that four years earlier she and other witches had made a clay dolly representing the eldest son of the next Laird, that the work was done for Elspet Monro; that it was Keathren Sowter, who was burnt, who shot William Hay, brother of the last Laird of Park, instigated by Gilbert Kinley, but that it was the witch-poke that did for the last two Lairds of Park (Pitcairn 1833, III, 618). All the elite of Moray and all their witches seem to have conspired against the hapless Hays.

On the island of Bute, in the Firth of Clyde, witches at the same period were also making witch-pokes out of the flesh of an unchristened bairn, thread, and nails which they hid in stables or buried under the door sill where people or cattle passed to curse them. NcWilliame and her daughter Katherine laid a poke in the easing of the east side of the house outside, between the window and the door and NcConoche and Elspath Galie laid some pokes under the threshold of Donald McConochie's door and almost killed his wife. 'Whether it be ther yet or not she knew not but she suspects it be and though the pock or the clout [rag] it was in may be rotten yet the thing itselfe and vertue might remaine' (MacPhail 1920, 25-26). The power of the curse might remain even when the poke was gone.

A witch-poke could also be a benevolent talisman designed to protect its wearer against witchcraft. In 1607 Bartie Paterson, a traditional healer of Newbattle, Midlothian, gave his client a herbal drink, rubbed him with ointments made of various green herbs, and got him to pray every night, three times nine times 'to ask his helth at all leving wichtis, aboue and vnder the earth, in the name of Jesus.' Finally he was to take nine grains of wheat, nine pinches of salt and nine pieces of rowan wood and to wear them continually on his person 'for his helth' (Pitcairn 1833, III, 535-536). Presumably he was to carry them in a little bag or wrapped in a piece of cloth.

A similar poke was known in classical Italy. As Leyland tells it, the goddess Tana loved a handsome youth named Endamone but she had a rival who was a witch, to whom he was indifferent. The witch clipped a lock of his hair. Then, taking a piece of sheep's intestine, she made it into a bag, into which she put the lock of hair, a red and a black ribbon bound together, a peacock feather and pepper and salt, over which she sang a very old curse. Tana could not break the spell but could come to Endamone in dreams. An archaic element also used at Auldearn is the sheep's intestine which is used instead of the red woollen bag found in beneficent magic. Red and black ribbons represent joy and sadness. A peacock's feather, *la penna maligna,* and pepper and salt occur in other spells, always to bring evil and cause suffering (Leyland 1899, 56-7).

Domestic Magic

In addition to dollies and pokes, every aspect of life that could be used for magical working was used, from birds, bones, cats and cattle to circles, cloth, iron, numbers, sarks, threads, sleeves, stones and water.

Bird magic. Helen Fraser commanded John Ramsay, being sick of a consuming disease, to sit down in a doorway, before the fowls had flown to their roost, and open his clothes so that when the birds flew over him he might receive the wind of their wings about his heart, to loosen his heart pipes, which were closed (SCM I, 1841, 105). In Orkney Elspeth Cursetter in 1629 told a client to 'get the bones of ane tequhyt [linnet]' and carry them in his clothes (Dalyell 1835, 150).

Bone magic. Magic bones, even saintly relics, are very rare in Scotland, probably because the Gaels understood that a patron saint was a non-material entity. An exception was the human skull, reputedly that of St Marnock, which was once preserved in the parish church of Aberchirder or Marnock in Banff. 'The head of this holy person was a relic of the highest value, used instead of the Bible when oaths were made. It was also washed every Sunday of the year amidst the prayers of the clergy and the water carried to the sick, who drank it and recovered their health' (Dalyell 1835, 151). Aberchirder was also noted for a very large standing stone (Mackinlay 1914, 76). When Innes of that Ilk mustered his clan in 1594 to join with the Catholic earls of Huntley and Errol, in the Battle of Glenlivet, they took with them the skull of St Marnan who was their patron (Grant 1854, 163). Innes was a client of the fairy man, Andrew Man (d.1597) and evidently an Old Pagan. We can trace, in this incident, an affinity between fairies (or witches) and Catholics: both were repositories of various pagan customs and relics. In 1590 the North Berwick witches instructed by the Earl of Bothwell, made a collection of small bones which were to be dried, ground to powder, and used in unspecified ways to work evil. Small bones are often missing from Scottish graves: is it possible they were removed by sorcerers?

The fourth charge in the dittay against Isobel Strathanchyn, alias *Scudder*, of Aberdeen in February 1597, concerned the use of dead men's bones to create holy water. In modern spelling it reads:

'Fourthly you are indicted for passing to the Church of Dyce and there gathering a number of dead folk's bones and boiling them in water, and taking that water and thereafter washing William Symmer in the Halton of Fintray (he then being lying deadly sick) and thereafter causing the said William's goodmother take the said bones and cast them in the River Don, which when she had done, the water rumbled in such a manner as [if] all the hills had fallen therein and this you can not deny' (SCM 1841, I, 180).

Cat magic. A cat was known as 'the thing that goes about the fire'. As well as referring to the cat's habits this is a pun linking the witch's cat with G. *cath* 'troop of hunters'. Hunters 'go by the fire', meaning they respond to the hunt beacon when lit. Hunting is implied in the significance of the cat to fishermen. In Shetland a fisherman would not go to sea if crossed by a cat but if a cat went along with him that was a good omen (Black 1903, 167). When James Davidson could get no fish, Marion Layland washed the feet of a cat in his bait water and threw the water after him when he went to sea again (Black 1903, 116). If this did not work the cat's head would also be washed and the water thrown on to the fisherman and into his sea caschie and his bait box. Andro Man (tried in 1597) cured Alexander Simpson in Fordyce by putting him nine times through a hank of undyed yarn, then putting a cat nine times backwards through the same hank, and saying a prayer to put the sickness on the cat. The cat immediately died while Alexander recovered. To raise a storm the North Berwick witches went to Beigis Tod's house in Longniddry and after they had drunk together for a while they baptised a cat by passing it three times through the iron crook above the fire and three times under the chimney, tying human bones to its paws, and throwing it into the sea (it swam ashore) (Pitcairn 1833, 237). They baptised a second cat at Seaton by passing it nine times through the iron gates of the manor house there before christening it *Margaret* (no Gaelic here!). Then they all returned to the Deanfoot where they had originally met and threw the cat to the Devil (Pitcairn 1833, 542-3). According to Murray, the conjuring of cats is recorded only in Scotland (1921, 167) but the conversion of G. *taghairm* 'summons' into a way of raising the Devil by roasting cats is an extreme example of fake folklore. What is more extraordinary is that this joke, a rather bad one, has been taken as literal fact.

Cattle magic. Cattle were of such enormous importance in the rural economy that any illness presaged disaster for the family. Since witches were always blamed, many trials are little more than a catalogue of the ills to which half-starved milk-cows kept in unhygienic conditions are prone.

Cloth magic. Christian Stewart was executed at Perth in 1596 for bewitching and killing Patrick Ruthven by a piece of black cloth. Patrick Lowrie in 1605 was accused of curing a child in Glasgow who had been sick for eight or nine years, by taking a cloth off the child's face, and saining and crossing the bairn's face with his hand, keeping off the cloth for eight days, then covering his face with it again; whereupon the child slept for two days and in five days more was cured. **Blanket magic** is recorded from Aberdeenshire in 1597 where Margrat OIg went early to the Burn of Bogloch, threw water over her head, took a blanket and with it swept all the dew off the green to her own house to get the benefit of the pasture (SCM 1841, I, 143). In Breadalbane in the Highlands the ritual known as 'gathering the dew' was witnessed at Morenish on Lochtayside about 1890 (Gillies (1938, 351-2). One should go out early on 1 May and draw a hair rope over the neighbour's dewy grass, repeating a charm in Gaelic to draw the neighbour's milk away from her. See also **Rope magic**.

Earth magic. Ewphame Mackalzane of Cliftonhall, Midlothian, one of the North Berwick witches, and Catherene Carrutheris, called Erisch Jonett (because she was a Gaelic-speaker) laid kirkyard earth ('mwilds') and dust where the victim would walk over it and she began to suffer palpitations and became ill (Pitcairn 1833 i, part ii, 251).

Hair and nail magic. Hector Munro of Fowlis in the month of August 1588 met over five days with three notorious witches (in fact charmers), John McConeill-gar, his wife, and John Bane's wife, in Little Alteis in John Murray's house in Bakine, when John was absent. They tried to cure Hector's brother Robert Monro using clippings of his hair and nails of his fingers and toes, but they complained he had delayed too long in sending for them, and they could do him no good. For fear of his father he conveyed them away again under silence of night, 'quhilk is notourlie knawin to the haill countrey' (Pitcairn 1833, II, 201).

Iron magic. Iron in any form was powerful, whether a ploughshare or a pin. Divination by the sieve and shears was used to raise the Devil. Divination by the riddle and shears was known in Bute and in Dingwall and no doubt in every place between. In 1649 Margaret Munro in Culcraiggie in Alness was charged with practising sorcerie by the turning of the sieve and the shears (Mackay, 1896, 156). The riddle was suspended from a pair of shears (the old type with two blades connected by a spring or bowl). One of the points of the shears was driven into the wooden rim of the sieve. The bowl of the shears was balanced on a finger and the riddle turned this way or that in response to the questions put. Elspet Bruce of the Forfar coven 'by turning the sive and sheires, reased the divell, who being werry hard to be laid again, there wes a meiting of witches for laying of him' (Murray 1921, 114, Kinloch 122). In Aberdour, Fife, in 1669 John Lister was accused of turning the riddle. To identify a culprit a charm was repeated, the sieve was suspended between two fingers and the name of the suspect was repeated. If the sieve turns, trembles or shakes he or she is reckoned to be guilty. Divination was also done by suspending the riddle by a thread, tying it to the points of a pair of scissors, giving it room to turn and naming the suspects as before. Similar cases might be resolved by putting a key into a Bible (Simpkins 1914, 115). David Wood of Kirkcaldy, a sailor, confessed that he could turn the key, and that he learned how to do so on an English ship. When one of the company wanted to identify a thief he put a key in a Bible and read Psalm 50, verse 18: 'When thou sawest a thief, then thou consented with him'. Then he named all the people in the ship, and when he named the guilty person the key turned. As a remedy it was immediately popular (Simpkins 1914, 116-7).

Jonet Reid, tried in 1643, took a pot with water in it, laid the tongs across the mouth of the pot, then laid a cushion above the tongs and set the head of the sick child on it. Then she took a sieve and set it on the child's head and set a coggie full of water on the sieve, and then laid a wool shear in the mouth of the coggie. Then she took lead and put it in an iron lamp and melted it and poured it through the shears three times, divining through the lead whether the child would recover or not. Finally she gave the child a drink of the water and said he would recover ('but as yit the child is not') (Black 1903, 102).

Iron was used in less specific ways. In 1597 Helene Frasser of Foveran, Aberdeenshire, used iron magic on behalf of Christane Hendersoune, henwife at Fovern. When 'the young foullis died thick; for remedie quhairof, the said Helen bade the said Christane tak the haill cheikennis or young foullis and draw tham throw the link of the cruik, and tak the heindnest and lay with ane fyrie stick, quhilk thing being practised, nane died thairefter that yeir' (SCM 1841, I, 107). A cruik was an iron pot-hook. Margrat Og was accused that when 'thy kow being in bulling, and James Farquhar, thy awin gude sone haulding the Kow, thow stuid on the ane syd of the kow, and thy dochter Batrix Robbie, on the vther syd. and quhen the bull was lowping the kow, thow tuik a knyff and keist ower the kow, and thy dochter keapit the sam, and keist it over to the agane, and this ye did thryiss, quhilk thou can nocht deny' (SCM 1841, I, 144). The Aberdeenshire witch, Margaret Riach, when she clipped her sheep, turned the bowl of the shears in their mouth (SCM 1841, I, 192). On Papa Stour, Shetland, an old razor was kept in the byre to ward off evil (Black 1903, 160). A pin or an old horse-shoe served the same purpose.

Ring magic. A sick person might be passed through a hoop of woodbine or a barrel hoop so that their entire body was covered by whatever the incantation proposed. Generally the ring or hoop was cut up into nine pieces and burnt at the end of the process. Where there was no ring, as in the dedication of a new witch, it was enough to put one hand on top of the head and the other under the feet.

Rope magic. The use of a hair tether to steal milk is attested in all parts of Scotland except the Outer Isles (Mackenzie 1894, 128) and is described for Breadalbane (above). Isobell Gowdie in 1662 described a related method: 'When we tak away any cowes milk, we pull the tow, and twyn it and plaitt it in the vrong way, in the Divellis name; and we draw the tedder (sua made) in betuixt the cowes hinder foot, and owt betuixt the cowes forder foot, in the Divellis name; and therby tak with ws the kowes milk. We tak sheips milk ewin so. The way to giev bak the milk again, is to cut that tedder' (Pitcairn 1833, III, 605). In the first half of the nineteenth century it was alleged that a witch in the village of Strathkinness (near St Andrews, Fife), on the last night of the year skipped in the open air swinging a cow-tether made of hair over her head while she repeated the charm: 'Hares' milk and mares' milk, and a' the beast that bears milk, come to me!' (Simpkins 1914, 56). By this performance she was believed to have acquired the milk of her neighbours' cows as well as securing her own. McNeill has a photograph of a hair tether from Comrie, Perthshire (1977 edition, I, 144). In Breadalbane a woman who wished to steal her neighbour's milk might go out early on 1 May and draw a hair rope over the grass to collect the dew, saying as they did so: *Bainne an te so shios, bainne an te so shuas 'na mo ghogan fhein.* 'The milk of that cow down, the milk of that cow up, in my own great coggie'. The ceremony was known as 'gathering the dew' and a blanket was also used (Gillies 1938, 351). See also **Blanket magic**.

Sark magic. It was common practice to treat a sark or short as if it represented the sick person. When Ewfame McCalzane of Prestonpans, a woman of standing who was tried as a witch in 1591, consulted Catherine Campbell, a Gaelic-speaking Highlander, seeking her help to cure her son Thomas, she sent her Thomas's sark and two 30p coins (Pitcairn 1833, II, 250). In 1597 Jonet Stewart, a wise woman living in the Canongate, Edinburgh, took the sark and cap off Bessie Inglis in the Cowgate in Edinburgh, washed them in south-running water, and put the wet shirt back on the patient at midnight, saying three times 'In the name of the Fader the Sone and the Haly Ghaist'. She also heated water, and burnt straw at the four corners of the bed, as she had been taught by the late Michael Clark, smith in Lasswade (Pitcairn 1833, II, 25-29).

Sexual magic. Sexual magic was by several accounts the most common field of magic in which witches were involved but information is scanty. Witches were believed to control male potency as well as female fertility. Janet Clark *alias* Spaldarg, of Cromar was found guilty of giving a secret member to John Coutis, giving and taking the power from several other men's members, and taking John Wattis' secret member from him, c.1597 (Pitcairn 1833, I, 206). The witch Scudder at Dyce 'wes ane commond mariage maker, betuixt qhuatsumever personis'. When consulted by the widow, Elspet Murray, Scudder asked her to lend her a penny, which she bent and took a rag and a piece of red wax and sewed the penny and the wax in the rag and enchanted it by pronouncing a spell over it. She then told the widow to wear it round her neck, and when she saw the man she loved best, she should take the rag with the penny and the wax and strike her face with it. Elspet claimed she had thrown the rag and its contents into the fire. There are complaints in Aberdeenshire at this time of witches arranging marriages with 'low-class thriftless harlots' against the desires of the family, and of alienating the affections of married men. Helen Fraser 'be wicthcrafte entyssed Gilbert Dauidsoune, sonne to Williame Dauidsoune, in Lytoune of Meanye, to luiff and marie Margaret Strauthachin, in the Hill of Balgrescho, directlie aganis the will of his parentis, to the wtter wrak of the said Gilbert' (SCM 1841, I, 107). It was in addition claimed that the witch made Gilbert's mother, Cathrene Fetchit, go mad with fury, so that she lost the power of her left side, and died, and that she bewitched the unfortunate father so that he also died in a fury. It was also alleged that Helen Frasser used witchcraft to transfer the love and affection that Andrew Tillideff of Ranistoune had for his wife Isobel Cheyne to Margaret Neilsoun (SCM 1841, I, 108). Isobel Robbie confessed that the Devil was in the bed between her and William Ritchie her harlot, and he was upon them both, and that if she happened to die for witchcraft, he should also die, for if she was a devil, he was too (SCM I, 1841, 192). Helen Frasser was blamed for the 'great luif' which arose between Robert Merchand, hitherto a happily married man, and Issobell Bruce (SCM 1841, I, 109). The enchantment could be reversed. In 1623 Isobel Haldane of Perth cured Patrick Ruthven, skinner in Perth, of being witchit by Margaret Horncleuch. She had come into his bed and stretched herself over him, her hands on his hands 'and so furth', mumbling some words (Pitcairn 1833, III, 537). In September 1649 Mauld Galt of Kilbarchan (Lochwinnoch) was accused of witchcraft as 'schoe had committed any vyle act in abusing ane of hir servants'. She was accused of abusing her servant Agnes Mitchel 'with ane piece of clay formed be hir to the lyknes of a mans privie members doing of quhat is abominable to think or speik of' (RPC 2nd ser vol 8, 198 et seq.). In September 1649 Mauld Galt of Kilbarchan (Lochwinnoch) was accused of commiting a vile act having abused one of her servants with 'ane peis of clay formed lyke the secreit member of ane man' (RPC 1649). Was this sexual magic or sexual perversion?

In other cultures there are many anecdotal examples of women's private parts being used to promote the fertility of plants and fields and even inanimate objects. Peasant women exposed their genitals to the growing flax, while saying: 'Please grow as high as my genitals are now.' A virgin was sent down a mine which was running low in iron ore in order to revitalise Mother Earth by exposing her vital female essence or energy to the earth. Female sexuality was used to control wind and weather. Pliny believed that hailstorms, whirlwinds and lightning could be calmed by a naked woman. On the coasts of Scotland some women made a living by selling favourable winds or sinking boats. Catalan fishermen believed the sea calmed down 'if it saw a woman's cunt' and so their wives displayed their genitals to the sea before their men went to sea. But a woman could cause a storm by urinating in the waves. In Madras, India, women could subdue dangerous storms by exposing themselves. It was believed that the vulva had power to drive out devils, avert vicious spirits, frighten carnivores and scare opposing warriors and threatening deities away. A sixteenth-century traveller in North Africa recorded the belief that lions will turn tail and run from a woman exposing herself. At funerals, women were hired as mourners, with the express aim of exorcising demons by displaying their private parts. When a bear appears out of the Russian woods, it can be put to flight by a young woman raising her skirt at it. In the good old dance Gillatrypes, long popular among the lower orders in Scotland, the men danced back to back with their partners and linked elbows so that they could raise their partners on their backs and expose their private parts. As suggested by the cover of Terry Pratchett's twenty-third Discworld novel, *Carpe Jugulum* (1998), the Gillatrypes move is also effective against vampires.

The erotic dance known as Gillatrypes was notorious. In 1596 three servant lasses in Elgin confessed to performing 'ane dance called gillitrype singing ane foull hieland sang' (McNeill 1977, vol. 1, 143). At Auldearn in 1662 the Devil danced it with the Maiden, and as late as 1731, still in Moray, Margaret Hay was charged by the Kirk Session of Essill with dancing a notoriously indecent dance called Gillatrypes. The name might mean 'lad of the hunting bands' and it was notorious for its 'indecent postures', in which the couple dance back to back and the man hoists his partner up on his back to expose her privities.

In an eighteenth-century edition of the fables of Jean de La Fontaine a young woman defeats the Devil and saves her village by exposing her genitals. Rabelais had his old woman of Pope-Figland rout the Devil in the same manner, and reproductions of this confrontation between the vagina and the Devil can be found on seventeenth century drinking mugs (much of this information comess from Blackledge 2003). In Egypt squatting on ground so that there is contact between the labia and the soil has the dual purpose of making the soil fertile and driving off evil spirits. Logically not only the female genitals but also menstrual blood should be equated with fertility. In Sicily menstrual blood is used as a love-charm and so equated with fertility. In recent years,

194

faced with a disastrous drought, the farmers of Bihar in north India asked their unmarried daughters to plough their fields naked after sunset, while chanting ancient hymns and helped by the elderly females of the village. It seems that fertile or pregnant females would draw off the necessary power, the reverse argument used by Scottish covens. The official explanation is that they hope to embarrass the Rain Gods so that they would give them the gift of rain but a much older logic links maidens and hags with the fertility of the earth.

The symbolic or magical treatment of female genitalia is now rare. In most of the world the idea of women showing their genitals in public is restricted to pornography and is not normally seen as a source of good luck. Most evolved cultures ensure that female genitalia are rarely seen except in connection with childbirth but that in itself might acknowledge their psychic power.

The links between the sabbat and fertility and between witches, fairies and hunters reflect the fact that until quite recently the whole of Scotland shared a similar Gaelic culture and lived by hunting. They stopped only when forcibly disarmed in the eighteenth century. Vast tracts of the country are still designated deer forest, where no other form of exploitation is possible. The universal preoccupation of the pre-feudal population with wild resources in the form of herds of deer explains the preoccupation of the old religion with fertility and sexuality. Witches appeared to believe that their sexual activities generated magical energy which contributed to the fertility of the herds and to the well-being of the community, the family and the individual witch. This primitive idea shows us the first illumination of the human mind, linking sexual activity with the magic of reproduction. Witchcraft represents the magical origin of all supernatural religions. Its focus was ritual sex. The emphasis on the sex act was not an expression of feminism or an enjoyable pastime, but a form of hunting magic which contributed to the capacity of the herds to reproduce themselves, year after year, and continue to support mankind. This magical connection, once understood, developed into a fertility cult which at one time involved the whole community, as it did at Inverkeithing in 1282, and as we will find at the Hebridean celebrations of Michaelmas.

Stone magic. In Lowlands and Highlands alike, dipping a stone, a coin, a brooch, even a human skull in water, was a standard remedy for sick people and sick cattle. Forespoken water was used for every problem. It was widely used to sain houses, boats and cattle especially at Hallowe'en (Black 1903, 142). Sometimes, as at the Holy Pool near Killin, Perthshire, or at the Isle of Loch Maree, the whole person was dipped. A human skull which was reputedly that of St Marnock, was kept within the church of Marnock at Aberchirder: 'The head, which was thought to give special sanctity to oaths taken in its presence, was washed every Sunday and the water was given to be drunk by sick people' (MacKinlay 1914, 76). Up to his death in 1833 people came from a great distance to consult Gregor Willox, the warlock of Gaulrig in Strathavon,

Banffshire, who owned a magic crystal of a type preserved in many Highland families (Stewart 1823, 216-223). Some of his contemporaries said he was an old fraud but he was no more of a fraud than other warlocks and wise men. Stones, crystals and other relics of Gaelic witchcraft survived the Reformation and some continue to serve today. There is a rock-crystal on the sceptre of the Scottish kings. No doubt at one time every important family had its magic stone.

Stones and pennies were not powerful in themselves but were part of a chain of power which passed from the Lady to the healer, from the healer to the stone, and from the stone into the water that worked the cure. Any stone could be charmed, though stones with holes or which were naturally rounded, were more powerful. To use an enchanted stone as part of a cure was a capital offence because it relied on power derived from the Devil for which the stone acted as a transmitter. This power was transmitted from the Devil to the sorcerer to the stone to the water which effected the cure. One of the four wise women tried in Edinburgh in 1597, had a stone that cured epilepsy if tied round the patient's neck and left for five nights (Pitcairn ii, 27). Isobel Robbie, tried in Aberdeen in 1597, worked magic by casting a number of stones into a tub of water, which thereafter were seen dancing (SCM I, 191). James Reid, a sorcerer in Midlothian in 1603, to curse a miller's crops, enchanted nine stones which his client threw on the miller's lands (Pitcairn 421-422). Water does not seem to have been involved.

Gregorson Campbell (1902, 93-94) tells of a round stone with six regularly arranged circles carved upon it, which was long in the possession of a family in Knapdale, and is now in Tiree. It was used for the relief of colic pains and other internal gripings, and was believed to cast a skin when put in the water to be used. It was called *Clach a Ghreimich*, the Gripe Stone. There was a companion stone of the same size for the cure of the Evil-Eye. Several hundred carved stone balls, usually surface finds, have been found in Aberdeenshire and may have been used in some kind of game like bowling or petanque by hunters waiting for the drive to begin. These carved balls are probably from the late Neolithic. Archaeologists plotting distribution maps may not realise that such objects might be regarded as magical objects and move great distances across the country.

'Mary Macintyre, the noted Fort-William witch, a native of Barra, had a stone called *Clach na Leig*, 'the pebble of healing virtues'. It had a hole in it, through which she thrust her tongue previous to making divinations. It was of a blue colour, and by means of it Mary could give young women accounts of their sweethearts, secure for seamen and others who came to Fort William with flesh and other commodities a sale for their goods, etc. There is a stone in Caolas, Tiree, called *Clach na Stormty*, the Storm Stone, almost entirely buried in the ground. If taken out of the ground, cleaned, and set upright, it will cause a storm to arise. The Ardvoirlich Stone (in Perthshire) was used for the cure of murrain in cattle. A person going for it must not speak, or sit, or enter a house, or be found outside a house after sunset. He must take up his quarters for the night before the sun sets' (Campbell 1902, 106).

Rock crystals were very popular as charms and quite common. McNeill (1957 I, 92 ff) describes a crystal ball belonging to the Stewarts of Ardsheal in Appin, Argyll; the Clach na Bhrataich, which belonged to the Chiefs of Clan Donnachie (Robertson); the jewel associated with the MacLeans of Duart; the Glenorchy Charm Stone which belonged to the Campbells of Glenorchy; two more rock crystals which belonged to the family of Mackenzie of Ardloch in Assynt and the charm stone of the Macdonnells of Keppoch, which is also rock crystal. The Stewarts of Ardvorlich still have the Clach Dearg which is not red but another rock crystal. Some of the crystals are equipped with chains for dipping. The Strathardle witches had a garnet stone, now in the Highland Folk Museum, and the witches of the Mearns had a toad-stone, a ball of brown and white marble. The Stewarts of Garth, Perthshire, once owned a prehistoric arrowhead.

The most famous talisman was the Lee Penny, a dark red unpolished stone, heart-shaped, set in a silver penny of Edward I and kept by the Lockharts of Lee. It was used to cure cattle and in cases of rabies. Isobel Young, wife of George Smith, portioner, in East Barns, East Lothian, was tried and executed in 1629 for using witchcraft when her husband's cattle became sick. First she and her servants tried to transfer the illness to a single beast. Her servant had heard that one could bury one of the sick oxen alive with salt, in a deep pit, and have the others walk over it. This was tried once or twice but other cattle continued to die, at which point they decided to go for the Lee Penny which was kept by the Lockharts of Lee, in Lanarkshire. The owners would not give it on loan but instead gave flagons of the water in which it had been steeped for the cattle to drink, which they did, this time with good results (SM 1845, II, 45). In their defense the herdsmen claimed that what they had done was ordinary practice by the best of husbandmen. The outcome in their case is not known – but 1629 was a bad year for those who believed in old practices.

In 1640 when Katherine Craigie of Orkney was charged with sorcery and divination relative to Robert Robson to find out 'whether it be a hill spirit, a kirk spirit, or a water spirit that troubles him', she found that it was a kirk spirit by putting three stones in the fire, then laying them under the doorstep and finally dropping them into a vessel of water. The cure was completed by his wife going with the witch round the Cross-Kirk of Wobuster and Wobusster Loch before dawn (SM II, 49-50).

John Brugh of Fossaway in Kinross-shire, who was executed in 1643, had been taught by a local witch, Neane Nikclerith. He was best known for using water in which he had dipped 'tua inchantit stanes' (Reid 1899, 67, 195). He and Neane Nikclerith once worked together to save the last of a herd of cattle. The surviving animals were driven past a tub of water containing the two stones and each was sprinkled with the water. One beast, which was by then too weak to walk, was pulled out of the byre and buried alive in a hole. All the other surviving cattle were driven over the place and were cured (Reid 1899, 196-7). 'Burying an animal alive to check cattle plague was an ancient Germanic rite. Near Stuttgart during an outbreak, an old woman advised that the parish bull should be buried alive, and, wreathed in flowers, it was led in ceremony into a pit... It was the custom in Karuthen to bury a sick animal alive if plague broke out, and in Scandinavia, a live cow was buried to prevent plague' (Spinage 2003, 371). A comparable story comes from Ardtalnaig on Lochtayside in Highland Perthshire, where 'once upon a time, when a pestilence raged among the cattle on the south side of Loch Tay, the people seized a poor wandering man who happened to come the way, bound him hand and foot, and placed him in the ford of the Ardtalnaig burn. They made all the cattle pass over his body until his life was crushed out. It is said that he was buried in the knoll now occupied by the graveyard' (Gillies 1938, 385). Wandering men were often fairy healers.

Sometimes any stone would do, if the magic was strong enough. In Orkney 'forespoken' or enchanted water was most potent if it was made with one black, one white and one coloured stone – red, green or blue. The word 'Sain' should be pronounced over it before the appropriate incantation. For cattle a suitable incantation was as follows:

> In the name of Him that can cure or kill,
> This water shall cure all earthy ill,
> Shall cure the blood and flesh and bone,
> For ilka ane there is a stone;
> May she fleg all trouble, sickness, pain,
> Cure without and cure within,
> Cure the heart and horn and skin.

Thread magic. Jonet Lucas at her trial in 1597 was accused of carrying in her purse thrums and threads of all colours that she used for witchcraft (SCM 1841, I, 149). Issobell Oige promised two women who had cloth to sell at the market that their cloth would sell before any other, and kept her promise by putting on the cloth a green thread which had previously been used to sew a winding-sheet (SCM 1841, I, 152). Isobell Gowdie in 1662 told a complicated tale of taking coloured threads from a dyer's vat, tying three knots in each of them, putting them back in the vat, and thus taking away the strength of the dye (Pitcairn 1833, III, 605).

Isobel Smith of Banchory was accused in 1607 of using 'a wolne thred and a slewof' or sleeve to work magic (Henderson 1890, 216-217). Elspeth Strachund in Wartheil in Cromar was accused of charming Mage Clark for the fevers with a sleeve and a thread (SCM 1841, I, 189). In Bute in 1662, 'Item that Jonet NcNeill did heale a bairne of Jonet Mans by putting a string with knots and beids about the bairne which the said NcNeill desyred the said Jonet Man to let it byde about the bairne 48 hours and therafter to tak it off and bind it about the catt quhich the said Jonet Man did and immediately the Catt dyed' (MacPhail 1920, 23). Also in 1662, Marjorie Ritchie of Forfar confessed that she had put a curse on the house of John Storrock by laying down a little oatmeal and a thread on the doorstep. Treatment for a sprain in Shetland involved the use of a wresting thread: a linen or black woollen thread with nine knots evenly space; each knot to be made while reciting the common charm for a sprain:

> Our Lord rade, and the foal slade;
> He lighted and he righted
> Set joint to joint, bone to bone and sinew to sinew.
> Heal in the Holy Ghost's name. (Black 1903, 144)

Water magic. Witches and ghosts cannot cross running water; in some cases any water. In this case there is a very simple explanation as the Cailleach or great witch is fire (G. *cail* 'to burn'). When the Cailleach is found in a place-name she is always on the site of an important local beacon. Such beacons as well as being important were dangerous and threatened the surrounding countryside. Where possible, they were sited where the danger of a conflagration was limited by water, on a small island or in a stone enclosure or 'fort' on a headland between two burns which was cut off on the landward side by a ditch. When a saint sits up to his neck in water chanting psalms he is a personified beacon lit on a moat or island for safety.

At St Monans, Fife, this was the method used to sink a boat. First put a tub, brimful of water, in some unfrequented place from which you have a clear view of the boat as she leaves the harbour; then take a wooden cup and float it on the surface of the water about the centre of the tub, and whirl it seven times round (no doubt widdershins), always watching the boat and fixing your mind on the purpose. When you think that the boat has gone far enough from the shore, then whummel the caup so that it sinks, and you will see that the boat sinks also (Simpkins 1914, 108). In Shetland (where the weather was often wild and stormy) it was enough to put a number of wooden cups to float in the tub and agitate the water. Campbell (1902, 21) reports an identical method from the Highlands: 'The usual way witches took to shipwreck a vessel was to put a small round dish (*cuach*) floating in a milk-pan (*measair*) placed on the floor full of water. They then began their incantations, and when the dish upset, the ship sank'.

Lastly, Alison Nisbet in Hiltoun in 1632 cured a woman by bathing her legs in warm water, running three times round the bed widdershins and uttering certain words in an unknown language, probably Gaelic, as well as a charm: 'The bones to the fire and the soul to the devil' which can be understood to mean 'The bones to the bonfire and the soul to paradise', reflecting the old belief in cremation liberating the soul. Alison had borne a child to a married man, perhaps a sacrificial wean (*SM* 1845, II, 62-63), and was certainly one of the good old sort. Hiltoun is a parish in Berwickshire, where Nisbet was a common surname among local witches: Black in his Calendar names five Nisbets, witches in Berwickshire between 1629 and 1698 (1938, 94).

12 BLACK MAGIC: THE BOYLED CHYLDE AND THE FLYING OINTMENT

Deluding the people was reprehensible but much worse things are reported from pagan Scotland.

A common apparition in fairy tales, though not properly a fairy, is the *còineachan* or fairy changeling. He appears as a screaming, withered child, sometimes with long teeth, who looks like a little old man and fails to thrive, no matter how much he is fed. He cannot be burnt or drowned and is an excellent piper, though he only plays when no-one is about, but eventually, tricked in some way to reveal his true nature and above all his great age, he flies away out of the window or up the chimney, screaming abuse (MacDougall 1910, 100-101, 116-117, 144-145).

Almost every word of the Gaelic reveals a pun or a hunting image. The tailor who got the better of the changeling was red-haired. G. *seargta* 'withered' is also 'blasted with heat, scorched', and is related to *cèir* 'wax' and *suire* 'syren'. G. *fiacail* 'tooth' is a pun on *fachail* 'strife, dispute (hunt, deer-drive)', *faicill* 'caution, guard, watchfulness', and *fiadh-cùil* 'deer-trap'. G. *còineachan* 'child stolen by the fairies' is related to *coinneachadh* 'meeting, assembly (hunt)'. In the original authentic text 'a child stolen by the hunters' was a poetic way of referring to a young stag, for deer were seen as the children of the Cailleach who were stolen from her by hunters. This would explain why the changelings are always male. By the sixteenth century it may have referred to real babies given up by their mothers to be sacrificed by hunters.

Ronald Black in his introduction to a new edition of John Gregorson Campbell, *The Gaelic Otherworld* (2005), postulates that the changeling stories incorporated the methods used to dispose of seriously ailing or handicapped children. It is certainly a fact that the symptoms match those of foetal alcohol syndrome but it seems more likely that the fairy changeling, at least in his magical abilities, is a figment of fake folklore. A general belief in otherworldly changelings would certainly justify the use of extreme ways of getting rid of defective children, particularly as they would also be able to recover their own normal children, but it is also possible that the starving infant was destined for sacrifice, that it was an unbaptised child stolen by the hunters or, like Bessie Dunlop's newborn, a healthy child bartered with the Fairy Queen.

The sacrifice of unbaptized babies by witches in other parts of Europe has been seen as a semi-mythical anti-clerical or anti-Catholic practice, whether in the popular imagination or in fact, but this does not explain its prevalence in Reformed Scotland or its association with Gaelic fairy traditions. Infant sacrifice was probably much more common than recorded examples imply but it would evidently be part of the secret fairy doings.

That it did occur is shown by a unique event described by Patrick Anderson (1575-1624) and hidden in the archives until uncovered by Dr Hazel Horn in 2014. He gives no source for his information but it presumably came from the local trial for witchcraft of one Jonet Lindsay in East Lothian. For once one cannot feel much sympathy for the witch.

In general Anderson is a reputable source for the late sixteenth century and reliable where he can be checked. He drew on contemporary local material for the last few pages of his *History of Scotland*, completed in 1596 and gave us the story of the Boyled Chylde. The women involved lived in Lothian, probably in Tranent, but there is no further information about them. The incident is not dated and might have been years before 1596, or it might be total invention. In short make of it what you will. But I think it has the ring of truth. The procedure was well-planned and evidently an established ritual. It marks, as well as any single incident could, the gulf between pagan and Christian practice at the end of the sixteenth century and the gap between public attitudes then and now. Anderson wrote:

> 'One Jonet Lindsay who got a chylde with another wytches husband, fled and went far to the north, and there was delivered. Being examined, she confessed, that she slit the wombe thereof after it was borne and with the midwifes consent, being allso a witch, did boyle the chylde, and made an ointment of the broth thereof, and annoynted them therewith, when they intended to walk invisiblie, or when they inten[ded] to transport themselves as in a transe to any farre parte to there conventions'. (Adv. mss 35.5.3, History, 1596, F.281, r and v)

This can be placed against the background, noted already, of a Gaelic or Highland influence in local witchcraft. From Anderson we also learn that in 1596 several of these Tranent witches were still using Gaelic spirit names: 'the devil gave them marks and signs with other names, as Wallidragle and the like. And[ro] Mudies wife in Tranent was called Knell'. As discussed elsewhere such names belong to the older Gaelic tradition of fertility magic practised by the fairy folk.

The sacrifice of a fatherless bairn was no doubt an important event in such circles but perhaps not very rare. The fate of such children is enshrined in Gaelic folklore as the Fairy Changeling, a howling misshapen object subject to all sorts of cruelty. Such unfortunate infants were apparently stolen but in the case of Jonet Lindsay, the mother knew in advance, probably even in advance of conceiving the baby 'with another witch's husband', what the plan for the infant was and where she could find a suitably discreet midwife. A newborn child was probably thought to have no soul and its brief existence may have been seen as a blessing. Infanticide is only rarely mentioned in the witch trials: an exception is the trial in 1590 of Meg Dow of Gilmerton, also in Lothian, who was convicted of witchcraft and sorcery and 'for the crewell murdreissing of twa young infant bairnes, the ane pertaining to Bessie Rae in Gilmertoun' (Pitcairn 1833, II, 186; Dalyell 1835, 373).

It is difficult to judge the scale of what was always a clandestine activity, at least in Christian times, but there are suggestions of infant sacrifice in several other places. All of them are linked to fairy folk or initiates into hunting magic. Accused in 1615, Jonet Drever had fostered a child to the fairy folk of Westray in Orkney. Elspeth Reoch of Caithness, tried in 1616, had several children out of wedlock, apparently for some occult purpose: she had a child by Magnus Sinclair of Sorne at the request of his wife. Bessie Dunlop of Lyne, Ayrshire, was asked at her trial in 1576 'Why were the fairy folk good to her? What was Thom Reid's interest in her?' She replied, apparently inconsequentially, that when the Queen of Elphen, a stout woman, had visited her when she was still in bed after the birth of one of her children, the Queen asked for a drink and got it. She told Bessie that 'the barne wald die, and that his husband suld mend of his seiknes' (Pitcairn 56). In other words, Bessie was favoured because she had agreed to a bargain with the fairies. The Queen had come to bargain for the newborn child and in exchange she undertook to cure Bessie's husband (Pitcairn 1833, I, part 2, 56). The drink (presumably of breast-milk) sealed the bargain as her milk or its essence would then go to the fairy folk and not to her doomed child.

This commerce would explain why the Church believed that newborn babies were at risk until they were baptised into the protection of the Christian faith before the whole congregation. Until then they had no souls and could be hidden. Highland fairies also abducted nursing mothers, perhaps to act as wet-nurses for the changelings until their sacrifice was needed. In folk-tales fairy changelings (G. *tacharan*) are invariably male which suggests that females were spared to follow their mothers into the religion while unbaptised male children were taken for magical workings. But to have a changeling in the house was a curse which could destroy the rest of the family. How to recognise that such a creature was a fairy and how get rid of it before it did too much damage is spelled out in fairy tales. The truth is disguised in fantasy. These creatures were extremely old, they played the pipes extremely well, they were sensitive to fire and to iron, when thrown into water they became old grey-haired men, they flew up the chimney when thrown on the fire. In Scottish folk-tales we get a hint of the cruel reality behind these fables.

According to a French source, the Devil had rights over the children of his witches (Murray 1921, 174). Those who are contracted to him 'offer him whatsoever is dearest to them; nay, are constrained to offer him their children, or else the Devil would beat them, and contrive that they should never arrive at the state of marriage, and so should have no children, by reason that the Devil hath power by his adherents, to hinder both the one and the other... So soon as they come to be able to beget children, the Devil makes them offer the desire which they have of marrying to his Honour: and with this all the fruit that may proceed from their marriage. This they promise voluntarily, to the end that they may accomplish their designs: for otherwise the Devil threatens to hinder them by all manner of means, that they shall not marry, nor have children.'

Ointments

The fat of a sacrificial child was an essential element in magic ointments. To travel rapidly and invisibly was desirable for anyone out at night on unlawful business. Information about the use of magical ointments is found in Somerset in the confession of Elizabeth Style of Bayford, Somerset, in 1664. She called her spirit 'Robin' ['hunter'] and alleged that before they went to their meetings the witches anointed their foreheads and wrists with oil brought by the spirit 'which smells raw', and then they are carried in a very short time, saying 'Thout, tout a tout, tout, throughout and about'. And when they go from their meetings they say 'Rentum Tormentum' and are carried to their several homes in a short space' (Glanvil 1700, 74).

In Scotland it appears that newborn babies were used in the manufacture of magical ointments whose main use was to confer invisibility or the ability to fly. Jonet Lindsay hoped to become invisible; others wanted to fly. However the use of poisonous herbs makes the experimental use of witch ointments hazardous without the support and guidance of a current tradition. As a German witch said about flying: 'Of course there is an ointment but it is dangerous to use it too often' (Pearson 1897, 23). From accounts of recent experiments it seems the results experienced may be influenced by the desires of the person using the ointment. People who expect to fly experience flying and those who wish to experience sex do so. It is also alleged that rubbing the body with a hallucinogenic ointment such as that brewed from ragwort (*Senecio jacobeae*) gives the illusion of flying, and that the witches' broomstick was a stalk of ragwort (but there are other explanations for the ragwort). As noted elsewhere, Scott was wrong when he said that witches rode on hemlock stalks (McNeill 1957, I, 195). Witches used hemlock as an ingredient in their ointments but they rode on ragwort, as Burns knew.

Recipes for magical ointments are ancient and unreliable. 'The powder of sympathy and the *unguentum armorum* were remedies highly esteemed by the credulous of later centuries for the cure of wounds and injuries. The former is described as composed of various ingredients, and partly of human fat, blood, and *mumia*: and it is said to have been the invention of Paracelsus' (Dalyell 1835, 320-1). We would now define it as sympathetic magic but at the time of the trials no distinction was yet made between the scientific and the irrational.

Before the period of the witch hunts, healers used poisons such as aconite, belladonna and hemlock. In Scotland a charge of killing someone by poison was equivalent to a charge of witchcraft. Most cases involve local healers employed by local gentry to kill their enemies. Janet Douglas, Lady Glamis, who was put to death in 1537, was accused of using poison to kill both James V and her husband. Violat Mar, perhaps one of the fairy folk, was executed in 1577 for attempting to poison the Regent. Also in 1577 Katherine Ross, Lady Fowlis, used rat-poison and killed one person in error but was acquitted. There was a pool of knowledge about poisons among the fairy folk and their friends. In 1613 a family of Erskines from Dun, near Montrose, got a poisonous herb from Janet Irving, a local woman who was by reputation a witch. They soaked it in ale and gave it to their nephews who would otherwise inherit; four of the family of Dun were put to death on the block, for their crime was not witchcraft but poisoning for monetary gain.

Another of its applications was in the making of ointments. The healer Alesoun Piersoun, convicted and burnt in 1588, had close links with the local fairies of Fife: she admitted that 'scho saw the guid nychtbouris mak thair sawes [salves], with panis and fyris, and that thay gadderit thair herbis before the sone rysing, as scho did' (Pitcairn 1833, I, 167). Jonet Stewart of Edinburgh, executed in 1597, used Allessander, red nettles, woodbine and fresh butter to make her ointments and as far as we know poisoned no-one.

In the middle ages there were several famous ointments, ranging from the therapeutic to the purely magical. Patrick Anderson, author of the *History* quoted above, was himself the inventor of a magical pill, the *Grana Angelica* or Scotch Pill. It was pure quackery but sold in vast numbers from 1630 onwards, particularly in London. *Unguentum armorum* or Weapon Ointment was a purely magical ointment which is said to have been invented by Paracelsus (1493-1541). Paracelsus is regarded as a competent physician but he mixed sympathetic magic with what we would now see as orthodox treatments. His ointment contained human fat, blood, and *mumia* and was used as an adjunct to healing. Having magical rather than medical properties, it was applied to the weapon, not to the wound. One might imagine this would raise a logistical difficulty since in most cases the weapon is retained by the aggressor and not by the wounded person. Nevertheless Dalyell states that *unguentum armorum* was 'highly esteemed by the credulous of later centuries for the cure of wounds and injuries' (1835, 320-321). It reflects the ancient practice of necromancy, which gave magical value to the human body and to the recently dead. Necromancy was eventually rejected by all but a few, not because it was irrational or wicked but because it failed to produce the desired effects.

Witch ointments varied in their ingredients and their effects. Professor A.J.

Clark, while in his last post as Professor of *Materia Medica* at the University of Edinburgh from 1926 until his death in 1941, gave three recipes, published by Margaret Murray as Appendix V (1921, 279).

> 1. *Eleoselinum*, water of aconite, poplar leaves and soot. First described by Giovan Battista Della Porta in 1558. The identity of Eleoselinum is not known for certain but it might be hemlock.

> 2. *Sium* or water parsnip; *Acorum vulgare* or sweet flag; *Pentaphyllon* or cinquefoil or tormentilla; the blood of a bat; *Solanum somniferum* or deadly nightshade, and *oleum* – oil or fat. The recipe is attributed to the rationalist Johann Weyer or Wier (1515-1588).

> 3. Baby's fat, juice of water parsnip (cowbane), aconite, cinquefoil, deadly nightshade and soot. This recipe is also attributed to Johann Weyer.

Giovan Battista Della Porta (1558), in *De Miraculis Rerum Naturalium*, II, Chapter XXVI, gave more information about the *Lamiarum Unguentum* or Witches' Ointment.

> 'Although they mix in a great deal of superstition, it is apparent nonetheless to the observer that these things can result from a natural force. I shall repeat what I have been told by them. By boiling the fat of an unbaptised baby in a copper vessel, they get rid of its water, thickening what is left after boiling and remains last. Then they store it, and afterwards boil it again before use: with this, they mix celery [hemlock], aconite, poplar leaves and soot. Or, as an alternative: sium, acorus, cinquefoil, the blood of a bat, nightshade and oil; and if they mix in other substances they don't differ from these very much. Then they smear all the parts of the body, first rubbing them to make them ruddy and warm and to rarify whatever had been condensed because of cold. When the flesh is relaxed and the pores opened up, they add the fat so that the power of the juices can penetrate further and become stronger and more active, no doubt. And so they think that they are borne through the air on a moonlit night to banquets, music, dances and the embrace of handsome young men of their choice.'

Reginald Scot (1584) repeated the second and third of these recipes but according to Murray he was 'as usual, extraordinarily inaccurate in his statements' (1921, 100, 279).

Professor A.J. Clark, then Professor of Pharmacology at University College, London, commented on these recipes (Murray 1921, 279-280). The essential ingredient in the flying ointments is a poisonous alkaloid dissolved in a fatty or oily medium. Aconite, deadly nightshade and hemlock are by the three most poisonous plants growing freely in Europe. Eye of newt and toe of frog were probably added to distract from the important features. The ingredient given as Fr. *ache*, Lat. *apis* or *apium*, is probably not water parsnip, which is inactive, but the poisonous water-hemlock or cowbane. Any fat content might facilitate the absorption of the active elements of the plant extracts through the skin and into the peripheral bloodstream. According to Professor Clark, such an ointment, if rubbed into the skin, 'would produce excitement and irregular action of the heart'.

From other accounts, aconite and deadly nightshade (belladonna), used carefully can produce vivid hallucinations when rubbed on the skin. The recipe published by Reginald Scot in 1584 might have brought this ointment into wider circulation in Scotland but its use was still restricted to the literate and it does not seem that something so powerful and dangerous and requiring such careful use could be within the normal range of folk remedies. One or another of these poisons might have been used to poison elf-arrows which were distributed by local Devils in Bute and in Moray where witches report the successful 'shooting' of people. Isobell Gowdie, whose statements are generally capable of rational explanation, stated as a matter of fact, and as something that she was not proud of, that she shot at and killed several people in her career as a witch with arrows given to her by the Devil. This fits with the fact that witches (ie, fairy folk) had a reputation as poisoners, to the point where poisoning was equated in law with witchcraft.

Aconite has been used to poison arrows in the Himalayas, China and by the Ainu in Japan and is no doubt one of the secrets of northern hunters. Hemlock also has been used to poison arrows; it is probably too dangerous to have been used in any other way. It is thought unlikely that hemlock, cowbane, henbane, water hemlock or fool's parsley were ever used by witches. They are lethal even in minute doses applied externally. Henbane causes blisters on mucous surfaces. The opium poppy is an antidote but its use is not reported in traditional witchcraft. Against this we can place the numerous mysterious illnesses which were resistant to mainstream medicine and attributed, rightly or not, to witchcraft.

Witches appear to have used an ointment to dull the senses in preparation for ritual intercourse. The most appropriate herb for this purpose is aconite (also known as monkshood, wolfbane or women's bane). Applied to the external mucosa it is said to cause tingling followed by long-lasting anaesthesia. Aconite ointment could also be applied by a stick inserted into the vagina, to induce vaginal anaesthesia. Holinshed reports the possible use of such an ointment in 1384, though he does not say the lady flew. Lady Alice Kyteler had 'a Pipe of oyntment, wherewith she greased a staffe, upon the which she ambled and galloped through thick and thin' (Henderson and Cowan 2001, 102).

On the other hand, sources agree that 'flying ointment' was made or distributed by the Devil. In France in 1652, 'when they wanted to go to dances, they rubbed on an ointment given to them by a sorcerer sent by the Devil. Then they went "comme ung vent" to the dance with the others' (Murray 1921, 101). This suggests that it was a learned secret, though perhaps a very old one. Unauthorised use would certainly be unwise and perhaps fatal.

In both cases it appears that the witches were already in a group when they anointed themselves and did not fly *to* the sabbat but flew *at* the sabbat. Again, the ointment was provided by the Devil and it produced a sensation of disorientation and amnesia, as they sometimes found themselves in a place without knowing how they got there. The fairy healer Alesoun Pearsoun confessed that many men and women came to her, and she passed away with them further than she could tell, and saw piping and merriness and good cheer.

A sixteenth-century authority states that the use of these ointments was linked to ritual intercourse: 'Sometimes when the witches seem afraid [the unguent] serves to encourage them. When they are young and tender they will thus be better able to bear the hateful embrace of Satan who has assumed the shape of a man. For by this horrid anointing he dulls their senses and persuades these deluded wretches that there is some great virtue in the viscid lubricant' (Delrio 1599).

More Black Magic

In 1590 Katherine Ross, Lady Munro of Foulis in Easter Ross, was accused of witchcraft by her step-son Hector. She was tried and acquitted in Edinburgh in 1590 but there is no doubt whatever about her guilt. In 1577 she had employed twenty-six local witches to rid herself of her sister-in-law and step-son by making and shooting at various dollies. When the dolly magic did not work they resorted to rat poison, with disastrous results. 'In the first, thow art accusit for the making of twa wax pictouris of clay, in the company of the said Christian Rois Malcomesone [also known by the Gaelic spirit-name *Gradoch*], and Mariorie Neyne McAllester alias *Laskie Loucart*, in the said Christian western chalmer in Tanorth – the ane maid for the destruction and consumption of the young laird of Fowles; and the vther for the young ladie Balnagown – to the effect that the one thairoff suld be put at the brigend of Fowles, and the vther at Ardmoir, for the destruction of the said young laird and lady: and this suld haif bene performit at Alhallowmes in the yeir of God 1577 yeiris. Quhilks twa pictouris being sett on the north syd of the chalmer, the said Leskie Loucart tuik twa elf arrow heidis, and delyuerit ane to the said Katherine, and the vther the said Christian Rois Malcolmsone held in her awin hand, and thow schott twa schottis with the said arrow heid at the said Lady Balnagown: and Leskie Loucart schot thrie schottis at the said young laid of Fowles. In the meane tyme, baith the pictouris brak, and thow commandit Leskie Loucart to mak of new vther pictouris, thairefter for the said persounes.' When shooting the next two dolls with the arrow-head did not work, Lady Fowlis sent William McGillevorich into the hills to get information from the fairy folk about how best to poison the young Laird of Fowlis and Lady Balnagoune (Pitcairn 1833, I, part 2, 196). Then they tried ale poisoned with rat poison. It killed at least two people, not those Lady Foulis had designated, and led to the execution of several local witches (Pitcairn 1833, I, part 2, 185, 191-204). Even when the young Lady Balnagoune and her company were given poison in a dish of kidneys, though she became very ill she did not die (Bain 1899, 163-167). Several of those who had worked for her were executed in 1577-78, including Magie Bawdem, the Great Witch of the Chanonry and Kenneth Odhar the seer, of whom tradition relates that he was burnt on Chanonry Point for witchcraft. 'That Catherine, Hector, and probably Catherine's brother, George, were all involved in occult practices ... seems likely. Catherine and her brother were related to Francis, fifth Earl of Bothwell, who in 1591 was himself to stand trial for witchcraft and treason; and some years later George was accused by King James VI of giving him shelter and support during his escape to Caithness' (Pitcairn 1833, I, 191-204; Sutherland 1977, 136-7). Bain suggests that the mysterious fairy folk lurking in the hills may have been refugee members of Clan Gregor displaced by penal sanctions (1899, 169).

The mock burial. Power was sought in liminal situations, between high and low water marks, at dusk between day and night, at midnight when time hung in the balance and there was a way open between the hidden world and Middle Earth. This is clearly shown by the spells worked on behalf of Hector Monro of Fowlis. Hector Munro, second son of Robert Mor Monro, 15th Baron, accused his step-mother of using witchcraft, but was himself accused, with equal justification. In 1588, he had communed with three notorious witches for the recovery of his step-brother, Robert; and the witches had 'pollit the hair of Robert Munro, and plet the naillis of his fingeris and taes' but Robert had died in spite of these charms. In January 1588 Hector became seriously ill. He sent for Marion McIngaruch, 'ane of the maist notorious and rank Wichis in all this realme', who gave him three drinks of enchanted water from her three famous stones but this apparently did not help him. When Hector himself became ill he consulted his foster mother, Cristiane Neill Dayzell, and Mariaoune M'Ingareach, 'one of the most notorious and rank witches of the country,' who told him that he would not recover, unless the principal man of his blood should suffer for him. This was found to be his older brother George Munro of Obsdale. George came several times to visit the sick man, according to plan, and for an hour Hector lay with his brother's right hand in his left while the magic worked. This went on for five days. Then, an hour after mid-night, the two women went to a piece of ground where two manors met, and dug a grave near the high tide mark. Hector, wrapped in blankets, was carried out of his sick bed, laid in this grave and covered with sods. No-one spoke until Cristiane had consulted the devil. Then the witch M'Ingareach sat down by him, while Cristiane Dayzell, with a young boy in her hand, ran the breadth of nine rigs or furrows, coming back to the grave, to ask the witch 'who was her choice'. M'Ingareach, prompted by the Devil, answered that 'Mr Hector was her choice to live and his brother George to die for him.' This ceremony was repeated thrice, and then they all returned silently to the house, Mr Hector carried in his blankets as before. George must die but Hector was cautious: he must not die immediately or suddenly as this would cause comment. They fixed on 17 April 1588. The magic worked, with a year's delay. In April 1589 George became ill and in June he died, eight months after his father. Hector Munro became 17th Baron Fowlis and Chief of Clan Monro on the death of his brother. In 1590 he was tried for witchcraft but was acquitted, like his stepmother, by a jury packed with his dependents. He died in 1603. (Pitcairn 1833, I, 201-204.)

The seven stones. 'It is, in plain English, a formula for giving one's self to the Devil'.

'The person wishing to acquire the witch's knowledge must go to the sea-shore at midnight, must, as he goes, turn three times against the course of the sun, must lie down flat on his back with his head to the south, and on ground between the lines of high and low water. He must grasp a stone in each hand, have a stone at the side of each foot, a stone at his head, a flat stone on his chest and another over his heart; and must lie with arms and legs stretched out. He will then shut his eyes, and slowly repeat the following incantation:

O Mester King o' a' that's ill,
Come fill me with the warlock skill,
An' I sall serve wi' all me will.

Trow tak me gin I sinno,
Trow tak me gin I winno,
Trow tak me whin I dinno.

Come tak me noo and tak me a',
Tak lights and liver, pluck and ga',

Tak me, tak me, noo I say,
Fae de how o' de head tae de top of de tae;

Tak a' dat's oot an' in o' me,
Tak hide an' hair an' a' tae thee.
Tak hert an' harns, flesh, bleud and banes,
Tak a' atween de seeven stanes,

I' de name o'de muckle black Wallawa!

'The person must lie quiet for a little time after repeating the Incantation. Then opening his eyes he should turn on his left side, arise and thrown the stones used in the operation into the sea. Each stone must be flung singly; and with the throwing of each a certain malediction was said. The informant professed to have forgotten the terms of the malediction but he rather suspected she considered the imprecations too shocking to repeat' (Black 193, 51-52).

A similar procedure is reported from Shetland. 'When it is full moon and midnight the aspirant after unhallowed power goes alone to the sea-shore and lies down upon the beach below the flood-tide mark. She then puts her left hand under the soles of her feet and the right hand on the top of her head and repeats three times, 'The muckle maister Deil tak what's atween dis twa haunds.' The devil then appears and clenches the bargain with shaking of hands (!). The woman is his slave and he gives her power on land and sea' (Edmondston and Saxby 1888, 206; Black 1903, 52).

Initiation by a barrel girth. The indictment of Euphame Macalyane in 1591 says that Catherine Campbell 'an Ersche woman and a notirious witch du-elland in the Canongait, causit ane vther wich quha duelt in Sanct Ninianis Raw [also known as Beggars Raw, a very poor part of this very poor district] inaugwrat you in the said craft with the girth [hoop] of ane grit bikar, turnand the same oft owre your heid and hek, and oftymes round about your heid' (Dalyell 1835, 232; Pitcairn ii, 251). A girth was a hoop from a beer-barrel (there were until recently important breweries in the Canongate) which was large enough to pass over the whole witch from her head to her feet three times or as often as needed.

Initiation with a blood oath. Helen Guthrie of Forfar, 1662, had papers which identified all the witches in Scotland. 'That if she sie any witch in Scotland she can tell whether they be witches or no after she has advysed 24 houres. And that she has thrie papers with blood upon them which helpes hir thus to know witches. And that she receaved these 3 bloody papers 14 yeares since from the said Joanet Galloway. And that she will never part with them until she goe to the fire. And that then she sall burn them hir selfe. And that if the minister wold take them from his before hir going to the fire that he wold wrong himselfe and the burgh and country about'. Joseph Anderson believed that the 'bloody papers' inherited by Helen Guthrie from her mentor in Kirriemuir were probably 'lists of past initiates whose names had been written in their own blood by the leader of the coven when they joined. The method was to prick the finger and use it as a pen. To an illiterate witch such a paper would have a purely superstitious value' (PSAS 1888, vol. 22, 241-262). It is perhaps more likely that the witch made her mark in blood as part of an initiation ritual administered by Joanet Galloway at a time before there was a coven at Forfar.

13: HUNTING MAGIC

There never was a merry world since the fairies left off dancing.

John Seldon 1584-1654.

Today, insofar as they exist at all, witches and fairies exist in different dimensions and yet at the time of the trials, for all practical, spiritual, legal and literary purposes, the two were interchangeable: 'The Devil and the witches entered freely into the fairy mounds, the Devil is often spoken of as a fairy man, and he consorts with the Queen of Elfhame' (Murray 1921, 237). A fairy practiced witchcraft; witches were often described as fairy folk. Witches were described in court and in faux folklore as fairies, and individuals described as fairies were regularly condemned for practicing witchcraft. Several witnesses stress that fairy folk were the same size as everyone else though perhaps more nomadic in their habits (hunters moved around a lot). They seem to have been a great repository of herbal medicine including the use of some very powerful poisons.

The beings now known by an accident of etymology as 'fairies' (from G. *faire* 'to keep watch') began their existence as deer-hunters who practiced the same fertility rites as the witches, give or take some major changes in their circumstances with the advent of feudalism and the decline of Gaelic culture. Much of their current divergence can be attributed to their different treatment by historians and writers of folk-fiction which began in the latter part of the seventeenth century, even before the trials came to an end. Since then 'fairies' have dwined away into a twilight world and are now reduced to tiny imaginary beings fit only for nursery stories in which they have supernatural powers and do impossible things. But though witches also claimed to have supernatural powers and held many of the same supernatural beliefs, they have remained in the light of day. This is largely due to the trials. The transcripts are flawed but leave us in no doubt that witches are flesh-and-blood creatures who are a valid topic for research by serious historians, while the *daoine-sìth*, 'the people of the mounds', have become a supernatural people of small stature, who lived inside fairy mounds rather than in the hills, and are so detached from reality that they are in danger of vanishing altogether.

Scott, who made a study of supernatural lore, believed fairy lore had contributed to witch lore but the link between fairy lore and witch lore is much closer than he envisaged. In the fifth of his *Letters on Witchcraft and Demonology* (1830, 172) he touches on many 'fairy' themes which are also 'witch' themes including fortune-telling; mystical cures; the accounts of Bessie Dunlop and Alisone Pearsoun, both healers with spirit guides or ghosts or familiars, as he called them; Hector Munro, John Stewart and Isobell Gowdie. He concluded that 'These instances may tend to show how the fairy superstition, which, in its general sense of worshipping the *Dii Campestres*, was much the older of the two, came to bear upon, and have connexion with, that horrid belief in witchcraft, which cost so many innocent persons, and crazy imposters, their lives, for the supposed commission of impossible crimes'. It seems relevant that the *Dii Campestres* were worshipped by cavalry with a rite that involved the sacrifice of a wild gazelle, not the usual hen or goat; it is a short step to see them as the Maiden, Mother and Hag, the Cailleach in triple form, worshipped by mounted hunters.

Margaret Murray skirted round a firm identification but recognised that there was 'a strong connexion between witches and fairies' (1921, 238) and devoted eight pages of small print to examples of this connexion, starting with Joan of Arc and going by way of Bessie Dunlop of Ayrshire and Alesoune Piersoun of Boarhills in Fife, to Donald McIlmichall who was executed in Inveraray, Argyll, in 1677 for his association with 'unworldlie' bodies who had danced on the Sabbath while he played his Jew's harp. As so often in this dim, distant and very different world, we may suspect that there is more to Donald's case than meets the modern eye for until recently (and still in some circles) dancing was a pagan activity used to raise the powers and bring luck to the hunt.

If we wish to demonstrate this equivalence of the fairy with the witch, the Scottish evidence from the trials is of particular value as in Scotland the fertility religion practiced by the old Gaelic deer-hunters, survived to c.1600 and was close enough to the surface to provide us with the outline of a structure. There are traces of the same evolution in other parts of Europe but it is also in Scotland that we can see quite clearly the rise of a standard type of coven after c.1620 and distinguish coven magic from older traditions. The argument is enhanced by the fact that certain aspects of the coven – particularly its conversion from a matriarchy ruled by the Queen of Elphin to a subservient group of women dominated by the Devil – are recent (post-1600) innovations. The main argument is that in many trials, most commonly in the earlier period and in the more remote places, fairies morph into witches who behave in very much the same way as the fairy folk. Where did the hundreds or thousands of coven witches come from? Who are they, if not members of a parallel universe peopled by fairy folk?

We can add to the argument for identity by looking at what we can recover of their magical activities. In reviewing Gaelic magic there are two difficulties to overcome. The culture of the deer-hunters as a whole left relatively little information and the little that did survive to be recorded was almost immediately garbled by invented explanations, like Isobell Gowdie's Little Horse. The Gaels of course were not literate and so we are often thrown back on Lowland sources, particularly from trial transcripts, to throw light on what was going on in the *Gaidhealtachd*. One justification for this approach is that many Lowland witches were still Gaelic-speaking c.1600.

The wise women and warlocks of Scotland, whether they are described as fairies or witches, whether they spoke Gaelic or English, whether they lived in the Highlands or the Lowlands, had similar beliefs and used similar techniques. The activities of the coven have their parallels in the activities of the native cult (this is clear from the Oda of the Hebrides.) But the covens represent a terminal phase when English replaced Gaelic, imported book-learning replaced native lore, and attempts to inflict evil replaced the kindly hope of curing and protecting. As covens took over after 1600, the old hunting culture and its religious rites became increasingly redundant so that the old reality faded very rapidly into fake folklore and fairy tales.

Before 1600 and probably for many years after, in the Highlands, as in the Lowlands, most people were practicing pagans. There was a general background level of magic with certain outstanding practitioners. One of the professional witches consulted by John Og Campbell of Cabrachan in Argyll in the 1590s, asked to supply reinforcements, declared that 'syndrie of hir neibor she knew to be perfit in witchcraft, the two NicRicherts, etc. etc.' (MacPhail 1914, 167). In Argyll at that time casting a good charm was a domestic accomplishment, like baking a good bannock. There was a darker side to witchcraft in Scotland.

Many pagan practices persisted in the Highlands and some of them persisted throughout the country until the 1950s and would persist today if the people had survived. People continued to celebrate the seasonal feasts, notably at Beltane (1 May) and at Samhain or Hallowe'en (31 October). Through the nineteenth century Highland housewives continued to devote the last day of the Quarter to saining rituals designed to protect their families and livestock from the evil eye and other malign influences. Charm stones and other magical objects were still used in many places to make healing water which was sprinkled over the domestic animals; tar was put on the horns and ears of cattle as a prophylactic (McNeill 1959, 2, 64). The housewife might also use her own secret charms involving cow's urine and red threads to preserve the health of her cattle and the supply of milk on which her family depended despite the fact that in Lowland Scotland as late as the eighteenth century such rituals could lead to a conviction for witchcraft.

The Gaels recognised three types of magical operations.

Sian or *Seun* (saining) was a charm to protect against danger (Campbell 1902, 58).

Eolas 'knowledge' was for the cure of disease and to avert the evil eye: *eolas a chronachaidh* 'the spell of the counter-acting' involved charms, coloured threads, and dipping stones in enchanted water. A person carrying such a cure was not to speak a word of any kind until he got home again.

Oradh or prayers were for securing gifts and were originally addressed to the Cailleach as a supplication beginning: 'Dear Lady, give us...' But according to Mackenzie (1894, 102), an *oradh* was a spell for evil-working which might be used to drown a foe, win a law suit, deprive a man of his virility on his wedding night, or to provoke unlawful love. Among the types of *oradh* Dwelly lists the death-spell, the spell to silence an opponent, the spell to lock an enemy's mouth, the wounding incantation, the spell to spoil another's brewing, the Friday spell, the charm to induce one cow to take the calf of another, and the spell to raise a storm to drown a foe. He gives no further details, which some might think is just as well. Those who complain about the lack of good Gaelic curses must have overlooked the *oradh*.

To judge by the *oradh* and its capacity for working evil, protective rituals were needed and were performed in every part of the Highlands where the eye of the Kirk Session did not reach. Good-luck rituals involving salt, egg-shells and horse-shoes persist today and divination rites at Hallowe'en continued into the twentieth century. Recorded cases of domestic magic were all worked by women, particularly by dairymaids. There is much less evidence for the masculine equivalent as the magic of hunters became obsolete with the advent of feudalism long before 1600 and dwindled away into nonsensical folk tales, but the fairy raids on the last night of every quarter are a memory of the great seasonal deer hunts, and the Lowland Sabbat retains some of the religious aspects.

As fake folklore replaced genuine hunting lore, the main target of saining became the fairy folk themselves, reduced to small but powerful magical beings with a habit of stealing oatmeal and milk. Dozens of nonsensical fairy tales began to circulate which instructed the housewife how to prevent these pestilential creatures from entering a house and, if they did gain a hold, they provided more nonsensical advice on how to get rid of them again. Like witches, fairies might enter houses and steal the substance (G. *toradh* 'dole') of the food stored there (Mackenzie 1935, 208). In fact the *toradh* was the normal support provided for hunters over the summer and in the great days of the hunts the invasion of houses by fairies over the summer was normal practice. In earlier days beyond memory hunters had been billeted on settled folk between Beltane and Samhain and lived on milk, cheese and oatcakes until hunting began again. Their legendary appetites were normal for healthy young men living active lives.

The features of fairy culture discussed below include dancing, divination, elf-arrows, flying, iron and horse-shoes, lights, milk, night-activity, saining, salt, shells, stealing the substance (*toradh*), urine, the wand, and water magic. The comparison is not exact but witches also danced; they also knew the method of the sieve and the shears to foretell the future; they also used elf-arrows;

they flew, though not through the air; they were superstitious about iron and horse-shoes and egg-shells; they refer to lights at the sabbat; they stole milk from women and from cattle; they were active at night; they stole the substance of food and drink. All these features are recorded in English in the trial documents but their origins are generally easier to explain in Gaelic.

* * *

Dancing. Fairies, like witches, were fond of music, and were particularly noted for pipe music. In the hey-day of the hunt, the great Highland war-pipe was used to co-ordinate the hunt and pass information. Good pipe-tunes are often attributed to the fairies or hunters or to fairy chanters. To fiddle also means 'to hunt' (G. *fiadh* 'deer'). Highland dances performed by horned or masked men or which encircle an individual who imitates a stag are a form of sympathetic magic representing the movement by which hunters hope to encircle and kill the deer. From this it seems possible that dancing was a word for the manoevres used to trap the deer. Dancing appears to be as old as the hills. It is a mysterious word with no close relatives and yet a word cognate with E. *dance* is found in Albanian, Basque, Catalan, Dutch, English, Finnish, French, Gaelic, German, Italian, Portuguese, the Scandinavian languages and Spanish, but not in Greek or Latin.

Since it is unlikely that any one of these nations waited to be taught to dance by any one of the others, such a distribution suggests that Europeans already danced in the Palaeolithic, before Europe was settled and such pastimes became fixed in a place. G. *ring* means 'dance, hop'; Ir. *rinnce teampuill* is a circle dance (Dalyell 1835, 572) which mimics a deer drive. G. *teampuill*, E. *temple*, is a variant of G. *timchioll* 'surround, encompass', used with the specific sense of a circle of hunters trapping deer. G. *teine* (W. *tan*) 'fire', G. *tinne* 'chain', G. *timchioll* and E. *dance* may be remotely related. There is also a link with G. *tannas* 'apparition, spectre, ghost' which is in some sense fire: *feuch tannas dorch air creig* – 'See the dark spectre on the rock' (Dwelly 1901, 931). Was fire seen as a dancing creature? Smoke was certainly seen as a ghostly emanation.

Highland dances and witch dances have much in common but in general Highland dances were for men only while the witch dances or country dances were for couples. Both had magical intentions, encouraging the capture of the deer and raising sexual powers. Both fairies and witches danced to the music of the pipes, or a Jew's harp, or whistled, or sang, or clapped their hands. According to *Newes from Scotland* c.1591, when the North Berwick witches arrived at the church, they 'tooke hands on the land, and daunced this reill, or short daunce, singing all with one voice,

216

Commer goe ye before, Commer, go ye;
Giff ye will not goe before, Commer let me.'

King James was fascinated by this detail and had them sing it specially for him before sending the singers to their death.

Witches in Aberdeenshire danced round a phallic stone or a cross; coven witches danced round the Devil himself, imitating a stag trapped by a ring of hunters. In Krishna's idyll with the gopis or milkmaids, they danced around him, in pairs or in a ring while he played the flute (Ghosh 1965, 104). Witches in France danced in pairs, in follow-my-leader fashion, and back to back. At the end of a dance they leapt as high as possible (Summers 1925, 123). In Lyons in 1608 it was said of witches that 'they dance two by two, sometimes one here and one there, the dances being similar to those of the fairies, who were real embodied Devils, who reigned not long ago' (Murray 1921, 242).

Scottish country dances are based on intertwining movements, reels of two, three and four, circles and wheels, advancing and retiring, all representing aspects of a deer drive. Scottish circle dances normally move to the left and back again with the circle facing inwards. In the Eightsome Reel a man in the centre of the ring imitates a stag by raising his arms, extending his fingers, and performing high leaps while the rest of the set dance round him and back. The ninth man in the Ninesome Reel is the Bumpkin or Devil who traditionally wears a cocked hat, perhaps in place of a horned headdress, as he also dances in the centre of the ring. *Na Tuilaichean*, the Reel of Tulloch, is danced by two men imitating stags. The Highland Fling and the Gillecaluim or Sword Dance are performed by a single man. (The sword of the name is fake folklore: G. *sùrdach* means 'to leap, skip, jump, spring, bound'.)

There can be little doubt that the original dances were much wilder than those now promoted by the Royal Scottish Country Dance Society, a douce and respectable body, founded in 1923 and the epitome of middle-class decorum. But according to a reliable rumour, in its early days the RSCDS had to defend itself against a charge of promoting paganism. Dalyell reports that in his day (1835) only a century earlier dancing was not yet respectable: 'The canon law did not prohibit dancing for personal recreation, but for mystical purposes. Yet, as lately as the year 1723, an assembly of gentry, for such public amusement, instituted at Edinburgh, was denounced as a violation of reverence due to the divinity. Previously, and since that time, even down to 1834, its practice has been associated with profanity' (Dalyell 1835, 573).

The back-to back dance known as Gillatrypes was the most notorious of the country dances. The second element in the name could be G. *treubh* 'tribe, family, clan, kin', *treubhas* 'bravery, valour, feat, exploit', *trùp* 'troop (of horses)', or *trùpair* 'romp'. Gillatrypes was notoriously obscene, by which it appears the men lifted the women in the air, back to back and linking elbows, to expose their genitals. Durer made a drawing of a peasant couple dancing back-to-back and evidently having a good time. In Elgin in 1596 three servant lassies, perhaps Gaelic lassies from the Hielands, confessed that they had been in 'ane dance called gillitrype singing ane foull hieland sang'. Fifty years later, the coven at Auldearn was still dancing Gillatrypes. The Devil always partnered Jean Martin, the Maiden of the coven, whose nickname was 'Over the dyke with it', for this is what he and she always said at a certain point... (Murray 1921, 133). In 1731 Margaret Hoy in Garmouth was disciplined for having assumed 'indecent postures in unseemly dances,' among them Gillatrypes (McNeill 1957, vol I, 143). Today these unseemly dances appear to be forgotten but the Royal Scottish Country Dance Society still dance the Fairy Dance (book 3.6).

The two favourite airs of Auld Clootie, the Devil at Tranent in East Lothian, in 1659, were 'Kilt thy coat, Maggie, and come thy ways with me', and 'Hulie, the bed will fa'. Hule is another name for the devil and both names suggest indecent activity. The tune played by the Devil of the Kirkliston witches in Midlothian was 'The silly bit chicken, gar cast it a pickle and it will grow mickle'. The words could be innocent but were probably not. If not Highland in detail they were certainly fairy dances in character.

Some Highland dances had a more serious ritual aspect, according to Dwelly (1901, 148, quoting Alexander Carmichael, *Carmina Gadelica* 1992, 593). At Michaelmas and at other festivals in the Highlands, a dramatic dance called *Cailleach an dudain,* said to mean 'Old Woman of the Mill-Dust' was performed by a man and a woman while they or the rest of the company sang. The Cailleach is both an old lady and a tribal beacon and whatever G. *dudain* means it is not 'mill-dust' but probably has something to do with deer (G. *dubh*) or fire (G. *teine*). The man holds a *slachdan druidheachd* 'druidic wand' or *slachdan geasagach* 'magic wand' in his right hand and he and his partner dance round each other, passing and repassing. When he touches the woman with his wand, she falls down as if dead. He laments her death but then breathes new life into her, one part at a time, until she jumps up and dances as vigorously as before. The wand is liable to be a phallic symbol as the replacement of a dead animal requires sexual input. Carmichael adds that the music of this dance was 'quaint and irregular' and the words 'curious and archaic' but does not give them, which probably means they were grossly indecent. The tune is still popular with musicians.

There were several similar dances or performances. Carmichael reported that the *Sean triubhas* once contained much more acting than it does now but gave no details (1992, 594; McNeill 1959, vol.2, 113). The name does not mean 'old trousers' but 'gathering the troops, or tribes', the second element as in Gillatrypes. Carmichael names four other ritual dances or mimes: *cath nan coilleach* 'combat of the cocks' *or* 'hunt of the deer forest'; *turraban nan tunnag* 'chase of the ducks'; *ruidhleadh nan coileach dubha* 'chase of the black cocks' or 'deer'; and *cath nan curaidh* 'hunt of the warriors'. Predictably these dances reveal a preoccupation with the success of the hunt.

Divination. Witches and fairies were believed to be able to tell fortunes and to recover stolen property. In prosaic fact, foretelling the future means only possessing the ability to read beacon signals which told of forthcoming events. Recovering stolen property was one of the responsibilities of the Dewars of Glendochart. As hunters have little or nothing to steal, we might guess that they were responsible for locating straying herds of deer and driving them back into Glendochart for the next hunt.

Elf-arrows. Elf-arrows are fairy magic and common elements of Highland folklore, probably because hunters used real arrows. They were used by witches in Moray and in Bute, both conservative Gaelic places with a known 'fairy' population. In 1662 Isobell Gowdie in Moray and various witches in Bute swore that they had killed several people with elf-bolts or stone arrows given to them by the Devil and Isobell also gave detailed and apparently accurate details of how they were made. 'As for Elf-arrow-heidis,' she said, 'the Devill shapes them with his awin hand, and syne deliveris thame to Elf-boyes, who whytiis and dightis them with a sharp thing like a packing needle. Thes that dightis theim ar litle ones, hollow, and boss-baked! They speak gowstie lyk... We haw no bow to shoot with, but spang them from the naillis of our thowmbes. Som tymes we will misse; bot if thay twitch [touch], be it beast, or man, or woman, it will kill, tho' they haid an jack [coat of mail] wpon them' (Pitcairn 1833, III, 607). The flints were probably poisoned: deadly nightshade and aconite are both known to have been used to poison arrows. The use of elf-arrows on Bute, whether for magic or as real weapons, fits into the same pattern. Isobell and the witches of Bute both tell of several deaths which they believed they had achieved in this way. We should perhaps take their claims at face value.

In Bute in 1662 an elf-arrow was used to 'shoot' a child of seven, who died immediately (MacPhail 1920, 19, 23, 27). It seems probable that deer-hunters, who were killing to survive, not for sport, used poisoned arrows and that this knowledge was passed down among the fairy folk to emerge with much else in the witchcraft trials. The sharp thing like a packing needle sounds very like the antler tool used by modern knappers for retouching flakes (Wickham-Jones 1994, 109, illus. 92D). It is generally stated that fairy arrows are prehistoric flints found by chance but Isobell gives a rational and first-hand account of how flint arrow-heads were made by the fairy folk or hunters of Moray in the seventeenth century. Before this is dismissed as fantasy, archaeologists recently found evidence on Eilean an Tighe, the largest of the Shiant Isles and an important way-station for Hebridean hunters, for stone-chapping and flint working dated as recently as the fifteenth century (DES 2004, 137). Flint is as sharp as steel and much easier to obtain in the Highlands. Traditionally fairies carried bows and arrows and spears (Henderson & Cowan 2001, 50), as one would expect of those after red deer. Pictish stones show mounted hunters armed with spears. The Devil handed the arrows to the witches of Auldearn with a blessing which might have come down from the fairy hunters: 'Shoot thes in [the Devil's] name and they sall not goe heall hame', said the Devil. 'I shoot yon man [stag] in the Divellis name, he shall nott win heall hame!' said the witch.

There are some plausible links to Gaelic hidden in the more obscure corners of Isobell's story about the elves and their arrows. She said the elves who made the arrows were 'hollow' and 'boss-backed' which is of course nonsense; and nonsense is a sign of a hunting pun. E. *hollow* may be a translation of G. *cosach* 'full of hollows' for which we can substitute *casach* 'involved with hunting'. G. *crotach* 'hump-backed' may be *cròthadh* 'enclosing in a pen or trap', another by-name for a hunter which is found in MacDougall's faux tale, *Croitean an doire Sheilich*, 'The Humpback of the Willow Brake' (1910, 204). The *doire sheilich* is the forest of the watching, or deer-forest.

Flying is fake folklore, metaphor not magic, meaning 'to go very quickly' (as in English today). Witches in English and fairies in Gaelic both departed in a whirl of wind or were carried by a blast of wind (Summer 1925, 121). A blast of wind was equated with the passing of an invisible host of fairy hunters. The coded meaning of whirlwinds, straws and bean-stalks in English is again derived from various Gaelic words meaning 'to move at speed, like a hunter'. There are two origins for the metaphor: the hunter himself, who was always in a tearing hurry, and the beacon signal which called him and whose light was the fastest thing known to prehistoric man (and still difficult to beat). The witches of Auldearn flew 'lyk cattis', in other words, like a band of hunters responding to a beacon signal (Murray 1921, 106). The Devil as a cat, particularly as a black cat, was the master of the hunt or *cath*. 'To depart in a whirlwind' is a punning way of saying: 'to go as fast as a beacon signal', for G. *iomghaoth* 'whirlwind' can also be understood to mean 'hunt light', from G. *iom* 'going round, encircling (as deer)' and *gath* 'ray of light (beacon signal)'. G. *sìth-ghaoth* 'whirlwind' is literally 'ray of the hunter'.

Ragwort in Gaelic is *am buagallan buidhe* 'gathering beacon of the troop' (G. *gal* 'blast or flame of straw; warfare; slaughter'); the stalk (G. *galan*) is a reduplication. This pun explains why Gaelic fairies sheltered beside ragwort on stormy nights, and rode astride a ragwort stalk when they travelled from island to island, or from Alba to Erin or Man and home again (Carmichael, 1992, note to item 400). In other terms, hunters sheltered beside a fire on stormy nights, and island was linked with island, and Scotland with Ireland and the Isle of Man, by a beacon system. *Senecio jacobaea* (St James Wort) has a cluster of large yellow daisy-like flowers on a tall stalk, so the pun evidently existed in Gaelic and is not an artefact of translation.

Iron was powerful everywhere. It could be used to create an exclusion zone into which the Devil could not enter. The best protection against evil spirits was a circle drawn around one's self on the ground with the point of a sapling or a dirk while saying *Crois Chriosd oirnn!* 'The cross of Christ upon us!' 'Iron, or preferably steel, in any form is a protection, though it is not obvious how or why, against the fairies, – an iron ring on the point of a staff is as good as a sword, but evil spirits are subdued by it only when made into a lethal weapon' (Campbell 1902, 185). The value of iron gave it prophylactic powers which were effective down to the level of a single pin. The minister of Weem once helped a local man defeat the Adversary by instructing him to carry a Bible and to stand within a circle cut with a double-edged sword and with a radius of at least six feet at his next confrontation, thus demonstrating his grasp of fairy magic. This is also how the herd-boy stole the Red Book of Appin from the Devil. The Devil, in an Irish tale, could not cross a circle drawn with a dirk and 'went away in a flame of fire' (Campbell 1902, 185-7). A sword in the bed could protect a mother from the fairies (MacDougall 1910, 196).

But when we read that a mortal could keep the door of the fairy mound open by planting his dirk in the door-post (McDougall 1910, 283-4) we are talking in code. G. *ursainn* 'doorpost' also means 'a muster of hunters'. E. *iron* is a pun on G. *earrann* 'province, tribal deer forest'. To keep the door of a fairy mound open by means of iron was originally a ban on entering the tribal deer forest or *fearann*. Lowland witches used iron pot-hooks and iron cauldrons when working spells – the fact that they were made of iron added power to the process. Five of the Prestonpans coven baptised a cat by putting it 'thryis throw the linkis of the cruik, and passit itt thryis vnder the chimnay' (Pitcairn 1833, II, 237.) (The chimnay must have been a hanging lum in the middle of the house.) On another occasion they drew a cat nine times through the iron gate of Seton (Pitcairn 1833, II, 542). The use of the pot-hook has a sexual implication as G. *crom-odhar* 'the crook of the fireplace' also means 'penis'.

Horse-shoes, G. *crudh an eich*, being made of iron, also represented the *earrann* or tribal deer forest, a defined exclusion zone which was the tribe's source of plenty. In the Highlands, a horse-shoe, which had to be found by chance, had great power to protect cattle against witchcraft (Campbell 1902, 12). The Red Book of Appin advised that the shoe of an entire horse be nailed on the byre door, to counteract witches (Dalyell 1835, 200). If animals in the Hebrides were believed to be under the influence of witchcraft, 'their milk was boiled along with certain herbs, flints, and tempered steel, that the witch, to relieve her own sufferings, might come to touch the vessel' (Dalyell 1835, 323). At Lammas, after lighting a fire with fagots of rowan or some other sacred wood, and dividing the ceremonial bere bannock among the family, the guidman put the embers of the fagot-fire, with bits of old iron, into a pot which he, followed by his wife and children, carried sunwise round the outside of his house and round his steadings and his flocks gathered in for the purpose (McNeill 1957, II, 99).

In the Lowlands and even in England it was reckoned to be the sign of a witch to have a horse-shoe on the door. Elizabeth Bathgate of Eyemouth in 1634 was accused of having 'ane horse schoe in ane darnet and secreit pairt of your dur' (Dalyell 1835, 200), but belief was varied. Aubrey, in his *Miscellanies* (chapter 15) reports that 'A Horse-shoe nailed on the threshold of the dore is yet in fashion: and nowhere so much used as in the west part of London, especially the New-buildings: it ought [Mr Lilly sayes] to be a Horse-shoe that one finds by chance on the Roade. The end of it is to prevent the power of Witches, that come into your house; and it is an old Use derived from the Astrological principle, that Mars is an Enemie to Saturne, under whom witches are. At Mr Ashmoles' threshold the hollow of the horseshoe pointeth into the house.'

Lights at night on the hills showed the fairy folk were active and were left strictly alone. In the 1950s a native of Argyll was making his way home over the hill on a bicycle. But he hit an obstacle, fell off and was unable to move. His front light survived the accident and was clearly visible in the village below but it was day-light before anyone was brave enough to investigate. Fairy lights were either torches or signal beacons such as those lit on the fairy knolls to announce a hunt or to organise the drive. To say that the light at the *sithean* was like the light of day was a compliment to the penetrating power of the beacon, an example of Gaelic exaggeration but also an encouragement to the fire, indicating that the signal was not always as visible or as long-lived as one might wish, and that it was difficult to keep a fire burning brightly in an exposed place. The watchman, G. *faire*, spent many weary hours peering into the dark, hoping to spy a transient glimmer in the dark. A man with enormous eyes which stare into the distance is a familiar motif in medieval carvings. The Kilpeck sheela-na-gig (Weir and Jerman, 1986, plate 5) and the Lewis chessmen are examples. It is incidentally clear from his staring eyes and from other parallels that the so-called Green Man is not spouting leaves but flames. Hunters used torches when travelling at night, probably the same as the torches known as *samhnag* which were distributed to young people as part of the Hallowe'en celebrations and at one time would be part of the preparations for the great hunt-gathering, like their blackened faces and dole of food. The northern lights, the G. *fir-chlis*, 'nimble men' or 'merry dancers', were believed to be the lights of hunters (MacKenzie 1930, 120). Red crotal melted by overnight frost was said to be fairy blood.

Milk was important to both fairies and witches reflecting its importance in the northern diet. The most common and serious allegation against witches was that they had stolen their neighbours' milk by milking the hair tether or destroyed their milk by cursing the cow. Fairies also stole milk: in other words, hunters helped themselves to milk over the summer. Sometimes a witch was accused of stealing milk when in the form of a hare, which is to say, a hunter, which brings us back to the fact that deer-hunters lived on milk when deer were out of season. The breast to which the changeling is so attached is G. *cìoch*. *Cìoch* and *cìocar* 'hungry, ravenous creature' are punned with G. *cìog* 'beast, animal, deer', an old word which is probably also found in G. *giogail* 'follow, pursue', in the *gòcaman* or *gocam-gò* 'spy, scout, sentinel', as *còig* 'fifth' and as *cuach* 'cup' in Lowland place-names such as Cochrane, Cockairnie, Cockenzie, Cockpen, Gogar, and Gogo. A further pun between G. *cìochd* 'breast', G. *cog* 'drink', and G. *cog* 'to hunt', is found in stories about fairy changelings. Once a nursing mother escaped being stolen by the fairies by offering in exchange the best mare under milk that her husband had (Gregor 1881, 62) which suggests that the Gaels milked the mares of the forest ponies. Like stories of milking deer – who cannot be red deer but must be reindeer – which must go back to the Palaeolithic, milking the forest ponies may go back many thousands of years.

Night flying. There is repeated emphasis on fairies, like witches, being active at night and dancing over the hills, often in rings. This can be explained by the fact that the chain of hunters moved into position high in the hills during the night to be ready to drive the deer down to the ambush site at dawn. It was a delicate and skilful operation as it was easy to disturb the deer. The signal to start was given by a cock crowing; which was also the signal for the end of the sabbat. Another parable with the same meaning is that fairies were busy at night in mills where they ground stolen corn. The archaic Gaelic *mill* 'gathering or hunt' comes from the same root as G. *mill* 'lay waste, destroy, ruin, violate', E. *mill* 'to beat severely', E. *mill* 'rob, steal', E. *mill* 'prowl, loiter', G. *milidh* 'soldier, champion, hero (hunter)' and E. *military*. As beacons had to be intervisible, those responsible for creating prehistoric communications systems also worked at night, testing positions and alignments by fire at night and confirming their observations the following day. This accounts for the many tales in Gaelic and in English of churches, chapels and castles, including Columba's church on Iona and Stirling Castle, which were built by day by fairies or by the Devil and cast down again by night.

Saining. In the Highlands the eves of the Quarter Days were marked by protective rituals or saining, by divination, and by the manufacture of ritual bannocks. Campbell (1902, 241) places these ceremonies on the Quarter itself but they must have taken place on the Eve to be effective, and he says so of Beltane (1902, 270). Rowan, elder or juniper was hung above windows and doors (McNeill 1959, vol.ii, 63). Juniper was burned in the cow-shed, tar was put behind the ears of the cows and at the root of their tails, charms were said at their udders, red and blue threads were put on their tails, and various rituals with plants and fire were undertaken. The door-posts and walls, and even the cattle, were sprinkled with urine, perhaps to disguise their scent. The making of butter and cheese was completed, the fire was kept alight all night, bannocks were baked, and requests to give fire or rennet out of the house were refused. The same rituals were repeated at Hogmanay (midwinter or New Year) and at Fastern's Een (Campbell 1902, 73, 242, 257, 270, 278). Much of this has degenerated into meaningless superstition, though fumigation no doubt served a purpose and tar is a disinfectant. Saining as a communal rite is a close parallel of the Lowland coven rituals in its purpose and its dates and both can be seen as surviving features of a more coherent cult.

Salt was used to preserve food and even to preserve hay but it was also used therapeutically. A woman might protect a baking by sprinkling it with salt and was careful to use up the last of the meal to make a *bonnach fallaid* ('remnant bannock') which she shaped by hand, made a hole in the middle (to keep away the fairies) and toasted on a stone in front of the fire. The practical (preventing mould in the meal bin) and the sacramental overlap.

Shells and sailing. Witches went to sea in creels, in sieves, and on dried cow-sherds. A witch could also fly or sail in an egg-shell, G. *ballan-uibhe*, unless the bottom had been punched out of it, a practice which is still observed by the faithful. Highland children with prudent parents were allowed to play with egg-shell boats only at Easter. The housewife in the tale used egg-shells as cauldrons to detect a fairy changeling (MacDougall 1910, 156). The *ballan-uibhe* represents *bal* 'the sun (a bonfire)' and *eibh* 'fire'. To fly in an egg-shell means 'to go as fast as light'. G. *ballan* can also mean 'broom, churn, tub, vat, udder' which explains the use of brooms and tubs by witches for the same purpose. A scallop shell, *slige-chreach*, was used as a cup by travellers or pilgrims. The word is a pun on *creach* 'to plunder, pillage (hunt)' and is supported by a visual pun as a scallop shell shows tracks leading to a central trap, or pilgrim trails converging on a shrine. Another Gaelic word for a shell is *creich*, a pun on *creach* 'to plunder, pillage (hunt)'. A scallop shell was used as a cup by travellers or pilgrims – being flat, it was easy to pack. A scallop shell shows tracks leading to a central destination.

In chapter 15 of his *Miscellanies* Aubrey deals with 'Cracking of Eggeshells or making holes in them'. He quotes Sir Thomas Browne's *Vulgar Errors*: 'To break an Egg-shell after the meat is out, we are taught in our Childhood. And the intent thereof was to prevent Witchcraft: lest Witches should draw or prick their names therein and veneficiously mischiefe the persons, they broke the shell.' Pliny referred to this same superstition. In Scotland the shell was broken to prevent witches using it as a boat, though why this should be important is not clear. A witch might also sail in a sieve, G. *criathar. Sùil na creachar* means 'beacon of the hunting forest', which is a hunting shout. The East Lothian witches said they had gone to North Berwick in sieves: this means they went in a great hurry, like a hunter seeing a light. 'The ruins of North Berwick church occupy a naked, dark, and rocky promontory, over-hanging the sea' (Dalyell 1835, 567), an ideal site for a coastal light.

Stealing the substance or *toradh*. It is said that witches, like fairies (hunters) might steal the substance of the food or drink, the milk from a cow, or a field of oats (Mackenzie 1935, 208) but this is a spurious concept. Isobell Gowdie's testimony makes it plain that the *toradh* was not a supernatural essence but a dole of food and drink raised by the whole community, originally to support hunters, and to which she and the other witches were entitled as full-time pro-fessionals. It was secured by a token harvest and collected later. She describes a ritual in the oat field which the coven is marking their interest: 'And quhan we tak away the fruit of cornis, at Lambes [Lammas, 1 August], we tak an wooll-sheeir, and cuttis or clips onlie thrie stakis [stalks] of it, and plaitis vther thrie rudis togither, and sayes: "We cutt this corner in our Lord the Divellis nam, And we sall haw the fruit of it ham!" And this thryse ower; and so we haw the fruit of that field'. By 'fruit' she means the portion allotted to the coven. She explains that they saved up whatever they took until Yule, Easter, or some other holy day, when they divide it all up and feast on it (Pitcairn 1833, III, 614). In the same context she said: 'When we goe to any hous, we tak meat and drink; and we fill wp the barrellis with owr oven pish' (Pitcairn 1833, III, 603). G. *toradh* 'produce' is related to G. *torachd* 'pursuit, chase' and to *toir* 'pursuit, chase'. This suggests that witches, like hunters, were subsidised by the community and given their share of any food available. Those who failed to support them were open to reprisals, though it is also possible that witches' urine was a prophylactic.

Urine. 'New Year's Day, like the first of every quarter of the year (*h-uile latha ceann ràidhe*) was a great *saining* day, i.e. a day for taking precautions for keeping away evil from the cattle and the household. Certain ceremonies were carefully observed; juniper was burnt in the byre, the animals were marked with tar, the houses were decked with mountain ash [rowan], and the door-posts and walls, and even the cattle, were sprinkled with urine' (Campbell 1902, 241-2). A possible explanation is that a door-post in Gaelic is *ursainn* which also means 'a troop of hunters'. Perhaps when the quarters were the dates of major hunts stale cow urine was used to disguise the smell of the hunters. Today deer-hunters in North America use urine of different types to disguise their own scent. In the Hindu religion cow urine is used in ceremonies of purification. In France in some places the witches used urine in place of holy water (Murray 1921, 148, 248) (or it may have been that the Church used holy water in place of urine). 'The Devil at the same time made water into a hole dug in the earth, and used it as holy water, wherewith the celebrant of the mass sprinkled all present' (Summers 1925, 154). Cow's urine is used in

Hindu ceremonies of purification, even drunk by the participants, and in the Highlands G. *maighistir*, stale or fermented urine, was a powerful protective agent in saining rituals, sprinkled on door-posts, on the threshold, and on cattle (Campbell 1902, 11). Before the cattle migrated to the hills at Beltane they were sprinkled with urine to keep them from fighting, which points to a practical purpose behind the ritual.

Wand. The wand is a symbol but of what? The leader of the coven carried a magic staff or wand, perhaps a peeled shoot of witch-hazel. Thom Reid, a fairy man or ghost living or at least seen in Ayrshire in 1576, carried a white wand. This appears to have been distinct from the staff, stick, wand, tree or broom used by witches to ride on at the sabbat. Druids shown on Pictish picture stones at St Vigeans, Angus (ECMS, 1903, 271) carry wands or sceptres bearing symbols. In the dance 'Cailleach an Dudain' described above the man held a *slachdan druidheachd* 'druidic wand' or *slachdan geasagach* 'magic wand'. This at least confirms the place of a magic wand in hunting or hunting magic. There is also the *bachal* or crook which is carried by hooded hunters on the Papil Stone and the Bressay Stone, both Shetland (ECMS 1903, 7, 12) and again at St Vigeans (ECMS 1903, 240). Bachals are said to be the pastoral crooks of various bishops or saints but they are evidently a pagan artefact used by hunters. Bachals were once preserved in Strathfillan and in Lismore by families of hereditary guardians or *deoirach*, a name which suggests a link with the deer forest or *doire*. The Dewars of Glendochart set out on their search for lost property (herds of wild deer or cattle?) armed only with their *bachal*. It was perhaps a sign of their authority. G. *slat* 'wand' also means 'penis' and is a pun on G. *slad* 'carnage, plunder (of the hunt)'. G. *bioran* 'stick' is related to *bairinn* 'firebrand'. The staff of the witches was also *an lorgan* (Campbell 1902, 6) which means 'tracker or searcher; a dog that follows by scent, bloodhound, foxhound'. It might also be that the rod represents the *simidh* or mallet, also known as a 'priest', used to stun animals before bleeding them. In 1618 John Stewart stated that in Galway the King of the Fairies gave him a stroke with a white rod on the forehead, which deprived him of speech and the sight of one eye for the space of three years. Speech and sight were restored to him by the King of Fairies and his company, on a Hallowe'en night, at the town of Dublin in Ireland and that since that time, he had joined these people every Saturday at seven o'clock and remained with them all night.

Water magic. Dwelly describes a strange pseudo-ritual, a native Gaelic equivalent of fake folklore. He says the *casan uchd* or *caisean uchd* is 'the breast-strip of a sheep killed at Christmas or on New Year's eve, and singed and smelled by each member of the family, as a charm against fairies and spirits'. MacAlpine in his dictionary confirms the practice, saying: 'In Islay at any time, but never for the sake of the fairies'. The meaning lurking behind the nonsense is 'incantation for the hunt' (G. *cas, casan* 'hunting', *uchd* intercession'). Another similar 'smell' ritual was to leave an old shoe to smoulder beside the fire; fairies did not like the smell and who can blame them? (Mackenzie 1894, 128). The water used in certain charms to cure illness was *uisge casan an t-sealgair* 'water of the hunter's feet'; the feet of a cat will do. The dirty water must be thrown out or the fairies will come in to the house overnight (Campbell 1902, 61). The logic is probably that hunters had to wash their feet before they came into a house, to remove all traces of blood. It was bad luck to keep dirty water in the house overnight, as it might attract wolves (who were predators, like hunters or fairies). The lexical link with the hunt is archaic G. *cas* 'deer trap' or *cos* 'hollow crevice' which gives *casgair* 'butcher, slay, massacre' and *cas-cailleach* 'shaft of a fir torch'. Finally, a magnificent archaicc Gaelic curse: *Casgairt ort!* 'May you go to the butcher!'

14: CURING AND CURSING

'Imbecility fosters fraud. Who would have ventured to sell the winds, had not folly prompted their purchase?'

Dalyell 1835, 623.

As noted earlier an appropriate charm was a most significant part of every magical ritual. Given the history of Gaelic in Scotland it is impossible to draw a line between charms in Gaelic and those in English. Some are in recognisable Gaelic, some in decayed Gaelic and others in English and some are recognisable as Catholic prayers. Healing by charming and magic was a professional skill which took several years to master and which forged a strong bond between teacher and pupil. In many cases the line of inheritance was by way of the fairy folk whose language so long as it survived was the archaic form of Gaelic used by hunters and by a few conservative witches. As mentioned above, one of the witches consulted by John Og of Cabriachan, Euphrick Nikceoll roy of Lismore, had been taught by old Mackellar of Cruachan who had learned his charming at the Priory of Iona. One might wonder at the strange mixture of pagan and Christian learning that survived at the Priory c.1500.

In William Mackenzie's introduction to 'Gaelic Incantations, Charms and Blessings of the Hebrides' (published as an article in *TGSI* in May 1879) he says: 'In connection with Charms and Incantations, it has to be pointed out that while it appears to be impossible to get the malific Charms, or such as are identified with what is usually termed witchcraft, there are numerous specimens which are really of a Christian character, and are intended by the invocation of the Trinity to defy evil agencies, or effect cures. In these cases the Charms are forms of prayer — a sort of ritual unauthorised by the Churches. Although the Churches might have laughed at them, those who practised them sincerely believed in them. A discussion on the domain of prayer forms no part of my subject, but I think the ordinary mind may find it difficult to see wherein lies the difference between the simple-minded peasant who, with implicit faith in its efficacy, mutters a prayer with the view of stopping the toothache or curing a colic, and the modern ecclesiastic who, by a prayer, hopes to stamp out the influenza.'

Campbell of Tiree also said he found it difficult to get hold of curses (1902, 57) but we have found a few and how many, after all, does one need? Isobell

Gowdie in her trial in 1662 provided copious examples of malefic charms in a kind of doggerel English but they are probably of no great age, unless translated from the Gaelic, and they are certainly lacking in vigour. From Aberdeen c.1600 comes a drowning curse: 'Lat never sie nor saut watter bear him'. A more complete version is recorded in Breadalbane in 1747 (and no doubt in Gaelic) when Margaret Robertson prayed that Archibald Cameron might have 'ill meeting and ill flitting, that ill might he thrive, and that he might be drowned by sea or water'. She also expressed the wish that 'the Devil might take them in the air that are the instruments of Patrick Tosach's removal' (Gillies 1938, 347). In the notes to *Carmina Gadelica* (volume 2, 1928 edition) Carmichael published the Curse of the Seven Elements: *Deireadh na seachd sionn ort:* 'The death of the seven elements be upon thee!' Carmichael thought they might be fire, air, earth, water, wind, snow and ice.

Nor should we forget the splendid curse with which Isobel Grierson of Prestonpans (1607) faced death: 'May the faggotis of Hell lycht on thee, and Hell's caldrane may thou seith in!' (Dalyell 1833, 33). Her name is given in Lowland form but, like many East Lothian witches, this woman was not only a Highlander but a member of the outlawed Clan Gregor who may have lost their name but still at that time had 'a religion of their own'. They terrified James VI who tried to exterminate the race in an early genocide.

Another good curse is given by Alexander Carmichael in his account of Hogmanay guisers. A guiser is a hunter in full gear or 'disguise' who went round the settlement before a hunt asking for a dole of food. If the housewife failed to provide properly for them, the troop walked three times widdershins round the fire, walked out stamping their feet to remove the dust, built a *carnan mollachd* or cairn of cursing at the door, and intoned the following curse (in Gaelic). As all the animals mentioned are scavengers the implications are extremely unpleasant (Carmichal 1900, I, 157, item 66).

'The malison of God and of Hogmanay be on you,
and the curse of the plaintive buzzard,

The hen harrier, the raven, the eagle, the sneaking fox,
the curse of the dog and the cat,

The boar, the badger, the *brugha* [graveyard pig?],
the hipped bear and the wild wolf,

And the curse of the foul foumart be upon you.'

Dwelly (1901, 169) and other sources confirm that a *carnan mollachd* or accursed cairn marked a house which had been cursed by violent unsained death and the body was exposed to be stripped by the waiting birds and beasts.

In Galloway Gaelic persisted for a long time after the report in 1560 that 'the people for the moste part speketht erishe' (Armstrong 1884, 4, 17). Gaelic charms were still in use in the eighteenth century as we can calculate from an article published in the *Gallovidian* newspaper in 1902 about a witch who had lived at Hannayston in the Kells in the mid-eighteenth century. Her alleged crimes were of the fake folk or fictional sort and can be ignored: she stole butter, caused cows to sicken, sucked their milk from them when in the shape of a hare, appeared as a cat walking on its hind legs, and drowned people she disliked by sinking a cup in her ale-barrel. The interesting fact from our point of view is that at that late date she still muttered her incantations in Gaelic (Henderson 2006, 36).

Once we know what to look for we find Gaelic lurking in many trials. In 1662, when the Duke of Argyll launched a witch-hunt among his tenants in Bute, the natives of the island, like those of the neighbouring districts of Arran, Kintyre and Cowal, were still Gaelic-speaking, as they were at a much later date (McPhail 1920, 3-30). Most of the accused have Gaelic names and used Gaelic charms. Janet Man, who was not a native, complained that Janet McNeill had used a charme to hir bairne, who was extremely sick of the Glack (Sc. *glag* 'a gurgling or choking noise') and that the said charme was in Gaelic which she understood not (McPhail 1920, 4). Margaret NcWilliam confessed to 'haveing the charme for ane ill ey [an evil eye] quhilk she repeated over in the yrish language but that she made no use thair of but to her selfe only' (McPhail 1920, 19). Margaret NcLevin 'confessed that she had ane charme for wristing or brising quhilk she repeitted in the yrish leuage begineing *Obi er bhrachaad* etc. Quhilk proved effectuall to all such as she applyed it to and that she laid the charme in tallow or herbs and applyed it. Item that she charmed John Mctyre the taylor therewith that hade ane sore shoulder... that she hes another charme which is good for preserveing from mischance quhilk she repeited in the yrish language.' This charm began *Er brid na bachil duin.* She put it in water or in a cloth or something similar and transferred the blessing to a material object which worked the actual cure. It appears that *Obi er bhrachaad* is not originally a charm for sprains but for styes (G. *ob* 'spell, incantation', *brachag* 'stye'). Her Gaelic charm for 'wristing or brising' was probably the common charm for sprains in horses found both in Scots and in Gaelic (see below). *Er brid na bachil duin* is a prayer to 'Noble Bride of the brown crook' (G. *earr* 'noble', *bachall* 'stick, crook', *donn* 'brown'). Bride was as popular as Mary among the Gaels (McPhail 1920, 5-9, 19).

* * *

Charm for milk

An old charm for milk from St Andrew's in Fife.

> Hares' milk and mares' milk,
> And a' the beasts that bears milk,
>
> Come to me!

'Mr Kelly tells of a hair rope too, which in the hands of a witch would yield milk, adding that it must be made from the hair of different cows with a knot for each cow. The following verse was sung by way of incantation on such occasions' (Henderson 1866, 21). Worth noting is the fact that the only deer ever milked in Europe is the reindeer.

> Meare's milk, and deer's milk,
> And every beast that bears milk,
> Between St Johnston [Perth] and Dundee,
> Come a' to me, come a' to me.

Charm for affections of the chest

Only the first line of this old charm is given by Campbell (1902, 68-69) in Gaelic as *Air son iomairt cléibh*. The mother of the son of the King of Iver was apparently a snake.

> I will trample on thee, tightness
> As on mountain dust tonight;
> On thyself be thy blackening, dwarfing power,
> Evil and painful is that.
> The charm which Patrick put
> On the mother of the son of the King of Iver
> To kill the worms [snakes]
> Round the veins of her heart,
> Of the four and twenty afflictions
> In her constitution;
> For the water of the running stream of her boundary,
> For the stones of the earth's waves,
> For the weakness of her heart,
> For jaundice and distemper/
> For withering and for asthma

Charm against danger

The *seun* 'charm for protection' (Scots. *sain*), was used for the protection of both man and beast from particular dangers, such as being taken away by an enemy, being drowned, or struck by sword, or arrow, or bullet in battle. It consisted of rhymes or talismans made with parti-coloured strings, or plants; in many cases its nature remains a mystery. The seun was said over cows and sheep when leaving them for the night; it was put round the necks of infants; given by the fairy mistress (*leannan-sith*) to her earthly lover; sewn by the foster-mother (*muime*) into the clothes of a beloved foster-son (*dalta*) who was about to leave her. After it was once given or said, the two, the giver and the recipient, must not see each other again. If they did the charm lost its power (Campbell 1902, 73).

The Creed. As Pitcairn points out (i, 234), the charm used by Agnes Sampsone, the wise woman of Keith, tried in 1590, is a doggerel paraphrase of the Apostles' Creed. It begins

> *I trow in Almychtie God that wrocht, Baith heavin and erth and all of nocht,*
> *In to his deare sone Chryst Jesu, In to that anaplie lord, I trow,*
> *Wes gottin of the Haly Ghaist, Borne of the Virgin Marie,*
> *Stoppit to heavin, that all weill thane, And sittis att hisfaderis rycht hand...*

Charm for arrow-shot. Bartie Paterson, an Edinburgh wise man, tried in 1607, used this charm to cure cattle that had been shot by the fairies.

> I charme thee for arrow-schot, for dor-schot, for wondo-schot, for ey-schot, for tung-schot, for lever-schot, for lung-schot, for hert-schot, all the maist, in the name of the Father, the Sone and Haly Gaist. Amen.

A bedtime prayer. Marion Cunnynghame of Dunfermline, Fife, in 1650 admitted using this prayer when she went to bed but denied using the last three lines (Simpkins, 1914, 94). It begins as a coherent Catholic jingle but the last two lines are a curse. She was accused of using prayers and incantations and suspended from taking Communion (Henderson 1879, 321). Old English *dryhten* 'lord, ruler of a warband' (master of a hunt), cf. G. *triath* 'lord, king, noble'.

> The day is fryday, I shall fast quhill I may, to hear the knell of Christ his bell,
> The lord god on his chappell stood and his twelve apostles good.
> In came Drightine dear lord of Almightine, say man or Ladie sweet

Saint Marie,

Qt is yon fire, so light, so bright, so far furthe fra me;

It is my dear sone Jessus, he is naild to the tre;

He is naild weill, for he is naild throw wynegare,

Throw toothe and throw tongue,

Throw liver and throw longue,

And throw halie harn pan [brainpan, head]...

I drank of this blood instead of wyne;

Thou shalt have mutifire all thy days syne;

The bitter and the baneshaw, and manie evil yt na man knawes.

The last two lines are a curse rather than a healing charm. The baneshaw was sciatica. 'Mutifire' might be leprosy, considering G. *muth* 'change, alter, begin to rot', and *mutan* 'stump of a finger'.

Charm against dangers in war (Campbell 1902, 75-76). This fine charm, recited by an old man in Glenforsa in Mull, includes Christian saints but retains archaic features. It is a charm for a hunter: 'war' was a deer-drive. Dorgill might be G. *toir* 'hunt' and *gille* 'servant, lad' but then who is Dorgill's daughter?

For himself and for his goods, the charm Bridget put around Dorgill's daughter,

The charm Mary put round her Son, between her soles and her neck,

Between her breast and her knee, between her eye and her hair;

The sword of Michael be on thy side, the sword of Michael on thy shoulder;

There is none between sky and earth can overcome the King of grace.

Edge will not cleave thee, sea will not drown thee,

Christ's banners round thee, Christ's shadow over thee,

From thy crown to thy sole, the charm of virtue covers thee.

You will go in the King's name, and come in your Commander's name;

Thou belongest to God and all His powers.

I will make the charm on Monday, in a narrow sharp thorny space [the deer ambush];

Go, with the charm about thee; and let no fear be on thee!

Thou wilt ascend the tops of cliffs, and not be thrown backwards;

Thou art the calm Swan's son in battle, thou wilt stand amid the slaughter [of deer];

Thou wilt run through five hundred, and thy oppressor will be caught;

God's charm be about thee! People go with thee!

Charms for sprains and broken bones in horses. A popular charm for sprains and broken bones in horses or people exists in a Christian version throughout the Lowlands, in a Gaelic version in the Highlands, and in medieval Germany where the agent is Woden. A pagan version is known from the second Merseburg Incantation, added at some time after the tenth century to a medieval German manuscript.

> Phol and Wodan rode into the woods,
> There Balder's foal sprained its foot.
> It was charmed by Sinthgunt, her sister Sunna;
> It was charmed by Frija, her sister Volla;
> It was charmed by Wodan, as he well knew how:
> Bone-sprain, like blood-sprain,
> Like limb-sprain:
> Bone to bone; blood to blood;
> Limb to limb – as though they were glued.

Janet Brown of Markinch, Fife, in 1643 used the Christian version.

> Our Lord forth raide;
> His foal's foot slade;
> Our Lord down lighted;
> His foal's foot righted;
> Saying flesh to flesh, blood to blood, and bane to bane
> In our Lord his name.

A variant comes from Orkney (Black 1903, 144).

> Our Saviour rade
> His fore-foot slade;
> Our Saviour lichtit down,
> Sinew to sinew, vein to vein,
> Joint to joint, and bane to bane,
> Mend thou in God's name!

Thread magic was often used at the same time: knots were tied in a coloured thread and wound round the affected part.

Alexander Carmichael published several Gaelic versions of this charm in *Carmina Gadelica*, his collection of Gaelic hymns and incantations. Here are two versions in the original Gaelic and in Carmichael's English transation (1992, nos. 128-132; II, 15, 19 etc).

Chaidh Criosd air each,
Bhrist each a chas,
Chaidh Criosd a bhan,
Rinn e slan a chas.
Mar a shlanuich Criosd sin,
Gun slanuich Criosd seo,
Agus na 's mo na seo ma 's e thoil a dheanamh.
Christ went on a horse,
The horse broke its leg,
Christ went down,
He made whole the leg.
As Christ made whole that,
May Christ make whole this.
And more than this, if it be his will to do so.
Char Bride mach, maduinn mhoch,
Le caraid each; bhris each a chas,
Le uinich och, bha sid mu seach,
Chuir i cnamh ri cnamh,
Chuir i feoil ri feoil,
Chuir i feithe ri feithe,
Chuir i cuisle ri cuisle;
Mar a leighis ise sin, gun leighis mise seo.
Bride went out in the morning early,
With a pair of horses; one broke his leg.
With much ado that was apart;
She put bone to bone,
She put flesh to flesh,
She put sinew to sinew,
She put vein to vein;
As she healed that, may I heal this.

At Auldearn before 1662 they used a garbled version of this common charm.

Owr Lord to hunting he [is gone]
. . . .
He pat the blood to the blood, till all vp stood;
The lith to the lith [joint], till all took with;
Owr Ladie charmed her deirlie Sone, with hir tooth and hir townge
And hir ten fingeris . . .

They repeated this three times, stroking the sore, and it healed.
In 1650 in Bute, for sprains in horses Archibald McNeill used a diferent

charm with the usual Christian gloss (Hewison 1895, ii, 268 and note). Hewison thought that G. *shiag* was for *sitheag* 'fairy'.

Eolus chuir shiag obi er crissadh er
Chliskadh er shiachadh er att er ith er
Ambhais nach deachie somo
Dhume no mobheach acht so
Leadhas dhia nan dule

'The charm which seven enchantments put

On shivering, on starting, on withering, on joint,
On the death that affected not my man nor my beast
But went under the healing of the Lord of Hosts.'

Charm for sciatica. For the bean-shaw or sciatica the Auldearn witches used a nonsense rhyme with some Gaelic content. Boneshaw is G. *bean-sith*, the banshee or female fairy, in archaic terms, a fire or beacon. E. *manner* might be G. *mainnir* 'fold on the hill-side for domestic animals'. 'Stoor' is G. *stor* 'treasure' is from G. *toir* 'pursuit, chase': a hunter's treasure is the wild herds. A spell for the evil eye in *Carmina Gadelica* refers to 'Three lovely little maidens, born the same night with Christ' (II, 56-57) who are Faith, Hope and Charity. A blue beaver is *dobhar-chu gorm* which translates back as 'noble water-dog' but must mean something else.

We are here three maidens charming for the bean-straw
[boneshave or boneshaw, ie, sciatica]
The man of the Middle-earth, blue beaver, land-fever,
manners of stoors,
The Lord flogged the Fiend with his holy candles
and yeird foot stone;
There she sits and here she is gone: let her never come here again!

Isobell Gowdie used a Gaelic phrase translated as 'bean-stalk' or 'bean-straw' as another way to describe travelling very rapidly; it is a pun for the signal sent by a fire, which also goes very fast. The link with sciatica could be the shooting pain. The three little maidens are the Triple Goddess, one maiden, one mother and one hag.

Charm for fever. In 1623 William Kerrow in Elgin, in Moray, used the following charm for cases of fever (Larner 1981, 140).

> The fever and the trembling fever,
> And the sea fever and the land fever,
> Bot and the head fever and the hart fever,
> And all the fevers that God creatit.
> In Sanct Johnes name, Sanct Peteris name,
> And all the sancts of heavin's name
> Our Lord Jesus Chrystis name (McPherson, 1929, 246).

In Auldearn, Moray, in 1662 they knew a variant.

> I forbid the quaking-fevers, the sea-fevers, the land-fevers, and all the fevers that ever God ordained,
> Out of the head, out of the heart, out of the back, out of the sides, out of the knees, out of the thies,
> Frae the points of the fingers to the nebs of the taes:
> Out sall the fevers go, some to the hill, some to the hope,
> Some to the stone, some to the stock,
> In St Peter's name, St Paul's name, and all the saints of heaven,
> In the name of the Father, the Son, and the Haly Ghaist!

Charm to protect the churn. Hunting charms were put to domestic use. This Gaelic hunting charm was used to protect the butter churn against witchcraft. It is given by Gregorson Campbell (1874, 12). The charm was written by the blind bard Ailein Dall or Allan MacDougall (1750–1829), a native of Glencoe and one of the last of the great Gaelic bards who is saidd to have 'gathered potent herbs on St Swithin's Day and studied magic with one foot in the chimney crook': in other words he was a devotee of the Lady and trained in the old wisdom. Ailein Dall was Glengarry's bard.

> *Badan de ni 'chaorruinn*
> *Thig o aodunn Ealasaid*
> *Cuir snaithn' dearg 'us streang as,*
> *Cuir sid an ceann a chrathadair.*
> *'S get thigeadh buidseach Endor,*
> *Gun ceannsaicheadh Ailein i.*

Campbell gives the following translation.

> A tuft of rowan twigs
> From the face of Ailsa Craig,

Put a red thread and a knot on it
And place it on the end of the sprinkler,
And though the Witch of Endor came,
Allan could manage her.

The hidden text is a hunt-charm:

The hunt of the blaze,
The blaze of the beacon site;
[Give] power to the hunters of the red deer,
[Give] power to the hunters' trap in the forest.

The first two lines refer to the common superstitions of using rowan wood for luck and a red thread to keep witches away from the butter-churn but overall the rhyme barely makes sense. As in most cases of near-nonsense in Gaelic there is a second layer of meaning, for *caor* and *aodunn* in the first line are also words for 'fire'. The references to rowan twigs and a red thread belong either to a coded layer of meaning within the old language or to a bad translation of an obsolete hunting charm which has fed back more recently into Gaelic lore. The Witch of Endor is the Cailleach, who is also fire. In any such a recital, puns referring to fire and the chase form a kind of descant which the educated ear can recognise behind the surface meaning.

Charm against the evil eye. A peculiarity of the Evil Eye was that it could be laid on accidentally, without evil intention, but that it required charming to remove it or to protect against it. This old fire charm was used to protect against the influence of the evil eye by Marget McKirdy of Bute, suspected of witchcraft in 1649 (Black 1938, 57). In archaic Gaelic a reference to the eye (G. *suil*) is a coded reference to a beacon signal, seen as the single eye of the fire. The origin of the belief in the evil eye is no doubt in the worship or invocation of a beacon fire by hunters. Below is Sinclair's charm with its English version and a reinterpretation. Its hidden meaning is once again a prayer for the success of a joint hunt, announced by a beacon signal (*suil* 'eye').

Cuirrith mi an obi er hull
A hucht Phedir is Phoile
An obi is fear fui na yren
Obi thia o neoth gi lar
I will put an enchantment on the eye,
From the bosom of Peter and Paul,
The one best enchantment under the sun,
That will come from heaven to earth.
[Give us] power for a charm for the beacon signal,

The prayer of the hunter and his kindred,
The blessing of the fear-fuinn [hunters] of the district,
A charm for the sacred assembly

More Gaelic charms against the Evil Eye (Campbell 1902, 64-65). This charm for curing the Evil Eye must be made on Thursday or Sunday. It varies with the locality. The following, with slight variations on the part of different individuals, is the version used in Tiree. The words within brackets are omitted when the charm is for a sick beast.

> I will put salve on eye, The best salve beneath the sun,
> [The Son of God made for an angel of heaven]
> Throughout the world, for small eye,
> for big eye for my own eye, for the grey man's eye,
> For the eye of the nine slim fairy women,
> who never ate or digested aught, in yonder hill.
> Whoever has thee under lock of eye, or malice,
> or envy on themselves may it fall.
> On their goods, and on their children.
> On their juice, and on their fatness.
> On their long white ground, on their choicest herd,
> their whitebacked cows, their sheep and pointed goats.
> Each eye and each envy that lies on thee,
> A. B. in the very centre of the east.
> Talkative are folk over thee, Christ has taken away their likeness.
> Twelve eyes before every eye, strong is the eye of the Son of God,
> weak is the eye of the unjust.

Campbell says: 'The five last lines probably mean, that the fairies or elves, whom God has rendered invisible, are speaking among themselves over the sick person, and the succour of the twelve apostles and of Christ is more powerful than the injustice of man. Others use these lines

> 'The eye that went over, and came back,
> That reached the bone and reached the marrow,
> I will lift from off thee and the King of the Elements will aid me.'

'A woman in Islay worked wonderful cures with the following. It is a wretched specimen of superstition, but is given to show how ancient creeds accommodate themselves to modern modes of thought. The ancient charm, instead of being entirely abandoned, became a sort of prayer

'If eye has blighted, three have blessed.
Stronger are the three that blessed, than the eye that blighted
The Father, Son, and Holy Ghost
If aught elfin or wordly has harmed it.'

Margaret NcWilliam of Bute in 1662 confessed to 'haveing the charme for ane ill ey [an evil eye] quhilk she repeated over in the yrish language but that she made no use thair of but to her selfe only' (McPhail 1920, 19).

In 1857 in Rothesay an Irish woman used a charm against the evil eye to cure a child. Water was placed in a bowl, then salt, and a needle was dropped into the mixture. If it stood upright this meant there would be a cure (Hewison 1895, ii, 269).

Charm for a wind. The widespread idea that a witch can sell a wind is fake folklore. Campbell (1902, 19) gives the three traditional Gaelic 'knot'. Like so many magical scraps of obscure Gaelic they were originally hunting shouts, passed around the district to alert hunters when a distant beacon fire was seen.

One knot: *thig gu fòill* 'Come gently', for a gentle breeze.
Originally: 'Come to the hunt.'

Two knots: *teann na's fhear* 'Come better', for a stiff breeze.
Originally: 'Come to the fire of the hunter.'

Three knots: *cruaidh-chàs* 'Hardship' for a storm fierce enough to wreck the boat. 'The red fire is burning.'

Charm for good hunting. This is another example of a hunting charm garbled in Gaelic and nonsensical in English (Campbell 1902, 27). The Mother of the Corpses was the Lady; the corpses were those of her deer killed at the ambush.

Di–luain a dheirich a ghaoth
S thog i orra fraoch us fearg.
Us innis do mhathair mo chuirp
Gur h-e na m-uile a rinn an t-sealg.
 - On Monday arose the wind
 - And gathered its fury and rage.
 - Tell the mother of my body
 - 'Twas the evils made the hunt.
On Monday arose the sharp signal
And gathered the watching men
Give us, Mother of the corpses [of deer],

Power in the whole country of the hunt.

A cure for the Universal Gout: originally a fire charm. *Satan's invisible world discovered*, compiled by George Sinclair in 1685, contains a splendid collection of charms in archaic Gaelic. He said: 'Charms and spells have been first taught to men and women in confederacy with the Devil, many of which are received by Tradition and used by Witches and ignorant Persons too. The vertue of curing, must be from the Devils active invisible application of them, to such or such a disease, as the curing of an Universal Gout by this unintelligible Charm.' He noted the adoption of Catholic prayers as pagan charms. 'Besides this, there are Prayers and Avies among the Highlanders, wherein they think there lays great vertue, as in repeating the Lord's Prayer in Latine thus: Paidder nohter kish in sheali....'

Sinclair's *Cure for the Universal Gout* is in well-preserved phonetic Gaelic. It was originally a fire-charm used by hunters to ensure that their beacon burned brightly. The association with the stabbing pains of gout may come from G. *pèac* 'any long sharp pointed thing'. This interpretation shows 'Etter sheen etter sock' as given by Sinclair, a possible Gaelic version, and its probable meaning.

Etter sheen etter sock
Aodhair sìan, aodhair suaigh (*su* 'gather', *aigh* 'deer')
Roaring fire, fire of the deer gathering (also 'prosperity'),
Etta leur etta pachk
Aodhair léir, aodhair pèac,
Far-visible fire, sharp-pointed or piercing fire,
Wipper sicaan easemitter in shi
Uipear seicean easmaidh an sìth,
Churl of the hide bag [the fire, carried in a leather pouch], a sharp
signal in the forest,
Fo leish in shi corne
Follas an sìth corne,
Send out the news into the deer forest of the traps
[V-shaped deer traps],
Orn sheip twa till ane
Orn sèap tuathaile àin,
Slaughter great quantities, light of the folk,
Curht mach a mainfhore [printed as *mainshore*]
Curaidh mach a min-fheur
Champion of the deer plain of the fine grass.

This prayer has a very archaic feature: it is addressed not to the Lady (who was the personification of fire) but to the fire itself, the beacon which governed all activity within the deer forest, to encourage it to burn brightly so that its signal would be seen far and wide.

Sinclair published two further Gaelic charms. 'There is in some Part of Galloway a Charm for curing a disease called the Ling, in these words, *Cathari Duni Chini Brini*. Another there is, which some use for effectuating that, which others do by casting three knots, *far si far, fa far fay u, far four na forty Kay u Mack straik it a pain four hun creig weil Mack smeoran bun bagie.*' He says 'This language cannot be interpreted' but with a little ingenuity it can.

The Ling, like the Glaick and the Mutifire, is an illness unknown to modern lexicographers but from Sc. *link* 'joint', it was perhaps arthritis. This charm also appears to be in origin a prayer addressed directly to a fire without the intervention of the Cailleach or any of the saints. Cathari Duni Chini Brini might be *Cathair daoine cinnich brionn* 'Watchman *or* Guardian of the people, grow bright!' It might also have begun as a hunting shout: 'A bright fire on the signal post!' (G. *cathair* 'the fairy mound').

The third charm, like casting three knots, was used for relief in child-birth but it appears to be a collection of hunting shouts calling the community's attention to a distant beacon.

> *Far si far, fa far fay* - 'Fire, see fire! The watch sees fire!'
> *U far four na forty kay* - 'The gathering fire in the far distance!'
> *U mack straik it a pain four hun* -
> 'Out of the hunting plain flashes the fire of the hunt!'
> *Creig weil mack smeoran bun bagie* -
> 'Plunder of the hunt in the deer forest of the warlike fire!'

Charm for love. Many of these charms are remarkable but perhaps the most remarkable of all is the love charm given by Campbell (1902, 82) and ascribed to Allan MacDougall (c.1750-1829), Glengarry's bard, a native of Glencoe, who was known throughout the Highlands as Ailean Dall or Blind Allan. I have been unable to find the original Gaelic version from which we could deduce the coded version but even as it stands it has some archaic features, notably the magical qualities attributed to the ashes of human bones. From a legend preserved at Kilmallie on Loch Eil the bones of dead warriors were preserved there prior to cremation at the Annat, probably at Hallowe'en, the feast of the dead.

> That is not a love-charm which is a charm of wisps and straws,
> But one to draw with warmth the love of the man you like.
> Rise early on Wednesday and go to a broad level flag-stone,

Take with you the people's blessing, and the priest's cowl,
Lift then upon your shoulders a wooden shovel,
Get nine stalks of fern cut with an axe,
And three bones of an old man taken from a grave;
Burn that in a fire of brushwood till you reduce it all to ashes,
And shake it in your lover's fair bosom against a north wind,
And I will go twice security that man will not leave you.

Glossary for charms

aodh 'fire'.

aodunn 'face, steep rock', for *aodhan* 'fire'.

aoibhneas 'pleasure, gladness'; *badan* 'twigs' for *baidean* 'flock'. Related words: *badh* 'vulture'; *baideal* 'ensign, standard (signal)'; *baidheach* 'champion (hunter)'; *baiteal* 'battle (hunt)'; *bat* 'club, cudgel'; *bath* 'slaughter, massacre, death'. It appears that archaic *bad* or *baidh* means 'hunt' or 'gathering'. The Great Witch of the Chanonrie in Easter Ross in 1577 was known as Maggie Bawdem – perhaps Maggie of the Herds.

bagach 'warlike'.

caorann 'rowan' and *caor* 'berry of the rowan' are puns for *caoir* 'firebrand, blaze of fire'. The red berries of the rowan were used as fire-lighters. *caoirean* 'plaintive song' is related – the Little Washer (the Queen of the Fairies) sang a plaintive song as she washed the shirts of the dead.

ceann 'head', for *ceann* 'trap'.

crathadair 'churn' for *creachadair* 'plunderer, despoiler, robber (hunter)'; *creach* 'plunder, booty, spoil; host, army (of hunters)'. The important part played by the 'churn' in fake folklore is due to this important pun.

creach 'plunder'.

cruaidh chàs for *cruach* 'red' and *cas* 'hunt'; *fear* 'man'. A fearie-man was a hunter, a man of the beacon-fires.

cu-ibhe 'gathering fire'.

cum 'battle, fight (hunt)'.

cur 'power, virility'.

dearg 'red', also 'red deer'.

Ealasaid 'Ailsa Craig' an isolated rock and beacon stance in the Firth of Clyde is also known as *Allasan* 'place of glory', from *allas* 'glory, brightness' which may be derived from *eallach* 'battle (hunt)'. G. *eala* 'swan', found in early Irish fiction and on Pictish stones, is a related pun.

earrann 'land, district, region, tribal deer forest'.

far 'far', 'fire'; *faire* 'look-out'; *foir-thìr* 'distant'; *four* 'fire'.

fear fui na yren: *fear-fuinn* na earrann, or 'men of the tribal forest' – a body of men who went about singing carols (to bring good luck to their neighbours). G. *fear* 'man' may have been a fearie-man or hunter.

fòill 'mild, soft', for *foil* 'steal, pilfer (hunt)'.

freiceadan 'guard, watch'.

gath 'arrow, a clear sharp beacon signal'.

lar 'mould, soil' may refer here to *lathair* 'assembly' (of hunters).

magh 'deer forest, hunting plain'.

mheil 'of the hunt', G. *mill* 'lay waste, despoil, hunt'.

neoth 'heaven' but also *naomh* 'deer forest (a sanctuary or holy place with restricted entry)'.

ob 'spell, charm'; *obag* 'witch'.

painnthear 'place of snares (deer-forest).

Phedir 'Peter' for *peithir* 'hunter'.

Phoile 'Paul' for *fuil* 'blood, kindred' or 'blood-shed' (desirable in hunting).

reann 'country'.

sid 'place', for *sid* or *sith* 'deer forest, mount, hill'; *sith* 'fairy, hunter'.

smeuran 'berries (archaic 'fire').

snathainn 'thread': probably for *snaidh* 'lop, hew, cut up (butchered?) or

244

snuath 'blood'. Related puns are *sneachd* 'snow'; *snathad* 'needle'; *snio* 'to spin (to entrap deer)'.

sreang 'knot': probably 'trap, snare'. G. *srann* 'to make a whistling noise' and *sreann* 'whirlwind' are elements of witch and fairy lore.

strad 'flash, sparkle'.

suil 'eye' in the old language *suil* 'fire, beacon'.

teann 'come' for *teine* 'fire'.

ua 'out of'.

ucht 'bosom' or 'intercession'.

* * *

The Three Winds is a traditional Gaelic verse linking Connan with fire. Connan is a name for a hunting fire, for the Devil and for lust. G. *aisling chonnain* is a sexual dream. Kilichonan in Rannoch was the site of a hunt muster. Cill Chonain in north Skye (NG 2261) was a beacon site close to Dun Borrafiach ('fire of the deer'), and a broch (NG 2363). A traditional verse links Connan with fire.

> *Ma tha gaoth an ifrinn fhuar,*
> *A Chonnain, cuir 'nar deaghaidh i,*
> *'Na tonnaibh 's 'na taosgaibh;*
> If there be a wind in cold hell,
> Devil, send it after us,
> In waves and surges;
>
> *Gaoth tuath bho ifrinn fhuair,*
> *A thionnd'as am muir ri aon uair,*
> *A Chonnain, cuir 'na deaghaidh,*
> *'na sradan tein' on teinntean"*
> A north wind from the cold hell,
> That in one hour drives the sea upwards from the bottom;
> St Conan push it on in sparks of fire, as from the hearth.

We can convert this nonsense into a punning incantation for luck in the hunt.

'[Give] a light at the beacon site, death [of deer] during the hunt of the fire.

'May the gathering-fire burn as powerfully in sparks of fire as a bright fire in a hearth.'

Glossary *aon* for *ain* 'fire'; *cur* 'power' (common in incantations); *gaoth* 'wind', a pun on *gath* 'arrow (signal)': both are sharp and go very fast; *ifrinn* 'hell', not normally a very cold place but *fuar* may mean 'fire'; *muir* 'sea' for *mar* 'hunt'; *toinn* 'twist (catch, trap)'; *toinneamh* 'death'; *uair* for *ur* 'fire'.

15: A FEW MORE FACTS ABOUT FAIRIES

There are fairies, and brownies, and shades Amazonian,
Of harper, and sharper, and old Cameronian,
Some small as pigmies, some tall as a steeple:
The spirits are all gone as mad as the people.

James Hogg, *Royal Jubilee*, 1822.

One point of entry into the fairy world is by way of the terminology used. The small supernatural fairy or elf was probably brought into Scotland by English story-tellers and has inadvertently created a barrier to understanding as historians find it difficult to cope with irrational evidence. The Gaels liked the new stories, which derived much of their content from the equally fantastic witch stories, and went on to introduce more puns and fantasies of their own. To these inventive tales we owe the common elements in witch-lore and fairy-lore such as shape-changing, prophylactic iron and salt, flying by night, elf-arrows, magic water, malicious cats and magical hares.

And so before 1700 fairies lost their link with reality and became a mystery, although it is evident from the earlier trials that fairyland and the fairfolk were as real as the witches and in many ways interchangeable with them. All of them flew by night, celebrated at Hallowe'en by feasting and dancing, and were supposed to have supernatural powers. What may have been the critical difference was that covens recruited among settled farming folk, while fairies were nomadic or semi-nomadic hunters who lived largely apart from settled families.

Much can be deduced from the terminology, particularly in Gaelic. The authentic native 'fairy' as a term for a hunter arises out of an unfortunate pun on Gaelic *faire* 'sentinel, guard, watch, watch-hill', which takes us back to the hunting band and the fairy knoll. In the Lowlands, fairies might be known as the good neighbours, or as the *seely court*, or the *seely wights*, from G. *seall* 'to see, behold, look', which is related to G. *seilg* 'hunt, chase, hunting'. All these words derive from the same underlying fact: fairies were hunters who kept watch on the fairy mounds or outlook posts. The *Scots Thesaurus* (1990) still lists them as little folk and as supernatural beings; they are neither.

Another pun which may have influenced understanding is that fairies lived in the *monadh* – not a mound but high pasture or remote deer-forest distinguished from farmland. They flew to join the muster. There is nothing supernatural about their origins. But by 1700 fairies whatever they were called had become a fantastic small people who could fly through the air and lived in a world apart from reality.

Fairy lexicon

As noted above we can learn something of witchcraft in the Highlands by way of the words used. The most interesting link is between E. *sabbat* 'a witches' midnight meeting' and G. *sabaid* 'fight, fray, hunt'. The sabbats took place at the Quarters and so, according to John Gregorson Campbell, did the fairy raids or communal deer drives. Witches who attended the Lowland sabbats at the Quarter days and fairies who gathered on the same dates in the Highland deer-forests were following very closely in the footsteps of deer-hunters who gathered on the nights of the full moon to take part in communal deer-drives. In both cases the most important dates were the eve of Beltane (now 30 April) and the eve of Samhain or Hallowe'en (now 31 October) (1874, 18). The main change which confusion in the dates shows quite clearly, was from a lunar (hunting or pagan) cycle to a solar (farming or Christian) date.

The sabbat had a widespread and ancient ancestry. Hebrew *sabaoth* 'hosts, armies' may originally have referred to armies of hunters. Greek *sabai* 'a Bacchic yell' may have been a hunting shout, sent around the neighbourhood to alert hunters to a distant signal. Greek *sabaktes* 'destroyer' was a mischievous domestic goblin who destroyed pots but originally he was a killer and perhaps a hunter. French *sabotage* 'deliberate damage' could mean the damage inflicted by hunters. The French *sabot*, like the English *clog*, would be a block of wood or shackle used by hunters to immobilise an animal. The *sabbat* in the Highlands retained its original form as a communal hunt or *sabaid* presumably preceded by good-luck rituals, including ritual intercourse, and followed by a feast.

The late evolution of the coven in Lowland Scotland and its absence from Highland Scotland, where we find only loosely-organised groups of healers, charmers and possessors of the second sight, may explain why there is no Gaelic term equivalent to the Lowland 'witch'. Or so it is said, but in fact there are several words. G. *baobh* was 'a wicked, mischievous female, who invoked a curse or some evil on others.' The *baobh* seems to have been a solitary charmer with evil tendencies who was not a member of a coven or subject to a demonic pact.

Another Gaelic term is *buitseach* or *buidseach* 'witch, wizard'. Maclennan (1925, 59) says this is the Gaelic spelling of English *witch*. He may be right, as the *buidseach* of Gaelic folklore was an evil hag devoted to raising storms, causing shipwrecks, causing illness and taking milk from cows (Campbell 1874, 54), an image borrowed from the fake folklore of Lowland Scotland.

However if *buidseach* contains G. *buidhe* 'yellow, fire' this would give the word a Gaelic etymology as a name for the Cailleach as a signal-fire. Another word which is more certainly related to *buidhe* is G. *buidheann* 'troop (of hunters)', ie, a band of people responding to a beacon signal. This would give E. *witch* the plausible origin which at the moment it lacks. Moreover, Gaelic *buidseach* is the non-aspirated version with initial B, which must be older than English *witch*, with its aspirate Bh or W.

A third Gaelic term which is translated by 'witch' but which is not at all the Lowland 'witch' is G. *cailleach,* a wonderfully comprehensive word. According to Dwelly it may mean 'woman, single woman, old woman, old wife, childless woman, or a nun'. In origin the Cailleach was a bonfire or beacon, from G. *cail* 'to burn', hence the expression 'Burn the witch!' meaning 'Light the bonfire!' The Cailleach might also be 'a supernatural or malign influence dwelling in dark caves, woods and corries, a coward, a spiritless, heartless man, the last handful of standing corn on a farm, a circular wisp on top of a corn-stack, or a coal-tit'. In the recent vernacular *cailleach* was the normal word for an old woman but in Gaelic folklore of respectable age, she was a supernatural female, larger than life, who controlled the weather and the herds. She was never confused with a human being but when her memory had faded people thought that they saw her in the form of a cat or a hare (both Gaelic puns for a hunter). She was also confused with a witch in the worthless pseudo-folklore of the nineteenth century. In Stewart's collection, *Bean-a-Laggan,* the Goodwife of Laggan in Strathdearn was an evil witch who died after being attacked by a hunter's dogs while she was in the form of a hare (1823, 189-98). MacDougall (1910, 230-233) collected another equally lurid version of *Sealgair Shrath Eirinn is a' Chailleach* 'the Strath Dearn Hunter and the Witch'. *Bean-a-Laggan* was not an evil witch of local imagination but the old hunt-beacon at Laggan. In confirmation we find hunters in both versions.

In an equally foolish story about the tragic drowning of MacLeod of Raasay in 1671 (Stewart 1823, 184-189), the tragedy is attributed to a gathering of malevolent witches in the shape of a gang of cats who hung around the boat. This again is commercialised fantasy, as indeed are all Gaelic tales which depict the witch as an agent of evil or identify her as a hare, a cat, or any other animal. From a more reliable source we learn that the death of Raasay was caused by drink. He had gone to Lewis to witness the baptism of a child of the Earl of Seaforth, and had indulged in a great drinking bout with his host on the shore before embarking. 'Drunkenness did the mischief', said James Fraser (Sutherland 1977, 134) and this rings truer than the witches as cats.

Gaelic *briosag* or *briosaid* is an obsolete word meaning 'witch, sorceress'. The word is also rare, having no evident parallels in English and few in Gaelic. Given the popularity of flyting competitions where barbed insults are exchanged, *briosag* may be 'one who mocks', from G. *brios* 'mockery'. G. *briosaid* can also mean 'belt, girdle' which brings to mind the use of belts in

Scottish witchcraft. G. *eolasair* 'necromancer', from *eolas* 'knowledge, science, enchantment, spell, incantation', *eile* 'prayer, entreaty', is also peculiar to Gaelic.

When we turn to the warlock we find a remarkable thing. A hunter traditionally referred to himself as a robber or thief as he stole her children from the Lady. G. *mèirleach* is one such word. But G. *mèirleach* 'thief' is structurally identical with E. *warlock* as initial M aspirates to Mh, which is pronounced F or V. Of E. *warlock,* the OED says that the word is related to but not dependent on OE *wǣrloga* 'a breaker of an agreement, a devil' and that 'some other word, lost or not discovered, has perhaps influenced both form and sense.' Like 'witch', E. *warlock* is restricted to Britain. We have now found this missing word in a place where OED would never think of searching. The English meaning may refer to his crime against the Lady. The old lost word **mar* 'hunt' is related as it represents the aspirated form E. *war*.

The druid, G. *druidh,* is rare in recent Gaelic tradition but he was a learned person responsible for hunting ritual and for *draoidneachd* 'sorcery'. Andro Man, a learned man who lived beside the beacon of his clan, was almost certainly a druid. According to Dwelly a witch was a *ban-druidh* or female druid. G. *drùidh* 'pierce, drain, pour forth the last drop' is likely to be related and suggests that druids were responsible for ritual slaughter, a line of business that leads on the one hand to butchers' shops, striped aprons and black puddings, and on the other to priestly pretensions, organised religion, holy books, and black masses. The perverted use of the blood and fat of children for ritual purposes may at one time have mimicked the slaughter of young stags, who were poetically described as the children of the Cailleach. Like the death spell, G. *or bas,* it was not evil in origin, as the death so earnestly sought by a hunter was the death of his prey.

The English *fairy* probably owes her origins to the Persian *peri,* a small fiery creature who watched at the doors of paradise. The theme of guarding access to the deer forest by fire was probably already old in the Palaeolithic. The fairy/peri migrated to Europe, perhaps in the baggage of the Crusaders, before the thirteenth century, when the Fairy Queen replaces the Cailleach in tales about the seer or druid, Thomas the Rhymer (Henderson & Cowan, 2001, 8). In England in the thirteenth century the fairy had little competition from native sources but in Scotland hunters and hunting lore survived in places for some centuries more. Since Scottish fairy lore is derived from archaic hunting lore, the word *fairy* was introduced into Scottish tales from outside and appears to be due at least in part to a pun on G. *faire* 'to keep watch'. But the introduction of the English *fairy* into Gaelic folklore displaced the native memories of hunters and created insoluble contradictions.

The Gaels had many other names for these people who lived apart in the wilderness, whom they sometimes heard and saw moving around at night as they went from one site to another, on foot and on horseback. The bands of roving hunters, the troops or gangs of victorious soldiers, brave heroes and champions who owed allegiance to the Cailleach were known collectively and individually as *ruagaire, stalcair, meirge, ceatharn, buidheann, freiceadean, milidhean, sealgair, sìthichean, sithean, sliochd, sluagh,* and *ursainn.* They were also the *daoine-sìthe* or *sìth-bhruthaich* 'people of the fairy hills or beacon sites', *daoine matha* 'good folk', *sluagh math* 'the good troop', and the *tuilleach* 'fire people' (G. *tul* 'fire, hearth'). These names are said to be equivalent but at one time there must have been as much complexity in the ranks of the hunters as there is in the organisation of a modern army. G. *math* means 'skilled, powerful, prepared, prosperous' rather than simply 'good' and matches the Scots term *skeely wights* 'skilled people'. G. *sìthionn* 'venison' provides a link between fairies, fairy hills and hunting. G. *seilg* 'to hunt' also means 'venison'. The Silkies of Shetland were hunters.

G. *Daoin* 'Thursday' is the hunting day (G. *toir* 'to chase') and another Gaelic name for hunters is *daoine-sìth* said to mean 'men of peace'. The peace does not refer to some magical other-world but to the fact that there was a ban on interpersonal violence within the bounds of the deer-forest. Whatever the circumstances, any man taking part in a hunt accepted an enforced truce; in metaphorical or perhaps real terms he left his weapons at the door. This was necessary to avoid the disruption of the hunt by personal feuds. Those who took part in a communal deer-drive came from a wide area and might have to work alongside individuals with whom they had active feuds. Under the *sìth* or peace they could join the hunt in the certain knowledge that all personal feuds were for the moment suspended. This peace survived in the rights of sanctuary within the deer-forest of Applecross (Argyll), within the limits of the royal deer-park at Holyroodhouse (Midlothian), at MacDuff's Cross (Fife), and around the church of Luss on Lochlomondside. There must once have been many more of these sanctuaries. They preserve something of the nature of tribal muster-sites.

James MacDougall (1910), parish minister of Duror in Argyll, divided the fairies of fake folklore into social fairies and solitary fairies. The solitary fairies are easy to define: all of them are the Cailleach in disguise. The hunters who lived in the wilderness were of the social variety, living in green knolls like Tomnahurich. Mortals, if they had any sense, did not get involved but a man who joined them was committed to remain with them for a year and a day, or for ever.

Another solitary fairy of considerable age is the *Bean-Shithe* or female fairy. In some tales the Banshee is a beautiful maiden but in others she has only one nostril, one large protruding tooth, long pendulous breasts and one webbed foot. This is her original ugly shape as a tribal beacon, standing on a pole. She is also found as the fabulous Fachin who had half a head, half a body, one arm, and one leg on which it hopped with much agility. Like all other fabulous creatures which lack an eye or have any locomotory problems the Banshee and the Fachin are the personifications of hunt beacons hoisted on a pole or tree. The Desert Creature of Glen Eitidh (no. 38 in the Lay of the Smithy in Campbell's collection) had 'one hand out of his chest, one leg out of his haunch, and one eye out of the front of his face'. He was a giant, and a wood-cutter, and went at a great pace before the Irish king Murdoch MacBrian, who had lost sight of his red-eared hound, and his deer, and Ireland. Originally the Desert Creature was the Cailleach.

The Banshee is also identified with the sorrowful being known as the Little Washer, 'a female wraith or ghost, usually imagined to be of very small stature, who was seen at a loch or burn washing clothes when some person in the neighbourhood was about to die.' This fiction rests on a pun between G. *brònach* 'mournful' and *bronnach* 'bestowing, generous', epithets of the Lady, and another linking E. *sorrow* and G. *soraidh* 'blessings, happiness'. When Angus Mor peeked over the parapet of the bridge of the Easan Dubh he saw the Fairy Queen rubbing clothes on a stone in the water and singing to herself (MacDougall 1910, 139). The clothes, the washing, the bridge, the name of the river are all hunting or fire puns. G. *caol-shùil* 'peek' is also 'narrow place (deer trap) of the beacon'. G. *barran* 'parapet' is a pun on *bar* 'hero (hunter)' and barr 'fire'. G. *drochaid* 'bridge' is also a hurdle used by hunters to transport venison. G. *glanadh* 'cleaning' is also 'blazing, bright'; *aodaich* 'clothes' is a pun on *aodh* 'fire'; *easan* 'waterfall' is a pun on *essan* 'death', and *dubh* 'black' is also *dubh* 'deer'. With only a slight stretch from Angus to *aonach* 'great assembly', Angus Mor himself is a large hunt-gathering. G. *fùcadh* 'rubbing' remains to be decoded. Stories about a banshee who predicts a death in the family derive from the lighting of a hunt beacon which predicts a forthcoming hunt and the death of deer. The story of the Fairy Queen washing clothes in the Burn of Death is the remnants of an oration addressed by hunters to the Cailleach as the source of all good things, in the hope that she will provide her supplicants with a bright beacon and luck in the chase.

In Moray we can trace a link between the *Bean nighe* or washing-woman and a charm in practical witchcraft, used by Isobell Gowdie to raise or lay the wind on the coast of Moray. 'Quhen we rease the wind, we tak a rag of cloth, and weitts it in water; and we tak a beetle and knokis the rag on a stone, and we say thryse ower: "I knok this ragg wpon this stane, To raise the wind, in the Divellis name; It sall not lye vntill I please again!" Whan we wold lay the wind, we dry the ragg and say (thryce ower): "We lay the wind in the Divellis name, It sall not ryse quhill we lyk to rease it again!" If the wind will not lye instantlie we call wpon owr Spirit, and say to him, "Thieffe! Thieffe! conjure the wind, and caws it to lye"...' (Pitcairn, 1833, III, 607). That this began as a Gaelic supplication to the Cailleach is shown by G. *broineag* 'rag' used in place of G. *bronnach* 'bestowing, generous'.

There are also links with hunting. Hunting leaves few remains and so tends to be overlooked by archaeologists and others but it was a vitally important resource through prehistory. In the post-Roman period the Picts were a Gaelic elite who controlled hunting throughout Scotland; mounted hunters hunting with dogs are to be seen on many of their carved stones. Such an organisation could be, and apparently was, destroyed by disrupting their system of signal beacons. Under the feudal system the native deer-hunting culture collapsed and Picts and fairies disappear. Their disappearance seemed mysterious to those who came later. If feudal exploitation was disastrous for the native nobility it was even more disastrous for the herds of red deer, which had survived under careful management since the Mesolithic and now became extinct in one Lowland district after another.

Even the King was subject to the rules of supply and demand. In 1122 we find Alexander I deep in the heart of the Perthshire deer forests, staying with his Queen Sybilla on a crannog in Loch Tay (Gillies 1938, 35). David I (d.1153) hunted parked deer with his nobles in the artificial setting of Holyrood Park in Midlothian. William I (d.1214) built himself another deer-park further north at Kincardine in Angus. James IV (d.1513) found his sport among the native hunters of Highland Perthshire and sent back venison to his Queen at Linlithgow (Murray MacGregor, 1898, 41-2). Hunting was increasingly restricted.

But it was still important as a source of food in Lowland Scotland c.1600. When Andrew Penycuk of that Ilk (d.1603) succeeded his father, Sir John Penycuk, in 1591, the deed confirming his succession describes one of his feudal obligations as being 'Six blasts of a flowing horn on the common moor of Edinburgh, of old called the forest of Drunnselch, at the king's hunt on the said moor...' Selch is G. *seilg* 'hunt', hence the horn. Drumselch is an old name for the Boroughmuir to the south of the town.

As one would expect, a correct view of who the fairies were and what they did persisted for longest where hunting persisted for longest. In 1677 the Gaelic population of Appin in Argyll still knew for a fact that unworldlie spirits existed in the flesh; they saw unworldlie fairy folk moving around the district and they were bad neighbours, as we see in the case of Donald McIlmichall. His trial gives us our first and last view of native hunters in Argyll as a group of vagabonds, involved in cattle theft – they no doubt remembered the days when cattle and horses lived wild on the hills and were free for the taking – living in perilous circumstances on the fringes of an encroaching English-speaking society, breaking the law but still getting together to dance every Sabbath (MacPhail 1920, 36-38). But they are distant figures, apart from Donald. When the last of the fairy hunters were strangled and burnt or sank into beggary and vanished, they left many questions unanswered. Native ingenuity provided a great variety of answers, few of them with any bearing on reality.

Despite the heavy hand of feudalism we still find native huntsmen or 'fairies' managing the deer-forests of Atholl and Menteith in the sixteenth century. Two traditions suggest that the fairies of Atholl were an organised body of native hunters who acted as forest wardens on behalf of the feudal earls. 'Perthshire was of old a noted district for the intrigues of the fairies. The Clan Donnachaidh, or Robertson of Struan, were not generally favourites with them. During the minority of James V, this powerful clan committed bloody outrages over the district of Athole, at which the fairies were so enraged that they contrived means whereby the enemy waylaid the laird of Struan while visiting his uncle, and basely assassinated him in the presence of his relative' (MacGregor 1922, 25).

Another version of this episode is that William Robertson of Struan succeeded his grandfather Alexander in 1505 and took advantage of the interregnum of 1513-14, after the disaster of Flodden, to raid the property of his cousin, John Stewart, Earl of Atholl, with whom he was at odds. In 1516, when the Duke of Albany had restored some measure of law and order in the kingdom, William was captured with the help of the *sìth* or fairies or native hunters of Atholl, tried by the Duke, and heidit at Tulliemet, the justice seat of Atholl. What he had done to enrage the fairies and justify the death penalty is not explained but most probably he had destroyed the game on which the entire population depended and which the fairies were employed to protect.

That the fairies of Atholl were game wardens whose word had authority in the forest is also supported by the account given by Sir David Lyndsay of the Mount (1490-1555) of a great deer-drive in the Forest of Benchrombeg in the autumn of 1528, organised by the same John Stewart to entertain James V, his Queen, and the Papal Nuncio (who must have wondered what kind of savages he had fallen amongst). The King remained 'in this wilderness at the hunting three days and three nights' and there was killed 'thirty score hart and hynd, with other small beasts, as roe, wolf, fox and wild cats'. No sooner had the King left than the Earl, 'instigated by the fairies', burnt down the splendid wooden halls built for the reception of the King and his guests. The Earl explained that 'It is the use of our Highlandmen, though they be never so well lodged, to burn the lodgings when they depart.' The gesture was perhaps vainglorious; perhaps the wooden halls were built for an exceptional event but by burning everything, hunters made sure that nothing was left to attract wolves and other vermin (MacGregor 1891, 26).

A tradition, part fiction but based on a true memory about fairy hunters in the employ of the Earl of Menteith, also survives in south Perthshire, where Cnoc-an-Bocan or Bogle Knowe on the southeast shore of the Lake of Menteith was the headquarters of the fairies of the whole district. To give them employment one of the Earls asked them to make a road from the south shore to the middle of the Lake, a story inspired by the promontory known as Arnmauk which reaches into the loch from the south side. The Menteith beacon was probably on Ben Venue which was given to the local fairies by the Earl (Marshall 1881, 383-4). The Lake of Menteith has four crannogs or artificial islands, probably of late Bronze Age date. Dog Island is said to be where the Earl kept his hunting dogs (Henderson 1998, 273-292).

Sir David reported that the entrance to Fairyland was in a wilderness, inhabited only by wild animals. This is not fantasy: he was describing the forest of Atholl which he had visited. He knew, as did everyone else in his day, that there was nothing supernatural about the fairies who lived there. That Fairyland was remote and difficult of access was a plain fact and increasingly true. John Leyden who contributed the introductory essay to the 'Ballad of Tamlane' in Scott's *Minstrelsy* in 1802 echoed Sir David when he said that 'The entrance to the Land of Faërie is placed in the wilderness', that fairies were addicted to the chase, were attracted to places where blood was shed, and lived a restless life, moving about by moonlight. The *good folk* of the Isle of Man also lived 'in the wilds and forests, and on mountains' (1802, II, 291). These are plain facts plainly stated but the fable was more popular. Once launched it travelled as fast as a story-teller could walk from one township to the next, taking its newly-invented facts with it.

In Ireland there were legendary deer-hunters known as the *fianaibh* or Fian. After Brian Borumha had defeated the Danes in 1000 A.D, he recovered many treasures that had been plundered from places of importance. They included *diamhraibh dichealta ag fianaibh no ag sithcuiraib* – 'sanctuaries and solitudes belonging to the Fian or men of the *sith*' (MacRitchie 1890, 81-2). The bard glosses them as *sithcuiraibh* or fairy folk. G. *diamhladh* 'place of refuge, sanctuary' is synonymous with *dichealtair* 'deer-forest'. From this it is evident that the treasures recovered by Brian Borumha were the deer-forests.

This all tends to support the view that the *sith* or fairies of Scotland were guardians of the forest land, beyond agricultural settlement. They were the expert hunters who managed the beacon systems and the deer-drives. As farming encroached year by year on the wilderness and the feudal system of land-holding ran roughshod over native traditions, accounting for the fairies' reported aversion to ploughed soil, hunters were pushed into more and more remote regions or turned to farming or fishing. But deer had been essential to the survival of the people through the winter months and their loss spelled disaster for Gaelic society. This early feudal clearance converted a whole population of native men into landless serfs.

There is no mention in any of the trials of the fact that fairies were hunters, though it is implied by the fact that gangs of men under a master man had meetings with fairy women in desert places. Fairy men themselves were seldom targeted, Andro Man in Banff being an exception. Most of the fairy folk mentioned in the trials were solitary women: healers, vagabonds, or individuals of doubtful status who met with the fairies, like Jean Campbell of Rothesay. Many healers were condemned to death for confessing that the source of their knowledge was an unworldly fairy teacher. Only Andro Man and Alesoun Piersoun give a detailed account of fairy doings and both statements have become very confused during the process of transcription. The sense of a hidden but concrete reality is supported by the fact that all those described as fairies tell a similar story and yet only a few admit to having contact with fairies beyond their own districts. There is a sense of a very old religious and practical reality passed on by oral teaching among an elite and easily corrupted when the practice was no longer relevant. Only their relationships with ghosts takes us out of the normal.

When we equate fairies with hunters it becomes easy to perceive the alternative reality behind the false lore. It is like an optical illusion: nothing changes but we see an entirely different picture. Fairyland was the deer-forest, the desert place beyond settlement land, the rough bounds, a wild place which at the same time was the source of goodness and wealth, just as the Death Hag, when embraced in the sexual act, was revealed as a beautiful and generous maiden who gave hunters everything they needed. Fairies were not magical small creatures but bands of peripatetic deer-hunters who lived bachelor lives with 'neither wif ne childe' (though not without sex). The knolls or outlook posts of fairyland, the *sìthean* or *tomhan,* survive in their hundreds throughout Scotland and are discussed elsewhere. Most of them are unaltered natural features, of no interest to archaeologists, but The Downie Hill, the *sìthean* of Appin used by Donald McIlmichel's *unworldlie* folk in 1677, and hundreds of others can still be found on the map. The *sìth* or *faire* or watchman on his mound watched ceaselessly for a distant beacon announcing a hunt. Fairies lived in the hills but not inside the hills.

Settled folk retained vivid but confused memories of fairies gathering and dancing on the hills at night and knew to stay well out of the way, if they understood nothing more about it. In fact hunters had once relied on the light of the moon or on torches, as they got into position for the deer-drive that began at dawn, when the crowing of a cock dispelled sorcerers and en- chantments. This was not the farmyard cock but the black cock of the high tops, *an coileach dubh* – a pun on 'deer forest' (MacDougall 1910, 228) – and it gave the signal to begin the drive. Men and married women lived over the winter in separate communities, though several women who lived for longer or shorter periods in the deer-forests (in Fairyland) are mentioned in the trials, from Alesoun Piersoun onwards. Bessie Dunlop in 1576 refused to join the fairies despite their promise of power and knowledge since 'sche duelt with her awin husband and bairnis and culd nocht leif thame' (Murray 1921, 44, 241). She described the fairy troop as consisting of eight women and four men, the men dressed like gentlemen and the women with plaids and very presentable (Pitcairn, 1833, I, 52-53).

Isobell Gowdie (1662) was an initiated and experienced witch who had spent time in Fairyland. There was nothing imaginary about her experience. Her coven went one day from Auldearn to the far side of the Meikle Burn, expecting to meet up with a second coven there but found the other coven had gone ahead of them to the Downie-hills (NH 967582) near Darnaway Castle, seat of the Earls of Moray. To quote RCAHMS, this hill is 'an afforested knoll commanding extensive views in all directions' (Canmore Archive). Isobell's testimony states that the Auldearn coven also 'went in to the Downie-hillis; the hill opened, and we came to an fair and large braw rowme in the day tyme' (Pitcairn 1833, III, 603, 617) but the words 'the hill opened' are meaningless and presumably interpolated by the clerk, as can be deduced elsewhere in Isobell's testimony.

If you go east from Auldearn and cross the Meikle Burn, you enter the extensive park surrounding Darnaway Castle which in 1662 was the property of Alexander Stewart, fourth Earl of Moray, who seems to have been well-disposed towards the Auldearn witches. Isobell does not name the Quene and King of Faerie who met them there but she describes them in clear detail, down to the generous amount of food they provided. 'I was in the Downie-hillis, and got meat ther from the Qwein of Fearrie, mor than I could eat. The Qwein of Fearrie is brawlie clothed in whyt linens, and in whyt and browne cloathes, &c; and the King of Fearrie is a braw man, weill favoured, and broad faced, &c.' (Pitcairn, 1833, III, 604, 611).

As for fairies living inside hills, we still talk about 'going into the hills' without implying any troglodyte activity. Fairyland was the wilderness, the uplands beyond settlement, the deer forest. A 'rowme' was not a chamber in a house but an extent of grazing or a holding of land.

The presence at Auldearn of an active band of fairy hunters as late as 1662 goes far to explain the existence of the minor 'devils' Isobell describes in such compelling detail: 'There are thirteen in each coven, and each one of us has a Sprit to wait upon us'. Several more waited upon the Master Devil who was bigger and more awful than the minor ones. She knew these spirits in real life 'when they appear like a man'. Their costumes were black, yellow, sea-green, grass-green, or dun which suggests tartan plaids in 'hunting' colours. The names she gives are in English but they are heroic names: the Red Reaver, Robert a Jakis (with the coat of mail), Thomas a Fearie, the Roaring Lion, Thieffe of Hell and Robert the Rule who commands the rest (Pitcairn 1833, III, 613-618). Minor devils who partner the witches were a feature of certain French covens (Murray 1921, 228) and bands of fairy men are mentioned elsewhere in Scotland, in Bute, Aberdour in Fife, and Caithness.

Witches and fairies were both active at the Quarters of the year, both held their meetings at night, and events at a fairy gathering and at a witches' sabbat were very similar as far as one can judge in the absence of detailed information about the fairy raids; but we know that a successful hunt ended with a feast. Witches shared a communal meal with the best available food and drink, sang, danced, and enjoyed themselves while at certain times of year, at fairy mounds and in one case inside a mill, one could hear the sounds of great merriment, with music, dancing, fiddling, piping, singing, laughing and conversation (Douglas 1894, 124). Alesoun Peirsoune described the fairy folk as men and women who enjoyed piping, merriment and good cheer (Pitcairn

1833, I, 161-165). Sexual intercourse can be assumed by analogy with the sabbat and also deduced from stories of women who lived for a while with the hunters, from ballads in which the Queen elopes with her lover to Fairyland, and from the Michaelmas celebration or Oda in the Hebrides.

The most important of the sabbat feasts for both hunters and witches was Hallowe'en, 31 October, the eve of the Quarter, the start of winter, the best time to work magic, and a popular bonfire festival banned repeatedly by the Church. Now the date of Hallowe'en is fixed by the solar calendar but originally it was a lunar date calculated by reference to the autumn equinox (20 September) as Easter is still calculated by reference to the spring equinox (20 March). The Harvest Moon is the first full moon after the autumnal equinox, and the Hunter's Moon, which marked the opening of the hunting season and the old New Year, is the next again, at latest 29 October.

The Hallowe'en celebration had both practical and religious aspects. On the practical side the bonfire announced the change in the season and the forthcoming hunt. Its religious purpose was to bring good luck to the hunters by the usual sexual rites but of even greater importance, it was the time when the bones of the dead were cremated, freeing their ghosts to rise to paradise in the smoke. Worship of the dead persists in the Christian calendar as All-Souls (1 November) and All-Saints (2 November) and as requiem masses. Ghosts, spirits, dwarves, elves and fairies are all references to the supernatural aspects of hunting lore. Hallowe'en lanterns are now made of turnips or pumpkins but these are recent crops. Not long ago the lanterns were skulls, set aside because they do not burn well. The belief in ghosts evolved out of the use of dried bones as fuel in sub-Arctic climates. In Britain the practice persisted at important festivals, particularly at Hallowe'en and at Midsummer. Fairies, we know, had a particular concern for ghosts: Andro Man, burnt in 1598, told the Court that he 'kennis sindrie deid men in thair cumpanie [of the fairies] and that the kyng that deit in Flowdoun and Thomas Rymour is their' (SCM 1841, I, 121). The religious aspects of this gathering might explain the stern line taken by the Kirk when faced with what now appear to be harmless rural romps, and why witches seem to have been unaffected by the prospect of being burnt to ashes: it was the culmination of their religious beliefs.

One way of testing the proposal that fairies were hunters is to see what happens when we use it to interpret a traditional fairy tale. Most folk tales retain very little original material – invention has gone too far – but James MacDougall published one story which is close to reality (1910, 192-195). It is located in Morven. He called it *Na Sithichean ag Connsachadh*, 'The Fairies Wrangling', which we can translate as 'The Fairies Hunting', applying the general rule about a battle being a metaphor for a hunt. 'Some people of old believed that the fairies gathered now and again from every corner of the surrounding district to hold a meeting in an appointed place, such as Knock in Morven, and that one troop of them would side with the people of the farm, where their Fairy Knoll was situated, against a troop from any other farm or district ... Once a troop came from Mull to keep tryst with another troop from Morven, but on that occasion they met near the river of Acharn, instead of the usual place in Knock'. This is a statement of fact; troops of hunters came from Mull to hunt with local troops and while they waited at the muster site they played team games such as shinty. The story-teller needed to explain the wrangling and did so by inventing a man called Young John and a dispute about which team he was to join. The end of the story is that Young John went on his way and the fairy troops went to Acharn to dance.

In rational terms *sithichean* are hunters. G. *connsachadh* 'dispute, quarrel' is a communal deer-drive. Apart from the general rule that a confrontation or a battle is a hunt, G. *sach* has the same meaning as E. *sack* 'rob, pillage' and is related to G. *sac,* E. *sack* 'a bag'. Hunters on this occasion mustered near the river of Acharn where there was a beacon site: 'John' is phonetically equivalent to G. *aodhan* 'fire'. We learn that it was normal for hunters to travel considerable distances by land and by water to gather at prearranged places to take part in communal hunts and we might even guess that this organised by beacons for which they kept careful watch. This is the real story behind most Highland tales of conflict or battle.

We can deduce something about the internal organisation of the fairfolk from the trials and from fairy tales. They agree that the Fairy King was subordinate to the Queen, who represented the Cailleach or Lady. It is less clear that the King was master of the fairy folk or hunters, the master man who appears now and again. After the disbandment of the hunting troops, much the same position was filled by the man who led a coven which normally consisted only of women, though Isobell Gowdie reveals a more complex situation in Moray where her coven had equal numbers of men and women, perhaps an earlier feature, and a Maiden or Cailleach as well as a Master. Covens generally have residual hunting aspects including ritual sex and the pact confirming it, as well as some imported necromantic features which may have been in circulation from a much earlier date. In Bute in 1662 we see what may be a transitional phase where the Devil is both master of the hunt and master of the coven.

The 'fairy' trials reveal a world that is stranger than that of the covens but we can make sense of almost everything attributed to Andro Man and to Isobell Gowdie. There is one exception but it is not a supernatural riddle. She said that in the Downie Hills 'thair ar great bullis rowtting and skoyling ther at the entrie quhilk feared me.' These bulls are a puzzle. Did the Earls of Moray keep bulls of some improved breed in the fort on the hill? Were they fairy cattle with red ears, like the White Park breed? No herds of parked cattle are recorded from Moray but they might have been kept in the park at Darnaway. Were they the last of the aurochs bulls? The Gaels remembered the aurochs as the *uruisg*, a large hairy creature part man, part beast, who hung about the farmsteads and was pacified by milk-maids with libations of milk and cream. Aurochsen persisted in Poland until 1627 and a later survival in the isolated north of Scotland is entirely possible. Or were the great bulls carved on small stone slabs and used to mark the entrance to fairyland? There was a bull cult among the Picts of Moray a thousand years earlier. Auldearn is only 24 km (15 miles) from Burghead where more than thirty stones decorated with bulls were found in the course of the nineteenth century. Similar carvings are known from Grantown-on-Spey, Brodie and Glenferness.

16: FAIRY KNOLLS

The Elfin knight sits on yon hill,
He blaws his horn baith lowd and shrill

F.J. Child, *The English and Scottish Popular Ballads*, 1882.

It is doubtful if there is a parish in Scotland which did not once possess at least one
fairy hill, although these are being gradually forgotten; and in addition there was in
every region a larger hill where fairies from far and wide foregathered on the eve of
the Quarter Days and other high occasions.

Marion McNeill, 1956, I, 112.

But in the last days it shall come to pass, that the mountain of the house of the Lord
shall be established in the top of the mountains, and it shall be exhalted above the
hills; and people shall flow unto it.

Micah 4:1

Hunters were summoned to the muster by a distant beacon. When the watch-man or *faire* on his mound saw a faraway fire in the right place, he alerted local hunters by raising a shout which went round the neighbourhood. Many fragments of archaic Gaelic survive as hunting shouts, often in the shape of clan slogans or battle-cries. The Munro shout was *Casteal Folais an Teine!* 'Fire at Castle Fowlis!' and the shout of the MacGregors of Balquhidder was *Ard chaille!* 'Height of the fire!' Many were coded into folk tales. When Odhran was resurrected after three days he told Columba that hell was not as bad as he had expected. Hearing this blasphemy, the saint said:

'*Uir! Uir! air sùil Odhrain mu'n labhair e tuilleadh còmhraidh*'
'Earth! Earth! On Oran's eye that he may blab no more.'

(Henderson, 1911, 282.)

This has been inspired by a number of puns. What Columba actually said was probably:

'Fire! Fire! The beacon shows the hunter the signal for a joint hunt!'

Odhran's Eye or *Sùil odhrain* was presumably a beacon on Mull which was visible from Iona.

As soon as they heard the shout, wherever they were and whatever they were doing, hunters made their way with all speed (like the proverbial cats) to the prearranged muster site. Many muster sites are found today as moot hills, pillar-stones and abandoned graveyards. There is even, in Fossoway, a ball-green where local teams played at football as they waited. Clan chiefs built lodges and parish churches at muster sites, being the places where people were accustomed to congregate.

In fake folklore, the fairy hill is a green mound which opens to reveal a magnificent hall or room, brilliantly lit, within which small but beautiful supernatural creatures eat, drink, dance and make merry. Sex is implicit but the partner is usually a mortal man or woman of normal size. The door of the mound is open only at Hallowe'en, when a mortal man can freely enter and join the festivities but he can leave again only if he has planted an iron dirk or an iron pin in one of the door-posts.

In sober fact the fairy knolls found in every part of Scotland are prominent hillocks of variable height which in the great days of the *sith* were used as outlook points and muster sites, where beacons were lit to originate or relay a signal. The correct translation of 'fairy knoll' is 'outlook point' and their defining feature is a panoramic view. A handful appear to be man-made burial mounds adopted for secular purposes but the great majority are natural features with no relevant archaeology.

Many *sitheans* are unimproved natural features but we cannot reject a site for that reason, as RCAHMS does, for example, at Dull, Perthshire, where they say *Tom an t-Sidhean* (NN 841398) is 'a glacial moraine, not an antiquity'. A glacial hillock in a specific place with a specific outlook might be both a natural feature *and* an antiquity, if it served its purpose and had not been adapted. The significant feature of a *sithean* is its outlook, not its archaeology. Their history of use on the other hand is impressive: most of the sites listed below were in use by native hunters from prehistory, perhaps from the first settlement, until native use of the deer forests was banned with the advent of feudal law. As antiquities they are among the oldest in Europe, even when they are unaltered features of the Scottish landscape. Native land use in Scotland is notable for the absence of archaeological features.

The lexical link with the so-called fairies who used these knolls is G. *faire* 'to keep watch'. The Fairy Knolls covered the lower areas of the deer forest, the local hills, in contrast to the regional beacons on the high tops, such as Ben

Lawers, Ben Ledi, the Lomond Hills and Arthur's Seat, which belonged to a different period, or served a different purpose. Above all the *sithean* were used by deer-hunters.

A more realistic picture of fairyland can be found in the notes compiled by John Leyden and included by Scott in his *Minstrelsy of the Scottish Borders* (published in 1802 as an introduction to 'The Tale of Young Tamlane'). Leyden remarked that the door to fairyland was in the desert places 'where living land was left behind' and where fairies lived with 'neither wif ne childe'. They were addicted to the chase, were attracted to places where blood was shed, and lived a restless life, moving about by moonlight. In the Isle of Man, the *good folk* lived 'in the wilds and forests, and on mountains'. Elf-land was a terrestrial paradise but it also had sinister aspects for when a traveller had penetrated the fairy realm he would find himself wading knee-deep in blood:

'For a' the blude that's shed on earth
Rins through the springs o' that countrie'.

This is a complimentary exaggeration: the river of blood through which a traveller must wade describes the volume of blood shed at the end of a successful hunt.

Another more realistic view of a fairy hill in Speyside is given by Stewart (1822, 90-91).

'It is well known that the fairies are a sociable people, passionately given to festive amusements and jocund hilarity. Hence, it seldom happens that they cohabit in pairs, like most other species, but rove around in bands, each band having a stated habitation or residence, to which they resort as occasion suggests. Their habitations are generally found in rough irregular precipices and broken caverns, ... and so solid in their structure, as frequently to resemble "masses of rocks or earthen hillocks". Their doors, windows, smoke-vents, and other conveniences, are so artfully constructed, as to be invisible to the naked eye in daylight, though in dark nights splendid lights are frequently reflected through their invisible casements. Within these *Tomhans* or, as others term them, *Shian*, sociality and mirth are ever the inmates; and they are so much addicted to dancing, that it forms their chief and favourite amusement'.

The Speyside account suggests that the hollow hill of folklore was not a fairy knoll but may be a memory of these substantial stone bothies or huts. They appear to be larger and better-equipped than the bothies used by the milkmaids who went up to the shielings or summer pastures with the cows and calves in summer. They were built of branches overlaid with turf or heather on a stone

263

foundation but were only just large enough to sleep in. It is said, perhaps with truth, that these bothies were so low and mean and merged so closely with the hillside that a horseman could fall through a roof before he noticed it covered a dwelling.

Fairy knolls today are found on the map as *sìth, sithean, cnoc, cathair, tom* or *tomhan* and survive in inexhaustible numbers all over Scotland. Their archaeology may be negligible but as they are indestructible once mapped, they give us a most important geographical picture of Scottish deer-hunters at work.

The majority are known now only as place-names but a few, such as The Doon or Fairy Hill at Aberfoyle, Tomnahurich at Inverness and Tombuidhe Ghearrloch 'hill of the hunting troop of the Gairloch' which was inhabited by a dwarf (McRitchie 1890, 112), retain an association with fairies. In Strathtay the fairies danced on moonlit nights at Tom Challtuinn and migrated three times a year from Cnoc Forbaidh ('knoll of the ambush') to Creag Scraidhlain, presumably in the course of a deer-drive (Kennedy 1927, 46-7). The Fairy Knowe of Logie which 'still stands as an adornment to the Golf Course of Bridge of Allan' was visited at New Year and has a view which embraces the Vale of Menteith, Stirling Castle, the Forth and the distant Grampians (Fergusson 1912, VII, 58-9). More traditions no doubt remain to be dug out of the unindexed volumes of Scotland's local histories.

The listed sites came in the main from the Ordnance Survey Landranger 1:50,000 Gazetteer and RCAHMS Canmore archive. Some of the *sithean* are minor features shown only on the OS first edition six-inch maps; others are substantial hills. Almost two hundred sites are listed and several hundred more toms and tomhans are known but have not been listed. One often finds neighbouring place-names which may be of comparable age such as *eun* 'birds' a pun for *aodhan* 'fire', *loisgte* 'fire', *meadhon* 'a meeting place', *buidhe* 'yellow (fire)', and *teine* 'fire'. Survival has been affected by the preferential listing of features of interest to archaeologists. An unimproved natural site does not attract the high profile of a man-made site. The excellence of Watson's work in Ross & Cromarty underlines how many of these apparently unimportant sites have been lost in other areas.

Where there is enough background information, we find a very interesting continuity between prehistoric use by hunters, visitations by witches, and tribal musters of the historic period. It is not unusual to find a medieval baron court held on a fairy knowe. There are substantially more sites as one moves north and west but in most Highland areas there is little beyond the place-name, a striking demonstration of the effects of depopulation and a lack of literacy on the survival of native lore. References to fairies as supernatural beings also become fewer as one moves into the wilder areas of the Highlands.

Recognition must be qualified in the cases where sites are unaltered natural features, including some very large hills of 500 metres or more. However confusion is rare. Ben Shean at Strathyre in Perthshire is claimed to be the

Ben of the Fairies but is more likely to be named for the series of rocky knolls on the summit of the hill. The policy in compiling the list given below was to list every available name since misfits cannot easily be recognised without fieldwork and a great deal of delving into local histories.

The list includes a few sites that are associated with witches. Certain churches and churchyards were popular as muster sites, for reasons which go back far beyond Christianity, mainly because the earliest parish churches were built at existing centres where people were already accustomed to gather and which formed the nodes of the local communications networks. This was a factor in preserving the pre-Christian use of the place. It is common to find early churches with impressive stone towers (see *The Beacon Book*, in this series) which have a secular rather than a sacred function. Both hunters and witches met at the churches of Alloa, Alves, Auldearn, Elgin and Lanark but the pattern is very fragmentary. Also fragmentary but intriguing is the concurrence of *sitheans* close to Annats in Glenlyon, Lochtayside, Glenorchy, Kilbride in Skye, Loch Awe, Sutherland, and elsewhere.

The list includes a sample of SN names such as Sanquhar (NJ 0456) in Moray and Shantullich (NH 6353) in the Black Isle, Easter Ross. It seems likely that their first element is not G. *sean* 'old' but G. *sithean* 'outlook knoll'. Watson interpreted *Sian na h-Eileig* in Ross-shire as the *sithean* or beacon site of the *iolairig* or deer-trap (1926, 237). Gillies discussing Beinn Siantaidh in Jura (1906, 139) offers 'charmed or blessed hill' but it is once again a 'fairy' hill or hunting hill. The Shan names are typically high sites at the limit of cultivation and with wide-open views. There is a link with hunting at Sean-Mham (NM 4544), a gathering place high on Ben More in Mull.

Another rare term is G. *cathair*. Watson found several examples in Ross-shire and said: '*Cathair* in NW Scotland means a small knoll or "Fairy Seat", not "fort" as in other parts'. He translated it as 'fairy seat, like *sithean*' (1926, 222 note). G. *cathair* links the fairy knoll to the *cath* or band of hunters who kept watch there. All the examples found have been listed. Another relevant term is *tom* or *tomhan* but only four are listed out of three hundred and fifty in the OS Gazetteer.

Moray has fairly complete coverage from the fairy site at the Bin of Cullen (still in use up to 1597) to the area around Darnaway which still had a fairy population in 1662. There was easy contact along the coast, by land, by sea and by beacon so that one coven or band of hunters could easily join up with the next: from west to east: Nairn to Auldearn [10 km], Auldearn to Darnaway [9 km], Darnaway to Forres [9 km], Forres to Alves [10 km], Alves to Elgin [10 km], Elgin to the Bin of Cullen [27 km].

The Guidman's Croft is generally believed to be a patch of ground dedicated to the Devil but this appears to be fake lore invented by the Kirk. The Devil was not involved. It was said of Andro Man at his trial in 1597 that he had measured out and sanctified several small areas of land called Wards of the

Hynd Knight where it was forbidden to dig peat or plough. We see at Slains in Aberdeenshire, where there were three of these sanctuaries, that their correct designation was not to Satan or the Hynd Knight, but to the *guidmannis*, the fairy folk or hunters (Rust 1871, 32). The guidmannis crofts at Slains were not outlook posts but token areas of wilderness.

GAZETTEER OF FAIRY HILLS
AND SIMILAR SITES

Sites are filed under the old counties or under district names used in historical sources such as 'Hebrides'. The Ordnance Survey grid references ensure accuracy.

Aberdeenshire, Aberdeen. In 1597 local witches celebrated Hallowe'en by dancing around the Fish Cross in the middle of the city (NJ 944063). It stood on a fairy knoll known as St Catherine's Hill (NJ 942062), now removed. This saint was very popular with hunters (G. *cateran* 'hunter') as an acceptable Christian version of the Cailleach. The light on the hill marked the entrance to the harbour.

Aberdeenshire, Deeside. Sidhean Bealaidh (NO 0081) 'the signal post of the pass', being the pass linking the Chest of Dee with Glentilt in Atholl.

Aberdeenshire, Drumblade. Fairy Hillock (NJ 5740). Possible long barrow and round cairn, now destroyed. A place of execution in feudal times so presumably a moot-hill. Also known as Robin Height from some RB word meaning 'robber' or 'hunter'.

Aberdeenshire, Gartlie, Strathbogie. Shanquhar (NJ 5435), a remote upland place, is G. *sean-chathair* according to Watson. It is next to Corncatterach (NJ 5434), *Coire-na Cathrach* (Watson 1926, 222). Both refer to a local outlook position.

Aberdeenshire, Glen Ernan, Strathdon. Fairy Hillock (NJ 2712). Ernan (for Ethernan) means 'fire stance'.

Aberdeenshire, Huntly. Fairy Hillock (NJ 4536). A natural feature.

Aberdeenshire, Keig. Fairy Hillock (NJ 6020). 'Traditionally a meeting-place for fairies'.

Aberdeenshire, Lumphanan, Deeside. In 1597 local witches celebrated Hallowe'en by dancing round a standing-stone at the Hill of Craigleuch (SCM 1841, I), now Craiglich. The hill has a 'spectacular panoramic view over the countryside towards Mount Keen, Lochnagar and the Cairngorms'. See Aberdeen (above).

Aberdeenshire, Midmill. Fairy Hillock (NK0637). An abrupt eminence. Also known as the Witches' Pot.

Aberdeenshire, Moniack. Fairy Hillock, Reelig (NH 5543). A natural feature with vitrified material (a sign of a watch-fire) and a 4 metre spread of pebbles, probably to inhibit the spread of a watch-fire.

Aberdeenshire, Slains. Gaelic was still spoken there in 1650. Eight witches were executed at Slains in 1597 including Christen Reid, a vagabond, and perhaps also Erss Elspett aka Elspett Moiness, a Highlander, Hellie Pennie (mother of Katherine Gerard) (SCM i, 173), Christen Millar, Janet Degesses and Margrat Smyth. The local saint was Ternan for 'Ethernan', described as 'a long-famed voyager over the broad shipful sea'. The coastal light may have been at the Lykar or at the Chapel of St Ternan (NK041289). In 1620 the minister of Slains, not to be outdone by his parishioners, claimed he could identify a thief by making a cock crow under a cauldron (Mair 1876). In 1649 the Session discovered that three pagan holy places dedicated to the fairies were still in use. These uncultivated patches of ground or *garlets*, at Mill of Brogan (NK0130), Woodend of Balschamphie (NK0334), and at the Lykar Cairn 800 m. NNE of the church (Rust 1871, 32) (NK024336) were sacred to the fairies (G. *garlaoch* 'elf, fairy') and pagan rituals, such as exposing infants believed to be fairy changelings, continued at these places until late in the eighteenth century. In 1649 the Session ordered them to be ploughed up and banned the lighting of bonfires at Beltane, Midsummer, Hallowe'en and Yule.

Aberdeenshire, Tarves. Fairy Hillock (NJ 8934). Bones and urns reflect the use of human bones as fuel.

Angus, Carmylie. Fair-folk, Fairyfold, or Fairy Hillock (NO 5443). Finds include bones, charcoal, a brass ring, and the impression of a foot. Footprints cut in stone are found at several places; they had the practical purpose of positioning the watch-man in the correct spot and facing the right direction.

Argyll, Appin. Ardtur (NM 9016) was visited by fairy folk in November 1676, twenty days after Hallowday when Donald McIlmichael saw 'a great number of men and women within the hill'. He continued to visit them till twenty days before Christmas. He judged them not to be *wordlie* men or ordained of god; in other words, they were pagans or fairy folk. He had met them already in Lismore and at the Shian of Barcaldine (MacPhail 1920, 36-38). Dalnasheen (NM 9145) is 'the field of the fairy hill' (Henderson and Cowan 2001, 43).

Argyll, Ardchattan and Muckairn. Shian or An Sidhean (NM 907419), at Barcaldine, in Benderloch on Loch Creran. As well as the fairy mound a proliferation of cairns, standing stones, forts and Sgeir Cailleach 'the rock of the bonfire' (NM 9142). It was visited by fairy folk in 1676 (MacPhail 1920, 36-38).

Argyll, Ardnamurchan. Sidhean Mor (NM 4667), overlooking Sanna at the western end of the peninsula.

Argyll, Ballachulish. At Hallowe'en Donald the Post once met up with fairy folk at Corrychurachan (NN 0466). They threatened to take him with them. Then he noted on the hill above 'a large troop of fairies wheeling and dancing like the Merry Dancers', probably at Coire-Caorachan on Beinn Gucaig (NN 0565). The two troops then joined forces. This suggests the muster site was below, on the shores of Loch Linnhe.

Argyll, Barcaldine, Appin. *An Sidhean* (NM 909421). The *sithean* of Barcaldine was used as a camp-ground by fairy folk in 1676 (MacPhail 1920, 37). Both sides of Loch Creran have a dense network of beacon sites.

Argyll, Beinn Dorain, Glenorchy. Ais an t-Sithein (NN 3539). At an Annat.

Argyll, Cowal. Sidhean Mor (NR9669). Also Caisteal na Sidhe and Coille na Sidhe.

Argyll, Cowal. Sidhean Sluaigh (NS 0797), a hill of 435 m. overlooking Loch Fyne. Hut platforms in Glen Branter (NS 0996).

Argyll, Crarae, Kilmichael Glassary. Fairy Knowe (NR 9897) with a cairn, a cist with ashes (indicating a cremation site), a standing-stone and an earlier midden.

Argyll, Glenorchy. *Ais an t-Sithean* (NN 353392) 'the stronghold of the outlook posts', a former muster site near the Annait and the river Conghlais 'gathering fire', at the Annat on the south slopes of Beinn Dobhrain, a famous deer-forest which gave its virtue to the waters of *Allt na h'Annait* (NN 3438): in the words of Duncan Ban Macintyre, they were *iocshlainte mhaireann*, 'an unfailing remedy ... good manifold was wont to be got from it without purchase'. Also traces of an ancient burial ground (*Campbell, 1888, 47-49.*)

Argyll, Kentraw. Fairy's Hill (NR 2662). Inhumation dated to 1560 BC with food vessel and flint; cist burial.

Argyll, Kilmichael Glassary. Sidhean Beag (NR 9598), a hill of 261 m., used as a trig point.

Argyll, Kilmichael Glassary. (a) Sith More (NM 9200), a hill of 408 m. At the southeast corner of Loch Awe.

Argyll, Kilmichael Glassary. (b) Sith More (NM 9203), a hill of 326 m. At the southeast corner of Loch Awe.

Argyll, Kintyre, Skeroblingarry, Campbeltown. Fairy Knowe (NR 7126). A natural feature.

Argyll, Loch Awe. Craigtulloch (NN 0625). It has a view of the surrounding district and was used by fairies (MacDougall 1910, 190). Close to the Annat of Kilchrenan (NN 0322).

Argyll, Morven district. Tom an t-Sidhean (NM 8261) 'knoll of the fairies'; it overlooks Strontian (another *sidhean* name).

Argyll, Morven. (a) Sidhean (NM 6750) 'outlook hill', facing north over Loch Arienas.

Argyll, Morven. (b) Sidhean an Aoinidh Bhig (NM 6750) or 'Little Bonnet of Lorn', a second position a short distance to the south of (a).

Argyll, Morven. Sidhean Achadh nan Gamhna (NM 6848) 'outlook hill of the stags, or stirks'.

Argyll, Morven. Sidhean na Raplaich (NM 6351). A hill of 551 m. The archaic meaning of *raplaich* is probably 'butchery' or 'slaughter'.

Argyll, Sunart. Strontian (NM 8161). G. *Sròn an t-Sìthein* 'the point of the fairy hill'. Tom an t-Sidhein (NM 8261). There are 32 hut platforms in the glen to the northeast (DES 2002, 63).

Arran. Cnoc 'ic Eoghan (NR9127), McEwan's hill or 'the beacon hill of the son of the fire' (G. *aodhan*), at Druimaghinear (1773 *Drummaginar*, OS *Drimiginar*), used by hunters crossing to Northern Ireland. A possible fairy mound is shown as Cnoc Donn on the first edition OS six-inch map.

Arran. Shanochy or Shennachy (NR 9821) at the south end of the island from its name and the number of forts and cairns may have been an outlook station.

Arran. Sheeans (NR 9933). A hill of 373 m. used as a trig point.

Ayrshire, Barlaugh, Maybole. Fairy Hill (NS 3207), a round cairn, now destroyed. Barlaugh probably means 'hill of the light or signal fire'.

Ayrshire, Kilmaurs Hill. John Stewart of Irvine met the fairy queen there at Hallowe'en 1618. No other reference seems to have survived.

Ayrshire, Kirkoswald. Hollishean Camp on top of Prop Hill (NS 244061), a multivallate fort.

Ayrshire, Loudoun Hill. At Hallowe'en in 1605 Patrick Lowrie and Jonet Hunter assembled on the hill where they met 'ane devillische Spreit' who called herself Helene McBrune here (Pitcairn ii, 478). The hill is a prominent feature with a panoramic view and great strategic value. Scots *lowe* 'great fire'.

Borders. Eildon Hill (NT 5532), an outstanding fairy site, believed to be a hollow hill where Thomas met the Queen of Faerie (Henderson and Cowan 2001, 9) and where King Arthur sleeps with the Knights of the Round Table.

Bute, Kilmory. The Hill of Kilmory (NS 0560). A witches' meeting place next to an Annat.

Bute. The Knockane. Not located but a Knock (G. *cnoc*) is generally the site of a signal beacon.

Bute, Ambrisbeg. The fairfolk of Bute were believed to use a cave under Cnoc Alastair Drummer on the farm of Ambrisbeg (NS 0659). They emerged to help the local farmer at harvest-time. He rewarded them with bannocks and milk.

Caithness, Bower. Sinclair's Sithean (ND 1662), a long cairn with human remains, on a natural ridge.

Caithness, Clyth. Sidhean Fuar (ND 2641), overlooking valley of Clyth burn.

Caithness, Dunbeath. (a) Sithean Corr Meille (ND 0839) 'the outlook post of the wild peas'.

Caithness, Dunbeath. (b) Sithean na Gearra (ND 0838) 'the outlook post of the hares'.

Caithness, Halkirk. Sithean Harraig, a cairn (ND 0956).

Caithness, Halkirk. The Shean (ND 1455), a cairn with hut circles and smaller cairns.

Caithness, Latheron. Sith na Gearra, also known as Wag Mor (ND 083364). Cairn field and hut circle.

Caithness, Lower Dounreay (NC 99696772). Fairies Mound or Cnoc na h-Uiseig 'knoll of the hospitality', a chambered cairn of Orkney-Cromarty type, dating to the Neolithic, c.3400 BC and used for the storage of bones over many generations. They may have been ferried over to a beacon site on the adjacent coast.

Caithness, Reay (a). Shean Mor Brawlbin (ND 0657) and several other cairns. Brawlbin is probably 'height of the fire'; G. *braoil* is now 'a furious burst or a great noise' like burning wood.

Caithness, Reay (b). Sithean Buidhe (ND 0657), remains of a chambered cairn.

Caithness, Thurso. Cnoc nan Sithean (ND 0342), a hill of 195 m. on the river Thurso.

Caithness, Upper Dounreay. Na Tri Shean (ND 012653) 'the three fairy mounds', name of a chambered cairn (Henderson and Cowan 2001, 9). One of the mounds is known as *Cnoc Freiceadan* 'the beacon hill of the watch'. This area of Caithness has a proliferation of cairns, tumuli, and beacon sites reflecting intensive use by hunters.

Clackmannanshire, Alloa. Witches tried in 1658 confessed they had met with the Devil at the old Kirk of Alloa and at the adjacent Cuningar (an old rabbit warren), the sloping ground running down from the Kirk to the shore (Fergusson, *SHR* 1907, vol.4, 40-48). The location of St Mungo's old Kirk on the shore, its impressive tower, and the use of this location by the coven suggests it was once the site of a coastal hunt-beacon. There is no local Annat but this site has a landing-place, a coastal light, a notable church tower, a graveyard, and witches' cantraips which are all suggestive.

Clackmannanshire, Cauldhame (probably NS 8201), near Dunblane, is said to be a fairy palace (Simpkins 1914, 316).

Dunbartonshire, Dumbuck Hill (Henderson and Cowan 2001, 9). A fairy hill. Use by hunters is suggested by a cup-and-ring-marked stone (NS 419747). Open outlook to south and west.

Dunbartonshire, Glen Douglas. Sith Mor (NS 3096), a rocky summit on the side of Doune Hill (NS 2997), between Loch Long and Loch Lomond.

Dunbartonshire, Kilmaronock. Catter (NS 4787) was formerly *The Cathair*, seat of the Mormaers of Lennox. 'There is a large artificial mound of earth, where in ancient times courts were held' (OSA). Courts to settle disputes were generally held at muster sites. Catter Moot Hill is supposed to be a feudal motte but may have older origins.

East Lothian, Spott. The Doune-hill of Spott (NT 6875) was a meeting-place for local witches. Isobel Young was found guilty c.1628, of being with the Devil on the Doune-hill of Spott and convicted of witchcraft (SM 1845, II, 45). The Kirk Session noted that 'Many witches were burnt on top of Spott Law'. There is an Iron Age Fort and an Anglo-Saxon hall on the Doon Hill. The Witches' Stone is a standing-stone (NT 669753). St John's Well (NT 672756) indicates a prehistoric beacon site ('John' is a pun with G. *aodhan* 'fire'). E. *dod*, as in Spott Dod (NT 668744) is a name for a prehistoric beacon site.

East Lothian, Yester. Witches Knowe (NT 519635), a fortified knoll in a prominent position.

Forfar, Stracathro (NO 6265) c.1212 *Stracatherach* 'the strath of the camp or camps'. Watson thought that the *cathair* may have been the White Caterthun. White and Brown Caterthun are powerful Iron Age hill-forts in commanding positions on a high pass west of Brechin.

Forfar. Witches of the Forfar coven confessed in 1662 they had met with the Devil at 'the green hill near the Loch of Forfar', in the churchyard of Forfar, at Petterden midway between Forfar and Dundee (NO 4239), at Lapiedub half a mile east of Forfar, and at the Muryknowes a little west of Halcarton Mill (Anderson 1888, 248-253). Except for the churchyard, none of them appears to have any prehistoric importance.

Galloway, Dalry. The fairy knowe at St John's Town of Dalry (NX 6181) on the river Ken is a large and symmetrical structure. A great dragon used to coil around it in triple folds until he (she?) was killed by the blacksmith (Lang 1933, 37). Like most dragon tales this is probably fake news.

Galloway, Parton, on Loch Ken. A fairy knowe, probably artificial, is probably now known as Boreland Mote (NX 694709). The re-use of a prehistoric beacon site in the middle ages is common. The ruins of an ancient Catholic church on the old pilgrim route to St Ninian's shrine at Whithorn are at Parton (McNeill 1957, 185). Also known as the Green Tower motte, suggesting a pun between G. *uain* 'green' and G. *ain* 'fire'.

Hebrides and West Highlands. Dun Burg, Dun Bhuilg or Torr-a-Bhuilg are generic names for a hunt beacon and as such they appear at the climax of many fairy tales (for example, MacDougall 1910, 101). A beleaguered housewife is eaten out of house and home by invasive fairies, but gets rid of them by shouting 'Dun Bhuilg is on fire!' In other words the signal beacon for the hunters is alight, whereupon they all vanish in the twinkling of an eye, muttering hunting incantations as they go. This suggests that the duns of the Highlands were used as beacon sites by hunters. An actual example is Dun Bhuilg (NM 4226) at the extremity of Ardmeanach 'the height of the gathering' in Mull.

Hebrides, Benbecula, a fairy knoll and burial ground. Fishermen were guided by a light on a hill said to be in the island of Grimsay but more probably Sithean Rosinish (NF 8753) in Benbecula. The knoll was used for burial and bones to be used as fuel for the signal beacon were kept in a bee-hive hut. 'Clanranald used to have a summer shieling on one of the islets off Benbecula. He had a herd and a milkmaid there. They were both of them Catholics, and at the time of changing residence were in the habit of spilling a coggie of milk on the fairy-knoll.' Catholics were widely believed to be pagans. It is not clear if the fairy knoll was in Grimsay or Benbecula.

Hebrides, Colonsay. Sidhean Mor (NR 360916). A fairy mound where marriages were still conducted at the end of the eighteenth century.

Hebrides, Colonsay. Sithean Meadhonach (NR 359916), 'mound of the gathering'. A grassy mound 'not obviously artificial'. Also Sithean Beag (NR359916).

Hebrides, Eigg, Laig. Sidhean nan Cailleach (NM 470879), a long cairn with cist burials. The Cailleach links fairies, hunting and fire.

Hebrides, Eigg. 'A fairy hill called Cnoc na Piobaireachd, the Knoll of the Piping' (McNeil 1957, 110).

Hebrides, Harris. Sidhean Mor (NB 0307), a coastal hill of 96 m., in North Harris.

Hebrides, Iona. Pennant (1772) reported a small cairn inside a stone circle at Cnoc nan Aingeal 'knoll of the bright fire'. Later generations failed to find either feature on Iona but identified Cnon nan Aingeal with Cnoc an t-Sidhein (NM 272237). This is now dismissed as a natural feature but the traditional Michaelmas horse races (a remnant of hunting) took place at this knoll.

Hebrides, Islay, Kildalton and the Oa. Cathair na Maoil (NR269416).

Hebrides, Islay, The Rhinns.

Hebrides, Islay. An Sithean (NR 2566), in the Rinns of Islay, on the road between Loch Gorm and Gruinart, beside several hut circles and a field system.

Hebrides, Isle of Ewe. Sitheanan Dubha (NG 8489) 'outlook points of the deer', the extreme northern point of the island. Ewe represents G. *aodh* 'fire'. George Buchanan wrote in 1579 that the island was 'almost all covered with woods, and good for nothing but to harbour thieves, who rob passengers'. Being translated more correctly he had in fact been told that the island was a deer park and had resident hunters. Fairies (probably poachers) were seen there as recently as 1880.

Hebrides, Jura, Shian (NR 5387). A site near Shian Bay; not obviously a look-out site.

Hebrides, Kerrera. Sidhean Riabhach (NM 8129), on the north shore of the island, with a view of Lismore and East Mull.

Hebrides, Lewis. Sidhean an Airgid (NB 2513), a hill of 387 m. G. *airgiod* 'silver; riches', applied to deer.

Hebrides, Lewis. Sidhean Mor (NB 3833). West of Stornoway.

Hebrides, Lewis. Sidhean nan Creagan Gorm (NB 4340). North of Stornoway overlooking the river Coll.

Hebrides, Lewis. Sithean Airigh Murchaid (NB 4544). North of Stornoway. Perhaps a recent name. 'The knoll of Murdo's shieling'. NB The place-name element *sidhean* occurs in the names of several dozen shieling sites in Lewis. The word may simply mean 'mound' in local usage.

Hebrides, Lewis. Tom an t-Sealgair (NB 3840) 'knoll of the hunter'.

Hebrides, Lismore. A knoll at Allt Aogain (NM 836410) was reputed to be a favourite resort of the fairies (MacDougall 1910, 183). It is the most prom-inent part of the island, near Killean 'fire enclosure' (NM 8441) and other evidence for local beacons.

Hebrides, Mingulay. Tom a' Reithean (NL 5684) 'knoll of the quarters, G. *raith*', the northern end of the island of Mingulay in the Outer Hebrides, next to MacPhee's Hill. MacPhee is *Mac-dubh-sith* (Black), in archaic terms: 'son of the deer-hunter'.

Hebrides, Mull, Gribin. An Sithean (NM 4533), from six-inch OS map.

Hebrides, Mull. Sidhean Riabhach (NM 3324), in the Ross of Mull on the road to Iona.

Hebrides, North Uist, Cairinis. Cnoc nan Aingeal (NF 818605), a natural hillock with a cairn, 300 m. northeast of Teampull na Trionaid.

Hebrides, North Uist. Sithean Tuath (NF 719701) at Balranald, a fairy mound or sithean or perhaps a burnt mound which was the seat of the MacDonalds of North Uist in the sixteenth century.

Hebrides, Oransay, Argyll. Sithean Beag (NR 345890).

Hebrides, Oransay, Argyll. Sithean Mhurraig Bhearraig (NR 345889), a natural feature.

Hebrides, Oransay, Argyll. Sithean Mor (NR 346889).

Hebrides, Oronsay, Argyll. Sithean (NR 356875).

Hebrides, Raasay. Sithean Mor (NG 5947), at the north end of the island, overlooking Loch Arnish.

Hebrides, Scalpay. Sithean Glac an Ime (NG 6030). 303m.

Hebrides, Skye, Blackhill. Sithean Beinn a' Mhorrainn (NG 3649).

Hebrides, Skye, Broadford. An t-Sithean (NG 630226). The location given is close to Coire-chat-achan, once home to the Mackinnons of Strath, an ancient native family, to a chambered cairn (NG 627221), to the Annat at Kilbride (NG5820), and to the beacon hill Beinn na Cailleach (NG 6023) where the story of the fiddler is located.

Hebrides, Skye, Drynoch. Cnoc an t-Sithean (NG 3932). In a coastal position on Loch Harport.

Hebrides, Skye, Kyle Rhea. Sithean a' Coire Odhair (NG 7723), a hill of 507 m., immediately north of Beinn na Caillich (NG7723).

Hebrides, Skye, Portree. Sithean Bhealach Chumhaing (NG 5046) 'the out-look point of the narrow pass' (between two cliffs). A prominent coastal site above cliffs.

Hebrides, Skye, Sleat. Sithean Beag (NG 585084), site occupied by a modern farm building.

Hebrides, Skye, Sleat. Sithean Mor (NG 5907) and Sithean Beag (NG 5808).

Hebrides, Skye, Sligachan. Cnoc an t-Sithean (NG 4931). In a coastal position on Loch Sligachan.

Hebrides, Skye, Strath. An Sithean (NG 625225), overlooking the Broadford River. Stone settings.

Hebrides, Skye, Totaig. Cnoc an t-Sithean (NG 197497).

Hebrides, Skye. Cnoc an t-Sithean (NG 3621). On the west coast of the island south of Cnoc an Teine 'hill of the fire' (NG 3622).

Hebrides, Tiree. Sithean Beinn Ghott, Dun an t-Sithean (NM 0345). On OS 1:50,000 as 'Dun'. G. *goth* 'level'.

Inverness-shire, Abernethy. Sithean Dubh na Choimhead, also known as Tom na Choimhead (NJ 000100).

Inverness-shire, Alvie. Delfour, Alvie. (NH 845085), Delfour. According to RCAHMS, 'trial work showed An Sithean to be a natural mound. No evidence for human utilisation of this was found.' This should read: 'No *archaeological* evidence for human utilisation was found'.

Inverness-shire, Dores. Cathair Fhionn (NH 615336). Cairns.

Inverness-shire, Dundreggan. Sidhean Mullach fairy knoll (NH 329146). Perhaps also a medieval motte.

Inverness-shire, Duthil. Fairies were active at Mulinfenachan here (not located; perhaps Milton NM 9725) but left when the kiln at Tullochgriban (NM 9425) was seen to be on fire one night. In other words they moved to a position with a better outlook. Both sites are close to a local Annat (NM 9727) and Tullochgriban (NM 9625) has a notable view.

Inverness-shire, Inverness. Tomnahurich (NH 6543) 'hill of the yews', a prominent knoll with panoramic views over the Moray Firth to the north and down the Great Glen to the south. It was very famous as a fairy site and features in several tales such as 'Angus Mor and the Fairies' (MacDougall 1910, 132). In another tale, a fiddler is lured into playing at a fairy meeting there and emerges after one night (he thinks) to find that hundreds of years have passed. For 'fiddler' read 'hunter' (G. *fiadh* 'deer'). Is this intended to show that the life of a hunter was an endless round of pleasure?

Inverness-shire, Kilmonivaig. Tom Aingil (NN 307812) 'knoll of the fire'. Cille Choril on top is said to be a chapel to St Cyril but Cyril means 'beacon site' (G. *ceir* 'wax'). The knoll has good views along Glenspean.

Inverness-shire, Kilmonivaig. Tom an Teine 'knoll of the fire' (NN2179), part of the Annat complex at Kilmonivaig.

Inverness-shire, Kingussie. Sidhean Dubh (NH 5204), 'the signal post of the deer', an area in the Monadhliath Mountains. Less important than Sidhean Dubh na Cloiche Baine (NH 5001).

Inverness-shire, Kingussie. Sidhean Dubh na Cloiche Baine (NH 5001), 'outlook post of the white stone', a prominent hill of 756 m. deep in the Monadhliath Mountains. The site of the beacon was presumably marked by a white stone. Also Loch nan Sidhean.

Inverness-shire, Kingussie. Sidhean Liath (NH 5103), a knoll in the Sherramore Forest.

Inverness-shire, Newtonmore. Sidhean Mor Dail a Chaoruinn (NH 6900) 'fairy knoll of the glen of the rowans'. A prominent glacial knoll with extensive views of Glen Banchor and Glen Badenoch to which has been added a palisaded enclosure 38m. by 24m., perhaps a deer-park.

Inverness-shire, South Morar, Arisaig. Sidhean Mor (NM 7286), a hill of 600 m., a triangulation point.

Inverness-shire, South Morar, Glenfinnan. Sidhean Mor (NM 8783), an inland hill of 582 m.

Inverness-shire, Strathdearn. Sith Mor (NH 7117), a hill of 650 m. overlooking the upper valley of the Deveron near Coignafearn (NH 7017). There are several 'coig' names here which refer to hunting.

Kincardine-shire. A midsummer bonfire was lit on Cairnshee near Durris on 20 June (C. Hole 1973, 208).

Kinross-shire, Fossoway, Blairingone. Before 1662 the Crook of Devon coven sometimes met at Gibson's Craig at Palace Brae (NS 982975), in the southern part of the parish of Fossoway. 'The Rocky Pinnacle, now vulgarly called Gibson's Craig' is said to have been the rallying-rock of the Murrays of Tullibardine, later Earls of Atholl (OSA c.1790). A ball game was played at Ball Green, part of Palace Brae. Team games were played by hunters as they waited for the drive to start.

Kinross-shire. First edition OS six-inch map shows Witches' Knowe (NO 0405) near Warroch farm to the north of Fossoway.

Lanark. The witches of Lanark sometimes met at Lanark Hill, now an unknown name. Scott thought it might be Tinto (NS 9534), a great beacon hill. They also met at the old Kirk of Lanark.

Midlothian, Edinburgh. The Calton Hill between Edinburgh and Leith was the target of fake folklore published by Sinclair in his *Satan's Invisible World* (1685), the apocryphal story of the Fairy Boy of Leith whose supposed life was a generation earlier. If Calton Hill was ever the site of a hunt-beacon nothing has survived the fable to confirm this.

Moray, Alves, Laigh of Moray. The Knock of Alves, between Forres and Elgin (NJ 162627) was by reputation a fairy mound: 'Tis the land of the famed Knock of Alves, where fairies and spirits repair' sang the poet William Hay. There was music and dancing in the splendid fairy halls that opened off the Knock. According to McNeill (1957, I, 135) the witches of Forres met here. The Knock is also said to be where MacBeth met the witches but Hardmuir near Auldearn has a better claim. In 1602 two men were accused of going to Alves to consult 'ane vitche quha thaireftir wes brint in Darnevay' (*Records of Elgin* II, 96). A *cnoc* was the site of a local signal beacon.

Moray, Auldearn. Hill of Earlseat (NH 9554). The Auldearn coven met here (Pitcairn 1833, III, 603).

Moray, Auldearn. MacBeth's Hillock (NH 959567), a prominent natural knoll of 49 m. on Hardmuir 'near the old Toll House, a little off the road, marked by a few old pines', supposedly the blasted heath where MacBeth met the three witches. In more mundane terms this was probably a local beacon site used by the Brodies of Brodie (Brodie Castle NH 9857), a native clan wi' a lang pedigree. The symbol stone now in the grounds of Brodie Castle was found at no great distance in the churchyard of Dyke (NH 990584). It has several ogham inscriptions, one reading EDDARRNON or Ethernan 'fire site'. To judge by the Munro *duthchas* at Ferindonald the elite centre at Brodie would have a range of near-by sites for a variety of purposes. Johnson said the name Dyke usually marks an old camp (1934, 168). Brodie is from G. *brothach* 'little ditch'.

Moray, Banff, Aberdour. Cathair of Abbordobor (NJ 895649), at Dundarg Castle.

Moray, Banff, Aberlour. i Sheandow (NJ 2731) ii Sheandow (NJ 2739). iii Shenval (NJ 2638).

Moray, Banff. Bin of Cullen (NJ 4864), a coastal beacon and fairy knoll used in the 1590s by local witches and fairies. Andro Man, executed in 1598, lived at Darbreich (NJ 4863) on the southern slope of the hill and met the fairy folk there (*SCM* 1841, I, 120).

Moray, Banff. Longman Hill or Longman Cairn (NJ 737620). 67 m. (220 ft.) long. Not a natural feature but a large Bronze Age long barrow supplementing or heightening an existing mound or drum. It has a 360 degree view and is one of the distant points visible from the Bin of Cullen, so part of a coastal chain. Two secondary burials of cinerary urns support the use here of human bones as fuel in the beacon.

Moray, Dallas. Fairy Knowe, Fairy Loch (NJ 155495), perhaps a dun. Traditionally fairies camped at Fairy Loch.

Moray, Darnaway. The Doonie Hillock (in her testimony known as 'the Downie Hills' (NH 9658)). A meeting-place used by local fairy folk and the Auldearn coven. It has a good view and the remains of an Iron Age fort. The only Annat so far recognised in the area is at Logiebuchany (NH 9855) at Darnaway, taking Buchany to be 'shelter of the annat', as it is in Perthshire.

Moray, Edinkillie. Sidhean a' Tutach (NH 985408), 'the mound of the horn' (G. *dud*), or 'of the people' (G. *tuath*).

Moray, Forres. Forres had a bad name for witches but Black (1938) names only two, Isobel Elder and Isabel Simson, probably pricked, who 'died obstinat', probably innocent, on 4 May 1663. At Witch's Stone (NJ 043592) on the north side of Cluny Hill an inscription says: 'From Cluny Hill witches were rolled in stout barrels through which spikes were driven. Where the barrels stopped they were burned with their mangled contents. This stone marks the site of one such burning.' Whether this type of execution was in fact used for witches remains to be confirmed. According to Julian Goodare, there is no historical documentation of any such practice. When Dorothy Calder was put to death in Forres, early in the eighteenth century, she was burnt in the conventional way on top of Drumduan Hill to the east of the town using fifteen cartloads of peat. In 1825 human remains were found on Drumduan Hill which was the public execution ground; Hangman's Well lies below it to the north. Forres Castle (NJ 034587) might have been a motte. A fragment of a symbol stone (crescent and V-rod) was found in town (NJ 039588). Forres certainly has a long history but seems singularly lacking in lore.

Moray, Forres. Sanquhar (NJ 0456) is a *cathair* name: *Sean-chathair* 'the old fairy hill' or 'the fairy hill of the gathering', to the east of the river Findhorn, next to the territory of the Auldearn coven. There is a standing-stone with an ogham inscription here (NJ 039554).

Moray, Hill of Earlseat (NH 962543). A meeting place of the Auldearn coven; two of its members lived at the farm of Earlseat (NH 9554). Used as a trig point but it does not have a very impressive view.

Moray, Kirkmichael. Cnoc nan Sithean (NJ 157277). Name only.

Moray, Knockando. Fairy Hillock (NJ 2643) is a slight natural eminence. Outlook not known.

Moray, Knockando. Sidhean na Mannoch (NJ 1945), on the south slopes of Carn na Cailleach.

Moray, Nairn, Ardclach. Shian Hillock (NH 9141). A tumulus where human bones have been found.

Moray, Nairn. Shion Hillock (NH 916497), at Ardclach. Stone cists and human bones belonging to 'pagan interments'.

Orkney, Burrian. In 1773 an Orkney farmer told George Low that at the Broch of Burrian (HY 2918) near his house in Harray, on a Christmas morning, he had seen 'a large company dancing and frolicking, but upon his approach they all disappeared' (Henderson and Cowan 2001, 46). This may have been no more than the truth as Orkney was a stronghold of pagan belief and practice.

Orkney, Stromness, Sandwick. The Howans (little hills) of Hurkisgarth (HY 2517) on Mainland Orkney were a well-known fairy resort.

Peeblesshire, Minchmuir, near Peebles, was a busy place as both fairies and witches congregated there. They could be propitiated by an offering of cheese thrown into the Cheese Well (a double pun on G. *cas* 'hunt' and E. *chase*). Minchmuir was also the place where Mr Williamson of Cardrona carried off the Devil's book from witches dancing there. When they gave chase he abandoned it and so had nothing to show for his adventure except a good story (*Berwickshire Naturalists Club* xi, 265, quoted by Murray 1921, 197).

Perthshire, Aberfoyle. The Doon or Fairy Hill (NS 5199) is associated with the Rev. Robert Kirk but there is no evidence for fairies here before the early nineteenth century and the intervention of Walter Scott.

Perthshire, Balquhidder. Sithean a' Chata (NN 3516), 'fairy hill of the battle'. G. *cath* is 'hunt'. A battle or fight is also a hunt. It is between the west end of Balquhidder Glen and the north end of Loch Lomond.

Perthshire, Balquhidder. Tom nan Aingeal (NN 5321), a natural knoll immediately north of the church where fires were lit at Beltane and Samhain according to local tradition.

Perthshire, Blair Atholl. Sithean na Cluana (NN898649), a cairn containing a cist burial.

Perthshire, Dull. Tom an t-Sidhean (NN 841398). A small circular wooded knoll with steep sides, of glacial origin 12 m. (40 ft.) high. The name suggests this natural feature was used as an outlook post.

Perthshire, Glendochart. Sith a Bruaich, a short distance east of Bovain (NN 5430), home of the MacNab chief. A probable muster site for the MacNabs, a native family, a branch of Siol Alpin, who controlled the west end of Loch Tay and Glendochart.

Perthshire, Glendochart. Sithean Dubh, half a mile west of Bovain (NN 5430), on the north side of Glendochart. A probable muster site for the MacNabs, a native family who controlled the western part of Loch Tay and Glendochart.

Perthshire, Glenlyon. On the west part of Balnahanaid at Sithean a Bhaile-mheadhonaich (now Balmenoch, NN 6147) 'the outlook knoll at the meeting place' where there was a burial place for unbaptised babies (Campbell 1888, 48). See also Lawers.

Perthshire, Glenquaich. Dull. Easter and Wester Shian (NN 8439). Also Annatfauld (NN 8736) and a graveyard at Tom an t-Sidhean (NN 8439).

Perthshire, Inchyra. Witch Knowe (NO 189211), a burial mound with evidence for cremation (calcined bones, cinerary urns), implying use as beacon site where bones were used as fuel.

Perthshire, Killin. Tom nan Aingeil 'the hillock of the bright fire' (NN 573332), an outlook post and beacon stance behind the school in Killin, is an artificial hillock behind the school marked by a standing-stone. Its soil was believed to have magical qualities. It is close to Fingal's Grave (Victorian fakery?) which is also marked by a standing-stone. The megaliths appear to have been part of a stone circle now destroyed.

Perthshire, Loch Lyon, Glenmeran. Sith Tromaidh (NN 3943) (not found in the 1:50,000 O.S.).

Perthshire, Menteith in southwest Perthshire, famous for its fairies who gathered at Cnoc an Bocan or 'Bogle Knowe' (NS 584 996) and also at Coire na Uruisgeann on Ben Venue (NN 4807).

Perthshire, Milton of Abercairny, Fowlis Wester. A Fairy Knowe (NN 9123) to the west of two stone circles. Cinerary urns found here confirm the use of human bones as fuel.

Perthshire, North Lochtayside, Lawers. There was a *sithean* beside the old lint mill at Lawers (Gillies 1938, 338). Ben Lawers to the north was an important long-distance beacon, visible in the Low Country and handy both for the Annat on Lochtayside (NN 669379) and the Annat at Roro in Glenlyon (NN 623471). Campbell identified Balnahanaid in Glenlyon as a muster site: 'Here too there is an ancient burial place' (1888, 54). An iron hand-bell, since lost, was found in a farm building at Balnahanaid (Campbell 1888, 47-49).

Perthshire, Shianbank, Scone. Two stone circles (NO 1527) and a place known as Annatybank (NO 1628). The links with stone circles here and at Fowlis Wester point to calendar calculation at the circles.

Perthshire, Strathearn. Tullibardine (NN 9214) was originally *Catherlauenoch*, a name surviving as Carlownie Hill (NN9508) in the Ochils south of Auchterarder. G. *cathair* 'fairy seat' or outlook place is equivalent to *sidhean* (Watson, 1926, 223). *Lauenoch* is 'place of fire'.

Perthshire, Strathtay, Balnaguard. An Sithean (NN 9451) in the township.

Perthshire, Strathtay, Tullypowrie. There is a *sithean* or Fairy Knoll (NN 9153), 'behind the Roman Catholic Chapel and close by the seventh hole on the golf course' (Kennedy 1927, 17).

Perthshire, Strathtay. Tom Challtuinn was a knoll where the fairies of Grantully danced on moonlit nights. Its location is now uncertain but might be Creag a Challtuinne (NN 9347) or Tomchaldane (NN 865495) (OS First Edition six-inch Maps). The same fairies migrated from Cnoc Forbaidh to Craig Scriadhlain once in three years (Kennedy 1927, 46-7).

Ross & Cromarty, Achnasheen. Cnoc an t-Sidhean (NH 1553). An isolated cone-shaped hill of 372 m., where three glens meet. Achnasheen (NH 1558) probably refers to the same *sidhean*.

Ross & Cromarty, Applecross. Cnoc na Sithean, aka Camasdroi 'the bay of the druid' (NG 8257).

Ross & Cromarty, Ardross. Cnoc an t-Sidhean More (NH 5977) (658 m.) and Cnoc an t-Sidhean Beag (NH 6076) are in the same massif as Sidhean a Choin Bhan and overlook a prehistoric settlement and field system.

Ross & Cromarty, Ardross/Fearn. Sithean a' choin bhain (NH 5980) 'fairy hill of the white dog'. A remote hill marked by a cairn, on the watershed between Fearn and Ardross. The 'white dog' is probably 'gathering fire', with G. *ban* 'fire'. See also Cnoc an Sidhean Mhor (NH 5977).

Ross & Cromarty, Assynt, Oldany Island. Sidhean nan Ealachan (NC 0834) 'the outlook point of the fire stance', a hill of 104 m. Oldany is a tidal island off the north coast of Assynt, Ross & Cromarty. Oldany may be an Annat name. This was probably the site of a coastal beacon serving Assynt.

Ross & Cromarty, Black Isle, Munlochy. Shantullich, G. *an t-seann tulaich* (NH 6353). Shan is apparently *sithean* 'outlook knoll'. It is the site of a famous Clootie Well (NH 640537) known as St Curitan's Well or the Hill o Hirdie. Despite the ban of the local Kirk Sessions, unruly groups of young people of both sexes once visited such wells at the raiths of the year, particularly on 1 May, suggesting a link with fertility and of course with fairies.

Ross & Cromarty, Black Isle, Munlochy. The Feinne, who are legendary deer hunters, may be seen in the fairy mound of Craigacho or Craigiehow (NH 6852), on the coast near Munlochy, leaning on their elbows and waiting for the call. There is a Clootie Well at Craiguch (NH 67935318).

Ross & Cromarty, Braemore Forest. Sidhean na Sroine (NH 1977) 'the outlook post of the nose', overlooking Corrieshalloch.

Ross & Cromarty, Coigach, Wester Ross. Meall na Sithinn (NC 1904). Archaic G. *coig* 'deer'.

Ross & Cromarty, Freevater Forest. Sidhean Raireag (NH 3491), an isolated hill of 547 m. Perhaps G. *riarachd* 'distribution or sharing (of meat)'.

Ross & Cromarty, Gairloch. A' Cathair Bheag 'little fairy knoll or seat', now Kerrysdale (NG 8273) (Watson 1904, 225). Close to Sidhean Mor (NG 8171).

Ross & Cromarty, Gairloch. A' Cathair Dhubh 'black fairy knoll' (NG 7573), between Port Henderson and Loch nan Eun (Watson 1904, 222). Dubh is not 'black' but an archaic term for deer.

Ross & Cromarty, Gairloch. A' Cathair Ruadh 'the red fairy knoll', near Poolewe (Watson 1904, 229).

Ross & Cromarty, Gairloch. Cathair a' Phuirt 'fairy knoll of the harbour', near Big Sands. A harbour light. (Watson 1904, 227).

Ross & Cromarty, Gairloch. Cathair Chruchoille (NH 038622) 'fairy knoll of the horse-shoes', at a bend in Abhainn Bruachaig which resembles a horse-shoe (Watson 1904, 232). There was a burial ground on Eilean na Ghobhainn (NH 030626).

Ross & Cromarty, Gairloch. Loch na Cathrach Duibhe (NG 8990) 'the loch of the black fairy knoll' or 'the outlook place of the deer' (Watson 1904, 238).

Ross & Cromarty, Gairloch. Seanbhaile (NG 750806). An area north of Big Sand.

Ross & Cromarty, Gairloch. Sian na h-Eileig '*sithean* of the deer trap' (Watson 1904, 237). Between Slaggan (NG 8494) and Greenstone Point (NG 8698).

Ross & Cromarty, Gairloch. Sidhean Mor (NG 8171), part-way up a steep slope, southwest of Shieldag.

Ross & Cromarty, Gairloch. Sidhean Mor (NG 8374), a prominent rocky summit northeast of Shieldaig.

Ross & Cromarty, Gairloch. Tombuidhe Ghearloch 'knoll of the hunting troop (of fairies) of the Gairloch'. Not located. It was home to a *fuath* (a dwarf or ghost) (McRitchie 1890, 112).

Ross & Cromarty, Loch Broom. A' Cathair Dhubh (approximate position NH 1185) 'the black fairy knoll' or 'the outlook point of the deer', on the Strathbeg river (Watson 1904, 246).

Ross & Cromarty, Melvaig. Sidhean na Moine (NG 7587). An area of upland.

Ross & Cromarty, Migdale Rock (NH 6590). Fairies gathered there (*Tocher* 1978, 28/221, McLagan mss p.7391-2). From David Mackay, Creich: 'Old men said fairies used to be plentiful here, they used to live in the meal mill, Mullach nam Fuath [mill of the spectres] on Migdale'. Mills and millers are associated by pun with hunting, from G. *milidh* 'soldier, hero, (hunter)'; *mill* 'to lay waste (to hunt over)', etc.

Ross & Cromarty, Shieldaig. Sidhean a' Mhill (NG 7862). A hill of 222 m. used as a trig point.

Ross & Cromarty, Strathcarron. Sidhean an Radhairc (NH 5194), a hill of 396 m. overlooking the Annat at Amata tua (NH 4790). G. *radharc* 'view, prospect'.

Ross & Cromarty, Torridon. Loch Cuil Sithean (NG 828592).

Stirlingshire, Buchlyvie, Stirlingshire. A famous Fairy Knowe (NS 5894). A natural mound with extensive views and lots of archaeology including a first-century broch, a roundhouse, and human bones.

Stirlingshire, Kippen. A Fairy Knowe (NS 6494).

Stirlingshire, Lecropt, Hill of Airthrey, Bridge of Allan. The Fairy Knowe of Logie (NS 797981) 'still stands as an adornment to the Golf Course of Bridge of Allan'. It was visited at New Year, an important date for hunters, and its view embraces the Vale of Menteith, Stirling Castle, the Forth and the distant Grampians (Fergusson 1912, VII, 58-9).

Stirlingshire, Loch Chon. Coir-shian at Loch Chon (NN 4205), a mile above the source of the river Forth, is said to be a fairy knoll (probably by Patrick Graham, a contemporary of Walter Scott). No trace of this place has been found.

Stirlingshire, Stirling. Stirling Castle was built by a fairy whose secret name was Thomas son of Jock. He worked every day for a year except for quarter night when he went off to the fairy knoll. When his name was guessed, 'away he flew through the castle wall in a flame of fire, leaving behind him a hole which neither stone nor wood nor anything under the sun but horse dung can close' (MacDougall 1910, 169). This ending is remarkably similar to that of the riddling game, 'The Unco Knicht's Wowing': 'As sune as she the fiend did name, He flew away in a blazing flame' (Child 1882, 5, from Motherwell's MS, 647).

Sutherland, Assynt. Cathair dubh (NC 057259). A knoll of 79 m.

Sutherland, Assynt. Sidhean Mor (NC 0134), on the Point of Stoer. Site of a coastal beacon.

Sutherland, Bonar Bridge. Sidhean Mor (NH 6496), a hill of 242 m., north of Migdale Rock (NH 6591) where fairies gathered (*Tocher* 1978, 28, 221).

Sutherland, Cape Wrath. Sithean na h-Iolaireich (NC 2570), on the west coast. G. *iolarig* (E. *elrig*) was 'a v-shaped deer trap into which deer were driven and shot with arrows when they came out'.

Sutherland, Creich. Cathair bhan (NC 327126).

Sutherland, Edrachillis. Cathair dubh (NC 265332). At Loch Dubh.

Sutherland, Farr. Cathair dubh bo graideach (NC 816519). An enclosure 4 m. by 5 m. Perhaps 'The hunt-camp of the horse studs'.

Sutherland, Handa. Sithean Mor (NC 1348), a hill of 124 m., on Handa Island, West Sutherland. Trig point.

Sutherland, Invershin. Sidhean Mor (NH 5995), a height controlling the Kyle of Sutherland.

Sutherland, Kildonan. Cathair Donan or Suig Donan (NC 949187), Donan's Seat.

Sutherland, Kyle of Durness. Sithean Mor (NC 3562), looking north over the Kyle, close to the Annat of Durness (NC 3865), with the remains of a broch, a chambered cairn and several other cairns.

Sutherland, Kyle of Tongue. Sithean na Gearrsaich (NC 6054).

Sutherland, Lairg. Sidhean Achadh nan Eun (NC 6311), a hill of 317 m.

Sutherland, Lairg. Sidhean Ruighe na Beinne (NC 6307), a hill of 236 m., looking south over Lairg.

Sutherland, Loch Eriboll. Loch na Cathrach 'loch of the overlooking position or seat' (NC 4561), beside Cailleach a' Mhuillear (NC 464624), a beacon site. 'Miller' is a pun on G. *milidh* 'soldier, hero, hunter'.

Sutherland, Loch Laxford. Eilean an t-Sithein (NC 1751), at the entrance to Loch Laxford. close to the local Annat (NC2151) where bones were stored. Both sites are small rocks; the Annat is only 40 m. long.

Sutherland, Skinsdale. Cnoc an t-Sithean (NC7526), an isolated cone-shaped hill (290 m.) on the river Skinsdale.

West Lothian, Bo'ness. In 1679 the witches of Borrowstowness (now Bo'ness) met the Devil on the Links of the town, a port on the shores of the Forth opposite Alloa. Sometimes he met witches at St John's Well, now in the centre of town. Dedications to St John (G. *aodhan* 'fire') are often found at beacon sites.

17: THE PEOPLE WHO TALKED TO GHOSTS

The most unexpected and unexplained mystery that emerges when we look at the trials that specifically targeted fairy folk is the fact that several of these people talked to ghosts and were helped by them. So far there is no evidence that all the charmers and healers who were accused of witchcraft practiced necromancy, but there is often so little information overall that one might not know. However, though the practice is reported for an entire century (1576 to 1677), from Bessie Dunlop in Ayrshire to Donald McIlmichell in deepest Argyll, it appears to be an early feature which was dwindling away when records start.

The involvement of fairy men and women with the ghosts of the dead which is revealed by the trial evidence is one of the unsolved mysteries of the old pagan religion of Scotland. It does not appear to form part of coven activity – Isobell Gowdie does not mention ghosts – and it seems to vanish from the scene about 1600. It may be a purely Gaelic feature. Accounts of these encounters with ghosts are remarkably matter-of-fact and consistent which suggests that both the accused, their accusers and the public at large believed in the factual truth of their statements. To give the widest view of the ghost cult I have collected below all the information about fairy folk, whether or not they claimed a relationship with the dead. They show clearly enough that a ghost cult of considerable age was part of an accepted but very obscure cult or spiritual contact was a normal element of life in early Christian Scotland.

1576 Bessie (Elizabeth) Dunlop, of Lyne, Ayrshire. Bessie is one of the earliest and most intriguing fairy women on record. Her testimony is very puzzling. It is possible that the clerk is combining his own expectations with what Bessie actually said, but her account of the spirit world is coherent and supported by similar claims made by others of the fairy folk. They believed they got their learning from ghosts and had techniques for approaching them. Bessie said she got her learning from Thom Reid whom she described as 'ane honest wele elderie man, gray bardit, and had ane gray coitt with Lumbart slevis of the auld fassioun; ane pair of gray brekis and quhyte schankis, gartanit abone the kne; ane blak bonet on his heid, cloise behind and plane befoir, with silkin laisses drawin throw the lippis thereof, and ane qhyte wand in his hand' (Pitcairn 1833, I, 51). This seems quite sensible but she added that Thom Reid had died at the Battle of Pinkie in 1547, almost thirty years earlier. He was evidently a ghost, but he was also the father of a son, also Thom Reid, who

288

had taken his father's place as officiare or steward to the Laird of Blair, a local landed family. She said that Reid her mentor once took her to meet 'aucht wemene and four men: the men wer cled in gentilmennis clething, and the wemene had all plaiddis round about thame, and wer verrie semelie lyke to se' (Pitcairn 1833. I, 52-53). 'Thai baid hir sit doun, and said: "Welcum, Bessie, will thow go with ws?"' But she did not reply because Thom had forbidden her to speak to them (Pitcairn 1833, I, 53). Thom said they were 'the gude wychtis that wynit in the Court of Elfame' who had come to invite her to go with them. But she refused to join them, since 'sche duelt with her awin husband and bairnis and culd nocht leif thame' (Murray 1921, 241). They may also have been ghosts, in which case they were inviting Bessie to join them in the spirit world.

Thom Reid's mistress was the Quene of Elfame. There are parallels with Moray (below) where Andro Man's mistress was also described as the Queen of Elphame. Then the plot darkens. When Bessie was asked why Thom Reid should be so attentive to her, she replied, apparently inconsequentially, that the Queen of Elphen had visited her when she was still in bed after the birth of one of her children. 'Ane stout woman com in to hir, and sat doun on the forme besyde hir, and askit ane drink at hir, and sche gaif her'. As Bessie was in bed this suggests not a sup of ale or water but a symbolic suckling. This ritual is used to create or enforce a family link and there are many stories of fairies being suckled by a human mother whose child has been 'taken away by the fairies', as was the case here (MacDougall 1910, 142-147). By this act the Queen was diverting the milk that should have gone to the baby and by implication the child itself. She told Bessie that this new child would die but her husband would mend of his illness.

Bessie was in touch with other ghosts. As well as Thom Reid, elder, who had died in battle, she had seen the Laird of Auchinskeyth riding with the fair-folk (Pitcairn 1833, I, 55-57 and note). She declared that four years earlier she had seen him at a thorn beyond Monkcastle; which laird died more than five years earlier (Pitcairn 1833, I, 58). She was 'convict and brunt'. Hers is a very strange story but not unique.

1588 Alesoun Peirsoun of Boarhills, Fife. Alesoun was a notable fairy healer who had learned her craft from William Simpson, her mother's brother, who had died some years earlier. He had lived among the fairy folk and among the Egyptians or gypsies which is probably the same thing. She was convicted and burnt at Edinburgh. She features as the Fairy Queen in a satirical poem, *Legend of the Bischop of St Androis Lyfe.*

> *Ane carling of the Quene of Phareis, That ewill-win geir to Elphyne careis,*
> *Through all Braid–Albane scho hes bene, On horsbak on Hallowe-ewin;*
> *And ay in seiking certayne nyghtis, As scho sayis, with sur silly wychtis;*
> *And names out nychtbouris sex or sewin, That we belevit had bene in heawin.*

Scho said scho saw thame weill aneugh, And speciallie gude Auld Balcleugh, The Secretare and sundrie vther; Ane Williame Symsone, hir mother broth-er... (Pitcairn i, 161-195).

Scott explains this in his own way. 'Alison Pearson, the sorceress who cured Archbishop Adamson, averred that she had recognised in the Fairy court [among the dead] the celebrated Secretary Lethington and the old Knight of Buccleuch, the one of whom had been the most busy politician, the other one of the most unwearied partisans of Queen Mary, during the reign of that unfortunate queen. Upon the whole, persons carried off by sudden death were usually suspected of having fallen into the hands of the fairies and unless redeemed from their power, which it was not always safe to attempt, were doomed to conclude their lives with them. We must not omit to state that those who had an intimate communication with these spirits, while they were yet inhabitants of middle earth, were more apt to be seized upon and carried off to Elfland before their death' (Scott, 1830, 127-8).

Her dittay is of great interest and is given here in full, with the original spelling revised. What Thom Reid was to Bessie Dunlop, her cousin William Sympsoune was to Alesoun Peirsoun. Like Elspeth Reoch, her initiation took place when she was twelve years old and lasted seven years. Where Elspeth became dumb, Alesoun lost the power of her hand and foot. Alesoun was accused of associating with ghosts, particularly the ghost of her cousin William Simpson who taught her, and with the fairy folk or 'good neighbours', which was undeniably true.

Alesoun Peirsoun in Byrehill was dilatit of the pointis of Wichcraft eftir specifeit. This is an abbreviated and modified version of the original Dittay.

She was accused of using sorcery and witchcraft with the invocation of Devilish spirits, especially in the form of Mr William Sympsoune, her cousin and mother's brother's son, who, she claimed was a great scholar and a doctor of medicine, who had healed her of her disease in Lothian, within the town of Edinburgh, where she went to him, being twelve years old; and there coming and going by the space of seven years, when she was helped of her sickness, which she had when her strength and power was taken from her hand and foot; continuing thereby in familiarity with him, by the time aforementioned. She was also accused of dealing with charms, and abusing the common people with Wichcraft, for several years past.

(2) She had kept company with the fairies [gude nychtbouris], and the Queen of Elfame, for several years past, and had friends in that court, who were of her own blood, who had good acquaintance of the Queen of Elfphane, who might have helped her; but she was sometimes well, and sometimes ill, and at one time with them and at another time away, and never knew where she would be the next day. She had not seen the Queen for seven years. She had many good friends in that court, but they were all away now. And that it

was the *guid nychtbouris* that healed her under God. That she was coming and going to St Andrews, healing folk, for sixteen years.

(3) She was guilty of witchcraft, as the said Mr William Sympsoun, who was her grandfather's son, born in Stirling, his father was the King's smith, taught her her craft but was taken away from his father by a man of Egypt (a gipsy?), a giant, being only a child, who took him to Egypt, where he remained for twelve years before he came home again. And that his father had died in the mean time for opening a priest book and looking at it. Mr William healed her, soon after coming home.

(4) Being in the Grange Moor, with people passing by, she was lying down sick and alone when a man wearing green came to her and said: 'If she would be faithful, he would do her good'. She cried for help but no-one heard her. She asked him if he came in God's name and for the good of her soul but he went away. He appeared another time to her, a lusty man with many men and women with him, and she sained herself and prayed and went with them further than she could tell, and saw with them piping and merriness and good cheer, and was carried to Lothian and saw wine puncheons with wine-cups with them. And she declared she was fairly tormented with these things. And that she got a sore blow, the first time she went with them which took all the power of her left side from her, which left a blue mark which she did not feel and her side was much worse.

(5) She saw the guid nychtbouris making their ointments, with pans and fires, and they gathered their herbs before the sun rose, as she did. They came very threatening to her sometimes and frightened her and she cried when they came. They came maybe once in eight days and when she told of it last they had come to her and threatened her saying she would be worse handled than before, so they took the whole strength of her side so that she lay for twenty weeks afterwards. Sometimes they would come and sit beside her and promise her that she would never want if she would be faithful and keep her promise, but if she should tell of them and their doings they would martyr her. And Mr Williame Sympsoun is with thame, who healed her and taught her everything, and speaks and warms her of their coming and saves her; he was a young man only six years older than herself; she became afraid when she saw him as he appeared to herself alone before the Court came. He told her how he was carried away by them out of middle earth. And when we hear a whirl-wind blowing in the sky they will usually be with it or come soon after it, then Mr Williame will come and tell her so that she cannot be taken away with them again, for the tenth [teind] goes every year to hell.

(6) The said Mr Williame told her of every sickness, and which herbs she should use to heal them and now she should use them. He gives her direction at all times. And specially he taught her that the Bishop of St Andrews had many diseases such as the trimling fever, the palp, the rippillies and the flexus; and bade her make a salve to rub on his cheeks, craig, breast, stomach and

sides. And told her to use sheep's milk or waidraue with herbs, claret wine and some other things she gave him a boiled fown, and made a quart of sykelyk, gaif her directiounis to vse the yow mylk or *waidraue* with the herbis, claret wyne; and a boiled fowl, which he drank at two draughts.

1590 Agnes Sampson (Annie Simpson) of Nether Keith (NT 4564), East Lothian. Agnes was a great healer. She also had a familiar or devilish spirit who foretold the future. In rational terms the only thing that foretells the future is a signal beacon so it may be that her source of information was the beacon at the elite site of Keith Marischal, next to her home. If she was not herself a fairy, she and her landlord were in touch with the local fairy folk or hunters.

1597 Christian Lewingstoun, Leith, discussed elsewhere as a charmer, affirmed that her knowledge came from her daughter who met with the Fairie (which might mean she was dead) (Pitcairn 1833, II, 25-29).

1597 Christian Reid, a vagabond, probably a fairy woman. She cast a spell on a mill at Fedderat, near New Deer, Aberdeenshire, 'in the name of God and Christsunday' and was also known at Slains (SCM 1841, I, 172-4) where there were three guid-mannis crofts or pagan sanctuaries (Rust 1871, 32). Andro Man had installed several of these sanctuaries in Banff.

1597 Isobel Strauthaquhin alias Scudder, of Dyce, Aberdeenshire, and her daughter, perhaps Catherine Fergus, were executed in 1597. The daughter had learned her skill from her mother, who learned it from 'ane elf man quha lay with hir' (SCM 1841, I, 177-182). They were certainly fairy folk but the account is brief.

1598 Andro Man (c.1530-1598). The trial of Andro Man in 1597 gives us a unique view of native hunters in Banff (SMC 1841, I, 117-125) and provides more details of the lost world of the fairy folk. In January 1598 when he was executed for witchcraft and sorcery, Andro was at least sixty-five years old and had been involved with the fairy folk since childhood. He had learned his skills from a fairy teacher and was married to the Queen of Elfhame. He was active in the east of Moray, in Banffshire, near Gordonstoun and Duffus. It appears that in the sixteenth century some of these elite families still employed 'fairies' as huntsmen or game wardens. Andro Man's trial of 1598 reveals something of the life of a traditional wise man and other fairy folk.

Andro's initiation into hunting magic began when he was a boy and a woman calling herself the Queen of Elphen came to his mother's house where she was delivered of a baby. As it does in the similar case of Bessie Dunlop (above) this suggests that his mother was herself a wise-woman and midwife and an initiated member of the fairy community. The Queen promised Andro that he would become a healer who 'suld help and cuir all sort of seikness, except stand deid', and that he would never lack except at the end of his life, when he would have to beg for his food, like Thomas Rhymer (who spent seven years in fairyland). In other words Andro would pass a long apprenticeship in the field of traditional healing and would learn the skills he needed to support himself in the world of men. For thirty-two years he had been married to the Queen of Elphen, no doubt a successor to the Queen of his childhood, and had several children by her. The Queen and her company normally met at the Binn Hill (NJ 3065), near Cullen, and at the Binlocht, probably now Lochhill (NJ 2964). Though only 68 m. high, the Binn is visible at the elite sites of Duffus, Gordonstown and Elgin to the west and equally far to the east. It evidently functioned as a fairy hill or beacon site and look-out post and Andro was its keeper. In the transcript of his evidence the Queen's company are called 'elves', perhaps originally Gaelic *sithiche*, which is another word for hunters. Andro confirmed that they had shapes and clothes like men but were but 'shadows', reflecting the view of hunters as men who believed in ghosts and were instructed by them. The only mention of ghosts comes in a catalogue of unrelated crimes, 'Thow kennis sindrie deid men in thair cumpagnie, and that the king that deit at Flowdoun [James IV] and Thomas Rhymour is thair...'

Andro also met the Queen there with an angel or spirit or devil known as Christsunday – the clerk was unable to understand who or what this was. 'Chrystsunday rydis all the tyme that he is in thair cumpanie, and hes carnall daill with thame, and that all honest men and women, and he hym self, kissit his arse; also, that the men that cumis with thame hes do with the Quene of Elfane' (SCM 1841, I, 125). Much of this is nonsense invented by the court who believed that Christsunday was the Devil. G. *domhnach* 'Sunday' has apparently been confused with G. *domhan* 'world, universe', meaning a deer-forest or tribal domain, from G. *damh* 'stag'. In pedestrian terms *Christsunday* was the beacon of the tribal domain. Given the Scottish tendency to personify local beacons it is probable that Christsunday was not a person at all but the *aingeal* or beacon located on the Binn Hill. 'Christ' was popular as a beacon name as it has links with G. *ceir* 'wax', *crios* or *grioth* 'sun', *grios* 'heat', and *griosach* 'burning embers'. The most important local beacon hill was the Binn of Cullen (NJ 4764). Andro lived on its southern slopes at Darbreich (NJ 4863). The following points of difficulty are resolved if we take 'Christsunday' to be the name of the local beacon, a sacred but not a Christian entity and not a ghost.

Many details of Andro Man's life are laid out in the dittay against him. All the locations lie within a few miles of his home at Tarbruich, now Darbreich (NJ 4863), on the southern slopes of the Binn of Cullen, in the parish of Rathven (NJ 4465). Tarbruich refers to the beacon on the Binn: G. *toir* 'hunt' or E. *tor* 'hill' and G. *bruich* 'ruddy-faced, fiery'. His clients ranged along the coast between Lossiemouth to the west and Portsoy to the east. Angus (NJ 2557), Mains of Innes (NJ 2765), Buckie and Nether Buckie (NJ 4265),

Knock (NJ 5453), Fordyce (NJ 5563), and Durn (NJ 5865) are all mentioned. At Mains of Innes, Mains of Caddell and elsewhere Andro had installed and dedicated pagan sanctuaries known as Wards of the Hynd Knight, on behalf of local landowners. He measured out small areas of land, marked the corners with stones, and sanctified the whole, to preserve the land from the lunsaucht and all other diseases. It was forbidden to dig peat there or plough up this land. The Guidman's Croft is still a feature of some farms. The Church saw such plots as a home for the Devil but in the traditional view the wild herds were ruled by the Lady and the Guidmen's Croft was a sacrifice to the guidmen or fairy hunters.

We can deduce from Andro Man's dittay that hunters gathered at the Binhill and the Binlocht on certain days such as Ruidday-in-Harvest and Hallowe'en. The Devil was the court's name for the King of Elphen who the Queen's consort and hunt master. He appeared like a man and in the likeness of a black stag and there was carnal dealing between witches and the Devil and between the Quene of Elphane and members of her company: 'The Quene of Elphen was their, and vtheris with hir, rydand on quhyt haikneyes, and that thay com to the Binhill and the Binlocht, quhair thay vse commonlie to convene, and that they quha convenis with thame kissis Christsonday and the Quene of Elphenis airss, that the Quene is verray plesand, and wil be auld and young quhen scho plesissis; scho mackis any kyng quhom scho pleisis, and lyis with any scho lykis' (Spalding 1841, I, 119-121). As with the sabbat the purpose of the rite was to ensure the success of the forthcoming hunt.

To summarise the probable structure of the group who met periodically at the Binn, the Queen appointed a King to be her consort; he was probably also the hunt-master and the lord of the witches. A hunt-master is found in Caithness in 1616 where Katherine Caray met 'ane great number of fairie men' together with 'a maister man' (Dalyell 1835, 536) and a man who is at once the Devil of the witches and master of the hunt is found in Bute in 1662 (MacPhail 1921, 23). Andro was a senior officer or druid who kept the lore and ran the fire but overall control of the spiritual aspects lay with his wife, the Queen. The witches (probably younger than those cited, and more numerous) went through the ritual of the sabbat with the King while the hunters had sex either with the Queen or with the women of her Court. There would ideally be the same number of men and women at the sabbats (as Isobell Gowdie explained was the case in Auldearn). The purpose of the sexual activity was to bring success to the hunt.

The clerk did his best to fit it into what was understood of witchcraft in 1597, eking it out with a Devil, a coven, and two arses to kiss. These features appear to be imaginary. But we certainly we find a King of Elphame who had carnal dealing with the local witches while the Queen 'has a grip of all the craft' and had carnal dealing with some at least of the hunters. The trial of Andro Man gives us our most detailed view of the older religion of the fairies or deer-hunters.

1605 Patrick Lowrie, Halie, Ayrshire, was accused of cursing his neighbour's cows. He went with Janet Hunter, Catherine McTear and Margaret Duncane at Hallowe'en 1604 to Lowdon Hill, a prominent beacon hill in North Ayrshire (Scots *lowe* 'blaze'), where they met 'ane devillische Spreit in liknes of ane woman, and callit her selff Helen McBrune' (Pitcairn 1833, II, 478). He may have been the King of Elphame; Helen McBrune was apparently the Queen, and this was a typical Hallowe'en gathering.

1613 Margaret Reoch, a vagabond or fairy woman, sometime in Lumfannan, Aberdeenshire. Perhaps related to Elspeth Reoch, tried in Orkney in 1616, another fairy woman who led a wandering life.

1615 Janet Drever was one of the fairy folk of Orkney (Black 1903, 72-74). Ritual prostitution seems to have persisted there, for she was accused in 1615 of fostering a bairn in the hill of Westray to the fairy folk of Westray whom she called 'our guid nichtbouris, and in having carnal deall with hir [them] And haveing conversation with the fary 26 yeirs bygane'. If the fairy folk of Westray had sexual dealings with Janet over twenty-six years she stood in the same relationship to them as the Queen of Elfane did to Andro Man. 'Fostering a bairn' was not a humanitarian good deed in such a context; fairy changelings were destined for some important ritual. The Reformers' insistence on infant baptism was no doubt hoped to protect infants against the pagan indifference to their lives. On the other hand a pagan may have believed that an infant devoted to the Lady was a fortunate soul.

1616 Katherine Caray wandered among the hills of Caithness 'at the doun going of the sun' when she was met by a great number of fairy men or hunters, under a master (Dalyell 1835, 536; Rec. Ork. f. 94, f.63).

1616 Elspeth Reoch (MCM 1841, II, 187-190; Black 1903, 111-115), was daughter to the late Donald Reoch, piper to the 'Rough Earl', George Sinclair, 5th Earl of Caithness, 1566-1643, who was known as Wicked Earl George. She belonged to a far-flung family of fairy folk and is remarkable for the number of men who lay with her and the number of children she had by different fathers. She also communicated with ghosts. When she was twelve (and old enough to be initiated) she wandered out of Caithness where she was born to Lochaber to stay with her aunt, wife of Allan McKeldowie who was a skeely man (he was a fairy man with magical skills). In Lochaber while waiting for a boat she met two men who were in no way different from other men, 'ane clad in blak and the uther with ane grein tartane plaid about him'. The black man told her they were fairy men and gave her the gift of second sight. She had to roast an egg and take the sweat of it three Sundays, and on washing her hands she would see and know anything she might desire. In Strathspey she met James Mitchell at Kirk of Murthly in Balvenie, father of her first bairn (when she was fourteen) which was born at her sister's house in Strathspey. The black man that she met in Lochaber came to her in her sister's house and told her he was a fairy man who was once her kinsman John Stewart who was killed by McKay at the going-down of the sun, and so, neither dead nor living, was doomed for ever to wander between heaven and earth ('quha wes slane be Mc Key at the doun going of the soone And therfor nather deid nor leiving bot wald ever go betuix the heaven and the earth'). The black man dealt with her for two nights, not letting her sleep. The third night he lay with her she lost the power of her tongue and remained dumb despite violent treatment by her brother who hit her with a branks until she bled, wound a bow-string around her head and finally had her taken on several Sundays to be prayed for in church. Why was he so worried? Her loss of a faculty is similar to the story of Alesoune Piersoune and John Stewart of Irvine and appears to accompany a gain of supernatural powers. She also had a bairn to Magnus Sinclair in Sorne at the desire of his wife. At Yule the fairy man lay with her and told her to 'leave Orkney and go home to her awin countrey becaus this cuntrey was 'priestgone' by which he meant, there were too many ministers in it 'an gif she taryit she wald be hurt.'

Elspeth was involved with the Stewart earls. She had seen Robert Stewart, natural son of the late Patrick, once earl of Orkney, with Patrick Traill to whom she was with bairn and certain others with cloths about their heads in Edmond Callendar's house at their afternoon drink 'before the Earl of Caithness came to the cuntrey.' After the arrest of his father Patrick 'sumtyme earl of Orkney' for treason, Robert Stewart had rebelled against James VI in 1614 but was defeated by George Sinclair, Earl of Caithness, and hanged in Edinburgh on 14 November 1614. His father was executed in Edinburgh in 1615. The arrest of Elspeth Reoch the fairy woman in 1616 was liable to have had political motives.

1618 John Stewart. Recurrent features are the white wand, the loss of the power of speech and eyesight, and the care for the ghosts of those who have died a sudden or violent death. The sinking of the Irvine barque *The Gift of God* in 1618 off the coast of Cornwall on her way to France was attributed to three local women, Margaret Barclay or Dein who had a grudge against one of the owners, her good-brother, the Provost of Irvine, and two witches, Isobell Scherar alias Crawford and Isobel Insh, aided by John Stewart, a vagabond professing skill in palmestrie and jugglerie. News of the sinking was announced by John Stewart, probably reaching him by gossip or by another ship rather than by supernatural means. He admitted meeting the women at Hallowe'en (Scott 1830, 317-327). It being demanded of him by what means he professed himself to have knowledge of things to come, the said John confessed, that the space of twenty-six years ago, he being travelling on All-Hallow-Even night, between the towns of Monygoif and Clary in Galway, he met with the King of the Fairies and his company, the King of the Fairies gave him a stroke with a white rod over the forehead, which took from him the power of speech and the use of one eye, which he wanted for the space of three years. He declared, that the use of speech and eyesight was restored to him by the King of Fairies and his company, on an Hallowe'en night, at the town of Dublin, in Ireland, and that since that time, he had joined these people every Saturday at seven o'clock and remained with them all the night; also that they met every Hallow-tide, sometimes on Lanark Hill, sometimes on Kilmaurs Hill, and that he was then taught by them... He declared that he had seen many persons at the Court of Fairy, whose names he rehearsed particularly but which are not given, and declared that all such persons as are taken away by sudden death go with the King of Elfland (Scott 1830, 160). Stewart also describes seeing the devil in the form of a 'black litle quhalp' [whelp]. He committed suicide in prison.

This is the original version of John Stewart's account of how he acquired the power of prophecy.

> 'The said Jn. confest that about the space of twenty sax yeirs tharby, he being travelling on an hallowein betwixt the toun of Monygoiff and Clary, in Galloway. He foregetherit with the King of Pharie and his company, and that the King of Pharie gave him a straik with ane quhyt rod on the brow, at the quhilk tyme the power of his tung and his ane ey was tane frae him, and that he wantit the said power and sicht be the space of three yeirs; and that the said wus restorit agane to him be the said King of Pharie and his companie on ane hallow evin at the town of Dubling in Ireland; and that everie Setterday at evin he was with thame all that night sensyn, as also on everie hallowevin, and declarit thay met everie hallowday, sumtyme in Lanark Hill and sumtyme in Kilmaurs Hill, and was lernit be thame ... and declarit that he saw with the King of the Pharie sundrie personnes quhois name he rehersit particularlie; and that all sic personnes quho war tane away by suddane death went with the Pharie.'

1623 Isobel Haldane, **Margaret Hormscleugh** and **Janet Trall** lived in Dunning, worked together and were tried together in Perth in 1623. They were healers, not members of a coven, and the link defined by the court was not with the Devil but with the fairy folk. A fourth member of the group, Alexander Lokhart, seems to have got off scot free. Isobel Haldane confessed that ten years before she had gone to fairyland but her account appears to be in part a dream or an embellishment by the clerk. When she was lying in her bed, she was taken forth, whether it was by God or the Devil, she knows not; but she was carried to a hill side, 'the hill oppynit and scho enterit in... Thir scho stayit thrie dayis, viz. fro Thuirsday till Sonday at xii houris. Scho mett a man with ane gray beird, quha brocht hir furth agane'. She obtained all her information as to life and death from this man, whom she met among the fairy folk (that is, he was a ghost). Being required to declare if she had treated Andrew Duncan's bairn she answered, that according to the direction of Janet Trall, she went with Alexander Lokhart down to the Turret Port, and took water from the burn there, being dumb (silent). That she brought it to Andrew Duncan's house, and there on her knees washed the bairn in the name of the Father, Son, and Holy Ghost. Afterwards, accompanied by Alexander Lokhart, she took the water and the bairn's sark and cast both into the bum. Despite this the bairn died. Margaret Hormscleugh and Janet Trail also used south-flowing water and sark magic. Janet Trall also was involved with fairy folk who teased her. She said some were red, some were grey, and they rode on horses. Their leader was a bonny white man riding on a white horse and at other times dressed in green (Stuart 1843, xiii).

1628 Steven Malcome (also known as Steinie Maltman) of Leckie, Gargunnock, near Stirling, like Alesoun Pearsoun in Fife, Bessie Dunlop in Ayrshire, Christian Lewingstoun in Leith and others charged with charming and deceiving the public, had been initiated into the native theory of magical healing by 'the fairye folk quhom he had sein in bodilie schapes in sindrie places' (Fergusson 1907, 76). He charmed sarks (shirts) and used a drawn sword to protect against fairies, who could harm as well as cure, and an elf-arrow against 'the fairies shott'. He believed in the efficacy of south-running water or an elf-arrow rubbed on the body or boiled in south-running water. In one case he charmed one of the patient's sarks using the formula 'God be betwixt this man that aught this sark and all evills in name of the Father, the Sone and the Holy Ghost, and put on this sark thryse in the name of the Father etc,' then instructed the sick person to wash his body in south-running water and to cast out the water used for this washing in some desert place where no Christian soul repairs. He sent the patient a napkin to dry his body instructing him to throw it under his bed. If the illness was to be laid on a beast, it was to be paid for by the sick person. One lunatic was taken out alone on a winter night between nine and ten o'clock. Steven drew a circle round him with the point of a sword and then stood ready to repel the fairy folk who were responsible for his illness. Unfortunately the cure did not succeed. Sick people were taken out at night to where they thought they had got sick and instructed to pray to God 'and all unearthly wights' to be made well again. He never caused illness but he believed he could transfer it from one person to another, or to an animal, or to running water.

1629 Elspeth Cursetter, a wandering woman of Orkney, refused access to the house of a man in Birsay, sat down before the door and cursed the household, saying 'Ill might they all thryve, and ill might they speid' and within fourteen days his best horse died. She was probably insane and certainly a wicked old baggage.

1629 Jonet Rendall alias Rigga, probably from G. *ruaig* 'pursuit, hunt, chase', of Birsay in Orkney, was a poor beggar, dependent on alms, but with a Gaelic nickname she was probably one of the fairy folk. When she was refused charity in Rendall twenty years earlier a fairy man or Devil called Walliman, dressed in white, with a white head and a grey beard appeared and offered her the gift of healing to win alms. This was a common inducement to join the fairy folk. If one believes the indictment, Walliman and she were between them responsible for the deaths of an amazing quantity of livestock (Black 1903, 103-111).

1633 Issobell Sinclair of Orkney. It was alleged against her that during seven years, 'sex times at the reathes of the year, shoe hath bein controlled with the Phairie'. She was accused of firing a piece of linen cloth and a hair of the beast at Hallowe'en to preserve cattle (Dalyell 1835, 193 and note). Dalyell says that, as a cure, 'Hair is cut, or burnt, or cast aside'. She was also skilled in the second sight.

1662 Isobell Gowdie of Auldearn in Moray who joined a local coven in 1647, confessed at her trial in 1662 that she had killed various people by making witch-pokes, pronouncing charms, and shooting them with elf-arrows, all as instructed by the Devil. But she also had connections with the fairy world though not, apparently, with ghosts. Once she went to the Downie-hills where she met the Queen of Fearrie, who was bravely clothed in white linen and in white and brown cloth, the 'broad-faced' King of Fearrie and several elf-bulls. There were elf-bows making elf-arrows from blanks supplied by the Devil and 'ther wes elf-bullis rowtthing and skoylling wp and downe thair and affrighted me' (Pitcairn 1833, III, 602-616). The Downie Hillock (NH 9658) near Darnaway Castle is the site of a small Iron Age hill-fort with a panoramic view which evidently served as a look-out for hunters. She was impressed by the fact that she got more food than she could eat. She named ten of the thirteen male witches who belonged to her coven and whose aliases suggest they were fairy men or hunters. Swein, Rorie, The Roring Lyon, Mak Hector, Robert the Rule (who seemed to command the rest), Theiff of Hell, The Red Reiver, Robert the Jackis [coat of mail], Laing, Thomas a Fearie &c. She confirms that she would recognise them all 'quhan they appeir lyk a man' (Pitcairn 1833, III, 606). These aliases are not in the archaic Gaelic tradition but would be appropriate for hunters. 'Thomas a Fearie' is presumably Thomas the Rhymer.

1662 Jonet Morisoune of Rothesay in Bute 'declares that at the time she met with the devil quhen he was goeing by with a great number of men that she asked at him quhat were these that went by who answered they are my company and quhen she speired where they were going he answered that they were going to seek a prey' (MacPhail 1921, 23). This would be literal truth if the witch-master in traditional Gaelic society, like the King of Fairy in Banff, was also the master of the hunt. Bute was a purely Gaelic island in 1662, its links more with the Highlands than the Lowlands, and it seems to have had both a coven and a fairy (hunting) company. The witches' links were with the Highlands. Margret NcLevin told the court that 'in hervest last she was at a meiting in Lochfine with Donald McCartur, Kathrine Moore and a wife out of Kildavanane and Soirle McAllesters midmost son and severall other heiland people there (quhich she knew not) and one McKeraish out of Glendaroil (as she thought) quho was on a fisher boat and that the said McKeraish shot Robert McKomash after dinner being sitting on the craft' (MacPhail 1920, 10). The witches of Bute used witch-pokes, elf-arrows and Gaelic charms but the healers blamed the fairies for shooting sick people. Once her Devil gave Jonet 'an elf errow stone to shott [a child of seven] which she did ten dayes therafter that the child dyed imediately therafter'. Nevertheless Jonet declared the devil told her 'it was the fayries that took John Glas child's lyfe' (MacPhail 1920, 19, 23, 27). She used herbs to cure several people who had been blasted by the fairies. She explained that 'blasting is a whirlwinde that the fayries raises about that persone quich they intend to wrong quhich may be healed two wayes ether by herbs or by charming'.

1677 Donald McIlmichall, a homeless vagabond and probably a fairy man, was hanged in 1677 in the new burgh of Inveraray in Argyll, which at that time contained a cross, a court-house, a prison, a gibbet, a Reformed church, and a number of public houses. The Synod of Argyll met there for the first time in 1639. Donald was found guilty of 'that horrid cryme of corresponding with the devill.' His trial suggests that the different picture gained of paganism in Highland and Lowland Scotland is partly due to the lack of legal proceedings in the Highlands. This trial gives us a unique view of a troop of hunters in a Gaelic-speaking area at a late date. They seem to have been outcasts preying on settled folk, much as the Roma are now; at this late date it was still as much a crime to attend a fairy gathering as to attend a Lowland Sabbat. Donald was tried together with Donald dow McGregour in Dalavich on Loch Awe (NM 9612) for various counts of theft and for consulting sundry times with evil spirits. The first charge refers to his stealing a cow and selling it to waiting customers and was in itself a hanging business. In addition in November 1676 Donald McIlmichall had met with 'unworldlie folk' at various fairy hills in Appin and had played the Jew's harp while they danced (MacPhail 1920, 36-38). To be present at a fairy feast was evidently as serious a crime as to attend a sabbat or to steal a cow. Donald's trial confirms that fairies, despite their nomadic and ghostly tendencies, were as physically present in the real world as the witches of Lowland covens. We can follow his travels on the map, from the island of Lismore, where he had already stayed with the fairies, to the mainland of Argyll where they camped at the Shian of Barcaldine, which the editor in a note describes as 'a typical fairy mound, on the south side of Loch Creran, near the ferry to Appin' (MacPhail 1920, 38). 'And the said Donald being thereupon interrogat confesses judiciallie that on a night in the month of November 1676 he travelling betwixt Ardturr and Glackiriska at ane hill he saw a light not knowing quhair he was. And ther a great number of men and women within the hill quair he entered having many candles lighted, and saw ane old man as seemed to have preference above the rest and that sum of them desired to shutt him out and others to haev him drawine in And saw them all danceing about the lights and that they wold have him promise and engadge to come ther againe that night eight nights and for a considerable space thereaftir. Being interrogat what night it wes he mett first and quhair he went efter he parted with them Answers that it wes on the Sabath night and eftir he left them that night he went to Robert Buchanan his house in Glackiriskay and that he wes forceit to com againe the second tyme on the Sabath thereftir... That he entered 20 dayes eftir Hallowday and continowed till 20 days before Candlemes. That it was a woman among them that took the promise of him, and that he cannot weill tell quhat persons they er bot he judges them not to hae bein *wordlie* men or men ordayned of god, and that they enquyired if he wes baptized and that he said he wes, bot that they gave him no name nor that he told them his own name bot still called him by the name of that man...' He said he had met the same folk in Lismore and at the Shian of Barcaldine, a fairy hill or outlook post on the south side of Loch Creran (NM 9040) on Sabbath nights and played on the Jew's harp to them when they danced. The jury unanimously found him guilty of theft and consulting sundry times with evil spirits (MacPhail 1930, 36-38). Like Bessie Dunlop, Donald was guilty of dealing with stolen goods. 'Being interrogat as he consulted the devill and these evil spirits anent stolen goods answers that he went and enquyred anent stolen goods and it was told him especiallie of the stealling these twa horses from McAllister VcLauchlane in Ballegowine in Leismore. And that at other tymes loist goods wes told him without asking quhilk he wes discovering to the owners.'

It is possible that Donald was more involved with the local fairies than we learn from the bare record. Ardtur (NM 9146) is on Loch Linnhe opposite Lismore and the farm of Glackeriska (NM 9245) is on high ground between Ardtur and North Sheann on Loch Creran. Both appear to be ferry points. The distance between them is no more than a mile. Ardtur is near the north or seaward end of a fairly narrow coastal promontory, which suggests Donald had been ferried over from Lismore, guided by the light at the shian, in order to join in the Hallowe'en hunt. The hill where Donald met the fairies in November 1676 is probably Druim Dubh 'ridge of the deer', shown on the OS 1:50,000 map as a height of 36 m. It is near Dalnashean (NM 9145) 'meadow of the watch post' (probably *An Sidhean,* NM 908421). There is another Shean at Barcaldine (NM 9040), a typical fairy mound, on the south side of Loch Creran, near the ferry to Appin. In common with all fairy knolls this little hill has a wide view, ranging over Lismore and other coastal features.

The dates in his account are also of interest. Hallowday (1 November) and Candlemas (2 February) are both Quarter days which had special significance for Lowland witches and for Highland hunters. Candlemas was mid-way between the winter solstice and the spring equinox and reflects an old calendar which divided the year into eight parts. The native deer-hunters or *sidh,* known latterly as fairies following the English pun on G. *faire* 'to keep watch', were peripatetic but by 1676 it seems they were finding it difficult to maintain their mobile life-style. They had been excluded from the deer-forests and were arrested for poaching or theft if they went about their normal business. This case suggests that to survive they took to stealing cattle from settled farmers. Fairies came to occupy a hopeless marginal position in society much like that occupied now by gypsies. But they still danced every sabbath to the music of Donald McIlmichal's trumps.

VAGABONDS

Travelling folk, gypsies or vagabonds including those named below were regularly accused of charming and healing. **Alesoune Piersoun** (tried in 1588) learned her craft from William Simpson, her mother's brother who had lived among the fairy folk or among the Egyptians or gypsies. **Christian Reid**, a notorious witch and sorcerer, was tried in Aberdeen in 1597 (SCM I, 174). A member of a Borders gypsy family, **John Faw,** was tried in Orkney in 1612. Dalyell averred that 'the Egyptians indeed were undoubtedly the source of some of the Scottish superstitions'. Faw dealt in charming, fortune-telling and helping or hindering 'the proffeit of the milk of bestiall' (1835, 235). **Elspeth Reoch** (1616) moved from Orkney to Caithness, Lochaber, Speyside and back to Orkney, presumably as one of a band of fairy folk. **John Stewart** (1618) of Ayrshire was an itinerant juggler and fortune-teller who had got his knowledge from the King of the Fairies in Galway, Ireland. **Janet Rendall** of Orkney (1629) went from house to house begging. **Margaret Strudgeon** and **Isobel Gray**, vagabonds, were caught up in the trial of the Lanark coven in 1629. **John Phillips**, vagabond, probably known as Priep the Witch, was tried at Banff in 1631 on charges of sorcery and witchcraft. In 1643 **William Scottie** 'vagabond, warlache' was tried in Orkney. **Donald McIlmichel** (1677) was a vagabond who lived with the fairy folk in Lismore and in Appin.

18: THE FAIRY RELIGION

There is a story of a man on Lochrannoch-side who fought a bush, in mistake for a ghost, in a hollow, which had an evil name for being haunted. The conflict continued until dawn, when he was found exhausted, scratched and bleeding.

J.Gregorson Campbell 1901, 181.

The hand of the Lord was upon me, and carried me out in the Spirit of the Lord, and set me down in the midst of the valley which was full of bones. And caused me to pass by them round about: and behold, there were very many in the field; and lo, they were very dry.

Ezekiel 37:1-2.

It is difficult and perhaps impossible for a Western European living in the twenty-first century to enter into or even to imagine a world where medical science is taught by ghosts but we can consider one or two posssible points of entry. If we accept that irrational religious belief is a valid human attitude, it is from one point of view largely a question of definition and from another a matter of faith.

However there may be – there must be – some underlying reality for, in every country in Europe and as far as China and Japan, people have very similar beliefs about ghosts. They agree about their origins as the souls of the dead, they agree about their shadowy nature and their ability to interact with the living, though they treat this knowledge in different ways. The fairy folk of Scotland in the late sixteenth and early seventeenth century were involved in what would now be called necromancy, defined by Chamber's Dictionary as 'the art of revealing future events by calling up and questioning the spirits of the dead'. Like all religious concepts necromancy is imaginary or poetic but it was apparently taken literally both by the Kirk who persecuted necromancers, and by practitioners who believed they could traffic with the Devil. Bessie Dunlop, tried in 1576, was by her own account a highly successful medium whose spirit guide, Thom Reid, answered questions about the future which she put to him on her own behalf and on behalf of others. Some people still believe they can contact the ghosts or spirits of the dead by means of a spirit guide or medium and that these spirits can answer questions.

If we track the belief in ghosts back far enough we find that, like most superstitions, it has its origin in a rational activity. This is the use of bones as fuel. In the treeless landscapes of northern Europe at the end of the last glaciation, bands of hunters coordinated their movements by means of bonfires. In the absence of any other fuel, they collected dried bones from the tundra. There were apparently copious supplies of freeze-dried bones and this strategy worked very well. Even when shrubs and trees began to offer an alternative, hunters in the north continued for thousands of years to use bones as fuel in seasonal bonfires. This also had a practical reason. Wood is smoky but bones burn with a bright yellow flame which gives a good signal.

At first bones of all kinds were scavenged at random (hence the assortments found in bone caves) but the available bones must often have included the bodies of dead hunters. When the bones saved for the next bonfire included those of known individuals the personal began to outweigh the practical and an irrational or imaginary idea took hold. This was the concept of the ghost. An imaginative person swore he could see the ghost of someone who had recently died rising to heaven in the smoke. In a very short time everyone could see these wonderful ghosts and began to imagine the dead in heaven, hunting as they had done on earth, albeit in a shadowy invisible fashion (the afterlife was always a vague and variable location).

The discovery that bones were the seat of the soul gave them a religious significance which they have never lost. That this discovery was made a very long time ago is shown by parallels between the West and India. Hindus practise cremation because they believe that burning forces the soul to abandon its old body and move on to its next life. Since Hindus believe the soul resides in the head some of them encourage it to leave by cracking the skull prior to burning. Children are buried, not burnt, as they are felt to have not yet developed souls with a strong attachment to their bodies. In Scottish belief this may also have been true as they were often buried separately, in separate enclosures or to the north of the church. And as we have seen, witches felt no compunction about sacrificng newborn babies.

In Britain chambered tombs belong to an intermediate phase when the new ghost doctrine had been accepted and bones were respected but there was still a need for fuel for signal fires. The chambers served the practical purpose of storing bones in dry conditions until they were needed. The situation found on excavation reflects nothing more signficant than the inventory at the point where the local community changed its way of doing things or a better site was found for the beacon. Inhumations may identify individuals who were not eligible for cremation. Otherwise the selection and organisation of bones within the chambers reflects the practical business of running a bonfire. Long bones were set in tidy piles, like a well-managed wood-pile. Small bones were collected and kept in baskets, not for ritual purposes (as some witches did) but to use as kindling. Skulls may have been smashed to liberate the soul but also to encourage combustion and prevent explosions, as in India today.

It is a short step from recognising ghosts in the smoke of the cremation fire to the deduction that the souls of those who were not cremated, for whatever reason, would not rise to heaven but would remain in limbo, condemned to wander for ever between the living and the dead. This is the simplest explanation for a wandering ghost. But there was also an obligation on the living to restrict this very valuable privilege to reputable people who deserved it. Out of prudence the rite de passage normally excluded suicides, strangers, pregnant women, unbaptised children and drowned sailors. This gives force to the Gaelic curse that one's enemy should be drowned 'by sea or by water' and explains the efforts made to recover drowned bodies. It may even explain the Gaelic taboo on eating fish.

This link between cremation and the individual soul suggests a different way of looking at the two Bronze Age mummies of different periods which were uncovered at Cladh Hallan in South Uist. These two composite but complete skeletons, one male, one female, 'curated, trussed and mummified' had initially been preserved by brief immersion in a peat bog (using a technique used to preserve meat) and then kept on display for centuries before being buried under the floor of a Bronze Age hut (Parker Pearson 2005, 329-46). They had been repaired from time to time but remained essentially complete over the centuries. They were either very blessed or very wicked but as their bones were not burnt their souls remained earth-bound. The horror invoked by an unburnt skeleton is still lively and can be attributed to a residual fear of the undead and their restless souls. The wandering ghost became customary belief over most of Europe and the mummies of Cladh Hallan suggest it was already general in the Bronze Age. (A *cladh* is a pagan cemetery, probably at one time a cremation site as it is normally demarcated by a ditch.)

In view of what has been said about the treatment of children in India, it may be significant that at Cladh Hallan excavators also found the burials of many children and of a complete sheep. The sheep burial can be interpreted in similar terms, for the Gaels operated an embargo on burning the bones of sheep, thus preventing their translation to paradise: evidently hunters did not want the pesky animals disrupting the hunting in heaven as they had done on earth (Henderson 1911, 100).

The most famous but in certain ways the least typical medium in literature is the Witch of Endor who (to her own surprise and terror) raised the dead Samuel, wrapped in a robe and complaining about being disturbed so that Saul could ask him what to do (1 Samuel 28:3-25). Samuel had reason to be annoyed. Not only had necromancy recently been banned, and by Saul himself: he was not a lost soul. According to the law he had died without violence and been buried among his own people with all the proper observances (1 Samuel 25:1, 28:3). It appears that after the death of Samuel there was a resurgence of a ghost cult among the Jews and this is a moral tale designed to warn them that, though God had on this occasion made an exception and allowed

305

the dead to rise, He had done so only to show that meddling in necromancy did not pay, as Saul's subsequent history shows. The belief found in Classical Greece and in Europe up to the middle ages is that a restless ghost will haunt the living until it is given proper burial.

Restless ghosts

When we look in Scotland for restless ghosts we find many examples, not only in the trials but in folk literature. One Gaelic story, which cannot be of any great age, explains the situation in terms of the Fallen Angels (Carmichael vol.2, 1938, 352-353). The Proud Angel left heaven to found a kingdom of his own and other angels flocked after him, so many that heaven was in danger of being emptied. God ordered that the gates of heaven and hell should be closed and this was done immediately. Those who had reached hell were locked in but those who had left heaven but had not yet reached hell were the fairy folk and they were condemned to live in holes in the earth for ever. This was the song they sang.

Not of the seed of Adam are we, and Abraham is not our father.
But of the seed of the Proud Angel, driven forth from heaven.

It was widely known in Scotland that certain souls had been banished to fairyland, which was understood to be the land of the dead. There were many talented individuals who paid for their unusual abilities by giving their souls to the Devil or to the Fairy Queen. They include Michael Scot (1175-1232), Roger Bacon (c.1214-c.1292), Thomas Rhymer (d. c.1294), James IV (d. 1513), and Sir Robert Gordon (1647-1704). Another who is said to have paid the price of genius with his soul was Donald Mor MacCrimmon of Skye. According to legend MacCrimmon got a silver chanter from the Banshee of the Cave of Gold (the Cailleach or Fairy Queen) on condition that he would go with her into the Cave of Gold, *an Uamh Oir*, at the end of a day and a year. His disappearance is said to explain the story of the pibroch known as 'The Cave of Gold', said to have been composed by him in 1610.

Cha tig mise!
I shall never come back! I shall never return!
Before I come from the Cave of Gold
The kidling flocks will be goats of the rocks,
The feeble children will be warriors bold,
I am in woe, under spells to go;
I'll be for ever in the Cave of Gold.

This story is also told of a later MacCrimmon called Donald Ban who was killed at the Rout of Moy in 1746, which seems rather late for the genesis of a fairy story. Also in favour of an earlier date is the fact that the MacCrimmon pibroch is very similar to the lament, *Cha till mi tuill* 'I shall return no more', which was played at the funeral of Rob Roy MacGregor in 1734 and is found in the *Campbell Canntaireachd* manuscript of 1797. The Cave of Gold is the kingdom of fire ruled by the Cailleach, or the realm of death ruled by the cremation goddess. The name as usual is a pun. G. *uamh* is also the grave and G. *or* is also a spell.

The Bonfire

The bonfire moved from being a secular device to being a powerful religious ritual. Many local beacons went through further evolution into sacred entities, personified as patron saints, with protective and predictive powers. These aspects are shared with the saints or holy spirits of the Christian Church. Recently bonfires were lit at the quarter days but they are also associated with an earlier system which marked the solar seasons with major bonfires at mid-winter, midsummer and the spring and autumn equinoxes. The supernatural or ghostly aspect of these bonfires explains why the Church banned them again and again and why the people were so determined to keep them alive and keep the ghosts at bay.

All the recent quarter days or sabbats are associated with fire, though sometimes the tradition is frail. 1 February or Candlemas is the feast of Bridget whose perpetual flame was guarded at Kildare, and a bonfire called the Candlemas Bleeze was lit at Dornoch (McNeill 1959, II, 34). On 1 May the Beltane bonfires were lit on prominent sites at sunrise. The practice of lighting a bonfire at Lammas, 1 August, is now rare but persisted into the nineteenth century at Dalry in North Ayrshire, where the baal-fire or Tannel (G. *teine* 'fire') was still lit in 1843 (NSA; Paterson 1866, 144). Lammas is said to mean *hlaf-mas* 'loaf-mass' but is more likely to be from G. *laom* 'great blaze of fire', cognate with E. *flame*. It was not, as usually claimed, a harvest celebration, certainly not in Scotland where harvest (if any) was much later. In Ireland 1 August was Lughnasadh, the feast which the fire-god Lugh inaugurated in honour of his foster-mother Tailltiu. He buried her under a great mound at Tara where the anniversary, like any hunt gathering, was celebrated with bonfires, races and games (McNeill 1959, II, 94). According to one story, Tailltiu died clearing forested land for cultivation, which suggests a folk memory of a fire which got out of control. But the most important of the cremation events was Samhain or Hallowe'en, which was adopted into the calendar as the Feast of the Dead. Midwinter (the birth of Jesus and the feast of St John the Evangelist among many other beacon saints) and midsummer (the feast of St John the Baptist) were also celebrated with fire and were much more splendid and popular events.

From a story told by the minister of Latheron in Caithness in 1874 it seems the smoke itself had magical powers which might allow the powers of the dead to pass to the living (MacPhail 1898, 87). The focus of the tale is the ruined Neolithic chambered cairn near the Bronze Age stone setting at Achavanich (Achadh a Bheannaich, perhaps 'bone field', from G. *beann* 'bone'; ND 1742) in Latheron, which is associated with a cremation ritual. To the east of Achavanich there is a cairn overgrown with heather, in the middle of which is a small enclosure which we now know to be the collapsed roof structure of the cairn but which to the fancy of the age looked like a Druidical altar.

> When the principal Druid of that district had become so old and infirm that he could no longer perform the functions of his office, he was burnt alive on this altar as a sacrifice. While he was being offered, the young Druid who had been appointed his successor in office kept going round in the altar-smoke – *ex fumo dare lucem* – that he might catch the spirit of his predecessor as it took its flight.

We can probably discount the story of human sacrifice. According to a traditional tale collected by James Macdougall (1910, 202-203), the Gaels did not burn old people alive but exposed them when they felt the approach of death; but their dried bones were certainly burnt. This cremation story from Caithness appears to be a rare survival. The chambered cairn in which the local druid lived and died or where he at any rate worked is a round cairn of Orkney-Cromarty type which dates to the Neolithic (Henshall 1963, 257; Davidson & Henshall 1991, 89; Myatt 2004). Its forecourt (facing east) was possibly used for excarnation. The offering that was made to the fire was not a live victim but the old priest's bones which had been stored for months or perhaps for years in the chamber. That the stone setting may have had astronomical significance is suggested by Dr Euan MacKie (1975, 223) who pointed out that the peaks of Morven and Maiden Pap to the southwest and Ben Dorrery to the northwest provided ideal foresights for either solar or lunar observation.

The lighting of the seasonal bonfires remained a practical necessity but after the invention of the soul it was subsumed into the religious rite. The obligation to cremate explains the rarity of inhumation among the natives in prehistoric Scotland. Instead we find that bodies were stored in caves, in purpose-built chambers and at Annats and other sepulchral enclosures until they were needed. Temporary burial is also known. Beacons came to be at the centre of what are now seen as ritual landscapes but which originally had quite mundane purposes.

Even today some Christians hoard bones; the bones of Catholic saints have enormous value as magical relics. Nor is the Western attachment to bones restricted to Christian saints: consider the media frenzy when a skeleton supposed to be that of a king dead for more than six centuries is found in England, and the significance attached to the bones of the Unknown Soldier who represents whole armies of restless ghosts, appeased annually.

The Trials

The evidence from the trials, summarised in the previous chapter, suggests that hunters subscribed to a belief which involved communications between certain initiates or mediums and the ghosts of the dead, the *sluagh* or hosts. This was not ancestor worship which depends on notions of paternity and personal property. Hunters recognised paternity but did not live in nuclear families and all tribal property was held in common. The ancestors of the clan were a collective, the heroic old hunters. If their passing had been properly managed, they had been properly cremated, and their souls were safely in paradise and could sometimes be seen as the Wild Hunt passing overhead. Concern focussed more on the wandering spirits of those who had died violent deaths or whose bones could never be recovered. This is made explicit in the 1617 trial of Elspeth Reoch, a fairy woman in Orkney. She met more than once with a man dressed in black 'who callit him selff ane fairie man quha wes sumtyme her kinsman callit John Stewart quha wes slane be Mc Key at the doun going of the soone: And thairfor nather deid nor leiving bot wald ever go betuix the heaven and the earth' (Dalyell 1835, 536). The other John Stewart who died at Irvine in 1618 'made the usual declaration that he had seen many persons at the Court of Fairy, whose names he rehearsed particularly, and declared that all such persons as are taken away by sudden death go with the King of Elfland' (Scott 1830, 161). Unfortunately no-one recorded the names of these ghosts.

Several of those accused of sorcery stated that they had regular contact with the ghost of a named person who was trapped in fairyland and that when they needed answers to questions about the future, about life or death, or how to treat a sick person or animal, it was to these restless souls that they turned. These dedicated ghosts were helpful and protective, but perhaps in much the same way as a devout Catholic might view a patron saint. The details of their interactions with living people is impossible to define in rational terms, particularly as it involved treatment methods, though of course we do not exactly know that it did. Nor is it possible to say whether or not the fairy folk who practiced as mediums also took part in fertility rituals at the quarterly sabbat. It is a far cry from asking questions of the restless dead, which appears to be the older of the two practices, to having ritual intercourse with the Devil, which I have suggested was newly imported into Scotland c.1600, but there were common features. Even Isobell Gowdie met with the fairies of Darnaway (Pitcairn 1833, III, 610).

However, as one would expect if this change of practice from individual magic-workers to collective covens is authentic, ghosts are found only in the earlier trials (before c.1620) and in later trials of solitary initiates. A late example of a fairy-master who may have been a ghost is the man with the grey beard who was identified but not named by Isobel Haldane in 1623. As noted, none of these fairy men or women were associated with covens. Andro Man described the hunters under the rule of the Queen of Elphen as elves: in the real world these elves eat well, they play and dance and have shapes and clothes like men, and are stronger than men, 'but are bot schaddowis' (SCM 1841, I, 121). Has the clerk perhaps used E. *shadow* to translate one of the many Gaelic words for a member of a ghost cult?

It is not clear how rigorously the distinction was kept between fairyland as the resort of wandering souls between heaven and earth, and fairyland as the deer-forest. Sometimes it appears there was no distinction. In the satirical poem, 'The Legend of the Bishop of St Androis', Alesoun as Fairy Queen rides at Hallowe'en with her cousin and a crowd of ghosts including Auld Balcleugh and Maitland of Lethington 'that we belevit had bene in heawin'. She does not ride through the heavens but through Breadalbane, a famous hunting forest. This poem shows that the pagan association between fairies, hunters, ghosts, and the restless dead was a popular theme at the end of the sixteenth century.

The evidence suggests that hunters and their priests or druids (*faidh-dhraoidh*) believed that certain people were active as ghosts and could be interrogated by the living. The status of the undead was understood. Since they could not be cremated, their ghosts could not be liberated from their bones and rise to heaven. In the pagan scheme there was no hope of redemption; on the contrary, ten per cent went every year to hell; but this is an alien concept. It is probably significant that all the ghosts mentioned in the trials are of men who died violent deaths. They all have a historical context; indeed, it seems to have been rare for a ghost to outlive the memory of living people. They all seem to have been protective and helpful, not alarming or dangerous.

The evidence on which Andro Man of Banffshire was convicted in 1597 includes a mention of the link between fairy folk and the restless dead: 'the King that deit in Flowdoun and Thomas Rymour is there' in the company of the Queen of Elphin and Christsonday. The king that died at Flodden in 1513 was James IV, whose body was never found. Thomas of Ercildoun or Thomas Learmonth was a historical character, said to be a seer, who lived c.1220–c.1294 at Ercildoun, now Earlston, in Berwickshire. He went back to Fairyland with the Fairy Queen. Walter Scott wrote c.1800:

Some said to hill, and some to glen,
 Their wondrous course had been;
But ne'er in haunts of living men
 Again was Thomas seen.

Scott claimed that the return of Thomas of Ercildoun to fairyland was vouched for by local tradition and he was certainly legendary among the fairy folk of Banff in the sixteenth century. Nothing appears to be known of his death except that it was heralded by the appearance of a white hart and a white hind. A white deer was recognised throughout Scotland as a manifestation of the Cailleach or Fairy Queen so she had presumably come to claim her own. Decline in the power of pagan belief is suggested by the absence of any comparable legends in the case of the other great seer, Kenneth Ower of Easter Ross, who went to the stake in 1577-78, a victim of Lady Munro's cantraips.

At her trial in 1576 Bessie Dunlop described her mentor Thom Reid as an honest elderly man with a grey beard, a grey coat with old-fashioned Lombard sleeves, grey breeks, white stockings gartered at the knee with silk laces, a black bonnet and a white wand. This may seem too detailed for a ghost but in the same breath she states that he had died thirty years earlier, at the Battle of Pinkie in 1547 and whom she had never known in life (Pitcairn 1833, I, 51). In 1572 Bessie also saw but did not speak to the ghost of the Laird of Auchinskeyth who had died nine years earlier. She had seen him at a thorn beyond Monkcastell, riding with the fairfolk but his appearance appears to have been indistinct and she could not speak to him. At the desire of Lady Auchinskyeth, Bessie asked Thom Reid if 'a certain man' was among them (the fairy folk) and he answered that he was. Bessie and the man's widow seemed to find the transaction quite normal.

Aleson Piersoun (1588) gave a more confused account of her relationship with her cousin William Sympsoun, a young man only six years older than she was herself. He had 'gone abroad' or travelled with the Egyptians or fairfolk for twelve years. When he came back he had healed her (she complained of losing the power in her hand and foot, and at a later time the fairies deprived her of all the power of her left side). He also taught her, but had again been carried away with the Court of Elphane out of middle-earth – the world of men – and was now 'with thame', which seems to mean that he died a violent death. His ghost appeared only to herself and protected her. Whenever she heard a whirlwind over the sea she knew it announced the imminent arrival of the fairy folk but William came before them and warned her and kept her safe, so that she would not be taken away by them again, 'for a teind of them goes every year to hell.' She appears to distinguish between being in middle earth, being with thame, and being dead. Alesoun was perhaps tortured; her evidence is at least confused and melodramatic.

Isobell Gowdie in 1662 said nothing about ghosts but gave ten of the twelve spirit names used by the minor devils in her coven. All of them are in English, marking a break with fairy tradition, though they might have been translated from Gaelic. Isobell confirmed that she recognised them all 'quhan they appeir lyk a man' (Pitcairn iii, 606). She also met with the fairy folk on the Downie Hill. By her time it seems that the belief in restless ghosts was fading away with the rest of the fairy religion, though the fairy folk themselves lingered on the fringes of society for some time to come.

They were still lingering in Argyll in 1677 when the trial of Donald McIlmichall reveals the persistence of the traditional life of a fairy band in Appin. However it does little more. Donald gave his promise to a woman but the band was controlled by an old man, 'ane large tall corporal Gardman and ruddie'. One of the charges against him was 'corresponding with the devill and consulting him anent stollen goods and getting information for discoverie thereof'. Stolen goods were generally livestock, as in this case, and were normally recovered by consulting with trackers and not by supernatural intelligence. Donald was found guilty of theft and of consulting with evil spirits and hanged on the new gallows (MacPhail 1920, 36-38).

Survival

The concept of the wandering soul survives in Western culture in several forms, notably in the Catholic belief in purgatory and in patron saints and in the spiritualist belief that the spirits of the dead can and do communicate with the living. One major difference in both cases is the comforting doctrine that wandering souls are not doomed to wander for ever but can improve their standing, with the help of the living, until they achieve heaven.

In Roman Christianity belief in wandering souls finds expression in the doctrine of purgatory. The Catholic position on purgatory and the theological justification of prayers for the dead is uncertain but there is an implication that the living can intervene in the affairs of the dead, the reverse in fact of the pattern found in Scotland. Some Jews also thought that prayers offered for the dead helped those who had died to find pardon for their sins and a place in heaven. The Catholic Church defines purgatory as an intermediate state after physical death in which those destined for heaven 'undergo purification, so as to achieve the holiness necessary to enter the joy of heaven'. Saints (a relatively small number) are already redeemed or saved and at death go directly to heaven; the wicked (rather more numerous) go directly to hell, but the rest are only flawed or imperfect and go to an intermediate place between heaven and hell. When in this place they can still be saved by the prayers of the living or by the intercession of saints securely lodged in heaven – St Gertrude the Great, St John Macias and Our Lady are said to be particularly effective. Those who nonetheless fail to make the grade fall down into hell as lost souls. As a side issue, the individual can also ask for help in this world from the Holy Souls in Purgatory, a collective of wandering souls who have considerable powers to grant the prayers of the living.

This doctrine evolved in the middle ages and it is popular rather than scriptural. The main sources cited in support are few and flimsy: the apocryphal 2

Macabees 12:42-44 and 1 Corinthians 3:9-15, which appears to refer to the Church organisation, not to the individual soul, but the belief has many supporters and has at all times been profitable for the Church. This would not be the only Catholic doctrine contrived to appease the demands of worshippers attached to their pagan roots. The teind which goes every year to hell has found its place in the Catholic teaching which forsees that a few souls will prove impossible to save. The main difference with fairy doctrine is that lost souls can be recovered from purgatory by the efforts of the living; no such salvation is offered in the pagan version.

Dona eis requiem

There are no clues to the pagan rituals or liturgy, if any, used to bring peace to wandering souls. However, given the other parallels it is possible that they have contributed to the Requiem Mass, *Missa pro defunctis,* the Catholic service of blessing for the dead. Like its teaching on purgatory, the Requiem Mass seems to be an attempt by the Church to satisfy demand on the part of the living to improve the lot of the dead.

As one would expect for a late and improvised liturgy, its contents are ill-matched. Most of the prayers are addressed to God in the second person, as they should be, but a long hymn, the *Dies Irae* or 'day of wrath', which was added in the thirteenth or fourteenth century, is inappropriately in the first person. The *Offertorium* is 'theologically amiss' and significantly so, as it asks Michael the archangel rather than Jesus to rescue souls from hell. The last section, *Libera me,* also uses the first person, 'deliver me', when it is the sinner who should be delivered.

If these extraneous elements are removed we are left with six coherent prayers which may be original and which are summarised below. Of the six, four (1, 2, 4 and 5) are prayers for the dead which are found only in the *Missa pro defunctis* and the other two contribute an element of worship common to all masses. There is remarkably little that refers to Christian belief in the resurrection of the body; instead, the dead are to be freed from the jaws of the lion and brought out of darkness into the light, a rather less than orthodox view of the afterlife.

> 1 Give them eternal rest, O Lord, and let perpetual light shine upon them.

> 2 Lord Jesus Christ, king of glory, deliver the souls of all the faithful departed from the pains of Hell and the bottomless pit. Deliver them from the jaws of the lion, lest hell engulf them, lest they be plunged into darkness; let the holy standard-bearer Michael lead them into the holy light.

3 Holy, holy, holy, Lord God of hosts! (*Dominus Deus Sabaoth!*) Heaven and earth are full of your glory.

4 O Lamb of God that takest away the sins of the world, grant them eternal rest.

5 Let everlasting light shine on them, O Lord, with your saints for ever, for Thou art merciful. Grant them eternal rest, O Lord; and let perpetual light shine upon them with thy saints for ever, for Thou art merciful.

6 Deliver me, O Lord, from eternal death on that awful day when the heavens and earth shall be shaken and you shall come to judge the world by fire.

This rests on a vision of the dead as restless ghosts who already are or who may be plunged into darkness in the bottomless pit of hell from which Jesus (or Michael) can bring them into the light. If for 'light' we substitute 'fire' we come close to the hypothetical position of the ghost cult which hoped to rescue wandering ghosts from fairyland and complete their journey to heaven, by cremation at one or other of the bonfire festivals. Proof of such a transition was no more available to pagans than to Christians; there is no closure for ghosts, but the dead had to be known and vouched for, before they could be allowed into paradise.

Correct Burial

One very widespread and persistent element of this aspect of the ghost cult was the need to recover the body of a dead person by all possible means and to cremate or bury the remains in the right place, among its ancestors, beside his relatives, in the family plot. Today there is almost no popular reference to redemption or to the destination of the individual soul but the idea of a proper burial in the right place is still strongly held. It is a pagan belief which owes nothing to Christianity. When burial in the proper place is achieved there are no further problems; ghosts who have been properly buried or properly cremated do not walk.

Proper burial has been a powerful feeling for thousands of years. A Mesopotamian curse was: 'May the earth not receive your corpse!' The Jews attached great importance to proper burial and had a fear of being left unburied and those who breached the law were cursed in no uncertain terms: 'Thy carcase shall be meat unto all fowls of the air, and unto the beasts of the earth, and no man shall fray them away' (Deuteronomy 28:26). God put a terrible curse on King Jehoiakim: 'He shall be buried with the burial of an ass, drawn and cast forth beyond the gates of Jerusalem' (Jeremiah 22:19).

The widespread and persistent feeling that the dead should be buried in the proper place may reflect an obligation to bring the deceased or his bones back to the tribal beacon site for eventual cremation. Given the steady demand for bones as fuel, this in most cases would be the local tribal beacon but the great long-distance beacons must have had wider sources. The most familiar example is the removal of the bodies of Scottish kings from Lowland Scotland to Iona for burial. The steady flow of bones in the direction of Iona, using the bone caves or corpachs of Jura as temporary storage, suggests Iona was once known not for its saints but for its cremation rituals. Even Norwegian kings were buried there. A king, perhaps, had no tribe of his own but it was safe to cremate or bury such a powerful person with others of his kind. Put in other terms it would seem that Iona was the site of a particularly important long-distance beacon, whether one believed in Tír na nÓg or the resurrection of the body. But there are also annats or ossuaries close to the sites of major beacons such as Ben Nevis, Ben Ledi, Ben Lawers and Ben Dorain.

This dedication of the bones before death is seen, thinly disguised by Christian principles, in the story of *Murchadh Buidhe Nam Fiadh* 'Fair Murdoch of the Deer', collected by MacDougall (1910, 202, 326). Murchadh was a famous hunter whose favourite mountain was Beinn an Oir on Jura. When he was too feeble to hunt his son led him to the mountain and left him there to perish of cold and hunger. This now seems heartless but as it attracts no comment in the original it was presumably a normal event. It may not be a coincidence that his bones would be left conveniently high on the mountain near the site of the beacon. Whereupon Murdoch sang:

I am Yellow Murdoch of the Deer,
Left on the slopes of Beinn an Oir,
And though I am old and withered,
God can make me young once more.

He is not singing of his hope for a miracle cure but of his hopes of reaching Tír na nÓg, the Land of the Young, where he will hunt for ever, provided his bones are gathered together and his spirit is liberated into the smoke of the bonfire. It is not God but fire that will make him young again (God and fire are very close).

Fairy belief also survives as spiritualism. Spiritualists believe in the survival of the individual soul after death, in the ability of all souls to be increasingly purified after death, and in the ability of certain living people to contact the ghosts of the dead and ask them questions. It is closer to the fairy cult in allowing free contact between the souls of the dead and mediums. Anyone may become a medium through study and practice, but the dead are normally contacted at formal sessions or seances organised by mediums who can ask them for information. These spirits are protective and helpful. The afterlife is not static, but a place in which spirits are capable of growth and perfection, progressing through higher spheres or planes. This leads to the belief that spirits can provide knowledge about wider moral and ethical issues, as well as about God and the afterlife. Many mediums have 'spirit guides' whom they contact regularly and rely on for worldly and spiritual guidance. Many of those who were accused of witchcraft made an identical claim.

Shamanism

Several features of the ghost cult point to shamanism. A trained seer enters a trance in order to contact the spirit world and to channel the energies of the dead into this world for the purposes of divination and healing. There is in Scotland positive evidence for shamanism. In general it offers an answer to the question of how mediums such as Bessie Dunlop got into contact with the ghost or spirit guide who answered her questions for her.

The divination technique known as the *taghairm* described by Armstrong in his dictionary of Perthshire Gaelic, and quoted by Dwelly (1901, 920) is certainly shamanistic. This technique was for centuries hidden or disguised in an absurd folk fiction which interpreted the *taghairm* as a ritual involving roasting live cats, surely intended to be a joke.

'The divination by the *taghairm* was once a noted superstition among the Gael, and in the northern parts of the Lowlands of Scotland. When any important question concerning futurity arose, and of which a solution was, by all means, desirable, some shrewder person than his neighbours was pitched upon, to perform the part of a prophet. This person was wrapped in the warm smoking hide of a newly-slain ox or cow, commonly an ox, and laid at full length in the wildest recesses of some lonely waterfall. The question was then put to him and the oracle was left in solitude to consider it. Here he lay for some hours with his cloak of knowledge around him, and over his head, no doubt to see the better into futurity; deafened by the incessant roaring of the torrent; every sense assailed; his body steaming; his fancy in a ferment; and whatever notion had found its way into his mind from so many sources of prophecy, it was firmly believed to have been communicated by invisible beings who were supposed to haunt such solitudes'.

These invisible beings are the lost souls who haunted the wild realms of fairy-land. Although Armstrong makes this a general belief it may at least in part explain the lost religion of Clan Gregor and of other fairy folk.

The metaphysical or transcendental value of this account is not reduced by the fact that a similar technique, without any mention of divination, was used by the hunting tribes of Siberia when forced to spend the night out of doors: having killed a deer they slept wrapped in a hide: 'If a hunter managed to catch an elk or reindeer far from his camp in the evening, he slept right on the snow cover having wrapped himself up in the freshly-flayed skin' (Zaliznyak 1997, 80). Perhaps the use of the warm hide as a temporary refuge inspired shamanistic dreaming and visions.

A further hint of shamanism comes from elfish delusions, which might have resulted from an altered state of consciousness induced by drugs. One view is familar from popular fairy tales. According to this view, social fairies lived in green knolls and when the door was open, out came a light like the light of day and the sound of the sweetest music that ever was. On such rare occasions mortals could see 'fairy men and women in a circle in the middle of the floor, wheeling and dancing with mad energy' (MacDougall 1910, 132-3). But when the glamour was broken, 'the grand place was turned into a pit of red gravel, and the tall, handsome people that were in it into old creatures, small and ill-favoured' (MacDougall, 1910, 277).

A very similar account of fairy glamour which vanished overnight comes from the trial in 1597 of the druid Andro Man. He stated that when he met with the Queen of Elphen and her elves on the Binn Hill, the elves 'will mak the appeir to be in a fair chalmer, and yit thow will find thy selff in a moss on the morne; and that they will appeir to have candlis and licht, and swordis, quhilk wil be nothing else bot deed gress and strayes' (SCM 1841, I, 121-2). Perhaps hunters used hallucinogenic drugs to escape temporarily from the cold and the wet?

A further element of the fairy trials also suggests shamanism. Several of those tried report a loss of consciousness, or a transient loss of power or of sight and speech. Bessie Dunlop (1576) fell down and lay sick after meeting with the Court of Elphane and when meeting them could see their lips moving but could not hear them. Alesoun Peirsoun (1588) reported that her cousin William Sympsoun had healed her in Edinburghe, when she was twelve, when the power was taken from her hand and foot. The first time she went with the fairy court she got a hard blow from one of them which took all the power of her left side from her and left a blue mark. She also describes several episodes when she appears to have been in a trance and travelled a long distance without knowing how or where she was. Elspeth Reoch (1616) became dumb after dealing with a fairy man, which worried her brother so much so that he made her do penance in church and then applied torture in an attempt to cure her. John Stewart of Irvine (1618) lost the power of speech and became blind after the King of the Fairies struck him with a white rod over his forehead, on All-Hallow-Even night between the towns of Monygoif and Clary in Galway. After three years speech and sight were restored to him, also on Hallowe'en night, at the town of Dublin, in Ireland. These episodes could relate to some aspect of shamanism; they are found only in the confessions of those who dealt with the fairy folk.

The After-Life

An important aspect of the fairy religion is Tír na nÓg, the Land of Eternal Youth, the Otherworld or Paradise. In the terms of the ghost cult, a hunter became a ghost and went to live in Paradise when his bones were cremated and his ghost rose to heaven in the smoke. The big cremation event which retains its links with the dead was at Hallowe'en when (we are told) the barriers between this world and the next become thin. The link between Gaelic ghosts and fire comes from the terrifying crackling bonfires that periodically marked the passage of the ghosts and gave them new life.

There is at least one mention in the trials to middle earth which suggests that in some cosmological system there were also upper and lower levels, corresponding to heaven and hell. In one view, the upper level was Tír na nÓg 'Land of Youth', a heavenly place where the ghosts of champions and heroes went when their bones were cremated. However in the trial of Donald McIlmichall the record describes the fairy folk as 'not wordlie'. Does this imply that they belonged to a different world, neither above nor below middle earth but in a parallel universe of ghosts? Or are the unworldlie the unbaptised?

Several versions of the hunters' paradise exist, all of them offering a life free of earthly frustrations and fears, not to mention the problems of old age. Those who go to Tír na nÓg are 'warriors' or 'champions', and it is their ghosts hunting that one hears on stormy nights. Tír na nÓg is a far cry from the Flemish Lui Leker Land, the Land of Cockaigne, a high-calorie paradise, where rivers are made of chocolate, custard pies hang from the trees, and roasted chickens fly through the air but they have a common origin.

In another tradition, paradise is known as Fiddler's Green, a haven for deep-sea fishermen, where the weather is always fair, the skies are clear, and the cold coast of Greenland is far, far away. Fiddler's Green in the United States has become a pleasant limbo for old cavalry-men. From *We Remember*, publication of the American Cavalry Association it is put to music.

Halfway down the trail to Hell, in a shady meadow of green,
Are the souls of all good troopers camped, near a good old-time canteen
And this eternal resting-place is known as Fiddler's Green.

Neither version explains the fiddler. For that we have to go back to hunting deer and Gaelic. G. *fiadh* is 'deer' and a fiddler or *fiadhlear* is a hunter. Fiddler's Green is not a place where a fiddler plays while the dead dance but a deer-forest with abundant game. The pun has contributed to several stories in which fiddlers end up in the Otherworld and are unable to return. Two fiddlers who had played for the fairies for a night, as they thought, crumbled to dust when they left the fairy knoll. Bodies that crumble to dust or, even more significantly, to a thimbleful of black ashes (Briggs 1978, 19) after a prolonged stay with the fairies belong to the tradition of the ghosts rising in the smoke from the fire and to the deposits of calcined bones in cinerary urns found at almost every prehistoric beacon site.

The Wild Hunt is found as a folk belief throughout northern and western Europe, which points to a Palaeolithic origin for the concept of the soul as a shadowy body which continued to live in the sky. Details vary but in every case a cavalcade of ghostly hunters, mounted on ghostly horses and accompanied by ghostly hounds, chase ghostly deer through the endless wilderness of the heavens. To see or hear the Gabriel Hounds, the Ratchets, the Rout of Herla, or the Harlequin hounds was a death portent. They 'portend death or calamity to the house over which they hang... the cry of the Seven Whistlers was a death omen' (*Chambers Encyclopaedia* 1901). As usual the sense of the death portent has been inverted. In fact the Wild Hunt brought good luck as it anticipated the death of deer.

In Wales the otherworldly paradise was known as Annwn, and the Cŵn Annwn or Hounds of Hell took part nine times a year in a Wild Hunt, presided over by Gwyn ap Nudd, king of the fair-folk and ruler of the underworld. The Hounds hunted on the Feasts of St John, St Martin, St Michael the Archangel, All Saints, Christmas, New Year, St Agnes, St David, and Good Friday. With two adjustments these dates represents a hunt once a month from Samhain (31 October) to Beltane (1 May). This assumes that St John is the Evangelist at midwinter (27 December), not the Baptist at midsummer (24 June). Another problem is St Martin on 11 November which is too early in the month. Otherwise these dates span the winter season at monthly intervals, a reminder of the fact that hunts originally took place at every full moon over the winter.

1 October - Michaelmas 29 September.

1 November - All Saints 1 November.

1 December - Martinmas 11 November (too early).

1 January - Christmas 25 December, John 27 December, New Year 1 January.

1 February - Agnes 21 January.

1 March - David 1 March.

1 April - Good Friday, after the spring equinox.

1 May - Beltane is not listed. It was not itself a hunt but marked the end of the hunting season.

The Cŵn Annwn also escorted souls on their journey to the Otherworld. Sometimes the dead were accompanied or chased by a fearsome hag called *Mallt-y-Nos*, a Welsh Cailleach or Death Goddess (related to G. *malcta* 'rotten, putrid, cadaverous'), who took into her care the recently dead. G. *nos* also means 'white, pure'; for *Mallt-y-Nos* was also a beautiful virgin, a peri, a huri, a Valkyrie, a Fire Maiden. Like the Cailleach and the equally fearsome Kali, she represents the cleansing power of the cremation bonfires.

The Sleepers

In one of MacDougall's tales the social fairies are described as *seann duine mór, liath*, 'big, grey-haired, old men' (1910, 282-3). The One-Eyed Ferryman (*am Portair cam*), who suspected they were interfering with his cows, drove his iron dirk into the door frame to keep the door open which gave him 'a full view of the inside of the Fairy Knoll. It was lighted up with a brilliant light, and on the middle of the floor was a large fire with an iron caldron hanging over it; and around the fire was a circle of big old grey-haired men resting on their elbows'. This may reflect a genuine memory of old hunters, surviving by cattle-theft when they were no longer able to hunt. But G. *liath* 'grey' can also mean 'fire, light, smoke' and in the archaic language *seann duine mór, liath* also means 'the gathering-light of the great deer hunt', which sounds like a hunting shout. Another old grey man is found in a tale from northeast Scotland in which a grey horse changes into an old man with long grey hair and a long grey beard (Gregor 1881, 67).

Archaic ghost lore lingers on in the traditional belief in the Sleepers who wait to protect the Scottish nation in some future battle. This confirms a view of ghosts as protective spirits, like guardian angels. Like the ghosts commemorated by our fairy men and women the Sleepers were martial figures who had died in battle and who sleep the years away as they wait for the call to arms. Thomas the Rhymer and his company sleep in a cave under the Eildon Hills or perhaps under Dunbuck Hill, near Dumbarton. Arthur and his knights sleep under Arthur's Seat in Midlothian. The giants who sleep under Tomnahurich hill at Inverness are sometimes Fionn and his band of hunters and sometimes True Thomas and his band. The Feinne were enchanted but live on, 'leaning on their elbows in Craig-a-cho' (Mackenzie 1894, 101), a fairy hill on the coast of the Black Isle near Munlochy (NH6852). Another site associated with the Feinne and so with hunters, beacons and fairies is the Smith's Rock in Skye (Mackenzie 1931, 106-108). All of these places were the sites of long-distance beacons where year after year the bones of dead warriors were turned to smoke.

Second sight

A recent off-shoot of the ghost industry which evolved in the wake of populist ghost literature, is the capacity known as the second sight or double sight. Aubrey, who was accurate enough when reporting current superstitions, said that the second sight was a belief in ghosts, and that ghosts were fairies. 'They generally term this Second-sight in Irish Taishitaraughk [G. *taibhsearachd*?] and such as have it Taishatrin [G. *taibhsear*?], from Taish [G. *taibhse*], which is properly a shadowy substance, or such Naughty and Imperceptible thing, as can only, or rather scarcely be discerned by the Eye; but not caught by the hands: for which they assign it to the Bugles [bogles] or Ghosts, so that Taishtar, is as much as one that converses with Ghosts or Spirits, or as they commonly call them, the Fairies or Fairy-Folks' (Aubrey 1721, 211-212).

G. *taibhsearachd* is now understood to mean 'to believe in ghosts or to see them, particularly in connection with a forthcoming death' and G. *taibhse* can mean 'shadow of a departed person; vision, apparition, ghost, spirit'. Martin Martin paid great attention to the second sight 'in Irish called Taish' (1698, 321-348, 466-476) which he defined as the ability to see visions, both pleasant and unpleasant, which appeared as real as life. His accounts are almost entirely anecdotal. 'It was much more common twenty years ago than at present; for one in ten do not see it now, that saw it them' (1698, 330). There is in fact no evidence that anyone ever saw anything, except coincidentally, like modern dreams of getting on a doomed aircraft.

This amateurish necromancy is much inferior to the regular communion with the dead as practised by Bessie Dunlop, Elspeth Reoch and others. Mary Voir Nicvolvoire of Lismore, who was consulted by John Oig Campbell of Cabrachan in 1590, was neither a charmer nor a witch but could see into the future (MacPhail 1914, 166-167). Did she perhaps have a personal 'ghost' whom she consulted in cases of life and death, like the Great Witch of Iona, who was also consulted by the highest in the land as to their futures? The ghost has a much longer history, as we see from the number of related words (listed below) which show links with hunting and fire.

Necromancy was perhaps not rational but it had more practical value than repeated visions of funerals. The double sight which proliferated after 1700 was probably inspired by the ghost-cult but to foresee a death does not require any supernatural ability. A hunter foresaw death, but not his own, whenever he saw a beacon announcing a hunt.

Grey Ladies

The memory of a beacon lit to guide travellers or to regulate a hunt is the most rational explanation for apparitions which are seen at night, which are always seen in the same place, and which are associated with hunters or fairies. A particular manifestation of a ghostly spirit in Britain is the Grey Lady. Her colour is immaterial: she may also be white, green, blue, or even pink. Such ghostly ladies are relatively rare – there are no more than a dozen in the whole of Britain – and they are almost all at places old enough to have functioned as prehistoric beacons (Alexander 2002). The Ferry Boat Inn in the heart of the Fens is haunted by a White Lady and a slab of stone, now said to be her grave-stone, was once the stance for a beacon lit to guide travellers over the marshes. We can guess from the name of Leven Hall, Cumbria, (G. *liomh* 'polish, gloss (fire)') and from the Pink Lady and the Black Dog that are still seen there, that prehistoric hunters once mustered there. The Pink Lady is no doubt wearing hunting pink, a suitable colour for a beacon. The light which is sometimes seen at a high window in the fifteenth-century tower of Dilston Hall, Northumberland, was lit by Lady Derwentwater to guide her husband home. He was executed in 1716. Lights are also seen at Dunraven Castle in Mid Glamorgan, which is visited by a Blue Lady and where an early occupant is said to have used lights to lure ships to their doom. The most complete survival is at Glamis Castle, Angus, where a spectre is seen to float in a fiery glow above the clock-tower. It is the ghost of Lady Janet Douglas, widow of the 6th Lord of Glamis, who was accused of attempting to poison James V and was burned on a charge of treason in Edinburgh in 1537 to the lamentation of a great crowd.

Gaelic words for dwarfs, ghosts and spectres

The number and variety of these words point to a considerable body of lost lore. Many derive from words for hunting and fire. Names for hunters therefore merge with those for ghosts, spectres and smoke, referring to their former strong belief in cremation as the way to the afterlife. Words for the second sight are relatively isolated, suggesting a recent development.

abhag 'terrier; dwarf, spectre'. G. *eibh* 'fire'. Applied to a small hunting dog.

ailmse 'spectre'. Ogam *ailm* for A. G. *ailmh* 'flint stone; boundary stone'. A flint used to light a fire?

aingeal 'angel, messenger, fire, light'. G. *geal* 'bright, yellow'.

amh 'dwarf'. As G. *eibh*.

aog 'death, ghost, spectre, skeleton'. G. *aoigh* 'hero, skilful person, traveller, stranger, guest', a hunter summoned from a distance by a beacon.

arc 'dwarf; stag, hind'. Was the red deer a dwarf compared with the elk?

arrachd 'spectre, apparition, centaur, pigmy, dwarf, mannikin'. G. àr 'battle, slaughter (hunt)'. G. *arrachdan* 'fairy', or hunter.

baobh 'goblin, wizard, wicked mischievous female who invokes a curse or some evil on others, a she-spirit supposed to haunt rivers, witch'. G. *bo* 'gather', G. *eibh* 'fire', G. *biadh* 'meat, provender'.

bòcan 'hobgoblin, sprite, spectre, apparition, bugbear'. G. 'terrifying objects seen at night and taken to be supernatural.' G. *bochd* 'fire'. A *bòchdan* appears to be the layman's view of a cremation fire.

bodach 'carl, old man, an apparition seen at night'. *Bodach an Sméididh* 'the beckoning old man' (Campbell 1901, 187) is probably 'the old man emitting smoke' (G. *smùideadh*), like a signal beacon. E. *beacon* and E. *beckon* come from the same root. G. *bod* 'penis'.

brideach 'dwarf'. G. *breo* 'fire, flame'. Bride was a Fire Maiden. Perhaps a small fire.

càileireachd 'cremation of the dead'. G. *cail* 'burn', G. *cailleach* 'major beacon', Cailleach. the Black Lady.

corra-lòigein, a type of bodach or beacon, from G. *caoir* 'blaze' or G. *carraid* 'conflict, strife (hunting)' + G. *loisgeann* 'fire' (Campbell 1901, 187). G. *caoir* is punned with G. *corra* 'crane, stork'.

cruiteachan 'dwarf'. G. *cruth* 'phantom', G. *cruach* 'red', a beacon. The *Cruithen* or Picts were deer-hunters.

cruthlach 'ghost, fairy'. See *cruiteachan*.

dealbh 'spectre'. G. *dealan* 'flaming coal'. G. *dealt* 'dew'. The dew on May morning takes its magical or therapeutic properties from the smoke of the Beltane fire.

dreag 'a ghostly light like a comet, presaging the death of an important person'. A layman's view of a cremation bonfire.

eug 'ghost, spectre; death'.

faidh draoidh 'seer, prophet, druid'.

fàth 'ambush'.

fàthach 'giant, monster'.

fiosaiche 'fortune-teller, diviner'.

firean 'dwarf', from archaic G. *fir* 'fire'.

fo-dhuine 'dwarf, servant'. *Fo* may be an archaic 'fire' root.

fot 'giant', a major beacon, a long-distance beacon. The *lucht-fothach* or 'people of the wilderness' were hunters.

fuath 'aversion, hatred; goblin, scarecrow, diminutive insignificant person, spectre, ghost, demon, spirit, kelpie'. The main beacon of the island of Mull was a *fuath*: 'The name of the daring *fuath* was the bold, red, white-maned *Mhuireartach maol*. Her face was dusky, of the hue of coal, the teeth of her jaws crooked red; in her head there glared a single eye' (Campbell 1901, 188).

galoban 'dwarf'. G. *gal* 'blast of flame, smoke, kindred, warfare, slaughter, valour'. G. *gealach, gil* 'the moon' – the bright or yellow one.

gigean 'dwarf; term of contempt'. G. *cog* 'war, fight, deer'.

leibid 'dwarf'.

lucharan or *luch-àrnunn* 'pigmy', also found as G. *luchruban,* G. *luchorpan* and Ir. *leprachaun.* G. *lòchran* 'light, lamp, torch', G. *luachair* 'splendour, brightness', G. *leus* 'blaze, flame, light, ray of light', G. *luisne* 'flame, flash'. The island of Luchruban (NB 5066) is at the northern extremity of Lewis and was perhaps the site of a coastal beacon. It was joined to the mainland before the 17th century and it is still possible to gain access at low tide. It has the remains of round buildings. Mackenzie (1931, 131) said that G. *luchorpan* is equivalent to *corpach* 'a place where bodies were stored prior to burial or cremation'. Bones of oxen, young lambs, sheep, a dog and various birds were found there, perhaps to be used as fuel (Mackenzie 1905). The local saint is Frangus.

màileachan 'sprite, brownie'. G. *mal* 'king (beacon); champion, soldier (hunter)', G. *màilleid* 'wallet, bag'. G. *màilleach* 'armour, coat of mail'. *Mael-dubh* 'the Black Man' at the Annat of Kilmallie on Locheil was a bonfire.

monar 'dwarf'.

sibhreach 'fairy, spectre'.

sìochair 'dwarf, fairy-like person, contemptible fellow'.

sìodha 'fairy, hunter', from G. *sìth* 'mound, outlook point'. Fairies may be real or ghostly.

sìogaid 'lean, dwarfish, weakly fellow, starveling'. A hunter when hunting has failed.

sìogaidh 'fairy, pygmy'; 'twining like a serpent' or like a chain of hunters twining about the deer.

spiorad 'dwarf, ghost, fairy'. G. *speur* 'star'. E. *spirit*.

tachar 'dense volume of smoke'.

tachar 'fight, skirmish (hunt)'.

tàchar 'ghost' – 'a rare and almost obsolete word' found in *Sròn an tàchair* 'the ghost-haunted rock', between Kinloch Rannoch and Drumcastle, Perthshire, and *Imire tàchair* 'the ridge of the ghost' in Iona which leads from near the abbey to the hill.

tàcharan 'spirit, ghost, child left by the fairies, fairy changeling'.

taghairm 'gathering summons', a major hunt-beacon.

taibhs 'phantasm, object seen by a *taibhsear* or one with the second sight' (Campbell 1902, 123).

taibhs (pronounced ta-ish) 'the shade of a departed person; vision, apparition, ghost, spirit, phantasm, object seen by a *taibhsear*' (Campbell 1902, 123).

taibhseach 'silly, superstitious'.

taibhseachd 'pride, eloquence'.

taibhsear 'one with the second sight'.

taighleach 'bright'.

tail 'substance, product, wages'.

taileasg 'ghost (a hunter); sport, game, mirth (hunt); chess, backgammon, draughts'.

taimh 'death'.

taisdealach 'pilgrim, traveller, ghost'. Pilgrim and traveller are also words for a hunter.

taise 'dead bodies, relics of saints (bones)'.

taish na tailedh 'a funeral foregoing, a procession [of ghosts]'. Reality was a procession of hunters carrying dead deer on hurdles; their *tail* 'substance, product, wages'.

tamhasg 'the shade or double of a living person'. The only shade that was ever visible was the shade of a dead person rising to heaven in the smoke of the bonfire.

tannas or *tannasg* 'ghost, spectre, generally of the dead'. According to Campbell (1902, 123) a *tannasg* was more shadowy and spiritual than a *bòchdan*.

taracadair 'seer'.

tàradh 'noises heard at night through the house, presaging a coming event'.

taran 'the ghost of an unbaptised child'. Taransay off Lewis was a noted sepulchral island for infants.

tàsg 'ghost, apparition'. G. *taisg* 'deposit, lay up, hoard'. G. *tasgaidh* 'store, treasure'. G. *teas* 'heat, warmth'.

tasgaidh 'store, treasure'.

tàslach 'a supernatural premonition, felt or heard but not seen'.

tath 'slaughter'; *tathach* 'shade, ghost'; *tathach* 'guest, visitor, stranger' – a hunter; as *athach* 'giant, champion, monster' – complimentary terms for a hunter.

teas 'heat, warmth'. A very old root. Bones were used as fuel.

toir 'pursue, chase'.

torthair 'monster, dwarf'.

troichilean 'pigmy, dwarf'.

trosdan 'dwarf; trap'. *trost* 'dwarf'. Drostan and Tristan in place-names refer to hunting.

19: THE ODA: A FERTILITY
FESTIVAL IN THE HEBRIDES

In the hinder-end of harvest, on All Hallows even,
When our Good Neighours doe ryd, gif I read right,
Some buckled on a bunewand and some on a been,
Ay trottand in trupes from the twilight...
The King of Pharie and his court, with the Elfe Queen,
With many elfish Incubus was rydand that night.

Alexander Montgomery (1556-1610)

In the seventeenth century, the ministers and elders of the Reformed Kirk who investigated the relationship between the Devil and his witches may have been prurient and were certainly shocked but they did not flinch from asking their witches some pointed and personal questions which elicited some very odd facts. One of these was the critical role in the sabbat ritual of the sexual act, whether counterfeit or genuine. This was repeated in one account after another from one end of Scotland to the other. Given what the recorded accounts reveal of the importance of the sexual act in the activities of the coven, it is likely that it played an equally significant role in the charms, incantations, songs and dances and other rituals performed in the Highlands and Islands. However their Presbyterian counterparts in the nineteenth century were not only prudish: they destroyed or failed to record irreplaceable evidence of pagan rituals, which was a great deal worse. In view of this prudery we may assume that the role of sex was far greater than surviving evidence suggests. Thomas the Rhymer and the Queen of Elphane, enshrined in a ballad tradition, were too famous to be ignored and it is clear that they did not enjoy a platonic relationship.

In addition to the eighteenth-century fake folklore and the nineteenth-century censorship, a further barrier to the transmission of the secrets of hunting lore is that beginning in the twelfth century feudal law increasingly put the deer-forests out of bounds to native hunters. In consequence very few people had any knowledge of hunters or hunting. They were in any case Gaels and not literate. But one way of approaching this lack of direct knowledge is to construct parallels with the culture of the witches revealed in the trials.

One sign of the equivalence of witches, fairies and hunters is that many of the features of the Lowland sabbat are also present in the fairy raid of folklore which is a folkloric native version of the rituals associated with a communal hunt. Long before there were covens, the sabbat evolved into a pagan ritual designed to bring fertility to the herds and success to the hunters. The fairy raid of the tales is a memory of the hunt itself. The one thing that is needed to complete the equivalence is orgiastic or ritual intercourse in the Gaelic account. It is not missing from Andro Man's account of the fairy folk of Banff but in the Highlands elsewhere, as reported in the nineteenth century, the sexual aspects of the sabbat are missing or at least they are not mentioned.

As noted already, this is likely to be the result of avoidance on the part of contributors and over-zealous editing on the part of collectors rather than an actual absence, for despite all their care and duplicity certain clues survive. The obscene school-boy rhyme, *Ladhar Pocan* (discused below) is only a short step away from an equally obscene appeal to the Goddess. This rare surviving example of archaic sexual imagery confirms that sexual dealing was at the heart of hunting magic. It symbolised the rape of the goddess in the hunter's theft of her deer and it brought fertility to the herds by its re-enactment of the rut. Was this great secret ritual forgotten when hunting died? This seems unlikely, as many aspects of the sabbat and thinly-disguised fertility rituals persisted in agricultural communities throughout Lowland Scotland into the 1950s or later. We have only to consider the repeated bans attempted by the Reformed Church. The other possibility is that this aspect of pagan practice was so firmly suppressed by Calvinists that only a few surviving relics filtered out through a dense veil of Victorian prudery. This is much more likely.

With the march of scholarship it is now possible to say that several important Victorian collectors destroyed any mention of sexual activity as degrading or unseemly. The prime example of misplaced prudery is *Carmina Gadelica*, an impressive collection of incantations and prayers published in four volumes by Alexander Carmichael (1832–1912) and by his successors at intervals between 1900 and 1971, a time lag that suggests substantial editorial problems. Carmichael hoped his collection would raise the public image of the Gaels as civilised Christian folk but to achieve their posthumous conversion from paganism he destroyed or substantially rewrote an unknown quantity of pagan material and did so so thoroughly that the first three or four volumes of *Carmina Gadelica*, edited by Carmichael himself, are virtually devoid of archaic imagery – no archaic hunting puns here!

This is not a new observation. John McInnes, no mean scholar and a great Gael, wrote in his preface to the 1992 edition, on page 11, that 'more than one Gaelic reader felt some degree of uneasiness as he or she read through the volumes of *Carmina Gadelica*, especially volumes I to IV.' Since 1992 he has been persuaded that '*Carmina Gadelica* is not a monumental exercise in literary fabrication' but his first thoughts were better. With recent scholarly access to Carmichael's original notebooks our last hopes have gone. It is now quite clear that *Carmina Gadelica* is indeed a merciless exercise in literary fabrication which make the activities of Dr Bowdler seem quite insignificant and benign. Carmichael indulged in an exercise in deliberate falsification, fake folk on a stupendous scale.

A few topics only survived. Fortunately they include an independent and wonderfully detailed account of a Hebridean fertility festival, the Oda or Michaelmas celebrations. Other than the account of the Oda, what has been published in Carmichael's first four volumes, we can say with absolute certainty, is neither authentic nor archaic. The reasons are obvious. Victorian piety, prejudice and prudery have a great deal to do with why we know so little about a universal religion whose primary sacrament was the sexual act and whose primary icon was a grossly indecent female displaying her private parts. The sheela-na-gig was the idol of the deer-hunters (G. *seilg* 'hunt', archaic G. *coig* 'deer') and one such icon, much delapidated and defaced, survives high on a wall at St Clement's Church at Rodel, site of the Oda on Harris. But devout collectors knew sexual references belonged to the shameful pagan past and the shameful pagan religion of the hunters.

Dr Domhnall Uillean Stiubhart covers this point in his article, 'The Case of the Hebridean Michaelmas', which appeared in *Celtic Cosmology* (2014, 207-248) but reaches a different conclusion. Having studied and compared the published version with Carmichael's notes he concluded that 'the texts have been archaised and esotericised; new elements – sometimes startlingly so – have been inserted. As sources, Carmichael's printed texts are fatally compromised'. This is true of most of the published texts that make up *Carmina Gadelica* but the account of the Oda is not Carmichael's text and their archaism appears to be original and authentic.

Despite this problem, which cannot now be rectified, Carmichael's account of the Oda in the Isles, surprisingly, contains enough authentic pagan or sexual material to be a useful account of a widespread fertility festival, and Carmichael's pious interpolations are easy to recognise. The reason for this remarkable survival may be that, as Dr Stiubhart discovered, Carmichael got his information about it at the last moment, facing a deadline with his printers which left little or no time for invention or editing. This information came at his urgent request not from an illiterate crofter who might never have recognised ethnographic treason but from Father Allan McDonald of Eriskay, who certainly would. In favour of eventual survival in *Carmina Gadelica* or elsewhere the Oda was widespread and popular: the festival survived for a while even among migrants in Canada (Stiubhart 2014).

It is still true that the survival of most of the archaic Gaelic pagan material from the West Highlands and Hebrides, where we might expect it to be best preserved, has been dramatically and drastically affected by a nineteenth-century taboo enforced by a religious bigot. But by a kind of miracle this article on the Oda, the great orgiastic fertility festival of the western Gaels, appears to contain a large element of accurate fact.

The Oda of the West Highlands and Islands

One of the few topics to survive in unexpurgated form in *Carmina Gadelica* is Father McDonald's account of the Oda or Michaelmas celebrations. The persistence of the Oda is equally remarkable and points to its importance in Hebridean communities. It was a communal fertility festival which survived into the nineteenth century in the Hebrides and also in the West Highlands with many of its pagan features intact. It is quite reassuring to find that the Gaels did after all practise sexual magic. If we need a Gaelic equivalent for the sabbat we find it here.

Carmichael admitted its pagan elements but could hardly remove them without removing or rewriting the entire article which was of considerable length, taking up ten pages of his first volume (1900, 200-210). The reason for his unusual and indeed unique frankness in dealing with a celebration that was not only explicitly sexual but frankly immoral, was probably because he had not written it. As noted above the Oda material was sent to him by Father Allan McDonald of Eriskay (1859-1905) who had collected it at Carmichael's request from old people in remote islands who remembered the last of the festivals in their youth. This involvement of an independent scholar appears to have inhibited Carmichael's normal tendency to turn traditional lore into pious pap. He may well have introduced several pious elements such as prayers to Brigit, but it is not remotely possible that he invented the sexual aspects of this account, particularly those that describe promiscuous fornication and the fatherless bairns who were its desired consequence as cause for rejoicing.

Dwelly describes the Oda as a horse-race but horse-races were only one part of the fertility festival celebrated in the Hebrides at or about Michaelmas, 29 September. In Barra it took place on the feast of St Barr (25 September) and in Harris on the feast of St Clement (23 November). These dates were probably imposed by the Church. At one time it no doubt took place at Samhain or Hallowe'en, as Marian McNeill suggests in *The Silver Bough* (1959, vol.2, 148, note 6) or at the following full moon, for the Oda was in effect a sabbat or hunting festival which extended over two days and involved the entire community.

It survived into the nineteenth century but was banned in one place after another as the stern eye of the Presbyterian Church fell upon it. The last Oda took place in Islay and Mull c.1800, in Harris in 1818, in South Uist in 1820, in Barra in 1828, in Benbecula in 1830, and in North Uist in 1866. It was also reported from Lewis, Skye, Coll, Tiree, Lingay, St Kilda, Canna and the Western mainland (McNeill 1959, vol.2, 102-104). Nothing appears to be known of such an event in the rest of the Highlands.

In Iona there is a possible link with fairies or hunters. Pennant (1772) reported that men raced their horses sun-wise, round a small cairn inside a stone circle at *Cnoc nan Aingeal* 'knoll of the bright fire', a beacon site. Later visitors failed to find this cairn or the stone circle but identified the knoll as *Cnoc an t-Sidhein* (NM 272 237), a natural feature which was also, from its name, a fairy knoll and beacon site. It seems that the traditional Michaelmas horse-races took place at what is now known as *Cnoc an t-Sidhein*, 'the outlook hillock of the hunters'.

On the Eve (28 September) or on the Sunday before 29 September, *Domhnach Curran* or Carrot Sunday, the women went to dig up wild carrots (*Daucus carota*). No attempt was made to disguise the fact that the bannock and the carrots, G. *curran,* were sexual symbols; rather the contrary. The *struan* bannocks were generally triangular with the corners cut off, a shape 'which tradition associates with the female sex'. To extract the wild carrots the women dug a triangular hole or *torcan* 'little cleft' with a triangular trowel, in honour of the Trinity, as Carmichael has it, but a triangular shape is a universal symbol of the female sex. They sang explicit little ditties as they did so. Having harvested their carrots they tied them into little bundles with three-ply yarn, ideally red. The bundles were of a size that could be encompassed by thumb and first finger. This describes a *fascinum* or artificial penis.

The women also baked triangular bannocks or *struan* (in Islay the *sruan* is the triangular frame on which such a cake is baked). A lamb was killed; once no doubt it was a deer. On St Michael's Day activities focused on a pilgrimage on horseback to the cemetery or *cladh*, where there was a service and a circuit on horseback sunwise. A man might take any woman except his wife and he should use a stolen horse. Women went round the graveyard to ensure the safe delivery of children and mares in foal were blessed by being led round sunwise. The sunwise turns were followed by horse-races.

The Night of Michael was the night of the dances and songs, 'the merry-making and love-making and the love-gifts'. During the Night, dances of 'a curious and symbolic nature' were performed, as they were at the sabbat and women presented bundles of carrots to the men of their choice, saying 'Progeny and prosperity on thy lying and thy rising'. The man might reply: 'Progeny and peace on the hand that gave' or 'Pregnancy and prosperity to my love who gave'. There was much coming and going from the dance hall as the women went to replenish their supply of carrots. Family ties were ignored, as they were at the sabbat.

No Queen or King is mentioned in surviving accounts but the bannocks were made in each house by a Maiden and the Devil is represented by the archangel, known as Brian Michael. This was taken to mean 'the god Michael' but Brian was the god of evil or the Devil. The introduction of the archangel was no doubt eased by the fact that G. *aingeal* means 'bright fire, light, messenger' and Michael was a suitable name for a signal beacon. But the choice of the scriptural Michael in place of Brian the archetypal Black Man has hagiological justification as both had the cure of souls in transit. It seems that the Archangel replaced a pagan bonfire once personified as Brian.

A bonfire is also absent from the reported features except on Iona. The change from Brian to Michael was cosmetic. Where women had once prayed to Brian son of St Bride for children they now prayed to Michael. A child born 'opportunely' nine months after Michaelmas might be called *leanabh Micheil* 'child of Michael', *conail Micheil* 'procreated of Michael' (G. *conall* 'fertility') or *curran Micheil* 'carrot of Michael' (G. *cur* 'power, virility'). Such a child, conceived with the help of Michael on 29 September, would be born the following year, a few days before midsummer, the Feast of St John, a bonfire festival.

In Carmichael's version of the carrot song 'to endow' means to 'impregnate'.

Torcan fruitful, fruitful, fruitful, [*torcan* 'little cleft']

Joy of carrots surpassing upon me, [*curran* 'virility']

Michael the brave endowing me [with a child],

Bride the fair be aiding me [in child-birth].

Progeny pre-eminent over every progeny, progeny on my womb,

Progeny pre-eminent over every progeny, progeny on my progeny.

Forked carrots were particularly prized. If a woman found a forked carrot she sang:

Fork joyful, joyful, joyful, fork of great carrot to me,

Endowment of carrot surpassing upon me, joy of great carrot to me.

As McNeill said, 'the carrot is obviously a phallic emblem', but in 1959 this was not something one often saw in print (1959, vol.2, 148). Neither she nor Carmichael supplies the Gaelic word for a great forked carrot but it was probably G. *gobhal* 'fork' which also means the perineum.

McNeill thought the fertility aspects might have been transferred from Hallowe'en, 31 October, and she may be right. Michaelmas is not a popular date in the pagan calendar and it is also probable that the Oda, like a sabbat, was celebrated on a full moon, either the first or the second after the autumn equinox. The Oda and Hallowe'en are both important autumn events with rituals suggesting preparations for a hunt though there is no mention anywhere in the Hebrides of the bonfire which was an essential feature of Hallowe'en on the mainland. Hallowe'en is associated with the dead and the focus on the graveyard in the Oda suggests cremation rituals and ancestor worship. Hallowe'en retains guising with black faces, collecting doles of food, the bonfire, the celebration of the dead, some of which are moved to Midwinter, but apart from the witches' sabbat it has lost its sexual aspects. Many elements of the Oda also suggest preparations for a hunt: the search for a good horse among the wild herds, horse-races to test the mounts, games and trials of skill, magical dancing and mimes, the preparation of rations, and sexual intercourse to ensure the success of the foray.

By the early nineteenth century several elements of the Oda were no longer in their original form. In many Hebridean islands deer-hunting had died out long before and the hunt was reduced to a few unconnected activities: a procession, horse-races, tests of skill. The bannocks represent the provisions once taken by hunters setting off for a communal hunt and the lamb probably takes the place of a young stag but even so oats and sheep were introduced at earliest in the Bronze Age. The most intrusive element is the introduction of Michael and Bride into pagan prayers for fertility and good luck. Other than these minor omissions the festival was essentially pagan. Women raised their own power by ritual activity of which the end-point was sexual intercourse, which can be seen as an offering to the Lady and her consort or son Brian-Michael and the culmination a Michael child.

As a suggestion that the date was once calculated according to the moon, the date in recent times was quite variable. A date in late September suggests a link with the Harvest Moon which was the first full moon after the autumn equinox (20 September) rather than the Hunters' Moon which was the next full moon and marked the first hunt of the winter. The equinox was the fixed solar event in the series. By this scheme the Hunters' Moon or Samhain fell in late October or early November but was fixed by the Church at All-Hallows and All-Saints, 1-2 November. In Barra, as noted, the Oda was celebrated on St Barr's day, 25 September, and in Harris it was associated with St Clement, patron of Rodil in Harris, whose feast-day is 23 November. These may represent earlier hunt dates. The feast of Gabriel the Archangel on 9 September may also be significant. According to St Luke's Gospel it was Gabriel who notified Elizabeth the Hag that she would bear a son (Luke 1:19). We know that this visitation by the angel took place at the autumn equinox as John the Baptist was duly born at midsummer. Six months later Gabriel brought the same message to Elizabeth's cousin Mary the Virgin at the spring equinox, the result being a son born at the winter solstice. This scriptural story hides a pagan calendar myth of enormous age. A pagan version was preserved at the Annat of Locheil, where the fatherless son of the Maiden was known as the Black Lad son of the Bones who was a cremation bonfire. According to local tradition his immaculate conception by a maiden out of the ashes of the previous bonfire took place in the late autumn. It is this myth of the virgin conception of fire which the Oda and Hallowe'en both perpetuate. We can link the first hunt of the season and the beacon or *aingeal* announcing it with the regeneration of the Fire God or Black Man from the ashes of the previous bonfire. There is a great deal more seasonal mythology of a similar kind still to recognise.

Many Lowland burghs had their own annual celebrations with similar features, detailed in *The Silver Bough* by F. Marian McNeill (1956-1968). There was little reference to religion, if any. The local festivals and gala days which were once a great feature of social life in large and small places might include bonfires, torchlight processions, a dance, rolling bannocks and horse-races. There was often a Queen, sometimes a King, but never a Devil. In Dornoch the old sabbat of 1-2 February, redefined as Candlemas or St Bride's Day, was marked with cock-fights, a supper dance, a King (owner of the winning cock), a Queen, and a bonfire round which the children danced.

One other religious event in Skye is described by Martin Martin who wrote his account of the Hebrides at the end of the seventeenth century. This ritual took place at night, at Hallowe'en, at the church of St Mulvay in Lewis. The people sacrificed a cup of ale to a sea-god called Shony, who was asked to provide in exchange a copious supply of sea-weed which was used as fertiliser. Then they spent the rest of the night in drinking, dancing, and singing. Martin is not a very trustworthy source but this all sounds very familiar.

Further evidence for ritual sex in the *Gaidhealtachd* comes from a variety of sources.

Ladhar Pocan

A marvellously obscene address to the Cailleach is known as *Ladhar Pocan* 'the fork of the bag'. It survived despite being renowned for being indecent. McLagan reports his conversation with an old native affected with discretion. This decent old man refused to utter the words, though he knew them perfectly well. But he also said that 'it was like the secrets of the Freemasons' which suggests that the indecent words hid a quasi-religious secret.

> 'Now, Donald, will you give me the counting rhyme, be The Banners of the Fian in Gaelic Ballad tradition ginning 'Laura pocan?'
>
> 'Good G— — , you are an awful body.'
>
> 'Swearing, and you an elder in the church!'
>
> 'Worse than swearing you are, and you a teacher. Why, there's not a few vulgar words, indecent, too, in that rhyme.'

'I only want the good ones, and you know that. I'll put a cross down for the bad ones.'

Despite the old man's scruples, McLagan published several Gaelic versions and some notes on the lexical ambiguities though he stopped far short of an explicit English translation (1901, 92-96).

The Fork of the Bag is a supplication to the Cailleach for luck in the hunt which survived in school playgrounds up to 1900 or later. The Lady is not mentioned but her presence can be inferred from other similar orations. The references to fertility magic depend on the fact that the hunter's relationship with the *Cailleach* or Big Woman who controlled the deer was perceived as an extended sexual metaphor. The deer trap was her vulva, a bloody enclosure bristling with spears and she was periodically raped by hunters at hunts which coincided with the full moon. This sexual image is as old as the Palaeolithic, and there can be no doubt that sexual magic was the primary focus of pagan practice in Highland Scotland, just as it was in Lowland Scotland. The sexual metaphors go far to explain the abhorrence for pagan beliefs and for sex expressed through the centuries by orthodox Christians.

Ladhar Pocan like almost all surviving fragments of archaic Gaelic exists on two levels: garbled Gaelic, and a nonsensical English translation. We can reconstruct the original Gaelic (with some help from McLagan) as it is disguised or coded by a series of predictable Gaelic puns referring to hunting and sex. Some of these puns may be part of the original design: *slaid* 'gift' is a pun on *slat* 'penis' and both are appropriate. The first three lines may be older than the rest as they preserve a structure of linked and paired items which served as a mnemonic for those delivering a long incantation: '[Dear Lady, give us] the A of B, the B of C, the C of D...', and so on. It is also found in cumulative tales. This version was collected in Argyll (McLagan 1901, 96-99).

Lara pocan,
Pocan shepan,
Shepan sian,
Dughall Glas,
A legheil as,
A ceann sa chaolan,
Caolan slat an duine,
An duine so,
Na duine ud eile,
'S diuith dh'an dorus,
Crup a stigh do stock.

[Dear Lady, give luck to...]

Ladhar pocan – The crotch of the little bag *or* vagina [the deer ambush],

Pocan seipinn – The little bag of the snares *or* pin (penis) [the trap],

Seipinn seonaid – The penis of the good-luck charms [weapons? a spear?],

Da mheur mheadon – The deer (*damh*) of the deer-forest (*meadon* 'moor, forest'),

Meur mhic Iain – The hunting on the plain (*magh*) of the fire (*aodhan*),

Dughal Glas – The bright light of the deer [*dubh*],

A leig as – Lighting the fire,

A cheann 's a chaoil – the deer trap in the narrow place [The penis in the vagina],

Caol na slataig – The narrow place *or* vagina of the gift *or* penis,

An duine so – Of the young man *or* hunter,

Crup a stigh do stock.

The final line is found in different versions as *Crup a stigh, Stigh an dalmachd, Stock a stigh, Crup a stigh do stock, Stob a stigh,* and *Stop - stigh*. Campbell of Islay mentions a similar counting-out game (which he did not write out on account of its lack of decency) which ends with the words *Cuir stochd a staigh,* upon which the boy indicated had to stick his foot into the circle of players (Campbell, vol.iv, 1893, 289). The various combinations of *crup* or *crub* 'claw', *crub* 'deer trap', *cuir* 'put, place, lay, invite, influence', *staigh* 'within', and *stochd* 'wealth, store, cattle' are on the surface a prayer that the deer which are the wealth of the hunters and their people will be caught and held securely in the trap but *Cuir stochd a staigh, Stob a stigh* and *Stigh an dalmachd,* 'a stick in, a vigorous stick' is just as suggestive in Gaelic as in English. It is reminiscent of the party game Hokey-Pokey, which is also said to be indecent.

This analysis of one popular rhyme is evidently limited but it is typical of many others and supports the idea that the sexual aspects of hunting magic were well-known to the Gaels and that if there are few signs of ritual sex in Gaelic folklore this is due to the prudery of Victorian collectors, the prudence of publishers, and the discretion of their informants who wished above all else

337

to be respectable, like the old man. The lack of information is also an effect of the paucity of trials or any other information about witchcraft or magic within the Highlands. We have nothing to compare with the evidence gathered by the trials in the Lowlands, imperfect though it often is; and we might reflect that without the records of the trials we would know very little about the sexual aspects of the witch cult either. The underlying reason, as we saw in Perthshire, is that there were no organised covens in Gaelic-speaking areas, as a result of the language barrier, the scarcity of ministers, and the lack of interest on the part of proprietors, many of whom consulted witches themselves.

The natives knew that such rhymes were not respectable, and believed that they were not the kind of thing wanted by the gentlemen who collected Gaelic folklore. This was generally true. These gentlemen generally agreed that it was degrading or unseemly, and even when they did get their hands on obscene material they felt unable to publish it. There is virtually nothing in print about pagan practices in Highland Perthshire, for example, where still in the nineteenth century, or so it was claimed, Clan Gregor had a religion of its own (Jenner 1903, xxxiii). Campbell of Islay was one of the more intrepid publishers but his comments to his List of Stories are revealing: he wrote 'There is more but don't ask!' 'Good, but cannot be published.' 'Witty, and unfit for publication now-a-days.' 'There is more of it which should not be inquired for...' He does not suggest where an educated and fore-warned enquirer might inquire for the original of these stories but we live in hope of further discoveries and hope that in any future research the importance of the original explicit text is fully understood.

Sex and the Cailleach

Pious Victorians were not able to reform the entire Gaelic language and the lexicographer Edward Dwelly, whose Gaelic-English Dictionary was published between 1901 and 1911, printed every Gaelic word he could find. His dictionary in consequence contains a remarkable number of words for a licentious or deceitful woman and for lazy, dirty or violent men. They represent the Cailleach and the hunters who also followed her. These words stand out for two reason. First, the Gaels were not promiscuous and did not need several dozen names for an immoral woman. However such terms would apply to the Cailleach. Secondly, several of these abusive terms have alternative and arguably earlier meanings of an entirely different quality. G. *caile* 'vulgar girl, hussy, strumpet' is in Irish a neutral term for a woman or a girl. The root is G. *cail* 'burn' and it appears to be one of a large class of words which identify a girl as the person who looks after the fire. G. *dràicheal* means a 'slattern, drabbish, unthrifty person' but *dreachail* means 'comely, good-looking, handsome'. A *glaistig* was 'a she-devil or hag in the shape of a goat' but she was also and probably originally a beautiful female fairy, again a description of the Cailleach. This suggests that these Gaelic names for licentious women were once honorific descriptions of the Cailleach which have been modified by puritanical Presbyterians. They might also describe the fairy women who served the hunters as sacred prostitutes in imitation of the Cailleach. Even as they stand these are appropriate praise-names for a fertility goddess in a religion where the holy sacrament was ritual sex and the Queen of Faerie slept with anyone she liked. The following lists are offered as a starting point for a glossary of archaic sexual Gaelic related to the worship of the Cailleach and hints of sacred prostitution in the pursuit of successful hunting.

1 The Lady in current Gaelic as a sluttish and promiscuous woman

abarrach 'indelicate female'.

ap 'shameless woman, any little creature, ape'.

bodag 'heifer, bawd'; *bod* 'penis'; *bodagac* 'a heifer looking for the bull'; *bodach* 'old man'; *bodachail* 'churlish, boorish, clownish, inhospitable; slovenly'. *Bodamair* was a love of Fionn, the hunter. *Bodhmhall* was the nursemaid of young Fianna, who were probably in this context fawns. As a name of the Cailleach *bodag* means 'penis-ward' or 'penis-bag', a metaphorical reference to a deer trap. The second element in *Bodhmhall*, G. *maille* 'delay, hindrance' is an ML word which also suggests a deer trap. G. *mal* 'bag' in such a context is likely to be a word for the vagina. *Pell-mell* describes the *hurley-burley* or *shambles* of the killing or butchery. The game of Pall-Mall involved a mallet, a ball and iron rings and is one of many games played by hunters to hone their skills and pass the hours while they waited for the hunt to start.

botramaid 'slut, slattern, drab, trull, slovenly woman'. See *bodag*.

bréineag or *breunag* 'slut, dirty female, slattern, drab; turbulent female; lying woman' (the Lady sometimes failed to provide). G. *breun* 'stinking, foetid, putrid, filthy, loathsome, nasty, corrupt' may describe conditions at a kill site where remains were not burned or buried. Helen McBrune was a name of a spirit seen on Lowdon Hill, Ayrshire, at Hallowe'en, 1605. Her name appears to be roughly equivalent to 'fire at the deer trap'.

brinneach 'hag, old woman, mother.' As *bréineag*.

cabag 'strumpet, toothless female'. G. *cab* 'mouth ill-set with teeth' is a form of *gob* 'mouth'. Any reference to the mouth, lips or teeth is a reference to a deer ambush and to the vulva of the Cailleach.

caile 'vulgar girl, hussy, strumpet'. Ir. *caile* 'country woman, maiden, girl'. G. *ceal* 'muliebre pudendum', *ceallach* 'war (hunting)', *cail* 'to burn', and the Cailleach herself. Callioch was a witch alias in 1622. It is significant that the Irish term is neutral while the Scottish one is a sexual insult.

draimheas 'foul mouth' most probably refers to a narrow ravine used as an ambush site.

dreachail 'comely, good-looking, handsome', but *dràic* or *dràicheal* 'slattern, drabbish unthrifty person'; *draig* 'spendthrift'; *draighilc* 'trollop, draggle-tail'. *Draig* 'dragon' and *draigh-bhiorasg* 'fuel' take us to the hunting forest, and *drùidh* 'penetrate, pierce' takes us to butchery and druids, who were hunt officials. A dragon, rare among the Gaels, was a beacon. W. *draig* 'dragon', *dragio* 'to tear, mangle', *dragon* 'leader in war (hunt master)', and *dreigio* 'to lighten or flash at a distance'. Gr. *drakontion* may be related to *derkesthai* 'to look'. G. *dreach* 'to polish', *dreag* 'fight, wrangle (hunt) and 'give notice (send a signal)' and *dreug* 'falling star, fireball, corpse-candle' all refer to hunt-beacons and the pending death of deer. The witch name Wallydragle now means 'slut' but was once complimentary.

drùthanag, *drùth* 'harlot, bawd'. G. *droch* 'death', *drùidh* 'penetrate, drain (blood?)', *druidh* 'hunt official'. G. *droch-shùil* 'the evil eye' is literally 'death-bonfire', a cremation fire. Ir. *drúth* 'foolish girl, harlot.'

fuachaid 'jilting strumpet'. When the hunting failed the Cailleach was blamed.

gaorsach 'wanton girl; slut, bawd, drivelling prostitute'. G. *gaorr* 'gore, filth; thrust, pierce, gore, fight; glut', so associated with hunting. G. *geàrr* 'hare' is a shape much used by the Cailleach. G. *gearr* 'trap, fish-weir'.

giabhair 'prostitute'. Ir. *giabharacht* 'harlotry'.

glaisrig or *glaistig* 'a she-devil or hag in the shape of a goat; a beautiful female fairy, usually attired in a green robe, seen at the bank of a stream and engaged in washing, also known as *maighdean uaine*, the 'green maiden'. In older language the *glaistig* may have been a beacon signal (archaic G. *glas* 'brightness, light, fire'). G. *uaine* 'green' is a regular pun for G. *aodhan* or *aìn* 'fire', notably in fairy lore. Ir. *glaise* 'green' is the colour of hunters or of fairies; again it means 'fire'.

gogaid 'light-headed woman, coquette, giddy female, silly trull'. Archaic G. *gog* 'deer'.

greiseag 'wanton woman'.

leirist 'slovenly woman, slut, foolish, senseless person'. G. *léir* 'power of seeing;

wound, steal, pierce (hunt)'. Ir. *léiriste* 'beetle, hammer, mallet', used to kill animals.

liobasdair 'sloven'. Related to *liobh* 'love, attachment', *liobair* 'person with thick lips', *liobard* 'leopard (hunter)', E. *love* and E. *leper*. St Fillan was a leper or white man or beacon symbol. In pagan terms, the lips were the labia of the Cailleach which enclosed the entrance to the deer ambush, an image enhanced by the sharp teeth which figure so prominently in some medieval carvings.

liùsh 'sluttish, untidy woman', also 'a woman's tattered skirt; anything that hangs in a loose and slovenly manner'. The *liùsh* may have been made of skins. It is an LS 'fire' word, like G. *loise* 'flame' and *lùchar* 'light'.

màrach 'big ungainly woman'. Archaic Gaelic *mar 'to hunt'.

meirdreach 'concubine, courtesan, harlot'. The MR 'hunting' root is found also in G. *mèirleach* 'robber'.

muine 'whore'. The name of the letter M in the ogam alphabet.

pùiceach 'female that accepts bribes'. G. *pùc* 'ram, cram, push', E. *fuck*.

raipleach 'filthy or slovenly woman'. The RB 'hunting' root found in E. *robber*, *rape*. Ir. *raipleachán* 'a term of abuse'. The Raploch or 'dirty place' below Stirling Castle may have been the shambles where deer caught in the neighbouring parks were butchered.

rapach 'nasty, dirty, slovenly, foul-mouthed'; *ròib* 'filth, slovenliness, filth about the mouth, overgrown or squalid beard, circle of hair, pubes.' This suggests an unkempt and unsavoury deer ambush surrounded by bloody undergrowth. Ir. *ropach* 'violent attack or assault' appears to derive from hunting.

rasaiche 'lewd woman'.

ribhinn 'beautiful female, queen'; *rib* 'to snare, entangle'. The origins of *ribhinn* and *rapach* are identical.

salach 'foul, dirty, filthy, nasty, unclean'. E. *salacious* 'lustful, lecherous'. A link between salt and dirt is shown by G. *sàl* 'sea', Fr. *sale* 'dirty' and Fr. *sel* 'salt'.

sgiùnach 'bold, forward, impudent or shameless woman'. A *sgiùnach* is now also a fishing charm.

sgleòid 'silly man or woman, one easily imposed upon, slovenly man or woman, drab, slut, one who indulges in idle talk, heavy clumsy lifeless female; filth'.

G. *sgleò* 'vapour, mist, romance, spectre, struggle, misery, dimness of the eyes, romancing of one who sees imperfectly and consequently misrepresents facts'. Related to *sgeil* 'loud and rapid utterance, gabble' and *sgeul* 'narrative; tale, fable, story; false or malicious report, falsehood; news, information, tidings.' The original *sgeulachd* was hunting lore. Ir. *scleo* 'pompous words', *scleoid* 'silly person, sloven, slattern', E. *slut*.

sgliùrach 'slut, slattern, gossip, female tattler, whore, clumsy person'.

siùrsach 'prostitute, whore', a cognate of E. *whore*. Ir. *siúr* is a neutral word meaning only 'sister, female relative, kinswoman, darling'. Tom na Hurich, Inverness, is in one source Tom na Shirich, for *sibhreach* 'fairy, spectre' (McRitchie 1890, 147). These words are linked: the Great Whore was the Cailleach.

slaodag, *slaodaire* 'slut, slovenly woman'. cf. G. *slaid* 'booty, theft, robbery, munificent gift' and *slat* 'penis'. Ir. *slaodadh* 'dragging or trailing after one, slipping, sliding' is used for a sledge used to carry venison.

strabaid 'whore, harlot'. Lat. *stuprum*.

straill 'harlot', *straille draic* 'sloven'. Ir. *straille*, *strailleog*, *straillín* 'an untidy female' and E. *trull* are both milder expressions. G. *straill* can also mean 'to tear in pieces'. The archaic sense of *straille draic* is 'radiating light'.

strìopach 'strumpet, whore'. G. *strì* 'strife, contention, battle (hunt)'. Lat. *stuprum*, Fr. *strup*.

struidhleach 'wicked woman who acts from evil motives', cf *straill* (above) and *struidhe* 'extravagance, profusion'.

tàsan 'sloven', also 'slow, tedious, plaintive, monotonous discourse' in which may well be a contemporary view of a druidic incantation. Also 'wrangling (hunting)'.

teallach 'concubine'.

truth 'vile beast; beastly thing; shrew, sloven', *truthdar* 'slattern'.

2 Hunters as lazy, dirty and violent men

There is a corresponding stock of words for thieves and robbers. Hunters described themselves as robbers because the deer belonged to the Cailleach and they robbed her whenever they killed one. G. *ceatharnach* in one word shows the decline in the status of a hunter: 'soldier, guardsman, hero, stout trusty peasant, strong robust man, freebooter, outlaw, boor'. Any description of a hunter as a robber, thief, brigand or despoiler is a reliable clue to archaic content. In 'The Shifty Lad, the Widow's Son' – *Gille charaich mac na Bantrach* – the widow gives her son a good schooling and hopes he will choose a respectable trade, but he is set on being a thief (a hunter) and tricks her into sending him to the Black Rogue – *an Gadaiche-Dubh* – to be trained. G. *carach* 'cunning' is also 'circling, winding, turning', like a chain of hunters winding up a hill to trap deer, so the Shifty Lad or *Gille-charaich* was a hunter. The Thief, *An gadaiche-dubh*, is one who steals deer (G. *dubh* or *dubhan*) from the Lady. The *Bantrach* or widow-woman is of course the Cailleach.

buaileadair 'assailant', from *buail* 'strike, beat, smite, thrash; beetle, as lint'. A beetle or mallet was used to stun deer before cutting their throats.

ceatharnach 'soldier, guardsman, hero, stout trusty peasant, strong robust man, freebooter, outlaw, boor'; from *cath* 'battle, struggle, hunt; company of soldiers'. There are an inordinate number of references to *cats* in Gaelic folklore. McLagan has nine references to cats, against three to dogs and one to a horse. A cat is always a telltale of hunting lore.

coigreach 'stranger', ie, a hunter who came from a far distance. G. *coigchreach* 'plundering, sacking, pilfering' is a by-word for 'hunting'. Both words derive from G. *coig-crich* or *comh-chrioch* 'confines, border, edge, march', which incidentally identifies *coig* 'to gather, hunt'. All the many Gaelic words for a border, margin, edge, etc. define a hunting-forest. It appears that the *coig-crich* was normally exploited by a combined force of 'strangers' coming from a distance in response to a pre-arranged beacon signal.

creachadair 'plunderer, freebooter, spoiler, robber'; as *creach* 'plunder, booty; host, army; to plunder, spoil, pillage, rob, ruin' – the word used for cattle-lifting and for its proceeds.

cùiltear 'smuggler, skulker'. G. *cùil* 'corner, angle, recess, niche' is a word for a deer trap among rocks or in a ravine. Place-names in *cùil* have been converted into early church sites by Christians intent on enhancing their importance. Other related words include *cùilbhean* 'cup-shaped whirl in a stream'; *cuilbhear* 'musket'; *cùilbheartaich* 'craftiness, wiliness, trickiness, deceitfulness, cunning', referring to the skills of the hunter and E. *culvert* 'stone drain', probably from an original **cùilbheart* 'deer trap'.

dibheargach 'robber, fugitive (hunter)'. In Ireland the *dibheargach* or 'two-horned' were bands of young men who took vows and lived in the wild places between settlements, presumably by hunting. G. *diabhol* an entity with horns, hooves and a tail; *damh* 'stag'; *diobhail* 'loss, destruction, ruin, robbery'; *diobhall* 'old, ancient, antique'; *diobhanach* 'outlaw'; *diobhraice* 'warlike, destructive'.

falachair 'one who hides, conceals, skulks'. G. *falach-fuinn* as Ir. *fulach fiadh* as used by the Irish contributors to VB 1990 and in the Irish Sites and Monuments Record (SMR), or *fulachta fiann* 'burnt mound', Daithi O hOgain, BA 1987, 215. The remains of a field-kitchen used by deer-hunters, with G. *fiadh* 'deer'; *fàl* 'circle; wall, hedge, dike; guarding'; *falaisg* 'moor-burning'; *falchaidh* 'lurking, concealing, dissembling; secret, concealed'; *falchaig* 'raid, foraging expedition'; *faoil* 'hospitality, generosity'; *faoileach* 'holidays, feastdays, carnival'.

gadaiche 'thief, robber'; *gad* 'withe, twisted stick', probably a noose or snare; *gadag* 'rope of twigs'; *gadanach* 'causing a continued noise'; *gadhar* 'lurcher-dog, mastiff' – also as *gaoir* 'noise', *gaoir-chatha* 'battle-cry, war-cry, shout set up when engaging in battle' (the shout made by beaters at the start of the deer-drive, both to startle the deer and to coordinate their movements); *gaoth* 'theft'.

geòcair 'glutton, spendthrift, parasite, vagabond, rebel, debauchee'.

grisean 'one of a rabble'.

ionradhach 'plunderer, depopulator', from *ionradh* 'plundering, laying waste, devastation'. The first element corresponds to *aodhan* 'fire'.

làdar, *ladran* 'robber, thief'.

luidealach 'lazy fellow, slovenly lounger, bumpkin'.

mèirleach 'thief, robber, rogue, rebel'; the same root is found in *meirghe* 'banner, standard, flag, troop, company, band'; *méirneal* 'merlin, a type of falcon'. The same word applied to a blackbird, Sc. *merl*, Fr. *merle*, provides a well-known Irish pun or joke while *meirdreach* 'concubine, harlot' is a late and unfriendly view of the forest guardian or Fairy Sweetheart. They all come from the archaic MR 'hunting' or 'gathering' word used *mar*, also for the sea as *muir*, gen. *mara*, seen as a great gathering of the waters; E. *more*, *moor* 'a hunting place', *morass* 'a bog where deer were caught'. G. *mèirleach* appears to be the origin of E. *warlock*.

milleadair, *milltear* 'destroyer, waster, spendthrift'; *mill* 'spoil, hurt, mar'; *milidh* 'warrior, champion (hunter)'. As E. *military*.

ràbair 'litigous, troublesome person; roarer; wrangler'; *rabal* 'noise, bustle'; *rabh* 'warn, guard'; *rabhachan* 'warning, advertisement, beacon'; *rabhadh* 'alarm, hue and cry'; *raobhachd* 'gluttony, excess'; *reub* 'tear, rend, pull asunder; wound, mangle'; E. *rabble*, *robber*, Lat. *raptor* 'robber, plunderer'.

reubair 'robber, violent person, tearer, bruiser': see *rabair*.

sladaiche or *slaidear* 'robber, plunderer, thief'; from *slad* 'steal, rob, deprive of strength; havoc, carnage'; cf also *slagan cùl a'chinn* 'hollow at the back of the neck' (resembling a deer trap); *slaid* 'munificent gift or present; booty'; probably as E. *slash, slaughter*; cf *slaightear* 'rogue, rascal, knave, blackguard'. *Slaod-theine* 'a great fire in which many people were consumed' – was this a bonfire?

spionadair 'one who tears or snatches away', from *spion* 'to snatch, take away by force or violence'. Also *spiontag* 'currant, gooseberry'.

spùilleadair 'brigand, robber', in Dwelly also as *spùinneadair*, but the *l* form is supported by *spall* 'beat, strike'; *speal* 'sword; to mow, cut down; short spell of vigorous exertion'; *speil* 'drove, herd of cattle or swine'; *speilean* 'ball game like Cat and Bat played in Uist'; *spòld* 'piece of a joint of meat'; *spòltadh* 'hacking, hewing, slaying, slashing, massacring'; E. *spoil*, Sc. *spulzie* 'depredation, plundering' and Lat. *spolium* 'skin stripped from an animal'.

stig 'sneaking fellow'; *stìgear* 'mean abject skulking fellow'.

trustar 'debauchee', cf. *trusgan* 'man's private parts'. Drostan is found as a place-name element in Perthshire in Ardtrostan and Craigchrosten (NN6723) where it may refer to a deer ambush.

20: FLYING BY NIGHT

This connexion of the witches and fairies opens up a very wide field; at present it is little more than speculation that the two are identical, but there is promise that the theory may be proved at some later date.

Margaret Murray 1921, 14.

We cannot claim to have proved anything but the main conclusion of this study of witches, fairies and hunters is that they coincide, not completely of course but essentially. Charmers who appear in the trials were often called fairy folk or witches; witches visited the fairy folk for help; the coven witches followed an evolved and rather decadent variety of the old fertility cult practiced by the fairy folk such as Andro Man or by the whole population in the Oda. In the century of the witch trials from 1570 to 1670 Scots law did not distinguish between charmers, fairy folk and witches.

However we found a marked distinction between the activities of witches in the Lowlands and the role of charmers in the Highlands which was not entirely due to the language difference. This also is shown by the trials. Those tried before c.1620 were mainly individuals while after c.1620 the trials increasingly deal with larger groups of witches who had given an oath of allegiance to their Lord or, as the Church saw things, to the Devil. These new covens were managed by literate gentlemen who were known to the courts as 'Devils'. As we saw in Perthshire, the coven movement began in the eastern Lowlands c.1600-1620 and spread rapidly north and west as interest in the old religion spread among the literate. Earlier large groups like those in Easter Ross and in East Lothian were temporary assemblies of individuals who worked together for elite clients with difficult demands.

The trials provide many examples of individual women of uncertain status who interact with 'fairies'. The ability of witches and fairies to co-exist is shown by events in Bute in 1660 when the Session heard that Jean Campbell of Rothesay 'gangs with the faryes' (Hewison 1895, II, 264). She was called before the Presbytery of Bute charged with 'frequenting with the company of spirits'. According to the trial record Jean suffered from indigestion but had found relief using an ointment which she had got from a fairy healer and was telling everyone how good it was. She was warned to have no more dealings with the fair folk and not to try to cure others (which suggests that she herself was a healer with links to the old people). A year later she was again charged with claiming to cure desperate diseases by herbs 'and such-like' and was again warned not to do any more curing or she would be charged with witchcraft. That she survived even one such warning suggests she had influential friends as this was no idle threat. Two years later twenty members of the Rothesay coven were arrested and tried. Four women were executed and a fifth, Janet McNicol, fled to Ayrshire only to be caught and executed when she came back to Bute in 1673, twelve years later. The main charge against them was meeting with an evil spirit on the shore at a place called Butkee in Rothesay and having engaged themselves in his service. Who these witches were is unclear but all twenty had Highland names and one used Gaelic charms (MacPhail 1920, 3-30). Meanwhile the fair folk of Bute, like those of other Lowland areas, continue with their herbal remedies unmolested, eventually to vanish into the background or join the local coven. To judge by the reaction of the authorities in Bute, it seems that they considered fairies to be a mild irritant but that co-ven witches, who were members of an organised group and who were thirled to the Devil by the demonic pact, were a threat. There were also hunters or fairies in the native background: the witch Jonet Morisoune of Bute, tried in 1662, 'met with the devil when he was going by with a great number of men, that she asked at him quhat were these that went by, who answered they are my company, and quhen she spiered where they were going he answered that they were going to seek a prey' (MacPhail 1920, 23). For 'Devil' in this case we should perhaps read 'Fairy King' or hunt-master.

A Family Business. We have seen that occult learning ran in families and by personal instruction and that learning was attributed to ghosts. As recorded at several of the trials in the witch century it was generally passed on in the female line but sometimes to a husband (Moress Elder of Andro Man's circle learned from his wife; old Mackellar of Cruachan had learned his charms at the Priory of Iona in the sixteenth century and he in turn taught others) (MacPhail 1914, 166). Andro Man was taught by the Queen, his wife, or an unrelated man (as in the case of John Brugh). Alesoun Piersoun got her learning from a ghost, William Sympsoun, her maternal cousin, probably in a dream or under the influence of drugs. At the trials a family link was often enough to condemn a man or woman: Thomas Leys followed his mother, Janet Wischert, to the stake in 1597; she was by all accounts a great vitche but he appears to have been blameless. The pattern persisted into the last years of the witch-hunt in Scotland which saw two brothers, George and Lachlan Rattray, probably fairy folk, executed in 1706 in Inverness for the 'horrid crimes of mischievous charms, by witchcraft and malefice, sorcery or necromancy'. The last Scottish witches whose executions were authorised by the Privy Council were those of the Ratters in Shetland in 1708, two sisters and a brother, said to be vagabonds, who were 'great deluders and abusers of the people' (Hill 2013, 222-223). They also look like fairy folk or hunters and pagans.

'A Great Number of Men'. One would expect to find more women than men but in the better managed covens like Aludearn and in the facts as reported by Andro Man numbers appear to be even. We are accustomed to groups of women but in the trial transcripts we get occasional glimpses of groups or gangs of men, often accompanied by one or more women. These men wear green or brown clothes which were perhaps plaids in a muted or 'hunting' tartan. In 1576 Bessie Dunlop of Ayrshire met eight women and four men and was told they belonged to the Court of Elphane. In 1588 Alesoun Peirsoun of Fife met a man in green on Grangemuir, when she was lying there ill and once she met him again with 'mony mene and wemen with him'. In 1616 Katherine Caray stated that she was once met among the hills of Caithness 'at the doun-going of the sun' by a great number of fairy men under a master man (Rec. Ork. f.94, f.63; Dalyell 1835, 536). In 1622 Helen Cumine of Aberdour in Fife saw a great number of women, 'shee thought above fortie but ther was so great a mist betweixt her and them that she could not know them; lykways shee saw a great number of men in another place but ther was a great mist betwixt her and them too' (RPC 1896, I, xiii, 48-50). Isobel Sinclair of Orkney, tried in 1633, had been 'controlled with the Phairie six times at the reathes of the year' (Murray 1921, 243). Isobell Gowdie in 1662 named ten of the thirteen minor fairy men attached to her coven: Swein, Rorie, The Roring Lyon, Mak Hector, Robert the Rule (who seemed to command the rest), Theiff of Hell, The Red Reiver, Robert the Jackis [a coat of mail], Laing, Thomas a Fearie &c. These nicknames suggest a link with hunting. In other words they were hunters. Donald McIlmichall tried in Inveraray in 1677 confessed that he had seen 'a great number of men and women within the hill quair he entered having many candles lighted, and saw ane old man as seemed to have preference above the rest' (MacPhail 1920, 37). Fairies, as we have seen, gathered on fairy knolls. Sometimes we glimpse a sacrificial infant. In Orkney where there was an active fairy population, Jonet Drever in 1615 was accused of having carnal dealings with 'the fary xxvj yeiris bygane', and of fostering a bairn in the hill of Westray to the fairy folk. This bairn was probably destined for sacrifice, like those of Bessie Dunlop, Janet Lindsay and Elspeth Reoch.

One question to which we can now offer an explanation is the unsatisfactory status of men in what Pearson called the mother-age. He was struck by the fact that in his day (c.1900) the male element in the German rural population was idle. Men did little or no productive work – they did not even help with the heavier agricultural work, but left it all to their wives. He put it down to laziness but this does not seem to be an adequate explanation. The history of Scotland provides similar examples of idle males which we can attribute to the failure or abandonment of communal hunting. In Scotland the loafers and vagabonds were unemployed hunters, playing games to sharpen their skills and to pass the hungry hours while they waited for the beacon to give the signal for the next deer-drive. By 1600 such men and their skills were redundant, chased into extinction by feudal landlords. Within the next century vast numbers of single men emigrated to the Lowlands, to England, to the new colonies to seek for land. Many went into the British Army. Hunters make excellent soldiers.

From the evidence of the trials, as far as we can judge, fairies and witches were different names for initiated members of the same pagan population; in the Highlands this included every member of society. Fairies and witches have many features in common. They performed magical rituals on the quarters, notably at Hallowe'en (or at the nearest full moon), when they sained themselves, their families and livestock and as coven witches blessed the whole community. They danced on the hills at night, performed fertility rituals and had a feast – originally to celebrate a successful hunt. All of them are noted for flying at night – in other words, they travelled very rapidly to a designated meeting place.

This kind of hunting magic is extremely old. The earliest works of art that survive in Europe date back to the Palaeolithic and include several very stout women, the oldest dating to 40-35,000 BP and a well-endowed dancing priest who is wearing antlers, an animal hide and nothing else. The Lion Man from the Hohlenstein Stade region of Germany dates to 32-28,000 years ago and again represents a male priest in the guise of an animal – not, in fact, a lion but a lioness. In Banff in 1600 we find hunters devoted to a Big Woman and priests disguised as animals. For all that time, the Devil has danced at the full moon, wearing an animal pelt, and mated with a stout and fertile woman. These Palaeolithic aspects of a pan-European religion must have been brought into the country by the first settlers at the end of the last glaciation as this is the last time there was free cultural exchange throughout Europe. Through subsequent times until the introduction of feudalism there has been no significant change in the religious rituals in Scotland (see *Possibly Palaeolithic*, in this series).

With the imposition of the feudal system the old way of life came to an end but fairies persisted with their peripatetic way of life and observed their own pagan religion for as long as they could. Pagans were said to be still active in Breadalbane at the time of Viscount Dundee (d. 1689) when the Clan Gregor was neither Catholic nor Protestant but had a religon of its own (Jenner 1903). Still in the seventeenth century in most of Lowland Scotland, even in the largest towns, healers visited the elves, were taught by them how to kill and cure, passed time in fairyland and paid the penalty. We have found dozens of cases. Bessie Dunlop who died in 1576 had given her newborn baby to the Queen of Elphane to save her husband's life; Bessie described her as a stout body. Andro Man of Banff-shire who died in 1598 had been initiated into the fairy religion as a small boy and later married the local Queen and had several children by her. Elspeth Reoch, tried in 1616, had contacts among the fairy folk of Orkney, Caithness, Speyside and Lochaber. Her career began when she when she was twelve and old enough to be initiated (*MCM* II,

187-191; Murray 1921, 242-3). The Queen and her consort at Darnaway gave Isobell Gowdie and the rest of the Auldearn coven more than they could eat, a revealing and perhaps unique event in her life. The Queen here also was described as stout. In 1662 the fairy folk of Bute co-existed with a new coven. In 1677 Donald McIlmichall played his trump for the fairy folk of Benderloch and was found guilty of trafficking with the Devil. The trials opened a window on a world that is normally concealed, showing us fairy activity from one end of Scotland to the other.

Dalyell in 1835 summarised current beliefs about fairies, some of which have a grounding in fact. 'They can become invisible'. Invisibility was achieved not by magical ointments but by disguise. Hunters survive also as the bands of guisers who emerge on feast days and holidays, with their faces blackened, clothed in skins, carrying sticks or swords, singing and dancing, and equipped with a bag to receive presents of food or money. 'They are addicted to merriment: they are seen dancing, and are dressed in green'. These are literal facts. 'Animals from the flocks and herds, shot with elf-arrows, serve for their banquets'. This also is a plain fact, but the animals come from the wild herds.

The Fairy Raid. There is much in common between the sabbat of the coven witches and the fairy gathering of Gaelic folklore. Both witches and fairies assembled at preordained places at the Quarter Days, notably at Hallowe'en. In many cases their meeting-places were old tribal beacon sites where hunters had once gathered. They both passed the time in drinking, feasting, music and dancing. The sabbat culminated in ritual intercourse, a fact not mentioned in fake folklore but implicit in the general outline of the raid. The gatherings described by Andro Man of Banff (died 1593) certainly involved promiscuous sex and so did the Oda. The scarcity of any mention of the sexual aspects of Scotland's fairy religion can be attributed to the failure of oral lore, to the ban on pagan activity after 1600, and to the self-imposed censorship of nineteenth-century collectors. Failure to record does not imply it did not exist: without the evidence from the trials we would know nothing about the sexual aspects of witchcraft either.

There is no evidence in the Highlands for organised covens holding sabbats at the start of every new quarter, though they were beginning to spread north into Lowland Perthshire towards the end of the period. Much later collectors found memories of charming and cursing and a tradition of celebrations around the seasonal bonfires, where local farmers, farmers' wives, their children and their servants, danced round the fire and went in fear of ghosts. It is now easier to understand why the Kirk tried to ban these great seasonal festivities and why they failed to do so. Going further back into the mists of fake lore we find repeated stories about bands of fairies making merry at night in fairy hills, raiding settled folk, stealing their milk, dancing, riding in procession. The bonfires, the games, the dancing, the music and the ritual intercourse 'for luck', which is implied but never defined, represent the preparations for a deer-hunt, when food was collected, a reliable pony selected from the wild herd, a black face and an animal pelt adopted, the elf-arrows sharpened (and probably poisoned), the necessary rituals attended to.

Continuity with Christianity. The Church in Scotland, as elsewhere in Europe, regarded the earlier pagan religion as heresy. However the Church itself continually accommodated pagan practices. It rejected ritual sex, child sacrifice and cremation but kept the care of ghosts, lights, vigils, relics, bones and feasts. Mary replaced the Cailleach. The Christian liturgy retained the pagan prayers of confession, atonement, supplication, intercession and thanks-giving that were once addressed by hunters to the Lady. In many churches the congregation continued to kneel to pray, as witches did when addressing their Lord. Instrumental music and choral singing have survived as elements of worship, though very few people now dance or play ball in church. The Reformed Church also influenced the witch ritual. When Bothwell gathered his witches at North Berwick, a roll was kept, attendance was enforced, prog-ress was monitored, and backsliders were punished, just as they were in the Reformed Kirk.

Another coincidence is in the frequency of communion. In the Roman Church the sacrament is celebrated daily (in special circumstances three times a day) but in the Church of Scotland from 1560 onwards the recommended frequency was four times a year. The Reformers rejected the daily Mass but then fell in with the witches, whose communion with the devil also took place four times a year. The Reformers banned all feasts except Easter, which is the most pagan of all the Church feasts, but their dating method still follows the pagan calendar. Sabbats took place at the eves of the Quarter Days or Reaths of the year, on 1 February, 1 May, 1 August and 1 November but the Forfar witches met on the Christian feasts of Candlemas (2 February), Ruidday (3 May), Lambesmas or Lammas (1 August) and Hallowmas (31 October) (Anderson, 1888, 258). This again is reminiscent of the pattern of worship in the Reformed Kirk, with its weekly services on the Sabbath and three or four Communion seasons in the year. The Feast of the Dead on 1 November is a notable survival.

The Reformers also banned all seasonal bonfires, pilgrimages, carol singing, plays and mumming, dancing, drinking, music, sex outside marriage, and many more of the pleasurable aspects of life, all of which we can recognise to be features of pagan religion. But the people continued to celebrate the spring equinox, the birth of St John the Baptist at midsummer (23-24 June), Samhain or Hallowe'en (31 October) and Christmas or midwinter (25 December).

The master of the witches was identified by the Reformed Kirk with the Biblical Devil but the witch-hunts largely ignore these Devils. In the earlier trials he is not distinguished from the Fairy King or the master of the hunt. It seems that his position as the master of a coven of thirteen witches may have been influenced by imported ideas. We get more authentic information from fairy folk such as Andro Man (1597) and Patrick Lowrie (1605) though their own position is not clear.

The Boyled Chylde. There can be little doubt that the fairy folk trafficked in newborn children. One is reminded of the Hindu belief that children below the age of five have no souls. But when an archaic Gaelic text talks about the death of 'children' or 'sons' it generally means young stags, as deer were reckoned to be the children of the Cailleach. There is an obscure Gaelic saying: 'When Beltane falls on a Thursday many a woman loses an infant son' which may refer to a hunt late in the season which would target young deer. If such a saying were taken literally by credulous priests who had forgotten its true meaning they might well insist on sacrificing human infants. From the sacrifice of Isaac onwards the history of religion has many examples of bizarre beliefs based on the mistaken reinterpretation of obsolete secular instructions. Irrational doctrines and superstitions can very largely be attributed to a breakdown in the transmission of rational learning.

Karl Pearson believed that traces of a 'primitive cannibalistic sacrifice have even remained in the ceremonial of the most developed religions of highly civilised peoples' (1897, 62, note). It certainly seems that the Church of Rome practises token cannibalism but the original Easter festival involved not cannibalism but killing a lamb to celebrate the new season and the ewes coming into milk. Another myth with similar roots is the Slaughter of the Innocents which is celebrated on 28 December and which represents the midwinter hunt. In Scotland it seems possible that some similar lore was kept in memory but misinterpreted as we have evidence for a clandestine traffic in unbaptised children and their use in magical ointment in 1596 and for cannibalism at Forfar in 1661, when Helen Guthrie and four others raised the body of an unbaptised infant and made it into a pie 'that by this meanes they might never make a confession (as they thought) of their witchcraftis' (Murray 1921, 159). (The charm did not work.)

Thus, before 1600, in Highlands and Lowlands, we find skilful women and a few men who practise herbal medicine, use enchanted stones, know about effective poisons, use incantations and magical rites to protect against evil, who could impose or remove the evil eye, and recover or take away the milk of women and cows. These charmers were also believed to control the weather and the winds and give fishermen good catches. (Scottish fishermen were in origin landless hunters.) Compared with the coven witches these local charmers were benign. It seems safe to assume that this benevolence reflects the primeval character of the witch cult whose main purpose was to ensure the fertility of the herds and good luck in hunting, and that the Good Neighbours deserved their name. The principle of evil fairies and the Devil appears to have evolved with Christianity and in Scotland after the Reformation.

Pearson conjures up May Day celebrations in Germany, with ribald choral dances, feasting and drinking, fires on the hill-tops, and unregulated sex (1897, vol. ii, 40). Group marriage in which all the adult men and women participated is known in Scotland only from the Michaelmas celebration or Oda but this festival was both widespread and fully documented. What is less evident is that in the local festivals of Lowland Scotland (McNeill 1968) we also find all the elements of a sabbat or hunt muster. Sex is the unspoken extra but the festivities include ball games, horse-races, foot-races, competitive sports, the crowning of a Queen, the selection of a King, a procession on horseback or on foot, riding the bounds or marches, a bonfire at the traditional local site, fireworks, a free meal, guising with men dressed as women, singing and dancing. Pearson added tribal debate and law-making at such events (1897, vol.ii, 47). Disputes were certainly settled at hunt meets and several courts continued to meet on fairy knolls.

The Catholic Church tolerated obscene singing and dancing, playing ball, dancing around the church, eating and drinking in the church on Sundays. Medieval sources mention that the clergy played ball games in church at Easter (Houston 1829, vol. 4, 45). This is a relic of the ball games played by hunters while they waited for the hunt to begin. Medieval churches were generally built at existing muster sites where a bonfire was lit. Gibson's Craig, one of the places where the witches of Crook of Devon met, had also been used as a muster site by the Murrays of Tullibardine and had its own football pitch or ball green.

The Witches' Dole. Even municipal hospitality can be traced to the witches' dole which represents food supplied for the hunters and those who support them. Isobell told the Court in 1662 that the witches of Auldearn saved their doles of food and drink for the great festivals when they shared them out and feasted (Pitcairn 1833, III, 612-614). These grants of food seem to have been a recompence for their activities on behalf of the community as a whole. Sometimes they went through a ritual to secure their share but at other times it seems they simply helped themselves. It is evident from this that cattle in 1662 were exceedingly small.

'We wold goe to seuerall howssis, in the night tym. We wer at Candlmas last in Graingehill, quhair we got meat and drink anewgh. The Divell sat at the heid of the table, and all the Coven abowt... We killed an ox, in Burgie, about the dawing of the day, and we browght the ox with ws hom to Auldearne, and did eat all amongst ws, in an house of Auldearne, and feasted on it' (Picairn 1833, III, 612-3).

'And quhan we tak away the fruit of cornis, at Lambes [1 August], we tak an wooll-sheeir, and cuttis or clips onlie thrie stakis of it, and plaitis vther thrie rudis togither, and sayes

'We cutt this corne in our Lord the Divillis name,
And we sall haw the fruit of it hame

'And this thryse ower; and so we haw the fruit of that field. Ewin so,
quhan we tak keall or the lyk' &c. And we lay all up till Yewll, Pace, or
Halit dayes; and pairtis it among us, and feastis on that togither' (1833,
III, 614).

Pearson notes that three ears of corn were sacred to the Virgin Mary as the
Mother Goddess (1897, 42).

'When we tak cornes at Lambes we tak bot abowt two sheawes, whan
the cornes ar full; or two stokis of keall, or therby, and that giwes ws the
fruit of the corn-land, or keall-yaird, whair they grew'.

This is not, as Pitcairn says, 'a symbolic mode of taking the fruit, crop, or
produced of land, etc.' but an actual payment in kind. Isobell continues:

'And it maybe, we will keip yt while Yewell or Pace [Christmas or
Easter] and than devyd it amongst ws... When we goe to any hous,
we tak meat and drink and we fill wp the barrellis with owr oven pish
again... We were in the Earle of Murreyes hous in Dernvay, and ve gott
anewgh ther, and did eat and drink of the best, and browght pairt with
ws... I was in the Downie-hillis and got meat ther from the Qwein of
Fearrie, mor than I could eat...' (Pitcairn iii, 603-4).

Pearson also recognised that 'the old human sacrifice is a marked feature of
the religion of which witchcraft is the fossil. Witches, we are told, kill and eat
children, especially the unbaptized. They boil them down, as all early sacrifical
feasts appear to be boilings and not roastings. Remarkable in this respect is the
offering of wax figures of babies at shrines of the Virgin Mary as thank-offer-
ings for easy birth' (1897, 32-33). As we have seen, in Scotland infants were
indeed boiled, to make an ointment (Anderson 1596).

Raising the power. The men who ran the covens believed that magic worked,
if they could only find the right ritual, and that they could control it and
exploit it to their personal advantage by harnessing the power of local witches.
But Isobell Gowdie also believed that the coven got their power from this
man; 'when we seek it from him we call him "Owr Lord!"' (Pitcairn 1833, III,
605). To do so they followed a set ritual. When the witches had made a clay
model to destroy the male children of the Laird of Park, they gave it its power
by pronouncing an incantation over it. The Devil taught them the words 'and
quhan we haid learned them, we all fell downe wpon owr bare kneyis, and
owr hair abowt owr eyes, and owr handis lifted wp, looking steadfast wpon

the Divill, still saying the wordis thryse ower, till it wes maid' (Pitcairn 1833, III, 612).

Willy Matheson (1968, 76) identified Coinneach Odhar (Kenneth Ower) with the great warlock who became involved in the cantraips of Catherine, Lady Munro, in 1577 and was put to death for witchcraft by burning at Chanonry Point. He distinguishes between prophecy and the second sight which is 'represented as an involuntary gift – even as an affliction – whereas in the case of Coinneach Odhar what lies at the heart of the legend is a power deliberately cultivated and sought after by means of occult practices and sinister rituals, though this aspect has come to be considerably glossed over and played down in the course of oral transmission. Even so, the use of a magic stone to see into the future is clearly something that would not be considered appropriate in an account of the second sight...' Matheson plays it down. This cultivated power is at the heart of witchcraft, invisible but deeply felt. It is one of the last secrets, not investigated by Kirk Sessions, not recognised by James VI.

The covens failed, one after another, not primarily because they were persecuted but because their power and skills were not renewed over the generations and they did not have the power to survive persecution. Isobell Gowdie lamented her loss of power but she stated that it had passed back into the collective of the coven: 'The witches yet that are untaken [at liberty] haw thair awin poweris, and owr poweris quhilk we haid befor we were takin, both. Bot now I haw no power at all' (Pitcairn 1833, III, 605). It was on this conserved power, passed from one witch to another, that covens ran through the seventeenth century and survived, barely, into the eighteenth.

The witch's pact. Helen Frasser of Foveran, north of Aberdeen, 'a common vitche be oppin voce and common fame', was tried and executed in April 1597. One of the accusations made against her by the parish minister, Mr Thomas Tilideff, was that she had told Christane Hendersoune to put one hand to the crown of her head and the other to the sole of her foot, and deliver up whatever was between them to the Devil, and she should want for nothing that she would know or desire (SCM 1841, I, 107). This is word for word the demonic pact used at a later date by the masters of covens when recruiting new witches. We may assume that this dedication had once been administered to Helen Frasser by her teacher Maly Skein, 'brutit to be ane rank witche', and that it was indispensable in the making of a witch. The Devil is found in other formulae for gaining supernatural powers and may even have been the Queen of Elphane. He was not the Satan of scripture, whatever Mr Tilideff imagined. So the question remains: to whom did the new witch imagine she was dedicating herself?

The Fairy Organisation. We can now sketch out a provisional outline of the fairy organisation. The best source, though bedevilled by clerical confusion, is the dittay assembled against Andro Man who was tried in Aberdeen in 1597/1598 (the year changed at the equinox). He was a famous healer who was married to the Queen of Elphen, 'on quhom he begat dyveris bairnis'; leaving no doubt that the Queen was a real woman. The balance of power lay with her: 'scho mackis any kyng quhom scho pleisis, and lyis with any scho lykis' (SCM 1841, I, 121). The men who interrogated Andro Man in 1597 evidently expected to encounter the Devil controlling a horde of witches, on the lines made familiar by Francis Stewart and James VI and had difficulty in making sense of a group led by a female. They must also have been confused by the fact that the King of Elphan, who appeared like a man and like a stag, was subordinate to the Queen. The account of the trial is consequently difficult to understand.

The Queen is the key figure. Originally the Lady was the tribal fire personified, but as far back as we can go we find her also as a fertility goddess, an Earth-Mother who was at the time generous and treacherous. As the goddess of the hunters she was a night-riding Hag who could give luck in the chase or withhold it. In Wales the Hag rides with the Wild Hunt. In real life the Queen controls the hunters and all the other officers, who constitute her Court. In several places from Bute to Orkney we have found bands of hunters, fairy folk or elves, both men and women, who are subject to the Queen but under the control of the King or Hunt Master who is often called the Devil.

In Ayrshire also in 1576 Bessie Dunlop's master Thom Reid was subject to the Quene of Elphame and the eight respectable women wearing plaids and the six men in gentlemen's clothes who waited on her and invited her to join them were fairy folk from the Court of Elphame (Pitcairn 1833, I, 49-58). This probably means they were ghosts who invited her to the realm of the dead but the interaction between the normal world (Middle Earth) and the fairy world and between the living and the dead is not familiar or clear-cut. In the seventeenth century the witches of Auldearn were entertained by the Queen and King of Faerie at Darnaway and they were certainly real people.

Still relying on Andro Man's testimony, it is clear that the guidman was a priest. The name comes from G. *guidhe* 'to pray, entreat, beseech' which suggests he was responsible for organising ritual activity and for sacrifices. A separate officer was the hunt-master or Fairy King who appears at the head of his men in various places.

The King was the Queen's choice, which implies that he could be replaced. But he also appears to be the master of the hunt, the 'master-man'. Women as a rule do not enter the deer-forest, which is the territory of the Cailleach. Dairymaids lived in designated areas with their cattle and the hunters normally lived apart in the deer-forest. In reports of witch-trials before 1590 the witches do not appear to have a leader. They pass on their wisdom to selected pupils, most of them female, and inaugurate them one by one into the craft. The Devil is the Protestant Devil or the Court's name for the leader of a coven. Which raises, once again, the question: to whom did the witch at her inauguration dedicate herself? How do we reconcile the Muckle Black Wallawa with the worship of the Cailleach? Is 'the Devil' a euphemism for the Queen?

The relationship between deer-hunters and the Cailleach was conceived in vividly sexual terms. Hunters raped the goddess when they attacked her deer but at the same time her vulva, representing a deer-trap, was the ultimate good-luck symbol. If the primary function of a female witch was to enhance the fertility of her community by performing a sexual ritual, it would be logical for hunters to observe a parallel ritual which would replicate their rape of the Lady, representing the earth and her resources, and the death of the deer. Worship of the female icon is 'reported from the Indus Valley civilisation and from the Tantric levels of Hinduism: 'The goddess is worshipped in the form of a vulva and her menstrual cycle celebrated by adorning the icon with red powder' (Flood 2004, 192-3). In Assam in June pilgrims worship at a large cleft in the bedrock. There is a notable cleft in a rocky outcrop at St Bride's Chapel in southern Perthshire. In the original fairy version of this ritual the red powder is replaced by the blood of deer trapped at the ambush site, a cleft among the rocks which serves as a trap.

An objection to having a fertility ritual performed within the deer-forest is the reported jealousy of the fairy sweetheart, the *leannan sith*, towards any other woman but the trial evidence shows that numerous women did enter the deer-forest and stayed there for a period. Isobell Haldane was in the fairy hill from Thursday to Sunday at noon; Alesoun Peirsoun was sometimes with the fairies and sometimes not; Janet Drever of Orkney was convicted in 1615 of having carnal dealing with them over twenty-six years; the Auldearn coven and the Darnaway coven met the fairy folk on Downie Hill. This suggests that there were certain initiated women or groups of women who represented the Cailleach to the men of the hunting band, and who took part in ritual prostitution.

MacDougall collected the story of the four *glaistigs* who visit four hunters in their bothy in the semblance of their true sweethearts. A *glaistig* is either a she-devil or a beautiful female fairy. One of the men keeps his visitor at bay by sitting up all night and threatening her with his dirk. At cock-crow when the glaistigs vanish, he finds his companions with their throats cut and every drop of blood drained out of their veins (MacDougall 1910, 256-262). If this is not simply a Hallowe'en ghost story it could be a warning against ritual intercourse with a fairy sweetheart on the eve of a hunt but it also assumes that hunters might be visited by women in the forest.

Most of those executed in Scotland before 1620 were independent charmers or healers whose wider links, where we know anything about them, were with the fairy world. They got their knowledge from a ghost, or from the fairy people, which probably means the same thing. It is safe to assume that those who admitted to meeting with the fairies or being taught by the fairies were themselves fairy folk; that a woman who met a great number of fairy men had gone in some official capacity with other dedicated women to a well-known place where she had gone many times before.

What we learn of the fairy gatherings from the trials is like a sabbat expanded to accommodate both sexes. After 1620 the development of the coven moved the emphasis from a group of men backed up by a group of women to a large group of women controlled by a solitary man identified by the Kirk as the Devil but by the witches as their Lord. The Devil in Scotland appears to be a recent invention. Henri Boguet stated that the Devil had carnal relations with the female witches in his own shape but assumed a female shape to pleasure the male witches (Summers 1925, 97). It would be more normal, certainly in Scotland, which was always very conservative, for this female shape to be made flesh in the form of the Queen of Elphen who 'lyis with any scho lykis' and who had carnal dealings with the fairy men or elves 'that cumis with thame' (SCM 1841, I, 125).

I believe that Margaret Murray was correct to identify the witch-cult as a prehistoric sacred tradition, though what we find in Scotland is probably much older than she envisaged. Independent invention can be ruled out. It is not likely that the illiterate, static and isolated peasants of a thousand different rural settlements in northern Europe invented by chance the same package of beliefs and practices. There are plenty of examples of local invention in the field of belief and ritual in Europe and they are all divergent: midwinter rituals in Scotland or Greece are very different from midwinter rituals in France or Italy. Common features such as lighting a fire for good luck can safely be attributed to common inheritance from a shared past, before populations split up into separate groups and settled. Pan-European features go back to the Palaeolithic. It is remarkable that fairy belief lasted so long despite this separation.

We have tentatively assembled some elements of the early native cult from the Scottish evidence, bearing always in mind that in Scotland the difficulty of local communications and the collapse of the oral tradition would tend not only to preserve archaism but to produce local variants. The cult included worship of the Cailleach as fire, personified as a maiden. It taught that individual souls survived and rose to heaven in the smoke of the great seasonal bonfires. It recognised the Cailleach as a source of fertility and the source of all good things. The testimony of Ando Man at Banff in Aberdeen in 1597 reveals that fertility magic, sexual rituals, spirit guides and beacon lore were all part of the worship of the fairy folk. The links are explicit when apparently supernatural statements are revealed as archaic or coded Gaelic.

We have seen that after c.1620 the trials begin increasingly to target covens – often of thirteen witches – as well as independent practitioners.

This is thought to be because before c.1600 there were no covens to target. The similarity of all the later covens in Lowland Scotland as revealed by the trials suggests learned input from the same or several similar sources. Further analysis suggests that they were created by a network of literate enthusiasts anxious to emulate Bothwell's experiments in 1590 or by their own experiences at Continental universities to acquire supernatural powers, and that their techniques were either inherited from the earlier pagan cult, like the demonic pact, or inspired by literary sources. We know that leaders of covens (the so-called 'Devils') recruited existing adepts who brought their knowledge and their powers with them: Bothwell recruited the leading witches of Lothian; the Devil in Fossaway recruited John Brugh the warlock; the Devil in Forfar recruited Helen Frasser. Isobell Gowdie told the Court in 1662 that since her arrest her powers had left her and gone back to the other members of the coven (Pitcairn 1833, III, 605).

By the end of the seventeenth century whatever justification there had once been for trying charmers and coven witches as agents of the Devil was rapidly being overtaken by a disreputable welter of superstition, witch's marks, hares and magic bridles. As late as 1703 an elder of the Kirk, Robert Bainzie of Oyne, was accused of charming but he was merely rebuked. The last coven to be comprehensively destroyed was at Torryburn in West Fife at about the same date.

Before the rise of covens in the Lowlands there seems to have been little or no difference between Highland and Lowland witchcraft. Sources reveal many common features such as enchanted stones, enchanted water, iron magic, bone magic, milk magic (using a tether, a blanket, sweeping the dew), divination by the key or by turning the riddle (reported from Fife and from Tain), healing wells, infant sacrifice, clay or wax dollies, charming, using elf-arrows. Taking the power (G. *toradh*) from food or drink is probably fake lore inspired by the witches' entitlement to a dole. Healers in both places provided a service to farmers and their families, in which they were often successful in producing a cure, and they also fulfilled political projects for the elite.

The native religion, as far as we can judge, was propitiatory and syncretic. It persisted with its own old liturgies but did not reject novelty. Christianity was a source of powerful charms, not a threat. The polarisation of the situation is clearly due to the attitude of the Reformed Church. It was responsible for the confrontation created by the theological divide between Christ and the Devil, and between criminals and the state. This must have been very foreign to a religion that aimed to balance natural forces for the general benefit. Supplication and atonement were its natural voices. But there were also deeper and darker secrets as well as the focus on sexual intercourse which supported the view of demonology set up to challenge the Church.

The divide between Highland and Lowland witchcraft was not caused by different magical practices, or between Gaelic and English, or even according to where the Church was established and where it was not, but between areas which were equipped with a judicial infrastructure of literate clerks, an educated elite, prison, courthouse, church and gallows, and those which were not. It was possible to try the Gaelic-speaking witches of Bute in 1662 because Rothesay had been a royal burgh since 1401; it was possible to try Donald McIlmichall in 1677 at Inveraray as it had been a royal burgh since 1648 and in 1677 consisted of a tower-house, a prison, a courthouse, a church, a school, a gallows, a stone cross and forty-three alehouses. We can see from the shenanigans in Easter Ross that language made little difference: the cult in the Gaelic-speaking community was essentially the same as the cult in the English-speaking parts of Scotland, that a network of wise women, charmers, healers, and the occasional warlock had preserved the lore in an unbroken tradition. But we only know about them because the legal documents were written in English by professional clerks employed by the local justice of the peace.

That the fairy religion is based on archaic hunting lore and represents the remnants or fossils of an archaic hunting religion is suggested by several factors. With the exception of some recent literary fictions, the evidence from the witch trials in different European countries shares many features, usefully summarised by Margaret Murray (1921). Trials for sorcery began in France, England and Germany in the fourteenth century, and in Switzerland and Italy in the fifteenth century. In Scotland it became a capital crime in 1563 and remained so until 1736. The last legal execution in Western Europe is believed to be that of Anna Goelid in Switzerland in 1782 but two witches were burned in Poland in 1793 and the Irish statute was not repealed until 1821 (Summers 1925, 46, n.). French witches in the fourteenth century, Scottish witches in the sixteenth century, and Polish witches in the eighteenth century confessed to very similar activities. In pursuit of their various arguments, scholars quote indiscriminately from witch trials in Scotland, England, France, and Germany. There was no particularly Calvinistic form of witch belief (Larner 1981, 158). The impression of a shared inheritance is reinforced by the geographical spread of the witch hunts in Western Europe and by their persistence. But it seems to be much older than even Murray supposed.

There are a limited number of mechanisms which produce convergence between different cultures. The least common is coincidental independent invention and it can be rejected here. It is very unlikely that similar beliefs and practices arose among the illiterate peasants of several different countries by chance. Borrowing from a common source such as a recent missionary movement can also be ruled out; it might have affected the coven movement but it implies literacy and witches were not literate. Borrowing is most often from the trials themselves, a fertile source of novel ideas which influenced popular belief. It cannot explain the origin of these novel ideas. The only convincing explanation is that Scottish witches shared a pan-European tradition which was part of their common Palaeolithic heritage. Its main features are reflected in the antipathy of the established Church to consulting ghosts, eating and drinking, music, dancing, and orgiastic sex.

This investigation of witchcraft in Lowland Scotland has shown a network of autonomous individuals who organised very similar local rituals designed to enhance the fertility of animals, particularly deer and cattle. They retained a considerable body of traditional hunting lore and a knowledge of herbal medicine. The probability of archaic survival in Scotland up to 1560 is enhanced by the fact that the Catholic Church appears to have been indifferent to deviant rituals among its Gaelic-speaking flock. It did not even get greatly agitated about the scandalous behaviour of its own parish priest in 1282 (Stevenson 1839). The fact that the priest was not disciplined suggests that fertility festivals were, as he claimed, commonplace among the Gaelic-speaking population of Lowland Scotland at that date.

The sexual activities of the covens are well reported as they were taken as proof of the diabolic pact, but are rare in the earlier trials of charmers and healers. There are very few mentions of carnal dealing in Gaelic folklore with the exception of the Carrot festival (McNeill 1959, II, 102-115) which happily breaks all the rules. This silence may be due to the language barrier: fairies were observed and described from the outside, as a mysterious people living within their own rules. This is true not only of sexual rituals but of Gaelic culture as a whole. In addition, Gaelic culture was oral. The clearest evidence for sexual activity comes from the Gaelic language, which has great numbers of words defining sluttish women (the Cailleach) and randy or violent men (the hunters), pointing to a vast area of ritual activity which is otherwise hidden.

Hunters attached specific and detailed sexual imagery to the deer ambush or trap. This is no longer evident in English but it is clear in archaic Gaelic. G. *iolairig* 'deer trap' is defined as 'a V-shaped structure, not necessarily artificial, wide at one end and narrow at the other, into which deer were driven, and shot with arrows as they came out'. In rocky or mountainous areas there were plenty of natural ambush sites. Hunters saw the narrow bloody cleft as the vulva of the goddess, whose fickle nature required careful management by way of obedience to her rules, and prayers of supplication and atonement. The Roman Mass preserves the enforced fast that preceded the hunt, now enforced as a form of discipline, and the communal feasting on flesh and blood that marked its successful conclusion.

Other incantations use sexually-explicit language and were regarded as a potent source of good luck in the primitive deer-hunting society of the Gaels. The imagery linking the deer-trap and the female vulva was reinforced by converting the spear into a phallic symbol. The spear in the Grail romances which drips blood into a bowl or cup has just raped the virgin goddess by killing a deer. This imagery is further enhanced by the monthly nature of the hunts that shed blood at this sacred and dreadful place. The menstrual imagery acquires a further dimension as hunts generally took place at or near the full moon. These images of fire, blood, supplication and gratitude still inform the poetic subconscious in its dealings with sex, blood, death, and rebirth. The equation of guilt and atonement with blood, death and supernatural generosity survives even within Christianity, a most unnatural religion.

Hunting is never mentioned in the trial evidence but during the century of the trials it was still an important source of food over the winter in the uplands. By the end of the seventeenth century the law was leaning heavily on the last of the native hunters. We glimpse the last of the fairy folk of Argyll in 1677 – landless vagabonds, living on stolen cattle and borrowed time. The prison, the courthouse and the gallows of Inveraray were made for such as they were.

Certain individuals throughout the Lowlands reveal a familiarity with Gaelic and provide a link with the Highlands and Islands where ritual observances were commonplace but witchcraft was seldom prosecuted. In consequence there are few contemporary records to match those of Lowland Scotland, and several developments since the seventeenth century also work against this expectation – the decline of Gaelic oral culture after 1600, the dislocation of rural life after 1700, and massive depopulation, a vicious attack by the Presbyterian Church on every aspect of Gaelic culture and effective censorship in key areas.

Scottish fairy lore is a fictional view of an obsolete hunting culture. It represents a variety of attempts to explain surviving sayings, beliefs, scraps of instruction, and distant memories of hunters, transformed very often into small people. Whether these fictional reinterpretations arose spontaneously or were inspired by imported English fairy-stories with supernatural elements – fairies also fly by night – the idea arose among the Gaels that the *daoine-sith* had been a supernatural people and they forgot about the deer-hunters whose way of life no longer existed. There was no single philosophy or consistency in this little proto-religion but this new method of analysing Highland fairy tales shows that there is a single underlying reality, that the main themes survive in several different forms.

We are faced, finally, with the problem of irrational belief. Book-based religious speculation and fake folklore have in their different ways conditioned us to accept the existence of supernatural and irrational things that we know have no real existence. We feel no need to question miraculous events in such sources. When we try to understand the origins of witches, fairies and ghosts this irrational conditioning seems to stop logic in its tracks. Montague Summers believed in the real existence of powerful and evil witches as agents of a real Devil. There is no such entity. Norman Cohn and Kirstie Larner go closer to the truth: they did not believe that witches had real powers but assumed that a belief in witches with real powers had once been a real element in society. This is also Katherine Briggs' approach to fairies but it still requires the acceptance of irrational events: people once believed fairies were real just as they believed in the miracles of the New Testament. But neither Briggs, Purkiss, Henderson, Cowan, Black, nor any other writers on witchcraft has questioned the reality behind the myths, just as good Christians never doubt the reality of events described in the New Testament. Our tolerance of irrationality is a difficult lesson to forget.

The witch cult preserves a fertility ritual whose background was hunting. Nothing else can explain how the practices of Galician peasants in the seventh century, French peasants in the fourteenth century, Scottish peasants in the sixteenth century and Polish peasants in the eighteenth century were all so very similar. The witch cult of northern Europe may have been the oldest continuous tradition in the world.

We get a last glimpse of the *sìth* or fairy men in the Highland cadgers who worked as cattle drovers and lived on the streets of Edinburgh, waiting for a drove going south. They were extremely hardy, strong, sturdy, rough, but honest and disciplined, living under a captain or master-man, and famous for their unbreakable code of honour. Though penniless they could be safely entrusted with large sums of money. When all else failed, they worked on the golf links of Leith and Boroughmuir as caddies or kiddies, or descended, not without dignity, to beggary; to cadge is 'to pick up a living on the streets, to beg'.

> *Gone are the green-coated fairies that brightened the hillside of old*
> *The witches that rode on the tempest, the urisk that haunted the fold.*
> *The life of the days that have fleeted, comes back not with vision or spell;*
> *So rest ye, dim shadows of cloudland- ye fairies, for ever fare-well.*

Alexander Nicolson (1827-1893).

APPENDIX 1 - CALENDAR

The Gregorian calendar began to replace the Julian in the sixteenth century. 24 November became 6 December so eleven days were 'lost'.

St Luke's Day, 18 October, was close to Old Hallowe'en (31 less 11 = 20 October) but only if St Luke's Day did not move.

Calculation is not made easier by the practice of counting inclusively; ie, counting eight days from one Sunday to the following.

Local beacons were used to announce communal events. This is shown very clearly by the seasonal pattern revealed by a study of the patronal dates of 285 of the parish churches in the department of Creuse, France. Only 70 fall in the four months from April to July, a monthly average of 18. The least popular month is July (14), followed by May (16). But 215 feasts fall in the eight months from August to March, on average 27 per month. The most popular is March (39), followed by November (29), December (28) and January (29). This clear preference for a winter feast appears to reflect the fact that hunting took place over the winter, from October to March. Its abrupt stop in April coincides with Lent, 'the empty season', when adult animals were too thin and the newly-born too small to be worth eating. It is not a coincidence that Easter is celebrated in many places with roast lamb. There is a general focus on the winter solstice but no sign in Creuse of special activity at Midsummer or Hallowe'en. They may be northern festivals but a superficial analysis of northern saints shows that in Ireland also the most popular months were January, March, August, November and December. It is perhaps evident that people will celebrate when food is most abundant. March appears to be the exception, a last fling (*carnival* means 'meat eating') before the hard time of Lent.

THE HUNTING CALENDAR

Since the fourth century the Western calendar has been tied to a solar year of twelve months divided by solstices and equinoxes into four equal parts. Hunters are tied to the solar seasons followed by their prey animals but they hunt by the light of the moon. Uncorrected lunar feasts progress through the calendar from summer to winter and back again and are only sustainable in rich agricultural societies such as Egypt where events outside the temple precincts were governed by seasonal factors. Hunters, like farmers, must remain in touch with the real world. Consequently they need to calibrate their calendar at least once a year, setting the start of a new lunar year by reference to a solstice or an equinox. The date of Easter is still calculated as dates were calculated in pre-Christian times, by reference to the moon. Therefore it varies by several days from year to year. If uncorrected, a lunar date will progress backwards through the calendar and within a very few years will lose touch with the life of the herds. The most popular calibration points are the spring solstice and midsummer, when the sun is likely to be visible.

Whatever else they did, the monuments of the Neolithic and Bronze Age provided a guide to solar events. The dates they provided did not need to be very accurate if everyone in the district agreed to follow the same authority. When the date was established it was broadcast by lighting a bonfire in a central place visible over the relevant area. This avoids the confusion which would invariably arise if every place made its own calculation. One such central place may have been the stone-setting at Lundin Farm (NN 882505) in Strathtay near Grandtully as Burl notes that it has 'a marvellous view westwards towards Ben Lawers' (1976, 202) which is the major long-distance beacon for Lochtayside. Stone settings in Scotland are also often associated with cremations and with cupmarks, showing where hunters waited for moonrise. Grinding one stone on another may in itself have created a signal. At every site several things come together: visibility, calendar alignments, and cremated bone pointing to a local bonfire which marked the annual arrival of the important date.

The need for calibration explains why there have been several different dates for the new year, including the spring equinox, the autumn equinox, Hallowe'en and midwinter. Modern folk festivals and church festivals are a mish-mash of solar events, lunar events and other ways of dividing up the calendar. But for a preliterate population solar events are easy to observe and offer an accessible and reliable way of calibrating the lunar year to within a few days. A gain or loss of two or three days or even a week or two would have no significance so long as everyone in the area followed the same calendar.

The sabbat was originally a lunar feast but most recently it was celebrated on the solar Quarter Days, 1 November or All-Hallows, 1 February or Candlemas, 1 May or Beltane, and 1 August or Lammas. This introduces a further complication as these are not the old natural quarters which were marked by midwinter, spring equinox, midsummer and autumn equinox but a month behind them. This suggests they have been calculated, like Easter, according to the next full moon. In other words, although the Quarter Days are now solar dates, at one time, like all hunting feasts, they were movable events which took place at the next full moon. This method is still used to establish the date of Easter, which is the first Sunday after the first full moon on or after the spring equinox. Beltane was also a lunar date calculated from the spring equinox. By analogy, Samhain or Hallowe'en was not fixed on 31 October but celebrated on the first full moon on or after the autumn equinox.

This old rhyme is a reminder of how the date of Easter (and of other lunar feasts) was calculated. It gives Lent far more than its normal forty days.

First comes Candlemass, syne the new mune;
The neist Tyseday aifter that is aye Festern's E'en.
That mune oot an the neist mune fou [*or* the neist mune licht]
The first Sunday aifer that
Is aye Pasch true.
(McNeill The Silver Bough vol. 2, 46).

The number forty appears to represents one and a half lunations. There seems to be no name for this period but in the Bible 'forty days' is used to mean 'a very long time, as far as we can count'. The Israelites wandered in the desert for forty years; Moses spent forty days on Mount Sinai; Elijah spent forty days and forty nights walking to Mount Horeb; prior to the Flood it rained for forty days and forty nights and Jonah gave the city of Nineveh forty days to repent or be destroyed. It is forty days from Jesus' birth to Candlemas on 2 February, now the Feast of the Purification of the Virgin. Jesus fasted in the wilderness for forty days. The Lenten fast lasts for a nominal forty days from Ash Wednesday to Easter Sunday though it is generally more as Easter may be as much as six days after the full moon. Jesus flew up to Heaven forty days after Easter. A period of forty days or six weeks is also the term of Orthodox funerary rites. As the calendar now stands, Hallowe'en falls forty days after the autumn equinox. It was regarded as the start of a new year or at least its winter half.

Christianity was unable to change the underlying logic of the pagan calendar. Easter remained attached to the spring equinox. Midsummer became the Feast of St John the Baptist (24 June) but the bonfires continued. Midwinter was devoted to his cousin Jesus and other beacon saints or old fire gods, including St John the Evangelist, and more bonfires. Samhain became the Feast of All Saints and All Souls but it retained signs of the pagan ceremonies when the bones of the dead were burned and their souls sent on their way to heaven.

The two dates which are mentioned most often as sabbats, Beltane (1 May) and Samhain (31 October), marked the age-old division of the year into summer and winter and the transition between hunting and pastoral occupancy of the uplands. Between Samhain and Beltane the wilderness was devoted to hunting, giving Hallowe'en its enduring reputation as a great witch festival. There was believed to be a particular danger at Beltane from witches who went in the shape of hares to take their produce from the newly-calved cows. Interpreted, this means that after Beltane hunters depended on the dairy-maids to support them during the summer.

However they calculated the dates, Scottish witches at least in principle met four times a year on specific dates. In the sixteenth-seventeenth century, sabbats in Scotland were held on the Quarter Days which by then were associated with Candlemas (2 February), Beltane or Rood Day (30 April-1 May), Lammas (1 August) and Hallowmas or Samhain (31 October-1 November).

At Maybole in Ayrshire the four annual fairs or markets were held on these days, probably for legal reasons rather than to support local witches.

As one might expect there are some puzzles. In 1633 in Orkney it was alleged against Isobel Sinclair that during seven years, 'sex times at the reathes of the year, shoe hath being controlled with the Phairie' (Dalyell 1835, 470). (A 'reathe' is G. *ràidh* 'quarter, season'.) Does this mean she met with them only six times in that period or that the Phairie met six times a year?

The pagan nature of seasonal festivals has always been recognised but they have generally been attributed to farmers. In Scotland we can trace their origins to the earlier hunters and herders. The most significant relic is guising. Guisers are bands of young men or children who wear old clothes and masks, or have their faces blackened. They go from house to house at Hallowe'en and at New Year, performing ritual songs and dances 'for good luck' and are rewarded with gifts of food, once their provisions for the hunt, which they carry off to a private feast or distribute to the poor.

THE FESTIVALS

Candlemas, 1-2 February, a quarterly sabbat, a Scottish quarter-day, a fire festival, forty days after Christmas, or after the winter solstice; midway between the winter solstice (21 December) and the spring equinox (21 March); the festival of Brigit as the fire goddess. She was 'the daughter of Ivor' which means the fire in the hearth (G. *eibh*) – hence the charm: 'I will not touch the daughter of Ivor and she will not touch me.' (McNeill 1959, vol.2, 27). This allows us to identify the serpent of a second version of this charm and the queen (*righinn*) of a third version with 'fire'. 'Serpent' was the name of a devil. G. *ribhinn* 'nymph, maid; beautiful female; serpent; queen' refers to the Lady in various of her guises. Bride was celebrated with ceremonial bannocks and with rituals which, performed correctly, promised fertility in family, flock and field for the coming year. Candlemas was calving time and the Irish milk festival of Imbolc was celebrated on 2 February. In pagan Rome this date was celebrated with burning torches and candles in honour of Februa, mother of Mars ('fire, mother of hunting'). It was adopted by those who constructed the Christian year as the Feast of the Purification of the Virgin, when Simeon (a hunter, from *sim* 'to gather') prophesied that the infant Jesus would be 'a light to lighten the Gentiles'. Jesus was known as Christ, the Annointed as bonfires were annointed with oil to make sure they burned brightly. In France 2 February is La Chandeleur, a candle festival when pancakes are eaten. Scottish schoolchildren appointed a Candlemas King and Queen who reigned for six weeks or forty days. Ball games were played at Kelso and Jedburgh. In Dornoch c.1800 the celebrations included a cockfight, the crowning of the King and Queen, a procession through the streets led by a piper and a drummer, a supper dance for adults, and a bonfire round which the children danced. The date has attracted a cluster of 'fire' saints: Adamannus, Caornan, Aedan, and Mittan on 31 January (G. *aodhan* 'fire, *caoir* 'firebrand, blaze of fire', *meadhon* 'hunt gathering'); one-eyed Brigit and Darlugdach 'hunting light' on 1-2 February; Lawrence on 2 February; Blaise on 3 February; Modan 'gathering fire' on 4 February.

Shrove Tuesday, a moveable feast. Also known as **Fasten's Een** ('the eve of the fast') preceded the forty-day fast of Lent, counting back from Easter. 'Shrovetide' was also 'the first Tuesday of the spring light' [this must refer to the full moon before the Easter moon]. 'Shrovetide was one of the great days for saining cattle, juniper being burned before them, and other superstitious precautions were taken to keep them free from harm' (Campbell 1902, 256-257). Communal ball games were played on Candlemas in the West of Scotland and on Fastern's Een in the East. At Kilmarnock there were horse-races, a typical pre-hunt exercise. Also reminiscent of a hunt is the custom of having beef for dinner so that the cattle would thrive. Special bannocks or pancakes were baked.

Spring Equinox. 21-22 March. Up to 1600 in Scotland, later in England, 25 March marked the start of the New Year. As *Latha na Cailleach*, 'the day of the Cailleach', it was marked by beacons.

Easter was a lunosolar feast celebrated on the first Sunday after the full moon on or after the spring equinox. A communal fertility ritual took place at Easter in Inverkeithing in Fife in the thirteenth century. Easter games: ball games as well as tipcat, the cat being a small block of wood, were played in the Highlands.

Hock-Tide, a movable feast, was a lunar festival celebrated in England on the second Tuesday after Easter Sunday when women captured and tied up men in a simulacrum of the hunt.

Beltane or May-Eve, 30 April, **May Day,** 1 May, **Rood Day,** 3 May. A bonfire festival, quarterly sabbat, Scottish Quarter Day, and the first day of summer. On 1 May dew had magical properties and wells were visited. When Beltane fell on a Thursday, 'many a woman lost an infant son', as young stags were hunted. (The Slaughter of the Innocents, celebrated on 28 December, has a similar origin.) In Finland on 1 May hill-tops were crowded with witches (or hunters). The practical aspects of Beltane relate to the removal from the winter township to the summer sheilings but protective rituals are appropriate to any flitting. The ritual bannock for the children's dinner was prepared by hand and handed to them directly. In various places in Lowland Scotland there were horse-races, processions, morris dances (in Perth by 13 dancers decorated with bells), communal ball games and May plays of a mixed pagan-Christian nature. There was a maypole on Arthur's Seat. In Germany 30 April was Walpurgis Night when the witches gathered in high places, particularly on the Brocken in the Harz, to dance. Walpurgis was adopted as a Christian saint whose feast was celebrated four times a year.

Midsummer, 20 June, celebrated at St John's Eve, 23-24 June, feast of the birth of John the Baptist (G. *aodhan* 'fire'). His is one of the only three births so celebrated for reasons now almost lost in the fog of Catholic hagiology, the other two being those of the Virgin and Christ. John's death is celebrated in the normal way as the Decollation of St John on 29 August. The creation of a second feast at midsummer was part of an elaborate scheme which allowed the Church to adopt the summer solstice into its calendar. The Christian feast was once marked, like Christmas, with three masses. 'The whole history of St John the Baptist was, by our ancestors, accounted mysterious, and connected with their own superstitions' (Scott 1931, 299). This was mainly because midsummer served as a universal calendar mark which was confirmed universally by lighting bonfires. One of the last midsummer fires was on Cairnshee, the 'fairy hill' at Durris in Deeside. Lit at dusk, the smoke and flames were visible for many miles. Bonfires on St John's Eve or St Peter's Eve (28-9 June) were banned in the sixteenth century. St John's Wort, *eala-bhuidhe* 'light of the fire', like ragwort, a plant with clusters of starry yellow flowers, was used to ensure fertility. On St John's Eve fern seed and elderberries also had significance. In Orkney and Shetland a bone was added to the bonfire.

August: Lammas, 1 August, Lugnasa, a harvest festival, a sabbat, a fire festival, and a Scottish quarter-day. The date has no Christian associations but the Gaels performed saining rituals and a magical bannock called *Moilean Moire* was baked. The last Tannel (G. *teine* 'fire') or Lammas bonfire was lit in Ayrshire on the last day of July in 1843. Traditionally there was a piper and people danced round the fire. Ladybirds, known as Lady Tanners, were caught and used in divination. 1 August was the Irish Lugnasa or feast of Lug. Lug or 'light' invented horse-races, ball games and chess. As he was a beacon figure he closed one of his eyes when performing protective magic while his grandfather, Balar 'fire place', had a destructive eye which was opened only during a battle: in other words they were both beacons. The marriage market at the Tailtenn Fair at Lugnasa perpetuated 'an earlier promiscuous love-making ... or [had] the object of magically assisting the fruitfulness of the soil' (McNeill 1959, vol 2, 94-5). Fertility magic also worked for the wild herds.

September: Rood-day in Harvest, 14 September. In 1597 on Ruidday in harvest, Andro Man 'saw Christsonday cum owt of the snaw in likeness of a stag' (SCM vol I, 1841, 137-138). Snow in September is unlikely. The word translated as snow was probably G. *cathaich* 'to hunt (fight)', mistaken for G. *cathadh* 'falling snow, snow-drift'. Roodmas was when the deer rut began (McNeill 1959, 143).

September: Michaelmas, 29 September. Michaelmas was a type of Gaelic sabbat with ceremonial food, horse-racing, 'many curious dances', and explicit sexual aspects. It is discussed in detail elsewhere.

October: Hallowe'en or **Samhain**, 31 October, was an important sabbat, a Scottish quarter-day and a beacon festival marking the beginning of winter. 1 November was once New Year and its importance persists. From a single point in Buchan one could see sixty or eighty bonfires and from Cluny Rock in Strathtay seventy or seventy-five were visible (Kennedy 1927, 59). They indicated that the master beacon had been seen and its message understood. There are many traditions concerning witches, fairies and fire. In many parts of Scotland hundreds of torches or *samhnag* were prepared so that people could run round their farms to keep them safe and to protect mothers and young babies against the fairies. As 'fairy' is a name for a hunter, the underlying lore relates to the fact that Samhain marked the opening of the hunting season, when hunters could kill young stags. There was a prejudice against Hallowe'en falling on a Wednesday, perhaps because some hunting date had to be postponed as a result. 1 November, in Christian terms All Saints, and 2 November, All Souls, are the Feast of the Dead when cemeteries all over Europe are filled with flowers and there were horse-races, games and dances (as always when people met up in numbers). In St Kilda the ceremonial bannock was 'in the form of a triangle furrowed' (Martin, quoted by McNeill vol.31961, 21). In Shetland bands of guisers known as Grülacks (G. *grullagan* 'circle, ring of people' in other words, band of hunters) or Skekklers (G. *sgeig* 'to mock, ridicule, deride') under a leader or Skuddler (G. *sgud* or *sgath* 'hew down, destroy') and equipped with a fiddler and a bag-man, went from door to door collecting food, as hunters once collected supplies before setting off for the hills. Like male witches, the Grülacks hid their faces behind veils. Elsewhere Hallowe'en guisers blackened their faces to make themselves invisible to the spirits of the dead (to be invisible as they advanced on the deer). Hallowe'en coincides with the feasts of the beacon saints Fillan and Aeda. The Night-Hag rides at Hallowe'en. It is suggested elsewhere that the bones of the illustrious dead were burned in the Hallowe'en bonfire while their ghosts rose to paradise in the smoke. The illuminated death's-head, skeletons, ghosts, witches, and bonfires associated with Hallowe'en are not modern inventions. Hallowe'en was once a lunar feast. *Gealach an t-sealgair* 'the hunter's moon' was the second moon in autumn (after the autumn equinox, 21 September) and the next was the last moon in harvest which extended for a month before Hallowe'en. Hallowe'en was therefore the second full moon after the equinox (Campbell 1902, 306-7).

But Campbell also says that Hallowe'en 'being the night preceding the first day of a lunar month was always dark' (1902, 286). If he is right, Hallowe'en was celebrated at the dark moon, not the full moon, though still calculated from the autumn equinox on 20-21 September. This would be closer to its modern date at the end of October. It is however more probable, given the fact that Hallowe'en was a sabaid or communal hunt, with much nocturnal activity, that the original festival took place at the *full* moon. Fairies or hunters also were abroad that night. Fairy mounds were open that one day in the year, which is to say that the October full moon marked the opening of the hunting season, when the bands were recruited. After Samhain the wilderness was devoted to hunting.

November: Martinmas, 11 November, Old Hallowe'en. A link with hunting is suggested by G. *mart*, an animal killed for winter provisions, originally deer, later cattle. Corresponds to Whit. A song sung at Hallowe'en around bonfires:

This is Hallaevan, the morn is Halladay

Nine free nights till Martinmas, and sune they'll wear away. It was essential that blood should be shed at Martinmas (it was the date of a hunt). Martinmas is associated with the ancient New Year festivals of early November.

St Lucy, 13 December, Festival of Lights. In Sweden known as Little Yule, once the shortest day.

December: Midwinter, the major annual festival encompassing the winter solstice (22 December), Christmas or Yule (G. *geal* 'fire') (25 December), Hogmanay or Calluin (31 December) and New Year (1 January). It has absorbed many elements from Hallowe'en, the old New Year. The Slaughter of the Innocents, which the Church celebrated on 28 December, commemorated the killing of all male children under the age of two, by which we may understand a cull of surplus young stags, killed while there was still a mouthful on them. At Hogmanay, 31 December, there were once universal bonfires or torch rituals which survive at Burghead, Campbeltown, Newton Stewart, Minnigaff, Dingwall, Stonehaven, Comrie, Biggar and many other places. On Hogmanay juniper was used to fumigate the byres and the dwelling-house (C. Hole 219). 'Kissing for luck' is no doubt a euphemism for more significant sexual activity. On Hogmanay housewives undertook the kind of fundamental cleaning associated with a removal or flitting. Fairies are said to flit on New Year's Eve (but this may refer to Hallowe'en). Some authorities locate a sabbat on a movable date soon after Christmas, probably the first full moon after the winter solstice. In the Highlands a Yule log was identified with the Cailleach. Yule was noted for over-indulgence in eating and drinking, for mistletoe (G. *nuaudhulig* 'all-heal'), for sports, for circle dances (the original *carols*) which sometimes took place in churches, and for guising. In Greece at St Nicolas the

Kalikantzari, or evil spirits, were kept at bay by burning a log or by lighting bonfires and ringing bells. The Grülacks or guisers in their straw disguises were out again in Shetland, as at Hallowe'en. On North Ronaldshay, Orkney, towards the end of the eighteenth century, people still danced round a standing stone by moonlight, singing to provide the music. On 1 January the Iomain Mhor or great shinty match was played in every Highland community, a communal ball game was played in Kirkwall, and bowling matches took place at East Wemyss and Kirkcaldy. A major football match takes place in Glasgow. The season is marked by a galaxy of fabulous beacon saints, all notifying the mid-winter hunt. The series begins with Nicholas on 6 December (followed by Lucy, Drostan, Methvanna, Flannan, Samthainne (*sam* 'together + G. *teine* 'fire'), Thomas, Finan (the longest night), Ethernaisc, Stephen (Fr. *Etienne*, G. *teine* 'fire'), John the Evangelist (*aodhan*), Enan and Ethbin (*aodh*), not forgetting Christ (annointed with oil) on 25 December. There is abundant evidence at midwinter for beacons, fire worship, hunting, feasting and fertility rituals. Nicolas raised three 'boys' or young stags pickled by a butcher. In the Outer Hebrides, the *Gillean Callaig* was dressed in the hide of a bull, complete with horns, hooves and tail, and perambulated through the township while his followers beat on the hide with sticks. In Lochaber a hide which served as a drum was worn by one man while the others beat at it with sticks, shouting 'Calluin of the yellow sack of hide' (or 'Calluin of the leather sack of the fire'). At one time these were hunters collecting a levy of food to sustain them through the forthcoming hunt. In Sutherland King Geigean ('deer fire'?) was a man who presided over 'death revels' (a hunt). 'A tub of cold water was poured over his head and down his throat, after which his face and neck were smeared with soot. When he had been made as formidable and hideous as possible, a sword, scythe or sickle was placed in his hand to serve as an emblem of office' (Carmichael, *Carmina Gadelica*, 2nd edition, II, 300-1). In other words, the Geigean was disguised and equipped as a hunter. In Rome on the day preceding the last full moon of the old year, a date that would normally be associated with a hunt, a skin-clad man representing Old Mars was beaten with long rods and driven out of the city. In seventh-century England, on the first of January, men went about wearing the horns and hides of stags or bulls (Summers 1925, 6). In Austria at St Nicolas (5-6 December) farms were visited by guisers known as Krampus who wore huge fleecy coats and masks with horns and long red tongues.

Yule's come and Yule's gane An we hae feasted weel.

Now Jock maun tae his flail again and Jennie tae her wheel.

* * *

Calendar sayings

Beltane and Samhain, 1 May and 31 October

*Duair is Ciadaoineach an t-Samhain is iarganach fir an domhainAch 's
meirg is mathair dha 'n mhac bhaoth 'd uair is Daorn dh'an Bhealltain*
['When the Wednesday is Hallowmass, restless are the men of the
deer-forest;
But woe the mother of the foolish son when Thursday is the Beltane'.]

The men of the deer-forest are deer who are restless if Samhain falls
on a Wednesday because they recognise preparations for the big hunt
of the season which takes place the following day.

*Is iomadh te bhios gun bhacan baoth dar is ann air
Di'rdaoin bhios a Bhealltainn*
[Many a woman will be without an infant son, when Beltane falls on a
Thursday.'] If Beltane falls on a Thursday, there will be one more hunt
before the end of the season and young deer will be at risk.

Candlemas, 1-2 February, a sabbat. Purification of the Virgin; Imbolc; a hunt
in Scotland.

Là Fhèill Brìghde bàine, bheir na cait an connadh dhachaigh

[On fair St Bride's Day the cats will bring home the brushwood.]

'On bright Bride's day, the hunters will carry fuel for the fire
homewards.'

Là Fhèill Brìghde, thig an rìbhinn as an toll; [*tul* 'fire'] *Cha bhean mise
dhan rìbhinn, 'S chan bhean an rìbhinn rium* [*ribe* 'trap, ambush'].

[On St Bride's Day the nymph/queen/snake will come out of the hole;
'I won't touch the nymph and she won't touch me'.]

'On St Bride's Day the fire is lit at the ambush site.

I will not touch the fire and the fire will not harm me.'

Seachdain ro Fhèill Brìghde, thig nighean Iomhair as an tom [*tom* 'fairy
knoll, signal stance'];
Cha bhi mise ri nighean Iomhair, 's cha mhò bhios nighean Iomhair rium –
[A week before St Bride's Day, Ivor's daughter will come out of the
knoll;

I will not touch the daughter of Ivor and the daughter of Ivor will not hurt me.]

G. *nighean Iomhair* 'the maiden of the holy place (deer-forest)'; the Cailleach

Spring Equinox, 7 March

On St Patrick's Day, cats bring home the brushwood
Meaning: at the spring equinox, hunters bring home kindling for the signal fire.

Spring Equinox, 21 March OS.

Là Fhèill Math-Cheasaig bithidh gach easgann [easan] torrach –
[On St Kessog's Day every eel is pregnant]
'At the spring equinox a large fire announces the hunt'.

G. *bibhith* 'a very large fire'; *eis* 'troop'; *aos* 'fire'; *toir* 'pursuit, chase'.

Tom a Cheasaig is a fairy knoll or outlook post beside the river Teith, in Callander, Perthshire.

Summer solstice (Midsummer), 20-21 June, the longest day.

Là Fhèill Eòin as t-Samhradh, theid a' chuthag gu taigh Geamhraidh –

On St John's Day in summer, the cuckoo goes to her winter home.

Là Fhèill Eòin, their iad aighean ris na gamhna –
On St John's Day they call the stirks heifers.

Summer solstice (Midsummer), 20-21 June, longest day. Fern seed became visible on St John's Eve at the moment when the Baptist was born, was under the protection of the Queen of Faëry, and gave its possessor the power of becoming invisible 'at will. This is a hunting pun. Fern seed is G. *iarmart na raineach* which may mean 'progeny of the deer forest'. G. *raineach* 'fern' is a pun on G. *rann* 'portion of land (tribal deer forest)' which is also found as *fearann* and *earann* 'fire-portion'. The original saying refers to a master beacon lit at Midsummer.

Lammas, 1 August (a sabbat).

Latha Lùnasdal caillidh chreithleag an leth shùil

[At Lammas the gad-fly loses one of his eyes.]

At Lammas the hunt beacon burns at half-strength [?]

Possible solutions: G. *cailleach* 'bonfire'; *creath* 'corpse, dead body'; *creach* 'spoils of the chase', *suil* 'bonfire'.
An leth-shuil means literally 'with half an eye'.

* * *

APPENDIX TWO - CONFESSIONS OF A COVEN: FORFAR, 1661

Joseph Anderson, PSAS, 5th ser. vol 22, 1888, 246-255, from the original MS in the Society's Library.

Followeth the Confessions of certain persons inhabitants within the Burgh of Forfar incarcerat in the Prison House thereof for Witchcraft, September 1661.

The Confession of Helen Guthrie Spouse to James Howat in Forfar.

(1) First, the said Helen Guthrie confesses that she has been a verie drunk-ensome woman, a terrible banner and curser and of a very wicked life and conversatione.

(2) She confesses hir selfe to be a witch, and that she learned to be a witch of one Joanet Galloway who lived near to Kerymure.

(3) That when she gave her malisone to any persone or creature it usually lighted.

(4) That if she sie any witch in Scotland she can tell whether they be witches or no after she has advysed 24 houres. And that she has thrie papers with blood upon them which helpes hir thus to know witches. And that she received these 3 bloody papers 14 yeares since from the said Joanet Galloway. And that she will never part with them until she goe to the fire. And that then she sall burn them hir selfe. And that if the minister wold take them from his before hir going to the fire that he wold wrong himselfe and the burgh and country about.

(5) That she can tell the malefices which many other witches does though she hir selfe be not present with them:– as when Elspet Alexander wronged Baillie David Dickyson, and Helen Alexander wronged David Walker, and Joanet Stout wronged John Couper, and John Tailzour wronged Andrew Watsone, and Ketheren Portour wronged James Peirsone, toune clerk and George Sutty by witchcraft; that she knew assuredly all these things though she was not present at the acting of them.

(6) That on the 15 of September instant about midnight, the divill cam unto hir prison, and laboured to carry her away, and that she was carried up from the earth thrie or four foot heigh at leist, hir head being among the jestes [joists] of the house, and that she had been caried away by the divill, were not the watch-men being stout did opose and strike at hir with their swords, and did prevent it. The treuth of this last confession was testified by thrie men which wer on the watch that night, the fourth watchman being absent in the meantime. [J.A. It appears from the burgh records of Forfar that the town was divided into eight districts, each of which furnished a 'gaird for the witches' of six men nightly and daily. Their function may have been to prevent the witch sleeping. This account appears to be a hallucination or nightmare.]

(7) She declared that she had many other things to confess, and that she will confes them befor she will goe to the fire.

This confessione was maid before the undersubscribers whin some few dayes [after] she was aprehended, and renewed several tymes sinsyne, and lastly befor the m[inisters] of the Prebitry of Forfar on the 25th of September 1661 instant.

Mr Alex. Robertsone, minister. Da. Dickson, baillie. Charles Dickeson. Jo. Gray. A. Scott, provest. James Benny, ealder.

13 Nov. 1661. Helen Guthrie confest before Jonet Stout that she was ane witch a long tyme since and that she went abroad with the Egyptians she being a witch then.

[J.A. The 'bloody papers' which Helen Guthrie inherited from Joanet Galloway of Kirriemuir were probably lists of past witches whose names had been written in their own blood by the leader of the coven when they joined. The method was to prick the finger and use it as a pen. To an illiterate witch such a paper would have a purely superstitious value. SMcG. These papers could not have been generated inside the coven; as Helen said, she and Joanet Galloway were trained in the older 'fairy' tradition. It is more probable that this was part of an initiation administered by Joanet Galloway using the witches' mark.]

> *The Confession of Joanet Huit, daughter to James Huit in Forfar,* maid at Forfar on the [25] day of September 1661, Before Mr. Alex. Robertsone minister, Chairles Dickyson baillie, Thomsa Guthrie lait baillie, John Gray, Thomas Robertson, notars, and William Cuthbert merchand in Forfar.

The said Joanet Howit confessed as followeth,

(1) First that about the beginning of the last oatsied [oatseed] tyme Isabell Syrie did cary hir to the Insch within the Loch of Forfar, and that ther the said Isabell Shyrie presented her to the divill, and that the divill said What sall I doe with such a little bairn as [this]? And that the said Isabell answered she is my maiden take hir to you. Further the said Joanet confesses that she saw at this tyme about threteen witches with the divill, and that they daunced togither, the divill being all in black, and that hir selfe was called by the divill the Pretty Dauncer, and that besyd hir selfe and the said Isabell Syrie, Mary Rind, Helen Alexander and [Isabel] Durward nicknamed Noblie *alias* Ouglie wer present; as for the rest she did not know them.

(2) That about four weeks after the foresaid mieting in the Insch the said Isabell Shyrie carried her to ane other mieting to Muryknowes, a little bewest Halcartounmiln, and that at this mieting ther wer about twenty persones present with the divill, and that they daunced togither and eat togither having bieff bread and ale, and that she did eat and drink with them hirselfe bot hir bellie was not filled, and that she filled the drink to the rest of the company, and that at this mieting the divill kyst hir and niped her upon one of hir shoulders, so as she had greate paine for some tyme thereafter. And that the said Mary Rind and Isabell Durward and Helen Alexander wer present amongst the rest.

(3) Thirdly, about sex weeks after this second mieting the divill cam to hir, he being all in grien at a place called Lapiedub halfe ane myle be-eist Forfar, and that then the divill calling hir his bony bird did kisse her, and straiked hir shoulder which was niped with his hand, and that presently after that she was eased of hir former paine.

(4) That one tyme she was with hir owne mother [Helen Guthrie] at a place called Newmanhill hard by Forfar about midnight. And that then she saw the divill have carnal copulation with hir mother. And that the divill having done, rode away on ane blacke horse. And that she followed him a little way until he directed her to return to hir mother. And that when she was returned to hir mother, hir mother forbade her to tell hir father of what she had seen that night.

(5) She confesses that at the foirsaid mieting at Muryknowes, the divill spoke to hir, saying that if she would do his biding she should nevir want, and that he bade hir renunce hir God, and she answered Mary shall I.

[Little Joanet was presented not by her mother but by Helen Guthrie who was apparently the senior witch. The devil's unwillingness to accept her is attributed by Murray to the fact that she had not yet come to puberty, reckoned to occur at twelve years. Until then she was not fertile, could not be initiated and could not add to the power of the coven. Joanet claims once to have seen at one time thirteen and at another time twenty witches. The evidence suggests that the Forfar coven consisted of the Devil plus thirteen women (EA, ID, JH, HG, KP, MR, IS, JS, CW, HA, CW, IS and EB) and three men (JT, GE, AW). The average attendance appears to have been less than half the total. Compared with the coven at Auldeart, Forfar was not well managed.]

The confession of John Tailzeour made at Forfar the . . . dayes of September, before Mr Alexander Robertsone minister, Charles Thornton and James Bennie younger, burgesses in Forfar.

John Tailzeour confesses as followeth

(1) That about bearsied [barley-sowing] tyme last, the devill apeared to him near to Halcarton, that he haid ane broun horse and that upon his apearance the beastes in the pleugh began to feare and that the divill told him that he knew he was going to some mercates, and that he wold len him money. But he refused to medle with his money.

(2) He confessed that at ane other tyme the devill appeared to him at Petterden but he refused to have anything to do with him.

[The Devil appears to have been actively recruiting in 1660-61. How did he identify potential recruits? From other sources it appears that John Tailzeour did more than he admits here.]

The confession of Isobell Shyrie, made at Forfar on the fyftein day of September 1661, being the Sabbath day between sermones Before David Dickieson baillie whom she sent for, Alex. Scott lait baillie, John Dickieson merchant, John Gray, Chairles Thorntoun and William Cuthbert, burgesses of Forfar.

(1) She confesses that she is a witch, and tooke on hir the guilt of witch craft.

(2) That amongst several other meetings she did meet with the devill at the green hill near the Loch of Forfar, within these 20 days or ane month last past, wher ther were present John Tailzeour, Helen Guthrie, Mary Rind, Elspet Alexander, Joanet Stout and Joanet Howatt. And that the divill haid ther carnall copulatione with hir.

(3) That she wronged Baillie Wood by braying to powder two toads' heads and ane peece of ane dead man's scull and ane peece dead man's flesh which the divill perfumed. And having condiscended with the divill therewith to be Baillie Wood's death, the divill declared that within a moneth or 20 days as shee pleased he sould die. And that shee went therefter to Baillie Wood's house, and inquired for a pan which was before that time poinded fra her for

cess. The baillie called on hir and gave hir a drinke, and before she delyvered the cup to him againe she put the powder in it, and he died within the time prescribed.

(4) That she hade wronged Thomas Webster in his meanes by casting ane cantrop [charm, spell] before his doore, but could not have power of his person.

'There is an unamended copy of this confession taken 'between sermons', and signed by Mr Alexander Robertson, minister, along with the other signatures. It has the words before the third item of the confession:– 'And being inquired if shee hade done any malefice to any, shee answered that she wronged Baillie Wood &c.' as above' (J.A.)

The Confessione of Elspet Alexander, spouse to Jon Muffit in Forfar, maid at Forfar on the 17th of September 1661, before the minister, Charles and David Dickson baillies, Thomas Guthrie lait baillie, Charles Thorntoun and James Beny burgesses, Thomas and John Robertson notars in Forfar, and William Cuthbert merchant there.

Elspet Alexander confesseth as followeth,

(1) First, that about thrie halfe yeares since she was at a mieting of witches with the divill at Peterden midway betwixt Forfar and Dondie, and that ther amongst others ther wer present beside hir selfe Isabell Shyrie Helen Guthrie Joanet Howit John Tailzeour and Joanet Stout. And that at the said mieting they daunced together and that they received new names from the divill, vizl, she hir selfe was called Alyson, Isabell Shyrie was called The Horse, Helen Guthrie was called The White Witch, Joanet Howit was called The Pretty Dauncer, John Tailzeour was called Beelzebob; further she confesses that the divill marked hir selfe that night on the left shoulder.

(2) She confesses that about four weekes after this mieting at Petterden she was at ane second mieting at the Muryknowes, and at this second mieting the divill and the witches did drinke together, having flesh bread and aile, and that the persones in the first mieting were lykeways present at the second mieting. Further she confesses that the divill straiked her shoulder with his fingers and that after that she had ease in the place formerly niped by the divill.

(3) She confesses that she was present at ane third mieting with the forenamed persones near Kerymure and that the divill and the said witches daunced togidder, and that the divill kissed hir selfe that night and that it was ane cold kisse. She confesses that Mary Rynd was at one of thir meetings and that she was called The Divill's Dau[ghter]. She confesses hir selfe guilty of witchcraft and that she is willing to suffer deith for it.

380

The Confessione of Jonet Stout.

Joanet Stout confesseth as followeth,

(1) First That about thrie halfe yeares since she was at a mieting with the divill and other witches at Petterden in the midway betwixt Forfar and Dondie. And that beside hir selfe ther wer present at this mieting Elspet Alexander Isabell Shyrie Helen Guthrie Joanet Howit and John Tailzeour. And that at the said mieting the divill and the said witches daunced togither and that the divill kissed sundrie of them bot did not kiss hir selfe because she stealled behind the backes of the rest. And that they received new names viz. Elspet Alexander was called Alesone, Isabell Shyrrie The Horse, Helen Guthrie The White Witch, Joanet Howit The Pretty Dauncer, John Tailzour Beelzebob and for hir own name she had forgot it.

(2) That she was at ane other meiting with the divill and the said witches at the Mury Knowes about four or six weeks after the first mieting at Petterden and that this second meeting the divill and the said witches did eat and drinke, having flesch bread and aile upon ane table as she thought, and that the said Joanet Huit was capper and filled the drinke.

(3) That she was at a third mieting with the divill and the said witches, and that they daunced at the said mieting which was near to Kerymure.

(4) She confesses that the divill appeared to hir two severall tymes at the well of Drumgley and told hir that she sould not want.

(5) She confesses hir self guilty of witchcraft and that she is willing to suffer deith for it.

This confession was maid on the 17th September before the under-subscrivers and ratified befor the ministers of the Presbitery of Forfar on the 25th day of the said moneth of September instant. Mr Alex. Robertsone &c (as before).

[To a second copy of this confession is added, under the signatures:–

'The said Jonet confest before John Hepburne James Esplen and George Renney that she had carnale copulation with the divill at Petterden'. Did the earlier investigators forget to ask about this?]

The confession of Kethern Portour maid at Forfar on the day of September 1661 before the subscribers [as before] and ratified at severall tymes befor severall other persones.

Ketheren Portour confesseth as followeth.

381

(1) First That about . . . . hir selfe and two other wome who are now both dead did meet at the quarrie near the buter wall and that the divill met them there and haid some discourse with the other two women, bot for hir selfe she was feared and did haist away.

(2) She confesses that at any other tyme the said women being present with hir selfe the divill came to them at the bleachin grien hard by the toune of Forfar and haid discourse with the said two women who are now dead. Bot for hir selfe she reproved them and told them if they wold not com away that she being blind wold goe be hir selfe allon as she could.

(3) That after that, the forsaid two women tooke hir furth to Ferytounfields near to Forfar to get ane sour coug and quhill they were togither in the said Ferytounfields the divill came to them and that although she was a blind woman for many yeares before, yit at that time she had some sight so far as she saw the divill and he hade ane blacke plaid about him and that the divill tooke hir by the hand and that his hand was cold and that therupon she haistened away.

(4) That she hes been a great banner and a terrible curser, and a very wicked woman.

[The preamble suggests that the Forfar witches were subjected to repeated interrogation.]

The Confession of Agnes Sparke, maid at Forfar the 26th September 1661, before Mr Alexander Robertsone minister, Charles Dickyson baillie, James Webster, Thomas Robertsone and Thomas Scot, notars in Forfar.

The said Agnes Sparke confesseth as followeth, first, that in August last Isobel Shirie cam to hir about midnight, and carried her away to Littlemiln or thereabout, and that ther she did sie about ane dusson of people dauncing, and that they had swet musicke amongst them and as she thought it was the musicke of ane pype, and that she hard that people ther present did speake of Isabell Shirie and said that she was the divill's horse, and that the divill did alwayes ryde upon hir, and that she was shoad like any mare or ane horse, and that night the said Isabel Shirrie went aside fra hir for some tyme, and that the divill (as she supposed) had then carnal copulation with hir. And that she did see Joanet Howit there, and that she was called the pretty dauncer. And that Isabel Shirie carried hir back again to hir owne house. That the nixt day after, she went to see the said Isabell, and that she fund hir lying on hir bed, and that she did ly all that day. And that hir hands were very sore and that she plucked the skin off them and maid great moan and said that it was no wonder that she had so sore hands seeing she was so sore tossed up and doune, and the said Agnes answered hir If you haid not been at such worke yesterevin as you was at, you wold not have been lying in your bed this day. And that Isobell said Have ye nothing to doe with that and speake nothing of it to anie bodie. That the said Isobell used many entysing words to draw hir on to the divill's service, and said it would be ane great joy to hir to be in such service. But she refused to hearken to hir.

[Agnes Sparke's hearsay evidence was inspired by the popular lore of the day. If the devil ever 'rode' Isobell it was in a sexual sense.]

Ane further Confession made be Helen Guthrie, prisoner in the Tolbooth of Forfar for witchcraft on the 28 of October 1661, before Mr Alexander Robertsone minister, Alexander Scot provost, Thomas Guthrie and David Dickesone baillies, Charles Dickesone lait baillie, Charles Thorntoun, James Benny elder, and James Benny younger, John Auld, William Cuthbert and Alexander Benny, burgesses of the said burgh of Forfar.

(1) First, the said Helen confesses that about the tyme that St Johnstounes bridge wes carried away she murdered her mother's dochter callit Marget Hutchen, being hir halfe-sister about sex or seven yeares of age, and that for the said murther hir mother did give alwayes hir malison to hir, yea and upone hir deathe bed continued to give her malison notwithstanding the said Helen's earnest request and beseikings in the contrair, and that she strak hir said sister at that tyme till she bled, whilk stroak was afterwards her death.

(2) That about thrie years before the last ait seed tyme, she was at a meitting in the church yard of Forfar in the holfe thereof and that ther wer present ther the divell himself in the sahpe of a black iron hewed man, and these persons following Katheren Porter, Mary Rynd, Isobell Shyrrie, Elspet Alexander, Jonet Stout, Cristen Whyte, Andrew Watsone, John Tailzeor, George Ellies, and that they daunced together, and that the ground under them was all fire-flaughts, and that the said Andrew Watsone had his usuale staff in his hand altho he be a blind man yet he daunced alse nimblie as any of the company and made alse great mirriment by singing his old ballads, and that the said Isobell Shyrrie did sing her song called Tinkletum Tankletum, and that the divil kist every ane of the women and for herself the divell kist onlie her hand.

(3) That about ane yeare efter the forementioned meitting betwixt the ait-seid and the beir-seid she was at ane other meitting at the pavilione-holl and that ther wer present the divell himselfe in shape as befor, and the persones of the first meitting, viz. Mary Rynd, Isobell Shyrrie, Elspet Alexander, Jonet Stout, Christen Whyte, Catheren Porter, Andrew Watsone, Johne Tailzeor, George Ellies and besydes them there were also Helen Alexander living in Forfar, Catheren Wallace in the parochin of Forfar, Isobel Smith in the paroch

of Oathlaw, and that they daunsed a whyle togidder till they were skaired by some people coming by and that thereupon they were fryghted and [fle] suddenly.

(4) That this same year, betwixt the oatseid and bearsied shee was at a thrid meitting in the church yeard of Forfar in the holfe thereof about the same tyme of the nyght [as they used to hold] meittings, viz., at midnyght and that there were present the divell himself [and all the] persones mentioned in the first meitting together with Helen Alexander and hey they daunced togither a whyle and then went to Mary Rynds house and sat downe at the table the divell being present at the head of it, and that some of them went to John Bennyes house he being a brewer and brought ale from thence and that they [went] threw in at a litle holl lyk bies and took the substance of the aile, and others of them to Alexander Hieches and brought aqua vite from thence and thus made themselves mirrie, and that the divell made much of them all but especiallie of Mary Rynd and that he kist them all except the said Helen herself whose hand onlie he kist, and that at the said meitting they agried togidder to undoe the aforesaid John Benny in his meanes, and that she and Jonet Stout sat opposite ane to another at the table.

(5) That at the first of theis meittings Andrew Watsone, Mary Rynd, Elspet Alexander, Isobell Shyrrie and herselfe, went up to the church wall about the south easst doore, and the said Andrew Watsone reased a young bairne unbap-tized, and took severall pieces thereof, as the feet the hands a pair of the head and a pairt of the buttock, and that they made a py thereof that they might eat of it, that by this meanes they might never make a confession (as they thought) of their witchcraft. And that she knowes that Elspet Bruice and Marie Rynd and severall other witches went to see the King's coronation.

(6) That the beginning of the last oatsied tyme, Elspet Bruice in Cortaquhie, now prisoner upoun the suspitione of witchcraft, hade a webb of cloath stollen from her and that thereby by turning the sive and the sheires she reased the divell who being werry hard to be laid againe ther was a meiting of witches for laying of him and that amongst others she hirselfe and Janet Stout and the said Elspet Bruice were present; for the rest she knew them not. And that at this meitting they hade pipe musick and dauncing as they used to have at all other meittings. And that at last they went to the bridge of Cortaquhie with intentione to pull it doune and that for this end she hirselfe, Jonet Stout and others of them did thrust their shoulders aganest the bridge, and that the divell was bussie amang them acting his pairt, and that ther wes ane extraordinary great wind reased so that the boords of the bridge flew to and fro at a great distance and that at this meitting the divill kist them all except herself and that he kist her hand onlie.

(7) That about a week before St James's day [25 July] last hirselfe Isobell Shyrrie and Elspet Alexander did meit togither at an aile-house near to Barrie a little before sunsett and that efter they hade stayed in the said house about the space of ane houre drinking of thrie pints of ale togidder they went foorth to the sands, and that ther thrie other women met them and that the divell was ther present with them all in the shape of ane great horse, and that they concludit the sinking of ane shipp lying not farr off from Barrie, and that presentlie the said company appoynted hirselfe to tak hold of the cable tow and to hold it fast until they did returne and she hir selfe did presentlie take the said cable as she thought and that about the space of an houre therefter they returned all in the same likeness as before except that the divell was in the shape of a man upoune his returne, and that the rest wer sor traiked and that the divill did kiss them all except herselfe and that he kist her hand onlie, and that then they concludit another meitting to be at the nixt Hallowmes, and that they parted so late that night that she could get no lodging and was forced to lie at ane dykesyde all nyght.

(8) That the last summer except one she did sie Johne Tailzeor sometymes in the shape of a todde and sometimes in the shape of a swyn and that the said Johne Tailzeor in these shapes went up and doune among William Millne, miller at Hetherstakes, his cornes for the destructione of the same, because the said Williame had taken the mylne over his head, and that the divell came to hir and pointed out John Tailzeor in the foresaid shapes unto hir and told her that that wes Johne Tailzeor.

(9) That she the said Helen Guthrie knowes assuredly that Elspet Pigot's cleath which wes in wanting laitlie, wes taken away by a gentleman's servand who lodgit in the house at ane certain tyme and that she wes assured of this by a spirit which she has besyde other folkes yea besyde all the witches in Angus.

* * *

APPENDIX 3 - ENGLAND

Dalyell in 1835 summarised beliefs current at that time for which we can now offer a rational explanation.

1 They partake of human and spiritual nature: their size is diminutive.

By-gone peoples were always imagined to be very small. Fairies were real people of normal size.

2 They perpetuate their race: and offspring descends also of their intercourse with mortals. Fairies were normal people. Some of those tried, including Alesoun Peirsoune and Elspeth Reoch, were fairy folk.

3 They can become invisible.

Invisibility was achieved not by magical ointments but by disguise. Hunters survived in spirit as the bands of guisers who emerged on feast days and holidays, with their faces blackened, clothed in skins, carrying sticks or swords, singing and dancing, and equipped with a bag to receive presents of food or money. In every detail they replicated bands of hunters ready for the chase. Such groups became even more significant when they contained a man disguised as a woman.

4 They are addicted to merriment: they are seen dancing, and are dressed in green.

These are taken as literal facts.

5 Animals from the flocks and herds, shot with elf-arrows, serve for their banquets.

This also was plain fact, only the animals came from the wild herds.

6 The influence of fairies is greatest on Friday; at noon and at midnight.

Fairies hunted on Thursday. Friday would be the day when the spoils were distributed and they feasted. Insofar as they were seen as supernatural beings, heirs to the old witchcraft, its powers were always greatest at the cusps, at noon, at midnight, at dusk, between two lairds' lands, between high and low water-mark.

ENGLAND

Most supernatural black dogs are about the size of a calf and have burning eyes.

Rutterkin, a witch's cat.

Micol, a name for the Queen of the Fairies in England in the time of Charles I. (Dalyell 1835, 537.) It is similar to Michael in Gaelic ritual and to Scots *mickle* 'great'.

Barguest in the North of England, is a black dog with horns. G. bearg 'champion, G. *barrachas* 'curly-haired', *barrachd* 'superior, pre-eminent', *barg* 'red-hot', *barr* 'top, head (beacon site)'.

Familiars.

Domestic familiars are known only from England but resemble the shape-changing animals found elsewhere. A familiar was an animal used for divination or for carrying out instructions and was understood to be either the Devil or the witch herself in disguise. One English witch had as her familiar a dog called Tom. When, as she believed, he had done her bidding, he would come and bark, then 'I did stroake him on the backe, and then he would becke unto me and wagge his tayle as being therewith contented' (Murray 1921, 213).

Perhaps surprisingly, most of the species respond to decoding in terms of the Gaelic already used to interpret the Scottish shape-changing animals; in other words, their names represent old hunting puns. Ten of the seventeen species – cat, crow or raven, dog, fly, frog, hare, hen, mouse, rat and toad – are also found as characters in fake folk tales. The moth and the maggot occur in an Irish shape-changing sequence which appears to involve late multilingual puns.

Bee G. *beach*. Kate McNiven said to appear as a bee.

Cat or **Kitten** G. *cath* 'battle (hunt)'. By far the most common animal in England or in Scotland. Cats could kill cows and pigs, which is to say that a hunt could kill wild cattle, wild boar and deer.

Crow G. *cathag*, as *cathaich* 'fight, strive (hunt)'. The black crow has been seen as a diabolical alternative to the pure white Christian dove (M. Summers 1925, 41) but as a symbol of death the crow or raven is considerably older than Christianity.

Dog G. *cu* 'dog', AG. *cu* 'to gather, hunt'.

Ferret   G. *coinneas*. cf G. *coinnich* 'assemble'.

Fly G. *cuileag*. AG. *cùile* 'deer trap'. The Devil once appeared like flies round a candle.

Greyhound Known only from an invented story in Lancashire, c.1634.)W. Scott, *Letters on Demonology and Witchcraft*, 1830, 250.)

Frog G. *losgann*. G. *loise* 'flame'. The Queen of the Fairies once appeared as a frog in a Gaelic story.

Hare G. *labhran* 'hare' is a pun on G. *leòb* 'big lips'.

Hedgehog Perhaps a pun between E. *urchin* for G. *ursainn* 'ranks of a battle (a muster of hunters)'.

Hen G. *cearc* for G. *céir* 'wax (fire)'. In one Scottish folk tale, the Cailleach appears in the form of a huge hen. (J. MacDougall 1901, 231.)

Moth G. *leòman* for G. *lìomh* 'polish, gloss, colour (fire)'. G. *mùth* 'kill, destroy'. A moth appears in an Irish shape-changing sequence.

Mouse G. *luch* for AG. *lus* 'light'. JGC p.63, *An luchaidh san tom* 'A light on the hill', in a charm to avert evil.

Rat G. *radan* may be a pun on G. *ràidh* 'rank of soldiers (hunters)'. Cf. E. *raid*.

Toad G. *màgach* which in turn may be a pun on E. *maggot*. G. *spiantag* appears in an Irish shape-changing sequence. Toads had the power to 'plague men in their bodies'.

Wasp G. *connspeach*.

Weasel G. *neas* or *nios*. G. *nais* 'hearth, furnace (beacon site)', *naisg* 'bind, make fast (capture in hunting)'. Weasels were believed to have the power to kill horses.

* * *

The fairy shared its red or gold hair with many other personified beacons. Commodus, the Roman emperor, had crisp yellow hair that shone like a flame in the sun. Comaetho ('gathering fire') had golden hair which glowed like fire. The hair of Servius Tullius, as a child, was seen by many people to be on fire. Flames encircled the head of Lucius Martius in the glory of his triumph over the Carthaginians. Pages in Arthurian romance all have golden or red hair. Christ had a halo or glory round his head and in some traditions his hair and beard were red (Dalyell 1835, 440-442). *Christ* means 'anointed with oil', like a beacon ready for lighting: Gr. *chrisma* is a CR 'fire' word like G. *ceir* 'wax'. Messiah is another word for 'annointed'. The Church taught that red hair, particularly on a woman, brought bad luck but also that Judas Iscariot had red hair (Mackenzie 1894, 106).

We can recover some slight memories of deer-hunters from the tissue of puns and metaphors that came to pass for fairy lore. One story mentions a slender, red-haired fairy – *fear caol ruadh* – (MacDougall 1910, 126-7). He was *caol* 'slender, narrow' because G. *caol* 'the narrow place' is a deer trap and red-haired because he was a messenger. Red hair was typical of those who sent signals.

APPENDIX 4: INDEX OF INDIVIDUALS

INDIVIDUAL REFERENCES

The spelling of first names has been standardised. The date is generally that of the trial: events described may have taken place thirty or more years earlier. Aberdeen and Banff are covered in a separate chapter.

Agnes Brugh, Gooselands, Crook of Devon, 1662. R.B. Begg, 1888, 211-220.

Agnes Grant, Auldearn, Moray, 1643. Executed for the murder of the Laird of Park and his two sons. Register of the Privy Council, 2. series, vol.7, 595-596.

Agnes Mullikine alias Bessie Boswell, Dunfermline, Fife, 1563. Pitcairn, vol 1, part 1, 432. Banished.

Agnes Murie, Kilduff, Crook of Devon, Kinross, 1662. Strangled and burnt. R.B. Begg, 1888, 211-220.

Agnes Pittendreich, Tullibole, Crook of Devon, Kinross, 1662. R.B. Begg, 1888, 211-220.

Agnes Sampson, Nether Keith, Lothian 1590. Pitcairn vol 1, part 2, 230-241. Properly Annie Simpson.

Agnes Spark, Forfar coven, 1662. J. Anderson, 1888, 252.

Alexander Drummond, 1628, a native healer in Strathearn. A.G. Reid, The Annals of Auchterarder, 1899, 67-75.

Alexander Quhytelaw, 1590. One of those who met at North Berwick. Pitcairn, vol.1, 245-246.

Alison Balfour, Orkney 1596. Pitcairn vol 1, part 2, 373-377.

Alison Peirsoun, Byrehill (Boarhills) Fife, 1588. Scott B.M. 308-311. Pitcairn vol 1, part 2, 161-165.

Andrew Man, Tarbruich, Rathven, Banff, 1598. Spalding Club Miscellany I, 119-125.

Andrew Watson, Forfar coven, 1662. J. Anderson, 1888, 246-262. A blind man.

Anne Rychesoun, 1590. One of those who met at North Berwick. Pitcairn, vol.1, 245-246.

Anne Tailzeour alias Rwna Rowa, Orkney, 1624. RPC 2nd series, v.8, 360-364.

Barbara Erskine, Alloa, 1658. The Scottish Antiquary, Vol. 9, no. 34.

Barbara Naipar, Edinburgh, tried in 1591 but cleared by the assize. James VI claimed the jury was in error and got another one which also aquitted her. Pitcairn vol 1, part 2, 242-244.

Bartie Patersoun, Newbattle, Lothian, 1607. Pitcairn 535-6.

Beattie Lang at Pittenweem, Fife, 1704, H.E. Simpkins, 1914, 104-106.

Beigis Tod in Lang-Nydrie, Lothian, 1608. Pitcairn vol 2, 542-544.

Bessie Aikin, Leith, Lothian 1597-8. Pitcairn, vol 2, 22-29, 52-53. Pardoned and banished.

Bessie Boswell, 1563: see Agnes Mullikine. Could Mullikine be a witch-name?

Bessie Broune, 1590. One of those who met at North Berwick. Pitcairn, vol.1, 245-246.

Bessie Cowan, 1590. One of those who met at North Berwick. Pitcairn, vol.1, 245-246.

Bessie Croket, Forfar coven, 1662. J. Anderson 1888, 258

Bessie Dunlop, Lyne, Ayrshire, 1576. Pitcairn, vol.1, 49-58.

Bessie Henderson, Crook of Devon, Kinross, 1662. R.B. Begg, 1888, 211-220.

Bessie Neil, Gelvin, Crook of Devon, Kinross, 1662. R.B. Begg, 1888, 211-220.

Bessie Paton, Alloa, 1658. The Scottish Antiquary , Vol. 9, no. 34.

Bessie Thomsone, Lothian, 1590. One of those who met at North Berwick. Pitcairn, vol.1, 245-246.

Bessie Wrycht, 1590. One of those who met at North Berwick. Pitcairn, vol.1, 245-246.

Catherine Caray, Orkney, 1616. Dalyell 1835, 118, 126, 536.

Catherine Duncan, 1590. One of those who met at North Berwick. Pitcairn, vol.1, 245-246.

Catherine Gray, 1590. One of those who met at North Berwick. Pitcairn, vol.1, 245-246.

Catherine McGillis, 1590. One of those who met at North Berwick. Pitcairn, vol.1, 245-246.

Catherine Portour, Forfar coven, 1662. J. Anderson 1888, 246-262.

Catherine Renny, Alloa, 1658. The Scottish Antiquary, Vol. 9, no. 34.

Catherine Ross, Lady Fowlis, Easter Ross; tried 1590 in Edinburgh. Pitcairn vol 1, part 2, 185, 191-204.

Catherine Shaw, Carnwath, Lanark. Dead before 1644. RPC 2nd series, vol.8, 1908, 148.

Catherine Wallace, 1590. One of those who met at North Berwick. Pitcairn, vol.1, 245-246.

Catherine Wallace, Forfar coven, 1662. J. Anderson 1888, 246-262.

Christian Grahame, Glasgow 1622. Pitcairn vol 3, 508-536.

Christian Grieve, Crook of Devon, Kinross, 1662. R.B. Begg, 1888, 211-220.

Christian Keringtoune alias Likkit, 1590. One of those who met at North Berwick. Pitcairn, vol.1, 245-246.

Christian Saidler in Blakhous, Lothian 1597, an associate of one of the fairy folk. Pitcairn vol.2, 22-29.

Christian Stewart, Nokwalter, Perth 1596. Pitcairn 399-400.

Christian Whyte, Forfar coven, 1662. J. Anderson 1888, 246-262.

Christian Wilsone, Lothian 1661. Pitcairn vol. 3, 601.

Cristian Lewingstoun, in Leith, Lothian 1597. All her knowledge she had was by her daughter, who met with the Fairie. Pitcairn vol.2, 22-29.

Donald McIlmichall, Appin, Argyll, 1677. J.R.N. MacPhail (ed.), Highland Papers vol.III, 1920, Scottish History Society, 36-38.

Donald Robesoune, 1590. One of those who met at North Berwick. Pitcairn, vol.1, 245-246.

Duncan Buchquhanne, 1590. One of those who met at North Berwick. Pitcairn, vol.1, 245-246.

Edmund Robinson, [Lancashire], Scott Letters 250-252.

Edward Kyninmonth alias Lowrie, Forfar 1576. Pitcairn vol 1, part 2, 70.

Elizabeth Dick, Fife, 1701; J.E. Simpkins, 1914, 101.

Elspeth Alexander, Forfar coven, 1662. J. Anderson 1888, 249-250.

Elspeth Bruce, Cortachy, Forfar coven, 1662. J. Anderson 1888, 261. Ane prettie woman.

Elspeth Reoch. Orkney, 1616. G.F. Black, County Folklore 3, Orkney & Shetland Isles, 1903 (reprinted 1994), 102-119; (Maitland Club Misc. 187-191.)

Elspeth Williamson, Torryburn, Fife, 1704. J.E. Simpkins 1914, 103.

Ewfame McCalzane, Lothian 1590. Pitcairn vol 1, part 2, 249-50. One of those who met at North Berwick.

Geilis Duncan in Prestonpans, 1590. One of those who met at North Berwick. Pitcairn, vol.1, 245-246.

Geillis Johnstoun, Lothian 1661?. Pitcairn vol 3, 600-1.

George Ellis, Forfar coven, 1662. J. Anderson 1888, 246-262.

Gilbert McGill, 1590. One of those who met at North Berwick. Pitcairn, vol.1, 245-246.

Grissel Anderson, Torryburn, Fife, c.1703, burnt as a witch. Webster, Tracts on Witchcraft, 138.

Grissell Gairdner, Fife, 1610. Pitcairn vol 3, 95-98.

Helen Alexander, Forfar coven, 1662. J. Anderson 1888, 246-262.

Helen Cothill, Helen, Forfar, 1661-2. J. Anderson 1888, 259-60.

Helen Guthrie, Forfar coven, 1662. J. Anderson 1888, 246-262. Known as 'the White Witch'.

Helen Lauder, 1590. One of those who met at North Berwick. Pitcairn, vol.1, 245-246.

Helen Quhyte, 1590. One of those who met at North Berwick. Pitcairn, vol.1, 245-246.

Helen Stewart, Carnwath, Lanark, prior to 1644. RPC 2nd series, vol.8, 1908, 148.

Isobel Durward, Forfar coven, 1662. J. Anderson 1888, 246-262.

Isobel Gowdie, Auldearn, Moray, 1662. Pitcairn vol.3, 602-616.

Isobel Greirsoune, spous to Johnne Bull, in the Pannis, Lothian, 1607. Pitcairn 523-526.

Isobel Griersoune, Prestonpans, Lothian 1607. Pitcairn vol 2, 523

Isobel Gylloun, 1590. One of those who met at North Berwick. Pitcairn, vol.1, 245-246.

Isobel Haldane, Perth 1623. Pitcairn, vol. 2, 537-538.

Isobel Haldane, Perth, 1623. Pitcairn, Criminal Trials, 537-8.

Isobel Lauder, 1590. One of those who met at North Berwick. Pitcairn, vol.1, 245-246.

Isobel Rutherford, Crook of Devon, Kinross, 1662. R.B. Begg, 1888, 211-220.

Isobel Shyrie, Forfar coven, 1662. J. Anderson 1888, 248-262. Known as 'Horse' as she was messenger to the coven.

Isobel Smith, Banchory, 1607. J.A. Henderson, History of the Parish of Banchory-Devenick, 1890, 216-217.

Isobel Smith, Isobell, Oathlaw, Forfar. PSAS 1888, 256-258.

Isobel Smith, Oathlaw, Forfar, 1662. J. Anderson 1888, 246-260.

James Hudston, Alloa, 1658. The Scottish Antiquary, Vol. 9, no. 34.

James Kirk, James, Alloa, 1658. The Scottish Antiquary, Vol. 9, no. 34.

James Mure, Ayr, 1609. Pitcairn vol.3, 68-69.

James Reid, Musselburgh, Lothian 1603. Pitcairn vol 2, 421-2.

Janet Anderson, Fife, 1650. J.E. Simpkins, 1914, 95.

Janet Blak, Alloa, 1658. The Scottish Antiquary or Northern Notes and Queries, Vol. 9, no. 34.

Janet Boyman, 1572, Canongate, Edinburgh, spouse to Williame Steill. Pitcairn vol 1, part 2, 38.

Janet Braidheid, Auldearn, Moray, 1622. Pitcairn's Criminal Trials vol.III, 616-618. She mentions the previous executions of Kathrine Sowter and Agnes Grant. (20 years earlier?)

Janet Brugh, Crook of Devon, Kinross, 1662. R.B. Begg, 1888, 211-220.

Janet Campbell, 1590. One of those who met at North Berwick. Pitcairn, vol.1, 245-246.

Janet Douglas, Lady Glamis. Executed 1537. Scott Letters REF.

Janet Gall, 1590. One of those who met at North Berwick. Pitcairn, vol.1, 245-246.

Janet Grawie, Lothian 1597, one of the fairy folk. Pitcairn vol.2, 22-29.

Janet Howit, a child, daughter of Helen Guthrie, known as 'the Pretty Dauncer', Forfar coven, 1662. J. Anderson 1888, 247-248.

Janet Lockie, Carnwath, Lanark, 1644. RPC 2nd series, vol.8, 1908. 146-154.

Janet Logan, 1590. One of those who met at North Berwick. Pitcairn, vol.1, 245-246.

Janet Lyndsy, Tranent, Lothian, 1594. P. Anderson NLS MS, vol.3, F281 r and v.

Janet Millar, Tullebodie, Alloa, 1658. The Scottish Antiquary, Vol. 9, no. 34.

Janet Nicolsoun, 1590. One of those who met at North Berwick. Pitcairn, vol.1, 245-246.

Janet Paistoun, Lothian 1661. Pitcairn vol 3, 601.

Janet Paton (1), Crook of Devon, Kinross, 1662. R.B. Begg,1888, 211-220.

Janet Paton (2), Crook of Devon, Kinross, 1662. R.B. Begg, 1888, 211-220.

Janet Reid, Jonet, Alloa, 1658. The Scottish Antiquary or Northern Notes and Queries, Vol. 9, no. 34.

Janet Rendall alias Rigga, and her Devil Walliman, Orkney, 1629. G.F. Black, 1903, 103-111. He was claid in quhyt cloathes with ane quhyte head and ane gray beard.

Janet Stewart in the Canongait, Edinburgh, Lothian 1597. Pitcairn vol.2, 26-29.

Janet Stout, Forfar coven, 1662. J. Anderson 1888, 246-262.

Janet Straittoun, 1590. One of those who met at North Berwick. Pitcairn, vol.1, 245-246.

Janet, Lady Glamis, Forfar, 1532-37. Pitcairn vol 1, part 1, 158, 187-199.

Jean Lachlane, Carnwath, Lanark, 1644. RPC 2nd series, vol.8, 1908, 146-154. A charmer (healer) for twenty years.

Jean Weir, Jean, Edinburgh, Midlothian. Scott B.M. 308.

John Brugh, Fossaway, 1643. A.G. Reid, The Annals of Auchterarder, 1899, 195-208.

John Cunningham alias Fian, Presonpans, Lothian, 1590. Pitcairn vol 1, part 2, 209-230? Leader of the North Berwick witches.

John Gordoun alias Grey-meill, Prestonpans, Lothian, 1590. One of those who met a North Berwick. Pitcairn, vol.1, 245-246.

John McGillis, 1590. One of those who met at North Berwick. Pitcairn, vol.1, 245-246.

John McNeill, Dingwall, Easter Ross, 1577. He supplied an elf-arrow.

John Mullar, Fife, 1585. Pitcairn vol 1, part 2, 167.

John Stewart, Master of Orkney, Orkney, 1596. Pitcairn vol 1, part 2, 373-377.

John Tailzour, Forfar coven, 1662. J. Anderson 1888, 246-262. Known as 'Beelzebob'.

Kenneth Odhar, Easter Ross, 1577, accused with thirty others including Catherine Lady Munro. Exchequer Rolls vol. 20 1568-79. GRH 1899, 522-3. Identified with the Brahan Seer.

Lillias Adie, Torryburn, Fife, 1704; J.E. Simpkins, 1914, 101-104, quoting Webster, Tracts on Witchcraft 134-137. Webster, Tracts on Witchcraft, 139-144.

Mailie Pattersone in Carnwath, Lanark, 1644. RPC 2nd series, vol.8, 1908. 146-154.

Majorie Ritchie, Marjorie, Forfar, 1661-2. PSAS 1888, 261.

Malie Geddie, 1590. One of those who met at North Berwick. Pitcairn, vol.1, 245-246.

Manie Haliburton, Dirlton, East Lothian 1649. Pitcairn vol 3, 599-600.

Mar, Earl of Mar. Scott Letters, 284.

Margaret (Meg) Bogtoun, 1590. One of those who met at North Berwick. Pitcairn, vol.1, 245-246.

Margaret Aichesoun, 1590. One of those who met at North Berwick. Pitcairn, vol.1, 245-246.

Margaret Demperstoun, Margret, Alloa, 1658. The Scottish Antiquary, Vol. 9, no. 34.

Margaret Duchall, Alloa, 1658 (died in prison). The Scottish Antiquary, Vol. 9, no. 34.

Margaret Halket, Dysart, Fife, 1691. J.E. Simpkins 1914, 100-101.

Margaret Huggon, Crook of Devon, Kinross, 1662. R.B. Begg, 1888, 211-220.

Margaret Litster, Kilduff, Crook of Devon, Kinross, 1662. R.B. Begg, 1888, 211-220.

Margaret Nicol, Forfar coven, 1662. J. Anderson 1888, 258.

Margaret Tailzeor, Alloa, 1658. The Scottish Antiquary, vol. 9, no. 34.

Margaret Thomsoun in Striveling, 1590. One of those who met at North Berwick. Pitcairn, vol.1, 245-246. 1590.

Margaret Wallace, Glasgow, Lanark, 1622. Pitcairn vol 3, 508-536.

Margaret Watson, Carnwath, Lanark, 1644. RPC 2nd series, vol.8, 1908, 146-154. Margaret Watson (2) her aunt, was also a witch.

Marion Bailzie, 1590. One of those who met at North Berwick. Pitcairn, vol.1, 245-246.

Marion Congiltoun, 1590. One of those who met at North Berwick. Pitcairn, vol.1, 245-246.

Marion Cunninghame, Fife, 1650. J.E. Simpkins, 1914, 94-95.

Marion Lenchop, Leith, Lothian, 1590. One of the North Berwick witches. Pitcairn REF.

Marion McIngareach, Easter Ross, 1577 REF. to Hector, not 1577; his nurse.

Marion Nicolsoun, 1590. One of those who met at North Berwick. Pitcairn, vol.1, 245-246.

Marion Peebles alias Pardone, Hildiswick, Shetland, 1644. Pitcairn vol 3, 194.

Marion Richart alias Layland, Sanday, Orkney 1633. G.F. Black, 1903, 115-119.

Marion Schaw, 1590. One of those who met at North Berwick. Pitcairn, vol.1, 245-246.

Marjory Blaikie, Fife, 1585. Pitcairn vol 1, part 2, 167.

Marjory Ritchie, Forfar coven, 1662. J. Anderson 1888, 260-61.

Mary Paterson, 1590. One of those who met at North Berwick. Pitcairn, vol.1, 245-246.

Mary Rind, Forfar coven, 1662. J. Anderson 1888, 246-262. Known as 'The Devil's Daughter'.

Masie Aichesoune, 1590. One of those who met at North Berwick. Pitcairn, vol.1, 245-246.

Patrick Lowrie, Ayr, 1605. Pitcairn vol.2, 477-479.

Robert Greirsoun, 1590. One of those who met at North Berwick. Pitcairn, vol.1, 245-246.

Robert Wilson, Crook of Devon, Kinross, 1662. R.B. Begg, 1888, 211-220.

Robert, Annas, Isobel and Helen Erskine, Forfar 1613-1614. Pitcairn vol 3, 260-269.

Thomas Brounhill, 1590. One of those who met at North Berwick. Pitcairn, vol.1, 245-246.

Stine Bheag the witch of Tarbat (1738) sold winds to sailors. H. Miller 1835.

Thomas Greave, Falkland, Fife, 1623. Pitcairn, 555-558.

William Simpson, cousin or uncle of Alison Pearsoun,

* * *

APPENDIX 5 - AULDEARN, 1662 - THE MORAY TRIAL OF 1662

Confessions of Issobell Gowdie, spous to John Gilbert, in Lochloy.

(1.) Issobell Gowdie's first Confession.

At Aulderne, the threttein day of Aprill, 1662 yeiris. In presence of Master Harie Forbes, Minister of the Gospell at Aulderne; William Dallas of Cantrey, Shereffe deput of the shereffdom of Nairn; Thomas Dunbar of Graing; Alexander Brodie Yr of Leathin; Alexander Dunbar of Boath; James Dunbar, appeirant therof; Henrie Hay of Brightmanney; Hew Hay of Newtowne; William Dunbar of Clune; and David Smith and Johne Weir, in Auldern; Witnesses to the Confession efter specifeit, spokin furth of the mouth of Issobell Gowdie, spous to Johne Gilbert, in Lochloy.

The quhilk day, in presence of me, John Innes, Notar Publict, and Witnesses abownamet, all under subscryvand, the said Issobell Gowdie, appeiring penenent for hir haynows sinnes of Witchcraft, and that she haid bein ower lang in that service; without any compulsitouris ['indicating that no torture or compulsion had been resorted to for the purpose of extorting Confession; but that she came forward, and *voluntarily* made her Declaration, bewailing her former offences.' PP.] proceidit in hir Confessione in maner efter following, to wit.

As I wes goeing betwix the townes [farm-steadings] of Drumdewin and the Headis, I met with the Divell, and ther covenanted, in a maner, with him; and I promeisit to meit him, in the night time, in the Kirk of Aulderne; quhilk I did. And the first thing I did ther that night, I denyed my baptisme, and did put the on of my handis to the crowne of my head and the uther to the sole of my foot, and then renuncet all betuixt my two handis, ower to the Divell. He wes in the Readeris dask, and a blak book in his hand. Margret Brodie, in Aulderne, held me up to the Divell to be baptised be him; and he marked me in the showlder, and suked owt my blood at that mark, and spowted it in his hand, and, sprinkling it on my head, said 'I baptise the, Janet, in my awin name!' And within a quhill we all remooved. The nixt tym that I met with him

400

ves in the New Wardis of Inshoch, and haid carnall cowpulation and dealling with me. He wes a meikle, blak, roch [rough, hairy] man, werie cold; and I found his nature als cold within me as spring-well-water. Somtymes he haid buitis and sometymes shoes on his foot; but still his foot are forked and cloven. He vold be somtymes with us lyk a dear or a rae. Johne Taylor and Janet Breadhead, his vyff, in Belmakeith, ... Dowglas, and I my self, met in the Kirk-yaird of Nairne, and we raised an unchristened child owt of its greaff; and at the end of Breadleyis corn-field-land, just opposit to the Milne of Nairne, we took the said child, with the naillis [parings] of our fingeris and toes, pikles of all sortis of grain, and blaidis of keall [leaves of colewort] and haked thaim all verie small, mixed altogither; and did put a pairt thereof among the muk-heapes of Breadleyes landis, and therby took away the ffruit of his cornis, &c.; and we pairted it among two of our Coevens. Whan we tak cornes at Lambes [Lammas, 1 August] we tak bot abowt two sheaves, when the cornes ar full; or two stokis of keall, or therby, and that gives us the fruit of the corn-land, or keall-yaird, whair they grew. And it may be, we will keip it while Yewll or Pace [Christmas or Easter], and than devyd it amongst us. Ther ar threttein persones in my Coven.

The last tyme that owr Coven met, we, and an uther Coven, wer daunc- ing at the Hill of Earlseat betwixt Moyness and Bowgholl; and befor that we wes beyond the Meikle-burne; and the uther Coven being at the Downie-hillis, we went from beyond the Meikle-burne, and went besyd them, to the howssis at the Wood-end of Inshoch; and within a quhyll went hom to our howssis. Befor Candlemas, we went be-east Kinlosse, and ther we yoaked an pleughe of paddokis [frogs]. The Divell held the pleugh, and Johne Younge in Mebestoune, our Officer, did dryve the pleughe. Paddokis did draw the plewgh, as oxen; qwickens were soumes [the traces which linked the frogs to the plough were made of dog-grass], a riglen's horne was a cowter [the horn of a half-castrated ram was the plough-share], and an piece of an riglen's horne wes an sok. We two severall tymes about; and all we of the Coeven went still up and downe with the pleughe, prayeing to the Divell for the fruit of that land, and that thistles and brieries might grow ther.

When we goe to any hous, we tak meat and drink; and we fill up the barrellis with owr owen pish again; and we put boosomes [brooms] in our beds with our husbandis, till we return again to them. We wer in the Earle of Murreye's hous in Dernvay, and we gott aneugh ther, and did eat and drink of the beste, and brought pairt with us. We went in at the windowes. I haid a little horse, and wold say, 'Horse and Hattock, in the Divellis name!' And then we wold flie away, quhair we wold, be ewin as strawes wold flie upon an hie-way. We will flie lyk strawes quhan we pleas; wild-strawes and corne-strawes wil be horses to us, an [if] we put thaim betwixt our foot, and say, 'Horse and Hattock, in the Divellis nam!' An quhan any sies thes strawes in a whirlewind, and doe not sanctifie them selves, we may shoot them dead at owr pleasour. Any that ar shot be us, their sowell will goe to Hevin, bot ther bodies remains with us, and will flie as horsis to us, as small as strawes.

I was in the Downie-hillis, and got meat ther from the Qwein of Fearrie, mor than I could eat. The Qwein of Fearrie is brawlie clothed in whyt linens, and in whyt and browne cloathes, &c. ; and the King of Fearrie is a braw man, weill favoured, and broad faced, etc. Ther wes elf-bullis rowtting and skoilling up and downe thair, and affrighted me.

When we tak away any cowes milk, we pull the tow, and twyn it and plaitt it in the wrong way, in the Divellis name; and we draw the tedder (sua maid) in betwixt the cowes hinder foot [feet], and owt betwixt the cowes forder foot, in the Divellis name; and therby tak with us the kowes milk. We tak sheips milk evin so. The way to tak or giev bak the milk again, is to cut that tedder. Whan we tak away the strenth of anie persones eall [ale], and gives it to an uther, we tak a litle qwantitie owt of each barrell and stand of eall, and puts it in a stoup, in the Divellis nam; and, in his nam, with owr awin handis, puttis it amongst an utheris eall, and gives her the strenth and substance and heall of hir neightbouris eall. And to keip the eall from us, that we have no power of it, is to sanctifie it weill. We get all this power from the Divell; and when we seik it from him, we call him 'owr Lord!'

Johne Taylor and Janet Breadhead, his wyff, in Bellnakeith, Bessie Wilsone in Aulderne, and Margret Wilsone, spous to Donald Callam in Aulderne, and I, maid an pictur of clay, to distroy the Laird of Parkis meall [male] children. Johne Taylor brought hom the clay, in his plaid neuk; his wyff brak it very small, lyk meall, and sifted it with a siev, and poured in water among it, in the Divellis nam, and wrought it verie sore, like rye-bout; and maid of it a pictur of the Lairdis sones. It haid all the pairtis and merkis of a child, such as heid, eyes, nose, handis, foot, mouth and little lippes. It wanted no mark of a child; and the handis of it folded down by its sydes. It was lyk a pow [a roll of dough]; or a slain gryce [a flayed sucking pig]. We laid the face of it to the fyre, till it strakned [dried out]; and a cleir fyre round about it, till it wes red lyk a cole. After that, we wold rost it now and then; each other day ther wold be an piece of it weill rosten. The Laird of Parkis heall maill children by it ar to suffer, if it be not gotten and brokin, als weill as thes that ar borne and dead alreadie. It wes still putt in and taken out

402

of the fyre, in the Divellis name. It wes hung up upon an knag. It is yet in Johne Taylor's hous, and it hes a cradle of clay about it. Onlie Johne Taylor and his wyff, Janet Breadhead, Bessie and Margret Wilsones in Aulderne, and Margret Brodie, thair, and I, were only at the making of it. All the multitud of our number of Witches, of al the Coevens, kent [knew] all of it, at our nixt meitting after it was maid. And the Witches yet that ar untaken, hav their awin poweris, and our poweris quhilk we haid befor we wer takin, both. Bot now I hav no power at all.

Margret Kyllie in . . . . ., is on of the uther Coven, Meslie Hirdall, spous to Allexander Ross, in Lonheid, is one of them; hir skin is fyrie. Issobell Nicoll, in Lochley, is on of my Coevens. Margret Hasbein, in Moynes, is on; Margrat Brodie, in Aulderne, Bessie and Margrat Wilsones, thair, and Jean Marten, ther, and Elspet Nishie, spous to Johne Mathow, ther, are of my Coven. The said Jean Mairten is Maiden of owr Coven. Johne Young, in Mebestowne, is Officer to owr Coven.

Elspet Chisholme and Issobell More, in Aulderne, Magie Brodie, [thair] (ie in Aulderne)

IG (Pitcairn): 'The first woyage that ewer I went with the rest of owr cove wes to Plewghlandis'. They shot a man and a woman. This is well outside their normal area and may have been a commission, Plewlands (NJ1769) is near Duffus House (NJ1768) and Gordonstoun (NJ1868) (later tradition of sorcery). The Earl of Murray at Darnaway was also implicated. According to an unreliable tradition, the daughter of the owner of Castle Boorgie near Forres learned to be a witch from her nurse; the hag was burned and the girl bled to death. W.G. Stewart 210-211.

Some time before 1662 the witches dined once at Grangehill where the Devil sat at the top of the table. Was Grangehill his house? Known since 1749 as Dalvey, this house was a short distance east of Dyke church (NH9958). The owner of the Grangehill estate at that time was David Dunbar, born c.1630 and died 1691. There is another link. David was the third of four children of Ninian Dunbar of Grangehill, a distant relative of the old line of the Earls of Murray, and his first wife, Margaret Ogilvie. Ninian's second wife (David's step-mother) was Christian Dunbar by whom Ninian had a further two sons, Wiliam and John. Janet Breadheid of Auldearn reported that the Devil baptised her with her own blood and gave her the name 'Christian'. (M.A. Murray 1921, 84-85). Was the Devil who taught the witches of Auldearn and who spoke no Gaelic David Dunbar of Grangehill? Was the laird of Park his enemy?

Isobel Cameron, who gives no references, states (p.62) that Isobell Gowdie used 'moon paste' to help Jean Gordon of Gordonstown and that she used the same medium to bring sickness and death to the house of the Laird of Park.'

APPENDIX 6 -
FAIRIES WRANGLING IN MORVEN

If one arrives by sea one realizes the strategic importance of the sound as a waterway, and how bale-fires on the castles upon either side of it would flash warnings from end to end of it.

I. Grant 1935.

The importance of hunting in the lives of the Gaels cannot be overstated. When educated gentlemen first toured the Hebrides they found old men who had never tasted cereals but had lived all their lives on meat and milk. They also found young people who used the money they earned from such things as kelp-burning to buy oatmeal, a luxury imported from the Lowlands. Visitors also remarked on the vast resources of fish, exploited only by foreigners. The traditional Highland staples were red meat and milk; the oatmeal, the herring and the potato which are today seen as healthy traditional fare were short-lived expedients on which the people subsisted after their deer-forests had been taken over and destroyed by feudal gentry. By 1800 Gaelic culture was in a terminal state and by 1900 the population was facing extinction. Emigrants left in droves, drawn to new frontiers by the prospect of living free on their own land and hunting with their own guns. In most of the Highlands little of the Gael now survives except their place-names and a few archaeological sites, but the landscape has changed so little that in many places we can still recon-struct the time of the legendary *sith*, the days of the great deer-hunts. One area where the past is well preserved is Morven, a sea-girt peninsula between Ardnamurchan and Mull. The fairy tales, the place-names, the platforms, the monuments, the geography of Morvern, and its very restricted land-use all point to its exploitation through prehistory by transient bands of deer-hunters, the so-called 'fairies' who flit from place to place according to the signals sent by the hunt beacons.

In traditional lore Morven was associated with the legendary deer-hunters known as the Feiné or Fingalians, whose stories were popular throughout Gaeldom. One story is about the attempted abduction of the Flame Maiden by the Black Man or beacon, a common theme. One day a beautiful maiden, daughter of the king of *Tir-fo-Tonn* ('Kingdom under the Waves') arrived near Easroy in a large skin boat. She had come to seek the protection of the Feiné against Dyno-Borb (G. *duine-borb* 'barbaric man, churl'), son of the king of Ardnamurchan, who was attempting to capture her. Dyno-Borb soon appeared in pursuit of the maiden, his gigantic form of terrible aspect riding swiftly over the sea. He had a flaming helmet, a black curved shield, a single kingly eye, a great sword and two mighty spears. After many fights he was killed by Goll ('fire'), one of the Feiné and was buried with golden rings on all his fingers to show his superior status. That Dyno-Borb was a beacon is shown by his pursuit of the Flame maiden, speed of transit, flaming helmet, sharp weapons and, above all, his single eye. The story suggests conflict between the hunters of Morven and those of Ardnamurchan but it might also be a joke at the expense of Ardnamurchan.

Morven on the western seaboard, in northwest Argyll, is a triangular peninsula bounded by Loch Sunart, the Sound of Mull and Loch Linnhe. It is a typical Highland deer-forest, crammed with mountains. In the feudal period Morven and Ardnamurchan were peopled by the Macinneses or Clan Aonghais. Macinnes is taken to mean 'sons of Angus' but 'Angus' here and in Balquhidder may be G. *aonach* 'great assembly', a convocation of deer-hunters. The Macinneses were vassals of the Macdonald Lords of the Isles, who for centuries maintained a kingdom independent of the Scottish crown.

Before their subjugation by Clan Donald, Clan Aonghais had links with the Macdougals of Craignish, and supplied bowmen to the chiefs of Clan Fingon, the Mackinnons, part of the native grouping known as Siol Alpin 'people of Alba' which can be traced from the Inner Hebrides into Perthshire and as far as Strathspey. In historical times this relationship was acknowledged by the Mackinnons, Macphees, Macquarries, Maclivers, MacAulays, MacGregors, MacNabs and Grants. In 1671 Lauchlan Mackinnon of Strathordel signed a bond of friendship with the chief of Clan Gregor (Murray MacGregor 1901, 108-9), despite the danger of being charged with treason.

The Ailpeanach lived by hunting and used beacons to communicate over this enormous area. One chain linked the Hebrides with Perthshire: it went from the master beacon on Ben More in Mull to Ben Cruachan, Ben Dorain, and Ben Vorlich in Argyll, Ben Lomond in Dumbartonshire, Ben More in Glendochart, the other Ben Vorlich, and Ben Lawers in Perthshire. A more important chain was based on the greatest beacon hill of all, Ben Nevis (G. *naomh* 'holy, sacred'), the highest mountain in Scotland at 1344 metres (4409 feet) with a bare rocky summit found when a surface has been burned re-peatedly. Alexander Fraser, minister of Kilmalie c.1792, reported that from its summit he could see the Moray Firth to the north, Colonsay to the west, a total distance of 270 km (170 miles), and also had a good view of Mull and the Paps of Jura, the islands of Rum and Canna, the Cuillins in Skye, Loch Eil, the Great Glen, Loch Rannoch in Perthshire, the other beacons named above and even Ben Wyvis in Ross-shire, 144 km (90 miles) to the north. In fine weather, and in the clear air of the eighteenth century, all of this was visible by day with the naked eye, and visibility would be enhanced at night by the use of fire.

According to a long-established annual calendar, beacons were lit on certain hills on specific dates to notify hunters of a forthcoming deer-drive. Deer might be caught by trapping, netting, stalking and running down with hounds, but in the wilder parts of Highland Scotland they were driven by a chain of beaters into a prepared ambush, over a cliff, or into a bog. The elaborate activities of the chain appear to be the explanation for the dancing, spinning and weaving attributed to the fairy folk in many tales. In a wild area like Morven a deer-drive or tinchel ('fire-chain') might employ several hundred beaters. The more men, the better the chain.

When the watchers on their fairy mounds or look-out posts saw the light of a distant beacon blazing out at night they would acknowledge receipt by lighting a flare while a messenger ran through the settlement broadcasting the war-cry or hunting-shout. Then the troops would grab their weapons and make for the muster site, an event featured in the fairy tale, 'Fire on Dun Bulg!' The need to keep perpetual watch for the beacon is the link between G. *faire* 'to keep watch', E. *fairy* 'hunter' and the fairy mounds. Most men seem to have spent much of the year travelling to communal deer-drives in other areas. To go by boat gave them access to many areas inaccessible by land and allowed them to carry home a considerable weight of venison.

We learn about these events from a story which was collected by James MacDougall in the West Highlands in the nineteenth century (1910, 123, 192-5), *Na Sithichean ag Connsachadh* or 'The Fairies Wrangling', which is discussed elsewhere. It tells us that hunters from the surrounding districts (Mull and Ardnamurchan) gathered now and again in Morven to take part in a communal deer-drive (*connsachadh*). At these great gatherings or hostings the local lads sheltered, fed and entertained their visitors with dancing and competitive games until all the different troops had arrived and the hunt could begin. The visitors who responded to the beacon signal were known as *gall* 'foreigner, stranger', from G. *gal* 'blast or flame; kindred, warfare (hunting); slaughter; valour', or as *deòiridh* 'pilgrim, traveller, alien, stranger', from G. *tòir* 'pursue, chase'.

Until the feudal takeover communal deer-hunting was the primary form of exploitation in most of Scotland. The isolated uplands are suited to large-scale deer-drives and to little else. Otherwise the hills were used only by women and children who migrated annually to summer pastures with their cattle. Consequently we should interpret the archaeology of Morven in terms of hunting. It was well-adapted to hunts with landing-places, muster points, outlook points, and stances for signal beacons. Nothing else left its mark on this landscape.

It also catered for death. One of the most intriguing sites is a group of Bronze Age cairns at Kinlochaline, Claggan, and Acharn (Ritchie and

Thornber 1975). In Cairn 3 at Acharn (NM702504) the ashes of a young man of about twenty were buried in the Iron Age in a very rough little coiled pot, accompanied by five unworked flint flakes. The pot had been deposited in a Bronze Age cairn and the dead hunter had been sent on his way to Tír na nÓg

with his weapons or the making of them. Was this coincidence or continuity? Given the continuity of tradition in this area it is not impossible that the re-use of this site deep in a deer-forest for an identical purpose after several thousand years is due to continuous activity in Morven by deer-hunters from the Bronze Age and perhaps from the start of settlement at the Palaeolithic-Mesolithic interface.

In Morven we can relate every feature to its use by hunters (the 'fairies' of the tale). The translations given are not by any means guaranteed but these names are potentially the names used by hunters at the time they began to exploit this remote and difficult terrain. One can judge from the spread of archaeological features that they found it very much to their taste.

Most signs of prehistoric activity are in west Morven, facing Mull, the area of our folk-tale. They belong to a variety of cultures and range from Mesolithic flints and a chambered tomb to feudal castles. East Morven, facing Lismore, has fewer features and no fertile coastal strip. The lack of roads is now an inconvenience but was less so in prehistory when travellers went by sea, by horse or on foot. The paucity of archaeological features suggests that this area was less exploited by prehistoric hunters though large tracts of Highland Scotland are devoid of archaeology, despite place-names indicating prehistoric use. The third part of Morven, north of Kingairloch, is higher and has even fewer features, though it has at least one important beacon site.

Mesolithic flints and cairns are indisputable signs of prehistoric activity but place-names exist in much larger numbers and give even more information. They have been so abused that they are for most scholars a no-go area, but in their proper context they are an invaluable source of information for prehistoric activity in Highland Scotland, an area with a very simple settlement history. The proposal that Scottish Gaelic was used in Scotland from the dawn of settlement is gaining ground. Ewan Campbell (1999) has provided a sound archaeological argument for Gaelic as native to Argyll, which can be extended to the rest of the Gaeltacht, at least. It is a measure of their age that many names do not make good sense when translated into modern Gaelic but every place-name did once make perfect sense and had a practical value for those who used it. The interpretations offered here are consistent with what we know of human activity in this area. All the referenced sites are from OS Landranger sheets 47 and 49.

We can divide Morven into three areas.

I West of Loch Aline (38 sites)

II East of Loch Aline facing the island of Lismore (16 sites)

III North of Kingairloch, facing Appin (5 sites)

I West of Loch Aline (38 sites)

Acharn (NM7050) 'field of meat'? A butchery site? Acharn as a mustering place was accessible by small boat from Loch Aline and the Sound of Mull. The same name is found on the island of Carna (NM6259) off the north shore of Morven; it is possible that meat was collected and dispatched from here.

Aoineadh Mor (NM6451), Aoineadh Beag (NM6650), 'the large and small precipices'. These features form a cliff some 10 kilometres (6 miles) long and were almost certainly used as a deer drop. There is a comparable site near Ardtornish. The word may be related to G. *aineas* 'passion, joy; fury, frenzy; cruelty; bravery'.

Arienas, Loch, G. àiridh *Aonghais* with àiridh 'upland pasture'. The second element is also found in Morven as Tom Aonghais Ruaidh and in the name MacInnes and is probably G. *aonach* 'meeting, fair, great assembly', referring to the communal hunts which took place in this area. The hundreds of assembled hunters were no doubt accommodated in the 77 hut platforms on the northern slopes of the loch (Rennie, *DES* 1992, 42). MacInnes may also mean 'people of the island': see note on Loch Tearnait, below.

Auchindruineach, 'field of the piercing' or 'of the druids', a field at Kinlochaline, which may have been a butchery site. It was visited by Donald Gregory in 1831 (*Archaeologica Scotica* 4, 1857, quoted by Ritchie, 1988).

Beinn Bhan 'mountain of the fire' (NM6649), with a standing stone consisting of a basalt monolith 1.8m in height, aligned N-S, rectangular in section, straight-sided but with a pointed top. It commands extensive views over Fiunary Forest and the Sound of Mull and probably marked an observation point and signal station. The alignment tracked south would hit Sgurr Dearg in Mull (NM6634). It would also mark the equinoxes.

Beinn Bhuidhe (NM6053). Not 'yellow ben' but 'ben of the fire' or 'of the hunting troop'.

Cairn (NM6947), adjacent to Kinlochaline Castle. Cairns in general mark the exact site of a signal beacon.

Cairn (NM6949), on the route from Lochaline on the coast to Acharn (NM6950).

Cairn (NM698508) contained two cists and fragments of charcoal and cremated bone. It probably marked the position of a beacon used for cremation and then to dispose of the ashes.

Cairns (NM5849), near the coast, on a hill spur overlooking the Sound of Mull.

Cairns on Rubha Dearg, 'promontory of the red (fire)' (NM6644); three cairns on the shore were probably made to hold the poles of lanterns marking the landing place.

Carn Liath, the Grey Cairn (NM6455), a chambered cairn, probably a marker for a beacon site on Loch Teacuis.

Carn na Cailliche 'cairn of the Hag' (NM5850), a very large kerbed cairn 50 x 30m by 3-4 m in height. The Hag is an aspect of the Deer Goddess who also appears as a Maiden or flame and as such is the female counterpart of the Black Man or tribal beacon. Hence the common fictional theme of the elopement or capture of a maiden by a black knight or some comparable figure. It means only that a beacon was lit. In place-names *cailleach* is a beacon site. She was sometimes equated with a dragon (often female). G. *cail* 'to burn'.

Baile Geamhraidh 'winter enclosure' (NM6155). Hut platforms. Probably a hunters' camp; winter townships were generally on the coast.

Cnoc nan Saobhaidhean (NM6151), 'hill of the den of the wild beasts'. MacKenzie (1935, 109) tells of a giant in Morven who was a match for those in Mull; in other words he was the main beacon. He was once chased from Ardnamurchan round Loch Sunart to the eminence at Lon More, the Morven hill on which he lived. Lon More is not mapped but its probable location coincides with Cnoc nam Faobh (NM6051) or Cnoc nan Saobhaidhean (NM6151). This fits with all the other early features in Fernish.

Coire na Criche (NM6357), 'corry of the spoils'.

Doire nam Mart (NM6652) 'the deer-forest of the winter provisions'. The same name is found in Mull as Durinemast (NM6752). At the west end of Loch Arienas and along its north shore is a spread of seventy-seven recessed platforms (Rennie 1997, 112-3). There are similar platforms at *Baile Geamhraidh* 'winter settlement' (NM6155) and thirty more to the east of Loch Aline, between Ardtornish Bay and Inninmore Bay, facing Mull (NM6943 to

NM7241). Such platforms are in general found in isolated and secluded locations which are accessible by boat. These platforms have been a great puzzle as they are difficult to date. It is evident that such hut platforms, terraced into steep hillsides, which have been found in their hundreds in this area and in many similar remote areas, were camp-sites used year after year by itinerant deer-hunters. We find hundreds of hut platforms in Morven exactly where hundreds of men gathered periodically to hunt and it is reasonable to suppose that these were stances where they put up their tents.

Drimnin (NM5454), also known as Bonnavoulin. A fortified beacon site and outlook point on a ridge bounded by rocky cliffs. The castle was owned by Macleans in the 16-17th c.

Dun na Leiche (NM6248): a stone circle was reported here but not found by RCAHMS.

Eilean nan Eildean (NM6158), 'island of the hinds'.

Eiligeir (NM6746), 'a trap for large animals'; corresponds to Elrig in eastern Scotland.

Fernish (NM5750), an obsolete district name meaning 'fire land', i.e., a district controlled by a central beacon. One of its beacon sites was Carn na Cailliche q.v.

Gleann nan Iomairean (NM5950): glen of the gathering; see Castle, Kinlochaline.

Keil or Keills (NM6745) at 80 m. (260 ft.), an old church overlooking the entrance to Lochaline and the ferry port in Mull. The church of the ancient parish of Kilcolmkill, now part of Morven was dedicated to Columba and traditionally founded by him. 'Tradition further says that before fixing on this site, the saint surveyed the coast of Morven from an eminence, and that when he caught sight of what was afterwards known as Keil, he said to St Moluag, who was with him: 'That is the place'. The mark of the saint's foot on a rock, where he is reported to have stood, is still pointed out' (Mackinlay 1914, 54). The story is a good example of 'how to select a beacon site'. The footprint shows the observer where to stand and points him in the right direction. Stones at the church include a Class III cross with plant scrolls and dragons and several later elite graves with carved stones showing armed warriors, a hunt-follower wearing a kilt, and several stag hunts.

Killintaig (NM5653), a church or chapel and associated sanctuary explained as *Cill Dhonnaig* but dedicated to St Fintan, G. *fionn* 'white' and *teine* 'fire' (Mackinlay 1914, 71).

Killundine, castle on site of fort. Caisteal nan Con 'the castle or fort of the dogs' (NM5848) is also known as Killundine Castle. It was a key beacon site. The ruins are those of a 17c. castle inside a prehistoric fort, on a very prominent coastal knoll. From this spot the beacon on Ben More in Mull is visible. Further south Ben More disappears behind lower ridges but one still has a view of Ardtornish, Duart and the mainland near Oban (Grant 1935, 232). This may be *Kaille au inde,* a monastery founded by Columba (Watson 1926, 279). According to another tradition the folk from Aros Castle (NM5644) in Mull used it as a hunting-lodge when they came to Morven. Across in Aros one finds An Sean Caisteal, a broch (NM5449), many cairns and from another era a standing-stone. Also to the north a possible chapel (NM5750) at a landing place on a small beach (NM5750). No saint is known.

Kinlochaline (NM6947): the castle is a square turreted feudal construction of the 15th c. or earlier, on a rocky bluff at the head of Loch Aline. There is a little fireplace on the parapet, said to be to boil oil or water to pour down on attackers but more probably to keep a signal fire burning. It is locally known as *Casteal an Ime,* probably G. *imeachd* 'journey, circuit', not *im* 'butter'. The original occupants of this site were Clan Aonghais who lost their lands to Maclean of Duart in 1390.

Kinlochaline (NM697504): a flint scatter was left by Mesolithic hunters 'near Kinlochaline Cottages'.

Loch Arienas (NM6752-6851). There are 77 hut platforms on the north side of Loch Arienas, from the lochside up to 150 metres (500 feet) (Rennie, DES 1992, 42). They provided a base for hunters' huts or tents. A cave higher up on Beinn na h-Uamha (NM6753) no doubt provided accommodation at an earlier date.

Rahoy (NM6356): on the north shore of Loch Teacuis a small circular vitrified fort only 50 ft in diameter. In it were found a socketed iron axe and a modified La Tene Ic bronze fibular brooch pointing to use in the 3rd century B.C. (Stevenson 1966, 20).

Rahoy (NM6456): more than 100 hut platforms.

Sidhean (NM6750) 'outlook hill', facing north over Loch Arienas. A fairy knoll or outlook point.

Sidhean Achadh nan Gamhna (NM6848) 'outlook hill of the field of the stags'. A fairy knoll.

Sidhean na Raplaich (NM6351) 'outlook hill of the slaughter'.

Tom Aonghais Ruaidh (Gillies 1906, 107; not located): in place-names Aonghais is best interpreted as G. *aonach* 'muster, assembly', so this would be 'the knoll of the gathering of the deer'. A *tom* appears to have been a stance for a signal fire.

Tom nan Eildean (NM6057) 'knoll of the hinds'.

Tòrr na Faire 'watch hill' (NM6744) (Gillies 1906, 103) at the mouth of Loch Aline. As noted under Ardtornish, *torr* (like *cnoc*) appears to have been a name for a beacon hill.

II East of Loch Aline, facing Lismore (16 sites)

Allt an Doire Darach (NM7647), 'the burn of the oak-wood deer forest'. It runs into Loch Tearnait. There is another Doire Darach on the south coast of Morven.

Am Miodar (NM6844), a field at Ardtornish, from the name once a muster site. In stories told in eastern Scotland Midhir was the Fairy King or hunt-master.

Aoineadh Mor (NM7242) and Aoineadh Beag (NM6943), as in I (NM6451), cliffs several miles in length which could be used as deer-drops. Below there are 30 hut platforms and Ardtornish Castle. There is a similar feature on the north side of Glais Bheinn (NM7243).

Ardtornish Castle (NM6942). A 14th c. feudal tower on a highly visible site now shared with a light-house. It was once important though no more than 23 metres by 15 metres (75 feet by 50 feet). Gillies says 'Thor's ness' (1906, 103) but G. *torr* or *torran* appears to mean 'fire'; cf. G. *torn* 'kiln, furnace, oven' and *torr-leus* 'torch'. In the time of the Lordship, Ardtornish was one of a chain of beacon castles on the Sound of Mull which linked Mingary in Ardnamurchan, Rubha nan Gall in Mull, Drimnin, Caisteal nan Con, Aros, Ardtornish, Duart, Lismore, and Dunollie and Dunstaffnage on the mainland (Grant 1935, 226).

Cnoc nan Caorach (NM8146). G. *caoir* 'firebrand, blaze'. The word *cnoc* appears to identify a beacon hill.

Crannog, Loch Tearnait (NM7447). Said to have been built by one of the Lords of the Isles but Scottish crannogs generally date to the Iron Age (600 BC in Perthshire), though some continued in use into the 17th c. MacInnes can mean 'people of the island'. An isolated crannog can hardly be anything but a hunting lodge where the elite could feast, secure from wolves, bears and other carnivores. Hence perhaps its reputation as a 'sanctuary' for those fleeing from justice (Grant 1935, 232-3). The glen eventually reaches Glensanda.

Doire Buidhe (NM7150), 'hunting forest of the troop' (NM7150).

Doire Darach (NM7440), 'deer-forest of the oak wood'; a steep coastal strip which is still wooded. One would expect to find hut platforms here like those on the Ardtornish shore.

Glais Bheinn (NM7143), 'the shining mountain', a beacon site.

Gleann Geal (NM7250-7349), 'glen of the fire'.

Glensanda Castle (NM8246). Accessible by sea or by air. 'Sanda' may indicate a round-up or gathering, no doubt exploiting the glen behind, by which one arrives eventually at Loch Tearnait and its crannog.

Hut platforms (NM6943-7242), a group of 30, on the steep coast between Ardtornish Point and Rubha an Ridire 'the knight's point' (Rennie, DES 2002, 75). The coasts of Argyll have many other clusters in similar locations, pointing to their temporary occupation by large numbers of people arriving by sea.

Meal a' Chaorainn (NM7644), 'bald hill of the *caoir*' 'firebrand, blaze of fire', a widespread pun on *caor* 'sheep'.

Meall na h-Iolaire (NM8151): G. *iolaire* 'eagle' is a common but meaningless pun for *iolairig* 'deer trap'.

Monadh Meadhoin 'hill of the meeting or muster' (NM7153).

Rubha na Craoibhe (NM7541), 'the promontory of the fire or tree'.

III North of Kingairloch, facing Appin (5 sites). This area was evidently less popular with hunters.

Creach Bheinn, 'ben of the plunder' (NM8757), is 853 metres (2800 ft) high and 'a notable viewpoint'. It was probably the site of a long-distance beacon linking north Morven with Appin on the mainland.

Fuar Bheinn (NM8556), 'cold mountain'.

Beinn Mheadhoin (NM7951) 'Ben of the meeting or muster'. This name is common in deer forests where 'middle mountain' is meaningless.

Dubh Doire (NM8058), 'black wood', archaic Gaelic 'deer forest'.

Torr an Fhamhair (NM9358): 'the knoll of the giant (or beacon)'. A coastal beacon site, widely visible on the east side of Loch Linnhe.

APPENDIX 7 - GAELIC NAMES
AND THEIR MEANINGS

1 Gaelic Witch Names

> *'Many witches taken there who confessed many uncouth and strange things, and how the devil gave them marks and signs with other names, as Wallidragle and the like. And[ro] Mudies wife in Tranent was called Knell...*

Patrick Anderson, History, 1596.

The Gaelic origins of witchcraft in Lowland Scotland are most clearly shown by the nicknames attributed to witches in the records, as far as Orkney and Shetland. Witches gave them to each other and some masters of covens gave a witch a new name (but in English) when she or he joined the coven, renounced her original baptism and swore to follow him. Most of the aliases given in the trial records are complimentary names such as Greibok, G. *gribhach* 'heroic, warlike', Lykeas, G. *leigheas* 'healing, curing', and Premak G. *priomhach* 'favourite'. *Loskoir Longert* 'fire of the deer trap' in Easter Ross represents an archaic vein of Gaelic hunting lore. These names are evidence for a widespread cult operating in the Gaidhealtachd which was exposed, briefly, by the trials. On the basis of these names alone, I believe that Margaret Murray was right in identifying the witch-cult as a prehistoric sacred tradition, though what we find in Scotland is probably older than even she envisaged.

The continued use of Gaelic in Lothian up to 1600 is shown by the persistence of Gaelic names such as *Fian, Knell, Toppock, Wallydraggle* and *Winzit*. These names were part of a widespread cult operating in the Gaeltachd which might have remained invisible but for the trials. The Devil generally gave a witch a new name when she or he joined a coven but such names are invariably in English. The loss of the Gaelic naming tradition can be traced to the creation of covens by men who spoke only English: there is no known case of a Devil giving a new convert a Gaelic name. In 1640 when Janet Breadheid was initiated, the Devil at Auldearn was giving his witches English names and teaching them how to curse in English (Pitcairn iii, 618). Nevertheless, to judge by elements of Isobell Gowdie's confession, Gaelic was still spoken in Moray in 1662.

The names used by the Gaelic-speakers in Easter-Ross deserve special notice. Some thirty individuals were named in a Commission issued at Holyroodhouse on 25 October 1577 (Exchequer Rolls xx, 522-3, 1899). Their names were evidently compiled by an English-speaking clerk using information supplied orally by a number of people with local knowledge. In consequence the names are given in a variety of forms. The women's names are often Gaelic patronyms such as *Jonet Neyne Thomas McAllan*, 'Janet daughter of Thomas son of Allan', or *Jonetam Neyne Willelmun McClachan* 'Janet son of William McClachan'. In Caithness in 1719 we find *Margaret Nin-Gilbert*, 'Margaret daughter of Gilbert', instead of Margaret Gilbertson. This reflects the use of Gaelic as a spoken vernacular. A few individuals use surnames of Lowland type, such as Cattanach, Ross, Miller and Forbes. There are also Gaelic aliases such as Cassindonisch and Loskoir Longert. Cradoch Neynane McGillechallum and Christian Chactach are also listed. *Cradoch* and *Chactach* are neither personal names nor surnames but appear to be witch-aliases which have replaced their owners' original names. This kind of substitution is found elsewhere. A leader of the North Berwick witches is known as John Fean or Fiene (G. *fiann* 'giant, warrior (hunter)', but his real name was John Cunningham. In Aberdeenshire, one of the witches who danced around the Fish Cross and Meil Market of Aberdeen at Hallowe'en 1596 is known only as *Shuddack*. These names underline the widespread understanding of the Gaelic idiom among the witches.

Aunchtie. Katharine Nein Rob Aunchtie was tried in Easter Ross in 1629. This name is not listed by Black (1946) as a Scottish surname. Perhaps G. *anam-chaidh* 'brave'.

Bargans: 'a man called Bargans' was a fugitive from justice at Bo-ness, in Renfrew in 1650. The name is not listed by Black (1946) as a Scottish surname. It may be from G. *barg* 'red hot' (RPC 2 series, vol.8, 211-235).

Bean, the alias of Margaret Clerk executed in Aberdeen, 1597. G. *ban* 'white, bright'.

Berdock, alias used by Margaret Borthwick, Cousland, West Lothian, 1630. Perhaps G. *bearraideach* 'nimble, light, active'.

Brune, the alias of Katharene Rannald, Kilpunt, West Lothian, 1622. Mother of Barbara Home alias Winzit. Helen Mcbrune (below) may have been a local Fairy Queen.

Callioch, alias of Janet McIllwhichill in Ardoch, 1622. G. *cailleach* 'maiden'; she was perhaps the Maiden of the coven.

Cane, alias of Effie McCalzane, tried in Edinburgh in 1591 (Pitcairn 246). G. *cain* 'beloved, dear; clear, bright'.

Cassindonisch, the alias of Thomas McAnemoir McAllan McHendrik, Easter Ross, 1577. G. *cas* 'hunt', of the *dòmhnaich* 'deer forest' would be a hunting shout (cf Christsonday, below). It could also be *cas an donais* 'Devil's foot' but this is essentially meaningless.

Chactach, a probable witch-name recorded in Easter Ross in 1577: G. *chiatach* 'handsome, goodly'.

Dam. The first witch contacted by Katherine Ross, Lady Fowlis, was 'William McGilliewareycht-dame', William McGillievorich. This is probably not G. *damh* 'stag' but Dann or Daan, a place in Easter Ross.

Douglas, alias (or married surname?) of Barbara Napiar, Edinburgh 1590. G. *dubh* + *glas* 'deer light'.

Elva, one of the Devils in Bute in 1662. Perhaps G. *eala* 'sanctuary' or 'deer-forest'. E. *elf* may have a similar origin.

Feane, Fian, alias of John Cunningham, leader of the North Berwick witches. The Fian or Feinne were legendary deer-hunters (G. *fiadh* 'deer'). The word is related to G. *fionn* 'white'.

Galdragon, Shetland. 'Fire Master'. A traditional name for a witch or sorceress (Scott). cf Wallydraggle and W. *dragon* 'leader in war' or 'hunt master'.

Goilean. G. *goileam* 'fire, fire-kindling (Dalyell 1835, 540).

Gradoch. Neynane McGillecallum in Easter Ross in 1577. Gradock, the alias of Jonet Grant, 1590, Aberdeen. Gradoche Neinechat 'Beloved Maiden of the Troop', the name of a witch in Ross-shire in 1629 (Black 1938, 45). G. *gràdhag* 'esteemed, loved, admired'.

Gray-meal, the alias of John Gordoun, 'a silly old ploughman', who was door-keeper to the North Berwick witches, 1590 and evidently a Highlander. G. *greigh* 'herd' + *meall* 'beacon hill'.

Greibok, Griebik or **Grewik**, used by two Orkney witches: Katherine Bigland in 1615 and Jonet Thomesone in 1643. G. *gribhach* 'heroic, warlike'. Grapus is a name of the devil. Both are related to G. *gribh* 'warrior (hunter)', G. *grib, griobh* 'griffon', and E. *grab, grip*.

Greysteil, nickname of Patrick, third Lord Ruthven, father of William, first Earl of Gowrie and son of the Lord Ruthven who killed Queen Mary's favourite, David Rizzio. Greysteil was the hero of a metrical romance popular in the 15th-16th centuries. A Gaelic nickname meaning 'gallant warrior'.

Hattaraick, alias of Alexander Hunter, 'an old wizard' in Haddington, 1629. G. *càtharrach* 'fighting bravely or resolutely' (Summer 1925, 135).

Hauche, alias of Marion Johnestoun, Dumfriesshire, 1630. Perhaps G. *abhach* 'sportive, humorous, joyous'.

Helen Mcbrune. The name of a spirit (perhaps the Queen of Elphane) that appeared to Patrick Lowrie and Jonet Hunter at Hallowe'en 1605, on Lowdon Hill, Ayrshire, and gave him what sounds like a knitted glove (Pitcairn ii, 478). 'Brian' is a name of the devil and means 'fire'. At Hallowe'en on Lowdon Hill we would expect the fairy folk or hunters to light a bonfire.

Huthart was a familiar or spirit who informed the female soothsayer who predicted the imminent death of James I in 1436. G. *cutharthach* or *cobhartach* 'saviour, helper, comforter'.

Klareanough, the Devil who met Janet Morisoun at Knockanrioch, Bute, in 1662. G. *clàr-aodhanach* 'broad-faced' refers to a widely-visible fire (G. *aodh* 'fire'). A comparable word is *clàireineach* said to mean 'dwarf', but perhaps a small fire. The first element is related to G. *clearc* 'radiant, bright', E. *clear*, E. *clarion*, a type of trumpet used to send a signal. Isobel Gowdie said that the Fairy King at the Downie Hills was 'broad-faced'. This may have been the name of a beacon. The name Knockanrioach seems to be obsolete but in 1573 it was granted to Marion Fairlie, widow of Sheriff John Stewart together with Little Barone (NS0764) and Gartnakeilly (also NS0764), which are both a mile west of Rothesay. It may be the house now known as Larkhall.

Kna, Kna Donaldi 'daughter of Donald' was a witch in Easter Ross in 1577: G. *cna* 'good, bountiful, gracious, merciful'.

Knell, the name given to And[rew] Mudie's wife, a witch in Tranent, 1596. G. *gnèidheil* 'shapely, well-proportioned' (Anderson Adv. mss 35.5.3).

Lanie, Agnes alias Lanie Scot, tried in Aberdeen in 1536 (Black 1938, 21). G. *laineach* 'glad, joyful, merry'.

Leiris, listed in Easter Ross in 1577 as the husband of a witch. Perhaps from G. *leir* 'destructive, terrible', applied to a hunter.

Likkit or **Lukit,** alias of Christian Keringtoune of Prestonpans, tried in Edinburgh in 1591 (Pitcairn 246). G. *luchaidh* 'light'.

Loskoir Longert, alias of Mariota Neymaine (or Neyeane) McAlester, Easter Ross (1577). A hunting shout meaning 'fire at the hunting lodge' with G. *loisg* 'to burn' and *longhairt* or *luncart* 'hunting lodge'.

Lykeas, G. *leigheas* 'healing, curing'. On 16 October 1673, at the trial of Jannet McNicoll in Rothesay in Bute, it was stated that the devil, a gross lepper-faced man, gave her a new name of Mary Lykeas.

Micol, in English literature, a name of the Queen of Elfhame who could be summoned by calling, 'Micol, Micol queen of the pygmies, come!' (Dalyell 1835, 537).

Molach, Donald Molach was a notable witch in Morvern, 18-19c. (Campbell 1902, 10). G. *mol* 'assembly, flock', so, a hunter but also *mollachd* 'curse'.

Napeas or the fairie; G. *nàbaidh* 'neighbour' (Dalyell 1835, 539). Barbara Naipar, 1590 in Edinburgh, was **Naip,** perhaps a pun on her surname.

Naunnchie, alias of Katharine Mcinphersoun, Ross-shire, 1629. Perhaps G. *naomh* 'holy, sacred' + *sith* 'deer-forest'. Noance NicClerich was said to be sister's daughter to the witch of Monzie (see under Nic Niven).

NicAicherne, a witch in Morven; perhaps a beacon. Henderson, 2008, 7.

NicNiven or **Neven,** G. *nighean* 'daughter' + *naomhin* 'holy place (deer-forest)'. Cognate with Nemain or Neamhain, an Irish war goddess or battle fury (a hunting goddess) and with Gaulish *Nemetona*. Nemed was the husband of Macha, another war goddess, and of Cera ('light'), and father of Starn ('light'). There is probably also a link with Nine, as in Nine Maidens, G. *naoinear* 'nine persons', indicating a holy place or deer sanctuary. Nicniven was a frequent alias in Scotland, said to identify the Fairy Queen: 'Now Nicniven is the Queen of Elphin, the Mistress of the Sabbat' (Scott 1931, 300; M. Summers 1925, 7).

Sara Neven, the name of a trow at Quarff, Shetland, in the late nineteenth century. Sara in Gaelic is Mór, archaic *mar* 'hunt'. Archaic G. *naomhin* 'holy place (deer-forest)'.

Noance [Agnes?] NicClerich was sister's daughter to Nik Neiving, a notorious and infamous witch in Monzie who was burnt c.1565. She worked with John Brugh, the warlock of Fossaway (Reid, 1899, 202). Dalyell thought Nik Neiving of Monzie was the same as the witch called NicNiven who was burned at St Andros in 1569.

Kate McNieven, according to a story which has all the features of fake folklore, was nurse to the Laird of Inchbrackie, Perthshire, and was burned on the Knock of Crieff in 1715 for stealing a knife and fork while in the shape of a bee. This appears to be inspired by earlier events at Monzie with the addition of spurious fantasy (McAra 1881, 201). The date is disputed by Jamieson, minister of Monzie, in 'A southern outpost on the edge of the Highlands' (*Chronicles of Strathearn*, 1896, 333-340). Both Inchbrakie and Monzie are within two miles of Crieff. In *The Flyting of Montgomery and Polwart* Nicnevin is a generic (Irving and Laing (eds) 1821, 117). Then a cleir companie came soone after closse *Nicniven*, with her nymphs in number anew, With charmes from Caithness and Chanrie of Rosse, Whose cunning consists in casting a clew... Scott in talking of Celtic fairy lore mentions 'a gigantic and malignant female, the Hecate of this mythology, who rode on the storm, and marshalled the rambling host of wanderers under her grim banner. This hag ... was called Nicneven in that later system which blended the faith of the Celts and the Goths on this subject.' (Scott, Letters, 130). In *The Flyting of Dunbar and Kennedy* Dunbar pictures her at Hallowe'en, riding at the head of witches, fairies, sorceresses, elves and ghosts.

Nun. Janet Paton 'a great witch' of the Fossaway coven was called 'the Nun', perhaps for 'the Cailleach', which can have that meaning.

Pardone, name used by Marion Peebles, Shetland, 1644 (Pitcairn 194). G. *pairtean* '(having) abilities, or powers'.

Preip the Witch that wes brunt at Banff (Presbytery Book of Strathbogie 1843, 5). Perhaps G. *breab* 'kick, prance'. Black (1938, 48) says: Wrongly thought to be the alias of John Philip, vagabond, tried and executed in Banff, 1631, but if Preip the Witch was not John Philip, then who was?

Premak, alias of Isobel Thomson, Elgin, Moray in 1596. G. *priomhach* 'favourite' (Huie 1976, 290). Wrongly given as Preinak.

Rigerum, an alias of Margaret Craige, one of the Pollockshaws witches in 1676. Perhaps from G. *ruagair* 'hunter'. It is late to find Gaelic in daily use.

Rigga, Jonet Rendall, a poor vagabond, in Orkney 1629. G. *ruaig* 'pursuit, hunt, chase'. Her Devil was called Walliman. She blamed him for all the cattle who died: 'Giff they deit Walliman did it'.

Rossina, the new name given to Agnes Murie, Fossaway, 1661. G. *ros* 'pleasant, pretty, delightful' or from G. *rosachd* 'enchantment, charm, witchcraft' (Reid 1899, 220).

420

Runa Rowa, alias of Annie Tailyour, Orkney 1624. G. *run* 'beloved person or object' and *ruith* 'chase, pursuit, rout (deer drive)'. 'Beloved of the Hunt' was no doubt an honorific name of the Cailleach.

Scudder or **Sculdr**, alias of Isobell Strathaquin, Aberdeen, 1597. G. *sguideir* 'slut, whore', once an honourable attribute of the Cailleach.

Seweis, a suspected witch in custody in St Andrews, 1645. G. *seamhas* 'good luck, prosperity'. This is not known as a personal name or a family name. It corresponds to Lucky or Goody.

Shuddak, one of those who danced around the Fish Cross and Meil Market of Aberdeen at Hallowe'en 1596. G. *siodhach* 'a fairy, one of the fairy folk'.

Spaldarge, alias of Jonet Clark, 1590 (S.C.M. I, 140). Perhaps G. *spio-ladair* 'teaser'. Also as **Spalding.**

Spalding. See Spaldarge.

Stovd, alias of Barbara Thomasdochter, Shetland, 1616. Jakob Jakobsen gives *støvi* 'whirl of dust'.

Suppak or **Suppok**, alias of Helene Makkie in Aberdeen, 1597. G. *sopag* 'small bundle of straw', used to make a torch or send a signal. There are several other instances of a small bundle of straw or hay in witch-lore.

Swein, a male witch in Auldearn, in grass-green. Archaic Gaelic *samh* 'to gather' + *ain* 'fire'. It is the same as *Samhain* 'Hallowe'en'.

Todlock, alias of Margaret Ranie, Orkney 1643. G. *todhail* 'destruction'.

Toppock, alias of Elizabeth Steven, a female witch in Lothian c.1629. G. *tapaidh* 'clever, bold, heroic', or *taobhach* 'friendly, kind' (Summer 1925, 135).

Trachak, a witch in Aberdeenshire, with Spaldairg, 1597. G. *dreachach* 'fair, handsome' (Michie 1896, 38).

Wallawa, in Orkney a name of the Devil. The oath in part went: 'O Mester King o' a' that's ill, Come fill me with the warlock skill, An' I sall serve wi' all me will, in de name o' de muckle black Wallawa!' Probably the same name as Walliman (see below), an aspirated version of G. *baillie ban* meaning 'the person of the fire enclosure'.

Wallidragle, the name of a witch in Tranent, 1596 (Anderson. Adv. mss 35.5.3). G. *gal* 'flame, kindred, slaughter, valour (hunter)' or Sc. *wally* 'excellent, showy, ample' + *dreachail* 'comely, good-looking, handsome'. Probably an epithet of the hunting goddess 'the handsome one of the flame', degraded in Scots to *wallidraggle* 'slovenly woman'. It is related to the names Galdragon and Walliman, Jonet Rendall's Devil in Orkney.

Walliman, Jonet Rendall's Devil in Orkney. Perhaps from G. *baillie ban* 'of the enclosure of the fire'.

Winzit, alias of Barbara Home in Kilpont, West Lothian, 1622. G. *uinnseachadh* 'managing'.

2. Lowland names for the Fairy Queen.

See also names for the Cailleach. In Ireland the chief fairy was known as Mogh, Magh or Mabh.

Galdragon, an obsolete Shetland word for a witch or sorceress (Scott). 'Fire-master'.

Gay Carline. A name of the Cailleach. Probably for 'Gray Carline'. The same as the following.

Gyre-Carline. She lived on human flesh, which is a view of the Cailleach as a cremation bonfire.

Helen McBrune on Lowdon Hill, Ayrshire.

NicNevin. See above.

Queen of Elphame or **Elphin** 'ruler of the hill ground or deer-forest'.

3. Scottish Witch and Devil Names derived from English

Most of these names are from the later period or reflect early contact with English-speakers. The practice of giving witches Gaelic dedicatory or 'spirit' names persisted through the sixteenth and into the seventeenth century in most of Lowland Scotland. Then Gaelic names were replaced by English names. This reflects the spread of education in English and the control of local covens by educated Devils who spoke no Gaelic. On a wider scale the change reflects the retreat of Gaelic from Lowland Scotland.

The practice of giving witches new names when they renounced their

Christian baptism persisted after 1600 but in a degraded fashion. Pedestrian English names such as Margaret, David, Nan and Christian mark a break in the oral transmission of Gaelic lore, related to the spread of literacy in English, when the meaning and purpose of the Gaelic names (and no doubt many other features of the cult) were lost. This break corresponds with the spread of imported rituals and recipes learned from books and with the general spread of English at the expense of Gaelic.

Isobell Gowdie named several of the witches and ten of the thirteen devils belonging to her company at Auldearn as it was in 1662. The names she supplies are all in Scots – confirming that the Auldearn Devil was a member of the local elite who had been educated abroad, was not a Gaelic speaker, and who had acquired his interest in black magic from books. We can recognise the work of two different devils there, neither of them a Gaelic-speaker. The first, who was active c.1640, gave his witches very ordinary names such as Janet and Christian. The second had more imagination, but his names still have nothing in common with traditional Gaelic spirit names.

Able-and-Stout, alias of Bessie Hay, Auldearn, 1662.

Bandon is a figment found in the diary of Alexander Brodie of Brodie, in his entry for 30 September 1662: 'My Son went to Aldearn to see the trial of the witch *Bandon*; who adheard to her confessions, and was condemd.' His entry of 2 October: 'I heard much of her blaming Betti Hay as a teacher and partner in her witchcrafts.' Like Bessie Hay ('Able and Stout') 'Bandon' is in error for I. Gowdie. Only two members of the Auldearn coven were interrogated at that date: Isobell Gowdie and Janet Breidhead. Examination of the MS shows that Brodie made a mistake with the initial letter but corrected it without deletion to read 'IGaudie'. Apart from this it is easy to make 'owdie' out of the remaining letters.

Bawdem, the surname or alias of Maggie, the Great Witch of the Chanonrie, Easter Ross, executed 1577.

Bessie Bald, alias given to Elspet Nishe, Auldearn, 1662.

Broun, alias of Katharene Rannald in Kilpont, 1622. This is apparently not her married surname as her daughter's name was Barbara Home (see Winzie, above). Broun, as in Helen McBrune, is probably a 'fire' word and may represent Brian, a name of the Devil.

Christian, the name given to Janet Breadheid by her Devil, perhaps as early as 1640.

Hynd Knight, the Devil of Andro Man's coven, Aberdeen, 1587. cf. Hind Etin (above).

Janet, the baptismal name given to Isobell Gowdie by her Devil, some time before 1662.

Lanthorne, alias of Christian Wilson, a witch in Dalkeith, 1661.

Mak Hector or **MacKeeler** a male witch in Auldearn, a young man in grass-green.

Noblie, given as an alias of Isobel Durward, Angus, 1661. See Ouglie.

Norische or **Nurreych.** Marioun Wod, alias Erss [Highland?] Marioun, vtherwayes callit the Catnes norische (Aberdeen 1597). Bessie Roy, nurreych, Fetternear, Angus, 1590: both probably *nourrice* or wet-nurse. Was this an official position? Did they look after abducted infants?

Nun: Janet Paton, a great witch in Crook of Devon, was termed The Nun = G. *cailleach* (Reid 1899, 221).

Ower-the-Dyke-with-it, the name given to Janet Martin, Maiden of the Auldearn coven, 1662.

Pickle Nearest the Wind, name given to Margaret Wilson, Auldearn, 1662.

Rob the Rower, one of the North Berwick witches, 1590. He kept the roll or row. Robert was a popular name among devils and witches and means 'hunter' (as E. *robber*). Bobbie was a name for the Lowland Devil. This name reflects the influence of Frances Stewart, Earl of Bothwell, whose natural language appears to have been French.

Robbie o da Rees, a trow at Quarff, Shetland, late nineteenth century. The Rees may be the reaths or quarter-days.

Robert the Comptroller, the alias of Robert Grierson, North Berwick, 1590. This name has the same meaning as Rob the Rower.

Robert the Jackis, a male witch in Auldearn, 1662, an aged man in dune. For Robert see above. Sc. *jack* was a leather bag such as a saddle bag. Hunters carried provisions in leather satchels.

Robert the Rule, a male witch in Auldearn, 1662, who wore sadd-dun. For Robert see above. The second part is perhaps G. *ruladh* 'slaughtering, massacre (hunting)' but cf 'Rob the Rower'.

Rorie, a male witch in Auldearn, 1662, who wore yellow. *Ruairidh* was 'facetiously applied to the fox'. E. Dwelly 1026. A fox was one of the shape-changing animals; in other words, the Devil sometimes wore a fox-skin.

Roring Lyon, a male witch in Auldearn, in grass-green. The lion, as a great hunter and as a pun on G. *lion* 'gin, snare' and 'fill, replenish, satiate' was a very old and very popular hunting pun.

Samuel, the name used by the Devil of the Crook of Devon coven, 1662 (Reid 1899, 223).

Sanders, the Read Reiver, a male witch in Auldearn, in black. Sandie was a name of the Lowland Devil and appears to mean 'hunter'. A riever or robber was also a hunter. The root is found in G. *reubail* 'tear, mangle (kill, butcher)'. Red is perhaps G. *ruadh* 'deer'.

The Seelie Wights 'the skilful people', remembered as beautiful, happy people; G. *seilg* 'hunt'.

Serpent, the name of the leader of the coven at Inverkip, Renfrewshire. St Paul equated the serpent with the Devil.

Thieff of Hell, a male witch in Auldearn, 1662. A thief in any archaic context was a hunter. The Lowland Devil was known as the Auld Thief.

Thomas the Fearie, a male witch in Auldearn, 1662. G. *faire* 'to keep watch'. Thomas may be G. *tomhais* 'to measure, survey', which was originally done at night by aligning fires.

Throw-the-Cornyard, alias of Bessie Wilson, Auldearn, 1662.

Viceroy, the name used by Isabel Rutherford of the Crook of Devon coven, 1662.

In a notorious case that came to court in 1677 six members of an alleged coven at Pollockshaws near Glasgow were tried and condemned for attempting to cause the death of Sir George Maxwell. Their 'spirit' names are given by Sinclair in *Satan's Invisible World* (pages 4 to 10). As at Auldearn there is a change between the pedestrian English name *Landlady* and the obscure (invented?) Annippy or Enippa of 1677. Locas and Rigerum appear to be Gaelic in origin.

Ejoall or *Ejool*: the name given to himself by the Black Man at Pollockshaws. He wore black clothes, a blue band and white hand-cuffs with hogers and his feet were cloven.

Enippa or *Annippy*: the name given to Annabil Stuart (who had just been recruited) at Pollockshaws in 1677. This may be Scots *aneabil* 'single woman, concubine' or simply a version of her own name.

Jonat: the name given to John Stuart at Pollockshaws. It is unusual to give a man a woman's name.

Landlady: the name given to Jonet Mathie, mother of Annabil Stuart, at Pollockshaws.

Locas: the witch-name of Margaret Jackson at Pollockshaws. Perhaps G. *logais* 'awkward unwieldy person'?

Rigerum: the name given to Margaret Craige at Pollockshaws. It could be from G. *ruagair* 'hunter'.

Sopha: name given to Bessie Weir at Pollockshaws. This might be intended for Greek *Sophia* 'Wisdom', who is said to have created Lucifer; if so it points to some knowledge of the Classics on the part of the local Devil.

Dating the survival of Gaelic

The use of a Gaelic alias in any place shows the continued use of vernacular Gaelic among its witches within the previous generation. In the southwest and perhaps also in Ayrshire a knowledge of Gaelic lingered into the eighteenth century. There was more Gaelic than appeared as the leaders of covens generally spoke English and gave English names to their witches, regardless of their native vernacular.

1597: Aberdeen. Last Gaelic name on record: English also in use.

1618: Ayrshire.

1622: West Lothian.

1622: Wigtown.

1629: Easter Ross.

1629: East Lothian. English in use by 1661.

1630: Dumfriesshire. Gaelic still in use.

1631: Banff, Moray. But English was in use by the elite from c.1640.

1645: Fife. Gaelic still in use.

1645: Orkney. Gaelic names on record.

1662: Bute. Gaelic was still spoken in Bute in 1662 but by then the Devil was giving his witches pedestrian names like Janet, Catherine and Mary (MacPhail 1920, 6, 12, 13).

4. Names of the Cailleach

The following manifestations are all local beacons which were lit to announce communal hunts (Campbell 1902, 26, 51, ff). In the Highlands, despite her evolved identity as the goddess of deer and of life and death, and some late appearances as an evil witch, the Cailleach retained her original local identity as a tribal beacon. The following manifestations are all believed to be local beacons, lit to announce important communal hunts. The names show very nicely the distinction between meaningless literal translations and the archaic original Gaelic. At one time every local hunt had its own *cailleach*; these are only a few of the local names.

Fhua Mhoir Bein Baynac was a male ghost who lived in Glenavon, Banffshire. See Clashnichd Aulnaic.

Clashnichd Aulnaic was a female ghost who lived in Glenavon, Banffshire, and who often shrieked at night because Fhua Mhoir Bein Baynac had expelled her from her home (Stewart 1822, 6-8).

Ball odhar, Kintra, Ardnamurchan: G. *beoll* 'fire', archaic G. *odhar* 'fire place' or 'deer-forest'. G. *crom-odhar* 'the crook of the fireplace' or 'pot-hanger' also means 'penis', for obvious reasons.

Beire, a name of the Cailleach Bheur.

Cailleach Bheine Mhor lived in Jura at Larig Breac 'the pass of the deer'. When she saw that Mhic a Phie (a fairy man or hunter) had left her by a trick she slid down the side of Beinn an Oir on Sgriob na Cailich, the scree of the Big Woman, where you can still see her track (Campbell vol II).

Cailleach Bheur, the long-distance beacon on Ben Nevis. G. *beur* 'sharp,

427

loud (of a signal)'. Also known as Beire, the Gyre-Carline, the Gay Carline, and Mag Moullach. She heralded winter by washing her plaid in the Corrievreacain, a whirlpool which at times can be heard at a distance of twenty miles. It takes three days for the cauldron to boil and when the washing is done 'the plaid of old Scotland is virgin white'. The Cailleach Bheur had only one eye and lived on Ben Nevis where the Maiden Bride was imprisoned over the winter. She presided over the three months from Hallowe'en to Candlemas (McNeill 1959, vol 2, 20).

Cailleach Dhomhnuill Bhric, Lawers, Lochtayside. Donald Breac's Old Wife. Said to be the name of the Witch of Lawers; probably in fact the long-distance beacon on Ben Lawers (Gillies 1938, 350). Dhomhnuill or Donald is probably G. *domhan* 'world, universe (the tribal deer forest). G. *breac* 'speckled' normally refers to deer. Originally a Clan Gregor beacon.

Cailliach Mhor Chlibhrich, at Reay, Caithness. Campbell gives a spurious folk tale in which she milks the hinds.

Caiseart gharbh Ni'n an Aodhair, said to be one of the sisters of Glenforsa, Mull, but this is probably two names. 'The rough foot-gear of the daughter of the herdsman (or hunter)'. A.G. *cas* 'hunt', G. *casgair* 'butcher, massacre', A.G. *garbh* 'deer (rough ones)'. Nighean an Aodhair means 'woman of the beacon site'.

Cas a mhogain riabhaich, 'foot of the brindled footless stocking'. Perhaps one of the sisters of Glenforsa, Mull, but also said to have been in Glencoe. G. *cas* 'hunt, kill', *mùgh* 'kill, destroy', *riabhaich* 'deer (brindled ones)'. *An riabhach mòr* 'the great brindled one' is the Devil, seen as a great stag.

Corrag, daughter of *Iain Buidhe*, 'Yellow John' or 'Beacon of the hunting troop'. G. *corrach* 'fetter, shackle' is probably a deer trap.

Doideag, the famous Mull witch, *Na Doideag-un Muileach*, in the plural. In one story the Doideag lived in a house at Rutha Ghuirmean near Duart, no doubt to be handy for the MacLean chief. *Doideag-un* was a children's name for snowflakes, which are said to be the Mull witches on their way. Archaic G. *dòid* 'tooth' is cognate with the English word. The name may mean 'the sharp one' referring to the penetrating power of her beacon signal.

Gentle Annie, the anything-but-gentle storm-wife of northeast Scotland. G. *ain* 'fire'.

Gorm-shùil chrotach, Cràcaig, near Portree, Skye. Not: 'blue-eye humped one'. G. *crotach* 'hump-backed' is probably G. *cròthadh* 'enclosing in a pen or trap'. Isobell Gowdie described the fairy-boys who made the elf-arrows as hump-backed which means they were hunters.

Gorm-shùil mhòr, Moy, Lochaber. She was the leader of seven 'witches', leading to the memorable image of seven old crones dancing in a circle. She was stronger than all the witches of Mull – which means that her signal took precedence over those of the Mull beacons. But there may have been another *Gorm-shùil mhòr* on Mull, for according to Fitzroy MacLean her home was on Ben More and she was the most potent of the *Doideagan Muileach* or Grizzled Ones of Mull (F. MacLean, *West Highland Tales*, 2000, 116).

Gorm-shùil, Hianish, Tiree. Like all beacons she had but a single eye. Archaic G. *gorm* 'noble', *sùil* 'beacon'.

Gyre Carline, a name of the Cailleach Bheur (McNeill 1959, vol 2, 20). She lived on human flesh: in other words the Cailleach was a cremation bonfire.

Laorag, Tiree. G. *ladhrach* 'having large hoofs or claws'. A claw is a common metaphor for a deer-trap, as a feature which grips the animal so that he cannot escape. G. *ladhar* can also mean 'the single foot of a cloven-footed animal' and would be an appropriate name for the Devil.

Luideag of the Bens. 'A slovenly woman or slattern'. All sluts and whores are the Cailleach. So was Luideag, the shaggy filly of the folk tale, who comes to the magic bridge and should not be despised.

Mac Crauford, the witch of Arran. F.M. McNeill 1959, vol 2, 20.

Mac-Mhuirich nam buadh, said to mean 'Macpherson of power'.

Mag Moullach, the beacon of Clan Grant, also in Tullochgorum. F.M. McNeill 1959, vol 2, 20. G. *magh* 'plain, deer forest'. G. *mol* 'a bald place, a beacon site'.

Maol-Odhar of Kintyre. G. *mol* 'gathering, assembly; A.G. *mol* for maol 'beacon site', literally a bare place. G. *odhar* 'dun' probably for *aodhair* 'beacon site'.

Muileatach, Muileartach* or *Muireartach. Translated as 'Western Sea' and said to be the Witch of Lochlann ('hunting trap') but probably 'of Mull' (J.G. Campbell 1902, 188). A Mull or Maol was the site of a long-distance beacon; e.g., the Mull of Galloway, the Mull of Kintyre, and the island of Mull.

Nic-ill'-Domhnuich, Tiree: 'Daughter of the servant of Domnuich'. G. *gille* 'hunter', *damh* 'stag'; the pun between *dòmhnaich* 'of the deer forest' and *Dòmhnaich* 'Sunday' is discussed in the list of witch names. It probably means 'of the deer-forest'; Sunday was perhaps once a hunting day.

Nuckelavee. Douglas describes Nuckelavee as a fearsome creature, part man, part horse, with a large head, a large mouth, breath like steam from a kettle, and a single eye as red as fire (Douglas, 1894, 162). This is *Nic-ille-dhuibh* 'daughter of the black lad (deer hunter)' (cf Macgillewie for *Mac-gille-dhuibh*). Nuckelavee appears to be another name for the Cailleach as beacon. She is reported from Orkney.

Spoga buidhe: 'Yellow claws', from Meligeir on the east side of Skye. Also recorded as ***Spoga buidhe ni'a Douill 'ic Cormaig*** 'Yellow claws, daughter of Donald son of Cormac' which appears to be two names compounded. G. *spoga* 'deer trap', *buidhe* 'fire', *caoir* 'blaze of fire', *magh* 'plain, deer forest'.

5 Lowland names for the Devil

Oh thou! whatever title suit thee, Auld Hornie, Satan, Nick, or Clootie...

The original meaning of the word 'devil', as a Black Man or as lord of the animals, is fire. It is not surprising to find the Devil presiding over the magical aspects of hunting as he rules over Hell, the great fiery place. The Devil did not like church bells because they replaced his beacon as a source of information and system of control. Church bells were effective against lightning; but they were also effective against pagan beacons. This is confirmed by the story of St Quentin, who lamed the Devil at Llanblethian in the Vale of Glamorgan, Wales (Bord 2004, 114). Any lame or one-legged god or hero personifies a beacon on his pole. St Quentin is celebrated by the Church on 31 October, Samhain, no doubt at one time a hunt gathering at Llanblethian.

Names for God were limited to The Almichty, The Best, The Guid, and The Wye and they were not in popular use. There is a remarkable contrast with the plethora of irreverent and even affectionate names for the Devil, both in Gaelic and in English, suggesting that he was a familiar, respected and reassuring figure. They show a good many links with archaic Gaelic and with hunting but none with the Anti-Christ of the Presbyterians. They have little to do with the self-styled 'Lord' of the coven.

Many of the Lowland names would be appropriate nicknames for the leader or guidman of a witch coven but the Highland names (below) appear to refer more directly to a horned or hairy animal such as a bull or a stag. The prevalence of witch belief in Lowland Scotland suggest that these names arose among peasants whose immediate ancestors had spoken Gaelic and who were much more familiar with the pagan cult of the deer-hunters than with the Christian faith. They suggest a horned guidman who was responsible for hunting magic at local level. There appear to be no names referring to the devil's most prominent organ but they may remain to be recognised.

Black Lad, The. In archaic Gaelic, *an gille dubh*, 'servant of the deer'. An Gille dubh was the son of the Maiden, at Kilmallie. The witches of Auldearn talked about their devil disrespectfully as the Black Man.

Bobbie, Auld. Rob or Robin 'robber, hunter', a common name among witches and demons.

Chiel or **Chield, Auld**. Scots *chiel* 'lad' may be linked to G. *chùil* 'nook (deer trap)', as Hule. Sc. *chiel* and E. *child* may have been names for a young hunter.

Cloutie, Cloots or **Auld Cloutie**. Scots *cloot* 'hoof' reflecting G. *clùid* 'nook (deer trap)', both having a cloven shape.

Donald, Auld. 'From having assumed the shape of a Highlander'. More probably from G. *damh* 'stag'.

Gillatrypes. An obscene dance popular with witches in Moray. Probably 'servant of the herds'.

Grapus. G. *grib* 'griffon', E. *grab, grip*. G. and Sc. *grap* or *grape* 'three-tined fork' is a hunter's trident, once made of reindeer antler. The *Krampus* were guisers disguised as horned devils who paraded on St Nicolas (5-6 December) in parts of rural Austria.

Guidman, The G. *guidhe* 'beseeching, praying, intercession'. The Guidman's Croft or Acre was a piece of wild ground (residual deer forest) devoted to the Devil. Andrew Man (d.1598) dedicated several such reserves or wards to 'the hynd knicht quhom thow confessis to be a spreit, and puttis four stanis in the four nokis of the ward, and charmes the samen, and theirby haillis the guidis, and preservis thame from the lunsaucht [lung disease] and all vther diseasis, and thow forbiddis to cast faill or divett [cut turf] thereon, or put plewis therin; and this thow did in the Manis of Innes, in the Manis of Caddell, and in dyvers vtheris places' (SCM I, 120).

Halyman. The Halyman's Rig, like the Guidman's Croft, was left uncultivated in his honour but it was originally the plot of the guid mennis or fairies. Halyman is similar to Wallaway (a Shetland devil), Walliman and Wallidraggle. All probably derive from G. *gal* 'flame, kindred, slaughter, valour', so 'hunter'. The original guidmen were fairies and in the plural.

Hynd Knicht: see The Guidman.

Hind Etin was a fairy in a ballad. Perhaps G. *cinneadh* 'clan, tribe, kin' and *aodhan* 'fire'. The Red Etin was a giant (a beacon).

Hangie, Auld. G. *caingeann* 'prayer, supplication'.

Hornie, Auld Hornie. The Devil as a horned beast. The only example of a horned devil.

Hule. G. *chùil* 'nook (deer trap)'. Perhaps the same as Halyman (above).

Mahoun. Mohammed was believed to be an evil pagan god.

Mishanter, The. G. *mi-sheun* 'ill-luck, misfortune'. A curse: 'Go to the mishanter!'

Nick, Auld Nick. Is this G. *nighean* 'daughter'?

Nickieben. A female name, G. *nighean* 'daughter' + *ban* 'fire'. cf the witch alias NicNiven and the common 'devil' name Auld Nick.

Plotcock 'wee Pluto'.

Robin son of Artes, known in Ireland in the fourteenth century (Murray 1921, 154). G. *art, airt* 'God'.

Rougie, Auld. G. *ruaig* 'pursuit, hunt, chase'. Sc. *ruggair* 'depredator (hunter)'. Sc. *rugging* 'conveys the idea of rapacity in seizing and carrying off the property of others'. The *rugged* property was originally deer belonging to the Cailleach.

Ruffie, Auld. Sc. *ruffy* 'tallow candle, blaze used for fishing by night'.

Sandie, Auld Sandie. G. *seantaidh* 'primeval, primitive (hunting lore)'.

Sim, Simmie. G. *simid* 'mallet, beetle', used by hunters to stun animals prior to cutting their throats.

Smith, The Auld. G. *gobhainn* 'smith' is a regular pun on *gamhainn* 'stag, stirk'.

Sorra, The. This is more likely to be G. *soraidh* 'success, health, happiness' than E. *sorrow*.

Suitie, Sawtan, Sathan. A Biblical name, found in the Book of Job, where God speaks out of a whirlwind. The Gaels would understood it as *samh* 'to gather' + *teine* 'fire'.

Tary, The G. *tarbh* 'bull' or *tòir* 'pursuit, chase'.

Thief, the Auld Thief, the Muckle Thief. A thief was conventionally a hunter.

Thrummy or **Thrummy-Caip**. Scots 'shaggy cap', made of thrums or weavers' ends. Ellen Gray when in prison in Aberdeen was visited by 'an agit man, beirdit, with a quhyt gown and a thrummit hatt'. He told her she was 'ane evill trublit woman, who should forgif all creature and trust in God and a good assise'. He sounds more like a prison chaplain than a visitor from the Pit.

Wallaway or **Wallowae**, a name for the Devil in Shetland. Perhaps G. *galabhas* from *gal* 'flame' + *bàs* 'death', 'hunter', now 'glutton, flatterer' in a typical late inversion of the original sense. Wallowae is also cognate to *Gilledubh* 'servant of the deer'; perhaps a *gille* tended a fire. In Sanday c.1750 he was 'de muckle black Wallawa'.

Walliman, another version of the name of the Devil in Orkney. G. *gal* 'flame, kindred, slaughter, valour'. The same as Halyman, a Lowland name for the devil (below).

Wee Man, The.

Wirricow or **Wurricoe**, a demon or bogle. G. *mire-chatha* 'battle-frenzy'. G. *mire* 'play, pastime; mirth, sportiveness, merriment, rapture, ecstasy' describes the feelings aroused by the sabbat and by the hunt.

6 Gaelic names for the Devil (Campbell, 2001, 160 and many other sources)

Like his virgin mother the Cailleach, the Devil, with his blackness, roughness and burning eyes is an evolved personification of a hunt beacon. When he is vanquished in a Gaelic folk-tale he flies up the chimney in a puff of smoke or disappears in a flame of fire. Only two of those listed are Biblical in origin. It appears that the link between the Devil and the Adversary was not made by the Gaels until the Reformation. Several others are generic concepts for evil or misfortune which might be translated as 'Devil' in English but do not carry the same weight in Gaelic. G. *braman* 'misadventure', *breamas* 'mischief, mischance', *donas* 'mischief, harm, bad luck' and *mi-sheun* 'ill-luck, misfortune' are used in curses which mean 'Bad luck take you!' but which might be translated as 'Go to the devil!' Where the hero of a Lowland tale confronts and outwits a sinister black man with cloven feet, horns and a tail, his Gaelic counterpart faces a *duin-uasal* 'gentleman' or a 'shifty' or 'pranky' lad who plays tricks on him.

Abharsair E. *adversary*. Biblical.

Aibhisteir, An t- 'the one from the abyss', from *aibheis* 'an abyss, a depth' (the pit of Hell). Biblical.

Ainspiorad, An t- 'the bad spirit'.

Andras 'fury, devil'. G. *dreos* 'blaze'.

Aon fhear mor, An 'the one big one'.

Art, the father of an Irish devil. Said to mean 'god'.

Balkin 'lord of the northern mountains'; a beacon. According to Reginald Scot (1584), Balkin was an urisk in Sutherland, Caithness and the adjacent islands, 'who was reputed to be a giant and the father of the fairies.' He also says that the fairies of Orkney spoke an archaic form of Gaelic. Balkin is a diminutive of AG. *bal* 'fire' and of G. *ball* 'penis'. Giants are invariably beacons; the 'father' of the fairies was a hunt beacon.

Bidein 'biter', the serpent. G. *bid* 'fence, hedge' suggests the older meaning is 'deer-trap'.

Bochdainn 'poverty; trouble; mischief; bad luck; mishap'. G. *bochd* 'fire'.

Bodach 'old churl, bogle'. G. *bod* 'penis'.

Bradaidh 'thief; a hunter'.

Braman 'misadventure, mischief'.

Brian 'angel' (bright fire); archangel; god; god of evil'. Equated with the Black Lad of Kilmallie, Son of the Bones, a son of the Maiden who conceived him when impregnated by the ashes of dead men's bones. He is also said to be the son of Bride. Brian was also the name of St Michael's white horse. Brian was perhaps the most important manifestation of the Devil among the Gaels but was displaced or destroyed by the Archangel Michael.

Ciseal, from G. *cìs* 'homage, reverence'.

Connan 'hunting fire'. Kilichonan in Rannoch. G. *connan* 'lust' is secondary, hence *aisling chonnain* 'sexual dream'. Cill Chonain in north Skye (NG2261) was a beacon site close to Dun Borrafiach ('fire of the deer'), a broch (NG2363). A traditional verse, 'The Three Winds', links Connan with fire.

Dana 'the evil one'. As *Donas*.

Deamhan E. *demon*. G. *deamh* 'want, deficiency'.

Diabhal G. *dia* 'god' + AG. *bal* 'fire'. cf Lucifer 'light bearer'.

Dithean 'killer', from G. *dith* 'die, perish'.

Dolas mor, An 'great sorrow'.

Domhnall Dubh 'Black Donald', for AG. *domhnach* 'deer forest' + *dubh* 'deer'.

Donas 'wickedness, misfortune, bad luck' probably a recent evolution from G. *dòmhnaich* 'deer-forest, domain, world'. The witch alias Cassindonisch or *Cas-an donais* from Easter Ross (1577), said to mean 'Devil's foot' (Sutherland, 1977, 132) but closer to 'hunt of the forest or domain'.

Droch Spioraid, An 'the bad spirit'.

Fear dubh, Am 'black man' or 'man of the deer'.

Fear nach abair mi, Am 'the one I will not mention'.

Fear nach fhiach, Am 'the worthless one'.

Fear ud, Am 'yon one'.

Gille dubh 'servant of the deer'; the Black Lad.

Gille neumh 'holy lad' or 'servant of the deer sanctuary' (Campbell, vol. II, 318). 'A pranky man', full of tricks.

Glisoganach 'the shimmering one' of Strathtay. He was tall and dark and had a single glittering eye (Kennedy, 1927, 46) which identifies him as a beacon.

Goillin or **Goiline**, an Irish term for the Devil. Related to G. *goileam* 'to kindle fire', *goill* 'war, fight (hunt)', *goilean* 'greedy-gut'.

Mac an Rusgaich 'lad of the frays'. G. *ruisgeanta* 'fond of fighting (hunting)'.

Mac Mallachd 'the hairy lad', perhaps referring to a wild bull; also found as Mac mollachd 'the son of cursing' or G. *mol* 'assembly, gathering'. *Mac* may be *magh* 'plain' referring to the deer-forest.

Mogh, Magh or **Mabh** 'the chief fairy in Ireland'.

Muc Mhór Dhubh 'the big black pig' (Mackenzie 1935, 52), perhaps originally 'the big deer forest'. The equivalence of *magh* 'deer forest' and *muc* 'pig, devil' might explain the pork taboo in the Highlands. The Devil usually had a horse's hoof but sometimes he had a pig's trotter (Campbell, 1900, 290-2).

Muisean 'a mean or sordid fellow, ramscallion (hunter)'.

Piullaidh, for *peallaidh*, in Lewis. 'The hairy one' (Mackenzie 1935, 234).

Reabhach 'crafty, tricky person'. *an Riabhach mòr* 'the great brindled one' identifies him as a stag.

Rosad, An 'the mean mischievous one'.

7. Pagan personal names

Sources: Mackinlay 1910, 1914; Black 1946.

Three classes of Gaelic personal names can be identified: the Gille names, the Maol names and the Mac-Ean names. The first two belong to the late-pagan/early Christian period, when religion in Scotland was controlled by Culdee priests but under the influence of Christianity. They were sufficiently aware of Christianity to adapt in some ways, in particular by inventing a horde of local 'saints' such as Brandan, Ethernan, Marnan and Cyr who represented existing objects of worship such as local beacons. It is possible that in the tortuous evolution of early Christianity the creation of patron saints was inspired by the existing personification of tribal beacons as larger-than-life protective entities to be propitiated and supplicated. It is certainly true that the New Testament contains several 'saints' with 'beacon' names such as John, Jonas, Stephen, Agnes, Mary, Ann, Lazarus and Luke and that such names must be older than the books.

Beacon saints of both types survived into feudal times as parish patrons and many are still known today. Some come from written sources, showing that the Culdees acquired a degree of literacy. Mackinlay divides them in to Scriptural and non-Scriptural saints but in Scotland there is no essential difference. Their selection was in all cases based on a convenient pun. And in most cases the pun can be tied to an appropriate feature of a hunt.

The Gille names and the Maol names were dedicatory names appropriate to hunters and continued to be used into the middle ages by the Gaelic feudal elite and by more remote native clans. Their dedicatory nature is confirmed by the note given by Black in connection with the Maol name, Malise. It was used by a tanist of the MacLeans who is said to have had this name given him as his *ainm rathaid* or 'road name' (Black 1946, 578). More probably it was his *ainm raidh* 'name of his rank' as a hunter, from G. *raidh* 'rank, as of soldiers'. A Maol name marked him as the top-ranking hunter in his group.

7.1 The *Gille* names

The Gille names, a class of Gaelic personal name, appear to be dedicatory names given to hunters to mark their initiation, as 'great witches' were given new names when they were initiated. In time the Gille names became hereditary in families – in other words, they became standard surnames of English type – but early feudal records show that elite fathers and their sons each had a personal Gille name. Despite an occasional Christian gloss, which may reflect the syncretic tendencies of the Culdees, these are pagan names, used by hunters, which were still in use by the Gaelic elite in the middle ages. We can decode them in terms of hunting, fire and related topics.

The associated 'saints' may be local inventions based on hunting puns or they may be orthodox calender saints whose names create an appropriate pun with Gaelic, such as 'Cyric' and 'Constantine'. These native names reveal an unexpected degree of erudition. The survival of this host of spurious 'saints' shows that this pagan naming tradition and the organisation responsible for it (the Culdee priesthood) continued to be influential in the Christian period, even after the advent of the feudal church, despite the fact that its literacy was limited and its beliefs very unorthodox.

The *Gille* names are of unknown antiquity but were certainly used by the

Pictish hunters who ride with their hounds across the carved stones of the Dark Ages. Like the crosses and Biblical scenes on the stones, the Gille names demonstrate the persistence of pagan culture and the minor importance and irrelevance of the so-called Early Christian Church in Scotland. These hunters were not Christian, even when they were called Gillechrist. Christ was probably seen as a powerful patron. The persistence of pagan practice in early Christian Scotland is also shown by the number of *Gille* names used by churchmen whose names appear in early documents.

For the most part the saints of Gaelic Scotland are fabulous creatures who have no existence outside parish mythology. According to the fabulists, these early Scottish 'saints' were capable of even greater supernatural feats than witches and fairies: they could curse and cure, foretell the future, create light, fly through the air, sail across the sea on stones, control wind and weather, prophesy, see visions, and change shape. Now that we can begin to decode these elements we can see that the Lives of Scottish saints represent another redaction of the same archaic Gaelic hunting and beacon lore, but with added details that confirm they were compiled by people closer to the original source and undisturbed in their beliefs. As we see with the forced replacement of the White Hind of the Hopes with the equally spurious St Catherine, the replacement or conversion of native pagan elements into 'saints' still allowed pagan fire-worship and much else to continue virtually unchanged until the Reformation. The Gille names show a native Gaelic elite preoccupied with hunting and with beacons, not with religion.

The *Gille* names are relatively easy to interpret which suggests that they are relatively recent and that they were invented or created for each individual. Those listed below may be no older than the late pagan (Pictish) period when the native clergy, the Culdees, adopted several features of Christianity. But this did not include Christian names: the Gaels did not use sacred names as personal names.

G. *gille* is usually understood to mean 'youth, bachelor'. This probably derives from the Gille names which appear to be given to the elite of initiated hunters. But there are other GL words with more archaic meanings: *gal* 'smoke or blast of flame', *gal* 'kindred', *gal* 'hunting, slaughter', *gal* 'valour', *geal* 'white, bright, radiant' (E. *yellow*), *gile* 'whiteness', *goil* 'smoke; battle (hunt-beacon)'. Since the Gille names are associated with an elite they suggest a gille was a man who was responsible for maintaining and lighting a beacon. Analysis of the names supports this.

Gille-acad. G. *ach* 'hunt'. 'Servant of the hunt'.

Gille-adhamhnain, G. *aodhan* 'fire'. See Gille-eoin. Surname Macgillauenan.

Gille-aldan. G. *alltan* 'height (deer drop)'.

Gille-andrais, -endres. G. *ain* 'fire'; *dreos* 'blaze'. St Andrew. Surname Gillanders.

Gille-aodran. G. *aodhair* 'fiery conflagration'. St Ernan, Ethernan, Odhran.

Gille-assald. G. *aos* 'fire'; *alt* 'high place', so perhaps 'beacon site'.

Gille-bain. -vane, -vean, -waine. G. *bàn* 'white (fire)'. St Beathan or Bean.

Gille-baoithein. G. *baothan* 'young fellow, hunter' or *baith* 'lure, decoy'. St Baithene. Surname MacGilboythin in Dumfriesshire.

Gille-bar. Archaic G. *bar* 'fire'. St Barr, Finbarr.

Gille-baran, -vernan. Archaic G. *bar* 'fire'.

Gille-beorht. A Saxon rendering of G. *braight* 'hill used as a beacon site'. Cognate with Gille-vride.

Gille-barchane, -berchan, -bharquhane. G. *bearg* 'champion'. St Berchan.

Gille-bethoc, -beathag. G. *beath* 'blood'; *beathach* 'beast, animal (prey)'.

Gille-beil, -veil, -voyle. G. *boile* 'madness, rage, frenzy' applied to a fire, or G. *béillich* 'blubber-lips; having thick lips (an initiated hunter)'. The McGilveils were a sept of Clan Cameron.

Gille-brenenich, -vrenenich, -vrindie. G. *bhriananich* 'of the great fire'. Brian (not a saint).

Gille-bride, -vride, -vreed. G. *braight* 'hill used as a beacon'. St Bride. The new witch attending her first sabbat was 'the Bride' (W.G. Stewart, 1822, 173). See Gille-beorht.

Gille-buidhe. Archaic G. *buidhe* 'fire', buidheann 'troop (of hunters)'.

Gille-callum, -caluim, -callan, -colman. G. *gal* 'smoke; blast or flame of straw; kindred; warfare (hunting); slaughter; valour'. Sts Callan, Callin, Columba and Colman (there were 218 saints called Colman). Mac-ille-Challum is the patronymic of the Macleods of Raasay.

Gille-canniche, -whinnich. G. *coinneachadh* 'meeting, gathering'. St Cainnech or Kenneth was an invented contemporary of St Columba. See Gille-hench.

Gille-carrach, -garrich. G. *carraidh* 'conflict, strife (hunting)'.

Gille-catan -chatain. G. *cath* 'hunt'. St Catan. Clan Chattan were hunters.

Gille-catfar. Perhaps G. *cath* 'hunt' + **far* 'light', to give 'hunt beacon'. St Catfarch was a Welsh saint.

Gille-chad. G. *cadha* 'narrow pass (deer ambush)'. St Chad. He is associated with the *cadha* at Kenmore.

Gille-chomedy, -condad. G. *coimhead* 'watch, keep, preserve'.

Gille-chriosd. G. *crios* 'sun'. This name shows Christian influence but an enlightened Gael would understand *criosd* to mean 'bright light'. Surname Gilchrist.

Gille-ciar, -ciaran, -gar, -ger. G. *cèir* 'wax (fire)' or G. *ciar* 'dusky'. The 'Dusky Lad' of Gaelic fiction, also known as Brian, was fire personfied. St Ciaran. With or without a locative suffix.

Gille-clery. G. *clearc* 'bright, radiant, shining'. Gyloclery, father of Morgund, earl of Mar, 1171.

Gille-comgan, -conal, -congall, -cunil, -quhome. G. *comh* 'to gather' + *gall* 'fire'. Sts Comgal, Comgan, Congall, Connan. Connan was a name of the Devil. The Glengarry McDonalds worshipped an object known as the Coan, thought to have been a statue of their patron saint.

Gille-costentyn. Archaic G. *cas* 'hunt' (as E. *chase*) + *teine* 'fire'. St Constantine is an approximation.

Gille-crum. G. *crum* 'bent object (deer trap)'. The pagan figure known as Crom cruach 'trap of the round-up' or Crom dubh 'trap of the deer' was a pagan god, celebrated in Lochaber at Easter and in Ireland on the first Sunday in August. He was addressed as follows: *Di-Dòmhnaich crum-dubh, plaoisgidh mi an t-ùbh*. Literal English: 'On crooked black Sunday, I'll shell the egg'. Restored original version: 'Crooked one of the deer-forest, give me a spell for a blaze'. *domhain* 'domain, tribal deer-forest'; *plaosgadh* 'flash, blaze'; *ub* 'spell, charm, incantation'.

Gille-dawie, -due, -duff, -ghuie, -wie. Archaic G. *damh*, *dubh* 'deer'.

Gille-donagart. G. *domhnach* 'domain, tribal deer-forest' + *gart* 'enclosure, deer-trap'. St Domangart of Co. Antrim, Ireland, is a manifestation of this.

Gille-downie, -doneng, -duin. Either archaic G. *dubhanach* 'abounding in deer' or G. *domhnach* 'domain, deer-forest'. The Downie Hills were deer-forest. In Christian terms *domhnaich* 'of the Lord'.

Gille-ean. G. *ain* 'fire'. St John. Also Ewan, Ivan.

Gille-easpuig. G. *ess* 'death' + *buic* 'of the buck'. Somehow equated with E. *bishop*.

Gille-eis. G. *ess* 'death (of deer)'. Said to be Iosa 'Jesus'.

Gille-ethueny, -eoin, -eonain, -ewnan. G. *aodhan* 'fire'. St Adamnan, Ethny (mother of Columba), John, Iain, Ewen, Ethernan.

Gille-fad, -fod, -fud. G. *fad* 'kindle'; *faith* 'heat, warmth'.

Gille-faolain. G. *falanach* 'pertaining to blood'. St Fillan, son of Kentigeran 'Great Lady'.

Gille-feargain. Perhaps 'fire cairn'. St Feargna.

Gille-feddell. G. *feudail* 'booty, prey, spoil (of the hunt)'.

Gille-fedder. G. *fiadh* 'deer' + locative suffix; *fiadhaire* 'wilderness (deer forest). St Peter. The second element in Balquhidder 'settlement in the deer forest'. Surnames Paterson, Paton, Patullo, Peat, Peterson, Petrie, Butter, etc.

Gille-fersane. Archaic G. **fer* 'fire' + **san* 'to gather. Christianised as E. *parson* which is not entirely daft as a parson was also responsible for the local beacon.

Gille-fin, -gunnin, -guyn, -winnin. G. *fionn* 'white (light)'. Sts Findbar, Finnen.

Gille-girig. G. *greigh* 'herd'. St Cyricus or Cyrus, an orthodox Continental saint found in a calendar.

Gille-glas. G. *glas* 'light, bright (fire)'. The 'Grey Lad' of Gaelic fiction.

Gille-gorm. G. *gorm* 'great, illustrious'. Macgillegorm in Argyll and Arran. 'Gillegorm was a hero of the Maclennans' (Black 1946, 496).

Gille-grewer. G. *greigh* 'herd'. St Gregor or Gregory, an imported feudal name.

Gille-gunnin: see Gille-fin.

Gille-hagga, -hagie. archaic . *cag 'to hag or chop, to butcher (to hunt)', as Sc. haggis. St Mochuda. Some of the name were vassals to the Bishop of Glasgow.

Gille-haugh. From Eochaid 'Hugh'. G. *aodh* 'fire'.

Gille-helichy. G. *ceileadh* 'purloining (hunting)'; *ceileach* 'martial (to do with hunting)'.

Gille-hench. Probably G. *coinneachadh* 'meeting, gathering'. See Gille-cannich.

Gille-herran: see Gille-ciaran.

Gille-lane: see Gille-faolain. Gilbert McGillelane was Captain of Clan Connan in Galloway in reign of David II. Surname Maclellan.

Gille-magu. G. *magh* 'deer-forest'. St Mochuda. See Gille-hagga.

Gille-makessoc. G. *magh* 'deer forest' or *mo* 'to gather' + *ces* 'spear (beacon signal)' or archaic G. *cas* 'to hunt'. A hunting beacon. St Kessog. As his cult is limited to Luss, Dunbartonshire, and Callander, Perthshire, he probably represents a beacon on Beinn Bhreac (NS4296), midway between them, which was lit to announce a hunt in the Trossachs.

Gille-malloch, G. mal 'king, prince, champion, soldier'; the Mallochs of south Lochtayside were an elite family of Clan Gregor, ancestors of the Balhaldie line of chiefs. Or perhaps G. *mol* 'flock, assembly, gathering'; in both cases badly translated as *moloch* 'hairy, rough'.

Gille-manthach, -vantach, -mantic, -vantic. G. *meantachd* 'good luck, happiness, bliss'. Not *mannatch* 'stuttering'.

Gille-marnoch, -martin, -moire, -varnoch. Archaic G. *mar* 'to hunt'. St Marnock. See Gille-vernock.

Gille-màrtuinn. Gille-màrtuinn is the fox, a shape-changing animal. St Martin.

Gille-melooc. Archaic G. *mo 'to gather' and G. *loich* 'torch'. St Moluag.

Gille-michell. No evident Gaelic meaning. St Michael, may have replaced Brian. G. *aingeal* 'bright light, fire, messenger'.

Gille-min. G. *min* 'fine grazing'.

Gille-modan, -modyn, -motha. G. *meadhon* 'hunt gathering'. St Modan.

Gille-mour, -muir. Archaic G. *mar* 'hunt'. St Mary.

Gille-mowband. A fool in time of James V.

Gille-nain, -nein, -nef, -new. G. *naomh* 'holy, sacred (deer forest)'. St Ninian.

Gille-odran. Archaic G. *aodhairean* 'conflagration, beacon'. St Odran.

Gille-onie, -onvie, -onfhaidh. G. *ain* 'fire' + *fiadh* 'deer'. An old sept of Clan Cameron. Not 'servant of storm'.

Gille-patrick. G. *peithir* 'game warden, forester (hunter)'. St Patrick is a diminutive of Peter.

Gille-peddir. G. *peithir* 'game warden, forester (hunter)'. St Peter, equated with Patrick.

Gille-quhangzhie. G. *fang* 'fold, pen, prison'.

Gille-ravie, revie. G. *riabhach* 'brindled'. The Devil.

Gille-riach, -rie. G. *riadh* 'snare'.

Gille-roth, rowth, ruadh, ruth. G. *ruagh, ruith* 'pursuit, chase'. A legendary ancestor of the Camerons.

Gille-roy. G. *ruaidh* 'red'. A 'red-haired lad' is a signal fire.

Gille-schenoch. G. *seannach* 'fox; hunter (one who rounds up)'. St Seanoch.

Gille-seathain. G. *sithean* 'hunters'. Black locates the surname MacGhillesheathanaich in Jura, Islay and Seill. The late Hector Maclean of Islay understood Gillesheathanaich to mean 'servant of the hunter' (Personal and Tribal names among the Gaels, 11). St Seghine.

Gille-serf. G. *searb* 'theft, larceny'. A serf or servant was a hunt follower; the Gilleserfs were Culdees from St Serf's monastery on the isle of Loch Leven (12c).

Gille-talargyb. G. *tallair* 'thief, robber': a common name for a hunter. St Talorgan. Surname Taylor. The meaning appears to be 'butcher'.

Gille-thomas, -quham, -quhome, -wham. G. *tomhais* 'to measure'. St Thomas.

Gille-uras. G. *ur* 'fire' + *as* 'kindle a fire'. cf Gillefad.

Gille-vane: see Gille-bain.

Gille-vantic: see Gille-manthach.

Gille-veil, -voyle: see Gille-beil.

Gille-venna. Probably G. *bàn* 'white (fire)'. Black offers Meana which would mean 'hunt meet'.

Gille-vernock. Perhaps Gille-bhearnaig (Black, 515) then G. *bearnan* 'tribal lands, tribal deer-forest.' St Marnock, Ernan. See also Gille-marnock.

Gille-vie, -wie. G. fiadh 'deer'.

Gille-vray, -voray. G. *brath* 'destruction (hunting)', or 'conflagration'. Dwelly says the conflagration is imaginary, but he gives *brathadair* 'great fire, kindling, fuel'.

Gille-vrenenich: see Gille-brenenich.

Gille-vride: see Gille-bride.

Gille-whannell: see Gille-congall.

A small number of *Gille* names are not known as personal names.

Gille-boidhre 'the fox' (a hunter). G. *boidhe* 'yellow'.

Gille-caluim. A Highland dance (also known as the sword dance) in which the dancer imitates a stag.

Gille-cas-fluich 'servant wet-foot', the attendant of a chieftain who carried him across water.

Gille-bhrighde 'oyster-catcher', a black and white bird of the shore and field.

Gille-craigein 'frog, toad'.

Gille-driuchd 'sun-dew'. 'Servant of the druid'.

Gille-sguain 'train, tail (of hunters)'.

Gille-trypes 'servant of the troops, or herds'. The name of an indecent dance and 'ane foul Hieland sang' banned repeatedly in Moray in the eighteenth century. Not known as a personal name.

7.2 The *Maol* names

The Maol names are a subset of the *Gille* names which use *Maol* instead of *Gille*. Black rejects the interpretation of *Maol* as 'tonsured' in favour of G. *mal* 'king, prince, champion'. Four of the nineteen *Maol* names so far found do not have matching *Gille* names, but are not otherwise different. This suggests that the Gille names and the Maol names were in use at the same time, *Maol* being used by those of senior status and *Gille* by junior hunt-followers.

Maol-aechin. G. *aighean* 'deer (pl)'. Not found as a Gille name.

Maol-anfaid. cf Gille-on fhaidh.

Maol-beth. cf Gille-bethoc.

Maol-bride. cf Gille-bride.

Maol-colm. cf Gille-challum.

Maol-dubh. cf Gille-dubh.

Maol-donych. cf Gille-downie. Maoldomhnaich, G. *domhan* 'domain, deer-forest', not Domhnach 'Sunday'. Perhaps the original name of Christsunday. A favorite name of the early earls of Lennox.

Maol-girg. cf Gille-girig.

Maol-ise. G. Iosa 'Jesus'. Found among the old earls of Strathearn and in clan MacLean.

Maol-micheil. cf Gille-micheil.

Maol-modan. cf Gille-modan.

Maol-moran. G. *moran* 'great number' (of animals). Not found as a Gille name.

Maol-mure, -muir. cf Gille-muir.

Maol-otheny. cf Gille-ethueny. Mallethny was a serf of the Abbey of Dunfermline in the thirteenth century. His family origins may have been among the Culdees of Loch Leven.

Maol-otishok. G. *toiseach* 'leader'. Not found as a Gille name.

Maol-patric. cf Gille-patrick.

Maol-peter. cf Gille-peddir.

Maol-snecte. A pun between G. *sneachd* 'snow' and *snaidh* 'hew, cut, slash'. Not found as a Gille name.

Maol-pol. G. *beoll* 'fire'. Not found as a Gille name. St Paul.

7.3 The Mac-In names

The third category of Gaelic personal name with a ritual context is the Mac-In names. These names mainly identify families of professional men or craftsmen who worked in the late medieval period for native chiefs or for the feudal lords who replaced them. Many of them have a link with hunting.

Mac-in-ally. A member of a bardic family, G. *olaimh*.

Mac-in-dene, Denson. A member of the family of James MacGregor, Dean of Lismore, d.1540. The Dennisons were for at least five generations notaries at Fortingall.

Mac-in-deor. A Dewar, G. *deoir*, was the lay guardian of a sacred object, notably the five relics of St Fillan which were kept by five families of Dewars in Strathfillan, Perthshire.

Mac-in-esker: a member of the fishermen of Loch Tay. As the Gaels did not eat fish, this may refer to a special caste who supplied fish to the local Christian clergy as a penitential food.

Mac-in-espik. A member of the family of the bishop: but the original Gaelic meant 'watchman'; cf Gr. *episcopos* 'one who looks over'.

Mac-in-futtir. A professional hunter, G. *peither* 'forester, game warden'.

Mac-in-leich. A professional doctor or leech, G. *leigh*, used by members of the Beaton family.

Mac-in-leister. A professional arrow-maker, G. *leisdear*, borrowed from Fr. *flechier*. He used feathers.

Mac-in-malloch. G. *mol* 'flock, gathering', again professional hunters.

Mac-in-roy. G. *ruadh* 'red, fire'. A local family of watchmen or constables.

Mac-in-stalker. A professional hunter, G. *stalcair* 'hunter, fowler, deer-stalker; arrow-maker'.

Mac-in-taylor. G. *tallair* 'thief, robber (hunter)', probably a professional butcher; as Fr. *tailler* 'to cut, shape'. Equated with Mcintyre.

Mac-in-tosh. G. *toisich* 'leader, nobleman'. The Macintosh clan was a very old native group.

Mac-in-turner. Too early to be E. *turner*. Probably another family of hunters or butchers.

Mac-in-tyre. *Mac an-t-saoir* is always said to mean 'carpenter' but it means 'one who saws' and might also mean 'butcher'. In Perthshire it was equated with Taylor, G. *tallair* 'thief (hunter)'.

8 The Banners of the Fian

Another set of very archaic 'hunting' names is now known as the Banners of the Fian. None of them have anything in common with the nicknames of the witches but respond to interpretation in terms of archaic Gaelic. E. *banner* is from the same source as G. *bann* 'proclamation' and G. *ban* 'white, pale', in archaic Gaelic, a signal fire. A banner in an archaic or poetic context may be understood as a signal used by hunters in the form of a beacon or a hunting-shout. In Gaelic a banner is *bratach, suaicheantas* or *meirghe*. The first two terms are heraldic. G. *bratach* is a flag; the Fairy Flag of Dunvegan is *bratach-shith*. G. *suaicheantas* is a small flag or ensign. But G. *meirghe* has the same root as *meirle* 'robber, hunter' and can mean either 'flag, pennant etc', 'troop, band (of hunters)' or 'signal'.

Names come from *The Book of the Dean of Lismore* (c.1500), Donald Meek's article, 'The Banners of the Fian' (Cambridge Medival Celtic Studies 11, 29-48, 1986), and Dwelly's Gaelic dictionary (1901).

The Gaelic is archaic and fanciful, often obscure or open to more than one interpretation but guesswork is made more reliable by the predictable association of these names with hunting, for the Fian, whose banners they were, were deer-hunters. *Coinneal Chatha, Geal Ghreine* and many others may be hunting shouts (see below). A sun beam is a metaphor for a beacon signal. Though collected in Ireland, like the Fian these names are probably Scottish.

Aoin-Cheannach Oir. The banner of Raighne (Meek). G. *aodhan* 'fire', *ceann* 'deer trap'. *Ceann* is any round enclosure so also 'vulva'.

Aon Chosach, Aon Chasach Ruadh or **Ruagh** (Meek). G. *aodhan* 'fire' + *còs* 'recess (deer trap, vulva)' + *ruadh* 'red'. G. *caise* 'privy parts of a female' derives from G. *cas* 'deer trap (vulva)', related to E. *chase*.

Bearna an Réabhain. The banner of Osgar mac Garaidh (Meek). G. *beàrn* 'gap, crevice (deer trap, vulva)' of 'the crafty one' (the Lady); cf. *reabhair* 'crafty fellow', ie, a hunter.

Bhriachail-Bhròchuil: (Meek). G. *breac* 'the speckled ones (deer)' + *bròcail* 'mangle, spoil, lacerate (kill)'. Like Fr. *bric-à-brac* 'a collection of ancient objects of little value' and E. *helter-skelter, mish-mash, mixter-maxter, pell-mell, raggle-taggle, tapsalteerie, topsy-turvy* &c. it refers to the chaotic circumstances of the kill at the end of a successful deer-drive.

Brochaill 'banner of Gaul son of Morni' (Dwelly 1901, 126). G. *bròcail* 'mangle, spoil, lacerate (kill)'. As above.

Coinneal Chatha. The banner of Faolan (Meek). 'Light of the hunt'. G. *coinneal* is the same word as E. *candle*.

Craobh Fhuileach. The banner of Clann Mhic Lughaich (Meek). 'Fire of blood, or of the kindred'. In archaic Gaelic *craobh* is 'fire', in modern Gaelic it is 'tree'. G. *fuil* 'blood; family, tribe', *fuileach* 'bloody, gory'.

Dealbh-Ghréine. The banner of Fionn (Meek). 'Image of the sun or fire'. The reference is to a fire as bright as the sun. See Deo-Ghreine.

Deo-Ghréine 'sun-beam' (Meek). A ray of light from a beacon. Fionn's banner. See Dealbh-Ghreine.

Dubh-Nimhe 'deer-forest', the banner of Caoilte mac Reatha (Meek). G. *dubh* for *damh* 'stag' and *nimhe* 'sacred area', nemeton, exclusion zone, game preserve or deer-forest.

Dun Naomhtha, the banner of Oisean (Meek). The enclosure/beacon site of the holy place/exclusion zone.

Fhionn Chosach Ruadh: see Aoin-Cheannach Oir.

Fulang Doghra 'the banner of Goll' (Meek).

Fulang Dorrain 'the banner of Fergus, that is, the banner of one who could sustain a defeat, and play a losing game when necessary' (Dwelly 1901, 464). This interpretation rests on G. *fulang* 'patience' and *dorran* 'anger'. A *fulang* was also a prehistoric cooking place or camp kitchen, found as a mound of burnt stones. G. *dorrain* is probably from *doire* 'deer-forest'. The Gaels seethed their meat in the skin of the animal, using hot stones to heat the water.

Gath-Gréine (Meek). 'Sunbeam' but in archaic hunting terms 'beacon signal'. Also *Gath-Ghreine Mhic Cumhaill*.

Geal Ghreine 'Light of the sun'. To be as bright as the sun was a compliment to a fire.

Geal-Gheugach (Meek). 'Light of the deer'. G. *geug* 'young superfine female, nymph', the Cailleach, but also an archaic word for a deer or for 'a sunbeam', ie. a beacon signal. Also *Geal-gheugach Mhic Cumhaill* (Meek).

Làmh-Dhearg. The banner of Mac Ronain (Meek). 'Red hand' or perhaps 'red blade' referring to a weapon. But G. *lamhach* 'military manoevres, shooting' is 'hunting' in the older language.

Liath Luidhmeach, Liath Luineach or **Luidagach, Lia Luathnach** (Meek). G. *liath* 'grey', in archaic terms 'a light'. G. *luid* 'slovenly or filthy person' was an inverted epithet of the goddess related to *luideach* 'having long hair, like an animal'. The original meaning may be 'dressed in skins' or more simply 'deer'. G. *fogh-luidhe* 'robber, pirate (hunter)'. This might stretch as far as G. *loichead* or *loiche* 'lamp, light, torch'. See note on the witch Ludlam (below).

Lòch Luinneach. The banner of Diarmaid (Meek). G. *loch* is an old word for a V-shaped deer trap and probably also for the vulva.

Sguab Ghábhaidh. The banner of Osgar (Meek). G. *sguab* 'besom, broom', refer to a squat female, to a triangular shape, and to the Lady in the form of a vulva. Triangles play a major role in the decoration of prehistoric textiles and pottery. A candle-snuffer, G. *sguab*, is the same triangular shape. G. *gábhaidh* 'strange, wonderful, terrible, fearful' could also be an old epithet of the goddess.

9 Hunting shouts

Gaelic hunting shouts, once sent around the neighbourhood to alert hunters to a distant beacon, were later used to 'raise the Devil', in Calvinist terms. They survive in considerable numbers as elements of fake folklore but vary considerably in form. In his article on the Banners of the Fian (1986, 32) Professor Meek identifies the 'powerful shout' as a theme in folklore. 'In the course of his encounter, Caoilte emits a great shout which is heard in several of the most famous warrior-centres in Ireland. By this means he obtains a response from other warriors who are presumed to come to the aid of the Fian' and gives several references from Stith Thompson (1955-58) for powerful shouts, used to summon in Irish and other literatures. There is a link between the shouts and musters of hunters and also of rounding up cattle or deer. A remarkable herdsman in Irish myth sits shouting on a mountain top and cows [deer?] come from a great distance at his call (iii, 194 F679.1). A man's voice shakes the heavens in a Chinese story and a man's shout remains in the air for three days in an Irish myth. Noisy storms are giants shouting (iii, 196 F688). The Wild Hunt was heralded by the shout of the huntsmen (E501.13.5).

A bhuacharlain! Carmichael gives a nonsense rhyme about G. *buacharlain,* another name for ragwort which means 'fire plant'. It begins *A bhuacharlain! a bhuacharlain!* 'Fire, fire!' (vol. IV, 121 and note).

Banners of the Fian seem to be either the names of hunting troops, or their hunting shouts. They include **Coinneal Chatha** 'light of the hunt', **Craobh Fhuileach** 'Fire of the kindred', **Dealbh-Ghréine,** 'image of the sun'. **Gath-Gréine**, now 'Sunbeam' but in archaic hunting terms 'beacon signal', **Geal Ghreine** is 'light of the sun' which is a compliment to a fire (see above for several more examples).

Beannaich Aonghais ann san Oirrinn, the shout at Auchtubh in Balquhidder. Another word meaning 'blessed' is found in a place-name at Auchtubh at the east end of Balquhidder Glen in Perthshire. The complete name of this spot is *Beannaich Aonghais ann san Oirrinn,* said to mean 'the Blessing of Angus in the oratory' and it is said that anyone coming into Balquhidder from the east should repeat the words *Beannach Aonghais* at Auchtubh at the spot where Balquhidder glen first comes into view. However it appears to be a hunting shout. This is where a person coming into the glen from the east gets his first sight of the Kirkton where the gathering beacon was lit and where a watcher was posted to look for the beacon, the site being invisible from Auchtubh itself. The Blessing of Angus can be explained rationally as a hunting shout meaning 'The gathering beacon at the fire site!' G. *beannachd* is derived from *ban* 'fire' and *aonach* 'assembly'.

Benedicete Maikpeblis. According to Andro Man's testimony, the two magic words Benedicete and Maikpeblis conjure up Satan and dismiss him again (SCM I, 120, 124). If we take this as Gaelic, Satan can refer to a gathering fire (A.G. **sa* 'to gather' and *teine* 'fire'). To conjure up Satan is to light a beacon (or summon the coven) and to dismis him is to put it out again. *Maikpeblis* could be G. *magh* 'plain, deer-forest', and *pobull* 'tribe'. In that case 'Benedicete Maikpeblis' would mean 'Gathering fire of the tribal deer-forest', a hunting shout raised when the hunt beacon was lit to mobilise the troops. There has been learned editing.

Christsonday. It has been argued elsewhere that this was the name of the personified hunt-beacon on the Bin of Cullen in Banff in 1597. A pun with A.G. *crios* 'beacon, fire'and G. *domhan* 'the deer-forest or tribal domain'. G. *dòmhnaich* 'of the deer-forest' is punned with *Dòmhnaich* 'Sunday' which would give the original meaning 'Beacon of the deer-forest', a hunting shout. Sundayswell, Kincardine O'Neill, is found in Strathspey as *Tobar Domhnaich*. *Domhnach* can also mean 'the Church'.

Clan Munro's war-cry or slogan was *Caisteal Folais na Theine*, originally 'Fire at Casle Fowlis'. The slogans of the more authentic clans are generally their hunting shouts.

Loskoir Longert, alias of Mariota Neymaine McAlester, Easter Ross (1577) is a hunting shout meaning 'fire at the hunting lodge' with G. *loisg* 'to burn' and *longhairt* or *luncart* 'hunting lodge'.

Mult dhu an carbhail ghil. Walter Scott, source of so many wildly inaccurate and misleading stories, hung a whole clan battle on a Gaelic proverb: *mult dhu an carbhail ghil*, which he said meant 'The black wedder with the white tail (should never have been lambed)' (Scott 1893.a, 121). Scott promoted the idea that the theft of this animal by two travelling tinkers was the cause of the Battle of Glen Fruin between Colquhouns and MacGregors. In fact the grievance was the theft of Colquhoun livestock by members of Clan Gregor who had been prevented from hunting. Murray MacGregor (1898, 292) pointed out that the word is not *carbhail* but *earball* 'tail, troop of hunters', as E. *tail*. The first word is not *mult* but *milt* 'gathering, raid'; *dubh* is not 'black' but 'deer'; *geal* is not 'white' but 'fire'. The final result is 'The gathering of the deer by the troop of the fire!', a hunting shout or slogan, sent around the area to alert hunters to the fact that the hunt-beacon has been lit and they must report to the muster site. It has no necessary link with Glen Fruin.

Uir! Uir! air sùil Odhrain! The old name of the island, I, is probably G. *aodh* 'light, fire'. According to a nice old story, when building his church on Iona, Columba buried Odhran alive to secure the building. After three days he had the earth removed to see how Odhran fared. He was still alive and famously uttered the words: 'Chan eil am bàs 'na iongantas, no Ifrinn mar a dh'aithrisear', which is taken to mean: 'There is no wonder in death and hell is not as it is reported'. Columba reacted with passion, calling out, according to one version *Uir! Uir! air sùil Odhrain mu'n labhair e tuilleadh còmhraidh*, said to mean 'Earth! Earth! On Oran's eye that he may blab no more' (Henderson, 1911, 282). But it is a hunting shout: 'Fire! Fire! The beacon shows the hunter the signal for a joint hunt!' Among the puns is are *aodhair* 'fiery conflagration', *ùir* 'fire', *sùil* 'beacon, signal', *muin* 'shows, points out', *tul* 'fire', and *còmhraig* 'fight, hunt'. Odhran's Eye or *Sùil odhrain* was presumably a beacon on Mull which was visible from Iona. A hunting shout is less memorable than burying a man alive but covering a fire with earth is one way of putting it out.

10 The English witch Ludlam was a sorceress who lived, with her proverbially lazy dog, in a cave near Farnham, Surrey (Brewer 736). It is possible to explain her name in terms of G. *luid* 'slovenly or filthy person', an epithet of the goddess which refers to conditions at a butchery site. G. *luideach* 'having long hair, like an animal', links her with the *gruagach*. The original meaning of G. *lamhach* 'military manoevres, shooting' is 'hunting, deer-drive'. A related phrase is G. *luchd-lamhachais* 'archers (hunters)'. The dog is another pointer to Ludlam's link with hunting. G. *fogh-luidhe* 'robber, pirate (hunter)'. G. *cridhe luadhainn* 'heart of lead' was a way of divining by pouring molten lead into water.

Brewer also gives Lazy Lobkin, and Lazy Lawrence of Lubberland, said to be from a Scots word *larrence* 'laziness' but Lawrence has a host of links to the deer-forest as a source of plenty. It may be from G. *làrach* 'field of battle' (a deer-forest). Lubberland, an idealised deer-forest, appears to be from G. *lub* 'pudding' or 'roe'. The Land of Plenty is also known as Fiddler's Green, from G. *fiadh* 'deer'. As a 'fire' name, Lawrence can be linked to E. *flare,* and the lazy dog is from the same root as E. *blaze*. G. *lunndach* 'lazy' and *lunndair* 'lazy person' also have links with G. *lunndan* 'green meadow' and G. *lunndraig* 'thump, beat, strike'. The root is G. *lunn* 'to penetrate'. Lubberland, Fiddler's Green, the Dutch Luilekkerland, Fairyland, the Land of Cockaigne, the

Happy Hunting Ground, are all names for the tribal deer-forest which to a hunter was a land of plenty. We can refer Cockaigne to G. *cog* 'carry on war, fight (hunt)'. The same root has given us cakes and cookies.

11 The ùruisg or brownie.

The urisk was a large hairy creature, fond of milk, who is often heard bellowing in the woods, akin to an aurochs or wild bull. G. ùruisg 'being, supposed to haunt lonely and sequestered places, water-god, brownie, diviner, one who foretells future events, savage ugly fellow, sloven, slut, bear'. 'Bear' is an intelligent guess but the ùruisg is the aurochs, remembered from prehistory – or perhaps from quite recent history. A small herd of aurochsen survived in Poland into the seventeenth century where the last cow died in 1627 (Rokosz 2005). Similar animals may have survived later in Highland Scotland where for example they are said to have haunted the Cuillin Hills in Skye (Mackenzie 1935, 186) and Isobell Gowdie in 1662 reported two elf-bulls near Darnaway in Moray, which might have been surviving members of the breed. Some modern researchers believe Highland cattle are part-aurochs.

There were vivid memories of the great wild bulls which used to roam in the mountains of Breadalbane. Armstrong, reporting Perthshire tradition, noted that 'The ùruisg had a peculiar fondness for solitude at certain seasons of the year. About the end of harvest he became more sociable, and hovered about farmyards, stables and cattle-houses. He had a particular fondness for the products of the dairy, and was a fearful intruder on milk-maids who made regular libations of milk or cream to charm him off, or to procure his favour. He is said to have been a jolly personable being, with a broad blue bonnet, flowing yellow hair, and a long walking staff. Every manor-house had its ùruisg, and in the kitchen, close by the fire, was a seat which was left unoccupied for him. He was gainly and good-natured rather than formidable. He was known to perform many arduous exploits in kitchen, barn and stable, with marvellous precision and rapidity. Kind treatment was all he wished for and it never failed to procure his favour. The brownies seldom discoursed with man but they held frequent and affectionate converse with one another. They had their general assemblies too, and on these occasions they commonly selected for their rendezvous the rocky recesses of some remote torrent, whence their loud voices, mingling with the roar of the water, carried to the ears of wondering superstition.'

In other words, an ùruisg is the male of the aurochs, a more or less tame bull whose great interest in the farmyard and cattle-houses is explained by the tame cows who lived there. When he tended to bother the milk-maids, they distracted him by an offering of milk, which a bull likes as well as anyone. He probably did not wear a blue bonnet or sit beside the kitchen fire, but the roaring assemblies in the woods are authentic enough. Every township naturally had its own ùruisg as it had its more or less tame cows. They were let loose in the autumn, spent the winter in the forest, and were rounded up again in the spring, either about to calf or already in milk. There was an obstinate belief that anyone who needed a cow in the Highlands could simply go and catch one, a prehistoric attitude which left a long legacy.

The principal urisks of Breadalbane (Gillies 1938, 340-346).

An ùruisg (from G. *ur* 'fire' and archaic Gaelic *easg* 'to hunt') was originally an aurochs bull but the later memory of these huge creatures incorporates the names of deer traps and local hunters.

Adaidh of Glenlochan G. *aodh* 'fire'. The beacon of Glenlochan.

Amhlagan-dubh. G. *eibh* 'fire', *lagan* 'hollow, trap', *dubh* 'deer'. The fire of the deer trap.

Babaidh an lochan. The fringed one of the lochan.

Brunaidh an easain. G. *ess* 'death'. Beacon of the killing. A 'brownie' was a fire.

Brunaidh an eilein. Beacon ('brownie', burning one) of the island. Isle of Loch Tay?

Caobarlan of Lag an Tairbh Duibh on Drummond Hill. G. *cab* 'indent, notch, mouth ill-set with teeth (a deer trap)'; *eorlain* 'lower part of a glen that closes into a small space (a deer trap)'. The trap of the hollow of the black bull.

Carwhin: The urisk of Carwhin was a splendid weaver equal to six men.

Cas-luath leitir. 'Hunt-beacon of the hill slope.'

Catan ceann-liath. 'The hunt of the principal light'.

Cleitean. G. *cliath* 'battalion', a troop of hunters. In Lowland Scotland Clootie is the Devil.

Cludarlan. G. *clud* 'clout', *eorlain* 'lower part of a glen that closes into a small space'.

Fuath Coire Ghamhnain. 'The giant of the corry of the stags'.

Martain. G. *mart,* an animal killed for winter stores.

Paderlan a Fearnan. G. *peith* 'park, deer-forest'; *eorlain* 'deer trap (as above)'. Deer trap at Fearnan.

Patragan, Peadragan. G. *peith* 'park, deer forest'; *raighe* 'rank or file of soldiers (hunters)'.

Peallaidh an Spuit, a gathering at the Falls of Moness, Aberfeldy. G. *peallaideach* 'dressed in hides'; also *peallag* 'trollop, ragged woman' – a negative view of the Lady.

Sligeachan of Carwhin. G. *sluagh* 'troop of hunters'; *sligheach* 'cunning, sly'; (pun with *slige* 'shell').

Slochdail a chuirt. 'A gathering'. G. *sliochd* 'tribe, clan, hosts; troop of hunters'; *cùirteal* 'honourable, esteemed'.

Truibhas-dubh at Fartairchill. 'Troop of the deer' at Fortingall.

Uisdean or Hugh, for G. *aodhan* 'fire'.

Uruisg dubh more Eas-amhlagan. 'The great black aurochs of the fire-killing'?

12 Gaelic names of Cats (Campbell 1902, 27, 38 and note).

Names of famous hunting bands and hunters (G. *cath*) have been woven into tales about cats.

A Bhruchail Bhreac 'streaked brindled one'. The Foul Brindled one (also the Devil).

Bladrum 'thief', the little black kitten in the ash hole, *an toll na luath*. A black cat or *cat dubh* was a deer hunt, G. *toll* 'crevice, pit', *luath* 'light, fire'; so Bladrum was 'the hunt of the deer trap of or at the light.' G. *bleidir* 'thief'.

Bruc Riabhach 'streaked foul face'. The Foul Fiend (*riabhach* 'the Devil', E. *reiver*.)

An Iuchair Chath 'key of battle'. G. *iuc* 'notch', perhaps a V-shaped deer trap. The Hunt of the Ambush.

Maol Meanachan nan cat 'bald entrails of the hunt' or 'the beacon hill of the hunt'.

Righ nan Cat 'king of the cats'. King of the Hunts or Hunt-master.

An Urchuill earchaill mhor 'great calamity of the hunting trap'. G. *urchail* 'fetters'; *earchaill* 'hindrance'. The Great Fetters (Trap, Snare).

This is also the meaning of 'cat' in the following lines from Gregorson Campbell (Black ed. 192, 142.)

An tu 'n cat fiadht' a bh' aig Fionn, bha fiadhach o ghleann gu gleann?

Are you the untamed troop that Fionn had, that hunted from glen to glen?

No 'n tu bh'aig Osgar là bhlàr sguinn, no 'n tu dh'fhàg suinn fo dhochair ann?

Had Oscar you at the battle of Blair-sguinn, and left you heroes wounded there?

Glossary: *blàr* 'battle (hunt), plain, field (deer-forest)'; *dochair* 'wounded' (stags wounded by the hunt); *cath* 'troop of hunters'; *fiadh* 'deer'; *sguain* 'tail, crowd of followers'; *sonn* 'hero, champion'.

13 Names of English familiars.

The fantastic names given to their familiars by English witches also respond to decipherment in terms of Gaelic. They may be original relics of Gaelic in England or, more probably, they have been borrowed from Scottish sources by fake folklorists in England (cf. the Tewhit or linnet).

Elimanzar or Ilimauzar, 17c., a white dog. G. *eallach* 'battle, herd' + *maon* 'hero (hunter)' + *sar* 'noble, brave'.

Farmara 17c. cf Jarmara. 'who came in like a fat spaniel without any legs at all.'

Fillie, a white cat. G. *pealag* 'a felted cloak worn by hunters'.

Gibbe, a black cat. G. *gibeag* 'largesse, boon'.

Gille, a black cat. G. *gille* 'boy (young hunter)'.

Ginnie, 'a kitlyng or feende'. G. *gin* 'mouth (trap), E. *gin* 'trap'.

Greedigut. 17c. Grizel Greedigut. G. *greidh* 'herd of deer' + *guidhe* 'prayer'.

Hoult, 17c. who came in like a white kittling. G. *cùil* 'nook (deer trap)'. E. *holt* 'otter's den'.

Inges, a black and white cat. G. *innes* 'choice pasture for cattle or deer'.

Jarmara, a red and white cat. G. *iarmart* 'riches, offspring'.

Lierd, a red female cat or imp. G. *léireadh* 'tormenting, wounding, stealing (hunting)'.

Lightfoot, a cat. G. *lucht-fothach* 'people of the wilderness' or hunters.

Lunch, a toad. G. *luan* 'warrior (hunter)' or 'greyhound'.

Makeshift, a weasel. Perhaps G. *magh* 'field of battle, plain (hunting forest)' + *segh* 'wild ox, elk'.

Minny, a red and white dog. G. *minneachan* 'smooth place' ie, 'deer-forest'.

Newes 17c. 'Like a Polecat'. G. *niomhas* 'brightness, clearness'.

Peckin the Crown 17c.

Philip, a rat. As Fillie.

Pyewackett 17c. Perhaps G. *piobach* 'having pipes'. Or was the animal pied?

Robbyn, a toad. A hunter or 'robber'.

Sack n Sugar, 17c. 'like a black Rabbet'. A cat or imp. Perhaps G. *saigheadh-shìth* 'fairy arrow'.

Suckin, a black tom cat or imp. Perhaps the diminutive of G. *saigh* 'arrow'.

Tewhit, 'a yellow bird'. In Orkney it was believed that carrying the bones of a linnet in one's clothing preserved health (Dalyell 1835, 150). The yellow bird like others listed appears to be copied from a Scottish source.

Tissy or Tyttey. G. *titheach* 'pursuing keenly'.

Tom, a toad. G. *tom* 'mound', a fairy mound where signal fires were lit.

Vinegar Tom 17c. 'like a long-legg'd Greyhound, with a head like an Oxe.' Archaic G. *fionn* 'fire' + G. *gar* 'enclosure' + G. *tom* 'knoll'.

Wynoe, a black imp. Archaic G. *fionn* 'fire'.

14 The witches of Ross-shire, 1577

The Commission issued at Holyroodhouse against Catherine Ross on 25 October 1577 (Exchequer Rolls 1899, xx, 522-3) shows that at that date two different naming conventions were in use: Gaelic patronyms which were cumbersome but gave the person a detailed identity, and English surnames which required an address or some other distinguishing information. The Commission lists the names of thirty alleged witches from Easter Ross. Their names have been compiled by an English-speaking clerk using information supplied orally by a number of people with local knowledge. Women also used patronymics (using *Nic* instead of *Mac*) such as *Jonet Neyne Thomas McAllan*, 'Janet daughter of Thomas son of Allan' or *Jonetam Neyne Willelmun McClachan* 'Janet son of William McClachan'. A small minority have Lowland surnames such as Cattanach, Ross, Miller and Forbes. This is in striking contrast to a legal document of 1589 which accuses Hector Munro of Fowlis, step-son of Catherine Ross, of persecuting certain women. The background is still Easter Ross but now the accused women and the male jury all have English sur-names: MacKenzie, Bain, Glas, Cuthbert, Sutherland, Innes, Ross and Mowat (MacKenzie, 1898, 65). This does not mean they had all suddenly learned to speak English.

On 25 October 1577 a Commission of Justice from Holyroodhouse was issued to Walter Urquhart, Sheriff of Cromarty, and Robert Munro of Foulis (Exchequher Rolls vol.20 1568-79, GRH 1899, 522-3). It authorised them to arrest seven men and twenty-three women charged with 'diabolical practices of magic, enchantment, murder, homicide and other offences'. Their names and locations are given below. They acted on instructions from Catherine Ross, Lady Munro, to kill her step-son and sister-in-law by casting elf-arrows at images of butter and clay and, when this failed, using ratsbane (probably hemlock). Several people were poisoned including young Lady Balnagowan. 'The last name is that of Keanoch Ower – Coinneach Odhar as written by a Lowland clerk – who is described as "the leading or principal enchantress", no doubt due to the clerk's inability to distinguish between a male and a female Gaelic name.' He and several others (including Christiane Ross Malcolmson who is not mentioned in the Commission) were tried and executed at Chanonry, probably early in 1578.

Commissio justiciarie facta Waltero Urquhart, vicecomiti de Cromertie, et Roberto Monro de Foulis, conjunctim et divisim ad querendum,

perscrutandum, capiendum et apprehendendum omnes et singulas personas
subscriptas de diabolicis, iniquis, et odiosis criminibus artis magice, incan-
tationis, murthuri, homicidii, aliorumque horribilium criminum et offen-
sionum, infra bondes comitatus Rossie et dominii de Ardmanach ac aliarum
partium infra vicecomitatum de Invernes commissis, suspectus et delitatas,
videlicet.

Commission of justiciary addressed to Walter Urquhart, sheriff of Cromarty,
and Robert Monro of Fowlis, jointly and severally, to search for and apprehend
all or one of the various persons listed, who were accused of diabolical, iniquitous and odious practices of magic, enchantment, murder, homicide and other
offences: committed within the bounds of the earldom of Ross and lordship
of Ardmanach in the sheriffdom of Inverness.

A second commission was found among the Foulis papers.

Commission under the Quarter Seal appointing Lauchlin
Mackintosche of Dunnachtane, Colin Mackenzie of Kintail, Robert
Munro of Foulis, Walter Urquhart, Sheriff of Cromartie, Hugh alias
Hughean Ross of Kilraok, and Alexander Falconar of Halkartoun,
or one, two or three of them, conjunctly and severally, justiciaries
within the bounds of the Earldoms of Ross and Moray and Lordship
of Ardmanach, and other parts within the sheriffdoms of Innernes,
Elgin, Forres and Narne, to apprehend, imprison and try Kenneth
alias Kennoch Owir, principle or leader in the art of magic, [blank]
Neyeane McAllester alias Loskoloukart and Marjory Miller, daughter
of Robert Miller, smith in Assint, and all other men and women using
and exercising the diabolical, iniquitous and odious crimes of the art of
magic, sorcery and incantation within said bounds, who shall be named
by the ministers within the bounds foresaid each for his own parish.
At Halerudehouse 1577/8, 23 January

14.a Names and locations of the Easter Ross witches, 1577

The witches who worked for the elite of Clan Munro were illiterate Gaelic-
speaking natives living in Easter Ross. Their names are given in three forms.
There are Gaelic patronyms, Lowland surnames such as Bawden, Forbes,
Miller and Ross, and witch-names (listed below). William McGilliewareycht-
dane is so-called because he lived in Dune or Dane (NH6884), now Daan,
near Tain, and was evidently liable to be confused with another William
McGilliewareycht. Black gives the following versions of this name:
Mcgillieuorie-dam, McGilliveri-dame and McGillevori-dame. He was one of
those convicted and executed at the Chanonrie early in 1578.

Thomas McAnemoir McAllan McHenryk alias *Cassindonisch* [executed in 1577-78];

John McAne McThomas Cattanach;

William McGillevoir in Dune (Dane) [executed in 1577-78] (see note above);

Donald Gillevoir in Dune (Dane);

Marion Neynaine McAlester alias *Loskoir Longert* 'Fire at the hunt lodge';

Christian [Marjorie?] Milla[r], dau of Robert Milla[r], smith in Assynt [executed in 1577];

Cradoch Neynane McGillechallum, also listed as Gradoche Malcolmson;

Christian McColinstoun;

Katherine Ros, dau of David Ros [of Balnagoune];

Agnes Ros, servant of said Katherine;

Agnes Neynkeard;

Marion alias Mauld Neyne Donald McAndyour in Glastulie;

Jonet Neyne Thomas McAllan;

John McNoullar [McNellan];

Jonet Moir in Mylncraighous in Ardros;

Margaret alias Mage Bawden in lie Channonrie [the Great Witch of Channonrie];

Christina Neyn Andoy McGevin in Nig;

Agnes Roy there [condemned in 1577];

Christian Chactach in Tayne;

Moriach Neyne Yraschte there;

Margaret Neyne Govin there;

Margaret Neyn Velene [NicMillan] there;

Helen Neyne Alexander McConnochie in Logy Eistir;

Kna wife of Donald McConill Leiris there;

Isabella alias Ibbie ... in Calrossie;

Alexander McKessak;

Katherine Neyne Donald Roy;

Marian Neynewin ...;

Jonet Neyne William McClachan;

Isabella alias Ibbie Forbes, materfamilias of Ordhouse;

Keannoch Owir [executed in 1578], *ductricem sey principalem incantatricem,*

ac super iisdem juxta leges regni justitiam administrandum ac super iisdem juxta leges regni justitiam administrandum etc. 'leader and principal of the witches and of those persons subject to the laws of the kingdom'.

Christiane Roiss Malcolmson of 'Canorth' is mentioned in the trial in 1590 of Catherine Ross, Lady Fowlis (Pitcairn i, 193) and listed by Black (1938, 22). She was involved with Loskie Longhart in making clay dollies representing the young laird of and the young Lady Balnagowan and was one of those who shot at them with elf-arrows in her wester chalmer at 'Canorth'. 'These details seem to have been supplied from confession'. On 28 November 1577, she was tried in the cathedral church of Ross, convicted, and burnt (Pitcairn i, 193). In the Commissions she is listed under her witch name as *Cradoch* Neynane McGillechallum or *Gradoche* Malcolmson. Canorth is unknown; it is probably a misreading of Teanord, near Castle Fowlis.

14.b The locations of the Easter Ross witches

3 in Ardros (NH6174), at Millhouse near Ferindonald (the Munro duchthas).

2 in Assynt (NH5967), near Ferindonald.

4 in Calrossie (NH8077), next to Glastullich, near Tain.

1 in The Channonrie (NH7256), at Fortrose, on the south side of the Black Isle.

4 in Dane (NH6884), now Daan, near Tain.

6 in Glastulie (NH7976), next to Calrossie, near Tain.

2 in Logy Easter at Logie Hill (NH7676).

2 in Nig (NH8071), near Tain.

2 in Ordhouse, an English version of Teanord (NH5964), next to Castle Foulis.

4 in Tayne (NH7881), now Tain.

1 in 'Canorth', probably Teanord or Ordhouse (NH5964).

There were twenty witches in or near Tain, seven or eight near Castle Foulis, one isolated witch in Chanonrie on the south side of the Black Isle, and two more in Dingwall. Kennoch Owir or Coinneach Odhar may have been a vagabond like other fairy folk. According to Matheson's persuasive argument (1968) this warlock is the original of the so-called Brahan Seer, in Easter Ross, a century before his traditional date.

The pattern is very similar to that in East Lothian in 1590, where a member of the elite (the Earl of Bothwell) gathered together all the leading healers and charmers of the area, by word of mouth, using their own network, and employed them to make clay and wax models and to work other traditional magical rituals. In both cases several of the leading witches were executed and the elite person escaped justice.

14.c Gaelic nicknames from Easter Ross, 1577

Kna for G. *cna* 'good, bountiful, precious, merciful' (attributes of the Cailleach).

Leiris for G. *leirist* 'slovenly woman, slut' (also the Cailleach).

Chactach for G. *ciatach* 'handsome, goodly'.

Cradoch or Gradoch for G. *gràdhag* 'esteemed, loved, admired'.

Loskoir Longert for G. *loisgeach* 'burning' and *luncart* 'hunting lodge'.

Cassindonisch, a pun for 'Devil's foot', but G. *cas* is also 'hunt' and *dòmhnaich* is 'of the deer-forest'.

15 Prehistoric Banffshire

This survey shows the links between cremation rites (the Annats), the local beacon system, the carved stones associated with the Picts, and hunting. The landscape functioned as a single interactive continuous unit under the control of the local fairy folk or hunters.

Aberchirder. St Marnan's skull was kept in Marnock Church (NJ6068) (MacInlay 1914, 76). Oaths were adminstered on it and the holy water in which it had been dipped was given to be drunk by sick people.

Arndilly, Boharm. Pictish symbol stone (NJ2947) with rectangle and Z-rod and disk on stand (beacon symbol?).

Balneilean. Unfinished Pictish symbol stone (NJ1425) with circular disk enclosing three smaller disks (beacon symbol?) and unidentified curved lines.

Boyndie. Boyndie (NJ6463), with Boyndie Hills, Bay, Burn and Inverboyndie (NJ6664) is a possible Annat site (*buth* + **anaidach*). St Brandan's Stanes (NJ6061) are the remains of a recumbent stone circle. Eight cup marks were once visible and are associated with hunters waiting at a muster site (McGregor 2015). The name Brandan means 'fire'. The stanes at Boyndie probably mark another local beacon site.

Buckie. A probable Annat. Fordannet Bridge is on the Burn of Rannas (NJ 457 649). Many burial cairns near Bauds of Cullen (NJ4767) were removed when the land was brought under cultivation. There is a long cairn at Brankumleys (NJ4364), a name which may refer to a place where bodies were exposed and bones were stored prior to cremation.

Cullen. The Bin of Cullen (NJ4864), 320m., is visible as far as Longman Hill (NJ7362) to the east and Lossiemouth (NJ2370) 20 km (13 miles) to the west. Further possible links to the west include the Downie Hill with its Iron Age fort at Darnaway (NH9658). All these places were fairy hills, ie, look-out posts manned by native hunters, where pagan rituals took place and which formed a chain across the country.

Durn. The Hill of Durn (NJ5763), 199m., has an uncompleted Iron Age fort; it was one point in the chain of coastal beacons manned by hunters.

Forglen. An Annat is marked by Cairn Ennit (NJ678504) on the river Deveron. It is a ruined cairn, 25m. diameter, probably of Bronze Age date, probably marking the site of a beacon.

Glenlivet. Many relics of prehistoric religion including a probable Annat at Delhandie (NJ2224). Nevie 'holy place, nemet' (NJ2127) is the site of a chapel known as Nevin Christ 'holy place of Christ' (Watson 1926, 249) or 'holy place of the bonfire' (McGregor 2015). The Culdees hid their meaning behind puns.

Inveravon. Three Pictish symbol stones (NJ1837). A: eagle, beacon symbol (disk on stand), mirror and comb. B: head of a greyhound. C: crescent and Z-rod; cauldron; mirror and comb.

Logiebuchany, Darnaway, Moray (NH9855), site of an Annat and haunt of witches and fairy folk.

Monymusk. The Brecbannock or reliquary of Columba was kept at Monymusk on the river Don, Aberdeenshire, a long-lived centre of the Culdees or pagan priesthood. Like many Culdee churches in the eastern Lowlands it has a very early tower.

Mortlach or Dufftown. Auchanhandock (NJ3337) was probably *Auchnahannat* in 1546 *(Aberdeen Reg.* 1845: 1.432; cf.424, 444) and site of an Annat. Mortlach was an important pagan and Culdee centre. It has two Pictish symbol stones (NJ3239). The first has (i) faint traces of an eagle, a serpent and the head of a bull; at the bottom, a hunter on horseback accompanied by a hound; (ii) a plain cross of Christian proportions below two fish-monsters and above a small dog-like beast with no tail, no ears and webbed feet. The second shows an 'elephant' or greyhound above an ogival figure resembling the plan of a chambered tomb.

APPENDIX EIGHT –
MAMS: HUMPS OR HOLLOWS?

While browsing an article on Hebridean incantations reported to the Gaelic Society of Inverness by William Mackenzie in 1894 (TGSI xviii, 162-3) I came across two very curious rituals collected in the island of Colonsay and said to be part of a cure for boils in the armpit or the palm of the hand.

> 'A charm was used for reducing a swelling of the maxillary glands. The ceremony was efficacious only if performed on Friday, when certain magic words were muttered to the blade of an axe or knife (the more iron the better), which for the purpose was held close to the mouth, and then the blade applied to the sore place, the swelling crossed and parted into nine, or other numbers of imaginary divisions. After every crossing the axe was pointed toward a hill, the name of which must commence with 'mam'. In Mull the malady was transferred to any hill in that island, being a sound mountain'.

The Mam names used on Colonsay were recited in three groups of eight names (which are given), punctuated by 'Mam Mhor Dhuirach' (the Great Mam of Jura) at which point the charmer struck the floor with his axe. The Colonsay names are Mam Scriodain, Snodain, Dhoire Dhuaig, Chloiche Duinn, Sruthain, Siosair, Seilisteir, Shiaba, [Mam Mhor Dhuirach! once], Astal, Choireadail, Bhatain, Shraoisnich, Siobarsaich, Chataibh, Mororaig, Chloiche Gile, [Mam Mhor Dhuirach! twice], Doire Uaine, Doire Liath, Arichdhuairich, Choire-na-h-eirea'a, Ghribinn, Aisginis, Chlachaig, Choire Chriostal [Mam Mhor Dhiurach! for the third time]. The nine Knoydart Mams were Cloich-Airde, Uchd, Uidhe, Bharasdail (Barrisdale), Meadail, Odhar, Suidheig, Undulainn, and Lidh.

These two lists appear to be unique examples of oral hunting lore which has leaked into the secular world disguised as a magical chant. These lists make no sense whatsoever as used but might have been committed to memory by hunters as part of their education, so that they could make their way to a distant rendezvous (on a Mam) or follow instructions in the course of a hunt. They were not part of a magic ritual but essential knowledge relevant to their deployment among the high peaks. The structure of the mnemonic survives, the groups of eight names, punctuated by a dramatic blow on the floor with a weapon. One might imagine a hunter breaking his vows of secrecy to impress younger members of the family with his knowledge, reciting a list of names that no longer served any purpose. However the Mam lists became public property they certainly belong within the hunting world. However there is another curious feature of the Colonsay list.

It ought to have been straightforward to identify these sites in the 1:50,000 Gazetteer and this was the case with the nine Knoydart names. However it was not at all the case with the Colonsay names. Out of the twenty-five Colonsay names only two are on the modern map: Mam Chlachaig (NM5533) and Mam Choireadail (NM 5931), both in Mull. One or two others have tentative locations. Mam Mhor Dhiurach may be Mam an t-Siob (NR4973) at a great height among the Paps of Jura, and the learned gentlemen of Inverness noted a similarity between Mam Astal and Gleann Astaile in Jura, between Mam Mhor Dhiurach and Airigh Dhuairidh in Mull, and between Mam Scriodain and Loch Scridain in Mull. Even if these guesses happen to be right they account for only five or six of the twenty-five.

What are these unknown names? Since we can recognise among them crystal streams, yellow irises, snuff, an elf or hunters and the sabbat or hunt it seems clear that they were invented not recently but many centuries ago. If so solutions in the form of puns may remain to be found. That there was an original list of real names seems clear. So did the charmer, to preserve his power and observe an oath of secrecy, use the same old ritual but invent new names? Did someone along the line of transmission forget the real names and improvise new ones? Did the names change over the centuries? This did not happen in Knoydart or anywhere else where one can check. They seem to be invented names? If so, the people of Colonsay, like the members of the Gaelic Society of Inverness, did not know the difference.

A second more profitable discovery was the correct definition of the Mam as a landscape feature. According to every place-name book and Gaelic dictionary consulted, a *Mam* is a breast-shaped hill. Cameron Gillies defines G. *mam* as 'a round hill' (1906, 209). Dwelly proposes 'a hill of a particular form, slowly rising and not pointed, a large round hill'. However a search for Mams on the 1:50,000 OS Landranger maps immediately shows that they are not hills of any shape. A Mam is a negative feature, a rounded hollow or saddle, generally at a height, an area from which the ground typically rises steeply on two sides and drops steeply on the other two, an area recognisable even on a map without contours by the streams which drain away in all directions. Some have been defined as a 'gap', or a 'pass through mountains' but a pass is a *bealach*: the name 'Bealach of the Mam' underlines the difference. In 1870 Mam Lorn in the Forest of Lorn between Beinn a' Chaisteil and Beinn nam Fuaran (NN3637) was described as 'a magnificent *opening* and attracting to the eye from its regularity in the curve of the *pass*' and its meaning given as 'the Pass of Lorn' (OSNB, vol. 51, 59) – not quite right, as a pass leads from one approach or path to another while a Mam does not, but certainly not a hill. The *mam* is associated with the hollow of the armpit and with the hollow of the palm. G. *mam* is also 'a handful, as much as can be taken up by both hands together'. *Mam* can also mean 'hunt'. There is no excuse for persisting with the breast-shaped hill. Moreover the Mam is of some importance. For one thing it is a consistent and quite common landscape feature which can be recognised quite easily, even when the name has been lost, by studying the contours on the Landranger maps.

We can deduce that the Mam names were very early from the prolific occurrence of names such as Allt a' Mhaim which rely on an existing Mam to define secondary features such as an Allt, Bealach, Beul, Camus, Carn, Ceann, Clach, Cladh, Creag, Doire, Gleann, Lag, Loch, Lochan, Meall, Mullach, Sgor, Socach and Sron. These names confirm that the Mam came first and was used as a reference point for subsequent names. Only the Beinns are older. Qualified names such as Mam nan Calum and Mam nan Carn are unusual and probably arose out of a need to distinguish between two or more neighbouring Mams.

The Mam is revealed as 'a green hollow' among the hills, high up, often on a local watershed, sometimes the only level ground in an entire range. Some idea of their purpose can be deduced from the fact that the Mams are typically on or near high mountains, where level ground is at a premium, as in Glencoe or Jura. They might have served as camp-sites for hunters. We can imagine them wrapped in their muted plaids, unaware of cold and wet, watching for the signal telling them to get into position.

The name is found all over the west and southwest Highlands but proliferates in major uplands like Ben Nevis, Ben More in Mull, Kintail and Knoydart. Neighbouring names also suggests organised hunting, in particular *meadhoin* now 'middle' but originally a place where hunters mustered. In the Ben More massif in Mull we find Mam a' Bhadain, Mam Bhreapadail, Mam Choireadail, Mam a' Choir' Idhir, Mam Chlachaig, Mam Bhradhadail, Mam an Tiompan and Sean-Mham.

Gazetteer

Sites are listed under a qualifying name or under Mam. Sources include the OS 1:50,000 maps and Gazetteer, the Pathfinder Gazetteer, OS First Edition 6 inch maps, OS Name Books, and Mackenzie (1894, 162-3) who published the original lists in TGSI vol.xviiii. There is virtually no archaeology of any period other than a few hut foundations, in Barra, Glen Nevis and Loch Shiel. Rennie's hut platforms are in the same general areas, and probably served a similar purpose, but they have a different distribution.

Aisginis, Mam. 22nd in the Colonsay incantation. Not located.

Arichdhuairidh, Mam. 19th in the Colonsay incantation. Not found. cf. Airidh Dhuairidh in Mull.

Astal, Mam. 9th in the Colonsay incantation. Not found. Perhaps inspired by Gleann Astaile in Jura (NR4971).

Attadail, Mam (NG9434), Kintail, on a local watershed near Loch an Lascaigh and on a long-distance path from Attadale to Loch Long and Loch Duich. (6 inch, Pathfinder).

Ban, Mam (NN4367), Rannoch, on the watershed between Carn Dearg and Sgor Gaibhre.

Ban, Mam (NN5971), Glengarry, near Dalnaspidal. Now the name of a mountain of 918m. The Mam may be at NN5870. Pathfinder.

Barra, Bealach a' Mhaim Barra (NL6497), Barra to west of Castle Bay. RCAHMS reports a hut circle, a shelter and a clearance cairn. A very small Mam indeed.

Barrisdale: see Bharasdail.

Beag, Mam (NN1662), north of Kinlochleven, close to Mam Mor (NN1662) and south of Sgor Mam am Fhuarain (NN1864). (Pathfinder ref. NN1763).

Beag, Mambeg (NS2389), Gairlochhead. Also Mamore (NS2287). Now farm names. They are on a very small scale to be hunting names.

Bealach a' Mhaim (NM7936), at the south end of the island of Lismore.

Beathaig, Mam (NM8770), Sunart, on Beinn Mheadhoin (NM8769). (cf. OSNB Argyll, 68, 274).

Beul a' Mhaim, Allt Beul a' Mhaim (NN0674), Ardgour. A level plat-form at 267m. between Ceann Caol (480m.) and Meall an t-Slamain (467m.). (6 inch map, Pathfinder).

Bharasdail or Barrisdale, Mam (NG8501), Knoydart. The 4th Mam for Knoydart.

Bhatain, Mam a'. 11th in the Colonsay incantation. Not found.

Bhearna, Bealach Mam a'. Not located (OSNB 68, 255). The name means 'the pass of the pass of the pass', of which the Mam is the oldest element.

Bhlair, Mam a' Bhlair (NN0595), Lochaber north of Loch Arkaig. See Mam an Doire Dhuinn.

Bhradadail, Mam (NM6233), Torosay, Mull at 1399 ft. (OSNB 76,61). Allt, Doir' and Socach a' Mhaim (NM6133) on the watershed. A path leads up from Loch Spelve.

Bhreapadail, Mam (NM5832), Mull, at 390m. while surrounding hills are twice that. Also Coir' a Mhaim (NM5831) with a lochan, on west flank of Beinn Meadhoin. (6 inch map, OSBB 74, 83).

Bhuide, Mam Bhuidhe, (not located), Ardchattan & Muckairn, Argyll. (OSNB 49, 52). As Ardchattan includes Glencoe it may be the same as Mam Bhuidhe (NN1854; OSNM 50, 34) but there are two Name Book refs.

Bhuidhe, An Mam Bhuidhe (NN1569), Allt a'Mhaim Bhuidhe (NN1569), Kilmallie, on south slopes of Ben Nevis, in Glen Nevis. (6 inch map, Pathfinder, OSNB 38, 73).

Bhuidhe, Mam Bhuidhe (NN1854), Glencoe, on the ridge of Buachaille Etive Beag at 870m. Also Allt a' Mhaim Bhuidhe (6 inch, Pathfinder, OSNB 50, 34).

Bocan, Glac Mam (OSNB 67, 12). Listed in error for Glac nam Bocan (NR5083).

Calum, Mam nan Calum (NM9591), on Monadh Gorm, south of Glendessary. The Mam is clearly visible. (6 inch map, Pathfinder).

Car, Mam: see Charaidh.

Carn a Mhaim (NN9995), a mountain of 1037m. in Cairngorm to east of the Lairig Ghru. Location of the Mam perhaps along the ridge. (OSNB 17, 22).

Carn, Mam nan Carn (NN4007). Between Loch Katrine and Loch Lomond. Lochan Mhaim nan Carn on 6 inch map. Meall Meadhoinach (NN4108).

Carn, Mam nan Carn (NO0477). Flat-topped mountain of 986m, on bounds of Mar and Atholl. Pathfinder.

Carraigh, Mam (NN2841), Argyll, Inveroran, Glenorchy, between Glenfuar and Glenlochy. (Pathfinder).

Ceire, Mam na (NM7157), in Morven. (OSNB 72, 6). Also Meall Lochan na Ceire. *Ceire* 'fire'.

Chaill, Ghail or Hael, Mam a' (NM4967), Ardnamurchan, Argyll. Also Allt, Coire, etc. Beside Meall Mheadhoin. (OSNB 61, 27). G. *gal* 'fire'.

Chaill: see Ghail.

Charaidh, Mam (NH2733), Glen Cannich, Inverness-shire. On 6 inch map as Mam Car. (6 inch, Pathfinder, OSNB 51, 37).

Chataibh, Mam. 14th in the Colonsay incantation. Not identified. Said to be Caithness; this is unlikely.

Chatha, Mam a' Chatha (NH5741), The Aird south of the Beauly Firth. See also Mam Mor.

Chlachaig or Clachaig, Mam (NM5533), Torosay, Mull, where three tracks meet on a local watershed above Creag Mhic Fhionnlaidh. One leads down to Clachaig. Mam Clachaig is 23rd in the Colonsay incantation, one of only two identified. Listed by OSNB for Argyll, (74, 74), and by RCAHMS as the site of a cairn known as Carn Cul Righ Albainn 'the cairn of the Back of the King of Alba' or perhaps Carn Cul ri Alba' 'cairn turning the back on Alba'. It is traditionally the boundary between Alba and Dalriada but as one old source put it, 'this theory is susceptible to many objections.' On the 6 inch map but not in Pathfinder index. A hunter's perfect position is summarised in the story of *Iain Dubh Mor, Mac Righ na Sorcha* 'Big Black John, Son of the King of Sorcha (MacDougall 1910, 40-41): *An uair a rainig iad a' bheinn, shuidh iad sios air tolman boidheach uaine air chul gaoithe 's ri aodann greine, far am faiceadh iad gach duine, 's nach faiceadh duine iad* 'When they reached the hunting hill they sat down on a pretty little green knoll, behind the wind and before the sun, where they would see every man, and no man would see them'.

Chloiche Duinn, Mam. 4th in the Colonsay incantation. Not identified.

Chloiche Gile, Mam. 16th in the Colonsay incantation. Not identified.

Chluaindidh, Mullach Mam (NH0807), Ross & Cromarty. Creag a' Mhaim (NH0807) is named for the same Mam. On a path to Loch Loinn. Name comes from Loch Cluainie. (6 inch map).

Choire Chriostal, Mam. 24th in the Colonsay incantation. Not found.

Choire Idhir, Mam a' Choire-Idhir (NM5732), Mull, in the Ben More complex, above Coir a' Mhaim (NM5731) close to Mam an Tiompan and Mam Bhreapadail. (OSNB 74, 81).

Choire na-h-eirea'a, Mam. 20th in the Colonsay incantation. Not found.

Choireadail, Mam (NM5931), Mull, near Beinn Meadhoin, Mull (OSNB 74, 81). 10th in the Colonsay incantation. One of two or possibly three located in fact (see Clachaig and Mam an Siob).

Chreagain, Mam a' (NM9282): Moidart, a hill of 230m overlooking Glenfinnan. Pathfinder says NM9180 but this is at sea level. Not shown on Landranger map but listed in Pathfinder index and shown on the 6 inch map.

Chroisg, Mam (NH2607), Glenmoriston. A hill of 714m. Also Ceann a' Mhaim (NH2709) with two cairns.

Chroisg, Mam a' (NH2607). Pathfinder. Lochan a' Mhaim (NH2608). Ceann a'Mhaim (NH2708). Druim a'Mhain (NH2608). South of Glenmoriston.

Chuill Mhaim, Allt a', (no reference), Lismore & Appin (OSNB 72, 28). It may be Bealach a' Mhaim (NM7936), at the south end of Lismore. (6 inch and Pathfinder).

Chullaich, Mam a' (NM7443), Morven, a hill of 464m. Also Lochan Mam a Chullaich. (OSNB 72, 127).

Clach a' Bhadain, Mam (NM5032), Mull, in the Ben More complex. The Clach (300m.) is shown on the 1:50,000 map with the Mam unmarked between it and Maol Mheadhonach (481m.) (Pathfinder, OSNB 74, 69).

Clais a' Mhaim (NC7001), in Strathfleet, Sutherland. The Mam was probably at NC6901, a flat area between two hills reached by a path from Strathfleet.

Cloich-Airde or Chlach-Ard, Mam na Cloich-Airde (NM8994). Morar above Loch Nevis. Lochan a' Mhaim. The 1st Mam in the Knoydart incantation.

Coire Doimhneid, Mam, or Dhuinnid (NG9326), in Kintail, near Loch na Sithein, east of Loch Long on a long-distance path from Loch Long to Loch Duich. Close to Mam Dubharaiche (NG9523). Allt a'Mhaim (NG9325). Pathfinder. Coire an Easain, Mam (NN2649), Rannoch, Argyll, on Creag an Firich. Apparently distinct from Mam Coire Easain (NN2450) but this needs to be confirmed. (6 inch map, Pathfinder).

Coire Easain, Mam (NN2450), Rannoch, Argyll, on Meall a Bhuiridh; also Glen, Allt. (6 inch, Pathfinder, OSNB 50, 66). Apparently distinct from Mam Coire an Easain (NN2649 but this needs to be confirmed.

Crannlach, Mam na. Not located. Not indexed in Landranger, Pathfinder. (OSNB 68, 206).

Creag a' Mhaim (NH0807): see Mam a' Chluaindidh.

Croise, Mam na, Mull, Argyll (NM4932). Pathfinder. Maol Mheadhonach (NM5032).

Cumhann, Mam (NN1769); on southern slopes of Ben Nevis between river Nevis and Meall Cumhann. (6 inch map, Pathfinder).

Dhuirach, Mam Mhor (the Great Mam of Jura) is repeated three times in the Colonsay incantation after the 8th name, the 16th name and the 24th (last) name. The name is similar to Airidh Dhuiaridh in Mull. It may be Mam an t-Siob between Beinn an Oir and Beinn a' Chaolais in Jura.

Doire Dhuaig, Mam. 3rd in the Colonsay incantation. Not located.

Doire Dhuinn, Mam an (NN0495), Lochaber, north of Loch Arkaig, a hill of 564m. (Pathfinder). The correct name of this hill is Meall an Doire Dhuinne. Mam a' Bhlair (NN0595) is clearly visible on the Landranger map and named on the 6 inch map.

Doire Liath, Mam na. 18th in the Colonsay incantation. Not located.

Doire Uaine, Mam na. 17th in the Colonsay incantation. Not located.

Dubharaiche, Mam (NG9523), Kintail. A path leads down to Strath Croe and Loch Duich. (Pathfinder).

Eadail, Mam, the only Knoydart Mam not found; apparently an error for Mam Meadail (NM8497).

Fhuarain, Sgorr Mam Fhuarain (NN1864), now Sgorr an Fuarain, close to Mam Beag and Mam Mor (NN1662), to the north of Kinlochleven.

Fionna Mham (NM4430), Mull, at Ardmeanach (495m.). G. *fionn* 'white, fire'.

Ghribinn, Mam. 21st in the Colonsay incantation. Not located. Gribun is a coastal township in Mull.

Gualainn, Mam na (NN1162). A mountain of 796m. in Kilmallie north of Loch Leven. 'Mam' is used here as a hill name but the original feature is probably at NN0962 on a track leading north to Fort William. Tom Mheadhoin (NN0862) also refers to a muster of hunters. Allt a' Mhaim (NN1062).

Guibhais, Mam an (NH0256), Ross & Cromarty. On a long-distance path leading south to Loch Coulin. (6 inch map, Pathfinder, Watson 1904, 232).

Hael, Mam (NN0141): Abhainn Dalach is 'a considerable stream rising at Mam Hael and falling into Loch Etive at Dail' (OSNB 52, 10, 6 inch map).

Imriche, Mam na h-Imriche (NM8476), west side of Loch Shiel, below Beinn a' Chaorainn, not far above the loch (6 inch, Pathfinder).

Lidh or Li, Mam (NG8006), in Glenelg, Knoydart on a long-distance track. The 9th Mam for Knoydart.

Linne Beithe, Mam na (NM9370), Ardgour on south side of Glen Cona at a height of 389m. surrounded by hills of 450-550m, beside a wee lochan. (6 inch, OSNB 68, 185).

Lirein, Mam (NM6734), Mull, in Glen Lirein. (OSNB 76, 44).

Long, Mam nan (NM9790), Lochaber, Kinlocharkaig, on the north slope of Leac na Carnaig. (6 inch, Pathfinder).

Lorn, Mam (NN3537). In the Forest of Lorn between Beinn a' Chaisteil and Beinn nam Fuaran (NN3637) was described as 'a magnificent opening'. The route by way of Allt a' Mhaim Lorn (NN3636) leads down to the Annat of Beinn Dorain, another ancient site, shown on the 6 inch map of 1870, now vanished.

Lourie, Mam (NM9681). Pathfinder. (OSNB 68, 64).

Luirg, Mam na (NM8076), Moidart. Allt a' Mhaim (NM8276). (Pathfinder).

Luirginn, Mam na (NM7173), Moidart, north of Kinlochmoidart.

Mam Lic, Sgorr a' Mham Lic (NM9638). Benderloch, north of Loch Etive. G. *leac* 'stone slab, fire setting'.

Mam nan Carn, Lochan Mhaim nan Carn (NN3907), Trossachs, south of Loch Katrine, next to Meall Meadhonach (NN4108).

Mam-Ard, Sgeir a' Mhaim-Ard (NM4193), a sea-rock off the coast of Rum. Pathfinder; OS 6 inch.

Mam, Allt a' Mhaim (NN2156). Pathfinder.

Mam, Allt a' Mhaim (NR5068), Jura. The Mam is probably at NR4969 below Glas Bheinn.

Mam, Allt Carn a' Mhaim, Braemar, Aberdeenshire (OSNB 17, 21; 18, 43).

Mam, Allt Clach a' Mhaim (NH0758). Pathfinder.

Mam, Allt Coir' a' Mhaim, Kintail, Ross & Cromarty (OSNB 49, 67).

Mam, Allt Lian a' Mhaim (NM4246), Mull. The Mam is a platform below the summit of Beinn Bhuidhe. (Pathfinder).

Mam, Allt Linn a' Mhaim, Kilninian, Argyll (OSNB 44, 22). Not located.

Mam, Am (NG5218), Skye, Strathaird, on a long-distance track linking Strathaird with Sligachan.

Mam, Am (NH1230), Kintail, now used as a farm name. Allt Choire Mhaim (NH1231). (6 inch, Pathfinder).

Mam, Am, Kilmallie, Inverness-shire: see Sgurr a' Mhaim.

Mam, An (NH5675), Easter Ross, in Strathrusdale, inland from Alness; details obscured by planting.

Mam, An (NN0985), in the Locheil Forest, a hill of 389m. Allt a' Mhaim (NN0986). Pathfinder.

Mam, An (NR1230), now attached to a modern house on Loch Mullardoch, not the original site. Coire Mhaim (NR1131) is to the north; Allt Coire a' Mhaim (NR1231). In the same area as Mam Ruisgte.

Mam, An (NR4257), Islay. Appears to be used in the Landranger map as a hill name but it is not clear from the map if this is an error or a different local usage (6 inch map).

Mam, An: see Sac (NN2530).

Mam, Bealach a' Mhaim (NG4427), Skye; also Meall a' Mhaim, and Allt a' Mhaim (NG4326). Pathfinder.

Mam, Bealach a' Mhaim (NM7484), Arisaig or South Morar.

Mam, Bealach a' Mhaim (NM7936), south end of Lismore. (6 inch and Pathfinder). The smallest of all?

Mam, Bealach a' Mhaim (NN2507), north of the Cobbler; the Mam is at NN262070.

Mam, Bealach a' Mhaim (NN4344), between Loch an Daimh and Glenlyon. Here the Bealach *is* the Mam. Pathfinder.

Mam, Bealach a' Mhaim (NN6560). North of Kinloch Rannoch. Pathfinder.

Mam, Bealach a' Mhama (NM7485), South Morar. Also Gleann Mama (NM7484).

Mam, Camus Allt a Mhaim (NM1361). South side of Loch Leven; the Mam is not marked. Pathfinder.

Mam, Coir' a' Chuil Mhaim (NM8558), Allt a' Chuil Mhaim (NM8656). In Kingairloch near summit of Fuar Beinn (766m.). (Pathfinder).

Mam, Coire Mhaim (NR7973), Eas Coire Mhaim (NR7971), Kintyre. On a path leading to Ormsary on the west coast. (Pathfinder).

Mam, Creag a' Mhaim (NH0807), Loch Shiel, Moidart.

Mam, Creag a' Mhaim (NH0807): see Chluaindidh.

Mam, Gleann a' Mhaim (NS0781), Cowal. Bealach a' Mhaim (NS0781). (Pathfinder).

Mam, Lag a' Mhaim (NM8150), Lochan Lag a' Mhaim (NM8250), Kingairloch, on a long-distance track up from the coast (Loch Linnhe). (Pathfinder).

Mam, Loch a' Mhaim (NM6438), Mull, northeast of Ben More and northwest of Beinn Meadon (637m.), in a typical position on a watershed. No trace of the original name was found on the 6 inch map.

Mam, Lochan Coire Mhaim (NM5866), Ardnamurchan.

Mam, Lochan Dubh Mhaim (NM3899). Kinloch, Rum. Pathfinder. There is a probable Mam at NM3999.

Mam, Meall an Fhiar (Fhier) Mhaim (NM4843), Mull at 309m. (Pathfinder).

Mam, Sean-Mhaim (NM4544), Mull. 'The mam of the gathering'. Also Bealach a' Mhaim (Pathfinder.)

Mam, Sgurr a' Mhaim (NN1666), Kilmallie, Glen Nevis, a mountain of 1099m. Sron Sgurr a' Mhaim (NN1567), Allt a Mhaim. Close to Mam Bhuidhe and Mam Beag, on the north side of the river Nevis. RCAMHS report a charcoal-burner's hut (probably originally a hut platform used by hunters) (NN152671).

Mam, The (NH1108), Inverness-shire, on the south side of Loch Cluainie.

Mam, The (NO2797), north of the river Dee, near Braemar. Also known as The Maim, The Main and The Mime (with a Cockney accent). Where three hill routes meet. (6 inch map).

Mam: Allt a Mhaim (NN2156), Glencoe north of the river. There is a possible Mam at NN2157. (Pathfinder).

Mamag, Ross & Cromarty. Watson (1904, 183) says *mamag* is a diminutive and the site is 'beyond Coille righ opposite Carnoch'. Not found, not known to Pathfinder.

Maoime Bige, Bealach na Maoime Bige (NN6560) north of Kinloch Rannoch to Loch Errochty. Pathfinder interprets the name as Maime.

Maoime, Bealach na Maoime (NN6660) on a track north from Kinloch Rannoch to Loch Errochty.

Meadail, Mam (NM8497), Knoydart. The 5th Mam for Knoydart (reported as *Eadail*).

Mor, Mam (NH5742), Inverness-shire, in the Aird, south of the Beauly Firth. See also Mam a' Chatha.

Mor, Mam Mor (NN1663). North side of Loch Leven at Kinlochleven, beside Mam Beag. (6 inch map).

Mor, Mam Mor (NS2287), Gairlochhead. A farm name Mamore; cf. Mambeg (NS2389).

Mororaig, Mam na. The 15th Colonsay incantation. 'Of Morar', but not found.

Odhar, Mam (NH5823), in the Great Glen between Meall a' Ghuirmen and Carn Righear. (Pathfinder).

Odhar, Maman (1) (NM7687), Knoydart. The 6th Mam for Knoydart.

Odhar, Maman (2) (NM7969), Knoydart. Pathfinder. South of Loch Shiel, opposite the Annat. Immediately above a single large hut platform (NM793705), on south side of Loch Shiel. (OSNB 62, 63).

Phobuill, Mam an (NG5126), southwest of Loch Ainort, Skye.

Ruisgte, Mam (NH0934), Kintail, Ross & Cromarty. The Pathfinder ref. (NH0933) is on a steep slope. The 6 inch map shows Coire Mhaim (NH1131).

Sabhal, Mam, Ross & Cromarty (Watson 1904, 183). Not located. Watson suggests 'rounded hill of barns'. It was noted for its grass.

Sac, Mam an Sac (NN2530), also known as An Mam. On the watershed between Glen Orchy and Glen Lochy between Beinn Udlaidh and Beinn na Sroine. It is said that a well-known stream rising there flows into the Orchy north of Bochyle (OSNB 50, 147) but this stream was not identified.

Sac, Mam nan (NN2144), between Meall an Araich and Stob Ghabhar (1087m), on a path leading south to Clashgour and Glenorchy. (Pathfinder).

Scriodain, Mam a' Scriodain, perhaps in Mull. 1st in the Colonsay incantation. G. *sgriodan* 'a stony ravine; scree'. cf. Druim an Scriodain, Ardnamurchan (NM5468).

Seilg, Mam na (NH1004) and Allt na Mam na Seilg. Kilmonivaig, Inverness-shire. Pathfinder ref. is NH1003. On various long-distance paths.

Seilg, Mam na (NH1108). In Glen Shiel at 489m., south of Loch Cluanie. Related to Creag a' Mhaim (947m.) (NH0807). On long-distance path from Glen Loyne (now submerged by dam).

Seilisteir, Mam an t-Seilisteir. 7th in the Colonsay incantation. Not found. G. *seilisdeir* 'yellow iris'.

Shaiba, Mam. 8th in the Colonsay incantation. Not found. G. *sabaid* 'quarrel, fight, hunt'.

Shraoisnish, Mam. 12th in the Colonsay incantation. Not found.

Siob, Mam an t-Siob (NR4973), Jura. (6 inch, Pathfinder, OSNB 67, 139). Central to the Paps of Jura, between Beinn a' Chaolais and Beinn an Oir. Is this *a' Mam Mor Dhuirach*, the Great Mam of Jura?

Siobarsaich, Mam an t-Siobarsaich. 13th in the Colonsay incantation. Not located G. *siobhrag* 'elf, hunter'. cf. Mam an t-Siob (NR4973) in Jura.

Siosair, Mam an t-Siosair. 6th in the Colonsay incantation. Not located. G. *siosar* 'shears'.

Smiorasair, Mam (NH0066), southeast end of Loch Maree, Kinlochewe, on a long-distance track. Pathfinder.

Snodain, Mam an t-Snodain. 2nd in the Colonsay incantation. Not located. Perhaps G. *snoitean* 'snuff'.

Sodhail, Mam (NH1125), Kintail, Ross & Cromarty, between Loch Mullardoch and Glenaffric, a hill of 1181m.

Staing, Mam na (NG7813), Glenelg, on the mainland over looking Sound of Sleat, on western slopes of Beinn Mhialairigh, 548m. See also Mam nan Uranan.

Stainge, Mam na Stainge (NN0652), Duror, Argyll (Pathfinder ref. NN0552). The 6 inch map shows Mam na Stainge between Allt Chaorunn and Allt Tarsuinn where they fall into Allt Eilidh. It is linked by a track to Mam Uchdaich (NN0654) to the north and Glen Creran to the south.

Struthain, Mam an t-Struthain. 5th in the Colonsay incantation. Not identified. G. *sruth* 'stream'.

Suidheig, Mam (NG8101), Knoydart. The 7th Mam for Knoydart.

Suim, Mam (NJ0109), Cairngorm, on north side of Stac na h-Iolaire.

Tiompan, Mam an (NM6031), Torosay, Mull. Also Teanga an Tiompan (OSNB 76, 61). Pathfinder.

Trotanaich, Mam an (NM5625), Mull. Allt a' Mhaim (NM5527). On a long-distance path at a height of 1307 ft (6 inch, Pathfinder and OSNB 74, 141). RCAHMS report enclosures (NM551270).

Tuath, Mam (NM3799), Rum, on path leading to Kinloch. The Mam of the plebs.

Tuirc, Mam an (NG9826), Ross & Cromarty. The Mam of the wild pig.

Uchd, Mam (NG8396), Knoydart, on Beinn Bhuidhe. The 2nd Mam for Knoydart. Pathfinder.

Uchdaich, Mam (NN0654), Duror, south of Beinn Gulbin on a long-distance track leading to Ballachulish. Pathfinder. (OSNB 48, 32). See also Mam na Stainge.

Uidhe, Mam (NG7601), on a path from Inverie on Loch Nevis to Inverguseran on the Sound of Sleat. The 3rd Mam for Knoydart. (Pathfinder).

Unndulainn, Mam (NG8100), Knoydart, Glen Unndulainn. The 8th Mam for Knoydart. (Pathfinder ref. is NG8800).

Uranan, Mam nan (NG7916), Glenelg. Linked by a path to Mam an Staing (NG7813).

Vam, the Burn of (HY3906), a Gaelic place-name in Hobbister, Orkney Mainland.

Vamadale Mor, Knock (NB1435), Tacleit, Great Bernera. A hill of 46m.

* * *

FLYING BY NIGHT:
SCOTTISH WITCHES AND FAIRIES

REFERENCES AND SOURCES

Alexander, M. (2002). *A Companion to the Folklore, Myths & Customs of Britain.*

Alexander, W.M. (1952). *Place-Names of Aberdeenshire, Third Spalding Club.*

Anderson, D. (c.1859). *History of the Abbey and Palace of Holyrood.*

Anderson, J. (1888). 'Confessions of the Forfar Witches'. *P.S.A.S.* vol.22, 246-262.

Anderson, P. (1596). *Chronicles of Scotland.* Adv.Ms.35.5.3. F281 r and v.

Andrews, William (ed.) (1899). *Bygone Church Life in Scotland.*

Armstrong, R.B. (ed.). (1884). *Archaeological Collections relating to the Counties of Ayr and Wigton.*

Aubrey, J. (1696). 'Transportation by an Invisible Power', Chapter XIV, *Miscellanies,* 153.

Bahn, P. (1997). *Journey into the Ice Age.*

Bain, R. (1899). *History of the Ancient Province of Ross.*

Barrow, G.W.S. (1989) 'The lost Gàidhealtachd of medieval Scotland'. In W. Gillies (ed) 1989, 67-88.

Beith, M. (1995). *Healing Threads.*

Black, G.F. (1903). *Examples of Printed Folk-Lore concerning the Orkney and Shetland Islands.* County Folklore vol.3.

Black, G.F. (1938). *Calendar of Cases of Witchcraft in Scotland 1510-1727.*

Black, G.F. (1946). *Surnames of Scotland*.

Blackledge , C. (2003). *The History of V: A Natural History of Female Sexuality*.

Bord, J. (2004). *Footprints in Stone*.

Briggs, K.M. (1976). *The Encyclopedia of Fairies*.

Briggs, K.M. (1978). *The Vanishing People: a Study of Traditional Fairy Beliefs*.

Brimble, L.J.F. (1944). *Flowers in Britain*.

Brodie, A. of Brodie (1863). *Diary of Alexander Brodie*. Spalding Club.

Broedel, H.P. (2003). *The Malleus Maleficarum and the Construction of Witchcraft*.

Bruford, A. (1991). 'Trolls, hillfolk, finns, and Picts: the identify of the Good Neighbours in Orkney and Shetland'. In Narvaez, P. (ed.) (1991), 116-141.

Buchanan, George, *History of Scotland* lib.xiii. Anent fairies in Athole.

Buckley, V. (ed). (1990), *Burnt Offerings, International Contributions to Burnt Mound Archaeology*, Dublin.

Burl, A. (1979). *Rings of Stone: The prehistoric stone circles of Great Britain and Ireland*.

Burns Begg, R. (1887). 'Notice of Trials for Witchcraft at Crook of Devon, Kinross-shire, in 1662'. *PSAS* vol.22, 211-220.

Cameron, I. (1928). *A Highland Chapbook*.

Campbell, D. (1888). *The Book of Garth and Fortingall*.

Campbell, J.G. (1891). *The Fians or Stories, Poems and Traditions of Fionn and his Warrior Band*.

Campbell, J.G. (1900). *Superstitions of the Highlands and Islands of Scotland collected entirely from Oral Sources*.

Campbell, J.G. (1902). *Witchcraft & Second Sight in the Highlands and Islands of Scotland; Tales and Traditions collected entirely from Oral Sources*.

Carmichael A. (1992 edition). *Carmina Gadelica.*

Carver, M.O.H. (2009). 'Early Scottish Monasteries and Prehistory; a Preliminary Dialogue'. In *The Scottish Historical Review* vol. LXXXVIII, 2: No.226: October 2009, 332-351.

Chambers, R. (1858). *Domestic Annals of Scotland, Reign of Charles II.*

Child, F.J. (1882). *The English and Scottish Popular Ballads, part I.*

Cohn, N. (1975). *Europe's Inner Demons.*

Colcock, C.J. (1908). *Family of Hay.*

Cowan, S. (1904). *The Ancient Capital of Scotland; the Story of Perth from the Invasion of Agricola to the Passing of the Reform Bill.*

Cowan, E.J. and Henderson L. (2002). 'The last of the witches? The survival of Scottish witch belief'. In J. Goodare (ed.) *The Scottish Witch-Hunt in Context.*

Dalyell, J.G. (1835). *The Darker Superstitions of Scotland.*

Davidson, J.L. & Henshall, A.S. (1991). *The Chambered Cairns of Caithness.*

Delrio, M.A., S.J. (Louvain 1599). Quoted by Summers 1925, 122.

DES Discovery and Excavation in Scotland, published annually by the Council for Scottish Archaeology.

Douglas, G. (1894). In Henderson, W. (1866), *Witchcraft, Folklore and Charms of the Northern Counties.*

Dunbar, E.D. (1865). *Social Life in Former Days Chiefly in the Province of Moray* (1st series).

Edmonston, B. and Saxby, J.M.E. (1888). *The Home of a Naturalist.*

Dwelly, E. (1901-1911). *The Illustrated Gaelic-English Dictionary.*

Fergusson, R.M. (1907). *Scottish Social Sketches of the 17th Century.*

Fergusson, R.M. (1912). *The Ochil Fairy Tales.*

Fergusson, R.M. (1907). 'The Witches of Alloa'. *Scottish Historical Review* vol.4, 40-48.

Flood, G.D. (2004 ed.). *Introduction to Hinduism.*

Fountainhall: see Lauder.

Ghosh, O. (1965). *The Dance of Shiva and Other Tales from India.*

Gillies, W. (ed.) (1989). *Gaelic and Scotland: Alba agus a'Ghaidhlig.*

Gillies, W.A. (1938). *In Famed Breadalbane.*

Glanvil, J. (1636-1680). *Saducismus triumphans, or, Full and plain Evidence concerning Witch craft and Apparitions.* Edition of 1700.

Goodare, J. (ed.) (2002). *The Scottish Witch-Hunt in Context.*

Gorer, G. (1955). *Exploring English Character.*

Grant, J. (1854). *Philip Rollo, or The Scottish Musketeers.*

Graves, R. (1961). *The White Goddess.*

Gregory, D. (1857). *Archaeologica Scotica* 4.

Gregor, W. (1881). *The Folk-Lore of the North-East of Scotland.*

Henderson, E. (1879). *Annals of Dunfermline and Vicinity, 1069-1878.*

Henderson, G. (1911). *Survivals in Belief Among the Celts.*

Henderson, J.A. (1890). *History of Banchory-Devenick.*

Henderson, J.C. (1998). 'A survey of crannogs in the Lake of Menteith, Stirlingshire', *PSAS* 128, 273-292.

Henderson, L. (2006). 'The Survival of Witchcraft Prosecutions and Witch Belief in South-West Scotland'. In *Scottish Historical Review*, 85.1, 73.

Henderson, L. (2008). 'Witch-hunting and witch belief in the Gaidhealtachd'. In Goodare J., Martin, L. and Miller, J. (eds.) *Witchcraft and Belief in Early Modern Scotland.* Palgrave historical studies in witch-craft and magic.

Henderson, L. and Cowan, E.J. (2001). *Scottish Fairy Belief.*

Henderson, W. (1866, reprinted 2001). *Witchcraft, Folklore and Charms of the Northern Counties of England and the Borders.*

Henshall, A.S. (1963). *The Chambered Tombs of Scotland*, vol.1.

Hewison, J.K. (1895). *The Isle of Bute in the Olden Time*, 2 vols.

Hill, A. (2013). 'Decline and Survival in Scottish Witch Hunting 1701-1727'. In Goodare (ed.), *Scottish Witches and Witch-Hunters*, 215.

Hole, C. (1973). 'Some Instances of Image-Magic in Great Britain.' In Newall (ed.) 1973, 80-94).

Houston, G. (1829). *The Correspondent*, vol. 4.

Huie, C. (1976). *The Moray Book*.

Hunter, J. (1917). *Diocese and Presbytery of Dunblane, 1660-1689*.

Hutton, R. (2010). 'The Changing Faces of Manx Witchcraft'. In *Cultural and Social History*, vol. 7, issue 2, pages 153-169.

Irving, D. and Laing, D. (eds) (1821) *Flyting of Montgomery and Polwart*.

Jamieson, H.M. (1896). 'A southern outpost on the edge of the Highlands'. In *Chronicles of Strathearn*, 333-340.

Jenner, H. (1903). *Memoirs of the Lord Viscount Dundee*. The Russell Press, Stuart Series, vol.IV.

Kennedy, J. (1927). *Folklore and Reminiscences of Strathtay and Grandtully*.

Kieckhefer, R. (1976). *European Witch Trials*.

King, P.D. (1972). *Law and Society in the Visigothic Kingdom*.

Kingshill, S. (2012). *The Lore of Scotland; a Guide to Scottish Legends*.

Kinloch, G.R. (1848). *Reliquiae Antiquae Scotticae*.

Kirk, R. (1691, 1815, new edition 1893). *The Secret Commonwealth of Elves, Fauns and Fairies*.

Lang, A. (1893). Introduction to *The Secret Commonwealth of Elves, Fauns and Fairies*.

Larner, C.J. (1981). *Enemies of God; the Witch-hunt in Scotland*.

Larner, C.J, Lee, C.H. & McLachlan H. (1977). *A Source-Book of Scottish Witchcraft*.

Lauder, John (Lord Fountainhall) (1759, 1761). *The Decisions of the Lords of Council and Session from June 6th 1678 to July 30th 1712*. From the original manuscript, in the Library of the Faculty of Advocates.

Lawson, J.P. (1843). *History of the Scottish Episcopal Church from the Revolution to the Present*.

Lea, H.C. (1939, reprint) (ed.). *Materials Toward a History of Witchcraft*.

Leland, C.G. (1899). *Aradia, or, The Gospel of the Witches*.

Levack, B.P. (1980). 'The Great Scottish Witch Hunt of 1661-1662.' In *The Journal of British Studies* vol.xx/1.

Levack, B.P. (1987). *The Witch-Hunt in Early Modern Europe*.

Leland, C.G. (1899). *Aradia, or, the Gospel of the Witches*.

Linton, E.L. (1861). *Witch Stories*.

Lockhart, J.G. (1828). *Life of Robert Burns*.

Macara, D. (1881). *Crieff: Its Traditions and Characters*.

MacCulloch, J.A. (1921). 'The Merging of Fairy and Witch Beliefs in Sixteenth and Seventeenth Century Scotland'. *Folk-Lore* vol. 32, 227-244.

MacDonald, S. (2014). *Witches of Fife: Witch hunting in a Scottish Shire 1560-1710*.

Macdougall, J. (1910). *Folk Tales and Fairy Lore in Gaelic and English*.

MacGregor, A. (1891, edition of 1922), *Highland Superstitions*.

MacGregor, J. (1520). *Book of the Dean of Lismore*.

McGregor, S.A. (2018a). *Word-Lists, How Language evolved in Europe*.

McGregor, S.A. (2018b). *Bones and Bonfires, Cremation Rituals at the Annats of Scotland*.

McGregor, S.A. (2018c). *Possibly Palaeolithic, Prehistoric Survival in Highland Scotland*.

McGregor, S.A. (2018d). *First Settler Theory and the Origin of European Languages*.

Mackay, C. (1841). *Memoirs of Extraordinary Popular Delusions and the Madness of Crowds.*

Mackay, W. (ed.) (1896). *Records of the Presbyteries of Inverness and Dingwall 1643-1688.* SHS vol. 24.

McKenna, S. (1938). 'Pagan Survivals in Visigothic Spain'. In *Paganism and Pagan Survivals in Spain up to the Fall of the Visigothic Kingdom.*

MacKenzie, A. (1898). *History of the Munros of Fowlis.*

Mackenzie, G. (1678). *Laws of Scotland in Criminal Matters.*

MacKenzie, D.A. (1935). *Scottish Folk-Lore and Folk Life; Studies in Race, Culture and Tradition.*

Mackenzie, W. (1894). 'Gaelic Incantations, Charms and Blessings of the Hebrides'. In *TGSI* xviii, 97-182.

McKerrachar, A. (2000). *Perthshire in History and Legend.*

MacKie, E. W. (1975). *Scotland: An Archaeological Guide.*

MacKinlay, J.M. (1910). *Ancient Church Dedications in Scotland:* vol.1 *Scriptural.*

MacKinlay, J.M. (1914). *Ancient Church Dedications in Scotland:* vol.2 *Non-Scriptural.*

McLagan, R.C. (1901). *The Games and Diversions of Argyleshire.*

MacLennan, M. (1925). *A Pronouncing and Etymological Dictionary of the Gaelic Language.*

MacPhail, J.R.N. (ed.) (1914). *Highland Papers,* vol.1. Scottish History Society 2nd series V.

MacPhail, J.R.N. (ed.) (1920). *Highland Papers* vol.3. Scottish History Society 2nd series XX. Bute p.3; Appin p.36.

MacPhail, M. (1898) 'Folklore from the Hebrides', III. In *Folklore,* Vol. 9, No. 1. (March), 84-93.

MCM (1841). *Maitland Club Miscellany.*

McNeill, F.M. (1956-1968). *The Silver Bough.* Vols 1 to 4. Vol. One

(1956) Scottish Folklore and Folk Belief. Vol. Two (1959) A Calendar of Scottish National Festivals, Candlemas to Harvest Home. Vol. Three (1961) A Calendar of Scottish National Festivals, Hallowe'en to Yule. Vol. Four (1968) The Local Festivals of Scotland.

McPherson, J.M. (1929). *Primitive Beliefs in the Northeast of Scotland.*

Mair, T. (1876). *Records of the Parish of Ellon.*

Marshall, W, (1881). *Historic Scenes in Perthshire.*

Martin, L. (2002). 'The Devil and the domestic'. In Goodare (ed.) 2002, 78.

Martin, M. (1695). *A Description of the Western Islands of Scotland.* Birlinn ed. 1994.

Matheson, W. (1968). 'The Historical Coinneach Odhar and some prophecies attributed to him'. In *TGSI* 46 (1968), 66-88.

Maxwell-Stuart, P.G. (2001). *Satan's Conspiracy: Magic and Witchcraft in Seventeenth-century Scotland.*

Meek, D.E. (1986). 'The Banners of the Fian in Gaelic Ballad tradition'. In *Cambridge Medieval Celtic Studies* 11 Summer 1986, 29-44.

Melville. J. (1827). *Memoirs.* Bannatyne Club.

Michie, J.G. (1896). *History of Logie Coldstone and Braes of Cromar.*

Millar, J. (2004). *Magic and Witchcraft in Scotland.*

Miller, H. (1835). *Scenes and Legends of the North of Scotland.*

Murray, M.A. (1921). *The Witch-Cult in Western Europe; A Study in Anthropology.*

Myatt, L.J. (2004). 'Achavanich - A Re-Assessment'. In *Caithness Field Club Bulletin* no.4 http://www.caithness.org/caithnessfieldclub/bulletins/2004/achavanich.htm

Narvaez, P. (ed.) (1991). *The Good People: New Fairylore Essays.*

Neusner, J. and Green W.S. (1999). *Dictionary of Judaism in the Biblical Period 450 B.C.E. to 600 C.E.*

Newall, V. (ed.) (1973). *The Witch Figure: Folklore essays ... honouring the 75th Birthday of K.M. Briggs.*

NSA New Statistical Account (1845).

Obelkevich, J. (1976). *Religion and Rural Society: South Lindsey, 1825-1875.*

Ó Drisceóil, D.A. (1990). 'Fulachta fiadh: the value of early Irish literature'. In Buckley (ed.) 1990, 158.

OSA Old Statistical Account (1791-1796).

Parker Pearson, M. (2005). 'Evidence for mummification in Bronze Age Britain'. In *Antiquity* 79, 529-546.

Paterson, J. (1866). *History of the Counties of Ayr and Wigton.* Vol.III, Cuninghame.

Pearson, K. (1897). 'Woman as Witch'. In *The Chances of Death,* vol. II, 1-50.

Pennant, Thomas (1769). *A Tour in Scotland.*

Pitcairn, R. (1833). Ancient Criminal Trials in Scotland, *from A.D. 1488 to A.D. 1624.* Maitland Club.

Purkiss, D. (2000). *Troublesome Things; a History of Fairies and Fairy Stories.*

Rees, R.W. (1899). 'Witchcraft and the Kirk'. In William Andrews (ed.), *Bygone Church Life in Scotland.*

Reid, A.G. (1899). *The Annals of Auchterarder and Memorials of Strathearn.*

Reid, J.E. (1864). *History of the County of Bute and families connected therewith.*

Rennie, E.B. (1997). *The Recessed Platforms of Argyll, Bute and Inverness.* BAR British series, vol.253.

Ritchie, J.N.G. & Thornber, I (1975). 'Cairns in the Aline Valley, Morvern, Argyll. Proc Soc Antiq Scot 106, 15-30.

Rokosz, M. (2005). 'History of the Aurochs (*Bos taurus primigenius*) in

Poland'. *Antiquity* Website http://antiquity.ac.uk, 16 April 2005.

Rudgley, R. (1999). 'Witches' Ointments'. In *The Encyclopaedia of Psychoactive Substances.*

Rust, J. (1876). *Druidism Exhumed.*

SBSW (1977) *A Source-Book of Scottish Witchcraft.*

SCM Spalding Club Miscellany (1841, 1842).

SHR Scottish Historical Review.

SHS Scottish History Society.

SM Spottiswoode Miscellany (1844) Vol 1, (1845) Vol 2.

Scot, Reginald (1584). *Discoverie of Witchcraft.*

Scott, W. (1830 edition). *Letters on Demonology and Witchcraft.* The Family Library No. XVI.

Scott, W. (1931 reprint). *Minstrelsy of the Scottish Border.*

Scottish Antiquary or Northern Notes and Queries. Vol. 9, no. 34, Alloa.

Sharpe, C.K. (1819). *A Historical Account of the Belief in Witchcraft in Scotland.*

Shaw, C.B. (1988). *Pigeon Holes of Memory, The Life and Times of Dr John Mackenzie (1803-1886).*

Simpkins, J.E. (1914). *County Folklore VII: Fife.* Folklore Society.

Sinclair, G. (1685). *Satan's invisible world discovered.*

Smout, T.C. (1970, 2nd edition). *A History of the Scottish People, 1560-1830.*

Spalding Club Miscellany (1841). Vol I.

Spalding Club Miscellanh (1842). Vol II.

Spinage, C.A. (2003). *Cattle Plague - a History.*

Spottiswoode (1655, edition of 1855). *History of the Church of Scotland.*

Stuart, J. (ed.) (1843). *Extracts from the Presbytery Book of Strathbogie 1631-1654.* Spalding Club, Aberdeen.

Stuart, J. (ed.) (1848). *Extracts from the Council Register of the Burgh of Aberdeen*, Vol.II, 1570-1625. Spalding Club, Aberdeen.

Stevenson, J. (ed.) (1839). *The Chronicles of Lanercost*, Bannatyne Club.

Stewart, W.G. (1823). *Popular Superstitions and Festive Amusements of the Highlanders of Scotland.*

Summers, A.J-M.A.M. (1926). *The History of Witchcraft and Demonology.*

Sutherland, E. (1977). *The Brahan Seer.*

TGSI Transactions of the Gaelic Society of Inverness.

Thorne, T. (1990). *Bloomsbury Dictionary of Contemporary Slang.*

Todd, M. (2002). *The Culture of Protestantism in Early Modern Scotland.*

Turreff, G. (1859). *Antiquarian Gleanings from Aberdeenshire Records.*

Waddell, P.H. (1893). *An Old Kirk Chronicle* [Tyningham].

Watkins, C.S. (2007). *History and the Supernatural in England.*

Watson, W.J. (1904). *Place-Names of Ross and Cromarty.*

Watson, W.J. (1926). *The History of the Celtic Place-names of Scotland.*

Webster, D. (1820). *A Collection of Rare and Curious Tracts on Witchcraft.*

Weir, A. and Jerman, J. (1986). *Images of Lust, Sexual Carvings on Medieval Churches.*

Weyer, Johan (1515-1588), Protestant physician and demonologist, born in Basel, Switzerland, compiled an inventory of devils published in 1568. In his major work *De Praestigiis Daemonum et Incantationibus ac Veneficiis* (Basel, 1568), Weyer denounced witch hunters for extracting confessions under torture, pointing out that extreme hardships would force even the most innocent to confess themselves guilty. He claimed mental disease rather than demonic possession. See H. C. Lea (ed.) (1939, reprint), *Materials Toward a History of Witchcraft.*

Wilkin Rees, R. (1899). 'Witchcraft and the Kirk'. In Andrews 1899, 171.

Whitelock, B. (1682). *Memorials of the English Affairs*.

Wickham-Jones, C. (1994). *Scotland's First Settlers*.

Withers, C.W.J. (1989). 'On the geography and social history of Gaelic'. In Gillies, *Gaelic and Scotland*, 101-130.

Wormald, J. (1981). *Court, Kirk and Community, Scotland 1470-1625*, The New History of Scotland, vol. 4.

Wright, William (c.1591). *Newes from Scotland, Declaring the Damnable life and death of Dr Fian a notable Sorcerer, who was burned at Edenbrough in January last, etc.* James VI may have contributed to the text.

Zaliznyak, L. (1997). *Mesolithic Forest Hunters in Ukrainian Polessye*.

Printed in Great Britain
by Amazon

22066404R00284